For Cynthia
Of course, of course

Contents

Foreword

Mark A. Stoler

Over the past half-century the Second World War has engendered an historical literature of enormous size and complexity. That is hardly surprising given the scope, nature, and consequences of the conflict. World War II involved entire populations in total war efforts, and it resulted in an unprecedented death toll. It also refigured the world in ways we are still trying to understand.

The generation that fought the war clearly recognized the enormity and importance of the conflict, and it produced an extensive number of works seeking to witness and commemorate, as well as detail, explain, and understand, what had taken place. The children of that wartime generation were equally impressed by the war, even though they often disagreed with their parents' assessments, and throughout the 1970s and 1980s they added substantially to the existing literature. The results by 1989 were volumes numbered in the tens of thousands. That figure expanded enormously with the publication deluge accompanying the fiftieth anniversary of the war. Today the numbers are in six rather than five figures, and they continue to grow with each passing year.

Surprisingly, however, the enormous literature on World War II does not include any comprehensive historiographical analyses. This volume and its projected companion seek to rectify the gap and in the process provide scholars, students, and the general public with a broad, comprehensive overview of past histories, interpretive disputes, changes in emphasis, new approaches, and avenues for further research.

The sheer number of chapters and sections in this and the companion volume makes clear not only how extensive the literature is, but also how many areas of human endeavor the war encompassed. These chapters also make clear the numerous historical controversies and new approaches to the war that have developed over the past half-century, and the areas that still need to be researched. The nonspecialist may be surprised by the number of such controversies, new approaches, and areas still requiring research. The war, after all, is now approaching its sixtieth anniversary. Haven't all "the facts" been made clear and controversies resolved? Indeed, weren't they made clear and resolved years ago?

The answer, of course, is no. Although official documents began to be released even while the war was in progress and continued to be released along with official histories over the next three decades, nongovernmental researchers did not gain access to the extensive material relating to World War II within the British and American national archives until the 1970s. Other World War II archival records, most notably those of the Soviet Union, remained closed until very recently, and some still remain closed. Similarly, numerous personal manuscript collections of key individuals were unavailable until the 1970s and 1980s, and numerous memoirs were not published until that time.

The importance of such new material can be illustrated by the fact that in the 1970s this new material revealed the existence of Ultra, one of the last and best-kept secrets of the war. This in turn led to the development of the virtually new World War II subfield of cryptography. It also necessitated a wide-ranging reassessment of numerous aspects of the war. That reassessment is still in progress, but it has already altered previous conclusions regarding the reasons for Allied successes and failures in numerous specific air, land, and sea campaigns.

Release of new information offers only a partial explanation, however, for the continuing deluge of World War II histories. Equally important is the continuation of numerous wartime controversies that the new documentation has not been able to resolve, particularly those over military strategies, leadership, and decisions that chapters in this volume describe. Of perhaps even greater importance is the changing environment within which World War II history is written. Human beings look to history for roots to their contemporary problems and issues, thereby leading each generation to examine aspects of the war its predecessors had ignored. It also leads to new approaches within historical scholarship itself, most notably the development over the past two decades of social and cultural history as dominant forces within the profession.

The impact of these factors on World War II history can be most clearly seen in the development of women's history for the war—another subfield that did not even exist until the 1970s. It can also be clearly seen in recent analyses of cultural attitudes toward such controversial military strategies as the strategic bombing of civilians, and in both the explosion of Holocaust history and its integration into World War II history.

The essays that follow not only analyze the existing literature and interpretive disputes, but also explore probable future areas of research. They make clear that a large number of issues remain to be studied, and that evolving national and international environments are in the process of changing the very questions we ask about the war. Perhaps most notable in this regard is the end of the Cold War and with it our preoccupation with Soviet–American wartime relations. Instead we are already seeing, and are likely to continue to see, analyses revolving around our contemporary professional and national preoccupation with race, class, and gender. We are also likely to see more comparative analyses and more global, as opposed to strictly national, histories of the war—a result of the new international/cultural history within the profession and the growing economic interdependence of the world.

World War II is thus likely to remain one of the most studied events of modern history, albeit on terms appropriate to present and future generations rather than to the one that actually fought and experienced the war. This volume will provide the reader with an analysis of where we presently are in our study of the war, where we have been, and hopefully where we are going.

Introduction

Loyd E. Lee

There is, surprisingly, no comprehensive historiographic survey of the Second World War, due in part to specialization in the study of the war but also due to the massive literature on the many aspects of the conflict. This volume presents a reevaluation of basic aspects of the war in Europe and countries closely associated with Europe in order to focus each more clearly and to clarify connections among the topics.

To limit the scope of the work to a manageable length, primary emphasis is given to English-language material. Even with this limitation, mountains of material are left out. Here we strike a balance between the best-informed scholarship and an introduction of the reader to a broad variety of issues not reviewed elsewhere and not under the unified rubric of the Second World War.

Many bibliographies of the Second World War have appeared in English and other languages; these are discussed later. None are complete. Indeed, given what scholars consider to be the proper content of the topic "World War II," the vastness of the primary material, the multitude of publications and the large amount of nonprint material, artifacts in museums, photographs, films, and sound recordings, there may never be a single reference listing all that is available. There will likely never be a complete annotated bibliography.

This is the first comprehensive historiographic reference work by authorities in the main areas of scholarly and popular interest in the history of the war. The chapters collected here will interest experts of the respective topics as well as scholars and college teachers who want to know the historiography of the many war-related topics. It will also aid advanced students and serious amateurs who desire insight into the history of the war and its literature, whether on controversial topics (resolved or still contested), those areas where our knowledge has been expanded, and those needing further research.

Included are not only grand strategy and operational history, military and naval campaigns, and related matters of diplomacy, strategy, economic mobilization, and intelligence services but also resistance, collaboration, and the broad topics of the "home front." The chapters also reflect research on gender relations, race relations, prisoners of war, refugees, and the Holocaust. General introductory guides for individual research in archival, primary, and secondary sources are included in this handbook in addition.

The contributors, regardless of their topics, were asked to include, when possible, several common elements in their chapters. First, they were asked to describe the state of knowledge on the topic and to prepare a select bibliography of the most significant books, articles, dissertations, memoirs, and other material. Narrative chapters consider various aspects of their topics and relate each bibliographic reference to its themes and issues. Recent original scholarship is incorporated if it aids new understanding, and older works of enduring value find a place. Finally, contributors point out areas of needed research or topics yet poorly understood. Each chapter concludes with an alphabetized list of all cited works.

In the course of devising a workable scheme to organize this handbook and recruit its twenty-four contributors and the twenty-seven contributors to its companion volume, I relied on the expertise and helpful suggestions of several hundred scholars from around the world. Though unnamed here, their publications are cited in the following pages. I am very appreciative and thank them. During the past few years I have also had the pleasure of the advice and guidance of Robin Higham, advisory editor, without whose extraordinary knowledge of the literature, research, and scholars of the war, this endeavor would not have been possible.

Various libraries in the New York area were indispensable for planning and carrying out the project, especially the vast collections of the New York Public Library and its special World War II holdings, and the library of the U.S. Military Academy at West Point. Particular appreciation goes to the librarians of the Sojourner Truth Library at the State University of New York, College at New Paltz.

Abbreviations

ABBREVIATIONS USED IN TEXT

A/S	antisubmarine
ACTS	Air Corps Tactical School (United States)
ADC	aide-de-camp, a military assistant
AFB	Air Force Base
AFZ	Anti-Fascist Front of Women (Croatia)
APRA	Alianza Popular Revolucionaria Americana
BEF	Brazilian Expeditionary Force
BSC	British Security Coordination Service
CAF	Confederate Air Force (United States)
CBO	Combined Bomber Offensive
CIA	Central Intelligence Agency
CIO	Congress of Industrial Organizations (American labor organization)
CIS	Confederation of Independent States
COMINT	communications intelligence
CMH	Chief of Military History (United States)
CTM	Confederación de Trabajadores Mexicanos
DP	displaced person
EAM	Ethniko Apeleftherotiko Metopo, National Liberation Movement (Greece)
ELAS	Ethnikos Laikos Apeleftherotikos Stratos, National Popular Liberation Army (Greece)
GOU	Grupo de Oficiales Unidos (Argentina)

HUMINT	human intelligence
IGCR	Intergovernmental Committee on Refugees
IRO	International Relief Organization
LST	landing ship, tank (U.S. Navy)
MGFA	Militärgeschichtliches Forschungsamt (Military History Research Institute, Germany)
MNR	Movimiento Nacionalista Revolucionaria (Bolivia)
MPR	Mouvement populaire républicain (France)
M.P.R.	military participation ratio
NAM	National Archives Microfilm (United States)
NATO	North Atlantic Treaty Organization
OKH	Oberkommando des Heeres (German Army High Command)
OKW	Oberkommando der Wehrmacht (German Armed Forces High Command)
OMGUS	Office of Military Government of the United States for Germany
OSS	Office of Strategic Services (United States)
PCF	Parti communist français (French Communist Party)
PHOTINT	photographic intelligence
POWs	prisoners of war
RAF	Royal Air Force (Great Britain)
RCAF	Royal Canadian Air Force
RCN	Royal Canadian Navy
SA	Sturmabteilung (German Nazi paramilitary organization)
SHAEF	Supreme Headquarters, Allied Expeditionary Force
SIGINT	signal intelligence
SOE	Special Operations Executive (Great Britain)
SS	Schutzstafelln, protection squad of the Nazi Party
UNRRA	United Nations Relief and Rehabilitation Administration
USAAF	United States Army Air Force
USCG	United States Coast Guard
USN	United States Navy
USO	United Service Organization (United States)
USSBS	United States Strategic Bombing Survey
WAC	Women's Army Corps (United States)
WAFS	Women's Auxiliary Ferrying Squadron (United States)
WASP	Women's Airforce Service Pilots (United States)
WAVES	Women Accepted for Volunteer Emergency Service (United States)

ABBREVIATIONS USED IN CITATIONS

HMSO His (Her) Majesty's Printing Office
GPO Government Printing Office
NIP Naval Institute Press
UP University Press
PRO Public Records Office

The words Press, Publishing, Company, Limited, and Books are omitted. For titles which have been frequently reprinted the earliest and latest dates of publication are included. When the same work is published under different titles, that is noted.

PART I

General Histories and the International Background

1   Histories of the War in Europe and the Pacific

Donald G. Schilling

The momentous events of the twentieth century, most notably the two world wars, have never lacked fascination for historians. Challenged by the task of imposing order on the chaos of experience, of reducing inchoate images to a coherent, manageable narrative, of framing the questions and advancing convincing interpretations, historians first wrote general histories of these conflicts shortly after the fighting stopped. The human need to remember and commemorate the defining events of the past further stimulated historians. As we began to mark the half-century anniversaries of the Second World War, the appropriate volumes appeared with regularity. This particular past was once again engaged and reshaped from the perspectives of the present. Now we can assess the general histories of the war in the context of the earlier historiography, consider whether the writing of one- or two-volume histories of World War II has changed, and ask if the key historiographical issues are still those defined by writers like J.F.C. Fuller, Winston Churchill, and Chester Wilmot in their pioneering studies of the war.

At one level the war as defined and depicted in the late 1940s and early 1950s has remained strikingly consistent over the decades. As Sandhurst historian H. P. Willmott noted with some surprise in the introduction to his 1989 study, *The Great Crusade*, "our main themes of historical interpretation remain today much as they were when set down in the first glut of postwar memoirs and writings of the first generation of historians after 1945" (ix). Willmott is correct to some degree, but over the decades four major trends have marked the evolution of this historiography: the changing nature of military history, the effort to depict the war in its truly global dimensions, the increased attention to the roles of technology and intelligence in influencing the course of the war, and the belated recognition that not only the Holocaust but also other social phenomena should be included in the history of World War II.

THE SECOND WORLD WAR IN HISTORY

In 1956 Michael Howard began a long campaign to elevate the status and transform the nature of military history. Writing in *History*, he urged that military history become an accepted field of study for university faculty and no longer the exclusive purview of the gentleman scholar, the military journalist, or the scholarly soldier. This would require a shift in subject from "the technical aspects of combat and the lessons learned that could be applied to future operations" to the exploration of "its relevance to the nature and development of society as a whole" (186). Howard's critique, gradually reinforced by others in the field, contributed to such substantial growth in the "new" military history that Dennis Showalter could issue "A Modest Plea for Drums and Trumpets" in 1975. More recently, Paul Kennedy, echoing Howard, has articulated the challenge facing practitioners of the new military history:

No longer, it is argued, can a history of the war be confined to accounts of operations, generalship, and front-line combat. It must be widened to include the entire effort of the societies involved and thus to incorporate (among other things) the home fronts, political and propaganda aspects, ideology and race, social transformations, the changed position of women, culture, and art and literature. The historian taking this warfare-and-society approach is thus required to write what one might term *total* history. (*New York Times Book Review*, December 31, 1989, p. 10)

How do the one- or two-volume general histories of the war measure up to this standard? While it is perhaps unfair to judge the earliest works by a standard that had not yet been clearly articulated, especially when the first writers faced getting the basic story straight, the concept of total history provides a useful frame in which to understand an evolving historiography.

The war as a whole received early historical definition in 1948 with the single-volume works of Cyril Falls and J.F.C. Fuller. British writers on the First World War, these authors developed narratives grounded in the traditional conception of military history as the examination of strategy and operations. Their aims were appropriately modest. Falls in *The Second World War: A Short History*, the first of the venerated "short history" genre, attempted "a sketch of events" (285), while Fuller, publishing three months later, eschewed a "full-dress history of the recent war . . . because . . . on the data as yet available it is [not] a practical undertaking" (ii). If Falls wrote in a dry, factual style with little analysis or evaluation until the conclusion, Fuller's narrative bristled with judgments, etching the controversies of the war in acid and setting the agenda for subsequent debate. Typically, Fuller argued, "[I]rrespective of what your enemy does, it is more profitable to fight like a gentleman than like a cad; for a cad's war can only end in a cad's peace, and a cad's peace in yet another war, which to me seems to be silly" (13). Falls trusted that his British point of view had "not resulted in an incorrect estimation of the relative importance of events" (xii). His trust was somewhat misplaced as he helped establish a pervasive pattern for English-language writers of overemphasizing events in Western Europe, the Mediterranean, and, particularly, North Africa. He argued, for example, that "Alamein takes its place as a turning point as important as that of Stalingrad" (292) and gave short shrift to the Asian and the Pacific theaters, which were treated in isolation from the European.

Fuller was less guilty of this and did note, in passing, "the horrors of the concentration camps and gas chambers," about which Falls was totally silent. But Fuller made this reference only to emphasize that these horrors "will dim with the passing years," while "the ruined cities of Germany will stand as monuments to the barbarism of their conquerors ... [and] will remain to beckon generation after generation of Germans to revenge" (408). The convention of placing the Holocaust totally outside the purview of Second World War studies was established very early. Finally, both authors, products of a Victorian world, revealed biases that now seem curiosities. Falls, for example, concluded by lamenting the impact of modern life and the weakening of private enterprise on the quality of officers in the British army, the best of whom, he opined, had come through the British public school system (300–301). For Fuller the problem was "the disappearance of the gentleman—the man of honour and principle—as the backbone of the ruling class in England [for] political power rapidly passed into the hands of demagogues who ... created a permanent war psychosis ... to justify the massacre of civilian populations" (405). While subsequent writers remained horrified at the destruction, barbarism, and slaughter of the war, they rejected such facile explanations for their cause.

In 1948 Winston Churchill published the first of his six-volume tour de force and continued the story he had begun to tell about the Great War. Although not a short, general history, Churchill's *The Second World War* cannot be ignored, for this sweeping chronicle hangs the "discussion of great military and political events upon the thread of the personal experience of an individual" (I, iii). While not claiming to write history—that was for another generation—Churchill, nonetheless, put his distinctive stamp on the war, especially as it centered on Western Europe and the Mediterranean. With dramatically more space, Churchill had the luxury of treating issues in considerable depth, but he did not aspire to write the total history of this war; rather, he emphasized the interconnection between alliance politics and military strategy. In doing so he moved beyond the more limited conceptions of Falls and Fuller, but his own areas of involvement and interest led Churchill naturally to emphasize British policy and military activity, to give the Soviet theater only sketchy treatment, and to reinforce the silence on the destruction of the European Jews.

Writing during the height of the Cold War, the Australian journalist Chester Wilmot produced *The Struggle for Europe*, a masterful analysis of the war and grand strategy in Western Europe from the Battle of Britain to the defeat of Germany. A single issue drove Wilmot's 1952 study: "how and why, in the process of crushing Nazi Germany and liberating Western Europe, they [the Western Allies] allowed the Soviet Union to gain control of Eastern Europe" (xi). The implications of this approach for particular historiographical issues are considered later in this chapter, but for the moment it is sufficient to note that, its impressive qualities notwithstanding, Wilmot's treatment was neither global nor total.

The histories of the war appearing in the next two decades largely replicated the limitations of these early efforts despite the frequent publication of volumes in the various official histories. Providing a wealth of information and analysis on grand strategy, operations, particular campaigns, and the many other dimensions of total war, these works constituted a vital, but too frequently underutilized, source for the writers of general histories (for which see Higham, *Official Histories*).

Perhaps stimulated by the twenty-fifth anniversary of the war's end, the late 1960s and early 1970s proved a particularly vital period historiographically in two respects. First, substantive single-volume general histories of the Pacific war appeared. In 1968 Charles Bateson, *The War with Japan*, wrote a readable, if not particularly compelling, general overview of strategy and operations in all the Pacific theaters. This work was superseded within a year as Basil Collier admirably filled his purpose "to present, in a single volume, a concise account of the war which convulsed the Far East from 1941–1945" (xi). John Toland substantially enriched work on the Pacific war in 1970 with *The Rising Sun: The Decline and Fall of the Japanese Empire*. Not only did he move beyond the standard treatment of military operations to include both graphic personal accounts and the dynamics of diplomacy, but he also wrote from a Japanese point of view without ignoring other key participants. Despite the excellence of Toland's book, it largely ignored such topics as the economics of the war, home-front mobilization, occupation policies, and resistance. We must look to three other works in this period to find illustrations of Kennedy's total history.

The first was Gordon Wright, *The Ordeal of Total War, 1939–1945*, written in 1968 for the Rise of Modern Europe Series. This volume admirably fulfilled the mandate of the series, which was designed to provide the student and general reader with an "intelligent synthesis" and "a reliable survey of European history" that "went beyond a merely political-military narrative, . . . to lay stress upon social, economic, religious, scientific, and artistic development" (xi). Although he failed to exploit the relevant official history volumes, Wright claimed to be hampered by the lack of substantive monographic work on "economic and social developments, psychological warfare, [and] the impact of the war on intellectual and cultural life" (xiv). In addition, the page limitations of the series and its geographical focus forced Wright to truncate significantly his discussion of the military dimensions of the conflict (only three of eleven chapters examined military operations) and to ignore the Pacific theater.

Given these constraints, Wright produced a noteworthy history, but the French military historian Henri Michel, author of the second of these books, did even more to advance the cause of total history. Published in France in 1968 and available in English translation in 1975 as *The Second World War*, this book set the standard for the "heavyweight" category of general histories, that is, those tipping the scales at about five pounds and running to roughly one thousand pages in length. Michel, too, felt the time was right for a work of synthesis, although one marked by "an attempt to clarify rather than to explain, a factual account which poses more questions than it answers" (xx). He was unduly modest, for he brought to this project the benefit of his collaborative work as founder and general secretary of *Le Comité Français de l'Histoire de la Deuxième Guerre Mondiale*, which had the goal of making known the total history of the war. Employing the concept of total war, Michel probed all its dimensions from the key military campaigns in both Europe and the Pacific, to economic mobilization, occupation policies, and the destruction of the European Jews.

The British team of Peter Calvocoressi and Guy Wint wrote the third piece of this breakthrough triad in 1972. Writing for a general audience, they wrestled with the question of how much war to include in a book on World War II and concluded, "[W]e did not want to write a military or campaign history and were not qualified to do so, but . . . we felt it was essential . . . to show why particular campaigns were fought, when, and where they were fought, and also what happened behind . . . 'the lines' " (xvii). The result was an extremely readable book that gave substantial attention, as did Michel's, to all aspects of the total war, including its origins. If the treatment of the Asian–Pacific theaters, as written by Wint and revised for the second edition by John Pritchard, was more substantive than in many volumes, this was not a truly global history. After experimenting with an integrated global approach in early drafts, the authors concluded "that the wars in the two hemispheres were much less closely interdependent than we had first supposed" (xviii) and solved an organizational problem with what amounted to two separate books within one cover.

In 1970 one of the century's preeminent military historians, Basil H. Liddell Hart, had his study of the war published posthumously. Unlike the books just mentioned, Liddell Hart's work reflected the virtues of traditional military history. Engaging many issues of historiographical controversy in a strong narrative based on the analysis of strategy and operations in all the major theaters of the war, Liddell Hart brought his vast experience and knowledge to bear in rendering incisive, balanced judgments. If there was an area of weakness, it was his tendency to place too much faith in the testimony of the German generals whose perspective on the war he had recorded in *The Other Side of the Hill.*

A quarter of a century after the end of the war, then, historians had created the models for the general histories of the war. These books fall into three categories: (1) traditional military history with a primary emphasis on grand strategy and large-unit strategy and tactics (Falls, Fuller, Collier, and Liddell Hart); (2) a combination of traditional military history and serious examination of the diplomatic dimensions of the war (Churchill, Wilmot, and Toland); and (3) those that approached the goals of the total history (Wright, Michel, and Calvocoressi and Wint). Each of these categories in turn featured books that defined themselves as short histories and others that aspired to heavyweight status. Some fell into a middle range, such as Basil Collier's competent, but traditional, *The Second World War: A Military History.*

Following the spate of activity marking the twenty-fifth anniversary, general histories of the war were infrequent in appearance and often short in length. For example, James L. Stokesbury, a specialist in writing short histories of major wars, produced a readable, balanced general history in 1980, *A Short History of World War II.* To be sure, the treatment of the war was enriched during this period by specialized research in several areas. With the declassification of key documents beginning in the 1970s, participants in the "secret war" such as F. W. Winterbotham and Aileen Clayton told their stories while F. H. Hinsley began to produce his multivolume *British Intelligence in the Second World War.* These developments stimulated scholarly investigation of the roles of technology and intelligence and their impact on the course of the war. This work began to find its way into the general histories. For example, both M. K. Dziewanowski and Michael Lyons in their basic texts emphasized that they were filling an important gap by incorporating this evidence and, as Lyons writes, "demonstrat[ing] its role in achieving the eventual Allied victory" (xiv).

In the context of the more limited general histories on the Pacific war, this period did witness a veritable flurry of activity. A notable, though idiosyncratic, contribution by Saburo Ienaga surfaced in English translation in 1978. Rejecting a comprehensive history of the war as beyond his capabilities, Ienaga sought "to show the Japanese people the naked realities of the Pacific War. [And] . . . to stimulate reflection and self-criticism about the war" (xi). This he did admirably. In contrast John Costello returned to more standard purposes in his impressive *The Pacific War, 1941–1945*. Though inaccurately claiming that his was the first "single comprehensive volume . . . to trace the origins and to chronicle the course of one of mankind's greatest struggles" (v), Costello not only engaged the political, economic, and military dimensions of the Pacific war but also occasionally ventured new interpretations based on archival research. For instance, he argued that United States–British efforts to deter Japanese expansion in 1941 "can now be seen as possibly the prime cause of the Pearl Harbor disaster" (vii).

Unquestionably the best of the general histories of the Pacific war, *The Eagle against the Sun* by Ronald H. Spector appeared in 1985 in the series the Wars of the United States. In keeping with the mandate of this series, Spector emphasized policy, strategy, and operations, but he also "attempted to give the reader some sense of what the war was like for the men and women who fought it" (xii). Spector recognized that in seeking to capture the complexity of this immense conflict in one volume, he had to "slight not only units and individuals, but entire battles and campaigns as well as significant social and political events" (iii). Yet his interpretive narrative both preserved admirable balance and judiciously explored a number of controversial issues, among them the two-pronged strategy that is generally treated as a "useful compromise" but that he believed could "have led to disaster had the Japanese taken greater advantage of their opportunities" (xiii). Spector wisely grasped that the key to victory in the Pacific theater was less a matter of strategy than of logistics.

The armistice in the writing of general histories with a European or global scope was broken with a frontal assault in 1987–1990 as historians and others raced to capture the fiftieth-anniversary audience. By my count ten substantive general histories of the war appeared in these years, and several volumes followed before the commemorative events had ended in 1995. In addition, English translations of the most recent of the ambitious official histories, *Germany and the Second World War*, a projected ten-volume undertaking by the *Militärgeschichtliches Forschungsamt* (Military History Research Institute), began to appear with regularity with Wilhelm Deist et al., *Germany and the Second World War*. Confronted with this outpouring, we might ask, To what degree have these books enhanced our ability to apprehend the war as total, global history?

In the short history category, books by Michael Lyons, R.A.C. Parker, Loyd E. Lee, and Martin Kitchen merit attention. Writing in the framework of total history aiming "to present a balanced account that does justice to both the European and Pacific theaters of operations and the connections between them" (xiii), Lyons handled this task with considerable deftness and economy. Competing with Lyons for the university student audience with a book of similar scope, Kitchen offered a crisp, analytical narrative laced with bracing judgments. If Parker argued that "two separate wars made up the 'Second World War' " (1) and treated the European and Pacific theaters accordingly, his incisive analysis of "the decisive episodes of the war" (v) and his informed discussion of wartime economies, intelligence, morale, and the Holocaust made his one of the most stimulating of the short histories. Lee's *The War Years: A Global History of the Second World War* was distinguished by its self-conscious effort to present the war in both its total and global nature. In his short history, Lee achieved a genuine equality between the military and nonmilitary dimensions of the war and was more attentive to the global ramifications than most other authors, although his military analysis suffered as a consequence.

Four books also fall into the intermediate range, those by H. P. Willmott, John Ellis, John Keegan, and Len Deighton, the highly successful writer of spy novels. Deighton's *Blood, Tears, and Folly: An Objective Look at World War II* disappoints. Trumpeting his objectivity in both subtitle and preface, Deighton writes without irony to remind "ourselves how badly the world's leaders performed and how bravely they were supported by their suffering populations" (xvii). A curious blend of descriptive vignettes and technical detail, this idiosyncratic book seldom moved past 1941. In contrast, the other books in this category make important contributions.

Willmott, despite his long-held view "that it is impossible for a single volume history to do justice to the war against Japan" (xi)—let alone the war as whole—has written a truly provocative and engaging history. His forte is clearly the discussion of grand strategy and operational analysis, the staples of traditional military history, but Willmott adopted a chronological structure providing a bird's-eye view of the unfolding global conflict at given times and highlighting interconnections between the European and Pacific theaters often missed in other works. He did not try to evoke the experience of war or to write total history, despite the claim for completeness in the subtitle, but his global approach and his rethinking of the conventional judgments of military historians proved most refreshing.

Brute Force by John Ellis effectively explored the connections between economic production and battlefield success but eschewed total history. Further, by examining each theater from beginning to end, Ellis lost the benefits of a comparative global perspective. Ellis argued "that [Allied] commanders seemed unable to impose their will upon the enemy except by slowly and persistently battering him to death with a blunt instrument" (xviii). Ellis, especially hard on Bernard Montgomery and Arthur Harris, spared few Allied commanders his blunt criticism. While this gave his work an interpretive focus, it produced a monocausal analysis of Allied operations.

Not to be outdone by his competitors, John Keegan adroitly presented the central strategic and operational issues of the war in *The Second World War*. Realizing comprehensiveness was impossible, Keegan "decided from the outset to divide the story of the war into four topics—narrative, strategic analysis, battle piece and 'theme of war' and to use these four topics to carry the history of the six main sections into which the war falls" (5). Keegan's battle pieces, often enlivened with the telling anecdote or vivid example, illustrated the different types of warfare central to this global struggle, and the "theme of war" introduced such issues as production and supply, espionage and intelligence, resistance, and superweapons. If Keegan's judgments were more conventional than Willmott's, he combined the erudition of the military educator with a prose style profitably honed by his work in journalism.

The pattern of four prevails for those studies that reside in the heavyweight division. Two of these can be quickly dispatched: *Delivered from Evil: The Saga of World War II* by Robert Leckie and *The Second World War: A Complete History* by Martin Gilbert. The former emphasized traditional military history supplemented by diplomacy and biographical sketches of the great men all told in "a swiftly moving narrative" (947) that at times degenerated into parody: "His [Mussolini's] words ignited a train of gun powder that went flashing across the boot of Italy" (21). More troubling was Leckie's inability to discriminate among sources; he relied far too often on works lacking scholarly credibility.

Martin Gilbert is a much better historian; however, his "complete history" contains curious omissions and a chronological narrative strong on description but so weak on analysis that general patterns are lost. Although Gilbert was admirably sensitive to the fate of the European Jews and the suffering of common people and soldiers in total war, the absence of a conceptual framework drowned readers in detail.

Germany and the Second World War by Wilhelm Deist and others, on the other hand, has a conceptual framework, making its rich detail more comprehensible. Drawing heavily on the research of German scholars and emphasizing the German role in the war, this series "differs fundamentally from the old style of military history." Rather, it offers "an interdisciplinary and comparative approach, so that the work embraces political, economic, and social factors in a comprehensive account" (I, v).

Comprehensiveness is also evident in Gerhard Weinberg's monumental *A World at Arms: A Global History of World War II*. In this long-awaited work Weinberg has come closer to realizing the potential of both total and global history than any single historian. From his perspective, to treat the war from a national standpoint or in isolated theaters too often results in parochial history. Weinberg was particularly effective in integrating the Holocaust into the larger history of the war. He also made every effort to understand the war in the context of a world shaped by the First World

War and in which the Cold War and Vietnam had not yet happened. These perspectives, plus his extraordinary knowledge of archival sources, defined this distinguished book, a fitting culmination to fifty years of writing the war.

While not a general, narrative history of the war, Richard Overy's *Why the Allies Won* comprehensively deals with those issues taken up in general histories. Overy built on his extensive knowledge of various aspects of the war to present a thoughtful consideration of the reasons often offered for Allied victory. In doing so he developed his own explanation and analysis of the decisive factors such as combat, production, technology, politics, and morale which turned the "Unpredictable Victory," the title of the first chapter, into Allied military success.

BATTLING OVER THE WAR: HISTORIOGRAPHICAL DEBATES

Although the scope and nature of general histories can work against historiographic argument, over the years certain controversial issues have continued to engage the writers of these histories. Their willingness to do more than recount a story of the war not only made their work more stimulating but, along with the more specialized literature, contributed to the richness of scholarly debate. It is impossible to consider all the areas of debate, but the following seem most significant and contentious, as well as providing a brief introduction to issues taken up in more detail in subsequent chapters: (1) Germany's failure to achieve complete victory over the Soviet Union in 1941; (2) the establishment of the Second Front and the priority to be given the Mediterranean versus Northern European theaters; (3) wartime decisions contributing to the Soviet control of Central and Eastern Europe; and (4) the morality and value of strategic bombing and the use of the atomic bomb.

As noted earlier, Western, notably British, historians tend to shortchange the Soviet theater, especially in contrast to North Africa, and to underplay the particularly brutal nature of the fighting on this front. With the easing, then ending, of the Cold War, historians have been more willing to acknowledge the primacy of the Nazi–Soviet struggle in determining the outcome of the war and to appreciate its horrifying ferocity. As Willmott asserted, "In terms of scale the Nazi–Soviet conflict was unprecedented, and it was infinitely more important in deciding the outcome of the Second World War than any other theatre, perhaps even more important than all others combined" (146). However, even Ellis, who "regards the Russian contribution to Allied victory as absolutely fundamental," gave more attention to the Mediterranean than the Soviet theater, a fact he paradoxically noted "with some disappointment" (xix).

Despite these imbalances, the Nazi–Soviet conflict has long engaged analysts in the effort to explain why the German military, after stunning successes through the first months of the campaign, failed to capture Moscow and knock Russia out of the war in 1941. In contrast to Snyder, who labeled the German plan of attack "brilliant in both design and execution" (166), most historians have joined Wilmot in pointing out the strategic flaws inherent in the compromise between the drive on Moscow with the object of destroying the Red Army's military power and the focus on political and economic objectives evidenced by the northern and southern thrusts (80). Recent writers have emphasized that racial assumptions and flawed intelligence gathering caused the Nazis to overlook serious imbalances among their resources, logistic capabilities and objectives, and Soviet strength (Ellis, 37–46; Willmott, 135–39; Keegan, 174–81; Kitchen, 68; Weinberg, 190–91).

Stunning initial victories, due in part to Stalin's inept handling of the first stage of the war, seemed to open the door to a German victory. If that door was opened, what closed it? Explanations abound, driven by Germany's near miss before Moscow in late 1941. Assuming "General Winter" played a critical role, some authors argue that if only the Germans had launched their invasion of the Soviet Union earlier than June 22, they would have captured Moscow. Churchill, for example, believed Hitler's Balkan adventure in the spring of 1941 delayed the attack on Russia by five or six weeks and concluded, "It is reasonable to believe that Moscow was saved thereby" (III, 354). Liddell Hart concurred (152), but Keegan and other contemporary scholars disagree, arguing that the wet spring would have delayed the invasion in any case (174).

For many the critical moment came in August 1941, following the fall of Smolensk, when, after bitter debate with his generals, Hitler insisted that armored forces from Army Group Center, rather than refitting to launch an immediate assault toward Moscow, be dispatched to the northern and southern fronts. For Wilmot, writing in 1952, this was a critical decision, "for in the six weeks between the fall of Smolensk and the taking of Kiev the opportunity of seizing Moscow was lost" (82). If Michel indicated that German successes around Leningrad and Kiev "seemed to prove Hitler right" (219), Liddell Hart asserted, "The two wasted months . . . proved fatal to the prospects of reaching Moscow" (167), and Keegan agreed that the delay "may well have spared Stalin defeat in 1941" (194).

For Ellis, however, Hitler had the impossible task of trying to make four panzer groups do the work of six, thus rendering "much of this debate . . . essentially sterile in that it implies real strategic options, 'right' or 'wrong' decisions, when in fact neither the choices made nor their alternatives could have had much bearing on the fundamental cause of German failure—that the Wehrmacht was simply not powerful enough to conquer Russia" (59). In agreement Weinberg argued the Germans "could win further tactical successes on one or another of the front segments, but had already lost whatever chance they might theoretically have had to defeat the Soviet Union" (269). If most accounts stressed the impact of the early onset of the harsh Russian winter, a reason later emphasized by the German generals, Weinberg dismissed such claims as "ridiculous" and pointed out that "winter [is] not some extraordinary occasion which the Russians arrange to have in years when they are invaded" (274). The Germans failed before Moscow because they had not prepared like the Russians and had exhausted their offensive strength.

In examining the Russian theater more generally, a number of contemporary historians, especially Willmott and Weinberg, gave the Soviet military credit not just for the tenacity, courage, and sacrifice of the common soldier, which had always been recognized, but also for the increasing sophistication of Soviet tactical doctrine and reassessed the rosy view of German performance, so evident in the work of Liddell Hart, largely shaped by the self-serving memoirs and testimony of German officers. Willmott, for example, directly challenged "the popularly accepted, but pernicious, myth of German military excellence" (xi) and stated that in 1944 "the Wehrmacht was outfought at every level" (365). While Hitler undoubtedly had major weaknesses as a war leader, the best of the recent general histories emphatically argue that he was not the only reason the Germans lost on the Eastern front.

Part of Allied politics during the war and a subject of controversy ever since, the debates over the Second Front and the strategic choices made between the Mediterranean and Western European theaters are central to most of the general histories of the war. As one critically involved in the key strategic decisions of the war, Churchill was deeply embroiled in this controversy. On one hand, he was eager to assert his commitment to the Second Front in France and accuse his critics of misrepresenting his position. He wrote, "The following message . . . should incidentally, but I trust finally, dispose of the many American legends that I was inveterately hostile to the plan for a large-scale Channel crossing in 1943, and still more of the post-war Soviet assertions that I used the operation 'Torch' with the deliberate intention of preventing 'a Second Front in 1943' " (volume 4, 651; also volume 3, 379–80; volume 5, 128–29, 344, 582). On the other hand, Churchill continuously promoted the value of other strategic initiatives—the proposed invasions of Norway (volume 4, 322–25, 447–48) and Rhodes in the eastern Mediterranean to bring Turkey into the war (volume 5, 203–25, 344), as well as the actual invasions of North Africa, Sicily, and Italy (volume 4, 447–48, 650–51; volume 5, 154)—and emphasized the dangers of a cross-Channel invasion (volume 3, 379–80, 660–61). While he implied that these initiatives need not have jeopardized the invasion of France, in reality action in North Africa made Roundup impossible in 1943, and, if Churchill had prevailed, Overlord might not have occurred until 1945. Churchill was particularly frustrated that forces needed for the invasion of southern France (Anvil) were taken from Italy, where possibilities existed "of advancing through the Ljubljana Gap into Austria and Hungary and striking at the heart of Germany from another direction" (volume 6, 60–61).

Chester Wilmot, writing under the impress of Cold War conflicts and frustrations, shared Churchill's strategic fondness for Italy and the eastern Mediterranean, arguing that with the commitment to the cross-Channel invasion in 1944 "the Western powers had been diverted away from the area of Soviet aspirations" (142) and that the failure to exploit opportunities in the Mediterranean and the Balkans reflected the American inability to link military strategy to postwar political factors (714). With understated irony Gerhard Weinberg challenged this perspective:

The British were entirely correct in the belief that opportunities in Italy and in Southeast Europe were being sacrificed to the Americans' insistence on adherence to strategic priorities, though whether thld in the end have been that much happier if their troops had reached the Alps and the Western Powers had occupied Bulgaria while the Red Army liberated Belgium is at least open to question. (626)

If most analysts recognized that the Allies' Italian campaign tied down German divisions that otherwise could have been used against the Soviets or the Normandy landings, many shared Keegan's skepticism about the "soft underbelly" of Europe (319). In the end Willmott best articulated the underlying cause of this strategic debate:

[W]hat was at issue between the two allies was a fundamental difference of military philosophy. To the United States, wedded to a concept of war that stressed mass, firepower and shock action, the invasion of Europe was essential in order to meet and defeat the German army in the field; to Britain, a tradition shaped by maritime power and limited military resources decreed that the invasion should not be attempted until the enemy's defeat was assured. (197–98)

Many of the issues highlighted in the debate over the Second Front and Mediterranean are also reflected in the controversies over Allied strategic and political decisions that some historians claimed allowed the Soviet Union to dominate Central and Eastern Europe. Three specific issues are most relevant to this debate—unconditional surrender, the consequences of the Teheran and Yalta Conferences, and the virtues of the broad versus narrow front for the advance into Germany in 1944–1945.

Fuller laid down the gauntlet on unconditional surrender in 1948, asserting "that these two words were to hang like a putrefying albatross around the necks of America and Britain" and result in smashing the European balance of power so the Soviet Union could establish "an even more barbaric despotism" in place of Nazi tyranny (258–59). Though more restrained, Wilmot concurred and added that the Allied commitment to Overlord at the Teheran Conference ensured the extension of Soviet influence deep into Central Europe and the Balkans as well (142). For Liddell Hart the unconditional surrender demand unnecessarily prolonged the war and "proved of profit only to Stalin—by opening the way for Communist domination of central Europe" (volume 2, 713). In Wilmot's judgment the policy mistakes made in 1943 reached their logical and tragic culmination in the Yalta Conference, "Stalin's Greatest Victory" (628–59).

In contrast stood those historians who saw these critiques of Allied leaders and their decisions as ahistorical and misguided. From their perspective the argument against unconditional surrender was only "superficially plausible" (Willmott, 255). Rather than a major blunder, unconditional surrender logically grew out of total war and past historical experience and had little impact on the duration and outcome of the war. It may even have contributed positively to Allied unity (Calvocoressi and Wint, 398–99, 545; Michel, 424–25; Willmott, 255–56; Weinberg, 438–39). These historians articulated two primary counterpoints to the Wilmot thesis regarding Yalta. First, as Kitchen argued, "Yalta was one of the least important of the wartime conferences and it certainly does not deserve to be treated as Stalin's greatest victory over the gullible western leaders" (289; also Stokesbury, 180; Weinberg, 803). Second, battlefield realities dictated the extent of Soviet influence in Eastern and Central Europe, and the "United States yielded nothing that the Soviet Union did not already have or could take for herself without seeking American agreement" (Willmott, 447; also Snyder, 407–8; Michel, 677).

Consideration of battlefield realities points to the third of these linked issues, the debate over Allied strategy following the breakout from the Normandy beachhead. This debate was complicated by arguments over the respective merits of commanders. With Churchill demonstrating a diplomatic silence in this case, the running was again made by Fuller and Wilmot. Arguing that the mauling of the German army in France created the preconditions for ending the war in 1944, they blamed Eisenhower and the strategy of the broad front for the failure to exploit that opportunity. Had Eisenhower fully committed all available resources to either Montgomery or Bradley for a decisive and narrow thrust into Germany, the war would have ended in 1944 with profound consequences for the subsequent division of Europe (Fuller, 338–49; Wilmot, 468ff, 497, 614). But "either because he was a timid strategist or because he did not possess a strong enough personality to order one or the other of his Army Group Commanders to assume . . . a passive defence," Eisenhower rejected Montgomery's proposal and opted for the broad front policy (Fuller, 340).

Most contemporary historians, while acknowledging German vulnerability, suggest other reasons for failing to end the war in 1944. Liddell

Hart, Keegan, and Ellis emphasized that major logistical problems prevented the Allies from sustaining a rapid advance into Germany, even on a narrow front. Montgomery's "barely excusable" failure to clear the Scheldt estuary in early September 1944 perpetuated the logistical bottleneck, "the most calamitous flaw in the post-Normandy campaign" (Keegan, 437). Ellis charged, "Montgomery virtually forgot his actual mission, the opening up of Antwerp as a working port," and "began to indulge in renewed fantasies about hard-hitting mobile operations" (402). Willmott, finding the argument over the merits of individual commanders "sterile," identified the crux of the problem in another area: "[A]t no stage during the breakout from Normandy did the Allied High Command have a settled doctrine—in terms either of ensuring annihilation in the field or of advancing against geographical objectives of overwhelming strategic importance—to serve as the framework for the conduct of the *Overlord* campaign" (363). Consequently, the Western Allies missed opportunities to administer German forces even more decisive defeats.

If the postwar division of Europe was an underlying factor in the historiographical controversies just examined, questions of morality and military effectiveness and necessity have dominated the discussions of strategic bombing and the use of the atomic bomb. Fuller acknowledged the value of strategic bombing "directed against the sources of industrial and military energy and distribution" but vigorously condemned the "insensate bombing of cities and industrial centers" and its "Mongoloid destructiveness" (316–17). As a Victorian, Fuller believed that total war should not obliterate rules designed to preserve civilized behavior; as a military analyst, he judged the indiscriminate area bombing strategy of Churchill and Arthur "Bomber" Harris ineffective.

Fuller's moral critique has not been embraced by most subsequent writers. To be sure, Liddell Hart noted the strategic bombing campaign's "disregard for basic morality" (612), and Keegan concluded it was "certainly not fair play" (433), while Ellis was appalled at "the utter coarseness of soul that permitted, even compelled, Harris to persist with the most brutish offensive of a very brutal war" (221). More typically, this moral issue has become irrelevant in the face of the horrifying destructiveness of total war (Stokesbury, 287) or, in the case of Willmott, obviated by the reality of the Allied position: "[T]here existed in the war's middle years . . . no good moral consideration that would have justified the Allies denying themselves their only means of forcing Germany to respond to their initiative by a dissipation of battlefront strength and industrial effort" (277).

Like Fuller, most subsequent writers of general histories have recognized the problematic results achieved by strategic bombing. Even Churchill, a vigorous supporter of the Harris strategy, recognized that its zealous advocates claimed far more than could be delivered (volume 3,

507–8; volume 4, 552–53). Unlike Fuller, some have granted that strategic bombing, despite its failure to crack German civilian morale and other limitations, played a "vital part" in winning the war (Liddell Hart, 612; also Wright, 182; Michel, 550–51). Again, as on many other questions, Willmott's position intrigues. He argued, "Despite an obvious interdependence of efforts and air power's contribution to its own success in terms of the Americans' winning command of the air, Germany's naval and military defeat opened her to defeat in the strategic bombing offensive, not the other way around" (275).

As the war's ultimate weapon of indiscriminate destruction, the atomic bomb and its use have engaged historians in particularly heated and difficult issues. Cyril Falls addressed those issues in a thoughtful and dispassionate manner in 1948. He argued that while "there can be no shadow of doubt that Japan was utterly and hopelessly defeated before the dropping of the first atomic bomb . . . [and] was already making peace feelers," Japan was apparently prepared to use "the fanaticism of her troops and their power to inflict enormous casualties upon the Americans, before yielding" (280–81). While a demonstration of the bomb in an isolated area or the use of conventional bombing might have ended the war short of invasion, the Americans were "not absolutely sure of this" (283). Thus, they used the atomic bomb to end the war quickly and "save the lives of thousands" of their men (281).

For Fuller, however, this argument was specious: "Though to save life is laudable, it in no way justifies the employment of means which run counter to every precept of humanity and the customs of war" (392). Further, according to Fuller, Truman and Churchill could have ended the war in June if they had dropped the demand for unconditional surrender. Churchill, of course, disagreed and provided additional weight for the bomb's use when he asserted that fanatic Japanese resistance might well have cost "the loss of a million American lives and half that number of British" (volume 6, 638). For the Western Allies, the successful test of the bomb meant that "all this nightmare picture had vanished. . . . Moreover, we should not need the Russians" (volume 6, 638–39). Churchill's extreme casualty figures not only became part of the popular mythology of why the bomb was dropped but also found their way into some of the general histories. Even in his 1995 study of the Pacific war, Gailey repeats the million casualty figure (475).

In the years since these initial clashes, those accepting the decision to use the bomb have reiterated Falls' argument, though often providing greater insight into the role of the bombs in tipping the decision to end the war in favor of the Japanese government's peace faction. They also have stressed that while the atomic bomb was a horrifying weapon, the firebombing of Japanese cities was tremendously destructive of life and property and have suggested historians need to place themselves in the context of a total war and the tremendous momentum built up in the Manhattan project that created a strong presumption that the bomb would be used (Michel, 769–77; Spector, 540–59; Keegan, 576–78, 584–85; Weinberg, 885–91).

Fuller's moral critique has not been the standard position of those opposed to the use of the bomb, but they have agreed with his point that Japan had been defeated prior to its use. As Costello noted in 1981, "Astonishing new evidence . . . [reveals] the extent to which Allied war leaders were privy to Japan's desperate military plight in the summer of 1945. Inevitably this new intelligence must raise fresh doubts about the decision to drop the two atomic bombs" (vii). Critics have also cited the naval and air force leaders who believed the war could be won with conventional airpower and sea power, rendering both the bomb and invasion unnecessary, especially since the Soviet entrance into war would constitute another shock to the Japanese (Liddell Hart, 696–97; Ellis, 517). If the bomb was not really necessary to defeat Japan, then why was it used? While racism, revenge, and cost of the Manhattan project have been advanced as answers, the most frequent assertions concern the American desire to limit Soviet gains in East Asia and to strengthen America's hand in future diplomatic conflicts with the USSR (Liddell Hart, 697–98; Leckie, 944–45; Willmott, 466). If most writers of general histories believe that the bomb was necessary to move the Japanese government to accept defeat, the controversies over this issue, as others, are likely to defy resolution.

In numerous volumes generated over the course of fifty years, the writers of the general histories of the Second World War have not only provided clear, readable, concise overviews of military strategy and operations and often of other critical elements of total war but also applied their intelligence and knowledge to many of the controversies of the war. The general histories, especially of the short history variety, do not readily lend themselves to this, and some emphasize descriptive narrative, but the best of these works both engage and even shape the historiographical debates, enriching our understanding through adept synthesis and original insights. The general histories, foot soldiers in the battle to understand this century's most compelling global conflict, perform an essential, if unglamorous, function.

BIBLIOGRAPHY

Arnold-Forster, Mark. *The World at War.* New York: New American Library, 1973.

Bateson, Charles. *The War with Japan: A Concise History.* East Lansing: Michigan State UP, 1968.

Calvocoressi, Peter, and Guy Wint. *Total War: The Story of World War II.* New York: Pantheon, 1972.

Calvocoressi, Peter, Guy Wint, and John Pritchard. *Total War: Causes and Course of the Second World War.* 2d ed. 2 vols. New York: Pantheon; London: Viking, 1989.

Churchill, Winston S. *The Second World War: The Gathering Storm.* Vol. 1. Boston: Houghton Mifflin, 1948.

———. *The Second World War: Their Finest Hour.* Vol. 2. Boston: Houghton Mifflin, 1949.

———. *The Second World War: The Grand Alliance.* Vol. 3. Boston: Houghton Mifflin, 1950.

———. *The Second World War: The Hinge of Fate.* Vol. 4. Boston: Houghton Mifflin, 1950.

———. *The Second World War: Closing the Ring.* Vol. 5. Boston: Houghton Mifflin, 1951.

———. *The Second World War: Triumph and Tragedy.* Vol. 6. Boston: Houghton Mifflin, 1953.

Collier, Basil. *The Second World War: A Military History.* New York: Morrow, 1967.

———. *The War in the Far East.* New York: Morrow, 1969.

Costello, John. *The Pacific War, 1941–1945.* New York: Quill, 1981.

Deighton, Len. *Blood, Tears, and Folly: An Objective Look at World War II.* New York: HarperCollins, 1993.

Deist, Wilhelm, et al. *Germany and the Second World War.* Vol. 1, *The Build-up of German Aggression.* Vol. 2, *Germany's Initial Conquests in Europe.* Vol. 3, *The Mediterranean, South-East Europe and North Africa, 1939–1941: From Italy's Declaration of Non-Belligerence to the Entry of the United States into the War.* Trans. P. S. Falla et al. Oxford and New York: Clarendon Press, 1990–1995.

Dziewanowski, M. K. *War at Any Price: World War II in Europe, 1939–45.* Englewood Cliffs, NJ: Prentice-Hall, 1987, 1991.

Ellis, John. *Brute Force: Allied Strategy and Tactics in the Second World War.* New York: Viking Penguin, 1990.

Falls, Cyril. *The Second World War: A Short History.* London: Methuen, 1948.

Fuller, J.F.C. *The Second World War, 1939–45: A Strategical and Tactical History.* New York: Meredith Press, 1948.

Gailey, Harry A. *The War in the Pacific: From Pearl Harbor to Tokyo Bay.* Novato, CA: Presidio Press, 1995.

Gilbert, Martin. *The Second World War: A Complete History.* London: Weidenfeld and Micolson; New York: Henry Holt, 1989.

Higham, Robin, ed. *Official Histories: Essays and Bibliographies from around the World.* Manhattan: Kansas State University Library, 1970; 2d ed. forthcoming.

Howard, Michael. "Military History as a University Study." *History 41* (1956): 184–91.

Howe, Quincy. *Ashes of Victory: World War II and Its Aftermath.* New York: Simon and Schuster, 1972.

Hoyle, Martha Byrd. *A World in Flames: A History of World War II.* New York: Atheneum, 1970.

Ienaga, Saburo. *The Pacific War, 1931–1945.* New York: Random House, 1978.

Keegan, John. *The Second World War.* London: Hutchison, 1989; New York: Penguin, 1990.

Kitchen, Martin. *A World in Flames: A Short History of the Second World War in Europe and Asia, 1939–1945.* London and New York: Longman, 1990.

Leckie, Robert. *Delivered from Evil: The Saga of World War II*. New York: Harper and Row, 1987.

Lee, Loyd E. *The War Years: A Global History of the Second World War*. New York: Unwin Hyman, 1989.

Liddell Hart, Basil. *History of the Second World War*. London: Cassell, 1970; New York: Putnam, 1971; Perigree, 1982; and London: Papermac, 1992.

———. *The Other Side of the Hill*. London: Cassell, 1951. Revised and enlarged edition of *The German Generals Talk*. New York: Morrow, 1948.

Lyons, Michael J. *World War II: A Short History*. Englewood Cliffs, NJ: Prentice-Hall, 1989, 1994.

Michel, Henri. *The Second World War*. Trans. Douglas Parmee. New York: Praeger, 1975.

O'Neill, William L. *A Democracy at War: America's Fight at Home and Abroad in World War II*. New York: Free Press, 1993.

Overy, Richard. *Why the Allies Won*. New York and London: W. W. Norton, 1996.

Parker, R.A.C. *Struggle for Survival: The History of the Second World War*. Oxford: Oxford UP, 1989.

Showalter, Dennis. "A Modest Plea for Drums and Trumpets." *Military Affairs 39* (1975): 71–74.

Snyder, Louis L. *The War: A Concise History, 1939–1945*. New York: Julian Messner, 1960.

Spector, Ronald H. *The Eagle against the Sun*. New York: Free Press, 1985.

Stokesbury, James L. *A Short History of World War II*. New York: Morrow, 1980.

Toland, John. *The Rising Sun: The Decline and Fall of the Japanese Empire*. New York: Random House, 1970.

Weinberg, Gerhard. *A World at Arms: A Global History of World War II*. Cambridge: Cambridge UP, 1994.

Willmott, H. P. *The Great Crusade: A New Complete History of the Second World War*. New York: Free Press, 1989.

Wilmot, Chester. *The Struggle for Europe*. New York: Harper and Row, 1952.

Wright, Gordon. *The Ordeal of Total War, 1939–1945*. New York: Harper and Row, 1968.

Young, Peter. *A Short History of World War II, 1939–1945*. New York: Thomas Crowell, 1966.

2 The Origins of the War in Europe

Robert J. Caputi

On the autumn afternoon of October 19, 1781, Major General Benjamin Lincoln of the American Continental armies accepted the sword and surrender of the British garrison at Yorktown, Virginia, bringing to a close the successful colonial rebellion from the yoke of British rule. General Lord Charles Cornwallis, the ranking British commander, was absent, too distraught to attend the brief ceremony. A British band played a mournful tune, aptly titled "The World Turned Upside Down."

Almost two centuries later in a small schoolhouse in Reims, France, General Alfred Jodl, representative of the irrevocably shattered Thousand-Year Reich, affixed his signature to the unconditional surrender of all German armies in the West. Like Cornwallis, General Dwight Eisenhower, supreme commander, Allied Expeditionary Force, refused to attend the surrender, his hatred for Nazism having been well stoked by German atrocities at Malmédy, to say nothing of the recently liberated death camps. The dramatic, heartrending difference in May 1945 was that the entire world was truly turned upside down. Europe, which had dominated the world's history for centuries, would presently be shunted to the background. The Cold War, fueled largely by Stalinist megalomania on one side and American hysteria on the other, would divide the globe for the next half century.

The first half of the twentieth century represented the swan song of Europe's great power status. Those who so spectacularly gathered at King Edward's wake in 1910 believed with certainty that the European progress and stability that had spawned such glorious empires would continue, if not *ad infinitum*, at least for the next century. Few could or would foresee the undiluted years of calamity, the destruction of once-proud imperial families, the brutal regimes of fascist, Nazi, and communist extremism. The squalor of trench warfare that slaughtered not only many of Europe's best and brightest young men but also the mirage of liberal democratic government would be no more than a ghastly hors d'oeuvre to the bloody feast served up to Europeans, soldier and civilian alike, in the war of 1939–1945. The following details some of the most significant works of the last fifty years on the historiography of the origins of that war in Europe.

One of the four volumes of Winston Churchill's grandiloquent assessment of the Great War, *The World Crisis*, was entitled *The Stricken World*. For an author as wedded to historical romanticism and hyperbole as Churchill, his volume title could not have been more apt. Nearly thirteen million of Europe's sons perished on those soaked battlefields, with an innumerable remainder injured or lost. Four years of carnage cost Europe three of its greatest imperial entities. Romanov Russia, Germany, and the old Habsburg Empire had succumbed to the exertions of world war, with all its concomitant suffering. This, then, in another Churchillian phrase, was the charnel house that was Europe in early 1919. Ironically, a theme that many historians have ignored is that in the decade following the Versailles settlement, Europeans actually succeeded in binding up a great many of the continent's wounds.

The Locarno treaties, although fragile, were an important milestone on the way to international cooperation. The Kellogg Briand accord of 1928 evidenced the clear antiwar sentiment of most Europeans. The Dawes and Young financial plans were creative and enlightened alternatives to the futile and endless cycle of reparations. The resilience of the human spirit is an awesome thing, and after the biblical slaughter of the Great War, it miraculously appeared that in the late 1920s Europe might be settling into a peaceful and prosperous recovery. True, Russia had succumbed to the Bolshevik incubus, but with Lenin's early death it had severe internal problems after its own horrific civil war and could not directly threaten Europe's security. Italy became fascist in 1922, but many admired Mussolini's authoritarian hand as a bulwark against communist subversion. Germany's Weimar Republic, so dependent on American largesse, was led by as able and noble a statesman as Germany would see in this century, Gustav Stresemann. This pacific interlude, however, would be sadly short-lived. D. C. Watt, in *How War Came*, described this calm before the cruelest of storms when he alluded to the late 1920s: "Outwardly, Europe presented a view of peace, tranquillity and prosperity. But behind the facade, lurked the rats, ready, given half a chance, to kill and destroy, to remake the chaos and anarchy, the comradeship, dedication and adventure of war" (14).

ECONOMIC INTERPRETATIONS

Indeed, the sine qua non of the Second World War, without which it never would have occurred, was the Great Depression. A dark and troubling irony, for the United States at least, was that while it took the horror of the depression to bring on a European war, the European war and America's role as the great "arsenal of democracy" finally lifted the economic scourge from American shores. Deficit spending had at its heart governmental intervention and "priming the pump" to get the nation's economy going. Oddly enough, regimes as ideologically disparate as Nazi Germany and the United States employed massive public works programs and deficit spending in the 1930s, although one lusted for war and conquest, while the other remained staunchly isolationist.

John Maynard Keynes had initially gained fame with his withering critique of the Versailles Treaty, *The Economic Consequences of the Peace*. Published in 1920, it became a bible for those whose guilt over the way a defeated Germany had been humiliated led them to pursue treaty revisions. Keynes advocated a drastic reduction of the German war reparations and realized that what the German people needed were food, shelter, and hope for a better life, not open-ended revenge. He, unlike many others, could grasp the idea that if Germany were peaceful and prosperous, she would be no danger to the rest of Europe, and the Nazi Party would later have remained where it belonged, on the lunatic fringe of European politics. Keynes' work remains seminal to the understanding of the interwar years.

An appraisal that detailed many of the contributory reasons for the international economic collapse is Kindleberger's *The World in Depression*. He explained the need for the international economic and monetary system, during difficult periods, to have a world power to underwrite the world community, maintain a proper flow of investment capital, and take on bad debts. Britain had often performed this role through 1913; the particular virulence of the Great Depression stemmed partly from the lack of leadership of one dominant national state. In 1929, 1930, and 1931 Britain could not act as a stabilizer, and the United States would not. When every country turned to protect its national private interest, the world public interest went down the drain, and with it the private interests of all. The lack of leadership among the liberal states of the West fed the political extremism of regimes that eventually provoked war. One of the finest works on European economic diplomacy in the decade leading to the outbreak of war is Kaiser, *Economic Diplomacy and the Origins of the Second World War*. Kaiser discussed at length the great European powers and their rivalry in the economic expansion of Central and Eastern Europe. As early as 1914 he detailed the German plan for dominance of Central Europe *Mitteleuropa*. With the Russian collapse of 1917–1918, it seemed as if the dream would come to fruition as Germany seized Romania and Ukraine. However, as Kaiser noted, the sudden collapse of the German armies in late 1918 led this desideratum to be foiled with the Allied and associated victory. It was revived some twenty years later with the relentless Nazi quest for Lebensraum. Kaiser concluded that because the Western powers failed to defend the status quo in Eastern Europe, many of the weaker nations were forced into economic dependence on Nazi Germany, especially after the betrayal of the Czechs by their British and French allies at Munich. He reasoned that the democracies would pay heavily for these mistakes in judgment, and that they did, in a ruinous six-year war.

Carr addressed the Nazi drive for economic self-sufficiency in his *Arms, Autarky, and Aggression.* He noted that the idea of *Mitteleuropa* was updated by the Nazis into a new vision, the *Grossraumwirtschaft.* This economic order, stretching from the Atlantic to the Urals, was to be controlled by Germans who would take by force what they needed to sustain and increase their numbers (20). The frightening aspect of this concept was that it came to pass with the German conquest of Europe in 1940 and 1941, from the Atlantic to nearly the Urals, and indeed stripped the continent bare of a good portion of its resources. Carr detailed an August 1939 visit by Carl Burckhardt, the League of Nations commissioner for Danzig to Hitler, in the last few days of peace. The meeting revealed the tyrant's true motives and is expressly illustrative of his lust for economic autarky and Lebensraum in the East. As Burckhardt later quoted Hitler: "Everything that I have in mind is directed against Russia; if the west is too stupid and too blind to grasp this then I will be forced to come to terms with the Russians, to smash the west and after its defeat to turn against Russia with all my forces. I need the Ukraine so that we can't be starved out as in the last war" (116).

This economic orientation of cause and effect is compelling as a rationale for a military offensive, as in the German strike against Norway in April 1940 because British efforts to mine Scandinavian ports would have resulted in disruption of critical exports of Swedish iron ore to Germany. Carr later stated in *Poland to Pearl Harbor* that because of economic considerations, the real "point of no return . . . after which the Third Reich was irretrievably committed to war . . . occurred in the 18 months between the summer of 1936 and the spring of 1938" (37). The fact that Germany's rivals had begun rearmament, however halting, made the Nazi preparations for war a self-fulfilling prophecy in the late 1930s.

ADVOCATES OF APPEASEMENT

No individual among Europe's interwar leaders was more cognizant of the fragility of Britain's economic infrastructure than Neville Chamberlain. Elected to Parliament in 1918 at forty-nine, he rose rapidly into important cabinet positions, spent several years at the Ministry of Health, and was chancellor of the exchequer from 1931 to 1937. Chamberlain realized early on that the supreme exertions of the First World War had weakened the foundations of British power more than most Britons could or would imagine. As the chief of British finance for the six years before he became prime minister, he strongly advocated lessening the number of Britain's potential enemies. The commitments of empire were much too widespread for its dwindling resources, and it could not possibly envision fighting Germany, Italy, and Japan at the same time.

Chamberlain's two-pronged plan for European pacification included slow but steady retooling of Britain's overall defensive capabilities, with an overriding priority given to the Royal Air Force in construction of both fighters and bombers. The second part was a campaign to lessen the diplomatic tension in European affairs, a redress of all legitimate grievances that was known as appeasement. Reynolds, in *The Creation of the Anglo-American Alliance*, argued persuasively regarding appeasement:

Contrary to popular mythology, Chamberlain did not envisage piecemeal concessions to buy off the dictators, but comprehensive and durable settlements of all outstanding grievances on both sides. Munich was therefore a desperate aberration from appeasement rather than its culmination. He also insisted that rearmament was the indispensable counterpart to conciliation—stronger defences would deter war while diplomacy removed its causes. (8)

The ubiquitous financial concerns would obligate a slower rate of rearmament than was necessary to overawe the belligerent dictator states. Rock, in *Chamberlain and Roosevelt*, stressed that the British leaders, especially Chamberlain, were less than receptive to the idea of American meddling in European affairs. He cited Franklin Roosevelt's diplomatic initiative of January 1938, ostensibly to lessen European tension, and Chamberlain's brusque rejoinder:

He (Chamberlain) may not have been anti-American, but his attitude towards Americans generally, and Roosevelt in particular, was condescending and arrogant. Inclined to judge plans in the short run, . . . he did not appear to look beyond the Roosevelt plan itself (which might well have failed) to salutary consequences that might have sprung from it even in failure. (71)

However, Harrison, in "The United States and Great Britain," noted that American support was chimerical, more illusion than reality in a still stridently isolationist public opinion, though Roosevelt hoped for joint Anglo-American resistance to the German threat. Even sympathetic historians have tended to agree that Great Britain could not look across the Atlantic for meaningful support in confronting the expansionism of Germany, Italy, and Japan before World War II. To the extent that appeasement was a policy arising from the absence of alternatives, therefore, the behavior of the United States helped justify it.

Chamberlain eventually came to grief in his failed attempt to avoid another world war, a cataclysm that he knew would surely remove Britain from the ranks of the world's Great Powers. A work that should always be consulted for any real understanding of his turbulent years as Britain's leader is the initial biography, completed just four years after his death in November 1940, Keith Feiling's *The Life of Neville Chamberlain.* Fifty years later it remains of great consequence. Feiling utilized the private letters that Chamberlain wrote to his two spinster sisters every other week, respectively, for as long as he held influence in British politics, covering a quarter of a century. One of Feiling's main themes was that Chamberlain had so devoted himself to appeasement that he believed he could indeed come to a permanent peaceful accord by pacifying Germany; simultaneously, the Nazis thought only in terms of war and conquest. Once again, the most noble and virtuous of hopes turned out to be the worst possible policy in the face of systematic aggression.

The reality is that Chamberlain and his personal reputation have taken a brutal beating over the dismal failure of appeasement. Had the Nazis been rational men, and had a European war been avoided by peaceful conciliation and an honorable redress of grievances, Chamberlain's legacy would doubtless be an honored one in British history. Instead, he has been subject to the most vile of calumnies simply because his policies for European pacification ended in failure, and that failure led directly to Britain's entry into the European war in September 1939.

A source voicing the disillusion of the British public in the wake of the military disasters of 1940 was *Guilty Men.* Written by CATO, a pseudonym for a group of young journalists including future Labour Party leader Michael Foot, it accused Chamberlain's administration of "negligence and cowardice nearly tantamount to treason" and offered a long and detailed indictment of its wrongdoings in the face of the Nazi threat. Examples of other attacks upon appeasement in 1938 and 1939 were Rathbone's *War Can Be Averted,* Macgregor's *Truth and Mr. Chamberlain,* Seton-Watson's *From Munich to Danzig,* and Angell's *For What Do We Fight?* Many of the preceding recommended that some type of collective security arrangement ought to be constructed by Britain and its allies to combat the palpable danger of a Nazi-dominated Europe.

Conversely, notable publications from 1938 to 1940 supporting Chamberlain's appeasement of the dictator states included Walker-Smith's *Neville Chamberlain,* Hodgson's *The Man Who Made the Peace,* noted Nazi sympathizer Lord Londonderry's *Ourselves and Germany,* and Edward Carr's *Britain: A Study of Foreign Policy.* The Hodgson and Walker-Smith accounts credited Chamberlain for doing everything humanly possible to avoid war, a war that would doubtless spell the end of the empire and great power status for Britain. Carr based his reasoning on the relative weakness of Britain's military strength vis-à-vis that of the Germans. Carr believed that all policy ultimately entailed some element of risk of war, and the prudent statesman, in this case Chamberlain, "must balance the chances, and not pursue a policy which is likely to expose his country to war against equal or superior odds" (17). Carr concluded by insisting that Britain would fight in 1939 just as it fought in 1588 against the Armada, at Blenheim against Louis XIV, or at Waterloo against Napoleon, to keep the independent nations of Europe free from the domination of a single overwhelming power.

The failure of appeasement and Britain's entry into the six-year maelstrom of world war led Chamberlain's reputation to be savaged in the postwar historical reassessment of those perilous years. Among the accounts in support of Chamberlain were those whose authors had held positions in his three-year administration. The most cogent and persuasive of those was Viscount Templewood's (a.k.a. Samuel Hoare) *Nine Troubled Years*. Templewood insisted that appeasement had gained its negative stigma from its failure only because of German treachery and bloodlust and that Chamberlain's motives had been indisputably honorable throughout. Furthermore, he argued that British public opinion was solidly behind Neville Chamberlain's policies, as no one save the Nazis wanted war.

In conclusion, Templewood crafted a strong defense of his chief in the aftermath of the world's most apocalyptic struggle.

The devastation, political, material, and moral, that followed the failure of his crusade for peace does not prove that his policy was wrong, but rather that in the face of a world war it was right and necessary to try out every possible expedient for saving humanity from so terrible a catastrophe. (388)

Other accounts that strongly supported a very unpopular legacy in the wake of appeasement's failure were *Retrospect: The Memoirs of Sir John Simon*, written by Chamberlain's longtime ally and chancellor of the exchequer, and Viscount Maugham's *The Truth about the Munich Crisis*, which defended the sacrifice of Czechoslovakia as the lesser of two evils, the greater being war. A final source worthy of perusal is Foreign Secretary Halifax's *Fulness of Days*. Halifax admitted that the sacrifice of the Czechoslovak state was a "wretched but necessary business" and insisted that those who criticized the Munich agreement were flogging a dead horse; that opprobrium should be equally shared by all parties for the failure to stop the German march to war at the time of the reoccupation of the Rhineland in March 1936. He credited Neville Chamberlain for allowing the country and Commonwealth to be united as one in their righteous might when war finally did come.

CHURCHILL AND THE GUILTY MEN GENRE

Perhaps the most celebrated account of the origins of the Second World War came from the pen of one of the figures who helped most to ensure the Allied victory, Winston S. Churchill. The initial volume of his six-volume *History of the Second World War* was published in 1948, *The Gathering Storm.* Although essentially an outsider's view, Churchill's having suffered as a political pariah during his fabled wilderness years, it was widely accepted by the general public as an insider version of the actual events, doubtless due to the author's role as a national icon in the postwar years.

Churchill pontificated at length on the untold chances to forestall the cataclysm that were discarded by the West, when resolute action by Britain would almost certainly have stopped the dictator states in their tracks. Churchill referred to the Armageddon as the unnecessary war and severely castigated Chamberlain's decisions both to eschew American assistance in January 1938 and later to offer a blanket British guarantee to Poland after the Czechs had been abandoned to Nazi terror just six months before. Reflecting on the events that led to September 1939 and the outbreak of war with Germany, Churchill wrote, "[T]hat we should all have come to this pass makes those responsible, however honourable their motives, blameworthy before history" (346).

The hoary cliché that "history is written by the victors" is indeed central to Churchill's remembrances of the prewar years. The subtle inference that those who stood up to the folly of Chamberlain's leadership were alone prescient and patriotic is belied by the cold reality of Chamberlain's overwhelming personal and political popularity in 1938 and 1939. A postwar effort to settle accounts by one who had been cruelly ostracized during the interwar period is then understandable, even though hindsight often affords a convenient platform for criticism, and heroic conduct is in the eye of the beholder. Nevertheless, Churchill's contribution to the historiography of the war's origins carried a formidable weight and dramatically influenced not only his contemporaries but untold multitudes of future scholars and would do so until the beginnings of historical reassessment in the 1960s.

The fifteen years immediately after the war's end spurred a river of scholarship on the war's origins, which was dominated initially by a cadre of academic historians steeped in the postwar zeitgeist of the "guilty men" perspective. This rather simplistic view, with its Manichaean portrayal of good and evil, high moral tone, and lack of ambiguity, dovetailed well in the postwar West with an anticommunist fervor fueled by the Soviet subjugation of Eastern Europe and the "loss" of mainland China to communism. As the reasoning went, the West could dare not submit to any more "Munichs" lest appeasement of communist power start the world once again on the road to war. Incidentally, this specious analysis would be weighed in the balance and found wanting in the half century of post-war peace, from Korea to Suez, from Vietnam to the Persian Gulf.

Lewis Namier crafted a three-volume account of Britain's interwar diplomacy, *Diplomatic Prelude, Europe in Decay*, and *In the Nazi Era*. Utilizing captured German diplomatic documents and the Nuremberg trial to buttress his arguments, his strongly anti-German tone and staunch condemnation of Chamberlain's appeasers surely led his work to be more of an emotional than an empirical nature. In *Diplomatic Prelude*, Namier characterized the Munich agreement as nothing but a sham, a dark day in Britain's glorious history. Here is a sample of his prose referring to the Anglo-French guarantee of the rump of the Czech state after its summary emasculation at Munich: "Paper guarantees, feelingly accorded to the despoiled, merely add a sickening, humiliating touch, which no one who has been through such transactions can ever forget" (36). Namier concluded by offering that although Chamberlain would long continue to insist that what he had done at Munich was right and proper, the sad truth was that the "agonies of Czechoslovakia were the death rattle of appeasement as the guiding principle of British policy" (58–59).

Medlicott looms as another figure who occupied an important position in the discussion over war origins. In contrast to Namier, Medlicott employed a more dispassionate view of the failures of Chamberlain's policy. In *British Foreign Policy since Versailles*, he noted that in regard to the handling of the Nazi regime by the West, "neither a policy of unqualified concession nor one of unqualified resistance by foreign powers after 1933 would have removed the Nazi question from European politics" (220). The crucial arbiter remained the very efficacy of appeasement itself as a policy; that is, was it fundamentally viable, and had it any chance for success? It was difficult to envision, he stressed, how a different British policy during 1938 and 1939 could have secured peace on honorable terms. Medlicott concluded, after having carefully sifted through the existing evidence, that there indeed were few alternatives to appeasement save war or total capitulation to German demands.

A work that set the standard for scholarship of the Czech crisis of autumn 1938 is Wheeler-Bennett's *Munich: Prologue to Tragedy*. It appeared in print the same year, 1948, as Churchill's *Gathering Storm*, and both relentlessly condemned appeasement as a policy. Of Chamberlain's triumphant return from the partitioning of the Czech state at Munich, Wheeler-Bennett opined, "Had the British people been made aware that what Mr. Chamberlain had, in effect, brought back from Munich was not peace but a breathing space before war, the lamentable state of unpreparedness in 1939 and 1940 might have been repaired" (293). Indeed, of all of the errors listed on the general historical indictment of Neville Chamberlain, one of the most egregious was his continued and unalterable belief in appeasement's efficacy, well after any objective opinion would have ruled it shattered by Nazi perfidy. Wheeler-Bennett clearly evidenced to his readers the shame that emanated from Britain's weakness, a weakness that led it to sacrifice a smaller power to slavery.

A. L. Rowse was an Oxford academic and Labour candidate for Parliament in the 1930s whose work was a dramatic example of the tenacity of the "guilty men" genre of scholarship. His *Appeasement* was written in 1961, long after many of the works we have reviewed and at the beginning of the decade that witnessed profound alterations in the historical debate over the war's origins. Rowse detailed the usual litany of sins committed by the craven appeasers led by Chamberlain, the same charges that had been pending for nearly a quarter century by 1961. On appeasement, he stressed that it was "this spineless concessionism, when faced with blackmailers and murderers, that brought on the war . . . what is difficult to understand was why so many people did not, and would not, see it at the time" (65–66). Rowse concluded that the bitterly ironic legacy of the "men of Munich" was that while they allowed Nazi Germany to achieve a European dominance that was shattered only by war, the upshot was that the Nazi defeat presaged Soviet hegemony over Central and Eastern Europe for the next several generations, a cruel backwash of the Munich betrayal.

TAYLOR'S REVISIONISM

The catalyst for change and, arguably, the most controversial work ever published in the field of war origins touched off a violent historical debate and sparked significant levels of discourse and scholarship, a good deal in rebuttal of its rather revolutionary themes. In his 1961 *Origins of the Second World War*, A.J.P. Taylor rebuked the orthodox version of the events leading to war and raised a true firestorm of protest with a provocative broadside that the policy of appeasement represented "a triumph for all that was best and most enlightened in British life" (189). He insisted that many "historians do a bad day's work when they write the appeasers off as stupid or as cowards," stressing that they were realists who had to deal with a perilous international situation, all the while attempting to avoid a second European civil war.

The main thrust of Taylor's thesis was that the war had not been premeditated, thrust upon the West by a Nazi Germany lusting for world domination, but a mistake, the result of diplomatic blunders on both sides. Hitler, far from being a psychopathic demon, was simply an opportunistic statesman operating in the realm of a Bismarck or Metternich, always ready to exploit the weaknesses of external adversaries while at the same time gladly accepting bloodless diplomatic triumphs. In Taylor's words, "[I]n international affairs, there was nothing wrong with Hitler except that he was German," that he was "only the ordinary German writ large" (293). These inflammatory statements flew directly in the faces of those who espoused the long-held orthodox views of a war forced on the West by a systematic campaign of German aggression, from the reoccupation of the Rhineland to the *Anschluss*, from the seizure of Bohemia and Moravia to the undeclared invasion of Poland.

The orthodox view, initially voiced at the Nuremberg trials and then subsequently by Churchill, was that there existed a palpable German blueprint for aggression that would come to full fruition only with world conquest. Taylor debunked this thesis, portraying the Nazi leader as a passive figure who reacted to events and had no overriding master plan. Perhaps the most overtly infuriating aspect of Taylor's scholarship for orthodox historians was his belief that the Western Allies deserved some of the blame for the outbreak of the cataclysm. The impact of peaceful revision of grievances that had been appeasement's raison d'être had been "put forward as the way of avoiding war; yet it could be achieved only by methods which brought war nearer" (243–44). Because of their relative unreadiness for war, Chamberlain and his allies were obligated to shoulder at least partial blame for their diplomatic blunders that aided and abetted the conflagration. Taylor's contribution to the historiography, while indisputably flawed, was a watershed effort that rejuvenated the scholarly debate over the war's origins and thus in the long run was more positive than negative.

Surely a landmark work of revisionism like Taylor's *Origins* could not have long trodden in the no-man's land of scholarly criticism without the heavy artillery of the orthodox academic establishment crashing down hard about it. It had indeed cut the orthodox school to the quick, and response was dramatic. One of the more savage and immediate rejoinders was from Trevor-Roper, who demolished the Taylor thesis in "A.J.P. Taylor, Hitler, and the War." Trevor-Roper labeled the Taylor effort "utterly erroneous" and added that it would do "perhaps irreparable harm to Taylor's reputation as a serious historian" (95). Other efforts that served to reinforce the orthodox view and thereby opposed Taylor were *The Appeasers*, written by two of Taylor's former students, Gilbert and Gott, and a best-selling work from a nonacademic source, Shirer's *The Rise and Fall of the Third Reich*. Written by the longtime CBS journalist and colleague of the legendary Edward R. Murrow, Shirer's work was essentially an eyewitness account of his lengthy prewar European assignment. Its phenomenal popularity with the general public, in spite of scholarly criticism, was a testament to the durability of the orthodox perspective of the war's origins. It was contrary, root and branch, to Taylor's grand design and was absent in his bibliography.

Alan Bullock, who had supported the orthodox view of Nazi excesses that led to war in 1952's *Hitler: A Study in Tyranny*, continued to do so with his 1967 rejoinder to Taylor, *Hitler and the Origins of the Second World*

War, and would finally place the Nazi dictator in proper company with his cruel Soviet alter ego in the popular and scholarly *Hitler and Stalin*. D. C. Watt called for a scholarly reassessment of Chamberlain's appeasement policies in his watershed "Appeasement: The Rise of a Revisionist School?"

A number of edited anthologies responded to the Taylor thesis. Robertson, who had distinguished himself with the excellent *Hitler's Pre-War Policy and Military Plans*, edited a collection of essays a decade after Taylor's bombshell, aptly titled, doubtless out of respect for the original, *Origins of the Second World War*. Another collection was edited by Louis and titled *The Origins of the Second World War: A.J.P. Taylor and His Critics*. One of the more recent and perhaps the greatest testimony to Taylor's continued influence in the historiographic debate was edited by Martel, *The A.J.P. Taylor Debate after Twenty-Five Years*. That Taylor's arguably flawed but indubitably brilliant work should still be debated nearly thirty years after its release is reflective of its worth. Further progress on these issues necessarily awaited the opening of materials in the British archives in the 1970s and the full publication of the original, uncensored text of Woodward's official *British Foreign Policy in the Second World War*.

A journal article brilliantly summarizing the controversy over Taylor's work was Smallwood's "A Historical Debate of the 1960s." Smallwood reflected on the near immediacy of the postwar consensus reached by many Western European as well as American historians regarding the war's origins, that Hitler's long-term aims included not only European hegemony but eventual world domination and that he was aided and abetted by the endless vacillations of the Western democracies, particularly Britain. Smallwood referred to Seton-Watson's *From Munich to Danzig*, Namier's *Diplomatic Prelude*, and Wheeler-Bennett's *Munich*, along with Wiskemann's *Czechs and Germans* and *Prologue to War* and Arendt's *The Origins of Totalitarianism*, as representative of the orthodox view in the immediate wake of the war's end.

Smallwood also commented on some of the more notable works from the more recent past that were antithetical to Taylor's thesis. German historian Hildebrand's *The Foreign Policy of the Third Reich* blamed Nazi aggression for the war and added that Hitler's plans of conquest were not only European but also global in scope. In the same vein, Jaeckel, in *Hitler's Weltanschauung*, clearly contradicted Taylor's view that the Nazi tyrant was a passive opportunist; he planned for war, Jaeckel insisted, to gain his twin goals of Lebensraum and the total destruction of European Jewry. Smallwood also discussed the work of Fest, who wrote an extended biography of Hitler and portrayed him as demonic in nature. Smallwood concluded his review by noting that in light of the weighty array of scholarly evidence and support for the orthodox view, Taylor's work must be read with some skepticism. He reasoned that if Taylor's critics were the ignorant, the uninformed, perhaps one could arrive at different conclusions. But Taylor challenged a formidable host that included many of the most respected historians in the world. Indeed, he did, and the discourse and debate that ensued could have nothing but beneficial effects for the development of additional scholarly insight into humanity's most brutal struggle.

MUNICH'S LEGACY

In the wake of Taylor's shocking revisionism the parameters of the historiographic debate were altered. Thorne's *The Approach of War* discarded the inadequacies of the old "guilty men" interpretation of Britain's interwar foreign policy and replaced them with fresh insight into those events leading to war. Thorne envisaged appeasement's archpriest Neville Chamberlain as just as messianic as an earlier crusader for peace, Woodrow Wilson. In regard to the Munich agreement, Thorne critiqued the prime minister for his excessive optimism when there was no real basis for it and dismissed the "hollowness of recent attempts to proclaim Munich an exercise in *Realpolitik*. To a far larger extent it was a study in self-delusion" (21). As a man of peace, Chamberlain was out of his element amid the dogs of war, and a policy crafted to ensure peace sadly brought the Western Allies ever closer to war.

Robbins offered a fine analysis of the Munich agreement in his *Munich 1938*. He cautioned his readers to consider Munich not only as the product of a few years of British foreign policy but in the light of fifty years of European history. Chamberlain had definite hopes for a lasting peace in Munich's aftermath, one that would obviate the fears of a second war within one generation. Sadly, that was not to be, but Robbins declared that Munich itself was the "necessary purgatory" Britain had to pass through to emerge united for king and country in 1939.

The definitive work on the events that led to the loss of the Sudetenland to Nazi Germany was Telford Taylor's *Munich: The Price of Peace*. Taylor winced at the distorted image of Chamberlain that had come to fruition in the mirror of historical literature. He noted that "Chamberlain did what he did at Munich not because he thought he had to, but because he thought it right. For him, appeasement was a policy not of fear but of common and moral sense" (xiv–xv). Taylor did not see the Munich settlement as what Chamberlain would have desired, the first step on the road to a stable peace; he saw that the Allies felt they would somehow have greater success in an imminent war with the loss of the Czech state than they would have had with its aid in 1938.

Military historian Murray contemplated the Munich agreement and the true balance sheet of its aftermath in *The Change in the European Balance of Power*. Murray insisted that Chamberlain's true tragedy was that "having pursued a course that revealed the nature of Nazi policy, he refused to recognize that reality." Instead, after Bad Godesberg Chamberlain "threw everything away on the gamble that Hitler was trustworthy, that war would not come, and that Britain had no strategic interest in either Czechoslovakia or Southeastern Europe" (214). Murray noted that in his estimation, if the Western Allies had seized the initiative in September 1938 and gone to war in defense of Czechoslovakia, their efforts would "have led to the eventual collapse of the Nazi regime at considerably less cost than the war that broke out the following September" (263).

Murray was to detail further his perceptions of Munich's legacy in "Munich at Fifty." He repeated the assertion that with the abandonment of the Czechs in September 1938 the British gave away "nothing less than the strategic balance of Europe" and that, even more to the point, they avoided reality while seeking in vain to find some form of accommodation that might keep the peace and preserve the empire. "They failed to grasp that there is a difference between winning a war and losing one's empire and losing a war and losing one's national existence. The alternatives in 1938 were that stark" (25).

Weinberg took issue with the view that a Franco-British military defense of the Czechs in September 1938 would have been possible. In "Munich after 50 Years" he systematically debunked much of the old mythology accorded the historical lessons of Munich; he gave credit to the previously cringing British and French as the only powers that summoned up the courage to fight Germany in 1939, and he dismissed the great German "triumph" of Munich as a defeat because, in truth, Hitler did not get the war he wanted over Czechoslovakia. Finally, Weinberg claimed that the recent new archival openings prove that France would not have fought for the Czechs under any circumstance, and, perhaps just as important, the British Commonwealth would not have supported a war in 1938. This alone may have doomed any Anglo-French defense of Czechoslovakia, and Weinberg eloquently stressed that "as leaders contemplate the prospect of war, they would be well advised to make sure that their people, or at least a very large number of them, are prepared to make the relevant commitment and are ready to pay the price of sticking to it" (178).

Adamthwaite, in *France and the Coming of the Second World War*, offered a compelling perspective in *The Making of the Second World War*. He insisted that "there was nothing foreordained about the Second World War, and that the war in the way that it came about was an avoidable one" (25–26). He added that the conflict reflected a general breakdown in European society that had seen its origins in the years before 1914. In regard to Chamberlain's appeasement of the dictator states, he noted, "The appeasement pursued until March 1939 proved fatal because it was a policy of meeting German and Italian demands without insisting on firm reciprocal advantages" (26). An early classic account from the French view is

Baumont's *Origins of the Second World War.* Adamthwaite's writings on
French policy and the origins of the war should also be supplemented by
Alexander's *The Republic in Danger,* Young's *In Command of France,* and the
as yet untranslated *La Décadence* by Duroselle.

Lamb corroborated this view in *The Drift to War,* in which he traced the
melancholy path of events leading to the invasion of Poland. He strongly
believed, however, that at the time of the Munich Conference, the vaunted
German military might was more a product of diplomatic bluff than physical strength. Lamb pondered what might have been if the British and
French had stood fast over the Czech crisis and refused to capitulate to
Nazi demands. Like Adamthwaite, Lamb saw appeasement's impotence in
September 1938, when he noted that "Hitler was bluffing at Munich because his armies were too weak to fight in the east and west simultaneously, but Chamberlain hoped that appeasing him would turn him into a
peaceful animal. Such hopes were misplaced." Lamb echoed many of the
sentiments that had been uttered for a half century in the wake of Chamberlain's diplomatic failure that led directly to war.

Weinberg's *The Foreign Policy of Hitler's Germany* stated that the indisput-
able guilt for the war must be borne by Germany and its evil genius. He
attested, as had Hildebrand before him, that Hitler planned in advance a
series of short wars, with the ultimate goal being nothing less than world
domination. This thesis is a direct contradiction of Taylor, who saw the
Nazi leader as a passive, if not opportunistic, figure. In the same vein,
Rich's two-volume epic *Hitler's War Aims* details the step-by-step planning
of the Nazi high command for conquest. Chapter titles such as "War for
Lebensraum: Attack on Poland," "Security in the West: The Attack on
France and the Low Countries," and finally, "Final Drive for Lebensraum:
The Attack on Russia" evidence clearly to the reader the systematic pro-
gram of conquest, of limited war, to obviate the need for a wider conflict
that might be inimicable to German economic capabilities.

OTHER RECENT LITERATURE

For the complexities surrounding Munich as seen in the early 1980s
the reader should turn to Mommsen and Kettenacker's *The Fascist Challenge.* Contributions by twenty-eight scholars from five countries cover not
only the diplomacy of appeasement, but its military, economic, and domestic aspects within a wide international context.

Other examples of recent scholarship on those baleful locust years include Post's *Dilemmas of Appeasement,* Parker's *Chamberlain and Appeasement,*
and Adams' *British Politics and Foreign Policy,* all from 1993. Post offered
that the extended search for a coherent strategy of deterrence was both
Chamberlain's and Whitehall's, and the policy of appeasing Germany to
avoid war not only was Chamberlain's but was supported by every level of

the British government, not to mention public opinion. Parker, although attacking those whom he claimed sought to expiate Chamberlain's guilt for appeasement's failure, was evenhanded in his analysis of those fateful years. Reflecting on Churchill's postwar condemnation of the "guilty men," he noted, "The coming of war was more complicated than Churchill claimed and Chamberlain's errors are less simply explained than by his alleged ignorance and stupidity" (10). Adams desired to obviate the emotional nature of those accounts that sought only to condemn the British leadership for the six-year calamity of world war. On the appeasement of the dictator states to avoid war, he commented that "the appeasers did not pursue a course which led to such tragedy because they were weak, cowardly, stupid or wicked; whatever the reasons, what they were was wrong" (159–60).

An effort antithetical to the old "guilty men" synthesis was offered by Charmley in *Chamberlain and the Lost Peace*. He felt that "it is by no means clear that the results of the Second World War were commensurate with the sacrifices it entailed" (xiv). Charmley envisioned the end result of the war as disastrous for Britain; even in victory, the economic and diplomatic foundations of the empire would have been irreparably shattered, and a role as a satellite of the United States would have been Britain's only future. He surmised, in conclusion, the only proper legacy of Chamberlain's appeasement when he stated that "the venom of his enemies pursued him long, but his was the only policy which offered any hope of avoiding war—and of saving both lives and the British Empire" (212). The absence of the very customary moral judgments (in which a righteous Britain stood alone in defense of Western civilization against the foulest and most soul-destroying tyranny that has ever darkened and stained the pages of history) that have been a great part of the historiography of the origins of World War II made Charmley's *Lost Peace*, as well as a subsequent effort, *Churchill: The End of Glory*, unorthodox and thereby in many ways controversial.

CONCLUSIONS

Any work on the origins of the Second World War must attempt to define the reasons for it. Why a second deadly conflagration within a single generation? Why would Europe, which for so long had dominated the world's affairs, commit a form of suicide and abdicate its role as the icon of world civilization? A final review of relevant scholarship may allow some sense of understanding, some critical insight into this vexing conundrum. Lafore's *The End of Glory* is even now eloquent in various passages detailing the twilight of Europe's geopolitical independence. The rapid decline, Lafore insisted, began in 1914 with the destruction of imperial Europe.

In 1910 Europe had never been so rich, so fecund, so imperial. . . . Then, in 1914, Europe set about the work of destroying its own supremacy in the world. By 1945 the process was complete. Two wars, two decades of violence, hysteria, futility and hedonism, and the worst depression in history had carried the decline of world suzerainty to the point of extinction. The generation from 1914 to 1945 lived in one long, uneven nightmare of destruction, the sorry climax of a thousand years of European history. (11)

The depression was the true coup de grâce for Europe's fragile convalescence in the late 1920s and early 1930s, and one can imagine the 1939–1945 war never having occurred if the world's economy had not become so deranged.

Bell cited the curious dualism of the historical debate over the war's beginnings in *Origins of the Second World War in Europe.* He referred to the great controversy surrounding Taylor's *Origins,* noting metaphorically that "shot and shell flew round Mr. Taylor's head, and enough fragments could be gathered up from the battlefield to make more books in the years that followed" (39). According to Bell, that dualism over origins is evident in that "the idea of an inevitable war confronts that of an unnecessary war. The notion of a planned, premeditated war (even war by blueprint) stands against that of war by accident or improvisation" (41). Bell eventually concluded that the war was brought to fruition by, and only by, the inexorable aggression of Nazi Germany and that the debate over the war's origins is more complex than it need be: "All depended on the fateful premise that German expansion would not halt unless it was forcibly resisted. It is not surprising that most of the discussion on the origins of the Second World War in Europe continues to concentrate on the motives and forces behind the expansion of Germany" (301).

The updated edition of Calvocoressi, Wint, and Pritchard's classic *Total War* stressed that German responsibility for the outbreak of the Great War may well be doubted and debated but that "German responsibility for the Second World War in Europe is in a class of its own." Calvocoressi and his colleagues insisted, as had innumerable historians, including Murray, that Britain would have done well to stand fast at Munich and fight the inescapable war in October 1938 and not a year later.

There is reason to calculate that the avoidance of war in 1938 was not only a shameful act but an inexpedient and foolish one. The surrender at Munich, by postponing war, shaped its future course, ensured the defeat of France and, so far from buying time for rearmament, committed Great Britain to a battle which it nearly lost. (108)

British historians Overy and Wheatcroft rejected the usual blueprint for war thesis that has become such an integral part of the orthodox version of the war's origins. *The Road to War* made the laudable attempt to "retell the story of the interwar years without the benefit of hindsight, without the knowledge that there was going to be a war, in which the West would eventually triumph" (xii). They cited three great landmarks that dominated the skyline of the 1930s and so influenced the choices made by Western statesmen in that decade: the carnage of the Great War, the Russian Revolution of 1917, and the Great Depression of 1929–1939. One can begin to understand, in the face of these chaotic times, the vacillation and concern of those in power, which was all too often seen as cowardice and truckling in the relative safety of the postwar years. The authors noted the final irony of the dissolution of Britain's Great Power status after the Herculean exertions of war. "Britain lacked the means and the willingness to play the imperial role she had played at so little cost and with such profit before 1900. . . . Like the Habsburg Empire in 1914, Britain fought in 1939 to preserve an empire that could no longer be preserved" (103). Finally, Watt, whose scholarly influence for the last forty years has been profound and whose *How War Came: The Immediate Origins of the Second World War* has been lauded as definitive and a new standard by critics and contemporaries alike, stated in his Preface, in no uncertain terms, that "the Second World War was willed to happen." He mourned not only the loss of the millions dead and maimed by the conflagration but the ancillary destruction of such a tremendous percentage of Europe's unique cultural treasures, art, architecture, and historical landmarks, which in many cases had existed a thousand years, all shattered by the weight of war. Watt perceived four critical issues that dominated the outlook of the British cabinet under Neville Chamberlain in 1938 and 1939. They included the ghastly memories of the lost generations in the wake of the Great War; the economic collapse and political ramifications of the crisis of 1931; the dramatic disparity between Britain's commitments (Continental, imperial, and otherwise) and its actual resources; and finally the fact that the defense of "civilization" in early September 1939 overrode the great instinct to avoid war. Watt concluded that German aggression forced a war that no one save the megalomaniac in Berlin really wanted.

What is so extraordinary in the events which led up to the outbreak of the Second World War is that Hitler's will for war was able to overcome the reluctance with which virtually everybody else approached it. . . . The record of the British and French Cabinets, harried and hurried into guarantees that they could or would not implement, into a system of deterrence they did not understand, . . . is neither a happy nor an edifying spectacle. But it is really open to doubt whether any alternative course would have made any difference. (610)

Indeed, this may well be the case. So much of the historiography of the origins of the Second World War seems to play out like Greek tragedy, a cruel harbinger of Europe's demise as the center of world culture and civilization after centuries of dominance. To those whose hearts are in Europe, then, has not this century been a tragic decline since those languid days of the Victorian fin de siècle?

BIBLIOGRAPHY

Also see the chapters on the military and naval historiography of the European war for prewar aspects of those topics.

Adams, R.J.Q. *British Politics and Foreign Policy in the Age of Appeasement, 1935–1939.* Stanford, CA: Stanford UP, 1993.

Adamthwaite, Anthony. *France and the Coming of the Second World War 1936–1939.* London: Frank Cass, 1977.

———. *The Making of the Second World War.* London: George Allen and Unwin, 1979.

Alexander, Martin. *The Republic in Danger. General Maurice Gamelin and the Politics of French Defence, 1933–1940.* New York: Cambridge UP.

Angell, Norman. *For What Do We Fight?* London: Hamish Hamilton, 1939.

Arendt, Hannah. *The Origins of Totalitarianism.* New York: Harcourt and Brace, 1951.

Baumont, Maurice. *The Origins of the Second World War.* Trans. Simone De Couvreur Ferguson. New Haven, CT: Yale UP, 1978.

Bell, Philip M. *Origins of the Second World War in Europe.* London: Longmans, 1986.

Bullock, Alan. *Hitler: A Study in Tyranny.* London: Odhams, 1952.

———. *Hitler and the Origins of the Second World War.* London: Macmillan, 1967.

———. *Hitler and Stalin: Parallel Lives.* London: HarperCollins, 1991.

Calvocoressi, Peter, Guy Wint, and John Pritchard. *Total War: The Causes and Courses of the Second World War.* London: Viking, 1989.

Carr, Edward H. *Britain: A Study of Foreign Policy from Versailles to the Outbreak of War.* London: Longmans, Green, 1939.

Carr, William. *Arms, Autarky, and Aggression: A Study in German Foreign Policy, 1933–1939.* London: Edward Arnold, 1972.

———. *Poland to Pearl Harbor: The Making of the Second World War.* London: Edward Arnold, 1985.

CATO (M. Foot et al.). *Guilty Men.* London: V. Gollancz, 1940.

Charmley, John. *Chamberlain and the Lost Peace.* London: Hodder & Stoughton, 1989.

———. *Churchill: The End of Glory.* London: Hodder and Stoughton, 1993.

Churchill, Winston. *The Gathering Storm.* Boston: Houghton Mifflin, 1948.

Duroselle, Jean-Baptiste. *La Décadence, 1932–1939.* Paris: Imprimerie National, 1979.

Feiling, Keith. *The Life of Neville Chamberlain.* London: Macmillan, 1946.

Fest, Joachim. *Hitler.* New York: Harcourt Brace Jovanovich, 1974.

Gilbert, Martin, and Richard Gott. *The Appeasers.* Boston: Houghton Mifflin, 1963.

Halifax, Edward. *Fulness of Days.* New York: Dodd, Mead, 1957.

Harrison, Richard A. "The United States and Great Britain: Presidential Diplomacy and Alternatives to Appeasement in the 1930s." In David F. Schmitz and

Richard D. Challener, eds., *Appeasement in Europe: A Reassessment of U.S. Policies.* Westport, CT: Greenwood, 1990.

Hildebrand, Klaus. *The Foreign Policy of the Third Reich.* Berkeley: University of California, 1973.

Hodgson, Stuart. *The Man Who Made the Peace: Neville Chamberlain.* New York: E. P. Dutton, 1938.

Jaeckel, Eberhard. *Hitler's Weltanschauung: A Blueprint for Power.* Middletown, CT: Wesleyan UP, 1972.

Kaiser, David. *Economic Diplomacy and the Origins of the Second World War, Germany, Britain, France, and Eastern Europe, 1930–1939.* Princeton: Princeton UP, 1980.

Keynes, John Maynard. *The Economic Consequences of the Peace.* London and New York: Harcourt Brace Jovanovich, 1920, 1988.

Kindleberger, Charles. *The World in Depression, 1929–1939.* Berkeley: University of California, 1986.

Lafore, Laurence. *The End of Glory: An Interpretation of the Origins of World War II.* New York: Lippincott, 1970.

Lamb, Richard. *The Drift to War, 1922–1939.* London: W. H. Allen, 1989.

Londonderry, Lord. *Ourselves and Germany.* London: R. Hale, 1938.

Louis, W. Roger, ed. *The Origins of the Second World War: A.J.P. Taylor and His Critics.* New York: Wiley, 1972.

Macgregor, Steven. *Truth and Mr. Chamberlain.* London: Fore, 1939.

Martel, Gordon, ed. *The Origins of the Second World War Reconsidered: The A.J.P. Taylor Debate after Twenty-Five Years.* Boston: George Allen and Unwin, 1986.

Maugham, Viscount. *The Truth about the Munich Crisis.* London: William Heinemann, 1944.

Medlicott, W. N. *British Foreign Policy since Versailles, 1919–1939.* London: Methuen, 1940.

Mommsen, Wolfgang, and Lothar Kettenacker, eds. *The Fascist Challenge and the Policy of Appeasement.* London: George Allen and Unwin, 1983.

Murray, Williamson. *The Change in the European Balance of Power, 1938–1939.* Princeton: Princeton UP, 1984.

————. "Munich at Fifty." *Commentary* 86 (July 1988): 25–30.

Namier, Lewis. *Diplomatic Prelude, 1938–1939.* London: Macmillan, 1948.

————. *Europe in Decay: A Study in Disintegration, 1938–1940.* London: Macmillan, 1950.

————. *In the Nazi Era.* London: Macmillan, 1952.

Overy, Richard, and Andrew Wheatcroft. *The Road to War.* London: Macmillan; New York: Random House, 1989.

Parker, R.A.C. *Chamberlain and Appeasement: British Policy and the Coming of the Second World War.* New York: St. Martin's, 1993.

Post, Gaines. *Dilemmas of Appeasement: British Deterrence and Defense, 1934–1937.* Ithaca, NY: Cornell UP, 1993.

Rathbone, Eleanor. *War Can Be Averted.* London: Gollancz, 1938.

Reynolds, David. *The Creation of the Anglo-American Alliance, 1937–1941.* London: Europa, 1981.

Rich, Norman. *Hitler's War Aims.* 2 vols. New York: Norton, 1973, 1974.

Robbins, Keith. "Fifty Years On: Recent Scholarship on the Origins of the Second World War." *German History 8* (1990): 339–45.

———. *Munich 1938.* London: Cassell, 1968.

Robertson, Esmonde, ed. *Hitler's Pre-War Policy and Military Plans, 1933–1939.* London: Macmillan, 1963.

———. *Origins of the Second World War: Historical Interpretations.* London: Macmillan, 1971.

Rock, William. *Chamberlain and Roosevelt: British Foreign Policy and the United States, 1937–1940.* Columbus: Ohio State UP, 1988.

Rowse, A. L. *Appeasement: A Study in Political Decline.* New York: W. W. Norton, 1961.

Seton-Watson, R. W. *From Munich to Danzig.* London: Methuen, 1939.

Shirer, William. *The Rise and Fall of the Third Reich.* New York: Simon and Schuster, 1960.

Simon, John. *Retrospect: The Memoirs of Sir John Simon.* London: Hutchinson, 1952.

Smallwood, James. "A Historical Debate of the 1960s: World War II Historiography—The Origins of the War, A.J.P. Taylor, and His Critics." *Australian Journal of Politics and History 26* (1980): 403–10.

Taylor, A.J.P. *Origins of the Second World War.* London: Hamish Hamilton, 1961.

Taylor, Telford. *Munich: The Price of Peace.* New York: Doubleday, 1979.

Templewood, Viscount. *Nine Troubled Years.* London: Collins, 1954.

Thorne, Christopher. *The Approach of War, 1938–1939.* London: Macmillan, 1967.

Trevor-Roper, Hugh. "A.J.P. Taylor, Hitler, and the War." *Encounter 17* (July 1961): 88–96.

Walker-Smith, Derek. *Neville Chamberlain; Man of Peace.* London: R. Hale, 1940.

Watt, Donald Cameron. "Appeasement: The Rise of a Revisionist School?" *Political Quarterly 36* (1965): 191–213.

———. *How War Came: The Immediate Origins of the Second World War, 1938–1939.* New York: Pantheon, 1989.

Weinberg, Gerhard. *The Foreign Policy of Hitler's Germany: Vol. II. Starting World War Two.* Chicago: University of Chicago, 1980.

———. "Munich after 50 Years." *Foreign Affairs 67* (1988): 165–78.

Wheeler-Bennett, John. *Munich: Prologue to Tragedy.* New York: Duell, Sloan, and Pearce, 1948.

Wiskemann, Elizabeth. *Czechs and Germans.* London: Oxford UP, 1938.

———. *Prologue to War.* New York: Oxford UP, 1940.

Woodward, Llewellyn. *British Foreign Policy in the Second World War.* London: HMSO, 1970–1976.

Young, Robert J. *In Command of France: French Foreign Policy and Military Planning, 1933–1940.* Cambridge: Cambridge UP, 1978.

Part II

Research Aids, Sources, and Bibliographies

3 Reference Works: Bibliographies, Encyclopedias, Dictionaries, Atlases, and Chronologies

Eugene L. Rasor and Loyd E. Lee

This chapter discusses the most important, general, and up-to-date references, with an emphasis on the military.

BIBLIOGRAPHIES

General

Enser's *A Subject Bibliography* comprehensively lists books in English, categorized alphabetically by subjects, while Bayliss' *Bibliographic Guide* surveys reference materials. Bloomberg and Weber's *World War II and Its Origins*, Ziegler's *World War II*, and Funk's *A Select Bibliography* are standard bibliographies for books in English; the latter two are not annotated. The *Newsletter, World War Two Studies Association* (formerly the American Committee on the History of the Second World War) periodically publishes select, unannotated bibliographies of books and articles in English on a wide variety of topics relating to the war. *The Journal of Military History* (formerly *Military Affairs*) also publishes recent journal articles and dissertations in military history appearing in English. Bausum and Bausum, *The Journal of Military History Cumulative Index*, covering issues from 1937 to 1994, is an invaluable aid in using its resources. The *War and Society Newsletter* publishes bibliographies of articles in journals and essays in collected works in Western languages, including the social, economic, and cultural history of warfare and military organization. It also notes works in progress. For contemporary wartime periodical publications about the war, consult Spier, *World War II in Our Magazines and Books*.

Rohwer and Müller, *Neue Forschungen zum Zweiten Weltkrieg*, contains extensive historiographic essays from sixty-seven nations arranged by country of origin of the works discussed. Most are written in English; the bibliographies are in all languages. This is indispensable for the research of the 1980s, though the absence of a topical index makes it difficult to follow transnational research. For official histories, the indispensable reference is Higham's *Official Histories*, with a historiographical essay for each country participating in the project; a new edition is forthcoming.

An important resource is dissertations, and a large number of them focus on World War II. *Dissertation Abstracts International*, published since 1938, lists and briefly summarizes most disserations; it is also available on CD-ROM. Millett and Cooling, *Doctoral Dissertations in Military Affairs*, is supplemented in *Military Affairs*, now *The Journal of Military History*.

Armies

For American military history see volume 4 of Shrader's *Reference Guide to United States Military History*. It provides assistance in researching military organization, chronology, battles, biographies, and events. Higham's *A Guide to the Sources of U.S. Military History*, with three supplements in cooperation with Mrozek and a fourth in press, has extensive authoritative, historiographical essays introducing each section. Also see Controvich, *United States Army Unit Histories*, which provides detailed information about American army units at all levels.

For Britain see Higham's *Guide to the Sources of British Military History*, updated and supplemented by Jordan, *British Military History*. Dornbusch compiled an *Australian Military History* bibliography, *The Canadian Army*, and *The New Zealand Army*. Cooke's *The Canadian Military Experience* is also published in French. LaFrance and Jones' *Latin American Military History* is a thorough guide to primary and secondary sources for the region. Showalter, *German Military History*, is also thorough but needs to be updated. Smith's *The Soviet Army* is limited to English-language primary sources.

Basic for the Pacific theater is Ryan's *The War in the Pacific*, a bibliography of reference works. The U.S. Army Military History Research Institute's series of *Special Bibliographies* displays its extensive holdings.

Orders of battle for various armies can be found in Joslen, *Orders of Battle, 1939–1945: United Kingdom and Colonial Formations and Units in the Second World War*; Nafziger, *The French Order of Battle in WWII*; Mitcham, *Hitler's Legions: The German Army Order of Battle*; Madej, *The Italian Army Order of Battle, 1940–1944: Between Fascism and Monarchy*, and his *Japanese Armed Forces Order of Battle*; Conner's *Red Army Order of Battle*; and Stanton, *Order of Battle: U.S. Army, World War II*, with the full order of battle for ground units of all categories.

Some publishers have developed special reference guide bibliographic series with volumes relating to the war. Garland's Military History Bibliographies series is edited by Robin Higham and Jacob W. Kipp; Wars of the United States series is edited by Richard Blanco. Greenwood continues to add to its Bibliographies of Battles and Leaders series, with Myron J. Smith, editor, and other reference publication series. Write the presses for catalogs.

Navies

The standard bibliography is Albion's *Naval and Maritime History*. Annotations are brief, and American topics dominate; it is updated by Labaree's *Supplement.* Smith, *World War II at Sea: A Bibliography*, surveys English-language sources in general. For general American naval and Marine Corps history bibliographies, see Coletta, *A Selected and Annotated Bibliography of American Naval History* and *An Annotated Bibliography of the U.S. Marine Corps History*. Both include books, dissertations, articles, personal papers, fiction, and film. Moran's *Creating a Legend* is a very complete coverage of periodical articles as well as other literature about the U.S. Marine Corps, often with brief descriptions. For the U.S. Navy in the Pacific see Sbrega, *The War against Japan*. Also check the official *Annotated Bibliography of the United States Marine Corps in the Second World War* by O'Quinlivan and Hilliard.

For the British, see Law, *The Royal Navy in World War II*, a comprehensive, annotated bibliography. Rasor's historiographical essay, *British Naval History since 1815*, devotes fifty pages to the Royal Navy in World War II. For Germany in general consult Bird, *German Naval History*.

Brown's *Warship Losses of World War Two* incorporates a day-by-day listing of all surface combatant ship losses, including locations, for all nations and all causes from 1939 to 1945. *Lloyd's War Losses* covers details of the circumstances of all Allied and neutral merchant ships sunk and damaged in the war. Browning has a paragraph about each ship in *U.S. Merchant Vessel War Casualties*, while Motley and Kelly's *Now Hear This!* surveys American ships during the war with brief histories, photos, and an appendix of unit citations, commendations, and operations.

Air Forces

Cresswell and Berger, *U.S. Air Force History*, includes twenty pages on World War II, while Smith's *Air War Bibliography* covers sources. Also see Smith's *American Warplanes* and Angelucci's *Combat Aircraft of World War II* in eight volumes. Daniels provided *A Guide to the Reports of the United States Strategic Bombing Survey*. Homze's *German Military Aviation* covers the Luftwaffe. Maurer's comprehensive *Combat Squadrons* and *Air Force Combat Units* list lineages, assignments, stations, aircraft, and emblems, among other details.

Theaters and Campaigns

Smith, *World War II: The European and Mediterranean Theaters*, is a thorough, annotated bibliography of English-language materials. Though Baxter's *The Normandy Campaign* is extensive, it is unannotated. His *War in North Africa* contains seven historiographic essays, followed by a bibliography of all works cited.

For the Pacific theater, see Smith's campaign bibliography, *The Battles of Coral Sea and Midway*. Controvich, *The Central Pacific Campaign*, with brief annotations, is divided by topics, campaigns, and armed forces, with considerable information on unit histories. Additional bibliographies relating to the Pacific and Asian theaters are Rasor's *Southwest Pacific Campaign*, *China–Burma–India Campaign*, *General Douglas MacArthur*, *The Solomon Islands Campaign*, and *Earl Mountbatten of Burma*, the last two forthcoming. Corfield's *Bibliography of Literature Relating to the Malayan Campaign* includes annotations, while Netzorg, *The Philippines*, is an extensively annotated guide to the literature on the Philippines during the war.

Intelligence

For the period before the revelation of Ultra, the standard is Harris, *Intelligence and National Security*. Constantinides, *Intelligence and Espionage*, includes over five hundred entries from all periods of history; each is arranged by author, with a full page of analytical and critical information, an assessment of the topics' significance, and recommendations for further research. The focus is on British intelligence. Petersen's *American Intelligence* has brief annotated entries relating to cryptology, espionage, covert action, and intelligence-counterintelligence operations. House, *Military Intelligence*, contains a narrative introduction and annotated entries on all types of intelligence, including non-American.

ENCYCLOPEDIAS

At the head of the list is the *Oxford Companion to World War II*, edited by Dear and Foot, with essays by over 140 experts. Campbell, *The Experience of World War II*, includes a time chart and lists of wartime civilian and military leaders, plus graphs and many illustrations. Polmar and Allen's extensive *World War II: America at War* begins with a long chronology followed by over eight hundred pages of alphabetic entries, plus several appendixes. Ernest and Trevor Dupuy's *The Harper Encyclopedia of Military History* devotes over two hundred pages to World War II. Also see Dupuy et al., *Harper Encyclopedia of Military Biography*.

Wheal, Pope, and Taylor's *The Meridian Encyclopedia of the Second World War* contains extensive entries, campaign maps, and a chronology. Various editions of Keegan's *Encyclopedia of World War II* have essays on battles, weapons, and personalities. Perrett and Hogg, *Encyclopedia of the Second World War*, includes battles, campaigns, personalities, forces, weapons, intelligence, and code names. Parrish, *Simon and Schuster Encyclopedia of World War II*, with over four thousand short essay entries, covers much of the same material. French historian Baudot edited, with an international team of historians, *The Historical Encyclopedia of World War II*; it was published in French and English in 1977 and republished in 1989 in an updated and expanded English edition. It includes a chronology and bibliographies of documents, general bibliographies, official histories, memoirs, and films. *Louis L. Snyder's Historical Guide to World War II* has fewer entries, but most entries are longer and organized according to a uniform principle. Chandler and Collins' *D-Day Encyclopedia* is a superb guide to that great event.

Military and naval annuals such as *Jane's, Conway's, Combat Fleets, Weyer's Warships of the World*, and *Brassey's* are encyclopedic in detail about warships, aircraft, and weapons. The best of these are *Jane's Fighting Ships* and *Jane's All the World's Aircraft*, published annually and in special combination editions. *Conway's All the World's Fighting Ships, 1922–1946* has illustrations of every combat ship from all nations before and during the war, and *Conway's All the World's Battleships, 1906 to the Present* contains schematic and photographic illustrations and technical details about all battleships since HMS *Dreadnought*.

In addition to the extensive publisher annuals, other informative compilations are available. See Silverstone, *U.S. Warships of World War II*; Young, *A Dictionary of Ships of the Royal Navy of the Second World War*, an alphabetical listing describing over two thousand warships by class; Jentschura, *Warships of the Imperial Japanese Navy*, providing considerable detail and over three hundred illustrations; and Chesneau, *Aircraft Carriers of the World*, with over four hundred schematic line drawings. Bauer and Roberts' *Register of Ships of the U.S. Navy* includes thousands of ships, with technical details and some historical identification.

Green's *War Planes of the Second World War* includes descriptions and drawings of all military aircraft organized by type. A more recent compilation is Gunston, *The Illustrated Directory of Fighting Aircraft of World War II*; also see his earlier *Aircraft of World War 2* and the more recent *Jane's Fighting Aircraft of World War II*.

The U.S. Department of Defense's *Handbook on German Military Forces* and *Handbook on Japanese Military Forces*, first published in 1942, were reissued in 1995. They remain useful manuals on military planning and information and for research.

Code names used extensively in the war are defined in Chant, *The Encyclopedia of Code Names of World War II*.

DICTIONARIES

Boatner's *Dictionary of World War Two* is a general dictionary to the war. Also see Tunney, *A Biographical Dictionary of World War II*, and Keegan, *Routledge Who's Who in World War II*. Mason's *Who's Who in World War II* has many photographs. Ancell and Miller's *Biographical Dictionary* outlines the careers of all U.S. generals and flag officers. Bright, *Historical Dictionary of the U.S. Air Force*, alphabetically lists topics related to the history of the U.S. Air Force (USAF). Extensive cross-referencing assists the user, though provocative topics such as strategic bombing receive short shrift. DuPre, *U.S. Air Force Biographical Dictionary*, includes entries on all general officers, Medal of Honor winners, and aces. Schuon's *U.S. Navy Biographical Dictionary* and his *U.S. Marine Corps Biographical Dictionary* include Medal of Honor winners with only spotty coverage of leaders. Howarth's *Men of War* has thirty-one biographies of major naval figures from all sides of the war.

ATLASES

Banks' *World Atlas* is a comprehensive historical atlas of military history. Also see Natkiel, *Atlas of World War II*. *The Atlas of Modern Warfare* by Cook and Stevenson is folio-size with narrative and numerous illustrations supporting the maps, divided by regions.

Pimlott, *The Historical Atlas of World War II*, and Smurthwaite, *The Pacific War Atlas*, are fiftieth-anniversary commemorative publications. Other contributions are Goodenough, *War Maps*, a folio-size format with over two hundred maps, each supported by narrative; Keegan, *The Times Atlas of the Second World War*; and an earlier but solid rendering, Young, *Atlas of the Second World War*.

Stamps and Esposito's two-volume *A Military History of World War II* presents solid maps, but more thorough is Griess, *Campaign Atlas to the Second World War*; both are in a West Point series. Man's *D-Day Atlas and the Normandy Campaign* covers that invasion and campaign.

Two volumes combine maps with chronology: Messenger's *World War Two: Chronological Atlas*, with maps making up one-third of the space, and Pitt and Pitt's *Chronological Atlas*, providing a full-page spread for each month of the war pinpointing where major events occurred, with a journalistic narrative.

CHRONOLOGIES

Argyle, *Chronology of World War II*, serves as a sound general overview. *Keesings' Contemporary Archives* is a detailed description of key events in world history, published contemporaneously with events since 1931 and thoroughly indexed. In the official history of *The U.S. Army in World War*

II see Williams, *Chronology, 1941–1945*, a day-to-day tactical history of American ground force operations. Trevor Dupuy's brief *Chronological Military History of World War II* surveys the period 1937 to 1945 with European and Atlantic events on even-numbered pages and those dealing with Asia and the Pacific on odd-numbered pages.

The *Chronology and Index of the Second World War*, compiled by the staff of the Royal Institute of International Affairs, presents a detailed, day-by-day summary of the war from September 1938 to August 1945, all indexed. Montgomery-Massingberd, *The Daily Telegraph Record of the Second World War*, is an up-to-date chronology of the war from 1939 to 1945, with commentary. Originally in Italian, Salmaggi and Pallavisini's *2194 Days of War: An Illustrated Chronology of the Second World War* also includes many illustrations and maps.

Rohwer and Hummelchen's *Chronology of the War at Sea*, recently revised, details naval events worldwide. The official U.S. *Naval Chronology* can be supplemented by Kimble's *Chronology of U.S. Navy Submarine Operations in the Pacific*. The Royal Air Force (RAF) *Bomber Command War Diaries* was edited by Middlebrook. For the U.S. Air Force see Carter and Mueller, *Combat Chronology*, the companion supportive volume for the official *U.S. Army Air Force in World War II*, and Hammel's *Air War Europa: America's Air War against Germany*.

Peter Young, *Almanac of World War II*, and Goralski, *World War II Almanac*, are similar. Each gives a day-by-day accounting beginning in 1931 with the Mukden incident and concluding with the Japanese surrender in 1945. For the North Pacific see Hutchison's day-by-day chronology in *World War II in the North Pacific*.

Other than Ellis' *Statistical Survey* there is no systematic and comprehensive presentation of data, especially comparative data. A broader and more comparative aid providing statistics for the past 150 years is Singer and Small, *The Wages of War*, though recent studies indicate that earlier estimates of World War II war dead are too low.

Even fifty years after the war there is a continuing need to update basic reference works on World War II. As the torrent of writing on the war continues, keeping abreast of new research and publication is a major challenge. Without doubt there will never be a single, comprehensive bibliography of the literature of the war, even for one restricted to works in the English language.

BIBLIOGRAPHY

Albion, Robert Greenhalgh. *Naval and Maritime History: An Annotated Bibliography.* Mystic, CT: Maritime Historical Association, 1951, 1973.

Ancell, R. Manning, and Christine M. Miller. *The Biographical Dictionary of World*

War II Generals and Flag Officers: The U.S. Armed Forces. Westport, CT: Greenwood, 1996.

Angelucci, Enzo. *Combat Aircraft of World War II.* 8 vols. New York: Orion Books, 1987.

Argyle, Christopher. *Chronology of World War II: The Day by Day Illustrated Record 1939–45.* New York: Exeter Books, 1980.

Banks, Arthur. *A World Atlas of Military History, 1861–1945.* London: Seeley, 1978; New York: Da Capa, 1988; and other various editions.

Baudot, Marcel, et al., eds. *The Historical Encyclopedia of World War II.* New York: Facts on File, 1977, 1989.

Bauer, K. Jack, and Stephen S. Roberts. *Register of Ships of the U.S. Navy, 1775–1990: Major Combatants.* Westport, CT: Greenwood, 1991.

Bausum, Henry S., and David Bausum. *The Journal of Military History Cumulative Index: Vols. 1–58, 1973–1994.* Lexington: Virginia Military Institute and the George C. Marshall Foundation, 1995.

Baxter, Colin F. *The Normandy Campaign, 1944: A Selected Bibliography.* Westport, CT: Greenwood, 1992.

———. *The War in North Africa, 1940–1943: A Selected Bibliography.* Westport, CT: Greenwood, 1996.

Bayliss, Gwyn M. *Bibliographic Guide to the Two World Wars: An Annotated Survey of English-Language Reference Materials.* London and New York: Bowker, 1977.

Bird, Keith W. *German Naval History: A Guide to the Literature.* New York and London: Garland, 1985.

Bloomberg, Marty, and Hans H. Weber. *World War II and Its Origins: A Select Annotated Bibliography of Books in English.* Littleton, CO: Libraries Unlimited, 1975.

Boatner, Mark T. *Dictionary of World War Two.* New York: Holt, 1993; Novato, CA: Presidio, 1966.

Brassey's Annual: The Armed Forces Yearbook. Various.

Bright, Charles D., ed. *Historical Dictionary of the U.S. Air Force.* Westport, CT: Greenwood, 1992.

Brown, J. David. *Warship Losses of World War Two.* Annapolis, MD: NIP, 1990, 1995.

Browning, Robert M. *U.S. Merchant Vessel War Casualties of World War II.* Annapolis, MD: NIP, 1996.

Campbell, John, ed. *The Experience of World War II.* London: Harrap, 1989.

Carter, Kit C., and Robert Mueller. *Combat Chronology, 1941–1945: The U.S. Army Air Force in World War II.* Washington, DC: GPO, 1973, 1991.

Chandler, David G., and James Lawton Collins, Jr. *The D-Day Encyclopedia.* New York: Simon & Schuster, 1994.

Chant, Christopher. *The Encyclopedia of Code Names of World War II.* London: Routledge, 1986.

Chesneau, Roger. *Aircraft Carriers of the World: 1914 to the Present: An Illustrated Encyclopedia.* Annapolis, MD: NIP, 1984.

Coletta, Paolo E., ed. *An Annotated Bibliography of U.S. Marine Corps History.* Lanham, MD: America, 1986.

———. *A Selected and Annotated Bibliography of American Naval History.* Lanham, MD: America, 1981, 1988.

Combat Fleets of the World: Their Ships, Aircraft, and Armament. Annapolis, MD: NIP, various annual editions.

Conner, Albert Z. *Red Army Order of Battle in the Great Patriotic War: Including Data from 1919 to the Present.* Novato, CA: Presidio, 1985.

Constantinides, George C. *Intelligence and Espionage: An Analytical Bibliography.* Boulder, CO: Westview, 1983.

Controvich, James T. *The Central Pacific Campaign, 1943–1944: A Bibliography.* Bibliographies of Battles and Leaders series. Westport, CT: Meckler, 1990.

———, ed. *United States Army Unit Histories: A Reference and Bibliography.* Manhattan, KS: Sunflower UP, 1983, 1992.

Conway's All the World's Battleships, 1906 to the Present. London: Conway, 1987, 1988.

Conway's All the World's Fighting Ships, 1922–1946. London: Conway, 1980.

Cook, Chris, and John Stevenson. *The Atlas of Modern Warfare.* New York: Putnam, 1978.

Cooke, Owen A. *The Canadian Military Experience 1867–1983: A Bibliography.* Ottawa: Directorate of History, Department of National Defense, 1984.

Corfield, Justin, ed. *A Bibliography of Literature Relating to the Malayan Campaign and the Japanese Period in Malaya, Singapore and Northern Borneo.* Hull, U.K.: University of Hull, 1988.

Cresswell, Mary Ann, and Carl Berger. *U.S. Air Force History: An Annotated Bibliography.* Washington, DC: Air Force, 1971.

Daniels, Gordon, ed. *A Guide to the Reports of the United States Strategic Bombing Survey.* London: Royal Historical Society, 1981.

Dear, I.C.B., and M.R.D. Foot. *The Oxford Companion to World War II.* Oxford and New York: Oxford UP, 1995.

Dissertation Abstracts International. Ann Arbor, MI: University Microfilms, 1938ff.

Dornbusch, C. E., comp. *Australian Military History.* New York: Hope Farm, 1963.

———. *The Canadian Army, 1855–1965: Lineages; Regimental Histories.* Cornwallville, NY: Hope Farm, 1966.

———. *The New Zealand Army: A Bibliography.* New York: Hope Farm, 1961.

DuPre, Flint O. *U.S. Air Force Biographical Dictionary.* New York: Watts, 1965.

Dupuy, R. Ernest, and Trevor N. Dupuy. *The Harper Encyclopedia of Military History: From 3500 B.C. to the Present.* New York: HarperCollins, 1970, 1993.

Dupuy, R. Ernest, et al. *The Harper Encyclopedia of Military Biography: From 3500 B.C. to the Present.* New York: HarperCollins, 1992, 1993.

Dupuy, Trevor N. *The Chronological Military History of World War II.* New York: Franklin Watts, 1965, 1967.

Ellis, John. *World War II: A Statistical Survey.* New York: Facts on File, 1993. Also published as *The World War II Databook: The Essential Facts and Figures for All Combatants.* London: Aurum, 1993.

Enser, A.G.S. *A Subject Bibliography of the Second World War: Books in English, 1939–1987.* Boulder, CO: Westview, 1977–1990, various editions.

Funk, Arthur L., comp. *The Second World War: A Select Bibliography of Books in English since 1975.* Claremont, CA: Regina, 1985.

———. *A Select Bibliography of Books on World War II Published in the United States, 1966–1975.* Gainesville, FL: American Committee on the History of the Second World War, 1975.

Goodenough, Simon. *War Maps: World War II from September 1939 to August 1945:*

Air, Sea and Land, Battle by Battle. New York: St. Martin's, 1982; New York: Crescent Books, 1988.

Goralski, Robert. *World War II Almanac, 1931–1945: A Political and Military Record.* New York: Putnam, 1981; London: Hamilton, 1984.

Green, William. *War Planes of the Second World War.* 10 vols. New York: Doubleday, 1960–1967.

Griess, Thomas E., ed. *Campaign Atlas to the Second World War.* 3 vols. Wayne, NJ: Avery, 1989.

Gunston, Bill. *Aircraft of World War 2.* New York: Crescent Books, 1980.

———. *The Illustrated Directory of Fighting Aircraft of World War II.* New York: Prentice-Hall, 1988.

———. *Jane's Fighting Aircraft of World War II.* London: Studio Editions, 1990.

Hammel, Eric M. *Air War Europa: America's Air War against Germany in Europe and North Africa, 1942–1945: A Chronology.* Pacifica, CA: Pacifica, 1994.

Harris, William Robert. *Intelligence and National Security: A Bibliography with Selected Annotations.* 2 vols. Cambridge: Harvard UP, 1968.

Higham, Robin, ed. *A Guide to the Sources of British Military History.* Berkeley: University of California, 1971.

———. *Official Histories: Essays and Bibliographies from Around the World.* Manhattan: Kansas State University, 1970.

Higham, Robin, and Donald J. Mrozek, eds. *A Guide to the Sources of U.S. Military History.* With *Supplements I, II, and III.* Hamden, CT: Archon, 1975–1993.

Homze, Edward L. *German Military Aviation: A Guide to the Literature.* New York and London: Garland, 1984.

House, Jonathan M. *Military Intelligence, 1870–1991: A Research Guide.* Westport, CT: Greenwood, 1993.

Howarth, Stephen, ed. *Men of War: Great Naval Leaders of World War II.* New York: St. Martin's; London: Weidenfeld and Nicolson, 1993.

Hutchison, Kevin D. *World War II in the North Pacific: Chronology and Fact Book.* Westport, CT: Greenwood, 1994.

Jane's All the World's Aircraft. Annual. London: Jane's, various.

Jane's Fighting Ships. Annual. London: Jane's, various.

Jentschura, Hansgeorg, et al. *Warships of the Imperial Japanese Navy, 1869–1945.* Annapolis, MD: NIP, 1970, 1977.

Jordan, Gerald, ed. *British Military History: A Supplement to Robin Higham's Guide to the Sources.* New York: Garland, 1988.

Joslen, H. F., comp. *Orders of Battle, 1939–1945: United Kingdom and Colonial Formations and Units in the Second World War.* 2 vols. London: HMSO, 1960, 1968.

The Journal of Military History. (1989–). Formerly, *Military Affairs* (1937–1988).

Keegan, John, ed. *Encyclopedia of World War II.* New York: Gallery, 1977, 1990.

———. *Routledge Who's Who in World War II.* London: Routledge, 1995.

———. *The Times Atlas of the Second World War.* New York: Harper, 1989.

Keesing's Contemporary Archives. Edinburgh, London: Longman Group, 1931– .

Kimble, David L. *Chronology of U.S. Navy Submarine Operations in the Pacific.* Bennington, VT: World War II Historical Society, 1995.

Labaree, Benjamin Woods. *A Supplement (1971–1986) to Robert G. Albion's Naval and*

Maritime History, an Annotated Bibliography. Mystic, CT: Munson Institute of American Maritime Studies, 1988.

LaFrance, David G., and Errol D. Jones. *Latin American Military History: An Annotated Bibliography.* New York: Garland, 1992.

Law, Derek G. *The Royal Navy in World War II: An Annotated Bibliography.* Novato, CA: Presidio, 1988.

Lloyd's War Losses: The Second World War. 2 vols. London: Lloyd's, 1989–1991.

Madej, W. Victor, ed. *The Italian Army Order of Battle, 1940–1944: Between Fascism and Monarchy.* Allentown, PA: Game, 1981.

———. *Japanese Armed Forces Order of Battle, 1937–1945.* 2 vols. Allentown, PA: Game, 1981.

Man, John. *The Penguin Atlas of D-Day and the Normandy Campaign.* London and New York: Viking, 1994. Also published as *The Facts on File D-Day Atlas: The Definitive Account of the Allied Invasion of Normandy.* New York: Facts on File, 1994.

Mason, David. *Who's Who in World War II.* London: Weidenfeld and Nicolson; Boston: Little, Brown, 1978.

Maurer, Maurer, ed. *Air Force Combat Units of World War II.* Washington, DC: GPO, 1961, 1963, 1983.

———. *Combat Squadrons of the Air Force, World War II.* Washington, DC: GPO, 1969.

Messenger, Charles. *World War Two: Chronological Atlas.* New York: Macmillan, 1989. Also published as *World War Two Chronological Atlas: When, Where, How and Why.* London: Bloomsbury, 1989.

Middlebrook, Martin, ed. *The Bomber Command War Diaries: An Operational Reference Book, 1939–1945.* Rev. ed. London and New York: Penguin, 1990; Leicester, U.K.: Midland, 1996.

Millett, Allan R., and Franklin B. Cooling, eds. *Doctoral Dissertations in Military Affairs: A Bibliography.* Manhattan: Kansas State UP, 1972.

Mitcham, Samuel W. *Hitler's Legions: The German Army Order of Battle, World War II.* New York: Dorset, 1985, 1987.

Montgomery-Massingberd, Hugh, ed. *The Daily Telegraph Record of the Second World War: Month by Month from 1939–1945.* London: Sidgwick and Jackson, 1989.

Moran, John B. *Creating a Legend: The Complete Record of Writing about the U.S. Marine Corps.* Chicago: Moran/Andrews, 1973.

Motley, John J., and Philip R. Kelly. *Now Hear This! Histories of U.S. Ships in World War II.* Washington, DC: Zenger, 1947.

Nafziger, George F. *The French Order of Battle in WWII: An Organizational History of the Divisions of the French Army.* West Chester, OH: G. Nafziger, 1995.

Natkiel, Richard. *Atlas of World War II.* London: Bison Books; New York: Military, 1985.

Naval Chronology: World War II. Washington, DC: GPO, 1955.

Netzorg, Morton J. *The Philippines in World War II and to Independence, December 8, 1941–July 4, 1946: An Annotated Bibliography.* Ithaca, NY: Cornell UP, 1977.

Newsletter, World War Two Studies Association, previously *Newsletter, American Committee for the History of World War II,* twice yearly, 1968– .

O'Neill, James E., and Robert W. Krauskopf, eds. *World War II: An Account of Its Documents.* Washington, DC: Howard UP, 1976.

O'Quinlivan, Michael, and Jack B. Hilliard. *An Annotated Bibliography of the United*

States Marine Corps in the Second World War. Washington, DC: GPO, 1965, 1970.

Parrish, Thomas, ed. *The Simon and Schuster Encyclopedia of World War II*. New York: Simon and Schuster, 1978.

Perrett, Bryan, and Ian Hogg. *Encyclopedia of the Second World War*. Novato, CA: Presidio, 1989.

Petersen, Neal H. *American Intelligence, 1775–1990: A Bibliographic Guide*. Claremont, CA: Regina, 1992.

Pimlott, John. *The Historical Atlas of World War II*. New York: Holt, 1995.

Pitt, Barrie, and Frances Pitt. *The Chronological Atlas of World War II*. London: Macmillan and Toronto: Lester Orpen Dennys, 1989.

Polmar, Norman, and Thomas B. Allen. *World War II: America at War: 1941–1945*. New York: Random House, 1991.

Rasor, Eugene L. *British Naval History since 1815: A Guide to the Literature*. New York: Garland, 1990.

———. *The China–Burma–India Campaign, 1941–1945: Historiography and Annotated Bibliography*. Bibliographies of Battles and Leaders series. Westport, CT: Greenwood, forthcoming.

———. *Earl Mountbatten of Burma, 1900–1979: Historiography and Annotated Bibliography*. Westport, CT: Greenwood, forthcoming.

———. *General Douglas MacArthur, 1880–1964: Historiography and Annotated Bibliography*. Westport, CT: Greenwood, 1994.

———. *The Solomon Islands Campaign, Guadalcanal to Rabaul: Historiography and Annotated Bibliography*. Westport, CT: Greenwood, 1997.

———. *The Southwest Pacific Campaign, 1941–1945: Historiography and Annotated Bibliography*. Westport, CT: Greenwood, 1996.

Rohwer, Jürgen, and Gerhard Hummelchen. *Chronology of the War at Sea, 1939–1945*. 2 vols. New York: Arco, 1973; 2d ed. London: Greenhill, 1992.

Rohwer, Jürgen, and Hildegard Müller, eds. *Neue Forschungen zum Zweiten Weltkrieg. Literaturberichte und Bibliographien aus 67 Ländern*. Koblenz: Bernard and Graefe, 1990.

Royal Institute of International Affairs Staff, comp. *Chronology and Index of the Second World War, 1938–1945*. Westport, CT: Greenwood, 1990. Reprint of 1975 ed.

Ryan, Duane. *The War in the Pacific: General Reference Works Bibliography*. Carlisle Barracks, PA: U.S. Army Military History Research Institute, 1978.

Salmaggi, Cesare, and Alfredo Pallavisini, comps. *2194 Days of War: An Illustrated Chronology of the Second World War*. New York: Mayflower, 1977, 1979.

Sbrega, John J. *The War against Japan: An Annotated Bibliography*. Wars of the U.S. Series. New York: Garland, 1989.

Schuon, Karl. *U.S. Marine Corps Biographical Dictionary*. New York: Watts, 1963.

———. *U.S. Navy Biographical Dictionary*. New York: Watts, 1965.

Showalter, Dennis E. *German Military History, 1648–1982: A Critical Bibliography*. New York and London: Garland, 1984.

Shrader, Charles R., ed. *Reference Guide to United States Military History*. Vol. 4: 1919–1945. New York: Facts on File, 1995.

Silverstone, Paul H. *U.S. Warships of World War II*. New York: Doubleday, 1965, 1989.

Singer, Joel D., and Melvin Small. *The Wages of War, 1816–1965: A Statistical Handbook*. New York: Wiley, 1972.

Smith, Myron J., Jr. *Air War Bibliography, 1939–1945: English Language Sources.* 5 vols. Manhattan, KS: MA/AH, 1977–1982.

———. *American Warplanes, 1908–1988: A Bibliography.* Westport, CT: Meckler, 1991.

———. *The Battles of Coral Sea and Midway, May–June 1942: A Selected Bibliography.* Westport, CT: Greenwood, 1990.

———. *The Soviet Army, 1939–1980: A Guide to Sources in English.* Santa Barbara, CA: ABC-Clio, 1982.

———. *World War II: The European and Mediterranean Theaters: An Annotated Bibliography.* New York: Garland, 1984.

———. *World War II at Sea: A Bibliography of Sources in English.* 4 vols. Metuchen, NJ: Scarecrow, 1976–1990.

Smurthwaite, David. *The Pacific War Atlas, 1941–1945.* New York: Facts on File and London: HMSO, 1995.

Snyder, Louis L. *Louis L. Snyder's Historical Guide to World War II.* Westport, CT, and London: Greenwood, 1982.

Spier, Henry O., ed. *World War II in Our Magazines and Books, September 1939–September 1945: A Bibliography.* New York: Stuyvesant, 1945.

Stamps, T. Dodson, and Vincent J. Esposito, eds. *A Military History of World War II with Atlas.* 2 vols. West Point, NY: USMA, 1953, 1956.

Stanton, Shelby L. *Order of Battle, U.S. Army, World War II.* Novato, CA: Presidio, 1984.

Tunney, Christopher. *A Biographical Dictionary of World War II.* London: Dent and New York: St. Martin's, 1972.

U.S. Army Military History Research Institute. *Special Bibliographies.* Carlisle Barracks, PA: Collection, 1970–1977.

U.S. Department of Defense. *Handbook on German Military Forces.* Baton Rouge: Louisiana State UP, 1995.

———. *Handbook on Japanese Military Forces.* Baton Rouge: Louisiana State UP, 1995.

War and Society Newsletter: A Bibliographical Survey. Munich: Militärgeschichtliches Forschungsamt, annually since 1973.

Weyer's Warships of the World. London: Weyer, annually.

Wheal, Elizabeth-Anne, Stephen Pope, and James Taylor. *A Dictionary of the Second World War.* New York: Peter Bedrick Books, 1990. Also published as *Meridian Encyclopedia of the Second World War.* New York: Penguin, 1989, 1992, and as *The Macmillan Dictionary of the Second World War.* London: Macmillan, 1995.

Williams, Mary H., comp. *Chronology, 1941–1945. U.S. Army in World War II.* Washington, DC: GPO, 1960, 1989.

Young, John. *A Dictionary of Ships of the Royal Navy of the Second World War.* Cambridge, U.K.: Stephens, 1975.

Young, Peter, ed. *The Almanac of World War II: The Complete and Comprehensive Documentary of World War II.* New York: World Almanac, 1992, reprint of 1981 edition; various editions.

———, ed. *Atlas of the Second World War.* New York: Putnam, 1973, 1979; various editions.

Ziegler, Janet, comp. *World War II: Books in English, 1945–1965.* Stanford, CA: Hoover Institution, 1971.

4 Primary Published Sources and Published Documents

Eugene L. Rasor and Loyd E. Lee

Sources for the study of the Second World War are so extensive that several volumes would still be no more than an introduction. Manuscripts, memoranda, official documents, diaries, personal papers, photographs, films, recordings, and art are deposited at numerous archives and libraries throughout the world. Published sources also abound and continue to appear. As a consequence of recent fiftieth anniversaries of wartime events, many are being revised and reissued, especially serial publications of the air forces, armies, navies, and other services. Almost every country, even those not militarily involved in the war, has national and regional archives relating to the war years.

What follows is a brief outline of major archives and libraries of a general nature and those relating to civilian and military leaders and to the conduct of the war, with references to descriptions or guides to their contents. Also noted are selected published documentary sources and official histories. These are generally limited to English-language materials and are organized by country. For archives worldwide, with addresses, phone numbers, and key staff members, see the annual publication *The World of Learning*. For nongovernmental organizations, consult Baer, *International Organizations, Nineteen Eighteen to Nineteen Forty-Five*.

THE UNITED STATES

General

A general introduction to sources and resources for the history of the United States is Blazek and Perrault, *United States History: A Selective Guide to Information Sources*. The U.S. National Archives and Records Administration in Washington, as well as at its twelve regional branches and the

Presidential Libraries, and the U.S. Library of Congress are the institutions with the largest collections of original material relating to the war. Both are readily available to researchers and offer a wide variety of services. Bustard, "The World in Flames," outlined World War II documents in the U.S. National Archives. Mulligan's *Guide to Records* supplements and updates the 1950–1951 two-volume *Federal Records of World War II*, especially the second volume, *Military Agencies.* The archives also publishes special guides to documents on select topics. Major changes with significant relocation of documents are taking place among the archives' three facilities in and around Washington, D.C. *The Record,* a serial publication issued by the archives, contains news and information about recent acquisitions, declassifications, and publications.

The *Newsletter* of the World War Two Studies Association carries information about important archival holdings, acquisitions, and declassifications from its first publication in 1968 to the present, not only for the United States but for other countries as well.

A brief resource guide for World War II records at the Library of Congress is Rohrbach's *The Largest Event.* The libraries of the American air, military, and naval academies and the various war colleges and higher education centers at Colorado Springs, West Point, Annapolis, Maxwell Air Force Base (AFB), Carlisle Barracks, Newport, and Quantico are repositories of official, special, and personal collections associated with the war. Most also have extensive oral history collections.

The archives of most American states and those of many municipalities also have extensive collections, as do research libraries and many public libraries and universities.

Combined Chiefs of Staff and Joint Chiefs of Staff

An Anglo-American Combined Chiefs of Staff met regularly during the war to plan grand strategy. Its *Wartime Conferences* is available on microfilm. In the United States, military, naval, and air strategies and tactics were planned and controlled by the heads of the armed services, the Joint Chiefs of Staff. Its records are available on microfilm. An especially enlightening memoir on its work is *I Was There* by Admiral William D. Leahy, chairman of the Joint Chiefs of Staff and military assistant to Presidents Roosevelt and Truman.

U.S. Army and U.S. Army Air Forces

The U.S. Army maintains two important library and archival research centers in addition to the library of the U.S. Military Academy at West Point: the U.S. Army Military History Research Institute, Carlisle Barracks, Pennsylvania, and the Center of Military History in Washington. The director of the Army Military History Research Institute, Sommers, described its *Manuscript Holdings* in three volumes, with a recent update, while Aimone and Sibley covered those at West Point in "World War II Holdings of the U.S. Military Academy Library."

The primary U.S. Army Air Force (USAAF) resource center is the U.S. Air Force Historical Research Agency, formerly the Albert F. Simpson Historical Research Center, Maxwell Air Force Base, Alabama. Cornett's "Albert F. Simpson Historical Research Center" outlined its holdings and services.

U.S. Navy and U.S. Marine Corps

The primary facility for naval records is the Naval Historical Center, Washington Navy Yard, Washington, D.C. As a guide, see Allard, Crawley, and Edmison, *U.S. Naval History Sources in the U.S.* and *U.S. Naval Sources in the Washington Area.* More recently, Lloyd detailed the "World War II Holdings of the Operational Archives" of the center. The unpublished *Official Papers* of King, chief of naval operations on the Joint Chiefs of Staff, is available on microfilm. The papers of Halsey, King, and Knowles are at the Library of Congress, which has a published guide.

The U.S. Navy Department Library collected over three hundred unpublished histories of administrative and operational organizations such as the various bureaus, amphibious forces, and fleet commands. Heimdahl, *Guide to United States Naval Administrative Histories of World War II*, sorts out and describes these valuable primary sources.

Other naval repositories are the Library of the U.S. Naval Academy, Annapolis, Maryland, and the Naval Historical Collection at the U.S. Naval War College, Newport, Rhode Island. In the 1950s the Bureau of Personnel of the U.S. Navy sponsored detailed tactical and strategic analyses of major naval battles for the use of the Naval War College. Of these, Bates prepared *The Battle for Leyte Gulf*, the greatest naval battle in history; four of the seven studies written were published.

The Marine Corps' new, centralized academic and archival facilities are at its base in Quantico, Virginia. See Frank's *Marine Corps Oral History Collection Catalog* for its extensive holdings in that area.

The State Department and Executive Office

The most important printed primary sources on American diplomatic affairs are the annual series published by the U.S. Department of State, *Foreign Relations of the United States*, with several volumes covering each year by area and separate volumes for the Teheran, Yalta, and Potsdam summit conferences and other special topics. They are indexed by Aandahl. As these are selected documents governed by the perspectives of the date of publication, the files in the National Archives must also be consulted.

Ten Presidential Libraries house papers and associated materials of the presidents' administrations and contain research facilities for scholars, amateur as well as professional. Three stand out for the study of the war: the Franklin D. Roosevelt Library in Hyde Park, New York; the Harry S. Truman Library in Independence, Missouri; and the Dwight D. Eisenhower Library in Abilene, Kansas, though the latter is the most important. It contains records for all theaters. Six American presidents after Eisenhower were in military service during the war: John F. Kennedy, Lyndon B. Johnson, Richard Nixon, Gerald Ford, Jimmy Carter, and George Bush. Zobrist briefly described their resources in 1975; new material is continually being added to all these libraries. George described and documented civil records for the "United States Official Civil Histories of World War II."

Selected *Public Papers and Addresses of Franklin D. Roosevelt* were published with some annotation by the president himself. Sherwood edited four volumes of documents, *Roosevelt and Hopkins: An Intimate History* and *The White House Papers of Harry L. Hopkins,* influential associate of the president in a variety of diplomatic and military matters during the war. Essential for the study of Roosevelt's ideas and policies in foreign affairs, as well as his relations with the prime minister, is Kimball's *Churchill and Roosevelt: The Complete Correspondence.* For a guide to research on Roosevelt see Lester's *Roosevelt Research: Collections for the Study of Theodore, Franklin, and Eleanor.*

Private Archives and Libraries

The Hoover Institution and Library on War, Revolution, and Peace, founded in 1919 and located at Stanford University, has major collections on all aspects of the war throughout the world, including the papers of many prominent participants. For an introduction see Peterson, "World War II Holdings."

The New York Public Library in New York City has an extensive collection of manuscripts as well as wartime and postwar print material. The latter is detailed in the New York Public Library, *Subject Catalog of the World War II Collection,* the contents of which are not currently electronically online.

Important and unique repositories and research centers honor two great American generals of World War II, George C. Marshall and Douglas MacArthur, respectively, in Lexington, Virginia, on the campus of Virginia Military Institute and in Norfolk, Virginia. For Marshall's published papers see Bland's *The Papers of George Catlett Marshall; Selected World War II Correspondence.* The MacArthur Memorial Archives and Museum is an official agency of the city of Norfolk. For it see Boone's "Practicing the Historian's Craft" and "World War II Holdings of the Douglas MacArthur Memorial Archives." Each has elaborate facilities and extensive materials relating to the war; each conducts ambitious educational programs.

The Admiral Chester Nimitz Museum and Historical Center of Fredericksburg, Texas, described by Deac in "Admiral Nimitz Museum," collects material relating to the Pacific conflict.

GREAT BRITAIN

For an introduction see Foster and Sheppard, *British Archives: A Guide.* For archival material relating to World War II see *The Two World Wars: A Guide to Manuscript Collections in the United Kingdom* by Mayer and Koenig. The Public Record Office at Kew near London is the primary official repository for British government records. For its war records, see Cantwell, *The Second World War: A Guide.* For British foreign relations, consult Aster's *British Foreign Policy: A Guide.* The Public Record Office also has many unpublished mimeographed guides and other handbooks. Published diplomatic records do not extend into the war, though see *Principal War Telegrams and Memoranda.* Also see Nicholas, *Washington Despatches 1941–1945: Weekly Political Reports from the British Embassy;* the first drafts were written by Isaiah Berlin.

The documents of the Special Operations Executive (SOE), a combination secret service and intelligence agency, are being released for research. See Atherton's brief descriptions in *S.O.E. Operations in the Far East* and *S.O.E. Operations in Scandinavia.* Also see her *Top Secret: An Interim Guide to Recent Releases of Intelligence Records at the Public Record Office.* The footnotes of Hinsley's official history, *British Intelligence,* can also serve as a guide.

The Imperial War Museum has a massive collection on the war, including oral histories, letters, diaries, photographs, paintings, and sculptures. It is described by Jorré, "The Imperial War Museum," and Suddaby, "IWM: Rich Store for Writers." The facilities of the Royal United Service Institute for Defence Studies, founded in 1831 and located in Whitehall, London, are briefly described in Bidwell's "The Royal United Service Institute."

Based on generous foundation support, the Liddell Hart Centre for Military Archives, King's College, London, offers research opportunities and sources for scholars. It includes World War II material and the papers of Liddell Hart and many others involved in the war. Barnett, "British Military Archives," described the Churchill Archives Centre at Churchill College, Cambridge.

The British Library (formerly the British Museum Library), the Ministry of Defence Library, and the Portsmouth Public Library are other important centers for sources relating to the war. The Broadlands Archive at the library of the University of Southampton has the papers of Admiral

Lord Louis Mountbatten, including his personal diary; see Mitchell, *A Summary Catalogue of the Papers of Earl Mountbatten of Burma* and the Broadlands Archive, *Catalogues and Guides.*

Churchill quoted copiously from wartime documents in his six-volume *Second World War.* His papers for the first sixteen months of the war are in *The Churchill War Papers,* edited by Gilbert, and in volumes six and seven of James' *Winston S. Churchill: His Complete Speeches,* which covers all war years.

AUSTRALIA AND CANADA

The Australian War Memorial, the country's central museum and research facility for all wars, has *A General Guide to the Library Collections and Archives.* For printed material on Australian foreign relations during the war see Neale, *Documents on Australian Foreign Policy.*

In Canada, the National Defence Headquarters and Archives in Ottawa is the key archival depository; there are also relevant provincial and regimental archives. For a printed guide to public records, see O'Brien and Wright, *Sources for the Study of the Second World War.*

GERMANY

Many German documents were collected by American troops toward the end of the war. See the *Conference on Captured German and Related Records,* edited by Wolfe, for a discussion of this material. The originals have been returned to Germany, with microfilm copies kept in the U.S. National Archives, which previously published a series of guides. The records of the Berlin Document Center, now under German control, are also available in microfilm copies in the archives. For German foreign affairs see Kimmich's *German Foreign Policy, 1918–1945: A Guide to Research and Research Materials.* But the published, translated *Documents on German Foreign Policy, 1918–1945* is complete only to the end of 1941. For an English-language guide to German libraries and archives see Welsch, Danyel, and Kilton, *Archives and Libraries.*

Domarus' four-volume collection of Hitler's *Speeches and Proclamations* is being translated into English. Also see Hitler's *Table Talk.* Trevor-Roper's *Hitler's War Directives* contains the general guidelines for various campaigns, while Gilbert, *Hitler Directs His War,* contains translated portions from surviving texts of Hitler's military conferences.

OFFICIAL HISTORIES

Among the best published sources available on the war are the extensive series of official histories of the war sponsored by the various participating governments. See *Official Histories*, edited by Robin Higham, for a world survey and a forthcoming follow-up volume. National research and publication policies as well as authorial differences influenced the quality and importance of individual volumes. Nonetheless, their wide availability and scholarship make them essential for investigators. The official histories are also especially valuable, as their authors had access to official documents that were often collected and stored as a unit in archives and include worthwhile select narrative histories later condensed in the published volumes or never published. Though many were sanitized or censored for publication, in some cases later editions carry fuller texts. In any event, they can serve the researcher as a guide to existent archival materials.

The U.S. Army in World War II, the comprehensive green series, is exemplary. Its initial director, Kent Rogers Greenfield, chief historian of the army, wrote an account of the undertaking, *The Historian and the Army*. A *Reader's Guide* compiled by Adamczyk and MacGregor describes the series' contents. Craven and Cate's edited seven volumes of *The Army Air Forces in World War II*, though an official history, is less scholarly, less critical, and more partisan, compared to the army histories, and appeared much earlier. For the navy, S. E. Morison wrote most parts of the well-crafted *History of United States Naval Operations*. It includes the U.S. Marines, but a better introduction to the marines in the Pacific is Isely and Crowl's *The U.S. Marines and Amphibious War*.

The Military Series of the United Kingdom Official History was headed by James R. M. Butler. The British approach differed from the American. Instead of separate air force, army, and navy histories, the broad, comprehensive, interdepartmental approach prevailed. The series includes *Grand Strategy, The Mediterranean and Middle East, The War against Japan, Victory in the West, The War at Sea*, and *The Strategic Air Offensive*, as well as volumes on individual campaigns. Civil and Medical Series were also published, under the editorship of Keith Hancock and Arthur S. McNalty, respectively. Woodward's original one volume was later revised and expanded into a five-volume history of *British Foreign Policy*. A five-volume history in six parts of *British Intelligence*, essentially the original manuscript, was published under the direction of Hinsley.

The Australian official history in twenty-two volumes, *Australia in the War*, was overseen by Gavin Long. The forty-eight volumes of New Zealand's official history was undertaken by the War Histories Branch of the New Zealand Department of Internal Affairs. The official histories of Canada, as befits a federal polity, have a varied provenance. Pacesetting is Stacey's *Official History of the Canadian Army*. See Cooke, "Canada's Second World War," for other official volumes.

In 1979 the Military History Research Institute (Militärgeschichtliches Forschungsamt) of the Federal Republic of Germany began publishing a projected and massive ten-volume *Germany and the Second World War*, based on German archival and other sources. It is being translated into English. The Research Institute, now located in Potsdam, is a semiautonomous official body whose meticulous and critical research has received praise from scholars everywhere.

The official archives of Japanese military and civilian agencies were decimated, partly due to American bombing and partly due to systematic destruction by Japanese officials. Nevertheless, thirty thousand volumes of Japanese military records were seized, microfilmed, and later returned to the Japanese government. That process and its products are described by Morley, and a checklist is available by Young. Subsequently, several official efforts were made to reconstruct and formulate an official history. The Allied Occupation authorities, the Japanese government, and the Center of Military History in Washington sponsored major programs. One product was 185 *Japanese Monographs* on Japanese operations published by the U.S. Army. There is a *Guide*, and all is described, much of it reproduced, some in English translation, in Detwiler and Burdick, *War in Asia and the Pacific.* The equivalent official history of Japanese army operations in the "Greater East Asia War" is published in Japanese, in eight volumes, by Hattori.

BIBLIOGRAPHY

Also see chapters on specific topics for further discussion and references to sources and published documents.

Aandahl, Fredrick, comp. *The Cumulated Index to the U.S. Department of State Papers Relating to the Foreign Relations of the United States, 1939–1945.* 2 vols. Millwood, NY: Kraus, 1902.

Adamczyk, Richard D., and Morris J. MacGregor, comps. *United States Army in World War II: Reader's Guide.* Washington, DC: Center of Military History, U.S. Army, 1992.

Aimone, Alan C., and Judith A. Sibley. "World War II Holdings of the U.S. Military Academy Library." *Newsletter, American Committee on the Second World War 46* (Fall 1991): 22–33.

Allard, Dean C., and Betty Bern. *U.S. Naval History Sources in the Washington Area and Suggested Research Subjects.* Washington, DC: Naval History Division, Navy Department, 1965.

Allard, Dean C., Martha L. Crawley, and Mary W. Edmison, comps. *U.S. Naval History Sources in the U.S.* Washington, DC: GPO, 1979.

Arnold, Henry H. *Global Mission.* New York: Arno, 1949, 1989, among others. Different editions are of varying length.

Aster, Sidney, comp. and ed. *British Foreign Policy, 1918–1945: A Guide to Research and Research Materials.* Rev. ed. Wilmington, DE: Scholarly Resources, 1991.

Atherton, Louise. *S.O.E. Operations in the Far East: An Introductory Guide to the Newly Released Records of the Special Operations Executive in the Public Record Office.* London: PRO, 1993.

———. *S.O.E. Operations in Scandinavia: A Guide to the Newly Released Records in the Public Record Office.* London: PRO, 1994.

————. *Top Secret: An Interim Guide to Recent Releases of Intelligence Records at the Public Record Office.* London: PRO, 1993.

Australian War Memorial. *A General Guide to the Library Collections and Archives in the Australian War Memorial.* Canberra: AWM, 1983.

Baer, George W. *International Organizations, Nineteen Eighteen to Nineteen Forty-Five: A Guide to Research and Research Materials.* Wilmington, DE: Scholarly Resources, 1991.

Barnett, Correlli. "British Military Archives: Churchill Archives Centre." *Journal of the Society for Army Historical Research* (Summer 1983): 77–79.

Bates, Richard W. *The Battle for Leyte Gulf, October 1944: Strategical and Tactical Analysis.* Washington, DC: GPO, 1953–1958.

Bidwell, Shelford. "The Royal United Service Institute for Defence Studies, 1831–1991." *Journal of the United Service Institute 136* (1991): 68–72.

Bland, Larry I., ed. *The Papers of George Catlett Marshall.* 3 vols. Baltimore: Johns Hopkins UP, 1981–1992.

Blazek, Ron, and Anna H. Perrault. *United States History: A Selective Guide to Information Sources.* Englewood, CO: Libraries Unlimited, 1994.

Boone, Edward J., Jr. "Practicing the Historian's Craft: The MacArthur Papers." *Army Historian* (Spring 1985): 11–12.

————. "World War II Holdings of the Douglas MacArthur Memorial Archives." *Newsletter, American Committee on the History of the Second World War 46* (1991): 17–21.

Broadlands Archive. *Catalogues and Guides to the Archives.* Southampton, U.K.: Southampton, 1991.

Bustard, Bruce I. "The World in Flames: World War II Documents from the National Archives." *Prologue 23* (1991): 315–21.

Butler, James R. M., ed. *Grand Strategy.* 6 vols. London: HMSO, 1956–1976.

Cantwell, John D. *The Second World War: A Guide to Documents in the Public Record Office.* London: HMSO, 1972; Lanham, MD: UNIPUB, 1993.

Chandler, Alfred D., Jr., ed. *The Papers of Dwight David Eisenhower: The War Years.* 5 vols. Baltimore: Johns Hopkins UP, 1970.

Churchill, Winston. Vol. 1, *The Churchill War Papers: At the Admiralty, September 1939–May 1940*; vol 2, *Never Surrender May 1940–December 1940.* Ed. Martin Gilbert. New York: W. W. Norton, 1993–1995.

————. *History of the Second World War.* London: Chartwell and Boston: Houghton Mifflin, 1948–1953, and various other editions.

Cooke, O. A., et al. "Canada's Second World War." In Jürgen Rohwer and Hildegard Müller, eds., *Neue Forschungen zum Zweiten Weltkrieg. Literaturberichte und Bibliographien aus 67 Ländern,* 268–82. Koblenz: Bernard and Graefe, 1990.

Cornett, Lloyd. "The Albert F. Simpson Historical Research Center." *Aerospace Historian 25* (1978): 188–91.

Craven, Wesley F., and James L. Cate. *The Army Air Forces in World War II.* Chicago: University of Chicago, 1948.

Deac, Wilfred P. "Admiral Nimitz Museum." *Military History 10* (1993): 82–87.

Detwiler, Donald S., and Charles B. Burdick, eds. *War in Asia and the Pacific, 1937–1949.* 15 vols. New York: Garland, 1980.

Domarus, Max. *Hitler: Speeches and Proclamations 1932–1945: The Chronicle of a Dictatorship.* London and Wauconda, IL: Tauris, 1990.

Foster, Janet, and Julia Sheppard, eds. *British Archives: A Guide to Archive Resources in the United Kingdom.* New York: Stockton, 1982, 1995.

Frank, Benis M. *Marine Corps Oral History Collection Catalog.* Washington, DC: USMC, 1973, 1979.

George, Mary. "United States Official Civil Histories of World War II." In Robin Higham, ed., *Official Histories,* 620–32. Manhattan: Kansas State University Library, 1970.

German Military History Institute (Militärgeschichtliches Forschungsamt). *Germany and the Second World War.* Vol. 1, Wilhelm Deist et al.; *The Build-up of German Aggression;* vol. 2, Klaus Meier et al.; *Germany's Initial Conquests in Europe;* vol. 3, Gerhard Schreiber et al.; *The Mediterranean, South-East Europe and North Africa, 1939–1941: From Italy's Declaration of Non-Belligerence to the Entry of the United States into the War.* Trans. P. S. Falla et al. Oxford and New York: Clarendon, 1990–1995.

Germany. Auswärtiges Amt. *Documents on German Foreign Policy, 1918–1945, from the Archives of the German Foreign Ministry.* Washington, DC: GPO, 1949, published only to December 1941.

Gilbert, Felix, ed. *Hitler Directs His War.* Oxford and New York: Oxford UP, 1950; New York: Award Books, 1971.

Great Britain. Cabinet Office. *Principal War Telegrams and Memoranda, 1940–1943.* Nedeln, Liechtenstein: KTO, 1976.

Greenfield, Kent Roberts. *The Historian and the Army.* New Brunswick, NJ: Rutgers UP, 1954.

Hattori, Takushiro. *The Complete History of the Greater East Asia War.* 8 vols. Tokyo: Hara Shobo, 1953, 1955.

Heimdahl, William C. *Guide to United States Naval Administrative Histories of World War II.* Washington, DC: Naval History Division, Department of Navy, 1976.

Higham, Robin, ed. *Official Histories: Essays and Bibliographies from Around the World.* Manhattan: Kansas State University Library, 1970.

Hinsley, F. H., et al. *British Intelligence in the Second World War.* 5 vols. in 6 parts. New York: Cambridge UP, 1979–1993.

Hitler, Adolf. *Hitler's Secret Conversations, 1941–1944.* New York: New American Library, 1953, 1961. Also published as *Hitler's Table Talk.* London: Weidenfeld and Nicholson, 1953.

Isely, Jeter A., and Philip A. Crowl. *The U.S. Marines and Amphibious War: Its Theory and Practice in the Pacific.* Princeton: Princeton UP, 1951; Quantico, VA: Marine Corps Association, 1979.

James, Robert Rhodes, ed. *Winston S. Churchill: His Complete Speeches, 1897–1963.* Vol. 6, *1935–1942;* vol. 7, *1943–1949.* New York: Bowker, 1974; New York: Chelsea House, 1983.

Jorré, John de St. "The Imperial War Museum." *Military History Quarterly 3* (1991): 8–16.

Kimball, Warren. *Churchill and Roosevelt: The Complete Correspondence.* 3 vols. Princeton: Princeton UP, 1984.

Kimmich, Christoph M. *German Foreign Policy, 1918–1945: A Guide to Research and Research Materials.* Wilmington, DE: Scholarly Resources, 1984.

King, Ernest J. *Official Papers.* 10 reels, microfilm. Wilmington, DE: Scholarly Resources, 1991.

Leahy, William D. *I Was There: The Personal Story of the Chief of Staff to Presidents Roosevelt and Truman.* New York: Whittlesey, 1950.

Lester, DeeGee. *Roosevelt Research: Collections for the Study of Theodore, Franklin, and Eleanor.* Westport, CT: Greenwood, 1992.

Lloyd, Kathleen M. "World War II Holdings of the Operational Archives, Naval Historical Center: An Insider's View." *Newsletter, World War Two Studies Association 49* (1993): 26–33.

Long, Gavin, ed. *Australia in the War of 1939–1945.* Canberra: AWM, 1952–1977.

The Magic Documents: Summaries and Transcripts of the Top-Secret Diplomatic Communications of Japan, 1938–1945. 14 reels microfilm. Washington, DC: University Publications of America, 1980.

Marshall, George C. *The Papers of George C. Marshall: Selected World War II Correspondence.* 40 reels microfilm. Bethesda, MD: University Publications of America, 1992.

Mayer, S. L., and W. J. Koenig. *The Two World Wars: A Guide to Manuscript Collections in the United Kingdom.* New York: Bowker, 1976.

Mitchell, L. M., et al., eds. *A Summary Catalogue of the Papers of Earl Mountbatten of Burma.* Southampton: University Library, 1991.

Morison, Samuel Eliot. *History of United States Naval Operations in World War II.* 15 vols. Boston: Little, Brown, 1947–1962.

Morley, James W. "Checklist of Seized Japanese Records in the National Archives." *Far Eastern Quarterly 9* (1950): 306–33.

Mote, Frederick W. *Japanese-Sponsored Governments in China, 1937–1945: An Annotated Bibliography Compiled from Materials in the Chinese Collection of the Hoover Library.* Stanford, CA: Hoover Institution, 1954.

Mulligan, Timothy, comp. *Guide to Records Relating to U.S. Military Participation in World War II.* Washington, DC: National Archives and Records Administration, 1995.

National Archives and Records Administration. *Guides to German Records Microfilmed at Alexandria, Va.* Washington, DC: National Archives, 1958ff.

Neale, R. G., ed. *Documents on Australian Foreign Policy, 1937–49.* 9 vols. Canberra: Australian Government Publication Services, 1975–1988.

New York Public Library, Research Libraries. *Subject Catalog of the World War II Collection.* 3 vols. Boston: G. K. Hall, 1977.

Newsletter, World War Two Studies Association. Previously *Newsletter, Committee on the History of the Second World War,* twice yearly, 1968–   .

New Zealand Department of Internal Affairs, War History Branch. *Official History of New Zealand in the Second World War 1939–1945.* 48 vols. Wellington: War Histories Branch, 1949–1986.

Nicholas, H. G., ed. *Washington Despatches 1941–1945: Weekly Political Reports from the British Embassy.* Chicago: University of Chicago; London: Weidenfeld and Nicholson, 1981.

O'Brien, Jerome W., and Glenn T. Wright. *Sources for the Study of the Second World War./Documents sur la deuxième guerre mondiale.* Archives of Canada Public Records. Ottawa: Supply and Services Canada, 1979.

O'Neill, James E., and Robert W. Krauskopf, eds. *World War II: An Account of Its Documents.* Washington, DC: Howard UP, 1976.

Peterson, Agnes R. "World War II Holdings of the Hoover Institution on War, Revolution, and Peace." *Newsletter, World War Two Studies Association 50* (Fall 1993): 20–30.

Rohrbach, Peter J. *The Largest Event: A Library of Congress Resource Guide for World War II.* Washington, DC: Library of Congress, 1994.

Romanus, Charles F., and Riley Sunderland, eds. *Stilwell's Personal File: China–Burma–India, 1942–1944.* 5 vols. Wilmington, DE: Scholarly Resources, 1976.

Roosevelt, Franklin D. *The Public Papers and Addresses of Franklin D. Roosevelt.* 13 vols. New York: Random House, 1938–1952.

Seeley, Charlotte Palmer, comp. *American Women and the U.S. Armed Forces: A Guide to the Records of Military Agencies in the National Archives Relating to American Women.* Revised by Virginia C. Purdy and Robert Gruber. Washington, DC: National Archives and Records Administration, 1992.

Sherwood, Robert E., ed. *Roosevelt and Hopkins: An Intimate History.* 2 vols. New York: Harper, 1950.

———. *The White House Papers of Harry L. Hopkins: An Intimate History.* 2 vols. London: Eyre, 1948.

Sommers, Richard J., comp. *Manuscript Holdings of the U.S. Army Military History Research Collection.* 3 vols. Carlisle Barracks, PA: Military Institute, 1972.

———. "World War II Holdings of the U.S. Army Military History Institute." *Newsletter, World War Two Studies Association, 1992 47* (1992): 30–35.

Spector, Ronald H., ed. *Listening to the Enemy: Key Documents of the Role of Communications Intelligence in the War with Japan.* Wilimington, DE: Scholarly Resources, 1988.

Stacey, Charles P. *Official History of the Canadian Army in the Second World War.* 3 vols. Ottawa: Queen's Printer, 1955–1966.

Stilwell, Joseph W. *The Stilwell Papers.* New York: DaCapo, 1948, 1992.

Suddaby, Roderick. "IWM: Rich Store for Writers." *Army Quarterly and Defence Journal 124* (1994): 402–5.

Trevor-Roper, Hugh. *Hitler's War Directives, 1939–1945.* London: Pan, 1966.

U.S. Army in World War II. Official History. 78 vols. Washington, DC: GPO, 1949–1993.

U.S. Department of the Army. *Japanese Monographs.* Washington, DC: Office of the Chief of Military History, 1945–1960.

U.S. Department of State. *Foreign Relations of the United States: Diplomatic Papers, 1937–1945.* Washington, DC: GPO, 1954–1972.

U.S. Joint Chiefs of Staff. *Records of the Joint Chiefs of Staff: The European Theater.* 14 reels microfilm. Frederick, MD: University Publications of America, 1982.

———. *Records of the Joint Chiefs of Staff: Pacific Theater.* 14 reels, microfilm and guide. Frederick, MD: University Publications of America, 1983.

U.S. Library of Congress, Manuscript Division. *William Frederick Halsey, Jr., Ernest Joseph King, Herbert Bain Knowles: A Register of Their Papers in the Library of Congress.* Washington, DC: Library of Congress, 1983.

U.S. National Archives and Records Administration. *Federal Records of World War II.* Vol. 1, *Civilian Agencies;* vol. 2, *Military Agencies.* Detroit: Gale Research, 1950, 1982.

————. *Guide to the National Archives of the United States.* Washington, DC: Archives, 1987.

————. *Guide to the Federal Records in the National Archives of the United States.* 3 vols. Washington, DC: National Archives and Records Administration, 1996.

U.S. Navy, Naval War College. *Battle Analysis Series: Leyte Gulf, Coral Sea, Midway, and Savo Island.* 3 reels microfilm. Wilmington, DE: Scholarly Resources, 1988.

Wartime Conferences of the Combined Chiefs of Staff. 3 reels microfilm. Wilmington, DE: Scholarly Resources, 1984.

Welsch, Erwin K., comp. *Archives and Libraries in France.* New York: Council for European Studies, 1991.

Welsch, Erwin K., Jürgen Danyel, and Thomas D. Kilton, comps. *Archives and Libraries in the New Germany.* New York: Council for European Studies, 1994.

Wolfe, Robert, ed. *Conference on Captured German and Related Records: A National Archives Conference.* Athens: Ohio UP, 1975.

Woodward, Llewellyn. *British Foreign Policy in the Second World War.* 5 vols. London: HMSO, 1970–1976.

The World of Learning. London: European, published annually.

Young, John. *Checklist of Microfilm Reproduction of Selected Archives of the Japanese Army, Navy, and Other Government Agencies, 1868–1945.* 163 reels microfilm. Washington, DC: Georgetown UP, 1959.

Zobrist, Benedict K. "Resources of Presidential Libraries for the History of the Second World War." *Military Affairs 39* (1975): 82–85.

5 World War II Battlefields and Museums

Stephen T. Powers

While thousands of books have been published on World War II battles over the past half century, the battlefields and the monuments dotting them have received much less attention. Guides to only a handful of the most famous have been written, leaving those interested in walking the ground at a great disadvantage compared, say, to those interested in American Civil War battlefields. American and British Commonwealth interest in World War II battlefields has, of course, been muted by their distance from the battle sites. National official agencies as well as veterans' organizations and private groups, such as the Battle of Normandy Foundation, have made major contributions to the preservation and memorializing of battlefields around the world.

In practice, it is almost impossible to separate a discussion of a battlefield from the battle fought there or to describe a battle adequately without reference to terrain and maps. Many of the works cited later skate a thin line between the simple battle narrative and a wider view that takes into account the physical nature of the battlefield itself, both then and now. Compounding the ambivalence is the fact that some battlefields (or portions of them) have been carefully preserved and converted into shrines. These battlefield shrines, most notably Pearl Harbor, the Normandy beaches, Iwo Jima, and Hiroshima, have taken on symbolic meanings to national, and even international, groups that have elevated them above the many other battles, greater or lesser, that preceded or followed them.

Finally, there is physical change. Unlike the battle, which lives on only in memory, documents, and historical reconstructions, battlefields change constantly. Whether by suburban sprawl, jungle overgrowth, rust and marine encrustation, wind and rain, or the sprouting of stone monuments, the face of the battlefield is inevitably and continually altered. This is as true of the lovingly tended American cemetery at Omaha Beach as it is of the rusting hulks in the Truk lagoon.

Since museums with World War II exhibits abound, the coverage given them here is only cursory, brief introductions to those with significant collections throughout North America, Europe, and the Pacific and the literature describing them.

BATTLEFIELDS

The most comprehensive survey of World War II battlefields under one cover is Chandler's *Battles and Battlescenes of World War Two*, which includes descriptions of fifty-two land, sea, and air battles. Chandler's work is useful as a general introduction to the location of major World War II battlefields, although descriptions of the battlefields, as opposed to the battles, are limited.

Macdonald's 1984 *Great Battlefields of the World* broke new ground with computer-generated projections of battlefields from Cannae to Dien Bien Phu. This lavishly illustrated, large-format book contains chapters on four World War II battles—El Alamein, Kohima, Arnhem, and Iwo Jima. Macdonald followed it two years later with a similar work, *Great Battles of World War II*, with chapters on seventeen World War II battles, whose computer-generated battlefield projections certainly give the reader a greater appreciation of the actual terrain. Despite their coffee table format and lack of information on the battlefields today, Macdonald's books are another useful starting point.

Undoubtedly, the greatest source of information about World War II battlefields is the magazine *After the Battle*, published quarterly in London under the editorship of Winston G. Ramsey. Each issue contains an extended article on an individual World War II battle that highlights photographs of the battlefield taken during or shortly after the battle alongside recent photographs of the same scene. Although they declare adherence to the old adage that one photograph is worth a thousand words, the editors of the magazine often provide some of the longest and most informative captions in magazine history. The battle narratives conclude with a description (at much greater length in recent years) of the current status of the battlefield and its monuments. Well over eighty battles and battlefields have been dissected by the staff at *After the Battle*, making it an invaluable resource for those interested in World War II battlefields.

Over the years, *After the Battle* has also published a number of books on World War II battles and battlefields, ranging from a discussion of panzer operations in Normandy, to a day-by-day account of the London blitz, from an account of the Battle of Britain, to a description of the Eighth Air Force's airfields in England.

European Battlefields

A general introduction to the battlefields in Western Europe is Book-man and Powers, *March to Victory*. This work guides the reader on tours of selected battlefields and sites from the remaining Eighth Air Force bases in East Anglia, through London, to the Normandy beaches, on across France, Belgium, and Luxembourg, to the Rhine crossings. An appendix briefly describes the principal World War II museums in those countries. Holmes' *Army Battlefield Guide* covers northern France and Belgium. Denfeld's *World War II Museums and Relics of Europe* is a broader work that surveys, albeit incompletely, the major monuments, museums, and battlefields scattered across Europe, excluding the Soviet Union. For Canadian sites consult Copp's *A Canadian's Guide to the Battlefields of Northwest Europe*.

Two of the best books on the Eighth Air Force bases in England are Freeman, *Airfields of the Eighth*, and Kaplan and Smith, *One Last Look*. While the coverage in *Airfields of the Eighth* is more comprehensive, the lavish use of color then-and-now photographs sets *One Last Look* apart.

After the Battle's Ramsey has done another superb job in collecting material connected with the Battle of Britain in *The Battle of Britain*.

The city of London, especially its East End, was a vast World War II battlefield. Although dotted with monuments and plaques commemorating events of the war, London's trials as a battlefield had been neglected until the publication of Ramsey's *The Blitz*, Demarne's *London Blitz: A Fireman's Tale*, and Ziegler's *London at War*.

On the far shore, the Normandy beachheads have received a great deal of attention, first from Boussel's 1964 *D-Day Beaches Revisited* and more recently from Holt and Holt's *Holt's Battlefield Guides: Normandy-Overlord* and their *Visitor's Guide to Normandy Landing Beaches*; Florentin, *Gateway to Victory*; Evans, *Guide to the Beaches and Battlefields of Normandy*; and Man, *Penguin Atlas of D-Day and the Normandy Campaign*. Lefèvre, *Panzers in Normandy*, develops the Wehrmacht perspective on the Normandy battles and battlefields.

Although Paris was largely spared the ravages of direct military action during the war, the city is dotted with plaques that commemorate its liberation in 1944. Most of number 14 (1976) of *After the Battle* is devoted to that story. A more detailed discussion of the 1,553 memorial plaques connected to the war can be found in Sauber, "Traces Fragiles."

The Holts produced another in their Battlefield Guide Series on Operation Market-Garden to guide the traveler along the route of the Allied advance into Holland. Also useful in reconstructing the First British Airborne Division's fight for Arnhem itself is found in *After the Battle*'s article "Arnhem" in number 2 (1973). *After the Battle* revisited Market-Garden in a special 1990 issue, "Prelude to Market Garden."

Allied battlefield monuments are carefully noted and photographed in Pallud, *Battle of the Bulge*, even though the story of *Wacht am Rhein* is told from the German perspective; the battlefields of the 1940 blitzkrieg through the Ardennes are explored in his *Blitzkrieg in the West*.

Pacific Battlefields

Pacific battlefields are widely scattered and much less accessible than those in Western Europe. Still, these sites have seen a steady stream of visitors since 1945, first to assess bomb damage and recover the dead, then to scuba dive on the sunken ships and revisit scenes of the war. Recently, the gun emplacements at Tarawa have been restored in an effort to attract tourist dollars. The state of preservation of World War II sites in the Pacific and what should be done in the future are the subject of Spennemann's article "The Politics of Heritage."

Guides to the battlefields are few, and most information about them today must be gleaned from a small number of articles and books. Possibly the best general guide to Pacific battlefields, although that was not its primary intent, is Manchester's *Goodbye, Darkness*, wherein the author takes the reader on a cathartic tour of selected Pacific battlefields. Probably the two most famous are those at Pearl Harbor and Hiroshima. Both sites have been visited by the *After the Battle* team in numbers 38 (1982) and 41 (1983).

Historical sites on Oahu are covered by Keys in *Where Were You in 42?* The history of the USS Arizona Memorial is described in Wisniewski, *Pearl Harbor and the USS Arizona Memorial*, and Slackman's *Remembering Pearl Harbor*. Linenthal has interpreted the meaning of the Pearl Harbor battlefield and the controversies surrounding it in his *Sacred Ground*, while Delgado in "Memorials, Myths and Symbols" assesses the Arizona Memorial as "a naval memorial, a war grave, and a national symbol."

David Green takes the reader back to the Palau Islands in two *After the Battle* articles, "Palau 50 Years On" (no. 76, 1992) and "Peleliu" (no. 78, 1992). Other *After the Battle* issues feature "Tarawa and Operation Galvanic" (no. 15, 1977), "Corregidor" (no. 23, 1979), "Singapore" (no. 31, 1981), "Battle for Okinawa—A Marine Returns" (no. 43, 1984), "Battle of Hong Kong" (no. 46, 1984), and "Aleutians" (no. 62, 1988).

One of the more unusual World War II battlefields, Iron Bottom Sound off Guadalcanal, has been chronicled by Ballard's *Lost Ships of Guadalcanal* and the video of his underwater exploration to find nineteen of the approximately fifty ships sunk there in 1942–1943, *Lost Fleet of Guadalcanal*.

Iwo Jima, because of the myths surrounding the flag raising, has recently been the subject of two studies—Marling and Wetenhall, *Iwo Jima*, and Albee and Freeman, *Shadow of Suribachi*. *After the Battle* featured "Iwo Jima" in 1993 (no. 82).

From 1989 to 1992, *Pacific Magazine* published a series of brief articles by Hinz on some of the major Pacific battlefields and bases, most appearing under the general title, "Then and Now: Battlegrounds of World War II": Honiara (May/June 1989); Tarawa (September/October 1990); Guadalcanal (November/December 1990); Rabaul (January/February 1991); Saipan (March/April 1991); Truk (May/June 1991); Wake Island (July/August 1991); New Guinea (September/October 1991); Pearl Harbor (November/December 1991); Peleliu (January/February 1992); the New Hebrides (March/April 1992); Midway (May/June 1992); the Marshall Islands (July/August 1992); and Guam (September/October 1992). Thompson recently surveyed the Wake Island battlefield in "Wake Island."

After the Battle revisited the sites, from Oak Ridge to Nagasaki, connected with the wartime production and deployment of the atomic bomb in no. 41 (1983).

Battlefield Monuments and Cemeteries

One feature of modern battlefields, especially those of World War II, is the profusion of monuments that have sprung up near them. The first permanent monuments were put in place while the war was still in progress, and the dedication of new ones has continued steadily to the present, as the military buddies, family, and friends of those who fought and died all have sought to commemorate the sacrifices made at that time and place.

No comprehensive directory of World War II memorials exists. The aforementioned works by Bookman and Powers, Denfeld, the Holts, Florentin, Pallud, and Evans, together with many other articles and books cited, especially those published by Battle of Britain Prints, mention hundreds of monuments but are quickly outdated as the landscape of memory constantly changes.

The use of monuments, memorials, and military cemeteries to create the "Myth of the War Experience" is analyzed by Mosse's *Fallen Soldiers*. Ignatieff's "Soviet War Memorials" and Popov's "Reminders of Glory" both explore the role of the war monument in creating the myth of the Great Patriotic War.

Shortly after the war, permanent cemeteries were set aside, and the remains of the dead were moved to them. These cemeteries remain among the most visited World War II sites by the general public and, for many, define the human dimension of the war as no museum or battlefield can. Gibson and Ward's *Courage Remembered* contains a great deal of useful information on British Commonwealth cemeteries and the monuments associated with them. The Commonwealth War Graves Commission, the American Battle Monuments Commission, the Volksbund

Deutscher Kriegsgräbefürsorge, and the French Ministère des Anciens Combattants all publish brochures describing the cemeteries and monuments under their control.

MUSEUMS

Military museums form an invaluable aid to the understanding of battlefields, not only by preserving artifacts of the battle but by offering the viewer a means to envision and interpret the events in a more graphic manner. The large, scale model of Mulberry B (the floating dock off Gold Beach in Normandy) in the Musée du Débarquement at Arromanches comes immediately to mind. Without it, the wreckage of the real Mulberry, visible from the museum, is unintelligible. Possibly the most masterful use of a museum as an interpretive device is the Musée Mémorial at Caen, where the exhibits are arranged so as to enable the visitor to interpret D-Day and the Battle of Normandy in the context of the origins and course of the Second World War in Europe.

Four standard guides that are helpful in locating museums of all types are the American Association of Museums, *Official Museum Directory, The Directory of Museums and Living Displays, The Cambridge Guide to the Museums of Europe,* and *Museums of the World.* All index military and naval museums but do not identify those devoted exclusively to World War II. More tightly focused is Lundeberg's "Museum Collections as Historical Sources," which conceives of museum collections as including works on all eras of American military and naval history, especially as they relate to the matériel that finds its way into museums. Hoff's *Directory of Museums of Arms and Military History* is now badly out of date but still useful for its worldwide coverage. Although many of the museums with World War II exhibits publish catalogs or descriptive brochures describing their collections, the bewildering number of sponsoring agencies and museum types makes classification difficult.

American and Canadian Museums

Various appendages of the U.S. federal government maintain an impressive number of museums with World War II exhibits. For a brief overview read Ewing's "Military Museums and Collections." The Smithsonian Institution, despite the controversy surrounding its *Enola Gay* effort, exhibits World War II military aircraft at its National Air and Space Museum. Its holdings are described in Bryan's *National Air and Space Museum* and Oakes' *Aircraft of the National Air and Space Museum.* The National Museum of American History also contains significant exhibits dealing with the war, including a reproduction of the Fermi atomic pile.

U.S. Army museums, including the George S. Patton Armor Museum at Ft. Knox, Kentucky; the U.S. Army Ordnance Museum at the Aberdeen Proving Ground, Maryland; and four located in Germany are described in Phillips, *Guide to U.S. Army Museums*. The Eisenhower Center at the University of New Orleans plans to open a National D-Day Museum. A list of smaller, nonarmy-operated museums can be found in MacKenzie's "World War II Exhibitions and Collections."

Naval museums and surviving World War II warships in the United States and Canada are covered in Smith's *Naval Institute Guide to Maritime Museums of North America*. The Naval Historical Center's brochure-sized *Guide to U.S. Naval Museums* lists those museums maintained by the U.S. Navy.

The National Park Service operates the U.S. Arizona Memorial and Museum. A number of preserved warships, which are scattered around the United States, are described in Butowski's *Warships Associated with World War II in the Pacific* and Brouwer's *International Register of Historic Ships*. "America's Preserved Warships," *After the Battle*, no. 12 (1976), features the four battleships *Massachusetts, Texas, Alabama*, and *North Carolina* and the carrier *Yorktown*. The four Iowa-class battleships, now mothballed, are lovingly described in Muir, *Iowa Class Battleships*. The multivolume *Dictionary of American Fighting Ships* contains biographies of all U.S. Navy warships.

The Admiral Nimitz Museum and Historical Center in Fredericksburg, Texas, maintains the Museum of the Pacific War, which contains significant collections relating to the Pacific conflict.

The U.S. Marine Corps' principal museums are located at the Marine Corps Historical Center in the Washington Navy Yard and at the U.S. Marine Corps Land/Air Museum, Quantico, Virginia.

The Air Force Museum Foundation published a catalog of the collection at Wright-Patterson AFB. The museum is further described in Apple, *Air Force Museum*. There are also significant displays of World War II military aircraft (on loan from the Air Force Museum) at Barksdale, Beale, Castle, Lackland, and March Air Force Bases. The Confederate Air Force (CAF), based in Midland, Texas, maintains the American Airpower Heritage Museum, where it keeps 135 World War II military aircraft in flying condition. The CAF also publishes a quarterly magazine, *Dispatch*, that features articles about the museum's collection and displays.

The story of the Manhattan project is told in the Bradbury Science Hall and Museum at Los Alamos and the National Atomic Museum at Kirtland AFB in Albuquerque. Early rocketry is one focus of the Space Museum at Alamogordo.

Seven of the eleven Canadian military museums with major World War II collections are regimental museums; those, with the Royal Canadian Ordinance Museum in Montreal, the Royal Canadian Artillery Museum in Shilo, and the Canadian War Museum and National Aviation Museum in Ottawa, can be found in *Museums of the World.* Canada's newly rehoused national aviation museum in Ottawa is the subject of Molson's *Canada's National Aviation Museum.* There are also several dozen Canadian regimental museums and several naval vessels.

European Museums

All but the most recently opened European museums can be found in *Museums of the World;* the larger ones are described in the elegant *Cambridge Guide to European Museums* under the headings of military history, aviation, aviation history, and naval history.

England abounds with museums dealing with the war, many of which are identified by Bookman and Powers. Principal ones are the Imperial War Museum, the RAF Museum at Hendon, the D-Day Museum at Portsmouth, the Royal Armoured Corps Tank Museum at Bovington Camp, and the Museum of the Airborne Forces in Aldershot. *The Imperial War Museum Handbook* and Simkins' *Cabinet War Rooms* are useful guides to those respective museums. The Imperial War Museum's aircraft museum at Duxford is the subject of its *Duxford Handbook,* as is Raby's "Fighter Station to War Museum."

Bookman and Powers also list the principal museums in France, Belgium, Luxembourg, and the Netherlands. Florentin, Evans, and the Holts provide current lists of D-Day museums in Normandy, several of which opened during the fiftieth-anniversary celebrations. There are many important museums scattered across Western Europe, with the largest number concentrated in Normandy. Peck takes the reader along on his 1979 whirlwind tour of air museums in "Touring Europe's Air Museums."

Italy has World War II museums in Trieste, San Sabba, the Fosse Ardeatine (outside Rome), and Rome (the Museo Storico della Liberazione di Roma). Paladini's *Via Tasso* is a guide to the last-named museum. Many national museums and military museums throughout Europe have sections devoted to the war. In the former Soviet Union there are important museums in Moscow, Borodino, Minsk, and Volgagrad.

Holocaust Museums

The United States Holocaust Memorial Museum in Washington, D.C., opened in 1994 to mark the liberation of the death camps in 1945; it is described in Weinberg and Elieli, *The Holocaust Museum.* Other major Holocaust museums are planned for Boston, New York, and Berlin in addition to the nineteen or so that already exist worldwide. Israel's Yad Vashem maintains the major Holocaust museum outside the United States. The Association of Holocaust Organizations publishes a worldwide *Directory* of its members, including those that have museums.

Rooms in the Musée Mémorial in Caen, France, and the Oorlogsmuseum near Overloon in the Netherlands have exhibits exploring the dimensions of the Holocaust in those countries. The Amsterdam house that sheltered Anne Frank's family is open to the public. Most of the former camps maintain exhibits dealing with local events. James Young's *Texture of Memory* gives meaning to the amazing variety of Holocaust monuments that have been dedicated in the past half century.

Pacific Museums

Despite the vast nature of the Pacific conflict and the debris of war scattered across the area, museums commemorating the war are few.

The three principal Australian museums are the Australian War Memorial at Campbell, the Military Museum at Deloraine, and the Tuggerah Lakes Military Museum at Berkeley Vale. The first is described in Stanley, *Guide to the Australian War Memorial*, and its history is outlined in Inglis, "A Sacred Place."

The dropping of the atomic bombs on Japan is memorialized at the Hiroshima Peace Memorial Museum and the Nagasaki International Cultural Hall.

BIBLIOGRAPHY

After the Battle. Ed. Winston G. Ramsey. London: Battle of Britain Prints, 1973–present. Individual numbers are cited in the text.

After the Battle. *The Battle of Britain: Then and Now.* Ed. Winston G. Ramsey. London: Battle of Britain Prints, 1989.

After the Battle. *The Blitz: Then and Now.* 3 vols. Ed. Winston G. Ramsey. London: Battle of Britain Prints, 1987–1990.

Air Force Museum Foundation. *United States Air Force Museum.* Wright-Patterson AFB, OH, 1993.

Albee, Parker Bishop, Jr., and Keller Cushing Freeman. *Shadow of Suribachi.* New York: Praeger, 1995.

American Association of Museums. *The Official Museum Directory.* 24th ed. New Providence, NJ: R. R. Bowker, 1993.

Apple, Nick P., and Gene Gurney. *The Air Force Museum.* 6th rev. ed. Dayton, OH: Central, 1991.

Association of Holocaust Organizations. *Directory, 1995.* Ed. William L. Shulman. Bayside, NY: Holocaust Resource Center and Archives, 1995.

Ballard, Robert D. *The Lost Fleet of Guadalcanal.* National Geographic Society, 1993. Videocassette.

———. *The Lost Ships of Guadalcanal.* New York: Warner Books, 1993.

Bookman, John T., and Stephen T. Powers. *The March to Victory.* 2d rev. ed. Boulder: University of Colorado, 1994.

Boussel, Patrice. *D-Day Beaches Revisited.* Trans. F. M. Watkins. Paris: Librairie Po-
    lytechnique Béranger, 1964.
Brouwer, Norman J. *International Register of Historic Ships.* 2d ed. Oswestry, U.K.: A.
    Nelson; Peekskill, NY: Sea History, 1993.
Bryan, C.D.B. *The National Air and Space Museum.* New York: Abrams, 1988.
Butowski, Harry A. *Warships Associated with World War II in the Pacific.* Washington,
    DC: National Park Service, 1985.
The Cambridge Guide to the Museums of Europe. Comp. Kenneth Hudson and Ann
    Nicholls. Cambridge: Cambridge UP, 1991.
Chandler, David G. *Battles and Battlescenes of World War Two.* London: Arms and
    Armour, 1989.
Confederate Air Force. *The Dispatch: The Confederate Air Force Magazine.* Midland,
    TX.
Copp, Terry. *A Canadian's Guide to the Battlefields of Northwest Europe.* Waterloo,
    Ontario: Laurier Centre for Military Strategic and Disarmament Studies,
    1994.
Delgado, James P. "Memorials, Myths and Symbols: The Significance of the Ari-
    zona Memorial." *The Valley Forge Journal 5* (1991): 310–26.
Demarne, Cyril. *The London Blitz: A Fireman's Tale.* London: Battle of Britain Prints,
    1991.
Denfeld, Duane. *World War II Museums and Relics of Europe.* Manhattan, KS: MA/
    AH, 1980.
The Directory of Museums and Living Displays. 3d ed. Comp. Kenneth Hudson and
    Ann Nicholls. New York: Stockton, 1985.
Evans, David. *A Guide to the Beaches and Battlefields of Normandy.* London: Michael
    Joseph, 1994.
Ewing, Joseph. "Military Museums and Collections." In John E. Jessup, Jr., and
    Robert W. Coakley, eds., *A Guide to the Study of Military History,* 339–48.
    Washington, DC: GPO, 1979.
Florentin, Eddy. *Gateway to Victory: The Five D-Day Beaches.* Trans. Jacques Boyer.
    Paris: Tallandier, 1989.
Freeman, Roger A. *Airfields of the Eighth: Then and Now.* London: Battle of Britain
    Prints, 1989.
Gibson, T. A., and G. Kingsley Ward. *Courage Remembered.* London: HMSO, 1989.
Guide to U.S. Naval Museums. Comp. the Naval Historical Center. Washington, DC,
    1993.
Hoff, Arne, ed. *Directory of Museums of Arms and Military History.* Copenhagen: Töj-
    husmuseet, 1970.
Holmes, Richard. *Army Battlefield Guide: Belgium and Northern France.* London:
    HSMO, 1995.
Holt, Tonie, and Valmai Holt. *Holt's Battlefield Guides: Market-Garden. Corridor.* Lon-
    don: Leo Cooper, 1984.
———. *Holt's Battlefield Guides: Normandy–Overlord.* London: Leo Cooper, 1983.
———. *The Visitor's Guide to Normandy Landing Beaches, Memorials and Museums.*
    Ashbourne, U.K.: Moorland; Edison, NJ: Hunter, 1994.
Ignatieff, Michael. "Soviet War Memorials." *History Workshop Journal 17* (1984):
    157–63.

Imperial War Museum. *Imperial War Museum, Duxford Handbook.* Duxford, Cambridgeshire: Museum, 1988.

———. *The Imperial War Museum Handbook.* London: Museum, 1985.

Inglis, K. S. "A Sacred Place: The Making of the Australian War Memorial." *War and Society 3* (1985): 99–126.

Kaplan, Philip, and Rex Alan Smith. *One Last Look.* New York: Abbeville, 1983.

Keys, George F. *Where Were You in 42?* Honolulu, HI: Privately published, 1991.

Lefèvre, Eric. *Panzers in Normandy: Then and Now.* London: Battle of Britain Prints, 1983.

Linenthal, Edward. *Sacred Ground.* Urbana: University of Illinois, 1991.

Lundeberg, Philip K. "Museum Collections as Historical Sources." In Robin Higham and Donald Mrozek, eds., *A Guide to the Sources of United States Military History, Supplement III,* 374–426. Hamden, CT: Archon, 1993.

Macdonald, John. *Great Battles of the World.* New York: Macmillan, 1984.

———. *Great Battlefields of World War II.* New York: Macmillan, 1986.

MacKenzie, Beth F. "World War II Exhibitions and Collections." *Army History 24* (1992): 28–30.

Man, John. *The Penguin Atlas of D-Day and the Normandy Campaign.* London: Penguin, 1994.

Manchester, William. *Goodbye, Darkness: A Memoir of the Pacific War.* Boston: Little, Brown, 1979.

Marling, Karal Ann, and John Wetenhall. *Iwo Jima: Monuments, Memories, and the American Hero.* Cambridge, MA: Harvard UP, 1991.

Molson, Kenneth M. *Canada's National Aviation Museum: Its History and Collections.* Ottawa: National Aviation Museum, 1988.

Mosse, George L. *Fallen Soldiers: Reshaping the Memory of the World Wars.* New York: Oxford UP, 1990.

Muir, Malcolm. *The Iowa Class Battleships.* New York: Dorset, 1987.

Museums of the World: Museen der Welt. 3d rev. ed. Munich: K. G. Saur, 1981.

Oakes, Claudia M. *Aircraft of the National Air and Space Museum.* Washington, DC: Smithsonian, 1985.

Pacific Magazine, 1989–1992. (Honolulu, HI.)

Paladini, Arrigo. *Via Tasso.* Rome: Istituto Poligrafico, 1986.

Pallud, Jean Paul. *Battle of the Bulge: Then and Now.* London: Battle of Britain Prints, 1984.

———. *Blitzkrieg in the West: Then and Now.* London: Battle of Britain Prints, 1991.

Peck, Edward. "Touring Europe's Air Museums." *Aerospace Historian 26* (1979): 154–60.

Phillips, R. Cody. *A Guide to U.S. Army Museums.* Washington, DC: Center for Military History, 1992.

Popov, Vladimir I. "Reminders of Glory: Soviet War Memorials." *Cultures 2* (1975): 135–43.

Raby, Alister. "Fighter Station to War Museum: Duxford Airfield's Seventy Years in Aviation History." *Aerospace Historian 35* (1988): 137–40.

Ramsey, Winston G. See *After the Battle.*

Sauber, Mariana. "Traces Fragiles: Les plaques commemorative dans les rues de Paris." *Annales 48* (1993): 715–27.

Simkins, Peter. *Cabinet War Rooms.* London: Imperial War Museum, 1983.

Slackman, Michael. *Remembering Pearl Harbor: The Story of the USS Arizona Memorial.* 7th ed. Honolulu, HI: Arizona Memorial Museum Association, 1993.

Smith, Robert H. *Naval Institute Guide to Maritime Museums of North America.* Annapolis, MD: NIP, 1990.

Spennemann, Dirk H. R. "The Politics of Heritage: Second World War Remains on Central Pacific Islands." *The Pacific Review 5* (1992): 278–90.

Stanley, Peter. *A Guide to the Australian War Memorial.* Sidney: John Ferguson, 1986.

Thompson, Erwin N. "Wake Island: 50 Years Ago—and Today." *Periodical 17* (1990): 27–41.

Weinberg, Jeshujahu, and Rina Elieli. *The Holocaust Museum in Washington.* New York: Rizzoli, 1995.

Wisniewski, Richard A. *Pearl Harbor and the USS Arizona Memorial: A Pictorial History.* Honolulu, HI: Pacific Basin Enterprises, 1986.

Young, James E. *The Texture of Memory: Holocaust Memorials and Meaning.* New Haven, CT: Yale UP, 1993.

Ziegler, Philip. *London at War, 1939–1945.* New York: Knopf, 1995.

6 Personal Narratives of War Leaders

Loyd E. Lee

An important source for understanding and writing about the Second World War is the diaries, memoirs, letters, and interviews or oral histories of its principal leaders. Most useful are diaries that have not been altered to suit later political or military interests; especially valuable are those written only as a personal record, with no intention of publication. Such diaries are rare.

Many prominent diarists knew their involvement in decision making and leadership were historic and kept notes for the specific purpose of leaving a public record.

Other memoirs or autobiographies were composed after 1945; usually they were based, at least in part, on diaries and notes kept during the war. Of whatever type, they can be revealing or deceiving, sometimes dull, or interesting and incisive. At their best, memoirs offer a reflective retrospect of events in which the writer participated that may be absent in diaries. Many personalities, however, either did not keep diaries, could not turn what they had into publishable accounts, or chose not to make them public or even to bequeath them to manuscript collections for later historians. Described here are some of the most important published personal accounts by individuals who were political leaders and statesmen or close to such leaders, and senior officers in the armed forces. From the many published, the following account is selective and representative. The reader should consult appropriate bibliographies or national biographical dictionaries for other personal narratives.

BRITAIN AND THE COMMONWEALTH

Civilians

British wartime leaders have produced numerous personal accounts. Although not strictly a memoir, Churchill's six-volume *The Second World War* falls somewhere among a memoir, a collection of official documents, and general history; he described events in which he took part, using papers he had handled during the war. Anthony Eden, who resigned in February 1938 from Chamberlain's government, rejoined the government in 1940, first becoming secretary of state for war, then foreign secretary, in which capacity he traveled widely and accompanied Churchill to wartime conferences. *The Eden Memoirs* incorporates various official documents and parts of his own diaries. Dilks' careful editing of the extensive *Diaries of Sir Alexander Cadogan*, permanent undersecretary of state for foreign affairs and a close adviser of Churchill, covers the war years portion of his continuous journal from 1933 until the late 1960s. Churchill's secretary John Colville published portions of his diary in *The Fringes of Power*, indicating deletions and explanatory paragraphs. Conservative politician Harold Macmillan, British liaison to Eisenhower's headquarters in North Africa, played an important role in policy making, as found in his *Blast of War;* he also used official documents and other nonautobiographical material.

The massive second volume of *The Empire at Bay: The Leo Amery Diaries*, edited by Barnes and Nicholson, relates the public life of a staunch British imperialist, especially his parliamentary activities and his contacts with important personalities. Also see Pimlott's edited selections from *The Second World War Diary of Hugh Dalton*, British Labour leader and minister of economic warfare and the only Labour leader in the government to keep a diary.

Lord Casey kept a daily diary of his activities as Australian minister to the United States and British representative in the Middle East and India; he turned this long work into a narrative of his *Personal Experience, 1939–1946.* For the memoirs of the Australian prime minister for the first two years of the war, see Robert Menzies' *Afternoon Light.* The four volumes of the *Mackenzie King Record*, edited by Pickersgill and Forster, is a rather formal account by the Canadian prime minister of his official activities throughout the war, not a personal record.

Military and Naval

There are a large number of British military memoirs. The chief of the Imperial General Staff for the first nine months of the war, Edmund Ironside, reluctantly agreed to allow publication of extracts from his diary,

Time Unguarded. His successor, John Dill, who died in Washington in 1944 while on the Combined Chiefs of Staff, left no diary. Following him was the Viscount Alanbrooke (also Alan Brooke), whose *The Turn of the Tide* and *Triumph in the West*, edited by Bryant, are not quite diaries or autobiographies, as the full titles suggest. John Kennedy, director of military operations in the British Army's General Staff, differed with many military policies, though his *Business of War* (cut by half for publication) emphasized the administrative side of the conflict more than intramural controversies.

Henry Pownall, who held several commands, most in Asia before he retired because of ill health, wrote twelve volumes of his diary, not intending them for publication and never revising or editing them. Bond's two-volume selection from that diary in *Chief of Staff* omits some sections. Commander in Chief, Middle East, Wavell's *Journal* was edited by Moon; Churchill replaced him in July 1941, making him commander in chief, India, and in 1943 viceroy of India.

Montgomery's *Memoirs* describes his life from boyhood days to the establishment of the North Atlantic Treaty Organization (NATO), including his command in North Africa and invasion of Western Europe; they should be compared with his chief of staff de Guingand's *Operation Victory*. Horrocks, who served under Montgomery for most of the war from Dunkirk to Arnhem, gave his side of the controversies, along with much else, in *A Full Life*. Soon after the war, Wilson, Eisenhower's successor as supreme commander in the Mediterranean, published his *Eight Years Overseas*. Alexander, whose wartime career was also largely spent in the Mediterranean theater, succeeded him. J. North edited his wartime *Memoirs*. Slim's *Defeat into Victory* tells the Burma Fourteenth Army campaign story, which earned him general high respect as a field commander, but also see his more candid *Unofficial History*. Also see Commander in Chief, Southeast Asia, Mountbatten's *Diary* as supreme allied commander from 1943 to 1946. An important Australian general's memoirs are those of Blamey, who became Australian commander in chief of ground forces in 1939 but whose reputation sank thereafter.

Tedder, Eisenhower's deputy for Overlord, and a man often at odds with Churchill and noted for his supranational cooperativeness, titled his memoirs *With Prejudice*, by which he indicated that he had his own particular views on many issues of the war. In *Bomber Offensive*, Bomber Command's Commander in Chief Harris defended the still-controversial "area bombing," which, though briefly popular for a while, by war's end conflicted with Allied policy. Slessor's *The Central Blue* combines autobiographical reflections with a detailed history of the RAF in which he played a variety of key roles, from coastal defense, to the battle of the Atlantic and as commander of RAF Mediterranean forces.

Among naval leaders, see Cunningham's full, factual *A Sailor's Odyssey*, by the commander in chief of the British Mediterranean fleet at the start of the war and first sea lord after October 1943. *The Year of D-Day* is from the diaries of Ramsay, naval commander in chief for Neptune, the assault on the Normandy beaches; he was killed in a 1945 air accident.

GERMANY

Civilian

Hitler left no wartime diary, though briefly many outstanding authorities believed one had surfaced. For that farcical story see Hamilton's *The Hitler Diaries*. As partial substitutes, in addition to official documents and speeches, we do have *Hitler's Secret Conversations* (*Table Talk*), a record of his late-night ramblings in his bunker. The garrulous Goebbels, the Nazi propaganda minister, kept a detailed diary from 1924 to 1945, handwritten to July 1941, dictated after that. Only portions have been published in English: Lochner edited and translated selections, *The Goebbels Diaries*; Taylor's translated edition, *The Goebbels Diaries*, covers the period from late 1939 to July 1941; Trevor-Roper edited those for the last six weeks of the Third Reich and included details on the manuscript's history, an annex of speeches, a chronology, and gazetteer.

More extensive than Goebbels' diary are the various memoirs by Albert Speer, confidant of Hitler and minister of armaments and munitions from February 1942, beginning with *Inside the Third Reich*, written while in Berlin's Spandau prison. He also wrote *Spandau: The Secret Diaries*; while not a wartime diary, it includes many reminiscences and entries regarding the war. Its elaborate table of contents with brief summaries and dated entries makes it easy to consult. Many consider these to be little more than insincere attempts to dissociate himself from the Nazi regime. Von Papen, the 1932 German chancellor and later ambassador to Austria (whose annexation he helped prepare) and then to Turkey, was acquitted at Nuremberg. His memoirs and those of the generally uninfluential Nazi foreign minister after 1938, von Ribbentrop, are available in English.

Important and notorious are the postwar memoirs of Rudolf Hoess, *Commandant of Auschwitz*, written between October 1946 and his execution in April 1947 while in a Polish prison. *Death Dealer*, edited by Paskul, includes these memoirs plus final letters and other material. General Reinhard Gehlen directed the intelligence branch of the German High Command on the eastern front as well as that of the German Federal Republic after the war. See *The Service* for his memoirs.

Two important personal documents from leaders in German society and the German resistance are by Fabian von Schlabrendorff and Ulrich von Hassell. *The Secret War against Hitler* is by von Schlabrendorff, the officer who placed a bomb that failed to explode in Hitler's plane in 1943; though arrested, he managed to survive the war and write this firsthand account of the conspiracy. Ambassador to Italy before the war but pensioned in 1938 because of his opposition, von Hassell in his *Diaries* reflects the activities of a staunch conservative and monarchist closely involved in the military–civilian conspiracy to overthrow Hitler. Executed in 1944, his diaries were found hidden on his estate. Also of interest are the *Letters to Freya*, which Helmuth von Moltke wrote to his wife. The German edition is incomplete, and the English translation is even shorter; the letters include family matters as well as those relating to the conspiracy named after his Silesian estate Kreisau, where he brought together many resistance leaders.

Military and Naval

Military leaders writing memoirs after the war usually attempted to distance themselves from the regime that they once loyally served and from which they benefited. Von Manstein wrote *Lost Victories*, an account of the battles in Poland, France, and Russia; he served four years in prison after the war. Guderian in *Panzer Leader* covered his role in campaigns in Poland, France, and Russia. More important for understanding armored warfare are the memoirs of von Mellenthin, *Panzer Battles*.

For Kesselring, Luftwaffe officer who spent most of the war in the Mediterranean theater, see *Kesselring: A Soldier's Record*, written from memory. Rommel left no diary, but Basil Liddell Hart edited his letters, reports, and other materials as *The Rommel Papers*, including a narrative commentary for the campaigns in France, Africa, Italy, and the invasion of Western Europe.

Halder, chief of the Army General Staff from September 1938 until September 1942, kept a detailed war diary. Not intended for official use, it was published as *The Halder War Diary, 1939–1942* and in a one-volume abridged edition by Burdick and Jacobsen as *Kriegstagebuch: The Halder War Diary*, which eliminated family and personal material. Most important for understanding the workings of the German military headquarters is Warlimont's *Inside Hitler's Headquarters*; he served from September 1939 until September 1944 as deputy chief of operations staff of the German Armed Forces High Command, a position giving him close access to all wartime military leaders and the Führer. The memoirs include various appendixes and fragments of conferences. Lesser known but more frank is von Senger und Etterlin's *Neither Fear nor Hope*. A Rhodes scholar, a Catholic from southwest Germany, and writer on military affairs, he commanded a panzer division in Sicily in 1943 and the Fourteenth Panzer Corps, which defended Monte Cassino in Italy in 1944.

The memoirs of pioneer Luftwaffe ace Galland, *The First and the Last*, coincide with the German air force's wartime history. Written in the mid-1980s, *Panzer Commander* by von Luck, an apolitical Prussian aristocrat who rose to command a tank regiment at Normandy, is an honest recounting by a thoughtful officer. Raeder, German navy chief from 1928 until 1943, wrote *My Life*. The *Memoirs* of his successor, Donitz (also spelled Doenitz or Dönitz), covers his long career as submarine commander and as head of the German navy for the last two years of the war.

JAPAN

Memoirs of Japanese leaders in English are scarce. Shigenori Togo wrote his autobiography, *The Cause of Japan*, while serving a postwar sentence. Ambassador to Germany and then the Soviet Union, Togo became foreign minister under Tojo in October 1941; he favored peace with the United States and resigned two years later. Gordon Prange called Admiral Ugaki's diary, *Fading Victory*, the "best documentation of the last days of Japan's road to war in the Pacific and her conflict with the U.S. from the hand of any Japanese public official in any branch of the government" (Foreword). The original fifteen volumes are greatly reduced to 731 pages in the English translation.

THE SOVIET UNION

Few Soviet civilian leaders left memoirs. Chuev interviewed Molotov, second most powerful man in the Soviet Union during the war, over a period of seventeen years for *Molotov Remembers*. The Soviet Union's ambassador to Great Britain, Maisky, used his diary along with official documents, letters, and other memoirs to construct his *Memoirs of a Soviet Ambassador*. In 1943 he became deputy people's commissar for foreign affairs and attended the Yalta and Potsdam conferences. Gromyko, an agricultural economist by profession, became ambassador to the United States and attended several wartime conferences; the first chapters of his *Memoirs* describe these events.

Several Russian generals published memoirs after the war, many of which have very little personal content and are unclear as to their exact sources. One of the most celebrated Russian officers, Zhukov, whose wartime military career extended from defeating the Japanese in the summer of 1939 at Khalkin-Gol (Nomonhan) through various Eastern Front campaigns and the fall of Berlin, worked on his memoirs for many years before publishing them in Russian in 1969; a translation, *Memoirs*, followed in 1971. Bialer edited selections in *Stalin and His Generals*, which includes maps and an extensive biographical index with a paragraph each on forty-five officers. He also provided a useful bibliography and commentary on the politics and history of Soviet war literature.

THE UNITED STATES

Civilians

President Roosevelt left no diary, but his son edited *F.D.R. His Personal Letters*, a portion of which covers the war years. Many of those around Roosevelt, however, either kept diaries or wrote memoirs after the war. Leahy, a friend of the president since World War I, became his chief of staff and chair of the Joint Chiefs of Staff in 1942, from which he wrote soon after the war his insider's *I Was There*. Hassett, a presidential aide, began his diary in January 1942 at age sixty-one, published in 1958 as *Off the Record with FDR*. President Truman published a two-volume *Memoirs*; the volume *1945: Year of Decisions* gave his version of the initial months of his presidency, the growing conflict with the Russians, and the use of the atomic bomb against Japan, among other matters.

Several cabinet officials published personal accounts. Stimson, secretary of war, entitled his *On Active Service in Peace and War*. Another Republican and secretary of the interior throughout the Roosevelt years, Ickes kept a diary accumulating to some six million words, writing it over the weekends. Only a portion has been published, and only the third volume, *The Lowering Clouds*, relates to wartime. Secretary of State Hull, notoriously ignored by the president, tried to create a narrative of those years in volume two of his *Memoirs*, using memoranda, telegrams, and other documents as his basis. His successor in 1944 was Stettinius; his *Diaries* for the period October 1943 to June 1946 was edited by Campbell and Herring from a mass of copies of phone calls, end-of-the-day dictated summaries, and long reports of his various missions. A Wall Street financier with limited international experience, he served in various capacities for the president.

The tone of the memoirs of the war's last secretary of state, Byrnes, is discerned in its title, *Speaking Frankly*. Byrnes attended the Yalta conference (but as an outsider), becoming Truman's secretary of state in July 1945. He transcribed wartime Gregg shorthand notes, admitting that "writing is a profession," and "it is not my profession." Blum edited the *Morganthau Diaries*, of which two volumes, *Years of Urgency* and *Years of War*, cover the period. Morgenthau, a New York friend of Roosevelt's and secretary of the treasury, is most known for his proposed punitive Morgenthau Plan for Germany; he also played a key role in shaping the Bretton Woods conference and the postwar world economic order. Retired Rear Admiral Emory Land's *Winning the War with Ships* describes his return to government service in 1938 as chair of the U.S. Maritime Commission and later the War Shipping Administration.

There are several important memoirs from Americans involved in foreign relations during the war. An attorney by profession, Acheson became assistant secretary of state in 1941, the beginning of a decade of service in the State Department; the first part of *Present at the Creation* deals with the war period. The American ambassador to the Soviet Union from 1936 to 1938, Davies, in his best-seller *Mission to Moscow*, 1941, naively thought that "[n]o leaders of a nation have been so misrepresented and misunderstood as those in the Soviet Government during those critical years between the two world wars" (vii). Standley's memoirs, authored with Agerton, took a contrary view, depicting the chaos of American relations with the Soviet Union during his brief and, by some accounts, unsuccessful tenure as ambassador in 1942–1943. He was succeeded by businessman Harriman, whose *Special Envoy to Churchill and Stalin* is based on notes and letters of the time but written later with professional assistance.

Charles Bohlen, stationed in Moscow for most of the war and translator for Roosevelt at Tehran, wrote on his service under Roosevelt in the second part of his *Witness to History*, whittled down by his editor Phelps to about one-third its original, nearly indecipherable length. Kennan, State Department official in Berlin before the war and in Moscow as Harriman's adviser after 1944, covered Germany until 1941 and Soviet affairs to 1950 in his *Memoirs*. Murphy, another career diplomat, played a role comparable to Macmillan's in North Africa and the Mediterranean until late 1944, when he was assigned to Germany; his *Diplomat among Warriors* detailed his key role in many events.

Military and Naval

Several leading American army commanders in the European theater published personal accounts as part of a postwar debate over the conduct of the war. Eisenhower's ghosted *Crusade in Europe* avoided controversy. His *Diaries*, edited by Ferrell, begins with his years in the Philippines, but it is incomplete, as he kept it only sporadically, and portions are lost. Ferrell published the entire diary for January–July 1942, while some other portions can be found in Chandler and Galambos' edition of his *Papers*; there is nothing for the period December 1944 to December 1945. Also see *Ike's Letters to a Friend*.

Having served in the Mediterranean theater and commanded the First U.S. Army in Northwestern Europe, Bradley in *A Soldier's Story* and later in *A General's Life* delivered neither a diary nor strictly a memoir. He used the diary of his aide Chester B. Hansen as well as documents for events or decisions in which he was not involved. Critical of both Montgomery and Patton, he tried to explain the effect of patriotism and personalities among officers who had not been abroad before. Ridgway commanded the Eighty-second Airborne Division in Italy and Normandy; he too had assistance in writing his memoirs, *Soldier*.

Patton's *War as I Knew It*, edited by his wife, includes letters from Africa and Sicily, a narrative of Overlord, "Reflections and Suggestions," and selections based on his diary from July 1942 to December 1945. Blumenson edited *The Patton Papers*, which are largely from his journal. He left out tactical and operational material in order to reveal Patton's role but included letters to his wife and a few from her, as well as some extracts from the journal of his headquarters. Clark, primarily known as commander of the U.S. Fifth Army in Italy and subsequently supreme commander in the Mediterranean, accepted the German surrender in Italy and headed the American occupation of Austria. A talented and ambitious individual, he told his story in *Calculated Risk*.

Other important European theater personal accounts by American commanders include Collins' *Lightning Joe*, which reflects his role at Guadalcanal, Normandy, and the Battle of the Bulge, and Gavin's *On to Berlin: Battles of an Airborne Commander*. Gavin was responsible for the development of doctrine, training, and organization of airborne operations; he led the Eighty-second Airborne Division on D-Day. Immediately after the war, Butcher, an Eisenhower family friend and the general's naval aide, published *My Three Years with Eisenhower*, a near daily account and the first inside view of Eisenhower's headquarters.

MacArthur's presence overshadowed that of all others in the Southwest Pacific. Three of the ten chapters in his *Reminiscences* present his retrospective thoughts on aspects of his controversial wartime career. When he was withdrawn from Bataan in 1942, he left Wainwright behind to surrender; his *Story* relates three years of Japanese cruelty and draws policy conclusions for the conduct and treatment of future prisoners of war. Luvaas' carefully edited letters of Eichelberger to his wife, *Dear Miss Em*, frankly show his differences of opinion with other theater commanders. Kenney's *Reports* details his innovative and successful improvement of air operations as MacArthur's chief air officer. Another of MacArthur's commanders, Chase of the First Cavalry Division, Eleventh Corps, wrote an *Autobiography* of his wartime career, especially in the recapturing of Luzon in the Philippines.

For the China, India, and Burma theater see General Stilwell's *Papers*. Head of the U.S. military mission to Chiang Kai-shek, Stilwell's forthright criticism of incompetence and candid views, presented in his own words from his official papers and letters to his wife, reflects his turbulent two and a half years in East Asia. Also see the memoirs of his aide Dorn, *Walkout: With Stilwell in Burma*. Stilwell's successor, Wedemeyer, a China expert, was better suited to the difficult task, though his *Wedemeyer Reports!* is also often critical of Chiang Kai-shek.

On the American air war, see *Global Mission*, the aptly titled memoirs of Arnold, head of the U.S. Army Air Forces (USAAF) throughout the war. Two sections of LeMay's full life memoirs, *Mission*, cover his experiences in Europe and as commander of the air war against Japan in 1945.

Of different interest are the flamboyant Doolittle's memoirs, *I Could Never Be So Lucky Again*. Chennault's lengthy *Way of a Fighter* recounts organizing the American volunteer Flying Tigers and commanding the Fourteenth USAAF in China as well as his postwar criticisms of American policies toward that country.

The commander in chief of the U.S. Fleet from December 1941 and principal creator of the navy's victory plan, King wrote his memoirs in retirement. Nimitz, commander in chief, U.S. Pacific Fleet after Pearl Harbor, left no memoirs, but see Halsey's (and Bryan) *Story* as aggressive carrier commander in the Pacific campaigns. Other important memoirs are those of Clarke, *Carrier Admiral,* commander of the USS *Suwanee* in the invasion of Northwest Africa and of the new USS *Yorktown* after 1943, and Radford, *From Pearl Harbor to Vietnam*. Lockwood's autobiography, *Down to the Sea in Subs*, is about his three years as head of the Pacific submarine force; he has written widely on submarine warfare. A well-documented memoir by a submariner, Fluckey's *Thunder Below!* is based on logs (including those of the Japanese) and messages, letters, oral histories, and an illegally kept diary.

Grove's *Now It Can Be Told*, a memoir, recounts his controversial administration of the Manhattan District, the project that produced the atomic bomb.

OTHER NATIONAL LEADERS

The most important French memoir from the Second World War is that of de Gaulle, *War Memoirs*, beginning with his exile in England after the fall of France and his formation of the "Free French" armed forces, ending with his leadership of the French resistance and recognition in 1944 as head of the liberation's provisional government. Also noteworthy is Edouard Daladier's *Prison Journal, 1940–1945*. French premier at Munich, he headed the government until March 1940; arrested by the Vichy regime, he was tried and handed over to the Germans. His prison notes were found posthumously by his son and first published in France in 1991.

Mussolini's son-in-law and foreign minister from 1936 to 1943, Ciano, kept the only diary by a high Italian official available in English. Smuggled out of Italy by his wife and microfilmed in part, *The Ciano Diaries* appeared shortly after the war. The president of Czechoslovakia before and after the war, Benes focused his uncompleted *Memoirs* on the immediate post-Munich period, never forgiving the British and the French for abandoning his country. The Polish ambassador to the United Kingdom and foreign minister in the exile government, Raczynski, began his diary in 1934. Unlike the general European custom, he did not revise it into a memoir, except for occasional explanations; it covers the important war years from the Polish government in exile's view.

Eisenhower, Dwight D. *Crusade in Europe.* Garden City, NY: Doubleday, 1948.

————. *Ike's Letters to a Friend, 1941–1958.* Lawrence: UP of Kansas, 1984.

————. *The Papers of Dwight David Eisenhower.* Ed. Alfred Dupont Chandler and Louis Galambos. Baltimore: Johns Hopkins UP, 1970.

Ferrell, Robert H., ed. *The Eisenhower Diaries.* New York and London: W. W. Norton, 1981.

Fluckey, Eugene B. *Thunder Below! The USS Barb Revolutionizes Submarine Warfare in World War II.* Urbana and Chicago: University of Illinois, 1992.

Galland, Adolf. *The First and the Last: The Rise and Fall of the German Fighter Forces, 1938–1945.* Trans. Mervyn Savill. New York: Henry Holt, 1969.

Gaulle, Charles de. *War Memoirs.* Vol. 1, *The Call to Honour, 1940–1942*; vol. 2, *Unity, 1942–1944*; vol. 3, *Salvation, 1944–1946.* New York: Simon and Schuster, 1955.

Gavin, James M. *On to Berlin: Battles of an Airborne Commander, 1943–1946.* New York: Viking, 1978.

Gehlen, Reinhard. *The Service: The Memoirs of General Reinhard Gehlen.* New York: World, 1972.

Goebbels, Joseph. *The Goebbels Diaries, 1942–1943.* Ed. and trans. Louis Lochner. Garden City, NY: Doubleday; Washington, DC: Infantry Journal, 1948.

————. *The Goebbels Diaries: The Last Days.* Ed. Hugh Trevor-Roper; trans. Richard Barry. London: Book Club Associates, 1978.

————. *The Goebbels Diaries, 1939–1941.* Ed. and trans. Fred Taylor. New York: G. P. Putnam's Sons, 1983.

Gromyko, Andrei A. *Memoirs.* New York: Doubleday, 1989.

Groves, Leslie R. *Now It Can Be Told: The Story of the Manhattan Project.* New York: DaCapo, 1983.

Guderian, Heinz. *Panzer Leader.* London: Futura, 1952; New York: Da Capo; Washington, DC: Zenger, 1979.

Halder, Franz. *The Halder War Diary.* London: Greenhill, 1946; Novato, CA: Presidio, 1988.

Halsey, William F., and Joseph Bryan. *Admiral Halsey's Story.* New York: Whittlesey House, 1947; Washington, DC: Zenger, 1980.

Hamilton, Charles. *The Hitler Diaries: Fakes That Fooled the World.* Lexington: UP of Kentucky, 1991.

Harriman, W. Averell, with Elie Abel. *Special Envoy to Churchill and Stalin, 1941–1945.* New York: Random House, 1975.

Harris, Arthur T. *Bomber Offensive.* London: Collins, 1947.

Hassell, Ulrich von. *The Von Hassell Diaries, 1938–1944: The Story of the Forces against Hitler inside Germany.* Garden City, NY: Doubleday, 1947; Boulder, CO: Westview, 1994.

Hassett, William D. *Off the Record with FDR, 1942–1945.* New Brunswick, NJ: Rutgers UP, 1958.

Hitler, Adolf. *Hitler's Table Talk, 1941–1944; Secret Conversations, 1941–1944.* London: Weidenfeld and Nicholson; New York: Farrar, Straus, and Young, 1953.

Hoess, Rudolf. *Commandant of Auschwitz: The Autobiography of Rudolf Hoess.* London: Pan, 1974.

————. *Death Dealer: The Memoirs of the SS Kommandant at Auschwitz.* Ed. Steven

Paskul; trans. Andrew Pollinger. Buffalo, NY: Prometheus, 1992; New York: Da Capo, 1996, 1992.

Horrocks, Brian. *A Full Life.* London: Collins, 1960.

Hull, Cordell. *The Memoirs of Cordell Hull.* New York: Macmillan, 1948.

Ickes, Harold L. *The Secret Diary of Harold L. Ickes.* Vol. 3, *The Lowering Clouds, 1939–1941.* New York: Simon and Schuster, 1953.

Ironside, Edmund. *Time Unguarded: The Ironside Diaries, 1937–1940.* Ed. R. Macleod and D. Kelly. London: Constable; New York: David McKay, 1962.

Kennan, George F. *Memoirs 1925–1950.* Boston and Toronto: Little, Brown, 1967.

Kennedy, John. *The Business of War; the War Narrative of John Kennedy.* Ed. Walter Millis. New York: William Morrow, 1958.

Kenney, George C. *General Kenney Reports: A Personal History of the Pacific War.* New York: Duell, 1949.

Kesselring, Albert. *Kesselring: A Soldier's Record.* New York: Morrow, 1954; Westport, CT: Greenwood, 1970, 1988.

King, Ernest J. *Fleet Admiral King: A Naval Record.* New York: W. W. Norton, 1952; London: Eyre and Spottiswood, 1953; New York: Da Capo, 1976.

Land, Emory Scott. *Winning the War with Ships: Land, Sea and Air—Mostly Land.* New York: Robert M. McBridge, 1957.

Leahy, William D. *I Was There: The Personal Story of the Chief of Staff to Presidents Roosevelt and Truman Based on His Notes and Diaries Made at the Time.* New York: Whittlesley House, 1950.

LeMay, Curtis, with MacKinlay Kantor. *Mission with LeMay; My Story.* Garden City, NY: Doubleday, 1965.

Lockwood, Charles A. *Down to the Sea in Subs.* New York: Norton, 1967.

Luck, Hans von. *Panzer Commander: The Memoirs of Colonel Hans von Luck.* New York, Westport, CT, and London: Praeger, 1989.

MacArthur, Douglas. *Reminiscences.* New York, Toronto, and London: McGraw-Hill, 1964.

Macmillan, Harold. *The Blast of War, 1939–1945.* New York: Harper and Row, 1968.

Maisky, Ivan. *Memoirs of a Soviet Ambassador: The War: 1939–1945.* London: Hutchinson, 1967; New York: Charles Scribner's Sons, 1968.

Manstein, Erich von. *Lost Victories.* London: Methuen, 1958; Chicago: H. Regnery, 1958; Elstree, U.K.: Herts Greenhill, 1987, 1958; Novato, CA: Presidio, 1982.

Mellenthin, F. W. von. *Panzer Battles: A Study of the Employment of Armor in the Second World War.* Ed. I.C.F. Turner; and trans. H. Betzler. Norman: University of Oklahoma Press, 1956.

Menzies, Robert. *Afternoon Light: Some Memories of Men and Events.* London: Cassell, 1967; New York: Coward-McCann, 1967.

Moltke, Helmuth James Graf von. *Letters to Freya, 1939–1945.* New York: Knopf, 1990.

Montgomery, Bernard Law. *The Memoirs of Field-Marshal the Viscount Montgomery of Alamein, K.G.* Cleveland: World, 1958; New York: Da Capo, 1982.

Mountbatten, Louis. *Personal Diary of Admiral the Lord Louis Mountbatten, Supreme Allied Commander, South-East Asia, 1943–1946.* London: Collins, 1988.

Murphy, Robert D. *Diplomat among Warriors.* Garden City, NY: Doubleday, 1964.

Papen, Franz von. *Memoirs.* London: A. Deutsch, 1952.

Patton, George S., Jr. *War as I Knew It.* Boston: Houghton Mifflin, 1947.

Pickersgill, J. W., and D. F. Forster. *The Mackenzie King Record.* Toronto: University of Toronto, 1960.

Pimlott, Ben, ed. *The Second World War Diary of Hugh Dalton, 1940–45.* London: Jonathan Cape, 1986.

Pownall, Henry. *Chief of Staff: The Diaries of Lieutenant-General Sir Henry Pownall.* 2 vols. Ed. Brian Bond. London: Leo Cooper, 1972.

Raczynski, Edward. *In Allied London.* London: Weidenfeld, 1962.

Radford, Arthur W. *From Pearl Harbor to Vietnam: The Memoirs of Admiral Arthur W. Radford.* Stanford, CA: Hoover Institute, 1980.

Raeder, Erich. *My Life.* Trans. H. W. Prexel. Annapolis, MD: NIP, 1960; New York: Arno, 1980.

Ramsay, Bertram Home. *The Year of D-Day: The 1944 Diary of Admiral Sir Bertram Ramsay.* Hull: University of Hull Press, 1994.

Ribbentrop, Joachim von. *The Ribbentrop Memoirs.* London: Weidenfeld and Nicolson, 1983.

Ridgway, Matthew B. *Soldier: The Memoirs of Matthew B. Ridgway, as told to Harold H. Martin.* New York: Harper, 1956.

Rommel, Erwin. *The Rommel Papers.* Ed. B. H. Liddell Hart; trans. Paul Findlay. New York: Harcourt, Brace; London: Collins, 1953.

Roosevelt, Elliott, ed. *F.D.R. His Personal Letters.* New York: Duel, Sloan, and Pearce, 1947.

Schlabrendorff, Fabian von. *The Secret War against Hitler.* London: Hodder and Stoughton, 1966; Boulder, CO: Westview, 1965.

Senger und Etterlin, Frido von. *Neither Fear nor Hope: The Wartime Memoirs of the German Defender of Cassino.* Trans. George Malcolm. Novato, CA: Presidio and London: Greenhill, 1963.

Slessor, John. *The Central Blue: Autobiography.* London: Cassell; New York: Praeger, 1957.

Slim, William. *Defeat into Victory.* London: Cassell, 1956, 1972.

———. *Unofficial History.* London: Cassell, 1960; London: Transworld, 1970.

Speer, Albert. *Inside the Third Reich: Memoirs.* New York: Macmillan, 1970.

———. *Spandau: The Secret Diaries.* New York: Macmillan, 1976.

Standley, William Harrison, and Arthur A. Agerton. *Admiral Ambassador to Russia.* Chicago: R. Regnery, 1955.

Stilwell, Joseph. *The Stilwell Papers.* New York: W. Sloane, 1948.

Stimson, Henry. *On Active Service in Peace and War.* New York: Harper, 1948.

Tedder, Arthur William. *With Prejudice: The War Memoirs of Marshal of the Royal Air Force, Lord Tedder, G.C.B.* Boston: Little, Brown; London: Cassell, 1966.

Togo, Shigenori. *The Cause of Japan.* New York: Simon and Schuster, 1956; Westport, CT: Greenwood, 1977.

Trevor-Roper, Hugh, ed. *Final Entries 1945: The Diaries of Joseph Goebbels.* New York: G. P. Putnam's Sons, 1978.

Truman, Harry S. *Memoirs of Harry S. Truman.* Vol. 1, *1945: Year of Decisions;* vol. 2, *Years of Trial and Hope.* Garden City, NY: Doubleday, 1955; New York: Da Capo, 1986.

Ugaki Matome. *Fading Victory: The Diary of Admiral Matome Ugaki.* Ed. Donald M. Goldstein and Katherine V. Dillon; trans. Masataka Chihaya. Pittsburgh: University of Pittsburgh, 1991.

Wainwright, Jonathan Mayhew. *General Wainwright's Story: The Account of Four Years of Humiliating Defeat, Surrender, and Captivity.* Ed. Robert Considine. Westport, CT: Greenwood, 1946.

Warlimont, Walter. *Inside Hitler's Headquarters, 1939–45.* New York: Praeger, 1961; Novato, CA: Presidio, 1962.

Wavell, Archibald Percival. *Wavell: The Viceroy's Journal.* Ed. E. P. Moon. London: Oxford UP, 1973.

Wedemeyer, Albert C. *Wedemeyer Reports!* New York: Holt, 1958.

Wilson, Henry Maitland. *Eight Years Overseas, 1939–1947.* London and New York: Hutchinson, 1948.

Zhukov, Georgi K. *The Memoirs of Marshal Zhukov.* Ed. Harrison Salisbury; trans. Theodor Shabad. London: Jonathan Cape; New York: Delacorte, 1971.

7 Personal Narratives of Sailors, Soldiers, and Civilians

Loyd E. Lee

Thousands of ordinary participants in the Second World War, civilian as well as military, wrote about their wartime experiences, though apparently not as many as for the First World War. Such diaries, memoirs, letters, interviews, and oral histories generally shed little light on the grand issues of strategy, diplomacy, and politics. Instead, they provide insight into the varieties of impact those years had on ordinary people. Diary keepers were not run-of-the-mill individuals; they were generally better educated than most, often writing for themselves in order to reflect on their impressions.

There are far more diaries and letters from the middle classes than from workers, farmers, and enlisted men and women. While there were no general orders in the military against keeping diaries, it was widely rumored that the practice was disapproved (and in some cases was against orders). Other factors limiting the keeping of diaries include soldiers' mobility, the provisional nature of living at the front, and the absence of privacy.

Most valuable are diaries or letters published as written; ones edited soon after the war were subject to prevailing literary conventions and self-censorship that are no longer present. Memoirs written or rewritten after the war, more common for European than American writers, are also of interest as witnesses who were there and who had time to develop mature considerations regarding their experiences. Of the personal narratives constructed late in a participant's life, the most valuable historically use wartime documents, such as logs, after-action battle reports, and so forth, though the reader should weigh internal evidence against original sources and the writers' postwar careers.

One of the greatest needs for the study of personal narratives is comprehensive, annotated bibliographies to provide the groundwork for investigating the entire gamut of war experiences for individuals, social groups, and societies as a whole.

There are national bibliographies of diaries and memoirs, but none comprehensive or specific to participants in the war. In spite of growing interest in personal narratives, oral history, and war memoirs, only a few publishers have been willing to bring such works to the public, forcing authors either to finance self-publication or to donate their manuscripts to repositories.

Oral histories are collected by many libraries, universities, museums, and research institutes, but a comprehensive account of their records is lacking. Perks' 1990 *Oral History* is generally inclusive for Great Britain, but only selective for the rest of the world. It brings together sources in print and published recordings based on, or using, oral history. Dornbusch's *Histories; Personal Narratives; United States Army* is limited in scope and is out of date. Barnard's *Oral History* lists oral history transcripts, mostly from U.S. Army generals.

This chapter is very selective of many hundreds of published personal accounts, giving preference to a few that vividly portray some aspect of the war, are clearly based in wartime experience and/or documentation, and are devoted primarily to the war years. They also illustrate the diversity within this genre.

Descriptions of personal narratives by those in military service, organized first by nationality and then by service for the European theater and by service alone for the Pacific, are followed by those of individuals in civilian life. At the end are a few collected works and especially noteworthy oral histories.

MILITARY EXPERIENCE IN EUROPE

United States

Air Forces. Among the best American memoirs is Ardery's *Bomber Pilot.* He explained with engrossing detail his training experiences and the missions of the 389th Bomb Group against the oil fields of Ploesti, Romania, and targets in Germany. Also well written, but in a more forthright language, in this case by a navigator in the 379th Bomb Group, is Bendiner's *The Fall of Fortresses.* He flew in the first missions against Schweinfurt. Both returned to civilian life after the war. Colgan's personal account, *World War II Fighter-Bomber Pilot,* used official sources and personal recollection to recount his many combat missions and adventures in the Seventy-ninth and Eighty-sixth Fighter Groups in southern Italy, southern France, and Germany. A retired career air force flier, he included many photos. *The Lucky Bastard Club* by Fletcher is in two parts: first a narrative memoir of his training and combat and a second part based on letters to his wife from early 1944 to 1945. Also noteworthy is *Gabby: A Fighter Pilot's Life*, a memoir by Gabreski, a career airman and ace who shot down thirty-one German fighter planes. Fighter pilot Robert S. Johnson, an ace of the Fifty-sixth Fighter Group in Europe, penned *Thunderbolt!* Much more than just a personal story, this book also covers his training and combat.

Several airborne memoirs stand out. Webster's *Parachute Infantry*, by a Harvard English literature major, describes his training, his first jump, killing and being fired on, the bonds of comradeship, and his loathing of "chickenshit." Using his letters and official sources, his memoirs were published posthumously. A German Jew who emigrated to the United States in the 1930s, Gabel in *The Making of a Paratrooper* narrated his training and experience in Western Europe in the 17th Airborne Division. Also see Burgett, *Currahee!*, an account of his time in the 506th Regiment, 101st Airborne Division.

In a rare correspondence between husband and wife, the B-26 almost becomes a third partner in Allen's *The Martin Marauders and the Franklin Allens*. Their letters are lively and detailed; a career airman, Franklin tested the plane as well as flew it throughout the war in New Guinea and in the European theater, while Jeanne stayed at home working and thinking of how she could promote the war effort. The volume is replete with lavish illustrations and documents.

Army. Army men seem to have found it easier to keep diaries and maintain a lengthy correspondence with wives and families. Though discouraged—if captured, a man's diary might reveal important information—diary keeping was not consistently forbidden to Americans. There are more diaries than for other services, largely because of the greater number of soldiers. Memoirs that are uncommonly reflective of the authors' experiences include Toole's *Battle Diary*, Standifer's *Not in Vain*, Randall's *Dirt and Doughfeet*, and Cawthon's *Other Clay*. Toole, keeping a secret diary, reluctantly commanded a platoon in K Company of the Fifteenth Infantry, Third Division. Including graphic photographs, he used unreserved language to describe his march through Western Europe from October 1944 to September 1945. A rifleman from Mississippi, Standifer tried to put his memoirs into a larger context, reflecting on a wide variety of issues; he read academic literature about combat and official histories and invited comments from others in his unit before publication.

Awarded a Purple Heart, among other citations, Randall wrote an effective memoir of the rifle platoon he led, changing some names and other details to "prevent painful recollections." Cawthon's account, written immediately after the war, used letters home and notes he made while in the hospital. In the 116th Regiment of the Twenty-ninth Infantry Division, he captured the mood of war from D-Day through May 1945:

With others in it, I shared intense experiences of violence, boredom, exuberance, despair, comedy, and tragedy. In it, too, was spent a prodigious quantity of youth, gone and, of course, irredeemable. Now there remains a pride and nostalgia that lends those years an overall glow they rarely had at the time and, regarded objectively, probably do not deserve. (Prologue)

Among celebrated memoirs is Audie Murphy's *To Hell and Back*. He received twenty-eight decorations, including the Medal of Honor and the Distinguished Service Cross, and later starred in a film of his exploits by the same name. Zorns' *I Walk through the Valley* is the mature and sober reflections of a thirty-one-year-old husband on combat, wounds, imprisonment, and liberation, based on letters he and his wife wrote one another. A unique "personal narrative" is Egger and Otts' *G Company's War*. The authors belonged to the same rifle company in the Third Army but were only casually acquainted; their nearly day-by-day accounts, printed side by side, give two very different perspectives on the same events, from mid-November 1944 to V-E Day.

Winston's *V-Mail* contains both diary entries and letters written by a medic, one who saw the worst aspects of combat, in the 398th Infantry Regiment, 100th Infantry Division. Several other veterans assisted him with information. Movingly written, he shows that men did not see the war as the "last good war." Assistant Surgeon Huebner, 88th Division, Third Battalion, 349th Infantry Regiment, scribbled his experiences on the back of maps. His *Long Walk through War* devotes a chapter to each month of his work in North Africa and Italy from December 1943 on. Prosaic and avoiding mention of specific units or individuals, *Long Walk* concretely describes injuries, treatments, and evacuation. Most unusual are the interesting letters by a Japanese-American medic, Tsuchida, in *Wear It Proudly*; he served with the 71st Infantry in France from September 1944. Finally, among noncombatants' writings are the letters of General Patton's aide-de-camp, Codman, a well-to-do Bostonian, to his wife over a period of three years, collected in his book *Drive*.

Henry Giles' *Hello, Janice* is a Kentucky novelist's intimate and poignant letters to his wife. Joining the army to escape the depression, he serendipitously met her on a bus trip in 1943. Immediately off to Europe, he wrote profusely until returning in October 1945. As was usual among front-line troops, he discarded her letters, an unfortunate practice for today's reader. Of the same genre is Alper's sophisticated *Love and Politics in Wartime*, a very self-conscious analysis with strong visual details of the larger significance of his two years in Italy resettling refugees and dealing with prisoners of war (POWs); times of excitement contrasted with unbearable boredom. For his somewhat irreverent memoir, *When Duty Called*, Denney used some three hundred letters he wrote his wife, plus the memories his rereading them stimulated. The memoir covers only his overseas service, from April 1944 to June 1945.

For both sides of a married couple's correspondence see Taylor's *Miss You*, edited with Litoff and Smith. A southern lieutenant in the infantry, Charles wrote nearly every day to Barbara (over eight hundred letters), his bride of 1942. Hers survive because he wrote return letters on the backside. Though hardly ordinary people, their letters uncover the tensions and difficulties, but most of all the details, of a wartime marriage. This is one of several collections of letters superbly edited by Litoff and Smith. The correspondence of the Eastons, *Love and War*, another newly married couple from California, relates their daily concerns as he served in Europe, and she raised their babies, did volunteer work, and passed on family chitchat. Edited to preserve privacy and to clarify the context, it includes many photographs and a moving appendix on "The Black Volunteers."

Among memoirs written to affect their readers' thoughts on the nature of combat rather than to serve a personal desire to record is Gray's *The Warriors*. A professional philosopher, Gray provided insight into the experience of war within its larger cultural and intellectual context. Intensely interesting and insightful, it is somewhat cerebral, though easily accessible. The popular and controversial *Wartime* by Fussell, a professor of literature and a former lieutenant of a rifle platoon in the 103d Infantry Division in France, vigorously reiterated his own very negative military experiences. He found nothing redeeming about the war. He drew more on a wide, but highly selective, literature of diaries, novels, and poetry than on his own material to construct his memoir.

Historians are often skeptical of memoirs written long after the event, when the lenses of time blur and dislocate earlier experiences. To test the validity of this view, Alice Hoffman, an oral historian, interviewed, over a period of years, her veteran psychologist husband, Howard, regarding his wartime experiences, checking contemporary sources for their accuracy. Their *Archives of Memory* shows that most of his recollections were consistently remembered and could be verified.

Navy. The European theater led to fewer American naval memoirs than did the Pacific. An interesting account by historian Louis Harlan, *All at Sea*, clearly reflects his postwar experiences, though based on letters, selective memory, interviews, and a diary kept by his ship's captain, Harold Clark. Tolley's *Caviar and Commissars* is a perceptive, entertaining, and informative account of a naval attache stationed in wartime Moscow with a handful of Americans. Moffat, recalled to duty in 1939 as a naval reserve captain, reminisces in *A Navy Maverick Comes of Age* about his wartime service close to home along the New England coast.

Britain

Air Forces. Various editions of the Royal Air Force (RAF) fighter ace James Johnson's popular and excellent *Wing Leader* are available. Barclay's *Fighter Pilot* is his entire diary plus some letters and other material, including an account of his escape through France and Spain after being shot down in North Africa in July 1942. Equally exciting is *Hugh Dormer's Diaries*, which he did not live to revise; he parachuted into France before the invasion and was killed in a tank clash in July 1944 in Normandy.

Englishman Scott, *Typhoon Pilot,* trained and led a team of New Zealanders to fly these fighter-bombers during the Normandy invasion and campaigns in Northwestern Europe, especially against armor, missile launching, and radar sites. Spooner's *In Full Flight* is another classic personal account.

Army. Seton-Watson's *Letters and Diaries* is extraordinarily thorough observations of an artilleryman, covering the entire war from Dunkirk, to North Africa, to Italy. Though he published only extracts, Seton-Watson, son of a historian and himself a historian of Italy, put each section into context and included photos and good maps. Cochrane, *Charlie Company,* used his personal journal of North African and Italian campaigns plus letters to his wife ("remorselessly cheerful, and very properly uninformative about our serious activities," xi) to write his memoirs. *Recollections of Rifleman Bowlby* vividly recounts all aspects of military life for the same theater. Bowlby also edited Crimp's *Diary of a Desert Rat,* a private's engaging diary and notebooks from July 1941 to May 1943. Also from North Africa is McCallum's *Journey with a Pistol,* an introspective account written immediately after the war based on his letters and notebooks but put aside and "rediscovered" a decade later by a veteran for whom the war belonged to another age.

Mayhew's unique *One Family's War* originated from a stepmother's suggestion that all six Mayhews in service and two cousins each write to her, and she would recopy their letters for all the rest, a task she carried out from September 1939 to the end of the war. Not originally intended for publication, it has been edited to eliminate personal matters and to shorten it.

Navy. The novelist Nicholas Monsarrat published several accounts during and after his war service as first lieutenant on a corvette escorting convoys between 1940 and 1943; see especially the collected edition of his wartime trilogy, *Three Corvettes.* Whinney, *U-Boat Peril,* started the war in Shanghai aboard the *Duncan,* helped track down the *Bismarck,* and sailed in every ocean from 1943 as a commander until after D-Day. Agar devoted a third of his *Footprints in the Sea* to his command of the HMS *Emerald* and then the HMS *Dorsetshire* until the Japanese sank it in 1942. Destroyer captain Donald, *Stand by for Action,* took part in various battles aboard different ships throughout the war. A very full life at sea as a captain of several ships from 1939 to 1945 unfolds in Pugsley's *Destroyer Man.*

For below-deck autobiographies read Connell's *Jack's War,* with more on the noncombat side of service than on battles. Amusing incidents are the main substance of Greenwood's *Stoker Greenwood's Navy;* for other engrossing stories see Jones' *From the Fo'csle Messdeck to the Wardroom.*

An American who joined the Royal Navy before the United States entered the war, Cherry recorded his lengthy service on several ships and finally in Germany in *Yankee R. N.* Holt's *A Banker All at Sea* chronicles an Australian's rise from 1941 through the Royal Navy before returning home for service in the Royal Australian Navy as a first lieutenant. Lawrence, who began as a midshipman, became a career officer, and then an English teacher, wrote *A Bloody War,* memoirs of service in the Royal Canadian Navy, as catharsis: "[I]t is a love story, or rather, it is several love stories" (viii).

British Commonwealth

As a young junior officer Donald Pearce enjoyed his soldiering in Northwestern Europe: "[a] kind of trick life, almost daily improvisation" and "a Canadian's discovery of the Motherland" before moving to the Continent. Unfortunately, he burned half his clandestinely kept entries after V-E day, so his *Journal,* partly altered for publication, is incomplete. His countryman Frost in *Once a Patricia* recounted his experience as an infantry officer in the Mediterranean theater and Holland; he quoted at length from letters home and consulted official historians and regimental war diaries. Cederberg, who served in the Cape Breton Highlanders, wrote an interesting *Autobiography* complete with drawings, photographs, and maps. Infantryman and popular postwar author Farley Mowat based *Memories* on letters to his parents.

In a superb memoir, Peden, *A Thousand Shall Fall,* movingly reminisces about life as a Canadian pilot flying Stirlings in RAF Bomber Command. Thompson's *Lancaster to Berlin* is another memoir of a Bomber Command crewman from Canada.

Gullett's *Not as a Duty Only* narrates an Australian's confrontation with war and combat in North Africa, New Guinea, and then France. Burrell began the war in the Australian Royal Navy as director of operations and plans but also commanded two destroyers; *Mermaids Do Exist* recounts those years. Collins of the Royal Australian Navy spent half of *As Luck Would Have It* on his wartime captaincy of two destroyers in waters around Australia.

Though covering only a brief, but critical, time in the western desert, South African Crisp's *Brazen Chariots* is a straightforward, vivid retelling of a journalist and cricket player's experiences in tanks at the front and behind.

Germany

Overwhelmingly, personal accounts by non-English speakers in the military come from Germans. The most popular, gripping, and compelling is Guy Sajer's *The Forgotten Soldier*, by a Frenchman from Alsace serving in the German army on the Eastern Front. Kennedy in "The Forgotten Soldier" questioned its authenticity because of inaccuracies he found in the text, a claim that may be unprovable since the original sources are not publicly available.

The Outermost Frontier by Pabst, a law student, is a touching diary, filled with irony, that he sent to his parents in the form of letters from the French occupation in July 1941 to his death on the Eastern Front in September 1943. The unchanged English translation added background notes for the reader. An unrepentant Austrian Nazi and proud professional soldier, Lieutenant Pruller began his *Diary* in the Polish campaign in the summer of 1939 and continued it through campaigns in France, the Balkans, and the Soviet Union until the end of the war.

Diaries from the lower ranks on the Eastern Front include Kern's *War Diary*, a continuous journal from the invasion of the Soviet Union through retreat, and Bamm's *The Invisible Flag*, a memoir of a medic dragging his horse-drawn covered wagon and dispensary from the Crimea to East Prussia at war's end.

For a revealing air memoir, especially on the Russo-German front from a Luftwaffe pilot, Rudel's *Stuka* stands alone; he carried out 2,530 operational flights, becoming a wing commander at age twenty-eight. Another important memoir by an "ordinary" air ace is Knoke's *I Flew for the Fuhrer*, based on his diary from 1939, when he was nineteen, to December 1944.

MILITARY EXPERIENCE IN ASIA AND THE PACIFIC

Air Forces

John Smith, a career naval officer, recounted his training and flying experience aboard the USS *Suwannee* during the battle for Leyte Gulf amid the Japanese kamikaze tactics in *Hellcats over the Philippine Deep*, using published sources and personal and crewmates' recollections. P-38 pilot Rothgeb scattered diary quotations throughout his memoir, *New Guinea Skies*. For Americans under Chennault in the China theater see Scott's *God Is My Co-Pilot*, a wartime best-seller in the United States, and Bond and Anderson's much later *A Flying Tiger's Diary*. Felix Smith's *China Pilot* is an anecdotal, lively recollection of cockpit and ground action. A delightful

book on a remarkable career, *Herman the German* tells of Gerhard Neumann's rise from being an enemy alien to master sergeant under Chennault, American citizenship by act of Congress, and finally head of
General Electric's jet engine division. O'Brien's *Out of the Blue* reports in
three volumes on a British pilot's exploits, first in bombing the Germans
in Europe and later flying under Wingate in India.

Army

An early American army memoir from the southwest Pacific began with
Mellnik's *Philippine War Diary*, written immediately after the war from sur-
reptitiously kept notes by a soldier taken prisoner at Corregidor. A rare
two-year diary, Kahn's aptly titled and moving *Between Tedium and Terror*,
gives a ground-level view from the army's Transportation Corps. Hall's
edition of her uncle Samuelson's diary (1941–1945) and letters, *Love, War,
and the 96th Engineers (Colored)*, tells of a white captain's command of one
of the first Afro-American units to come under fire in New Guinea. History
professor Mathias' *An Army Bandsman* draws on some three hundred letters plus his reminiscences of the Thirty-seventh Infantry Division to explain how a small-town boy came of age and encountered the larger world
of people unlike himself. Atypical but evocative, infantryman Hogan's *I
Am Not Alone* is the letters of a deeply devout Christian, apocalyptic in his
vision, who fought from Kwajalein throughout the Pacific before being
killed in Okinawa.

Another Australian in New Guinea in addition to Gullet mentioned
earlier was Pinney, who kept an illicit and very much edited diary, *The
Barbarians*, to spite his lieutenant; its Aussie dialect requires some effort
by non-Australians, even with the aid of endnotes. *The War Diaries of Weary
Dunlop*, by a doctor in the Royal Australian Medical Corps, is a lengthy,
provocative account with over a hundred graphic photographs of his work.

Southeast Asia was the setting for several interesting diaries and memoirs. Masters' *The Road Past Mandalay* is the difficult, often painful life of
a soldier raised in India who fought in Iraq, Syria, and Iran before joining
Wingate and the Chindits in Burma. The English geographer and ex-
plorer Chapman fought the Japanese for three years behind the lines in
Malay, an adventure set forth in *The Jungle Is Neutral*. In *American Guerrilla*,
Roger Hilsman, West Pointer and member of the Kennedy administration,
recounted his adventures behind the lines in Burma and China for the
Office of Strategic Services (OSS).

Navy

Calhoun, a junior officer on the destroyer USS *Sterrett*, drew from his
letters and more than fifty contributions from crewmates in recalling his

experience fondly in *Tin Can* [i.e., destroyer] *Sailor* as the most "exciting, inspirational, and gratifying" years of his life. Raines' *Good Night Officially*, also by a destroyer crewman, reflects the personal eye of a successful, youthful Dallas journalist and the ardent letters to his wife the last year of his life before being killed in action in April 1945. Especially poignant is his seven-page letter written in 1944 to be given her in the event of his death. A richly detailed account of nearly five years in the U.S. Navy is Jernigan's *Tin Can Man*. Historian Leach's *Now Hear This* has little combat drama but rather attempts to show the quality of life aboard a destroyer escort, based on a month-by-month (eighty-nine weeks) memoir he wrote immediately after the war, plus letters, the ship's log, and the captain's official diary.

A classic American naval account is Fahey's *Pacific War Diary*, from notes he secretly kept from October 1942 to December 1945. He wrote frankly about shipboard daily life, wartime atrocities, racism in the service, and his trip to Hiroshima.

The relatively small number of submariners compared to other service branches has produced several worthwhile personal narratives. Beach's *Submarine!* is an early classic of the several submarines he commanded during the war. Schratz's readable memoir, *Submarine Commander*, is half devoted to his experiences in the Atlantic and the Pacific conflicts. Submariner Ruhe campaigned in the Pacific, all the while keeping a journal, against regulations, now the basis of his *War in the Boats*.

A remarkably literate, vivid, and moving memoir of service aboard an aircraft carrier, Kernan's *Crossing the Line* includes his December 7, 1941, experience on the USS *Enterprise* and Lieutenant Colonel Doolittle's raid when it launched from the USS *Hornet*, a ship he was still on when Japanese fire sank it. On V-J Day he was back to Pearl Harbor.

The Poultons' extensive letter writing, *A Better Legend*, cut to book length, seeks to bring out specific themes relating to their different war experiences. He enlisted in 1942 and served in the Seabees in the Pacific and in Japan. Jane found the letters after his death in 1987.

Mishler's two years in China, especially in cooperative intelligence operations with the Nationalists, are detailed in *Sampan Sailor*, based on letters and notes he kept. Another unusual navy memoir, *Torokina*, is by present-day historian Jackson, who never saw a battleship and only one wounded Japanese. He used some two hundred letters home and navy records to construct his story.

Marines

The must-be-read U.S. Marine memoir from the Pacific is Sledge's *With the Old Breed at Peleliu and Okinawa*. Later a biology professor, Sledge painfully described the transformation of a teenager into a seasoned veteran by terrifying Pacific combat, at the same time retaining civilized values and affection for his fellow warriors. The wartime *Guadalcanal Diary* by journalist Tregaskis directly narrates the invasion and the daily first six weeks of fighting. A different marine account is Levin's *From the Battlefield*; he emigrated from Russia at an early age to become an unemployed communist in the 1930s. As a marine combat correspondent from November 1943, he covered the last year and a half of the war. Farrington's *The Leatherneck Boys* is a brief account of a boyish-looking marine on Guadalcanal from August 7, 1942, to mid-January 1943, written while under fire.

Japan

The very few Japanese personal narratives we have are from the navy. A submarine commander who sank the USS *Indianapolis*, Hashimoto's professional and thoughtful *Sunk* is a memoir as well as an analysis as to why Japan lost the war. Hara recounted his captaincy of a *Japanese Destroyer*. Also see an important collection of seventeen articles by former naval and air officers in *The Japanese Navy*, edited by Evans.

THE CIVILIAN EXPERIENCE

Diaries and memoirs from prominent Americans include William Manchester, *Goodbye, Darkness*; David Brinkley, *Washington Goes to War*; William Shirer, *Berlin Diary*; and Eric Sevareid, *Not So Wild a Dream*. While strictly neither diary nor memoir, Mauldin's books, especially *Bill Mauldin's Army* and *Up Front*, illustrate his European Forty-fifth Division experiences.

To keep local servicemen up to date about the war at home, Mrs. Keith Frazier Somerville, who had a broad social and political background, wrote an uncommonly informative "Dear Boys" column for the *Bolivar Commercial* (Mississippi) from January 1943 to August 1945. Litoff and Smith edited excerpts and provided an excellent introduction to *Dear Boys*.

With the assistance of her soldier husband, Zelma Katin detailed her wartime work experiences in London as a tram conductress in *"Clippie,"* a rare glimpse into a working-class woman's life. The wartime *Diary* of the political radical, pacifist, and feminist Vera Brittain comes from a very different social world. Broad and Fleming edited and greatly reduced the wartime portion of Nella Last's diary, which she began in 1939 as a corespondent for Mass-Observation, a public opinion service. *Nella Last's War* is noteworthy for the regularity of the entries and her skill at social description. Two Englishwomen living abroad during the war left diaries. Christabel Bielenberg lived in Germany from 1934 to 1945 with her German husband. *Ride Out the Dark* depicts life in Berlin until 1943, when she moved to the Black Forest. Iris Origo, an Anglo-American author married to a Tuscan landowner, depicted daily rural life for *War in Val d'Orca, 1943–1944.*

Among Continental European women Ursula von Kardorff kept a partially revised *Diary of a Nightmare* for the last three years of the war in Berlin. In her *Berlin Diaries* émigré Russian aristocrat Marie Vassiltchikov described her service as linguist for the German foreign ministry broadcasting service and her friendships in high Berlin society, including members of the anti-Hitler plot. Marie-Louise Osmont's *Normandy Diary* covers the German occupation from August 1940 until mid-August 1944. The wife of a doctor, she lived three miles from the site of Sword Beach, thus finding herself in the middle of the Allied invasion, experiencing both Axis and Allied occupation.

Exceptional for its thoroughness and testimony to Polish wartime suffering is Zygmunt Klukowski's *Diary.* A trained gentile physician and hospital director in Szczebrzeszyn, Klukowski was an amateur historian determined to document the years of German occupation, a true chronicle of his city's wartime life.

Collected Works

In *Letters from Fighting Hoosiers* Peckham and Snyder published 1,131 letters of veterans selected from over 3,000 they collected, with an emphasis on graphic descriptions from all service branches and a wide variety of subjects. Litoff and Smith's *Since You Went Away* is a selection of letters from four hundred American women out of some 25,000 they received in a national appeal, while their *We're in This War, Too* brings together letters from American women in uniform. As with their other books, they provide thorough discussions of their methods and sources.

Tapert's *Despatches from the Heart* reproduces British soldiers' letters solicited through regional newspapers; her *Lines of Battle* does the same for American servicemen. Blythe's *Private Words* is from the Imperial War Museum's collection of letters. Vining's *American Diaries* includes twenty-four accounts from all the services, four being from prisoners of war. *Wings of War*, edited by Lucas, brings together many stories from throughout the globe (but notably not the Soviet Union) of airmen, many not previously published.

Oral Histories

The pacesetter for oral histories is Terkel's classic *"The Good War,"* arranged topically and covering primarily American veterans and civilians. It overshadows Hoopes' *Americans Remember* and Harris, Mitchell, and Schecter's *The Homefront*, as well as Satterfield's *The Home Front*. An excellent oral history from one locality in Texas is Fairchild's *They Called It the War Effort.*

Broadfoot's *Six War Years* did much the same for Canada as Terkel did for the United States, though he did not identify his collaborators. For Britain see Calder and Sheridan's selections from mass-observation surveys and Croall's *Don't You Know There's a War On?*

There are several oral histories of the Normandy invasion prepared for the fiftieth anniversary. Ambrose's *D-Day* brings together many personal recollections from the large Eisenhower Center collection at the University of New Orleans. Astor's *June 6, 1944* is excellent. Also see Drez's *Voices of D-Day* (also under the auspices of the Eisenhower Center), Miller's *Nothing Less than Victory*, Neillands and De Norman's *D-Day* and Neillands' *Conquest of the Reich*, and, for those in naval service, Stillwell's *Assault on Normandy.*

Mason's *The Atlantic War Remembered* draws on Columbia University's oral history collection and that of the U.S. Naval Institute. Carefully edited and presented, it includes the interviews of civilian men and women but mostly of high-ranking naval officers. His *The Pacific War Remembered* does the same for that theater.

Steinhoff, Pechel, and Showalter spent two years interviewing 157 Germans in the 1980s, roughly a cross-section of present-day society. *Voices from the Third Reich* is overwhelmingly the voices of men and women less than twenty-one years of age when the war ended, leaving the wartime generation out; it is arranged by topic.

The best insight into Japanese society, military and civilian, can be found in the Cooks' detailed *Japan at War: An Oral History.* Gibney's *Senso* (war) contains some eleven hundred letters out of four thousand published in response to the newspaper *Asahi Shimbun's* request for personal recollections of the war. Other valuable perspectives, but not an oral history, are in Cary's *War-Wasted Asia,* a collection of letters by nine well-trained and informed U.S. naval language officers in Japan and East Asia immediately after the war; most of them pursued lifelong careers studying Japan and East Asia.

BIBLIOGRAPHY

References to personal narratives can also be found in the chapters on primary published sources and documents; references to personal narratives are also often included in chapters dealing with specific topics. Also see this volume's inclusive index under the rubric "personal narratives."

Agar, Augustus. *Footprints in the Sea.* London: Evans, 1959.
Allen, Franklin. *The Martin Marauder and the Franklin Allens: A Wartime Love Story.* Manhattan, KS: Sunflower UP, 1980.

Alper, Benedict S. *Love and Politics in Wartime: Letters to My Wife, 1943–45.* Urbana: University of Illinois, 1992.

Ambrose, Stephen. *D-Day June 6, 1944: The Climactic Battle of World War II.* New York: Simon and Schuster, 1994.

Ardery, Philip. *Bomber Pilot: A Memoir of World War II.* Lexington: University of Kentucky, 1978.

Astor, Gerald, comp. *June 6, 1944: The Voices of D-Day.* New York: St. Martin's, 1994.

Bamm, Peter Kurt Emmrich. *The Invisible Flag: Memoirs of a German Army Surgeon.* London: Faber and Faber, 1956, 1962; New York: John Day, 1956.

Barclay, George. *Fighter Pilot: A Self-Portrait.* London: William Kimber, 1976.

Barnard, Roy S., comp. *Oral History.* 2 vols. Washington, DC: GPO, 1976–1977.

Beach, Edward L. *Submarine!* New York: Holt, Rinehart, and Winston, 1952.

Bendiner, Elmer S. *The Fall of Fortresses: A Personal Account of the Most Daring—and Deadly—American Air Battles of World War II.* New York: Putnam's Sons, 1980.

Bielenberg, Christabel. *Ride Out the Dark: The Experiences of an Englishwoman in Wartime Germany.* Boston: G. K. Hall, 1984. Also published as *The Past Is Myself.* Alexandria, VA: Time-Life, 1968, 1991.

Blythe, Ronald, ed. *Private Words: Letters and Diaries from the Second World War.* London: Viking, 1991; London and New York: Penguin, 1993.

Bond, Charles R., and Terry Anderson, Jr. *A Flying Tiger's Diary.* College Station: Texas A and M UP, 1984.

Bowlby, Alex. *The Recollections of Rifleman Bowlby.* London: Leo Cooper, 1969.

Brinkley, David. *Washington Goes to War.* New York: Knopf, 1988.

Brittain, Vera. *Diary 1939–1945 Wartime Chronicle.* London: Victor Gollancz, 1989.

Broad, Richard, and Suzie Fleming, eds. *Nella Last's War: A Mother's Diary 1939–45.* London: Sphere; Bristol: Falling Wall, 1981.

Broadfoot, Barry. *Six War Years: Memoirs of Canadians at Home and Abroad.* New York and Toronto: Doubleday, 1974.

Burgett, Donald Robert. *Currahee!* Boston: Houghton Mifflin, 1967.

Burrell, Henry. *Mermaids Do Exist: The Autobiography of Vice-Admiral Sir Henry Burrell.* Melbourne: Macmillan, 1986.

Calder, Angus, and Dorothy Sheridan, eds. *Speak for Yourself: A Mass-Observation Anthology, 1937–1949.* London: Cape, 1984.

Calhoun, C. Raymond. *Tin Can Sailor: Life aboard the USS Sterrett, 1939–1945.* Annapolis, MD: NIP, 1993.

Cary, Otis, ed. *War-Wasted Asia: Letters—Japan, China, Korea 1945–1946.* Tokyo and New York: Kodansha International, 1975. Published in paperback as *From a Ruined Empire,* 1975.

Cawthon, Charles R. *Other Clay: A Remembrance of the World War II Infantry.* Niwot, CO: UP of Colorado, 1990.

Cederberg, Fred. *The Long Road Home: The Autobiography of a Canadian Soldier in Italy in World War II.* Toronto: General, 1984.

Chapman, F. Spencer. *The Jungle Is Neutral.* New York: W. W. Norton, 1949.

Cherry, A. H. *Yankee R. N.: Being the Story of a Wall Street Banker Who Volunteered for Active Duty in the Royal Navy Before America Came into the War.* London: Jarrold's, 1951.

Cochrane, Peter. *Charlie Company: In Service with C Company; 2nd Queen's Own Cameron Highlanders 1940–44.* London: Chatto and Windus, 1977.

Codman, Charles R. *Drive*. Boston: Little, Brown, 1957.

Colgan, Bill. *World War II Fighter-Bomber Pilot*. Blue Ridge Summit, PA: Tab, 1985; Manhattan, KS: Sunflower UP, 1988.

Collins, John. *As Luck Would Have It: The Reminiscences of an Australian Sailor*. Sydney: Angus and Robertson, 1965.

Connell, G. G. *Jack's War: Lower Deck Recollections from World War II*. London: Kimber, 1985.

Cook, Haruko Taya, and Theodore F. Cook. *Japan at War: An Oral History*. New York: New Press, 1992.

Crimp, R. L. *The Diary of a Desert Rat*. London: Cooper, 1971.

Crisp, Robert. *Brazen Chariots: An Account of Tank Warfare in the Western Desert, November–December 1941*. New York: W. W. Norton, 1960.

Croall, Jonathan. *Don't You Know There's a War On? The People's Voice, 1939–1945*. London: Hutchinson, 1988.

Denney, James Baxter. *When Duty Called: The Journal of an Enlisted Man, British Isles to Northwest France, April 1944–June 1945*. Manhattan, KS: Sunflower UP, 1994.

Donald, William. *Stand by for Action: A Sailor's Story*. London: Kimber, 1956.

Dormer, Hugh. *Hugh Dormer's Diaries*. London: Cape, 1947.

Dornbusch, Charles E. *Histories; Personal Narratives; United States Army*. Cornwallville, NY: Hope Farm, 1967.

Drez, Ronald J., ed. *Voices of D-Day: The Story of the Allied Invasion Told by Those Who Were There*. Baton Rouge: Louisiana State UP, 1994.

Dunlop, E. E. *The War Diaries of Weary Dunlop: Java and the Burma–Thailand Railway, 1942–1945*. Melbourne: Nelson, 1986, 1989.

Easton, Robert, and Jane Easton. *Love and War: Pearl Harbor through V-J Day*. Norman and London: University of Oklahoma, 1991.

Egger, Bruce E., and Lee MacMillan Otts. *G Company's War: Two Personal Accounts of the Campaigns in Europe, 1944–1945*. Tuscalossa and London: University of Alabama, 1992.

Evans, David C., ed. *The Japanese Navy in World War II*. Annapolis, MD: NIP, 1986.

Fahey, James J. *Pacific War Diary, 1942–1945*. Westport, CT: Greenwood, 1963.

Fairchild, Louis. *They Called It the War Effort; Oral Histories from World War II, Orange, Texas*. Austin: Eakin, 1993.

Farrington, Arthur C. *The Leatherneck Bosy: A PFC at the Battle for Guadalcanal*. Manhattan, KS: Sunflower UP, 1995.

Fletcher, Eugene. *The Lucky Bastard Club: A B-17 Pilot in Training and in Combat, 1943–45*. Seattle: University of Washington, 1992.

Frost, Charles Sydney. *Once a Patricia: Memoirs of a Junior Infantry Officer in World War II*. St. Catharines, Ontario: Vanwell, 1988.

Fussell, Paul. *Wartime: Understanding and Behavior in the Second World War*. New York: Oxford UP, 1989.

Gabel, Kurt. *The Making of a Paratrooper: Airborne Training and Combat in World War II*. Lawrence: UP of Kansas, 1990.

Gabreski, Francis, as told to Carl Molesworth. *Gabby: A Fighter Pilot's Life*. New York: Orion, 1991.

Gibney, Frank, ed. *Senso: The Japanese Remember the Pacific War: Letters to the Editor of Asahi Shimbun*. Armonk, NY, and London: M. E. Sharpe, 1995.

Giles, Henry. *Hello, Janice: The Wartime Letters of Henry Giles.* Ed. Dianne Watkins. Lexington: University of Kentucky, 1992.

Gray, J. Glenn. *The Warriors: Reflections on Men in Battle.* New York: Harper and Row, 1970.

Greenwood, Sydney. *Stoker Greenwood's Navy.* London: Midas, 1982.

Gullett, Henry. *Not as a Duty Only. An Infantryman's War.* Carlton, Victoria: Melbourne, 1976, 1984.

Hall, Gwendolyn Midlo, ed. *Love, War, and the 96th Engineers (Colored): The World War II New Guinea Diaries of Captain Hyman Samuelson.* Urbana and Chicago: University of Illinois Press, 1995.

Hara, Tameichi. *Japanese Destroyer Captain.* New York: Ballantine, 1961.

Harlan, Louis R. *All at Sea: Coming of Age in World War II.* Champaign: University of Illinois, 1996.

Harris, Mark Jonathan, Franklin D. Mitchell, and Steven J. Schechter. *The Homefront: America during World War II.* New York: Putnam, 1984.

Hashimoto, Mochitsura. *Sunk: The Story of the Japanese Submarine Fleet, 1941–1945.* New York: Avon, 1954.

Hilsman, Roger. *American Guerrilla: My War behind Japanese Lines.* London: Brassey's, 1990.

Hoffman, Alice M., and Howard S. Hoffman. *Archives of Memory: A Soldier Recalls World War II.* Lexington: University of Kentucky, 1990.

Hogan, John J. *I Am Not Alone: From the Letters of Combat Infantryman John J. Hogan, Killed at Okinawa.* Washington, DC: Mackinac, 1947.

Holt, F. S. *A Banker All at Sea: Being World War II Naval Memoirs (1941–1946) of F.S. Holt.* Newtown, Australia: Neptune, 1983.

Hoopes, Roy. *Americans Remember the Home Front: An Oral Narrative of World War II Years in America.* Chapel Hill: University of North Carolina Press, 1979; New York: Berkley, 1992, abridged ed.

Huebner, Klaus H. *Long Walk through War: A Combat Doctor's Diary.* College Station: Texas A and M UP, 1987.

Jackson, Donald. *Torokina: A Wartime Memoir, 1941–1945.* Ames: Iowa State UP, 1989.

Jernigan, E. J. *Tin Can Man.* Arlington, VA: Vandamere, 1993.

Johnson, James Edgar. *Wing Leader.* London: Chatto and Windus, 1956; New York: Time-Life, 1956.

Johnson, Robert S., with Martin Caidin. *Thunderbolt!* New York and Toronto: Rinehart, 1958.

Jones, John Charles. *From the Fo'csle Messdeck to the Wardroom.* Lewes, U.K.: Book Guild, 1987.

Kahn, Sy M. *Between Tedium and Terror: A Soldier's World War II Diary, 1943–45.* Champaign: University of Illinois, 1993.

Kardorff, Ursula von. *Diary of a Nightmare: Berlin 1942–1945.* London: Rupert Hart-Davis, 1965.

Katin, Zelma, in collaboration with Louis Katin. *"Clippie": The Autobiography of a Wartime Conductress.* London: John Gifford, 1944.

Kennedy, Edwin L., Jr. "The Forgotten Soldier: Fiction or Fact." *Army History* (1992): 23–25.

Kern, Ernst. *War Diary 1941–45.* New York: Vantage, 1993.

Kernan, Alvin. *Crossing the Line: A Bluejacket's World War II Odyssey.* Annapolis, MD: NIP, 1994.

Klukowski, Zygmunt. *Diary from the Years of Occupation, 1939–44.* Champaign: University of Illinois, 1993.

Knoke, Heinz. *I Flew for the Fuhrer.* London: Greenhill, 1954; Novato, CA: Presidio, 1991.

Lawrence, Hal. *A Bloody War: One Man's Memories of the Canadian Navy, 1939–1945.* Toronto: Macmillan of Canada, 1979.

Leach, Douglas. *Now Hear This: The Memoir of a Junior Naval Officer in the Great Pacific War.* Kent, OH: Kent State UP, 1987.

Levin, Dan. *From the Battlefield: Dispatches of a World War II Marine.* Annapolis, MD: NIP, 1995.

Litoff, Judy Barrett, and David C. Smith, eds. *Dear Boys: World War II Letters from a Woman Back Home.* Jackson: UP of Mississippi, 1991.

———. *Since You Went Away: World War II Letters from American Women on the Home Front.* New York and Oxford: Oxford UP, 1991.

———. *We're in This War, Too: World War II Letters from American Women in Uniform.* New York and London: Oxford UP, 1994.

Litoff, Judy Barrett, David C. Smith, Barbara Wooddall Taylor, and Charles E. Taylor. *Miss You: The World War II Letters of Barbara Wooddall Taylor and Charles E. Taylor.* Athens: University of Georgia, 1990.

Lucas, Laddie, ed. *Wings of War: Airmen of All Nations Tell Their Stories, 1939–1945.* New York: Macmillan, 1983.

Manchester, William. *Goodbye, Darkness: A Memoir of the Pacific War.* Boston: Dell, 1987.

Mason, John T. *The Atlantic War Remembered: An Oral History Collection.* Annapolis, MD: NIP, 1990.

———. *The Pacific War Remembered: An Oral History Collection.* Annapolis, MD: NIP, 1986.

Masters, John. *The Road Past Mandalay.* New York: Bengal-Rockland, 1961.

Mathias, Frank F. *G.I. Jive: An Army Bandsman in World War II.* Lexington: University of Kentucky, 1982.

Mauldin, William. *Bill Mauldin's Army.* Novato, CA: Presidio, 1983.

———. *Up Front.* New York: Henry Holt, 1944, 1945.

Mayhew, Patrick, ed. *One Family's War.* London: Hutchinson, 1985.

McCallum, Neil. *Journey with a Pistol: A Diary of War.* London: Victor Gollancz, 1961.

Mellnik, Stephen M. *Philippine War Diary, 1939–1945.* New York: Van Nostrand Reinhold, 1968, 1981.

Miller, Russell. *Nothing Less than Victory: The Oral History of D-Day.* New York: Morrow, 1994.

Mishler, Clayton. *Sampan Sailor: A Navy Man's Adventures in WWII China.* London: Brassey's, 1994.

Moffat, Alexander W. *A Navy Maverick Comes of Age, 1939–1945.* Middletown, CT: Wesleyan UP, 1977.

Monsarrat, Nicholas. *Three Corvettes: Comprising HM Corvette, East Coast Corvette, Corvette Command.* London: Cassell, 1945.

Mowat, Farley. *My Father's Son: Memories of War and Peace.* Boston: Houghton Mifflin, 1992.

Murphy, Audie. *To Hell and Back.* New York: H. Holt, 1949.

Neillands, Robin. *The Conquest of the Reich: D-Day to VE Day—A Soldiers' History.* New York and London: Weidenfeld and Nicolson, 1994.

Neillands, Robin, and Roderick De Norman. *D-Day 1944: Voices from Normandy.* London: Orion; Osceola, WI: Motorbooks International, 1994.

Neumann, Gerhard. *Herman the German: Enemy Alien, U.S. Army Master Sergeant #105000000.* New York: William Morrow, 1984.

O'Brien, Terence. *Out of the Blue: A Pilot with the Chindits.* London: Collins, 1984.

Origo, Iris. *War in Val d'Orca, 1943–1944.* Boston: D. R. Godine, 1984.

Osmont, Marie-Louise. *The Normandy Diary of Marie-Louise Osmont: 1940–1944.* New York: Random House, 1994.

Pabst, Helmut. *The Outermost Frontier: A German Soldier in the Russian Campaign.* Trans. Andrew and Eva Wilson. London: William Kimber, 1986.

Pearce, Donald. *Journal of a War; North-West Europe, 1944–1945.* Toronto: Macmillan, 1965.

Peckham, Howard H., and Shirley A. Snyder, eds. *Letters from Fighting Hoosiers,* Vol. 2 of *Indiana in World War II.* Bloomington: Indiana War History Commission, 1979.

Peden, Murray. *A Thousand Shall Fall.* Stittsville, Ontario: Canada's Wings; Alexandria, VA: Time-Life, 1992.

Perks, Robert, comp. *Oral History: An Annotated Bibliography.* London: British Library National Sound Archive, 1990.

Pinney, Peter. *The Barbarians: A Soldier's New Guinea Diary.* Queensland, Australia: University of Queensland Press, 1988.

Poulton, Jack, and Jane Poulton. *A Better Legend: From the World War II Letters of Jack and Jane Poulton.* Ed. Jane Weaver Poulton. Charlottesville and London: UP of Virginia, 1993.

Pruller, Wilhelm. *Diary of a German Soldier.* Ed. and trans. H. C. Robbins Landon and Sebastian Leitner. New York: Coward-McCann, 1963.

Pugsley, A. F. *Destroyer Man, by A. F. Pugsley in Collaboration with Captain Donald Macintyre.* London: Weidenfeld and Nicolson, 1957.

Raines, James Orvill. *Good Night Officially: The Pacific War Letters of a Destroyer Sailor: The Letters of Yeoman James Orvill Raines.* Ed. by William M. McBride. Boulder, CO: Westview Press, 1994.

Randall, Howard M. *Dirt and Doughfeet: Combat Experiences of a Rifle Platoon Leader.* New York: Exposition, 1955.

Rothgeb, Wayne P. *New Guinea Skies: A Fighter Pilot's View of World War II.* Ames: Iowa State UP, 1992.

Rudel, Hans Ulrich. *Stuka Pilot.* Dublin: Euphorion, 1952.

Ruhe, William J. *War in the Boats: My WWII Submarine Battles.* McLean, VA: Brassey's, 1994.

Sajer, Guy. *The Forgotten Soldier: The Classic World War II Autobiography.* New York: Harper and Row, 1971; New York: Brassey's, 1990.

Satterfield, Archie. *The Home Front: An Oral History of the War Years in America: 1941–45.* New York: Playboy, 1981.

Schratz, Paul R. *Submarine Commander. A Story of World War II and Korea.* Lexington: UP of Kentucky, 1988.

Scott, Desmond. *Typhoon Pilot.* London: Secker and Warburg, 1982.

Scott, Robert Lee. *God Is My Co-Pilot.* New York: Scribner, 1944.

Seton-Watson, Christopher. *Dunkirk–Alamein–Bologna: Letters and Diaries of an Artilleryman, 1939–1945.* London: Buckland, 1993.

Sevareid, Eric. *Not So Wild a Dream.* New York: Alfred A. Knopf, 1976.

Shirer, William L. *Berlin Diary: The Journal of a Foreign Correspondent, 1934–1941.* New York: Alfred A. Knopf, 1941.

Sledge, E. B. *With the Old Breed at Peleliu and Okinawa.* Novato, CA: Presidio, 1981; Oxford and New York: Oxford UP, 1990.

Smith, Felix. *China Pilot: Flying for Chiang and Chennault: Adventures of a China Pilot.* Washington, DC: Brassey's, 1995.

Smith, John. *Hellcats over the Philippine Deep.* Manhattan, KS: Sunflower UP, 1995.

Spooner, Tony. *In Full Flight.* Canterbury: Wingham, 1965, 1991.

Standifer, Leon C. *Not in Vain: A Rifleman Remembers World War II.* Baton Rouge: Louisiana State UP, 1991.

Steinhoff, Johannes, Peter Pechel, and Dennis Showalter. *Voices from the Third Reich: An Oral History.* Washington, DC: Regnery Gateway; New York: Da Capo, 1994.

Stillwell, Paul, ed. *Assault on Normandy: First-Person Accounts from the Sea Services.* Annapolis, MD: NIP, 1994.

Tapert, Annette, ed. *Despatches from the Heart: An Anthology of Letters from the Front during the First and Second World Wars.* London: H. Hamilton in association with the Imperial War Museum, 1984.

———. *Lines of Battle: Letters from American Servicemen, 1941–1945.* New York: Pocket, 1989.

Terkel, Studs. *"The Good War": An Oral History of World War II.* New York: Pantheon, 1984.

Thompson, Walter R. *Lancaster to Berlin.* London: Goodall, 1988.

Tolley, Kemp. *Caviar and Commissars: The Experiences of a U.S. Naval Officer in Stalin's Russia.* Annapolis, MD: NIP, 1983.

Toole, John H. *Battle Diary.* Missoula, MT: Vigilante, 1978.

Tregaskis, Richard William. *Guadalcanal Diary.* New York: Random House, 1943.

Tsuchida, William Shinji. *Wear It Proudly: Letters by William Shinji Tsuchida.* Berkeley and Los Angeles: University of California, 1947.

Vassiltchikov, Marie. *Berlin Diaries, 1940–1945.* New York: Alfred A. Knopf, 1987; London: Chatto and Windus, 1985.

Vining, Donald, ed. *American Diaries of World War II.* New York: Pepys, 1982.

Webster, David Kenyon. *Parachute Infantry: An American Paratrooper's Memoir of D-Day and the Fall of the Third Reich.* Baton Rouge: Louisiana State UP, 1994.

Whinney, Bob. *The U-Boat Peril: An Anti-Submarine Commander's War.* Poole: Blandford, 1986.

Winston, Keith. *V-Mail: Letters of a World War II Combat Medic.* Chapel Hill, NC: Algonquin, 1985.

Zorns, Bruce C. *I Walk through the Valley: A World War II Infantryman's Memoir of War, Imprisonment and Love.* Jefferson, NC: McFarland, 1991.

PART III

The European and Mediterranean– North African Theaters of the War

8   The German Onslaught, 1939–1940

Jonathan M. House

Countless journalists, historians, and novelists have described the first phase of the war in Europe, the period from the invasion of Poland in September 1939 until Hitler turned east at the end of 1940. Traditionally, the theme of this period has been the success of German arms, a success marred only by the stubborn defense of Great Britain during the air battles of 1940. Certainly, Germany held the initiative throughout this period, but it is also important to determine how and why the Germans won and how their military machine fell short of absolute victory.

Before considering such issues, however, it is useful to review the general studies and primary sources of this period.

GENERAL ACCOUNTS

Winston Churchill not only played a major role in these events but also helped shape our perception of them through his brilliant memoir-history, *The Second World War*. The first two volumes, *The Gathering Storm* (to May 1940) and *Their Finest Hour* (for the remainder of that year), remain classics, although the author was naturally silent about the role of signals intelligence. Most of Churchill's contemporaries published less original accounts; of these, Baldwin produced the best popular military summary in *The Crucial Years, 1939–1941*. The monumental British official *History of the Second World War, United Kingdom Military Series*, edited by Sir James Butler, is still an excellent starting point for most issues. In *The Last European War: September 1939/December 1941*, Lukacs presented an illuminating overview of the entire period, although he repeated a few legends, such as the idea that the Polish air force was destroyed on its airfields.

More recently, the passage of time and the release of official documents have facilitated a second generation of accounts of the German victories.

Germany's Military History Research Institute has undertaken a major official history, *Das Deutsche Reich und der Zweite Weltkrieg*, now being published in English as *Germany and the Second World War*. Maier and his coauthors of the second volume, *Germany's Initial Conquests in Europe*, did a remarkable job integrating German records with previous scholarship. The general reader may be disconcerted, however, by the somewhat disjointed series of essays contained in this volume; able summaries of strategy and operations are interspersed with more obscure topics. Nevertheless, this series is a useful counterweight to the typical Anglo-French version of events.

Even British historians are reexamining events. The second edition of Bond's *Britain, France and Belgium* superbly analyzed the problems of the British Expeditionary Force from its inception in the mid-1930s to its evacuation at Dunkirk. In the process, Bond also reviewed the key French, German, and Belgian decisions of that era.

PRIMARY SOURCES

Because Germany held the strategic initiative throughout this period of the war, any study of that period should include the published German memoirs and records. Franz Halder, chief of the German General Staff from August 1938 to September 1942, left a massive diary that reflected both German successes and the increasing difficulties of working under Hitler's direction. An edited version has been published as *The Halder War Diary*. One of Halder's operations officers, Walter Warlimont, left a more thorough record of the army staff in *Inside Hitler's Headquarters*. Wilhelm Keitel, Halder's counterpart in the armed forces command (Oberkommando der Wehrmacht), composed his own memoirs just before being executed for war crimes. Published in English as *In the Service of the Reich*, this study is marred by the tendency, common in so many older German works, to overemphasize Hitler's role in all aspects of the war. The dictator's wartime orders have been published by Trevor-Roper as *Blitzkrieg to Defeat: Hitler's War Directives, 1939–1945*.

At a lower level, the memoirs of German armored leaders can still provide a wealth of detail on the conduct of the German offensives. Heinz Guderian, a founder of German armored warfare, depicted a realistic view of his early campaigns in *Panzer Leader*. Erich von Manstein, the staff officer who helped devise the crucial German strategy in 1940, recorded his role in *Lost Victories*. Erwin Rommel's disjointed memoirs, published as *The Rommel Papers*, illustrate the functioning of a single armored division in 1940. Equally interesting are *The Memoirs of Field-Marshal Kesselring*. Most such memoirs carry certain biases; the reader should be skeptical of explanations of the role of Hitler and of the responsibility for war crimes.

Macksey's excellent biographies *Guderian* and *Rommel* serve as a "sanity check" to the German accounts.

BLITZKRIEG

The period of 1939 to 1941 is often referred to as the period of blitzkrieg or "Lightning War," yet few contemporaries or historians have understood the true nature of this warfare. The traditional version is that the Germans had perfected a new form of warfare, a skillful blend of tanks, parachutists, and screaming dive-bombers that demoralized as well as destroyed their opponents. While there is some truth to this image, in 1939–1940 blitzkrieg was not so much a fully developed method of warfare as it was an immature set of weapons made more terrible by the exaggerations of German propaganda.

Throughout World War II, the vast majority of the German army—and indeed of most combatant forces—was composed of foot-mobile infantry with horse-drawn artillery and supply vehicles. Until at least 1940, Hitler tended to give production priority to aircraft rather than tanks, and many senior German commanders were skeptical of the idea of anything resembling blitzkrieg. The vaunted panzer (armored) force consisted of only a handful of divisions, with the majority of tanks being lightly armored vehicles more suited to training than to combat. Indeed, both the British and French armies produced tanks that were more heavily armored than their German counterparts. In addition, the early panzer forces lacked armored vehicles to protect the infantry, engineers, and artillerymen who had to cooperate with the tanks.

German parachute and air forces suffered similar equipment shortcomings, but the primary weakness of blitzkrieg lay in methodology rather than weaponry. To cite but one example, the Luftwaffe had not developed procedures to provide on-call air strikes to support the armored troops. In *German Air Force Operations in Support of the Army*, Luftwaffe General Paul Deichmann traced the slow development of air–ground cooperation. Recently, Boog gave us *Die Deutsche Luftwaffenführung* and edited conference proceedings on *The Conduct of the Air War*.

Given such weaknesses, why were the German offensives so successful? The short answer is twofold. First, the Germans had more experience than their opponents, having formed their armored units earlier in the 1930s than anyone except the Soviets. Second, most armies were accustomed to the slow, methodical battles of World War I and were unprepared to respond to the rapid changes of situation brought about by German armored penetrations and exploitations. Ferris summarized many of these problems in "The British Army, Signals and Security in the Desert Campaign," a superb essay describing the communications issues for a generation of commanders.

There is a cottage industry devoted to popular chronicles of blitzkrieg. Some books, such as Cooper and Lucas' *Panzer: The Armoured Force of the Third Reich*, help perpetuate Guderian's contention that, given a free hand in development and production, the German armored forces had the potential to conquer any foe. Others are considerably more critical. Readers can profit from Kaufmann's *Hitler's Blitzkrieg Campaigns*, Perrett's *A History of Blitzkrieg*, and Bauer's *La Guerre des Blindées*. Perhaps the most incisive example of this genre is *Blitzkrieg Story* by Messenger. Those interested in a comparison with the Italian mechanized forces should consult Sweet's *Iron Arm: The Mechanization of Mussolini's Army*.

POLAND AND THE PHONY WAR

Despite this widespread interest, there are remarkably few studies of the first blitzkrieg campaign in Poland. Most observers, including some Poles, seem content with the image of gallant Polish lancers charging German tanks instead of asking the hard questions of how Poland collapsed in three weeks. For many years, the best analysis of the campaign remained Kennedy's brief study, *The German Campaign in Poland (1939)*. Despite its title, Bethell's *The War Hitler Won: The Fall of Poland, September 1939* gives short shrift to events in Poland, choosing to focus on diplomatic and political events from the British perspective. Recently, Zaloga and Madej have corrected many misconceptions by describing *The Polish Campaign* from the viewpoint of the impoverished Polish army. An equivalent view of Polish air defense problems can be gleaned from the Polish Air Force Association's *Destiny Can Wait*.

In addition to Guderian's memoirs and the German official history, German authors have left several useful studies of the Polish campaign. General von Vormann wrote a fine operational description in *Der Feldzug 1939 In Polen*. More recently, Elble analyzed one of the key battles as *Der Schlacht an der Bzura im September 1939*.

The stumbling Soviet occupation of eastern Poland in late September 1939 has never received appropriate attention. One of the Soviet commanders, Andrei Eremenko, gave a glimpse of this forgotten struggle in his memoirs, *The Arduous Beginning*. More than fifty years later, Boris Yeltsin's government belatedly acknowledged Soviet responsibility for the massacre of more than fourteen thousand captured Polish officers. For details of this atrocity, see Mackiewicz's *The Katyn Wood Murders* and Allen's *Katyn*.

After Poland surrendered, Europe entered the strange period known as the "Phony War." The British and French were unprepared to take the offensive against Germany, while weather and other factors delayed a German offensive until May 1940. *The Phony War* by Schlachtman is a fair summary of events during this strange lull. Fonvieille-Alquier's *The French and the Phoney War* provides a review from a non-English perspective. Bédarida has edited the minutes of the British–French Supreme Council as *La Stratégie Secrète de la Drôle de Guerre.*

FINLAND, NORWAY, AND DENMARK

Meanwhile, international attention shifted to Scandinavia. From November 1939 to March 1940, Finland earned the admiration of the world by its determined defense against Soviet aggression. In *Finland's War Years*, Nyman published a bibliography of Western sources on this conflict. Eloise and Lauri Paannanen attempted an objective view in *The Winter War*, but perhaps the best study is Chew's *The White Death*. Chew furnished realistic assessments of both combatants and noted that the most significant result of the war was the loss of Red Army prestige.

More immediately, the Soviet–Finnish struggle prompted British, French, and German decision makers to focus on Scandinavia, which eventually caused the conflict to spread northward. As described by Kersaudy in *Norway*, Churchill and a number of others saw Scandinavia as an opportunity to strike a low-cost blow at the German economy. Swedish iron ore moved by railroad to Narvik on the northern Norwegian coast and by ship through Norwegian waters to German industry. Some Allied leaders advocated naval mines to interdict this trade. Others thought even bigger—the Allies could seize Narvik and cross the Scandinavian peninsula, ostensibly to provide aid to Finland. Yet, as described in Nevakivi's *The Appeal That Was Never Made*, the Finnish government did not give the Allies the excuse they sought.

While the British and French hesitated to commit overt aggression, the Germans played into their hands. The German ship *Altmark*, carrying hundreds of captured British seamen, attempted to reach Germany by sailing along the Norwegian coast. The British created an international incident by boarding the ship inside Norwegian waters. Several accounts of this incident have been published, including Wiggan's *Hunt the Altmark.*

After World War II, Admiral Erich Raeder and other surviving German leaders attempted to blame the Allies for the German invasion of Norway, arguing that Hitler was simply responding to the threat of Allied invasion there. Yet, quite apart from Allied provocations, Hitler's naval staff was urging him to occupy the Norwegian coast for bases for German ships, submarines, and aircraft to operate in the Atlantic. Gemzell has made the most detailed institutional history of this concept in two books: *Raeder, Hitler, und Skandinavien* and the more general *Organization, Conflict, and Innovation.* The process by which Raeder pressed Hitler on the Norwegian issue is well summarized in *Germany's Initial Conquests in Europe*, where Maier and Stegemann in their respective chapters suggested that Hitler made his decision independently of the ongoing British–French planning for a similar operation.

The Norwegian–Danish campaign itself has been the subject of numerous studies. Derry's *The Campaign in Norway* in the British official history is excellent, as is Moulton's *A Study of Warfare in Three Dimensions*. Ash, *Norway 1940*, emphasized the British role in this frustrating operation, while Kersaudy's book of the same title attempted to portray the role of French, British, Norwegians, and Germans alike.

FRANCE AND THE LOW COUNTRIES

The conquest of Norway and Denmark in April 1940 was only the prelude to the astonishing collapse of France and the Low Countries in May and June. In examining the conduct of this campaign, it is appropriate to begin with the German plans.

In the immediate postwar era, it was common to attribute the brilliant German strategy solely to Erich von Manstein, an interpretation that he encouraged in *Lost Victories*. More recently, observers have concluded that although von Manstein produced the detailed plan for "Case Yellow," Hitler and others were equally involved in the basic concept. The works of Jacobsen remain the most thorough studies of this planning. In *Fall Gelb*, Jacobsen traced the evolution of von Manstein's idea from December 1939 onward. He later edited a companion collection of records on the matter, *Dokumente zum Westfeldzug 1940*.

Contrary to the mythology of the era, the Maginot Line, a string of elaborate fortifications along the northeastern French frontier, was by no means a failure. The Maginot Line was designed to prevent a German surprise attack before France could mobilize and to provide an anchor for French field forces after mobilization was completed. The worst that can be said of the Maginot Line is that, psychologically, it discouraged the French army from taking the offensive.

Numerous historians have described the true purpose of the Maginot Line, yet the legend persists. One of the best brief summaries of the matter is Kemp's *The Maginot Line: Myth and Reality*. *Grandeur et Sacrifice de la Ligne Maginot* by Anthérieu is equally reliable, if more partisan. Giuliano's *Les Soldats du Béton* is a local history of one sector of the line, providing a fuller understanding of the line and of the one outpost (La Ferté) that was attacked by the Germans.

Even if funds had been available, the French government would not have constructed similar large fortifications along the common frontier with Belgium. French industry and mines were too close to the border to be protected in this manner, and both France and Britain felt a moral obligation to defend the Belgians. Yet Belgium insisted on a precarious neutrality, as chronicled by Kieft in *Belgium's Return to Neutrality*.

As a result, in 1940 the British and French armies concentrated their most mobile divisions on the Belgian frontier, waiting to rush forward to defend the Belgians once the inevitable German attack began. Of the many accounts available, perhaps the most sympathetic explanation of Allied strategy in Belgium is Gunsburg's superb study, *Divided and Conquered*. For a contrasting, critical view of the strategy, see Alexander's essay, "Repercussions of the Breda Variant."

Two other aspects of the Belgian campaign deserve notice. First, the reputation of German airborne forces was enhanced by the daring glider attack that neutralized the key Belgian fortress of Eben Emael. Mrazek's *The Fall of Eben Emael* is a solid starting point for the study of this stunning victory. Second, once the Belgian army was defeated, King Leopold III decided to share captivity with his troops rather than join his government in exile in Britain. Keyes developed an effective defense of Leopold's actions in *Outrageous Fortune*.

If Belgium has been the focus of intense interest in the 1940 campaign, the simultaneous occupation of the Netherlands has gone almost unnoticed by historians. One of the few exceptions is Maass, whose brief *The Netherlands at War* offers a tantalizing taste of unexplored aspects of this battle.

While Belgian and Dutch troops fought desperately, the key battles of the western campaign occurred along the Meuse River, where German mechanized forces defeated poorly prepared French troops and began a huge encirclement of British and French troops in Belgium and northern France. As a corps commander, Heinz Guderian (*Panzer Leader*) had an excellent view of this battle from the German side. General Marshall-Cornwall, *Wars and Rumours of Wars*, commanded a British division in the campaign. More recently, Doughty has used the archives of both sides to produce a superb study in *The Breaking Point*.

Jackson's *Dunkirk: The British Evacuation* is a reliable, general account of the evacuation, while Merdal has the French perspective in *Dunkerque*. Franks produced an anecdotal view of *The Air Battle*, while Martin's *Invisibles Vainqueurs* is an equivalent source for the French air force. Yet the principal historical issue remains how and why the British were able to escape. An enduring myth is the idea that Hitler deliberately halted his panzers short of the beaches, choosing to allow the British to escape in hopes of some type of negotiated peace. Both Jackson and Bond have been at pains to lay this rumor to rest. They argued convincingly that the German mechanized forces had to halt in order to refit prior to attacking southward into France. Hitler and Goering placed too much reliance on the ability of the Luftwaffe to interdict any evacuation. Instead, the German airmen, like their ground counterparts, were overextended and needed to refit. This, plus the extraordinary heroism of British seamen, allowed many soldiers to escape the Dunkirk trap.

Dozens of studies have attempted to explain the amazing collapse of the Western Allies, particularly France, in the spring of 1940. These explanations may be divided into technical and moral, psychological ones.

In *The War in France and Flanders*, the British official historian Ellis emphasized the lack of unified command, doctrine, and coordination among the Allied armies. This theme echoes in most British accounts of the campaign; the French had their own internal command problems. Gunsburg's *Divided and Conquered* is an excellent exploration of these problems, which centered around the French commander, General Maurice Gamelin. The title of Gamelin's memoirs, *Servir* (to serve, rather than to lead), summarized his failure to provide leadership. As Le Goyet noted in *Le Mystère Gamelin*, the French general did not give a direct order to his subordinates until a week after the German advance began! Yet command problems persisted even after Gamelin was replaced, as described by Bankwitz in "Maxime Weygand and the Fall of France." Weygand's own memoirs, *Recalled to Service*, are of only limited utility.

The romance of blitzkrieg has inevitably caused many students to focus on the role of armor in the different armies of 1940. Britain and France began mass production of tanks well after Germany; their problems have been recorded by Ross, *The Business of Tanks*, and by the controller-general of French military production, Jacomet, *L'Armement de la France*. Despite this late start, however, the Allies actually had more tanks than the Germans on the Continent in May 1940, as demonstrated by Stolfi's "Equipment for Victory in France in 1940." The problem lay not so much in numbers or design as in organization, experience, and tactics. Ferré was the first to make this case with *Le Défaut de l'Armure*. Bell produced a detailed account of the fate of the three French armored divisions in "Division Cuirassée, 1940." Clarke's dissertation, "Military Technology in Republican France," traces the history of French tank doctrine and organization leading to the defeat. More recently, Doughty analyzed the matter at length in *The Seeds of Disaster*. He argued that France was a victim of its own history, geography, and institutions.

Indeed, the reasons for French defeat go well beyond technical and tactical issues. Horne's *To Lose a Battle* is an excellent starting point for the general reader. Horne delineated the psychological and political problems that hamstrung France and made it unwilling to fight again. Despite the author's pro-German bias, readers can also profit from the classic study by Benoist-Mechin, *Sixty Days That Shook the West*. For an opposing view of what might have been, consider the memoirs of Premier Paul Reynaud, published in translation as *In the Thick of the Fight*. After the war, the French legislature held hearings on all aspects of the French defeat; they were published in a multivolume study with the unwieldy title of *Rapport Fait au nom de la Commission Chargée d'Enquêter sur les Événements Survenues en France de 1933 à 1945*.

The magnitude of the French collapse has obscured the fact that many

French soldiers fought bravely and effectively. This was particularly evident when Benito Mussolini tried to invade southeastern France. French forces stopped the Italians in a matter of hours. Azeau has covered this forgotten battle in *La Guerre Franco-Italienne: Juin 1940.*

GERMANY VERSUS BRITAIN

When France surrendered in June 1940, few observers expected that Great Britain could continue the war alone. Behind the legend of Churchill's rhetoric and the indomitable British will, three interrelated issues worked against the Germans: the recovery of the British armed forces after Dunkirk, the difficulties of mounting an amphibious invasion (Operation Sea Lion), and the air Battle of Britain itself.

Had Hitler been prepared to invade Great Britain in June or July 1940, there would have been very little to stop him. The British army had been saved from the beaches of Dunkirk, but it had left its heavy equipment behind. The story of how this defeated army was rearmed, reorganized, and retrained in 1940–1941 remains one of the neglected aspects of the war. The first volume of Hamilton's seminal biography, *Monty,* illustrates the role of Bernard Montgomery and other professional soldiers in rebuilding their army in 1940. Readers should also consult Postan's official volume on *British War Production.*

Meanwhile, across the Channel, the Germans belatedly planned for a possible invasion. German staff planners did not begin serious planning and preparations until late June. Moreover, the invasion of Norway had caused such catastrophic naval losses that the German navy was unable to support an invasion.

Despite these realities, observers both then and since have been fascinated with the possibility of an invasion of Britain. In *Operation Sea Lion* Wheatley argued that the Germans made a serious effort to prepare for such invasion but that the three armed forces failed to coordinate with each other. Fleming examined both German preparations and British defenses in *Operation Sea Lion* but concluded that such an invasion was not necessary. That, in fact, was apparently Hitler's belief. In *Hitler Confronts England,* Ansel argued that Hitler never made a serious commitment to Sea Lion but instead sought victory through airpower.

Pride of place therefore goes to the Battle of Britain, when the German Luftwaffe failed to cow the British or even achieve air superiority for an invasion. The best starting point for any study of this air campaign is Collier's official volume on *The Defence of the United Kingdom.* Collier not only set forth day-by-day statistics on the battle but traces the air defense system of Britain from 1918 through the war. Mason's *Battle over Britain* is also crucial to an understanding of British air defense. Hough and Richards took a similar approach in a more recent review of the subject, *The*

Battle of Britain. Contrary to most other historians, Hough and Richards contended that the time gained from the Munich Conference of 1938 to the onset of the battle was vital to improved British air defenses.

From the British perspective, Macmillan provided a good contemporaneous account in the first volume of *The Royal Air Force in the World War.* Price focused on the greatest losses in *Battle of Britain: The Hardest Day, 18 August 1940.* More recently, Johnson and Lucas edited a useful reconsideration of the battle, *Glorious Summer.* Air historians should also consult Cooling's *Case Studies in the Achievement of Air Superiority.*

The most thorough assessment of the RAF is Terraine's *The Right of the Line,* published in the United States as *A Time for Courage.* Terraine emphasized the tactical controversy that cost Air Chief Marshal Sir Hugh Dowding his job as head of air defense. Dowding had resisted the theory of the "Big Wing" or "Bader Wing," the idea that multiple squadrons of fighters should join up in the air before attacking the Germans in mass. Turner's *The Bader Wing* is predictably supportive of the concept and includes the record of the October 1940 conference on the matter. In *The Narrow Margin,* Wood and Dempster rejected this tactic as unmanageable, as do most other historians.

Dowding's central role in the battle is carefully analyzed by Ray in *The Battle of Britain* and by Wright in *The Man Who Won the Battle of Britain.* Wright also assisted Sholto Douglas in his own memoirs, *Combat and Command.*

Another controversy about the battle arose decades after the war, when the British ability to decrypt certain German radio messages became public. In his groundbreaking book *The Ultra Secret,* Winterbotham asserted that Churchill had advance knowledge of a German air attack on Coventry but did nothing for fear of compromising the secrecy of the code-breaking effort. By contrast, Longmate argued convincingly, *Air Raid: The Bombing of Coventry, 1940,* that Ultra did not yield clear advance warning of this attack, and thus there was no soul-searching debate about whether or not to warn the city.

Of course, the battle was not entirely a matter of fighter versus bomber. The British defenses included other elements, which must be included for a complete view of the struggle. Sir Frederick Pile, commander of Anti-Aircraft Command, described the ground defenses in *Ack-Ack: Britain's Defence against Air Attack.* In *Attack Warning Red,* Wood chronicled the ground observers who supplemented radar in warning of German attacks. Finally, as part of the British official history O'Brien addressed the structure of *Civil Defence.*

Sources on the German side of the Battle of Britain are much less accessible. Murray's *Strategy for Defeat: The Luftwaffe, 1933–1945* remains the best general history. Von Ishoven published an intelligent popular account of *The Luftwaffe in the Battle of Britain.* Baumbach, a veteran of the battle, emphasized the failures of German aircraft design in *The Life and Death of the Luftwaffe*. Indeed, most accounts are united in criticizing the lack of effective bombers and the frequent change in targets, which hamstrung the Luftwaffe and helped the British to survive.

HITLER TURNS EAST

Even if Hitler had intended to launch an invasion, the Luftwaffe never achieved the air superiority that was an essential precondition to that invasion. Instead, as early as September 1940, Hitler abandoned the idea at least temporarily and focused his attention to the south and east. The decision to invade the Soviet Union (Operation Barbarossa) is more thoroughly discussed in Chapter 10. However, long before Barbarossa was launched in June 1941, Benito Mussolini had led Hitler into involvement in the Balkans.

Knox wrote a brilliant analysis of Italian politics and strategy in *Mussolini Unleashed*. Knox emphasized the many political, economic, and cultural limitations that handicapped the dictator in his efforts to achieve national greatness. His seizure of Albania in 1939 was reasonable, but he overreached himself by attacking Greece in 1940. The best available discussion of this disaster is Cervi's *The Hollow Legions*. The Greek defense was summarized by its commander, Papagos, in *The Battle of Greece, 1940–1941*.

The consequences of this Italian adventure in Greece were immense. Both Germany and Britain felt compelled to enter the conflict to support their allies, diverting German resources away from Russia and British resources away from North Africa. Van Creveld persuasively analyzed the situation in *Hitler's Strategy, 1940–1941: The Balkan Clue*. He concluded that Hitler regarded Yugoslavia as much more important economically than Greece but that, once compelled to help the Italians in the latter country, he went on to seize Greece and Crete as a base for possible future operations in the Middle East. Similarly, Zapantis' monograph on *Hitler's Balkan Campaign and the Invasion of the USSR* argues that the Yugoslav invasion did not affect the Russian campaign but that the German involvement in Greece cost Hitler significantly in terms of time and troops for Barbarossa. Ansel sought to review the entire campaign in *Hitler and the Middle Sea*. Von Mellenthin included one of the few tactical accounts of German troops in Greece as part of his classic *Panzer Battles*.

The equally expensive British involvement in this struggle is chronicled in Higham's *Diary of a Disaster*. He ably integrated British politics, Ultra intelligence, and operational considerations, giving a full picture of the matter. Blau's older monograph on *The German Campaigns in the Balkans* is also useful, as is Playfair et al.'s second volume of the official *The Mediterranean and Middle East*.

The penultimate act of German aggression was, of course, the aerial seizure of Crete in May 1941. Although it handed the British yet another defeat, this attack also shattered the German airborne force. Several British historians have revisited this battle recently, including Stewart, *The Struggle for Crete*, and Beevor, *Crete*. Beevor is particularly effective, giving an evocative, human interest account from both sides before indicting the British commanders for failing to perceive the threat clearly when the Germans could easily have been defeated. Biographers Barber in *Freyberg: Churchill's Salamander* and Freyberg in *Bernard Freyberg, VC* both provided effective views of the defending commander on Crete.

FUTURE RESEARCH

Like so much else in World War II, the period of initial German conquest is well known in outline but not always completely fleshed out in detail. The previous discussion implies three different avenues for future research.

First, with the exception of France, the victims' perspective is under-represented. Beyond their native languages, little is available concerning the armed forces and combat experiences of Poland, Norway, the Netherlands, Yugoslavia, and other countries that fell to Axis attack. Second, the emphasis on the broad outline of strategy and operations has produced a relative dearth of serious tactical studies. Beyond memoirs and anecdotes, we know relatively little about the actual tactical operations of German or opponent units. Doughty's *The Breaking Point* on the Battle of Sedan needs to be replicated for a host of lesser-known engagements in order to understand exactly how the Germans won, and their opponents lost.

Finally, despite two decades of work on Ultra, the history of World War II still needs further work in the area of intelligence. In addition to integrating the problems and omissions of intelligence into tactical history, future historians need to address the structure and functions of intelligence organizations at all levels of warfare. Hinsley's *British Intelligence in the Second World War* is an example of what such studies could add to our understanding.

BIBLIOGRAPHY

Alexander, Don W. "Repercussions of the Breda Variant." *French Historical Studies* 8 (1974): 459–88.
Allen, Paul. *Katyn: The Untold Story of Stalin's Polish Massacre.* New York: C. Scribner's Sons; Toronto: Maxwell Macmillan Canada, 1991.
Ansel, Walter. *Hitler Confronts England.* Durham, NC: Duke UP, 1960.
———. *Hitler and the Middle Sea.* Durham, NC: Duke UP, 1972.
Anthérieu, Étienne. *Grandeur et Sacrifice de la Ligne Maginot.* Paris: Durassie et Cie., 1962.

Ash, Bernard. *Norway 1940.* London: Cassell, 1964.

Azeau, Henri. *La Guerre Franco-Italienne: Juin 1940.* Paris: Presses de la Cité, 1967.

Baldwin, Hanson W. *The Crucial Years 1939–1941: The World at War.* New York: Harper and Row; London: Weidenfeld and Nicolson, 1976.

Bankwitz, Philip C. F. "Maxime Weygand and the Fall of France: A Study in Civil-Military Relations." *Journal of Modern History 31* (1959): 225–42.

Barber, Laurie. *Freyberg: Churchill's Salamander.* Auckland: Century Hutchinson, 1989.

Bauer, Eddy. *La Guerre des Blindées; les Operations de la Deuxième Guerre Mondiale sur les Fronts d'Europe et d'Afrique.* 2d ed. 2 vols. Paris and Lausanne: Payot, 1962.

Baumbach, Werner. *The Life and Death of the Luftwaffe.* Trans. Frederick Holt. New York: Ballantine, 1967.

Bayer, James A., and Nils Orvik. *The Scandinavian Flank as History: 1939–1940.* Kingston, Ontario: Queen's University, 1984.

Bédarida, François. *La Stratégie secrète de la Drôle de guerre: le Conseil Suprême Interallié, Septembre 1939–Avril, 1940.* Paris: Presse de la Fondation nationale des Sciences Politiques, 1979.

Beevor, Antony. *Crete: The Battle and the Resistance.* London: Penguin, 1992; Boulder, CO: Westview, 1994.

Bell, Raymond E. "Division Cuirassée, 1940." *Armor 83* (1974): 25–29.

Benoist-Mechin, Jacques G.P.M. *Soixante Jours Qui Ébranlerent l'Occident, 10 Mai–10 Juillet 1940.* 3 vols. Paris: Éditions Albin Michel, 1956. Trans. Peter Wiles as *Sixty Days That Shook the West: The Fall of France.* New York: Putnam; London: J. Cape, 1963.

Bethell, Nicholas W. *The War Hitler Won: The Fall of Poland, September 1939.* New York: Holt, Rinehart, and Winston, 1973; London: Futura, 1976.

Blau, George E. *The German Campaigns in the Balkans (Spring 1941).* Washington, DC: GPO, 1986.

Bond, Brian. *Britain, France and Belgium 1939–1940.* 2d ed. London: Brassey's/ Maxwell Pergamon, 1990.

Boog, Horst. *Die Deutsche Luftwaffenführung 1935–1945; Führungsprobleme, Spitzengliederung, Generalstabsausbildung.* Stuttgart: Deutsche Verlags-Anstalt, 1992.

———, ed. *The Conduct of the Air War in the Second World War: An International Comparison. Proceedings of the International Conference of Historians in Freiburg im Breisgau, FRG, from 29 August to 2 September, 1988.* New York: St. Martin's, 1992.

Butler, James R. M. *Grand Strategy.* Vol. 2, *September 1939–June 1941. History of the Second World War.* London: HMSO, 1957.

———, ed. *History of the Second World War, United Kingdom Military Series.* London: HMSO, 1949–1978.

Cervi, Mario. *The Hollow Legions: Mussolini's Blunder in Greece, 1940–1941.* Trans. Eric Mosbacher. Garden City, NY: Doubleday, 1971; London: Chatto and Windus, 1972.

Chew, Allen F. *The White Death: The Epic of the Soviet–Finnish Winter War.* Lansing: Michigan State UP, 1971, 1990.

Churchill, Winston S. *The Second World War.* Vol. 1, *The Gathering Storm;* vol. 2, *Their Finest Hour.* Boston: Houghton Mifflin, 1948–1949.

Clarke, Jeffrey J. "Military Technology in Republican France: The Evolution of the French Armored Force, 1917–1940." Diss., Duke University, 1969.

Collier, Basil. *The Defence of the United Kingdom. History of the Second World War.* United Kingdom Military Series. London: HMSO, 1957.

Cooling, Benjamin F. *Case Studies in the Achievement of Air Superiority.* Washington, DC: Center for Air Force History, 1994.

Cooper, Matthew, and James Lucas. *Panzer: The Armoured Force of the Third Reich.* New York: St. Martin's, 1978. Also published as *Panzer Grenadiers.* London: MacDonald and Jane's, 1977.

Cruickshank, Charles. *The German Occupation of the Channel Islands.* Gloucester, England, and Dover, NH: Sutton, 1993.

Deichmann, Paul. *German Air Force Operations in Support of the Army.* Maxwell Air Force Base, AL: Air University, 1962; New York: Arno, 1968.

Derry, T. K. *The Campaign in Norway. History of the Second World War.* United Kingdom Military Series. London: HMSO, 1952; London and Nashville, TN: Imperial War Museum/Battery, 1995.

Doughty, Robert F. *The Breaking Point: Sedan and the Fall of France, 1940.* Hamden, CT: Archon, 1990.

———. *The Seeds of Disaster: The Development of French Army Doctrine, 1919–1939.* Hamden, CT: Archon, 1985.

Douglas, Sholto, and Robert Wright. *Combat and Command: The Story of an Airman in Two World Wars.* New York: Simon and Schuster, 1966.

Dutailly, Henry. *Les Problèmes de l'Armée de Terre Française (1935–1939).* Paris: Imprimerie Nationale, 1980.

Elble, Rolf. *Die Schlacht an der Bzura im September 1939 aus deutscher und polnischer Sicht.* Freiburg: Verlag Rombach, 1975.

Ellis, Lionel F. *The War in France and Flanders, 1939–1940. History of the Second World War.* U.K. Military Series. London: HMSO, 1953.

Eremenko, Andrei I. *The Arduous Beginning.* Moscow: Progress, 1974.

Ferré, Charles. *Le Défaut de l'Armure. Nos Chars, Pouvaient-ils vaincre en 1940?* Paris: Charles-Lavauzelle, 1948.

Ferris, John. "The British Army, Signals and Security in the Desert Campaign, 1940–42." *Intelligence and National Security* 5 (1990): 255–91.

Fleming, Peter. *Operation Sea Lion: The Projected Invasion of England in 1940—An Account of the German Preparations and the British Countermeasures.* Westport, CT: Greenwood, 1977.

Fonvieille-Alquier, François. *The French and the Phoney War, 1939–40.* Trans. Edward Sacrum. London: Tom Stacey, 1973.

France. (Serré, C., Rapporteur) *Rapport Fait au nom de la Commission Chargée d'Enquêter sur les Événements Survenues en France de 1933 à 1945.* 8 vols. Paris: Imprimerie de l'Assemblée Nationale, 1947–1951.

Franks, Norman L. R. *The Air Battle of Dunkirk.* London: William Kimber, 1983.

Freyberg, Paul. *Bernard Freyberg, VC: Soldier of Two Nations.* London: Hodder and Stoughton, 1991.

Gamelin, Maurice G. *Servir.* 3 vols. Paris: Plon, 1980.

Gates, Eleanor M. *End of the Affair: The Collapse of the Anglo-French Alliance, 1939–40.* Berkeley: University of California and London: Allen and Unwin, 1981.

Gemzell, Carl-Axel. *Organization, Conflict, and Innovation: A Study of German Naval Strategic Planning, 1888–1940.* Stockholm: Scandinavian University Books/ Esselte Studium, 1973.

————. *Raeder, Hitler, und Skandinavien; Der Kampf für Einen Maritimen Operationsplan.* Lund, Sweden: C.W.K. Gleerup, 1965.

Giuliano, Gerard. *Les Soldats du Béton: La Ligne Maginot dans les Ardennes et en Meuse, 1939–1940.* Charleville-Mezières, France: Terres Ardennaises, 1986.

Guderian, Heinz. *Panzer Leader.* Trans. Constantine Fitzgibbon. London: Arrow and Costa Mesa, CA: Noontide, 1990.

Gunsburg, Jeffery A. *Divided and Conquered: The French High Command and the Defeat in the West, 1940.* Westport, CT, and London: Greenwood, 1979.

Halder, Franz. *The Halder War Diary, 1939–1942.* London: Greenhill; Novato, CA: Presidio, 1988.

Hamilton, Nigel. *Monty: The Making of a General, 1887–1942.* London: Hamilton; New York: McGraw-Hill, 1981.

Higham, Robin. *Diary of a Disaster: British Aid to Greece, 1940–1941.* Lexington: UP of Kentucky, 1986.

Hinsley, Francis H., E. E. Thomas, C.F.G. Ransom, and R. C. Knight. *British Intelligence in the Second World War: Its Influence on Strategy and Operations.* Vol. 1. London: HMSO, 1979, 1988.

Horne, Alistair. *To Lose a Battle: France, 1940.* New York: Penguin; London: Papermac, 1990.

Hough, Richard, and Denis Richards. *The Battle of Britain: The Greatest Air Battle of World War II.* New York: W. W. Norton; London: Hodder and Stoughton, 1989.

Jackson, Robert. *Air War over France, May–June 1940.* London: Ian Allen, 1974.

————. *Dunkirk: The British Evacuation, 1940.* New York: St. Martin's; London: Mayflower Granada, 1976.

Jacobsen, Hans-Adolf. *Fall Gelb: Der Kampf um den Deutschen Operationsplan zur Westoffensive 1940.* Wiesbaden, Germany: Franz Steiner Verlag, 1957.

————, ed. *Dokumente zum Westfeldzug 1940.* Berlin and Göttingen, Germany: Musterschmidt Verlag, 1960.

Jacomet, Robert. *L'Armement de la France, 1936–1939.* Paris: Éditions Lajeunesse, 1945.

Johnson, James E., and P. B. (Laddie) Lucas, eds. *Glorious Summer: The Story of the Battle of Britain.* London: Stanley Paul, 1990.

Kaufmann, J. E., and H. W. Kaufmann. *Hitler's Blitzkrieg Campaigns: The Invasion and Defense of Western Europe, 1939–1940.* Conshohocken, PA: Combined Books; London: Greenhill/Lionel Leventhal, 1993.

Keitel, Wilhelm. *In the Service of the Reich.* Trans. David Irving. Briarcliff Manor, NY: Stein and Day, 1966.

Kemp, Anthony. *The Maginot Line: Myth and Reality.* London: F. Warne; New York: Stein and Day, 1981.

Kennedy, Robert M. *The German Campaign in Poland (1939).* New York: Military Heritage, 1988.

Kersaudy, François. *Norway 1940.* London: William Collins; New York: St. Martin's, 1991.

Kesselring, Albert. *The Memoirs of Field-Marshal Kesselring.* Trans. Lynton Hudson. London: W. Kimber, 1953; Novato, CA: Presidio, 1989.

Keyes, Roger. *Outrageous Fortune: The Tragedy of Leopold III of the Belgians, 1901–1941.* London: Secker and Warburg, 1984.

Kieft, David O. *Belgium's Return to Neutrality: An Essay in the Frustration of Small Power Diplomacy*. Oxford: Clarendon, 1972.

Knox, MacGregor. *Mussolini Unleashed 1939–1941: Politics and Strategy in Fascist Italy's Last War*. Cambridge: Cambridge UP, 1982.

Le Goyet, Pierre. *Le Mystère Gamelin*. Paris: Presses de la Cité, 1975.

Longmate, Norman. *Air Raid: The Bombing of Coventry, 1940*. London: Hutchinson, 1976; New York: David McKay, 1978.

Lukacs, John. *The Last European War: September 1939/December 1941*. Garden City, NY: Anchor/Doubleday, 1976; London: Routledge and Kegan Paul, 1977.

Maass, Walter B. *The Netherlands at War: 1940–1945*. London and New York: Abelard-Schuman, 1970.

MacDonald, Callum A. *The Lost Battle: Crete 1941*. London: Macmillan; New York: Free Press/Macmillan, 1993.

Mackiewicz, Joseph. *The Katyn Wood Murders*. London: Hollis and Carter, 1951.

Macksey, Kenneth J. *Guderian: Creator of the Blitzkrieg*. New York: Stein and Day, 1976. Rev. ed. published as *Guderian: Panzer General*. London: Greenhill; Novato, CA: Presidio, 1992.

———. *Rommel: Battles and Campaigns*. London: Arms and Armour/Lionel Leventhal; New York: Mayflower, 1979.

Macmillan, Norman. *The Royal Air Force in the World War*. Vol. 1, *1919–1940*. London: George G. Harrap, 1942.

Maier, Klaus A., Horst Rohde, Bernd Stegemann, and Hans Umbreit. *Germany's Initial Conquests in Europe. Germany and the Second World War*. Vol. 2. Trans. Dean S. McMurry and Ewald Osers. New York and Oxford: Clarendon, 1991.

Marshall-Cornwall, James H. *Wars and Rumours of Wars: A Memoir*. London: L. Cooper/Seckert Warburg, 1989.

Martin, Paul. *Invisibles Vainqueurs: Exploits et Sacrifice de l'Armée de l'Air en 1939–1940*. Paris: Michelet, 1990.

Mason, Francis K. *Battle over Britain: A History of the German Air Assaults on Great Britain, 1917–18 and July–December 1940*. Garden City, NY: Doubleday, 1970; Bourne End: Aston, 1990.

Merdal, Jacques [Hervé Cras, pseud.]. *Dunkerque*. Paris: Éditions France-Empire, 1960.

Messenger, Charles. *The Blitzkrieg Story*. New York: Charles Scribner's Sons, 1976. 2d ed., *The Art of Blitzkrieg*. London: Ian Allen, 1991.

Moulton, J. L. *A Study of Warfare in Three Dimensions: The Norwegian Campaign of 1940*. Athens: Ohio UP, 1967.

Mrazek, James E. *The Fall of Eben Emael*. Washington, DC: Luce, 1971; London: Hale, 1972; Novato, CA: Presidio, 1991.

Murray, Williamson. *Strategy for Defeat: The Luftwaffe, 1933–1945*. Secaucus, NJ: Chartwell, 1986.

Nevakivi, Jukka. *The Appeal That Was Never Made: The Allies, Scandinavia, and the Finnish Winter War, 1939–1940*. Montreal: McGill-Queen's UP; London: Hurst, 1976.

Nyman, Kristina. *Finland's War Years, 1939–1945: A List of Books and Articles concerning the Winter War and the Continuation War, excluding Literature in Finnish and Russian*. Helsinki, Finland: Society of Military History, 1973.

O'Brien, Terence H. *Civil Defence. History of the Second World War.* London: HMSO, 1955.

Paananen, Eloise, and Lauri Paananen. *The Winter War: The Russo-Finnish Conflict, 1939–1940.* London: Sedgewick and Jackson, 1985; Harrisburg, PA: Stackpole, 1992.

Papagos, Alexandros. *The Battle of Greece, 1940–1941.* Trans. Pat Eliascos. Athens: J. M. Scazikis, 1949.

Perrett, Bryan. *A History of Blitzkrieg.* New York: Stein and Day, 1983; Berkley, 1989; London: Panther, 1985.

Pile, Frederick. *Ack-Ack: Britain's Defence against Air Attack during the Second World War.* London: George G. Harrap; New York: British Book Center, 1949.

Playfair, I.S.O., F. C. Flynn, C.J.C. Molony, and S. E. Toomer. *The Mediterranean and the Middle East.* Vol. 2, *History of the Second World War.* London: HMSO, 1956.

Polish Air Force Association. *Destiny Can Wait: The Polish Air Force in the Second World War.* Ed. Mieczyslaw Lisiewicz; trans. A. Truscoe. London: William Heinemann, 1949; Nashville, TN: Battery, 1988.

Postan, Michael M. *British War Production. History of the Second World War.* London: HMSO, 1952.

Price, Alfred. *Battle of Britain: The Hardest Day, 18 August 1940.* New York: Scribner's 1980; London: Arrow, 1990.

Ray, John P. *The Battle of Britain: New Perspectives: Behind the Scenes of the Great Air War.* London: Arms and Armour; New York: Sterling, 1991.

Reynaud, Paul. *In the Thick of the Fight, 1930–1945.* Trans. James D. Lambert. New York: Simon and Schuster; London: Cassell, 1955.

Rommel, Erwin. *The Rommel Papers.* Ed. B. H. Liddell Hart; trans. Paul Findlay. New York: Harcourt, Brace and London: Collins, 1953.

Ross, G. MacLeod. *The Business of Tanks, 1933–1945.* Devon, England: Arthur H. Stockwell, 1976.

Schachtman, Tom. *The Phony War, 1939–1940.* New York: Harper and Row, 1982.

Stewart, Ian M. G. *The Struggle for Crete, 20 May–1 June 1941: A Story of Lost Opportunity.* Oxford and New York: Oxford UP, 1966, 1991.

Stolfi, Russel H. S. "Equipment for Victory in France in 1940." *History* 55 (1970): 1–20.

Sweet, John J. T. *Iron Arm: The Mechanization of Mussolini's Army, 1920–1940.* Westport, CT: Greenwood, 1980.

Terraine, John. *The Right of the Line: The Royal Air Force in the European War, 1939–1945.* London: Hodder and Stoughton. Published in the United States as *A Time for Courage.* New York: Macmillan, 1985.

Trevor-Roper, Hugh R., ed. *Blitzkrieg to Defeat: Hitler's War Directives, 1939–1945.* New York: Holt, Rinehart, and Winston, 1964, 1971.

Turner, John F. *The Bader Wing.* New York, Kent: Hippocrene/Midas, 1981; Shrewsbury: Airlife, 1990.

Van Creveld, Martin L. *Hitler's Strategy, 1940–1941; The Balkan Clue.* London: Cambridge UP, 1973.

Van Ishoven, Armand. *The Luftwaffe in the Battle of Britain.* New York: Scribner's; London: Ian Allen, 1980.

von Manstein, Erich. *Lost Victories.* Trans. Anthony G. Powell. Chicago: Henry Regnery, 1958. Reprinted, Elistree: Greenhill, 1987; Novato, CA: Presidio, 1994.

von Mellenthin, Friedrich W. *Panzer Battles: A Study of the Employment of Armor in the Second World War.* Trans. H. Betzler. London: Cassell, 1955; Norman: University of Oklahoma, 1982; New York: Ballantine, 1987.

von Vormann, Nikolaus. *Der Feldzug 1939 In Polen; Die Operationen des Heeres.* Weissenburg: Prince-Eugen-Verlag, 1958.

Warlimont, Walter. *Inside Hitler's Headquarters, 1939–45.* Trans. R. H. Barry. New York: Praeger, 1964; Novato, CA: Presidio, 1991.

Weygand, Maxime. *Recalled to Service: The Memoirs of Maxime Weygand.* Trans. E. W. Dickes. London: Heinemann; Garden City, NY: Doubleday, 1952.

Wheatley, Ronald. *Operation Sea Lion: German Plans for the Invasion of England, 1939–1942.* Oxford: Clarendon, 1962; Westport, CT: Greenwood, 1978.

Wheldon, John. *Machine Age Armies.* London and New York: Abelard-Schuman, 1968.

Wiggan, Richard. *Hunt the Altmark.* London: Robert Hale, 1982, 1990.

Winterbotham, Frederick W. *The Ultra Secret.* London: Purnell Book Services; New York: Harper and Row, 1974.

Wood, Derek. *Attack Warning Red: The Royal Observer Corps and the Defence of Britain 1925 to 1975.* London: MacDonald and Jane's, 1976.

Wood, Derek, and Derek Dempster. *The Narrow Margin: The Battle of Britain and the Rise of Air Power, 1930–1940.* London: Hutchinson, 1961; Washington, DC: Smithsonian, 1990.

Wright, Robert. *The Man Who Won the Battle of Britain.* New York: Scribner's, 1969.

Zaloga, Steve, and Victor Madej. *The Polish Campaign, 1939.* New York: Hippocrene, 1985, 1991.

Zapantis, Andrew. *Hitler's Balkan Campaign and the Invasion of the USSR.* Boulder, CO and New York: East European Monographs, 1987.

9 North Africa and the Mediterranean Theater, 1939–1945

James J. Sadkovich

GENERAL COMMENTS

Four major World War II belligerents fought for five years in the Mediterranean, but the theater has generated relatively few works in English, and these tend to focus on North Africa. This appears to be due to the belief that the Mediterranean was a secondary theater, important only when it affected Germany's war effort. Russian historians have even claimed that by exhausting the Germans, the USSR won the war in the Mediterranean, and Ceva argued in *La condotta* that Italy's involvement in Russia assured its defeat in Africa.

What is certain is that from France's capitulation in 1940 to Italy's surrender in 1943, Britain and Italy deployed massive naval, air, and ground forces in the Mediterranean. After 1943 Germany diverted fifty divisions to the theater and ultimately suffered 435,000 casualties there. Until 1945, the Americans and British deployed significant air and ground forces on the Italian peninsula and against targets as far east as Ploesti.

Because the Mediterranean absorbed Allied and Axis forces through 1944, it affected other theaters. Landing craft needed in the Pacific were used to invade Italy; Britain constantly diverted naval and air units to Mediterranean bases; the area siphoned German air units from Russia; and Italy's surrender forced Berlin to cancel operations in Russia in order to defend a southern flank previously held by its ally. The area remained the only battleground for Anglo-American and German ground forces until mid-1944. The Mediterranean was thus the major theater for Italy and Britain and integral to Axis and Allied war efforts.

But this has not been obvious. Most studies focus on a handful of individuals, one or two belligerents, a single phase of the war, a limited area, a single service, or a particular battle. However, detailed knowledge of a single aspect of the war, for example, armored warfare in Libya, does not explain such phenomena as civilian morale in Italy, Axis diplomacy in Spain, Arab unrest in Iraq, Allied maneuvers in Turkey, or antipartisan operations in the Balkans. But it does make such phenomena appear to be less important than they were, and it privileges particular points of view.

For example, although a good deal has been published on Britain's SOE (Special Operations Executive), America's OSS (Office of Strategic Services), and irregular warfare in the Balkans, OSS and SOE sources on the resistance in the Balkans are less than accurate regarding the internal politics of the region. Similarly, focusing on Britain's defense of Suez gives the impression that skirmishes along the Egyptian frontier were more important than protracted combat between Greek and Italian forces in Albania—hence the belief that the Italo-Greek war was a negligible event that acquired importance only after British and German units intervened.

Studies on the Mediterranean vary widely but can be grouped into those on the background of operations and those that examine the tactical and strategic foreground. The latter include battle histories, biographies of major figures, studies of alliance systems, and studies of wartime politics. Background studies can similarly be broken down into accounts of support activities, including economic mobilization and logistical organization; studies of technique, from electrical-mechanical devices like radar, to systems of intelligence gathering and propaganda; studies of social phenomena, including assessments of morale on the home front and analyses of the behavior of soldiers in combat; and integrative histories that establish and analyze the links between the various fronts and individual services.

These categories can be further divided into scholarly, popular, tendentious (hagiographic, apologetic, denigratory), parochial (narrowly national or nationalist), and overarching, or synthetic. The last is the rarest; two of the best examples are Howard's *The Mediterranean Strategy* and Faldella's revisionist *L'Italia e la seconda guerra mondiale*.

More common are works that focus on a battle or an individual, such as Mack Smith's critical treatment of *Mussolini*; Irving's biography of Rommel, *The Trail of the Fox*, which combines popular and biographical formats with a provocative analysis; or Schofield's partisan account of the British *Attack on Taranto*. There are works by participants and contemporaries, but few have been translated into English. Ciano's *Diaries* is indispensable for anyone who cannot read De Felice's Italian edition. Others include Villari's *Italian Foreign Policy*, a rationalization of fascist foreign policy; the head of Italy's General Staff until 1940, Pietro Badoglio's *Italy in the Second World War*; and the self-serving memoirs by the diplomat Alfieri, *Dictators Face to Face*. Maugeri's memoirs, *From the Ashes of Disgrace*, is by an officer from the fascist era who made a career after the war; and Caccia-Dominioni's *Alamein* is an impressionistic memoir on North Africa.

Official histories tend to concentrate on specific services, battles, or techniques. Among the exceptions are Playfair et al.'s five-volume *The Mediterranean and the Middle East*, Hinsley et al.'s *British Intelligence*, and those published by the Italian navy and army.

When Hinsley is read with Behrendt's *Rommel's Intelligence*, Bennett's *Ultra and the Mediterranean Strategy*, Knox's *Mussolini*, Lewin's *Rommel* and *The Life and Death of the Afrika Korps*, and Sullivan's "A Fleet in Being," the impact of intelligence on the Mediterranean war appears great enough to advise a thorough reevaluation in interpretations formulated before the 1990s—an example of technical background absorbing operational foreground.

Whatever their form, studies echo the polemics of the war and the immediate postwar period. Relatively few have succeeded in maintaining an impartial point of view, and those who have tried to do so have often come in for sharp criticism.

One historian's balance may, of course, be another's bias, especially since anything that seems to "rehabilitate" the Italian military or the fascist regime is suspect, and there is no lack of paladins ready to break a lance to preserve the dominant historical canons. De Felice's untranslated, multivolume biography of Mussolini therefore comes in for its share of criticism, yet it is basic to any discussion of the war. For critiques of this productive and provocative historian, see Painter's "Renzo De Felice and the Historiography of Italian Fascism" and Ledeen's "Renzo De Felice and the Controversy over Italian Fascism."

LANGUAGE AND BIAS

All studies are limited by the linguistic skills and geographical location of the researcher. Because until 1943 the war was an Italo-British duel, with the Germans and Americans reluctant seconds, the literature in Italian is basic, as Sadkovich noted in his comparison of "Italian and British Service Histories." But little of the Italian literature has been translated, and many who have written on the topic have not been able to read Italian.

Bibliographic material can be found in Cassels' *Italian Foreign Policy*, as well as Knox's *Mussolini Unleashed*, Ceva's *Africa Settentrionale*, and Sadkovich's *The Italian Navy*. For translated works using Italian sources see Bragadin and Fioravanzo's *The Italian Navy in World War II*, Fraccaroli's *Italian Warships*, Toscano's excellent *Designs in Diplomacy*, and Borghese's partisan *Sea Devils*, a history of the navy's special operations unit (X MAS), as well as translated memoirs noted earlier. Finally, there is the comprehensive, indispensable guide by Baxter, *The War in North Africa*.

If Italian studies are not usable by most researchers, this is also true of works in other languages. It is worth learning French to consult the *Revue d'histoire de la deuxième guerre mondiale et des conflits contémporains*, which began publishing articles on the war and warfare in 1950. Among French works in English are de Belot's solid *The Struggle for the Mediterranean* on the air-naval war and *The French Navy* by Auphan and Mordal.

So many German works have been translated that readers of English view the Mediterranean theater through both German and Anglo-American lenses. In addition to popular histories by Carell, *The Foxes of the Desert*; Heckmann, *Rommel's War*; and others, there are memoirs, histories, and edited papers by the chief of German operations in the theater, Kesselring, *A Soldier's Record*; the diplomat von Hassell's *Diaries*; and the German naval liaison to the Italian command, Ruge's *Sea Warfare*. For Rommel, see *The Rommel Papers* and books by his subordinates, Behrendt, *Rommel's Intelligence*; Schmidt, *With Rommel in the Desert*; and Bayerlein, "El Alamein." Basic are the twenty-five volumes of documents, *German Military Studies*, edited by Detwiler, Burdick, and Rohwer.

Because many writers have uncritically repeated stereotypes shared by their sources, biases and prejudices have taken on the status of objective observations, including the idea that the Germans and British were the only belligerents in the Mediterranean after Italian setbacks in early 1941. Sadkovich questioned this point of view in "Of Myths and Men" and *The Italian Navy*, but persistent stereotypes, including that of the incompetent Italian, are well entrenched in the literature, from Puleston's early *The Influence of Sea Power*, to Gooch's "Italian Military Incompetence," to more recent publications by Mack Smith, Knox, and Sullivan.

Wartime bias is apparent in early British and American histories, which focused on German operations, dismissed Italian forces as inept or unimportant, and viewed Germany as the pivotal power in Europe during the interwar period. For a discussion of this, see Sadkovich, "Anglo-American Bias and the Italo-Greek War."

Bias includes both implicit assumptions, evident in Knox's title "The Sources of Italy's Defeat in 1940: Bluff or Institutionalized Incompetence?" and the selective use of sources. Also see Sullivan's "The Italian Armed Forces." Sims, *The Fighter Pilot*, ignored the Italians, while d'Este in *World War II in the Mediterranean* shaped his reader's image of Italians by citing a German comment that Italy's surrender was "the basest treachery" and by discussing Allied and German commanders but ignoring Messe, whose *Come finí la guerra in Africa* is an account of operations in Tunisia, where he commanded the Italian First Army, which held off both the U.S. Second Corps and the British Eighth Army.

Like Young, whose *Rommel the Desert Fox* created the Rommel myth, authors can appear biased because they echo sources that reflect the prejudices and assumptions of the period. Indeed, many of our unconscious assumptions about the war have been shaped by documentaries like *Victory at Sea*, by sophisticated propaganda like Frank Capra's wartime *Why We Fight* films, and by Hollywood films, television programs, and popular fiction in general. Dependence on non-Italian sources compromised Murray's analysis of the Italian military in *The Change in the European Balance of Power*, it led Van Creveld to conclude in *Supplying War* that Italians were "useless ballast," and it caused Fraser, *And We Shall Shock Them*, to dismiss Graziani as an anxiety-ridden procrastinator but praise Wavell as a fearless problem solver. Liddell Hart's German sources led him to conclude in *The German Generals Talk* that Italian "jealousy of the Germans" had helped save Egypt. Such conclusions later led Mearsheimer to question Liddell Hart's objectivity, though Liddell Hart's history of British *Tanks* and his concise *History of the Second World War* remain useful, as do Jackson's *The Battle for North Africa* and Lewin's *Rommel* and *The Life and Death of the Afrika Corps*.

If stereotypes make it hard for readers of English to credit any acts of heroism or any display of competence or persistence by Italians, the official Italian service histories, De Felice, Faldella, and Sadkovich in works previously cited, have sought to set the record straight, particularly with regard to Italy's convoy operations, which registered few periods of heavy losses until 1943, when overwhelming Allied material superiority and accurate intelligence made it possible to target and sink Axis shipping. But the disparity in strength is often ignored, and the consequent compensation in willpower and courage demanded from the Italians is not generally acknowledged, especially if authors use non-Italian sources.

ENGLISH AND ITALIAN SOURCES

There are excellent studies and useful primary sources available in English, including Great Britain, Admiralty, *Ships of the Royal Navy*; Young's *A Dictionary of Ships*; official Commonwealth histories of the war in North Africa, Greece, and the Aegean; and Roskill's *The War at Sea*. Various document collections, especially the United Kingdom, Cabinet History Series, *Principal War Telegrams;* and the official histories of the British war economy by Payton-Smith, *Oil: A Study of War-Time Policy and Administration*, and Postan, *British War Production*, as well as Medlicott, *The Economic Blockade*.

Still useful are older works on naval and air operations, including Ansel's *Hitler and the Middle Sea*, Macintyre's *The Battle for the Mediterranean*, Seth's *Two Fleets Surprised*, an account of the skirmish off Cape Matapan, and Owen's *The Desert Air Force*.

The best work on German armor is Chamberlain's *Encyclopedia*. Italian armored theory and development are discussed by Sweet, *Iron Arm: The*

Mechanization of Mussolini's Army, and by Riccio, *Italian Tanks and Fighting Vehicles.*

The most useful reference works on aircraft are by Angelucci and Cucari, *World War II Airplanes*, and Thompson, *Italian Civil and Military Aircraft*. Basic to the discussion of naval weaponry are the excellent studies by Bagnasco, *I M.A.S. e le motosiluranti italiane*, the multivolume *Le navi d'Italia* published by the Italian navy; Rohwer, *Axis Submarine Successes*; and Dulin and Garzke, *Battleships*. For artillery and small arms, Benussi's *Armi portatili* is indispensable, while Chamberlain and Gander's *Anti-Aircraft Guns* is incomplete but useful.

Italian official histories cover a wide range of topics; Italy, Marina Militare Italiana, *La marina italiana nella seconda guerra mondiale*, includes volumes on naval and merchant shipping losses (volumes 1, 2, 3), operations (volumes 4, 5), submarine and antisubmarine warfare (volume 13 [1, 2, and Base of Italian Atlantic Submarine at Bordeaux (Betasom)]); convoys (volumes 6, 7, 8 for Africa and volume 9 for the Balkans), minesweeping and minelaying (volumes 18, 19), blockade runners (volume 17), antisubmarine warfare (volume 20), special units (volume 14), and organization (volume 21). The army also published useful bibliographies.

In addition to battle histories, studies of logistics, and doctrine, the Italian army (Italy, Esercito) published the *Verbali*, or minutes, of Axis liaison meetings on operations in the Mediterranean and is in the process of publishing the high command's war diaries, the *Diario storico*. The wartime directives of the Air Force's Historical Office are also in print. Works in Italian on the air force have not been translated, and Segré's excellent volume, *Italo Balbo: A Fascist Life*, ends with his death in June 1940.

THE BALKANS, CRETE, AND MALTA

Works in English on the Balkans are few and biased, but the Italo-Greek conflict was crucial to the Italian war effort in the Mediterranean, as Sadkovich in "Understanding Defeat" and *The Italian Navy* noted. Furthermore, partisan operations in the Balkans were enervating for the Axis. Discussions of Italian operations and Italy's occupation of the Balkans are available only in Italian, French, Serbian, and Croatian. Readers of Italian should consult the Italian army's histories on Yugoslavia and Greece, as well as the short work by Bianchini and Privitera, *6 Aprile 1941: L'attacco italiano alla Jugoslavia.*

If Yugoslavia was a running sore for the Axis from April 1941, Greece distracted the Italians from late 1940 and cost them considerably more than it did the British. Consult Cervi's detailed *Hollow Legions* for Italian operations; Higham's excellent *Diary of a Disaster*, an analysis of the British role; Bitzes' careful study of Metaxas, *Greece in World War II to April 1941*; and the account by the Greek chief of staff, Alexander Papagos, *The Battle of Greece.* Van Creveld's *Hitler's Strategy* and Presseisen's "Prelude to 'Barbarossa' " looked at the war's impact on the German war effort.

The few armored units sent to Greece by London and Rome were ineffective and insignificant owing to inhospitable terrain, described in Crisp, *The Gods Were Neutral.* Although the British navy was savaged by German and Italian aircraft in the Aegean during the spring of 1941, the British realized unintended strategic benefits because Italy's occupation of the Balkans further dispersed its forces and seriously compromised its war effort in North Africa, allowing the British to cut their losses and focus their full attention on Libya.

Moreover, the Commonwealth's unsuccessful defense of Crete cost the Germans so dearly that Hitler balked at seizing Malta a year later—and if the air war over the island cost both sides hundreds of aircraft, the presence of British air and naval units on Malta hindered the Axis convoy effort. There is no agreement regarding *how* important Malta was, but it was seen as crucial. Jellison's *Besieged: The World War II Ordeal of Malta* is critical of the British; Cameron's *Story of the Malta Convoys* is balanced; and Smith and Walker's *Malta Striking Forces* provides a useful survey of the island's naval units. Giorgerini's "The Role of Malta in Italian Naval Operations" is provocative but unconvincing; and the two volumes *Malta,* one by Shores, Cull, and Malizia, the other by Shores and Malizia, are crammed with data, but their detailed chronological format makes them hard to use.

The negative repercussions of the Italian attack on Greece continued to reverberate long after the Balkans were overrun in 1941, but they were not nearly so serious as those from Hitler's attack on the Soviet Union. Italy's action, triggered by Germany's dispatch of troops to Romania and fear of a postwar world dominated by Berlin, led to German appropriation of Italy's sphere of influence in the Balkans and an occupation marked by partisan warfare and atrocities on all sides, forcing Italy to maintain large forces in Yugoslavia and Greece, where irregular warfare and friction with German and Croatian forces wore down the Italians morally and materially.

Italy's surrender strengthened the partisans and weakened the Germans and their Croatian and Serbian allies. Tito's forces obtained armaments and recruits from six Italian divisions, while a seventh fought the Germans at Dubrovnik. An Allied landing in the Balkans was never a realistic option, and whether the Allies should have backed Tito's partisans rather than Mihailovic's Chetniks is moot, because, like the Ustasha, the Chetniks had collaborated with the Axis.

It is intriguing to speculate on the course that the war might have taken had Yugoslavia followed the Bulgarian, Hungarian, or Romanian models. Had there been no military coup by Serbian officers in 1941, and had Macek's autonomous Croatian province survived, there would have been no Axis attack, no genocidal civil war, and little partisan activity—freeing Italian troops, ships, and artillery for the war in Africa. In other words, the importance of the Serbian coup seems to have resided in its effect on the Italian, not the German, war effort, and its ultimate significance may lie in the subsequent civilian suffering that resulted from the military occupation of Yugoslavia by the Axis and their Balkan allies.

NORTH AFRICA IN CONTEXT

Battle histories are the most readable for the nonspecialist because they are straightforward, chronological accounts of a single battle or a constellation of battles within a period that can be seen as a discrete whole. But, if useful, this is a limited approach. For example, focusing on the Axis advance in North Africa in the spring of 1941 and the subsequent British counterattacks in May and June tends to reduce the convoy war and the conflicts in the Balkans to epiphenomena whose sole importance is their impact on the armored skirmishes in Libya and Egypt. The essentially integrated nature of the war effort is fragmented and distorted.

Nonetheless, historians have traditionally used the battles in North Africa as benchmarks to mark the progress of the war in the Mediterranean, and it remains convenient to do so. One of the best series of battle histories is put out by the Italian army, whose detailed monographs begin with the skirmishes along the Egyptian frontier during the summer of 1940 and end with the final British drive through Libya and the siege of Tunisia in 1942–1943. These volumes are useful for their careful analysis and their many detailed maps. None have been translated.

Italy's advance to Sidi el Barrani in September 1940 was followed by a period of inactivity, then a British counterattack from Marsa Matruh in December, which culminated with the destruction of the remnants of the Italian forces in Cyrenaica at Beda Fomm in February 1941. These events are usually so compressed chronologically that it appears that a small force of British troops defeated all of the Italian troops in Libya and that the collapse of Italian forces in Cyrenaica was sudden and unexpected, rather than a two-month ordeal that saw Graziani plead with Rome for more armor and aircraft. Traditional histories thus shift to German forces after their arrival in early 1941, though the reality was that Axis collaboration was haphazard and that Mussolini and the Italian high command resisted German efforts to take over the Mediterranean theater through mid-1943. Moreover, the British were not on the verge of victory in Africa in February 1941.

Focusing on British successes and Italian failures in North Africa neglects operations in Italian East Africa, British Somalia, and the Balkans. It also ignores the inconclusive naval encounter between British and Italian forces off Punta Stilo (Calabria) in July 1940 and Axis convoys. In short, the North African foreground has tended to overwhelm the Mediterranean background.

There is no simple explanation as to why the Italians could not exploit their apparent advantage in manpower, but lack of modern artillery, a dearth of vehicles and armor, and too few modern aircraft were certainly important. Crucial too were the loss of a third of its merchant fleet, the limited capacity of Libyan ports, and the belief of Italian civilian and military leaders that the war would be a short one. The chronic lack of cooperation among the Axis powers and their failure to exploit French anger after the British attack on Mers-el-Kébir in July 1940, Hitler's inability to bring Spain into the war, his refusal to invade Britain, his obsession with the USSR, Mussolini's decision to attack Greece, Ultra's ability to read German intentions from the spring of 1941, the inability of the Axis to control the oceans and cut supply routes to the Middle East, and American support—all enabled Britain to survive and rebound in 1940. It was not so much that the Italians frittered away their initial advantages, as that those advantages were largely illusory.

Italian submarines were diverted to Bordeaux at the request of the Germans, who had only twenty-six boats serviceable in August 1940. Thomas' *German Navy* and Bird's *German Naval History* are fundamental for the Germany navy, as are the official Italian histories and Sadkovich's writings for the Italian. Not only was Germany too weak to contest the British navy, but also it lacked the armor simultaneously to mount an attack on the Soviet Union and sustain operations in the Mediterranean.

If Italy's attack on Greece and the dispatch of air units to the English Channel in October 1940 helped ensure disaster in Africa, the setbacks of 1940–1941 were more embarrassing than conclusive. The Italians held in Albania, East Africa, and Tripolitania; they quickly refurbished all but one battleship damaged at Taranto in November; they replaced their infantry and upgraded their armor in North Africa; and they shepherded convoys carrying armor and troops to Africa.

By March, there were enough Axis troops and rear-echelon personnel to support an advance into Cyrenaica. But by racing the British to Tobruk, Rommel wore out his troops, used up his equipment, and precluded another Axis offensive. Sadkovich in "Of Myths and Men" is critical of his performance; Addington's "Operation Sunflower" and Irving's *Trail of the Fox* are less so; while Lewin's *Rommel* and Mitcham's *Triumphant Fox* are adulatory.

Mussolini's reasons for following Hitler into Russia are murky, but his decision to do so clearly undermined his effort against Egypt. In North Africa quiet followed the intense activity of early 1941, as events in Greece and Russia eclipsed those in Africa. Not until mid-November, when the British mounted a massive offensive code-named Crusader, was Libya again a major battleground. The air-naval war also heated up, with forays against Axis convoys. The balance began to tilt in the Axis favor just as the British mounted Operation Crusader; see Agar-Hamilton and Turner, *The Sidi Rezegh Battles*, Carver, *Dilemmas of the Desert War*, and works cited earlier, as well as the official histories. British material superiority guaranteed only a draw, and a month after Crusader sputtered to a close in January 1942, Axis forces advanced.

Writers have viewed the war in the Mediterranean as either an air-naval or an armored clash between Britain and Germany. Sadkovich in "Aircraft Carriers" argued that their importance has been exaggerated. Carriers were extremely vulnerable, and most fighters, reconnaissance aircraft, and torpedo bombers were land-based. The British avoided Italian capital ships and curtailed operations if their own battleships could not put to sea. Even such actions as the Italian loss of five warships off Cape Matapan in March 1941 have been the subject of debate, in this case involving issues of intelligence, air reconnaissance, inter-Allied cooperation, training, morale, and ship construction. Accounts such as Pack's *Night Action off Matapan* and Seth's *Two Fleets Surprised* are now dated because they do not view Ultra, poor Axis command decisions, lack of air cover, Royal Air Force (RAF) bases on Crete, and dumb luck as crucial and therefore present the action off Cape Matapan as typical of Italo-British naval encounters. The official histories and Ansel, *Hitler and the Middle Sea*; Bragadin and Fioravanzo, *The Italian Navy*; de Belot, *The Struggle for the Mediterranean*; and Macintyre, *The Battle for the Mediterranean*, are also dated but still useful.

Because the Germans were fully engaged in Russia, the Italians garrisoned the Balkans, a task that required six hundred thousand men and one hundred thousand draft animals in 1942. The cost of Hitler's attacks on *both* Yugoslavia and Russia was thus borne by Italy. Rather than debate whether Germany's Balkans attack delayed operations against the Soviet Union, it seems more sensible to ask whether the British could have survived had the Axis given the Mediterranean priority. Van Creveld in *Hitler's Strategy* and other scholars have shown that the Balkan campaign had little impact on operations in Russia, but the idea survives, perhaps because it rationalizes Germany's failure in the East and is useful propaganda for Balkan nationalists.

Montgomery's offensive in October 1942 succeeded largely because he enjoyed overwhelming material superiority—what Ellis correctly called *Brute Force*—and because he had the patience to use it. That the British finally discovered that the Axis powers were reading an American code undoubtedly helped disorient the Desert Fox, but in the end simple, crushing, quantitative superiority assured victory in North Africa. The retreat to Tunisia, the Axis buildup, and the desperate efforts by the Italian navy to supply the Axis forces there were essentially minor events in a prolonged denouement, scripted by Ultra, and Barnett included a discussion of its impact in his revised edition of *The Desert Generals.*

Operation Torch, the Anglo-American invasion of northwest Africa, failed to unfold as planned, but further added to Allied superiority. For British planning, see the official histories by Butler, *June 1941–August 1942,* and Howard, *Mediterannean Strategy,* while American planning can be traced in Matloff and Snell's *Strategic Planning.* On the American side Howe's *North West Africa: Seizing the Initiative in the West* expertly covers military operations, while Blumenson's *Kasserine Pass* is an objective narrative of the unnerving debacle the U.S. army suffered in February 1943. As to whether Operation Torch should ever have taken place at all, Sainsbury in *Churchill and Roosevelt at War* argued that the Allies should have devoted 1942 to preparing for an invasion of France in 1943. In *Desperate Venture,* Gelb summarized all aspects of the political and military controversies, also concluding that the invasion was a mistake. The role of General George Marshall, the U.S. Chief of Staff who advised Roosevelt against Torch, can be followed in the second volume of the thorough and authoritative biography by Pogue, *Ordeal and Hope, 1939–1942.*

Political events within Italy and in the Axis zones of occupation were important, but the ways in which they interacted with military events are not clear. Certainly, tension among the Axis commands was echoed and enhanced by clashes between Italian and German workers in Germany and Italian and German troops along the demarcation line in Croatia. From September 1943, the Italians fought not only the Germans but each other and the Allies, as two Italian states briefly existed under the tutelage of the major belligerents. The surrender of Italian troops in the Balkans was a complex matter that led to the resuscitation of partisan formations there and the siphoning of German troops from the eastern front to the Mediterranean theater, with consequences as serious as those resulting from the capitulation of Axis forces in Tunisia.

Nonetheless, the surrender of Axis forces in Tunisia in early May 1943 marked the end of the war in North Africa and of fascist Italy's war as well. Italian forces could not defend Italy, and if it took the invasion of Sicily to spur the king and the fascist Grand Council to deprive Mussolini of power, the regime had been discredited long before then. Strikes in the spring of 1943 were symptomatic of both the end of the regime and the birth of a mass antiwar movement that eventually took the shape of partisan formations that harried the Germans and raced the Allies to "liberate" northern cities and towns in the spring of 1945, just as Tito's troops raced the Allies to Trieste. That the second phase opened with clashes between regular German and Italian troops after the Italian surrender that left eighteen thousand Italians dead and hundreds of thousands en route to concentration camps or fighting with the partisans in the Balkans has usually been ignored or separated from the larger war of which it is an integral part and whose history has yet to be written and integrated into the larger story of the war.

From July 1943, the war in the Mediterranean theater reduced itself to a series of disconnected fronts after torturous negotiations that ended in a questionable armistice and "cobelligerency," discussed in Castellano's memoirs and the volumes published by the Italian navy and the Italian army on the 1943–1945 period. The army's chief of staff, Roatta, *Otto milioni di baionette*, and the army's *Le operazioni delle unità italiane nel settembre–ottobre 1943* criticize the Italian high command for bungling the surrender in September but imply that the Allies would have been wise to cooperate with the Italian command and land farther to the north. Certainly, as Armstrong showed in *Unconditional Surrender*, the Allied policy of unconditional surrender was ill advised in military terms; and if the invasion of Sicily was necessary to force an Italian surrender, it is not clear that sustaining heavy casualties at Salerno was wiser than risking a landing farther up the peninsula in 1943 or that the carnage at Anzio in 1944 shortened the war. In *Italy Betrayed* Tompkins depicted the Anglo-American failure to exploit Italy's willingness to cooperate in 1943 as an avoidable disaster.

FUTURE RESEARCH

There is no perfect history. Nor is there a perfect researcher who disposes of the time, money, and linguistic ability to write such a history of the war in the Mediterranean. Playfair et al. came close to doing this, and it is worth considering what a comprehensive multivolume and multiauthor study might comprise.

Such a study would have to integrate both topical approaches and historical and scholarly interpretations. It would place major personalities in a wide context and carefully correlate the introduction of technologies like radar and techniques like Ultra to the general progress of the conflict as well as to individual events. While battles might remain in the foreground, economic mobilization, civilian morale, internal political struggles, emergent nationalist movements in North Africa and the Middle East, logistical support, and the infrastructure of Southern Europe and Africa would have to be discussed and correlated to the outcome of battles. The effect of personal conflicts, biases, prejudices, and racial attitudes would also have to be considered. An effort to merge biography, which often tends to be hagiographic, with social history, both of civilian populations and military groups, would also be necessary. Such a history would then have to integrate air, sea, and ground operations and assess in detail their importance, interdependence, and impact according to area, phase, and force.

The perfect history would not simply be an analysis of "grand strategy."

It would incorporate the particular, tactical aspects of the conflict, as well as its more synthetic operational and strategic aspects. It would avoid the apologetic, tendentious approaches of national interpretations, while evaluating the roles played by unsteady alliance systems and competing national interests. Domestically, it would need to examine the impact on the war of inter- and intraservice rivalries, competition among government agencies and civilian firms for resources, the interplay and formulation of domestic and foreign policy, and relations between military and civilian leaders.

Any history meeting these criteria and successfully combining a narrative approach with topical analysis and utilizing all of the sources available—official, memoirist, popular, academic, and scholarly—would be necessarily revisionist, if for no other reason than that the weight given personalities, civilian populations, economies, geography, battles, services, and states would be redistributed. Meanwhile, we are left to sort through the data and argue over partial interpretations of a theater whose complexity will guarantee that no matter how much is published, consensus will always reside in the future.

BIBLIOGRAPHY

Addington, Larry H. "Operation Sunflower. Rommel versus the General Staff." *Military Affairs 31* (1967): 120–30.

Agar-Hamilton, J. A., and L.C.F. Turner. *The Sidi Rezeg Battles, 1941.* London: Oxford UP, 1957.

Alfieri, Dino. *Dictators Face to Face.* New York: New York UP, 1948.

Angelucci, Enzo, and Attilio Cucari. *World War II Airplanes.* New York: Rand McNally, 1978.

Ansel, Walter. *Hitler and the Middle Sea.* Durham, NC: Duke UP, 1972.

Armstrong, Anne. *Unconditional Surrender: The Impact of the Casablanca Policy upon World War II.* New Brunswick, NJ: Rutgers UP, 1966.

Auphan, Paul, and Jacques Mordal. *The French Navy in World War II.* Annapolis, MD: U.S. NIP, 1959.

Badoglio, Pietro. *Italy in the Second World War: Memoirs and Documents.* London: Oxford UP, 1948.

Bagnasco, Erminio. *Le armi delle navi italiane nella seconda guerra mondiale.* Parma: Ermanno Albertelli, 1978.

Bagnasco, Erminio, and Marco Spertini. *I mezzi d'assalto Xa MAS, 1940–1945.* Parma: Ermanno Albertelli, 1991.

Barnett, Correlli. *The Desert Generals.* Bloomington: Indiana UP, 1960, 1986.

Baxter, Colin F. *The War in North Africa, 1940–1943: A Select Bibliography.* Westport, CT: Greenwood, 1996.

Bayerlein, Fritz. "El Alamein." In Seymour Freiden and William Richardson, eds., *The Fatal Decisions.* New York: W. Sloan, 1958.

Behrendt, Hans-Otto. *Rommel's Intelligence in the Desert Campaign, 1941–1943.* London: Kimber, 1985.

Bennett, Ralph. *Ultra and the Mediterranean Strategy, 1941–1945*. London: Hamish Hamilton, 1989.

Benussi, Giulio. *Armi portatili, artiglierie e semoventi del Regio esercito italiano, 1900–1943*. Milan: Intergest, 1975.

Bianchini, Stefano, and Francesco Privitera. *6 Aprile 1941: L'attacco italiano alla Jugoslavia*. Milano/Varese: Marzorati Editore, 1993.

Bird, Keith W. "The German Navy in World War II." In James Sadkovich, ed., *Reevaluating Major Naval Combatants of World War II*, 99–127. Westport, CT: Greenwood, 1990.

———. *German Naval History: A Guide to the Literature*. New York and London: Garland, 1985.

Bitzes, John G. *Greece in World War II to April 1941*. Manhattan, KS: Sunflower UP, 1988.

Blumenson, Martin. *Kasserine Pass*. New York: Tower Publications, 1966; Boston: Houghton Mifflin, 1967.

Borghese, Junio Valerio. *Sea Devils*. Chicago: Henry Regnery, 1954.

Bragadin, Marc'Antonio, and Giuseppe Fioravanzo. *The Italian Navy in World War II*. Annapolis, MD: NIP 1957, 1980.

Butler, James R. M. *Grand Strategy, June 1941 to August 1942*. London: HMSO, 1961.

Caccia-Dominioni, Paolo. *Alamein, 1933–1962, An Italian Story*. London: Allen and Unwin, 1966.

Cameron, Ian. *Red Duster, White Ensign. The Story of the Malta Convoys*. New York: Bantam, 1960; London: F. Muller, 1959.

Carell, Paul (Paul Karl Schmidt). *The Foxes of the Desert*. New York: Dutton, 1961.

Carver, Michael. *Dilemmas of the Desert War. A New Look at the Libyan Campaign, 1940–1942*. Bloomington: Indiana UP, 1986.

Cassels, Alan. *Italian Foreign Policy, 1918–1945. A Guide to Research and Research Materials*. Wilmington, DE: Scholarly Resources, 1981.

Castellano, Giuseppe. *Come firmai l'Armistizio di Cassibile*. Rome: A. Mondadori, 1945.

Cervi, Mario. *The Hollow Legions. Mussolini's Blunder in Greece, 1940–41*. Trans. Eric Mosbacher. New York: Doubleday, 1971.

Ceva, Lucio. *Africa Settentrionale, 1940–1943*. Rome: Bonacci, 1982.

———. *La condotta italiana della guerra. Cavallero e il Comando supremo 1941–1942*. Milan: Feltrinelli, 1975.

———. "Macgregor Knox, Mussolini Unleashed 1939–1941." *Storia contemporanea* (1983).

Chamberlain, Peter. *Encyclopedia of German Tanks of World War Two: A Complete Illustrated Directory of German Battle Tanks, Armoured Cars, Self-Propelled Guns and Semi-Tracked Vehicles, 1933–1945*. New York: Arco, 1978.

Chamberlain, Peter, and Terry Gander. *Anti-Aircraft Guns*. London and New York: Arms and Armour, 1975.

Ciano, Galeazzo. *The Ciano Diaries, 1939–1943*. Ed. Hugh Gibson. New York: Doubleday, 1946.

Crisp, Robert. *The Gods Were Neutral*. London: Frederick Muller, 1960.

De Belot, Raymond. *The Struggle for the Mediterranean, 1939–1945*. Princeton: Princeton UP, 1951.

D'Este, Carlo. *World War II in the Mediterranean, 1942–1945*. Chapel Hill, NC: Algonquin Books, 1990.

De Felice, Renzo. *Mussolini. L'alleato.* 2 vols. Turin: Einaudi, 1990.

———. *Mussolini il duce.* 2 vols. Turin: Einaudi, 1985.

Detwiler, Donald S., Charles Burdick, and Jurgen Rohwer. *German Military Studies.* New York: Garland, 1987.

Dulin, Robert O., and William Garzke. *Battleships: Axis and Neutral Battleships of World War II.* Annapolis, MD: NIP, 1985.

Ellis, John. *Brute Force: Allied Strategy and Tactics in the Second World War.* New York: Viking; London: Deutsch, 1990.

Faldella, Emilio. *L'Italia e la seconda guerra mondiale. (revisione di giudizi).* Rocca San Casciano (Bologna): Cappelli, 1967.

Fraccaroli, Aldo. *Italian Warships of World War II.* London: Ian Allan, 1968.

Fraser, David. *And We Shall Shock Them. The British Army in the Second World War.* London: Hodder and Stoughton, 1983.

Gelb, Norman. *Desperate Ventore: The Story of Operation Torch. The Allied Invasion of North Africa.* New York: William Morrow, 1992.

Giorgerini, Giorgio. "The Role of Malta in Italian Naval Operations, 1940–43." In *New Aspects of Naval History.* Baltimore: NIP, 1985.

Gooch, John. "Italian Military Incompetence." *The Journal of Strategic Studies* (1982).

Great Britain. *Statistical Digest of the War.* London: HMSO, 1951.

Great Britain, Admiralty. *Ships of the Royal Navy. Statement of Losses during the Second World War.* London: HMSO, 1947.

Hassell, Ulrich von. *The von Hassell Diaries, 1938–1944.* Garden City, NY: Doubleday, 1947.

Heckmann, Wolf. *Rommel's War in Africa.* Garden City, NY: Doubleday, 1981.

Higham, Robin. *Diary of a Disaster. British Aid to Greece, 1940–1941.* Lexington: UP of Kentucky, 1989.

Hinsley, Francis H., E. E. Thomas, C.F.G. Ransom, and R. C. Knight. *British Intelligence in the Second World War.* 5 vols. London: HMSO; New York: Cambridge UP, 1979–1990.

Howard, Michael. *The Mediterranean Strategy in the Second World War.* London: HMSO; New York: Praeger, 1968.

Howe, George F. *North West Africa: Seizing The Initiative in the West.* Washington, DC: Center of Military History, 1957, 1991

Irving, David J. D. *The Trail of the Fox. The Search for the True Field Marshal Rommel.* London: Wiedenfeld and Nicolson, 1977.

Italy, Esercito, Corpo di Stato Maggiore, Ufficio Storico. *Verbali delle riunioni tenute dal capo di SM, generale.* 4 vols. Rome: Stato maggiore dell 'Esercito, 1983.

———. *Le operazioni delle unità italiane nel settembre–ottobre 1943.* Rome, 1975.

Italy, Marina Militare Italiana, Ufficio Storico. *La marina militare italiana nella seconda guerra mondiale,* 21 vol. Rome, various dates.

———. *Le navi d'Italia.* 7 vols. Rome, 1969–1980.

Jackson, W.G.F. *The Battle for North Africa, 1940–1943.* New York: Mason/Charter, 1975.

Jellison, Charles A. *Besieged. The World War II Ordeal of Malta, 1940–42.* Hanover, NH: New England UP, 1987.

Kesselring, Albert. *Kesselring: A Soldier's Record.* Trans. L. Hudson. London: W. Kimber, 1954.

Knox, MacGregor. "The Italian Armed Forces, 1940–3." In Allen R. Millett and Williamson Murray, eds., *Military Effectiveness,* vol. 3, *The Second World War,* 136–79. Boston: Allen and Unwin, 1988.

———. *Mussolini Unleashed, 1939–1941. Politics and Strategy in Fascist Italy's Last War.* Cambridge: Cambridge UP, 1982.

———. "The Sources of Italy's Defeat in 1940: Bluff or Institutionalized Incompetence?" In Carole Fink et al., *German Nationalism and the European Response, 1890–1945.* Norman: University of Oklahoma, 1985.

Ledeen, Michael A. "Renzo De Felice and the Controversy over Italian Fascism." In George Mosse et al., *International Fascism: New Thoughts and New Approaches.* London: Sage, 1979.

Lewin, Ronald. *The Life and Death of the Afrika Korps.* New York: McGraw-Hill, 1977.

———. *Rommel as Military Commander.* New York: McGraw-Hill, 1969.

———. *Ultra Goes to War.* New York: McGraw-Hill, 1978.

Liddell Hart, Basil H. *The German Generals Speak.* New York: Quill, 1948, 1975.

———. *History of the Second World War.* London: Cassell, 1970.

———. *The Tanks: The History of the Royal Tank Regiment and Its Predecessors, Heavy Branch, Machine-Gun Corps, Tank Corps, and Royal Tank Corps, 1914–1945.* London: Cassell, 1959.

Macintyre, Donald. *The Battle for the Mediterranean.* New York: Norton, 1965.

Mack Smith, Denis. *Mussolini. A Biography.* New York: Knopf, 1982.

———. *Mussolini's Roman Empire.* New York: Viking, 1976.

Matloff, Maurice, and E. M. Snell. *Strategic Planning for Coalition Warfare: 1941–1942.* Washington, DC: Department of the Army, 1953.

Maugeri, Franco. *From the Ashes of Disgrace.* New York: Reynal and Hitchcock, 1948.

Mearsheimer, John J. *Liddell Hart and the Weight of History.* London: Brassey's Defence; Ithaca, NY: Cornell UP, 1988.

Medlicott, W. N. *The Economic Blockade.* 2 vols. London: HMSO, 1952–1959.

Messe, Giovanni. *Come finì la guerra in Africa. La mia armata in Tunisia.* Milan: Rizzoli, 1960.

Mitcham, Samuel W., Jr. *Rommel's Desert War. The Life and Death of the Afrika Korps.* New York: Stein and Day, 1982.

———. *Triumphant Fox. Erwin Rommel and the Rise of the Afrika Korps.* New York: Stein and Day, 1984.

Murray, Williamson. *The Change in the European Balance of Power, 1938–1939. The Path to Ruin.* Princeton: Princeton UP, 1984.

Owen, Roderic. *The Desert Air Force.* London: Hutchinson, 1948.

Pack, S.W.C. *Night Action off Matapan.* London: Ian Allan, 1972.

Painter, Borden W., Jr. "Renzo De Felice and the Historiography of Italian Fascism," *American Historical Review 95* (1990): 391–405.

Papagos, Alexander. *The Battle of Greece, 1940–1941.* Trans. P. Eliascos. Athens: J. M. Scazikis, 1949.

Payton-Smith, Derek Joseph. *Oil: A Study of War-Time Policy and Administration.* London: HMSO, 1971.

Pike, David Wingate. "Franco and the Axis Stigma." *Journal of Contemporary History* (1982).

Playfair, I.S.O., et al. *The Mediterranean and Middle East*. 5 vols. London: HMSO, 1954–1973.

Pogue, Forrest. *George C. Marshall. Ordeal and Hope 1939–1942*. New York: Viking, 1963.

Postan, Michael Moissey. *British War Production*. London: HMSO, 1952; Nendeln: Kraus, 1975.

Presseisen, Ernst L. "Prelude to 'Barbarossa': Germany and the Balkans, 1940–1941." *Journal of Modern History* (1960).

Puleston, W. D. *The Influence of Sea Power in World War II*. New Haven, CT: Yale UP, 1947.

Riccio, Ralph. *Italian Tanks and Fighting Vehicles of World War II*. Henley-on-Thames: Pique, 1975.

Roatta, Mario. *Otto milioni di baionette, l'Esercito italiano in guerra dal 1940 al 1944*. Milan: Garzanti, 1946.

Rohwer, Jurgen. *Axis Submarine Successes, 1939–1945*. Annapolis, MD: U.S. NIP, 1985.

Rommel, Erwin. *The Rommel Papers*. Ed. Basil Liddell Hart. London: Collins; New York: Harcourt, Brace, 1953.

Roskill, Stephen W. *The War at Sea, 1939–1945*. 3 vols. London: HMSO, 1954– .

———. *White Ensign. The British Navy at War, 1939–1945*. Annapolis, MD: NIP, 1960.

Ruge, Friedrich. *Sea Warfare, 1939–1945*. London: Cassell, 1957.

Sadkovich, James J. "Aircraft Carriers and the Mediterranean: Rethinking the Obvious." *Aerospace Historian* (1987): 263–71.

———. "Anglo-American Bias and the Italo-Greek War." *Journal of Military History* (1994): 617–42.

———. "Italian and British Service Histories," In Robin Higham, ed., *Official Military Histories*. Westport, CT: Greenwood, 1997.

———. "Italian Morale during the Italo-Greek War of 1940–1941." *War and Society* (1994): 96–123.

———. *The Italian Navy in World War II*. Westport, CT: Greenwood, 1994.

———. "Of Myths and Men: Rommel and the Italians in North Africa, 1940–42." *International History Review* (1991): 284–313.

———, ed. *Reevaluating Major Naval Combatants of World War II*. Westport, CT: Greenwood, 1990.

———. "Understanding Defeat: Reappraising Italy's Role in World War II." *Journal of Contemporary History* (1989): 27–61.

Sainsbury, Keith. *Churchill and Roosevelt at War: The War They Fought and the Peace They Hoped to Make*. New York: New York UP, 1994.

Schmidt, Heinz Werner. *With Rommel in the Desert*. London: Harrap, 1951.

Schofield, B. B. *Attack on Taranto*. Shepperton: Ian Allan, 1973.

Segré, Claudio G. *Italo Balbo: A Fascist Life*. Berkeley: University of California, 1987.

Seth, Roland. *Two Fleets Surprised. The Story of the Battle of Cape Matapan*. London: Geoffrey Bles, 1960.

Shores, Christopher, Brian Cull, and Nicola Malizia. *Malta: The Hurricane Years, 1940–1941*. London: Grub Street, 1987.

Shores, Christopher, and Nicola Malizia. *Malta: The Spitfire Year, 1942*. London: Grub Street, 1991.

Sims, Edward H. *The Fighter Pilot, a Comparative Study of the Royal Air Force, the Luftwaffe and the U.S. Army Air Forces in Europe and North Africa, 1939–1945.* London: Cassell, 1967.

Smith, Peter, and E. Walker. *Malta Striking Forces.* Shepperton: Ian Allan, 1974.

Sullivan, Brian. "A Fleet in Being: The Rise and Fall of Italian Sea Power, 1861–1943." *The International History Review* (1988).

———. "The Italian Armed Forces, 1918–40." In Allan Millett and Williamson Murray, eds., *Military Effectiveness.* Vol. 2, *The Interwar Period.* Boston: Allen and Unwin, 1988, pp. 169–217.

Sweet, John T. T. *Iron Arm. The Mechanization of Mussolini's Army, 1920–1940.* Westport, CT: Greenwood, 1980.

Tedder, Arthur William. *With Prejudice. The War Memoirs of Marshall of the Royal Air Force, Lord Tedder.* London: Cassell, 1966.

Thomas, Charles S. *The German Navy in the Nazi Era.* Annapolis, MD: NIP, 1990.

Thompson, Jonathan W. *Italian Civil and Military Aircraft, 1930–1945.* Fallbrook, CA: Aero, 1963.

Tompkins, Peter. *Italy Betrayed.* New York: Simon and Schuster, 1966.

Toscano, Mario. *Designs in Diplomacy.* Baltimore: Johns Hopkins UP, 1970.

United Kingdom, Cabinet Office, Cabinet History Series. *Principal War Telegrams and Memoranda. 1940–1943. Middle East.* Nendeln: KTO, 1976.

Van Creveld, Martin. *Hitler's Strategy, 1940–1941. The Balkan Clue.* London: Cambridge UP, 1973.

———. *Supplying War: Logistics from Wallenstein to Patton.* New York: Cambridge UP, 1977.

Villari, Luigi. *Italian Foreign Policy under Mussolini.* New York: Devin-Adair, 1956.

Whittam, John. "The Italian General Staff and the Coming of the Second World War." In Adrian Preston, ed., *General Staffs and Diplomacy before the Second World War.* Totowa, NJ: Rowan and Littlefield, 1978.

Young, Desmond. *Rommel the Desert Fox.* New York: Harper, 1950; Berkley, 1971.

Young, John. *A Dictionary of Ships of the Royal Navy of the Second World War.* Cambridge: Patrick Stephens, 1975.

10 The Soviet–German War, 1941–1945

David M. Glantz

Although a vast primary and secondary literature exists about the Soviet–German war, the thoroughness and accuracy of this work have suffered from the inaccessibility of Soviet military accounts and the lack of Soviet archival materials. As a result, since war's end, most operational accounts have included only German detail, and opposing Soviet forces have remained a virtually featureless and colorless mass devoid of structure or personality. Quite naturally, then, the German perspective on, and interpretation of, the war have predominated. Understandably and with few exceptions, Western scholars and the reading public have treated existing Soviet or Soviet-based accounts of the war with suspicion and incredulity. In essence, while the German army lost the war, it won the initial stages of the historical struggle with relative ease.

The dominant German school of historiography emerged during the immediate postwar years. Its creation and growth were a perfectly natural phenomenon, since most available sources on the war were German in origin and perspective. The first group of source materials was produced by U.S. governmental agencies, which, as the victors, reaped the archival spoils of war. These agencies had the practical mission of analyzing the character of the war and those armies that fought in it, in particular the Red Army, so that the U.S. military could better understand and deal with future Soviet military threats. In subsequent postwar decades, these initial official accounts were first supplemented by an impressive array of German memoir materials prepared by a generation of former German senior commanders who were now unemployed and eager to share their unique wartime perspectives with the new enemies of their most bitter wartime rival, the Soviet Union. Later, an increasing number of historians wrote scholarly accounts of the war based initially on official U.S. governmental materials and German memoir literature and, later, on newly released German archival records. In time, this mass of German sources swelled with the addition of the memoirs of private soldiers and a steady stream of published German wartime unit histories. Although much of this material was written in German, Western historians were generally better equipped to master this language and more intellectually inclined to exploit these sources than to do so with similar Russian source materials.

From the very outset, three imposing barriers inhibited the utility of Soviet (Russian) historical accounts. The first two, Western historians' unfamiliarity with Soviet historical works and their general inability to read Russian, were basically mechanical in nature and would erode over time as more Western historians learned the Russian language. The third barrier, a deep-rooted and often justified distrust of Soviet historical credibility, was fundamental and more difficult to overcome, because the content of most readily available Soviet historical works was significantly and blatantly ideological. A more credible Soviet historical perspective would emerge only after Western historians were able to tap into a broader and more credible base of Soviet works and when they were able to test the veracity of Soviet sources against German archival accounts. The clearly limited value of Soviet works produced in the decade immediately following the end of the war also discredited the positive efforts the Soviets made during the late 1950s and 1960s to improve the quality and accuracy of their historical accounts. In fact, despite the efforts of a few superb Western historians to replace Soviet bombast with hard fact, the credibility of the Soviet school would not improve until the 1980s, when significant amounts of Soviet archival materials finally began to be released to the public.

GERMAN PRIMARY SOURCE MATERIALS

The German school of historiography predominated, first and foremost, because it was able to monopolize existing sources of wartime history, the bulk of the German armed forces archival records. More important, the Germans exploited and publicized these records at a time when the Soviets treated their archives (and captured German archives), as well as their history, as state secrets. Ironically, having emerged victorious on the battlefield, the Soviets abandoned the field of historical struggle to their former Allies and enemies.

The fodder historians used to reconstruct the history of the war on the German Eastern Front was provided by vast quantities of existing German archival materials. Much of this material was captured by the Allied armies at war's end, and U.S., British, and now German archival repositories have made most of this material readily accessible to historians. Extensive archival sources that fell exclusively into Soviet hands, however, remain inaccessible to Western scholars. Although the extent of this material remains somewhat obscure, it certainly includes the records of military formations that were destroyed or captured by the Red Army during the course of combat in Eastern and Central Europe. This includes, for example, the combat records of German Ninth and Sixth Armies, portions of which have now been shown, but not released, to Western scholars.

Among the most valuable German primary source materials are the postwar compilations of German archival materials issued in book form and the voluminous German military unit records maintained in Western archives, including the U.S. National Archives in Washington, DC, and the German Militärgeschichtlichen Forschungsamt (Military History Research Institute) in Freiburg and Berlin. Most, but not all, of the documentary materials that were captured by U.S. forces and gathered in the U.S. National Archives have been copied on microfilm and made available for scholarly use. The original document collections have since been returned to the custody of the German archives. These collections include several particularly extensive and valuable German sources.

Edited by Percy E. Schramm, the two-volume, so-called *OKW War Diary* is a comprehensive, chronological, high-level German record of the war from the perspective of the Oberkommando der Wehrmacht (the Armed Forces High Command—OKW). In September 1942, The Oberkommando des Heeres (Army High Command—OKH) received full responsibility for operations in the eastern theater, and the OKW received detailed reports on the Eastern Front situation and played a significant role in German strategic decision making in the East. Supplementing this work are the fragmentary diary of Colonel Walter Scherff, Hitler's official war historian, and Greiner's description of OKW wartime functions.

Surviving OKH records are fragmentary since the Soviet army captured many German unit war diaries, particularly later in the war, and some German forces destroyed their records to prevent their falling into Soviet hands. Still other unit records were destroyed by Allied fire while being removed from Berlin after the Nazi government's collapse. The mass of surviving archival material includes a significant number of personal diaries interspersed among thousands of unit records at every level of army command. The most interesting high-level diary is the diary of the chief of the German General Staff, Franz Halder, in which he recorded his impressions of the war in the East until Hitler removed him from office in September 1942.

Among the most valuable and unique OKH records are the OKH *Lage Ost* (Eastern situation) maps, which display a complete German order of battle and an intelligence assessment of Soviet order of battle daily throughout the war. These wall-size maps lay in the U.S. National Archives until the late 1980s, when they were returned to Germany, unfortunately without being microfilmed. Therefore, they are not available for research-ers' and the general public's use through the archives microfilm system.

Several critical series of OKH and German army unit records exist, par-tially or in full, which may be exploited in the U.S. National Archives or obtained in microfilm form. National Archives Microfilm (NAM) series T-78, the records of Foreign Armies East (*Fremde Heere Ost*), contains German wartime intelligence materials and assessments of all aspects of the Soviet armed forces and Soviet military-industrial activity. Most inter-esting are the assessments of Soviet (and German) military strength, stra-tegic and operational intentions, and industrial war production; Red Army order of battle, force composition, and morale; and biographical materials on the Soviet political and military leadership. The NAM series T-311 through T-315 contains the records of German army groups, armies, pan-zer armies, corps, and divisions. Although sometimes incomplete, these include periodic situation maps and logs of military activities, operational and intelligence assessments, operational studies, and correspondence be-tween major headquarters.

Valuable war diaries and special reports prepared by numerous senior and midlevel commanders are interspersed throughout the war diaries of forces above division level. These include, for example, the personal war diaries contained in the NAM records prepared by Field Marshals von Bock (Army Group South) and von Leeb (Army Group North) and Gen-eral von Mackensen (Third Panzer Corps). The most valuable aspects of the corps and divisional records are the unit's war diaries (*Tagebuch*) with extensive appendixes and their associated periodic operational and intel-ligence situation maps.

Even today, new primary source materials that will enrich existing German archival holdings are appearing. Hundreds of postwar memoir studies have lain fallow while accounts by more famous and popular German commanders occupied the historical limelight. These newly dis-covered memoirs and studies include massive manuscripts written during the immediate postwar years by less famous German military leaders under the auspices of U.S. military historical organizations, in particular, the Historical Division of U.S. European Command. Most prominent in this extensive group of German-language manuscripts is the extensive memoir by the German defensive specialist Colonel General Gotthard Heinrici, which has just been rediscovered and is now being prepared for publi-cation.

Supplementing these works are the personal memoirs of a host of German military leaders and private soldiers, which have been retained since the war in private family holdings. When released for publication or exploited by scholars, these promise to offer a far more personal view of the war from those who fought and suffered in it. In addition, extensive

Finnish, Hungarian, Italian, and Rumanian archival holdings supplement these German records.

GERMAN-BASED SECONDARY SOURCE MATERIALS

Secondary materials that, by virtue of the nature of their source material, fall into the German school of historiography include several series of "official" studies and histories prepared and published by national military historical organizations, primarily in the United States and Germany, personal memoirs, and other standard historical surveys of individual operations and the war in general. Understandably, the first official histories of the war, which military historical organs prepared on the basis of captured German archival materials, appeared in the United States. Later, after these archival materials had been returned to Germany, official German military history organizations prepared comprehensive histories of their own.

The first official U.S. studies on the German-Soviet war appeared in the Department of the Army Pamphlet Series, which was prepared and published during the late 1940s and early 1950s as a product of the extensive U.S. government effort to debrief former German military commanders and analyze the nature of combat on the German eastern front. The series included only a fraction of the material collected by the U.S. European Command in its postwar analysis and debriefing program. These pamphlets received wide dissemination and, even today, have been reprinted by the U.S. Army's Center of Military History for modern reading audiences. Typical of these pamphlets was the superb study of German campaign planning in 1941 written by George Blau.

While these pamphlets made valuable initial contributions to a better Western understanding of the war, the accuracy of many was suspect, since their authors, most of whom had been wartime German commanders and staff officers, wrote them largely from memory and without access to German archival materials. Thus, in addition to their natural German bias, they contained numerous errors in fact.

In the 1960s the U.S. Army's Office of the Chief of Military History (CMH) began preparing substantive studies of the German-Soviet war to supplement an extensive ongoing series of publications on the U.S. Army's role in the war. CMH commissioned three volumes, which were to cover the war chronologically. Ultimately, two of these volumes appeared; the first, written by Ziemke, dealt with the period November 1942 (Stalingrad) to 1945 (Berlin), and, the second, coauthored by Ziemke and Bauer, covered the period December 1941 (Moscow) to November 1942 (Stalingrad). While these studies incorporated as much Soviet source material as was readily available, that material remained minimal. In the 1980s, the German Military History Institute (Potsdam) also began preparing an extensive series of official works on the Second World War. Several volumes of this new and as yet incomplete series cover the war on the Eastern Front.

The second major genre of German secondary sources was the postwar memoirs by, or biographies of, prestigious German wartime military leaders, the most famous of which appeared in the late 1940s and 1950s. These volumes established the parameters of the German school, appearing at a time when it was both necessary and sensible to disassociate oneself from Hitler or Hitler's policies. Justifiably or not, the writers of these memoirs, who shared in the earlier success of Hitler's Wehrmacht, refused to shoulder responsibility for the failures of the same armies and essentially placed the blame for German defeat on Hitler. Among the most notable memoirs are works by Walter Warlimont (OKW), Erich von Manstein (Fifty-sixth Panzer Corps, Eleventh Army, and Army Groups Don and South), Heinz Guderian (Panzer Group 2 and Second Panzer Army), and F. W. von Mellenthin (Eleventh Panzer Division and Forty-eigth Panzer Corps). In addition, the historian Walter Goerlitz edited the memoirs of Field Marshal Keitel and a study of Field Marshal Paulus. Among the most notable and influential of the many works that appeared in the German language was the classic study by F. M. von Senger und Etterlin, *Der Gegenschlag* (The Encounter Battle). This work has played a considerable role in the education of a generation of German officers.

All of these authors wrote their memoirs on the basis of their memory or their personal notes or records. Interpretation aside, this absence of archival sources often left the accuracy of their work seriously flawed. Fascinating as they were, these popular memoirs and biographies described war against a faceless enemy, an armed host that possessed neither concrete form nor precise features. In short, other than sensing the size and power of their foe and the ferocity and inhumanity of combat, they knew not what they fought. Although a subsequent generation of talented Western professional military historians have left a legacy of superb works, their work remains firmly embedded in the German school. Try as they did to reconstruct the Soviet face of war, they failed in the effort, since much of their primary material remained, of necessity, German.

Beginning in the early 1960s, an increasing number of reputable, trained historians began producing accounts of war and operations on the German Eastern Front. Although these works were more thorough than those of their predecessors, since they were based primarily on German sources, they failed to achieve a respectable balance between the German and Soviet perspectives. The earliest of these volumes did contain some Soviet materials collected and preserved by German wartime intelligence collection organs, and later volumes incorporated some materials produced by Soviet authors in the early 1960s after Khrushchev loosened the reins on Soviet historiography. These works also included studies by

Westerners who had spent considerable time in the Soviet Union during the war.

Among the best and most substantive of these works were Clark's survey of the war, *Barbarossa*; Schroter's *Stalingrad*; Ziemke's *Stalingrad to Berlin* and later, with Bauer, *Moscow to Stalingrad*; Carell's more journalistic accounts, *Hitler Moves East* and *Scorched Earth*; Salisbury's *The 900 Days* (1969); and Seaton's *The Russo-German War* and *The Battle for Moscow*. Clark's book contained some operational data but typified many books of the period by devoting most of its attention to the first two years of war. This reflected an often expressed judgment that there was little reason to study operations after mid-1943 because, after that time, Hitler's interference in operational matters perverted the ability of German commanders to conduct normal and reasonable operations. Schroter's work was the first detailed study of a major operation.

Ziemke's volumes, which appeared in the CMH Series, made a commendable effort to overcome earlier interpretive imbalances by including limited available Soviet data, perspectives, and interpretations. He also questioned some of the most serious errors found in earlier accounts from the German perspective. Carell, writing under a pen name, tapped a wealth of personal wartime recollections by individual German officers and enlisted men to construct moving human narratives of the harrowing combat. All the while he consulted extensively with military experts on the war, whose contributions made his essentially journalistic accounts remarkably accurate, moving, and credible. Salisbury drew upon his personal experiences and contacts with the Soviet population to describe the incredible suffering of the Leningrad population during its wartime siege. Finally, Seaton added a new dimension to war histories by using selective German unit histories and memoirs to describe tactical operations at the lowest level. He too exploited Soviet sources whenever feasible.

In the 1970s and 1980s a wealth of new secondary literature appeared that fell into the German school. In addition to a new wave of German memoirs and unit histories, some of which have been translated into English (including the Josef Goebbels' *Diary* and Albert Speer's memoirs), operational accounts now routinely incorporate a limited quantity of Soviet materials. Among the best of these many works are the second volume by Ziemke and Bauer, Whaley's exhaustive study of Operation Barbarossa, Reinhardt's sound analysis of the Battle of Moscow, Tarrant's more recent study of the battle of *Stalingrad*, Neipold's account of the destruction of German *Army Group Centre* in 1944, and Le Tissier's detailed study of the *Battle of Berlin*. Specialized studies by Jones, Motter, Sydnor, Bartov, and Dallin have addressed such ancillary issues as Allied Lend-Lease to the Soviet Union, the role of Schutzstaffeln (SS) formations (protection squads) in the war, German occupation policy in the East, and the nature and impact of German wartime genocidal policies. Beyond the realm of narrative history, historians began to analyze the unique nature of combat on the German Eastern Front. Foremost among these efforts is Wray's detailed account of evolving German tactical methods.

SOVIET PRIMARY SOURCE MATERIALS

The Sources

The closed nature of Soviet society and ideological restrictions on the writing of history complicate the definition and classification of Russian-language sources and English-language sources based on Soviet materials. Prior to 1987, the Soviet government limited access to a handful of "official" historians of virtually all materials considered primary in the West. Where access was granted, it was carefully controlled. The Soviets limited their official "release" of archival materials to specially selected documents on specific themes, which Communist Party authorities cleared for publication and published to achieve desired political effects. The party permitted military historians to write on narrow topics from a restricted database of officially approved sources. While many of the facts contained in the many published military studies were accurate, certain topics, such as casualties, most defeats, and the actual correlation of forces between the warring sides were either severely proscribed or routinely distorted. History also served starkly utilitarian ends, such as the advancement of specific political aims or military education. Almost coincidentally and somewhat ironically, Soviet commitment to sound education in the realm of military science had the beneficial effect of producing even greater candor, although even here within severe constraints.

Because of the unavailability of archival materials, detailed military studies prepared for the purposes of military education and memoir materials, which the Soviets used as vehicles for discussing controversial military and even political issues, fell into a category midway between what Westerners considered primary and secondary source material. If properly juxtaposed against Western primary sources, these military studies and memoirs served as proxies for actual primary sources.

The Red Army General Staff Historical Section prepared a variety of studies during and after the war on the basis of archival materials. The Soviet army used these publications, which were classified as top secret and secret, in army education and training. In the main, these studies incorporated archival materials directly and accurately and were generally honest and primary in nature. Like their unclassified counterpart studies, however, they avoided controversial political issues and tended to avoid politically sensitive defeats. A few of these wartime studies fell into the hands of German intelligence during the war and, hence, into Western hands after the war ended.

Another category of primary sources is the numerous classified military publications used for educational purposes at the many Soviet military educational institutions, such as the Voroshilov General Staff Academy and the Frunze Academy. Although Soviet authors wrote these studies on the basis of archival materials, they were subject to the same general constraints as General Staff writers, and the studies varied in accuracy based on contemporary political exigencies. During the 1950s and 1960s, when historical *glasnost* prevailed, these studies were fairly accurate and consistent with archival materials. Ultimately, however, by the mid-1970s, after the Brezhnev regime had discarded *glasnost* (openness), the accuracy, candor, and value of these materials had declined to the level of standard secondary sources.

Given the long-standing archival problems associated with properly reconstructing the history of the German-Soviet war and the fact that Soviet archival materials are now becoming available, a brief survey of existing primary and secondary source materials on the war is necessary. Each category of primary source materials warrants fuller explanation and evaluation.

The "Archives"

The Soviet (Russian) military archives are voluminous but fragmented in nature. Besides the Central State Archives of the Soviet Army (Ts-GASA), located in Moscow, which contains army military records from 1918 to 1940, there exist numerous branch archives at other locations associated with various ministries and their subordinate entities. These include the Central Archives of the Combined Armed Forces (TsAOVS) (formerly the Central Archives of the USSR Ministry of Defense— TsAMO), located at Podolsk; the Central Archives of the Navy located at Gatchina; and other lesser archives.

The Central Archives (TsAOVS) is the largest storehouse of military documentation in Russia (and the Commonwealth of Independent States [CIS]). It contains more than eighteen million records with documents from other central military command bodies: the Stavka (Soviet High Command); force branches; armies, special force headquarters, operational commands, large formations, and units; and military institutions, organizations, and enterprises (excluding the navy). More than ten million of these records deal with the period 1941–1945. The Central Archives and that of the navy also supervise the work of the remainder of the military archival system.

The recent increased flow of Soviet and Russian materials from these archives to the West is heartening but must be viewed in perspective. Collectively, it represents only the tip of the iceberg, and the release has been selective in nature. Some of the materials have been accurate and candid. Others have been as inaccurate as some of the existing open-source materials published over the past forty years. All of this, of course, conveys the clear message that some "archival" materials are not really archival at all but are, instead, products of the system that was so effective at managing information and history.

Archival Materials

Military archival materials released thus far fall into several distinct categories. The first, most accurate, and most useful are series of works that various directorates of the General Staff prepared for publication during the period 1942 through 1968. While preparing these series, the Red Army (and Soviet army) General Staff made a genuine attempt to establish the truth about the course and consequences of wartime military operations and to harness that truth in the service of improving future Soviet army combat performance. For the most part, when these studies are compared with German and Japanese archival records, their general accuracy and candor are vindicated.

There were, of course, topics that the General Staff could not address, including some of the most sensitive failed operations, such as the Liuban operation in early 1942 with its Vlasov connection and Operation Mars, the companion piece to the Stalingrad operation (Operation Uranus), which occurred at the same time but which was forgotten since it was a bloody failure. Also prohibited were politically sensitive topics, such as discussions and disputes among Stavka members (Stalin in particular), the General Staff, and field commands, which were numerous throughout the war, and the motives for controversial political and military decisions. This sort of information remained in the domain of the infamous and illusive "Stalin Archives." A detailed discussion of the scope, content, and accuracy of these Soviet archives and other Soviet primary source materials can be found in Glantz, "Newly Published Soviet Works on the Red Army, 1918–1991."

Many books published in the Soviet Union during the 1920s and 1930s were suppressed by Stalin shortly after their publication and were, hence, unavailable in the West. These too essentially can be categorized as primary sources. Included in their number were controversial works by key interwar theorists such as A. M. Zaionchkovsky, A. A. Svechin, M. N. Tukhachevsky, E. A. Shilovsky, and G. Isserson.

During the Second World War, Voennoe Izdatel'stvo or Voenizdat (the Ministry of Defense publishing house) prepared and published a sizable number of classified books dealing with major wartime operations. Most of these were prepared under General Staff auspices. For example, see Shaposhnikov, *Razgrom nemetskikh voisk pod Moskvoi, t. 1–3* (The Destruction of German Forces at Moscow, volumes 1–3). Similar but shorter volumes also appeared on many of the lesser wartime operations. Some of these classified studies later generated unclassified versions available to the public.

Archival materials, primarily documents, have also appeared on a selective basis in Soviet and Russian open-source political and military journals. These were released to add an air of authenticity to accounts of military operations, and recent archival releases have tended to validate the truthfulness and accuracy of this earlier material. After 1987, Party First Secretary Gorbachev used public journals as the principal conduit for the release of archival holdings in support of his program of renewed historical *glasnost*. The most notable series of released archival documents appeared in the most famous and most widely distributed and read military journal, *Voenno-istoricheskii zhurnal* (Military-Historical Journal, abbreviated *VIZh*), and a newly created Party Central Committee journal. See, for example, the series "Pervyye dni voiny v dokumentakh" (The First Days of War in Documents), *VIZh*, nos. 5–9 (May–September 1989); "Voennye razvedchiki dokladyvali..." (Military Intelligence Reported), nos. 2–3 (February–March 1989); and "GKO postanovliaet..." (The Peoples Commissariat of Defense Decrees), nos. 2–5 (February–May 1992).

A new party journal established by Gorbachev, the now defunct *Izvestiia TsK KPSS* (News of the Central Committee of the Communist Party of the Soviet Union), also issued an extensive series of documents. See, for example, the extensive series of documents published under the rubric "Iz istoriia Velikoi Otechestvennoi voiny" in nos. 1–12 (January–December 1990) and nos. 1–8 (January–August 1991). Unfortunately, the failed coup and outlawing of the Communist Party ended the publishing life of this journal and this series of document releases.

An Assessment of Soviet Primary Sources

It is important to note that most of these materials, General Staff studies, books, and journals alike, although technically archival, are in some way *processed* and that process has often affected their content. In addition, these are *released* materials that have found their way to the West largely through commercial conduits. Although release of these materials is welcome, the larger question regarding direct archival access in the Western sense of the word remains unanswered. Although Russian authorities have frequently announced that the archives are open for foreign scholars, that access is still severely limited and in no way comparable to access to Western archives. When archival access has been tested and received the most publicity, such as in the case of the officially agreed upon U.S. search for Prisoner of war (POW) information, access has meant documents brought to researchers rather than researchers hunting for documents in the actual archive locations. Scholars who to date have claimed access normally have had access to peripheral materials or have been provided selected materials on request or through the intervention of an influential third party.

In general, classified or restricted Soviet studies published after 1968, which supposedly exploited archival materials, lacked the substance and accuracy of their wartime and postwar counterparts. In fact, they bore many of the characteristics of open-source operational and tactical literature published during the more recent period. While their operational and tactical details and their narrative account of events were generally accurate, they exaggerated enemy strength and covered up the worst aspects of Soviet combat performance, in particular, specific details regarding the many Soviet combat disasters. Moreover, their political content was far more pervasive and strident than found in the earlier General Staff volumes. This was particularly disturbing regarding educational materials used at the Voroshilov and Frunze Academies and may explain why many contemporary Russian officers remain less than enthusiastic about study of their operational experiences. They themselves understand that what has been taught has been less than the whole truth. In this sense, more extensive release of archival materials will also benefit the Russian military educational system.

Recently released archival materials about the war, published between 1965 and 1989, fall into three general categories: Institute of Military History publications and those of the Voroshilov and Frunze Academies. Undoubtedly, other studies exist, but their precise nature remains unknown. The general characteristics of all available material in these three categories are the same; it lacks the substance, quality, accuracy, and candor of the earlier work.

Since 1964, the Institute of Military History has published a number of short series under the rubrics "Bulletins" and "Notes." The former contained short articles (ten to twenty pages) on a wide variety of military subjects, and the latter were an attempt to create a journal of more substance. The attempt failed after two annual issues. The articles in both of these publications in no way compare with the more substantive work of earlier years, for they are sketchy in detail and higher in political content.

Voroshilov Academy publications, issued since 1942 in a variety of formats under the imprimatur *VAGSh*, include texts, studies, analytical works, and lectures delivered at the academy. Some of these are multivolume surveys of the history of war and military art, such as a two-volume work edited by the eminent military historian I. E. Shavrov, that was published in revised versions every few years. The most interesting and valuable are the wartime volumes and the collections (Sborniki) of wartime materials. In general, the Voroshilov materials are more scholarly in nature and, hence, less inaccurate and political. The studies and lectures from the period after 1968, however, contain the same inaccuracies that are found in other Soviet publications. Frunze Academy publications, which have not been released in as great a number as the Voroshilov materials, share the characteristics of their Voroshilov counterparts.

Particularly interesting are several special publications released by the Central Archives of the Soviet Army. The first of these are the mobilization regulations (Ustav), issued in the years immediately preceding the war and the Red Army's mobilization journal. Although these records cast considerable light on Soviet mobilization capabilities and procedures, the critical appendixes linking mobilization and war plans have been removed. The second striking document is the transcript of proceedings of the controversial December 1941 Conference of the High Command. Release of this lengthy document ends years of speculation regarding what was said and by whom at this critical session, which followed the completion of the last major Soviet war games before the German June 1941 attack.

Finally, the collections of selective documents published in recent journals seem to be authentic and represent a genuine effort to begin an increased flow of released archival materials. By their very nature, however, they are selective, and the flow of materials has noticeably decreased since the downfall of Gorbachev and the collapse of the Soviet Union. It remains to be seen whether this trend will be reversed.

Compared with the past state of Soviet historical work on the subject of Eastern Front operations, what has transpired in recent years regarding release of archival materials has been revolutionary. But, just as the new Russian revolution is in its infancy, so also is the revolution in historiography. The archival materials that have been released thus far appear prodigious compared with the meager archival materials previously available (through captured German records). They are, however, really very limited compared with what certainly exists behind still-closed doors. Thus, while there is much to celebrate, there is also much to anticipate.

We can call the Russian (Soviet) archives open only when the archival flow is complete and when scholars, Western and Russian alike, have physical access to the archival repositories themselves. Clearly, there will remain certain limits on what can be seen and used, just as there are in the West. But these limits should be well defined and well understood. In particular, access can be judged as adequate only when the records of Stavka and operating fronts, armies, corps, and other military organizations are made available to scholars. The task of negotiating this access has only just begun.

SOVIET-BASED SECONDARY SOURCE MATERIALS

Although relatively few of the many published Russian-language works have been translated into English, the vast array of Soviet secondary materials must be addressed because it served as the stimulus for subsequent Western scholarship on the subject. Since de-Stalinization, or roughly 1958, Soviet historiography has produced a massive number of survey histories, operational studies, memoirs, and unit histories associated with the war.

Included in this number were three major, officially sanctioned survey histories and several encyclopedia series. The first comprehensive study of the war was Platonov's single-volume *The Second World War*, which established the parameters of the Soviet interpretation of the war. The six-volume *History of the Great Patriotic War*, which appeared between 1960 and 1965, was a classic example of the de-Stalinization process and Khrushchevian *glasnost*. It introduced readers to hitherto forbidden topics, such as more detail on the 1941 catastrophe, and to a limited number of wartime defeats, such as the May 1942 Khar'kov disaster, which became the "Potemkin village" for failed Soviet wartime operations. Between 1973 and 1982, the Soviets produced a twelve-volume *History of the Second World War* (as *Istoriia vtoroi mirovoi voiny*) which, while according the Red Army and Soviet state the leading role in war, finally introduced Russian readers to Allied operations. Characteristic of the Brezhnev period, these volumes were less candid than their six-volume predecessor.

The most substantive effort to produce a comprehensive encyclopedia of military history took place during the period 1976 through 1980, when the Ministry of Defense produced the eight-volume *Sovetskaia voennaia entsiklopediia* (Soviet Military Encyclopedia), edited under the supervision of then Marshal I. V. Ogarkov. A companion single-volume encyclopedia of the Great Patriotic War appeared in 1985. Although of immense use to researchers, these volumes are in Russian and bear the same negative characteristics as other books published during the period. The Ministry of Defense began preparing a new, more candid version of the multivolume encyclopedia in 1990 but ceased publication of the work when the Soviet Union crumbled in 1991.

The best and least politicized of these secondary sources appeared during the height of the 1960's "thaw." Thereafter, works were of mixed value depending on the degree of license accorded each author and the sensitivity of the subject each addressed. As a general rule, those in favor were permitted to write with greater candor, as were those writing utilitarian accounts for Soviet army officer education. Regardless of historical license, certain topics, such as many combat defeats, correct correlations of forces, and politically sensitive operations, remained forbidden. On the other hand, wartime controversies that served current political needs were thoroughly aired (such as the Zhukov–Konev debate over the Berlin operation, which paralleled political infighting in the contemporary Soviet political hierarchy).

A limited number of these works, such as memoirs by senior commanders G. K. Zhukov, A. M. Vasilevsky, I. S. Konev, K. K. Rokossovsky, A. I. Eremenko, S. K. Meretskov, and V. I. Chuikov; an invaluable study of the General Staff at war by Shtemenko; and a few operational studies on politically safe operations, such as Grechko's account of the Caucasus operation and Parotkin's anthology on *The Battle of Kursk*, appeared in English translation. Soviet authorities, however, heavily edited all memoirs, and only today are the expurgated portions of these memoirs appearing. The best and most accurate operational and tactical studies, however, remained in the Russian language.

A few Western historians, by virtue of their wartime service, keen linguistic talents, or unique access to Soviet sources, were able to synthesize Soviet materials and present a unique picture of the wartime Red Army. In so doing, they formed the Soviet school of war historiography in the West. Foremost among this small group were Allen and Muratoff, who wrote the first history on the war on the Eastern Front from the Soviet perspective in 1946, and MacIntosh and Erickson, whose work in the 1960s began to etch a "face" on the hitherto featureless Red Army and added detail to equally shadowy Red Army operations. They did so shortly after Sovet historians began writing with greater candor about the war. MacIntosh's interest and knowledge of the Red Army resulted from his wartime association with it. Erickson's work resulted, in part, because of his unique access to senior Red Army commanders during the early 1960s Khrushchev "thaw" in Soviet historical writing when the term *"glasnost"* was first used. For many years, MacIntosh's single-volume history of the Red Army, *Juggernaut*, was the most reliable single volume on the subject. Erickson's seminal study, *The Soviet High Command*, appeared in 1962 and provided unprecedented detail about the Red Army's development from 1918 through 1941, and, later, his massive and classic tomes *The Road to Stalingrad* and *The Road to Berlin* provided rich details of Soviet participation in the war. Yet even Erickson would admit that although much of his work has withstood the archival test, he would have preferred to have had greater access to Soviet archives at the time he was writing his works.

Subsequently, other Western historians developed the trend initiated by MacIntosh and Erickson. In 1969 Bialer edited an anthology of biographical sketches of leading Soviet military figures, and two years later Chaney wrote a comprehensive biography of the leading Soviet military commander, Marshal G. K. Zhukov. The effort to add personality to a faceless Red Army has now culminated in the recent publication of Shukman's biographical anthology, *Stalin's Generals*, and Armstrong's *Red Army Tank Commanders*.

In the 1980s, fueled by improved access to Russian-language sources, increased Soviet historical candor, and intensified interest in Soviet affairs by Western scholars, the Soviet (Russian) school of historiography has matured. More important, scholars have been able to integrate Russian materials with, and test them against, German and Japanese archival sources to produce a more balanced interpretation of the war. Among those whose efforts have stood out are Bellamy, Dunn, Duffy, Adair, Hardesty, Glantz, Jukes, Fugate, Parrish, and a growing number of younger historians.

During the early 1980s, the U.S. Army War College contributed to a greater understanding of the nature of combat on the Eastern Front when it sponsored three symposia on Soviet wartime operations. Assisted by German veterans of the war, Glantz exploited Soviet sources to create a unique and detailed view of specific wartime operations. The results of these symposia and a fourth, later sponsored by the U.S. Army's Soviet Army Studies Office, were then published in four extensive volumes. The symposia then fostered additional valuable work, including Duffy's study of the final year of war, Adair's analysis of the Belorussian operation, and more extensive research and writing by Glantz.

Based on his earlier work on Soviet 1945 operations in Manchuria and new materials uncovered in the War College symposia, Glantz prepared studies of Soviet wartime intelligence and deception operations, which opened new vistas on an understanding of the nature and impact of wartime military operations. He further exploited Soviet and German archival sources to prepare subsequent volumes assessing Soviet tactics, operational methods, and wartime strategy. This work culminated in his preparation with House of a comprehensive survey history of the war, *When Titans Clashed*, which exploited both German and Soviet records to uncover previously forgotten major operations and cast new light on those which were already well known. Assisted by even more extensive Soviet archival releases and more thorough analysis of German archival sources, new volumes in preparation promise to alter fundamentally traditional accounts of the war. A blueprint for this new analysis, entitled "The Failures of Historiography: Forgotten Battles of the German-Soviet War," appeared in a recent issue of *The Journal of Slavic Military Studies* and in a Russian Academy of Science reassessment of the war, entitled *The Second World War* (in Russian).

Meanwhile, Bellamy prepared his comprehensive assessment of wartime Soviet use of artillery, *The Red God of War*, while Jukes, Fugate, and Gebhardt provided more detailed accounts of Operation Barbarossa, the titanic Battle of Kursk, and the Petsamo-Kirkenes operation in the Soviet far north. Parrish paved the way for the work of all of these historians by preparing massive and seminal bibliographical studies of Soviet historical materials on the war. While little work has been done on the Soviet navy, Hardesty published *Red Phoenix*, the first thorough account of the Red Air Force at war. Additionally, new vistas on Soviet force structuring, organization, and order of battle have been opened by Dunn's seminal study, *Hitler's Nemesis*, which covers Soviet wartime combat forces and will be followed by a similar work on support and logistical forces and by Poirier and Conner's *The Red Army Order of Battle.* Finally, Orenstein has applied his keen translation and editorial talents to preparation for Western consumption of many of the volumes in the imposing and extensive Soviet General Staff archival series, as well as a two-volume documentary work on Soviet operational art. Many of these Soviet archival studies have been serialized in *The Journal of Slavic Military Studies.*

Tangentially, additional light has been cast on Soviet participation in the 1939 Polish and 1939–1940 Finnish wars. While many accounts of these formerly obscure wars have appeared by Finnish historians and, more recently, by Polish historians, among the best English-language sources are Chew's *The White Death* and Zaloga and Madej's *The Polish Campaign 1939.*

DEBATES AND INTERPRETATIONS

It was inevitable that warfare on so colossal a scale and with so decisive an influence on the ultimate outcome of the Second World War would generate heated controversy on both sides. Although many critical issues have already been defined, shaped, and debated, striking changes in the availability and exploitation of archival materials (particularly Soviet, but also German) now necessitate extensive revision of what are now considered to be classic accounts and interpretations of the war. That revisionism is now only beginning. When complete, it will likely fundamentally change the face of the German-Soviet war.

The most pervasive and extensive debate on the German side has been, and continues to be, the question of wartime leadership and the analogous issue of who was responsible for military defeat—Hitler or his generals. Fueled by German memoir materials, to a greater or lesser degree, most of those in the German school tend to side with the latter and conclude that Hitler's policies, if they did not deprive Germany of victory, certainly hastened defeat. The best of these works, such as that of Ziemke and Seaton, debate the issue with an understanding that, regardless of blame, the German military effort against the Soviet Union was probably beyond Germany's means.

A second major debate, more recent in nature and fueled by inflammatory writing based on Soviet sources, rages over responsibility for the war in the first place. This debate swirls around a claim made, ironically, by a Soviet émigré writing under the pen name Viktor Suvorov that Germany's invasion of the Soviet Union was preemptive in nature and responded to Soviet plans to invade German territory in the summer of 1941. This claim, which was a virtual by-product of political turmoil in the Soviet Union shortly before its fall, was quickly embraced by many extreme reformers who, through their intense hatred of the communist system, sought to discredit all things Soviet in general and Stalin's policies in particular. While most reputable Soviet scholars in the West and contemporary Russian historians reject the claim, understandably it has found fertile ground among a growing number of German historians.

Extensive debates have also occurred within the Soviet historical community since the late 1950s, when the lid was taken off strict Stalinist censorship. These debates have generally occurred within the context of contemporary political debates or power struggles (such as de-Stalinization) and the changing political fortunes of key military figures (such as Zhukov). The most important issues were the role of Stalin in decision making, the nature and causes of surprise in June 1941, blame for subsequent military defeats (those few revealed), and debates over the operational conduct of the war (like the Zhukov–Konev controversy). Soviet reform historians have also become embroiled in the debate over the origins of the war.

Future debates will likely be fueled by the inevitable and necessary revision of accounts of the Red Army's conduct of the war. Already, controversy rages over Soviet wartime losses, and a few Russian historians are finally lifting the veil on long-forgotten or suppressed military defeats. More extensive exploitation of German archival sources, together with more significant Russian archival releases, will permit and require a virtual rewriting of the history of the war.

CONCLUSION

Although thousands of works have been written in German, Russian, and English about the German-Soviet war, historiographical coverage of the war remains woefully inadequate. While German archival materials have been available for decades and have been skillfully exploited, Soviet archival materials have been frozen in a historical limbo. Without the latter, full exploitation of the former cannot occur. Already the testing of German materials against Soviet open-source accounts and the limited existing quantity of Soviet archival materials has produced a strikingly different picture of the war. When that comparison and testing can be done in full measure, the results will be even more significant. In essence, on the eve of the twenty-first century, we stand not at the end of historiography on the war but rather at the threshhold of a new beginning.

BIBLIOGRAPHY

Adair, Paul. *Hitler's Greatest Defeat: The Collapse of German Army Group Centre, June 1944*. London: Arms and Armour, 1994.
Allen, W.E.D., and Paul Muratoff. *The Russian Campaign of 1944–1945*. Harmondsworth, England: Penguin, 1946.

Armstrong, Richard N. *Red Army Tank Commanders: The Armored Guards.* Atglen, PA: Schiffer, 1994.

——, ed. *Red Army Combat Orders: Combat Regulations for Tank and Mechanized Forces 1944.* Trans. Joseph G. Welsh. London: Frank Cass, 1991.

Bartov, Omer. *The Eastern Front, 1941–45: German Troops and the Barbarisation of Warfare.* New York: St. Martin's, 1986.

Bellamy, Chris. *The Red God of War: Soviet Artillery and Rocket Forces.* London: Brassey's, 1986.

Bialer, Seweryn, ed. *Stalin's Generals.* New York: Pegasus, 1969.

Blau, George. *The German Campaign in Russia—Planning and Operations, 1940–1942.* In Department of the Army Pamphlet 20–261a. Washington, DC: GPO, 1955.

Boevoi sostav Sovetskoi armii, 3 T. (Combat Composition of the Red Army, 3 vol.) Moscow: Voenno-nauchnoe upravlenie General'nogo Shtaba (Military-Scientific Directorate of the General Staff), 1963–1972. Classified secret, declassified in 1964. Available in the West since 1993.

Carell, Paul. *Hitler Moves East, 1941–1943.* Boston: Little, Brown, 1964. Published in England as *Hitler's War on Russia 1941–1943.* London: Harrap, 1964.

——. *Scorched Earth: The Russian-German War 1943–44.* London: Harrap, 1970.

Chaney, Otto P. *Zhukov.* Norman: University of Oklahoma, 1971.

Chew, Allen F. *The White Death: The Epic of the Soviet–Finnish War.* East Lansing: Michigan State UP, 1971.

Chuikov, V. I. *The Battle for Stalingrad.* New York: Holt, Rinehart, and Winston, 1964.

——. *The End of the Third Reich.* Moscow: Progress, 1978.

Clark, Alan. *Barbarossa: The Russian–German Conflict 1941–45.* New York: William Morrow, 1966.

Craig, William. *Enemy at the Gates: The Battle for Stalingrad.* New York: Dutton, 1973.

Dallin, Alexander. *German Rule in Russia, 1941–1945.* New York: St. Martin's, 1957.

Das Deutsche Reich und der Zweite Weltkrieg. 10 vols. Stuttgart: Deutsche Verlags-Anstadt, 1981–1995. Six volumes published, three are translated into English as Deist, Wilhelm, et al. *Germany and the Second World War.* Vol. 1; *The Build-up of German Aggression.* Vol. 2; *Germany's Initial Conquests in Europe;* Vol. 3; *The Mediterranean, South-East Europe and North Africa, 1939–1941: From Italy's Declaration of Non-Belligerence to the Entry of the United States into the War.* Trans. by P. S. Falla, et al. Oxford and New York: Clarendon Press, 1990–1995.

Duffy, Christopher. *Red Storm on the Reich.* New York: Atheneum, 1991.

Dunn, Walter S., Jr. *Hitler's Nemesis: The Red Army, 1930–1945.* New York: Praeger, 1994.

Eremenko, A. I. *The Arduous Beginning.* Moscow: Progress, 1966.

Erickson, John. *The Road to Berlin.* Boulder, CO: Westview, 1983.

——. *The Road to Stalingrad.* London: Weidenfeld and Nicolson, 1975.

——. *The Soviet High Command 1918–1941.* London: Macmillan, 1962.

Fugate, Brian I. *Operation Barbarossa: Strategy and Tactics on the Eastern Front.* Novato, CA: Presidio, 1984.

Gebhardt, James F. *The Petsamo-Kirkenes Operation: Soviet Breakthrough and Pursuit in the Arctic, October 1944*. Leavenworth Paper no. 17. Fort Leavenworth, KS: Combat Studies Office, 1989.

Glantz, David M. *August Storm: The Soviet 1945 Strategic Offensive in Manchuria*. Leavenworth Paper no. 7. Fort Leavenworth, KS: Combat Studies Institute, 1983.

———. *August Storm: Soviet Tactical and Operational Combat in Manchuria, 1945*. Leavenworth Paper no. 8. Fort Leavenworth, KS: Combat Studies Institute, 1983.

———. "The Failures of Historiography: Forgotten Battles of the German–Soviet War (1941–1945)." *The Journal of Slavic Military Studies 8* (1995): 768–809. Reprinted in Russian in O. A. Rzheshevsky, ed., *Vtoraia mirovaia voina: Aktual'nye problemy* (The Second World War: Actual Problems). Moscow: Nauka, 1995.

———. *From the Don to the Dnepr: Soviet Offensive Operations, December 1942–August 1943*. London: Frank Cass, 1991.

———. *A History of Soviet Airborne Forces*. London: Frank Cass, 1994.

———. *The Military Strategy of the Soviet Union*. London: Frank Cass, 1992.

———. "Newly Published Soviet Works on the Red Army, 1918–1991." *The Journal of Slavic Military Studies 8* (1995): 319–33.

———. *The Role of Intelligence in Soviet Military Strategy in World War II*. Novato, CA: Presidio, 1990.

———. *The Soviet Conduct of Tactical Maneuver: Spearhead of the Offensive*. London: Frank Cass, 1991.

———. *Soviet Military Deception in the Second World War*. London: Frank Cass, 1989.

———. *Soviet Military Intelligence in War*. London: Frank Cass, 1990.

———. *Soviet Military Operational Art: In Pursuit of Deep Battle*. London: Frank Cass, 1991.

———, ed. *The Initial Period of War on the Eastern Front, 22 June–August 1941*. London: Frank Cass, 1993.

———, ed. *1984 Art of War Symposium. From the Don to the Dnepr: Soviet Offensive Operation, December 1942–August 1943*. Carlisle, PA: U.S. Army War College, 1984.

———. *1985 Art of War Symposium. From the Dnepr to the Vistula: Soviet Offensive Operations, November 1943–August 1944*. Carlisle, PA: U.S. Army War College, 1985.

———. *1986 Art of War Symposium. From the Vistula to the Oder: Soviet Offensive Operations, October 1944–March 1945*. Carlisle, PA: U.S. Army War College, 1986.

Glantz, David M., and Jonathan House. *When Titans Clashed: The Red Army and the Wehrmacht, 1941–1945*. Lawrence: Kansas UP, 1995.

Goerlitz, Walter, ed. *The Memoirs of Field Marshal Keitel*. New York: Stein and Day, 1966.

———. *Paulus in Stalingrad*. New York: Citadel, 1963.

Great Patriotic War of the Soviet Union 1941–1945. Moscow: Progress, 1974.

Grechko, A. *Battle for the Caucasus*. Moscow: Progress, 1971.

Greiner, Helmuth. *Aufzeichnungen ueber die Lagevortraege und Besprechungen im Fuehrerhauptquartier vom 12. August 1942 bis zum 17. Maerz 1943*. Published in English as *Greiner Diary Notes*. Historical Division, U.S. Army, Europe, MS # C-065a.

Guderian, Heinz. *Panzer Leader*. New York: Dutton, 1952.

Guide to Foreign Military Studies 1945–54. Historical Division, U.S. Army, Europe.

Guide to German Archival Records Microfilmed at Alexandria, Va. Washington, DC: National Archives and Records Administration, 1974–1979.

Halder, Franz. *Kriegstagebuch.* Stuttgart: W. Kohlhammer, 1964. In translation as *The Halder Diaries: The Private War Journals of Colonel General Franz Halder.* Boulder, CO: Westview, 1976.

Hardesty, Von. *The Red Phoenix: The Rise of Soviet Air Power 1941–1945.* Washington, DC: Smithsonian, 1982.

Heinrici, Gotthard. *The Campaign in Russia.* London: Frank Cass, 1995.

History of the Great Patriotic War. 6 volumes. Moscow: Institute of Marxism Leninism, 1960.

Istoriia vtoroi mirovoi voiny 1939–1945, 12 T. (A History of the Second World War 1939–1945, 12 vols.). Moscow: Voenizdat, 1973–1982.

Jones, Robert H. *The Roads to Russia: United States Lend-Lease to the Soviet Union.* Norman: University of Oklahoma, 1969.

Jukes, Goeffrey. *Kursk: The Clash of Armour.* London: Purnell, 1968.

Konev, Ivan. *Year of Victory.* Moscow: Progress, 1969.

Kozlov, M. M. *Velikaia Otechestvenniai voina 1941–1945: entsiklopediia* (The Great Patriotic War 1941–1945: An Encyclodepia). Moscow: Soviet Encyclopedia, 1985.

Le Tissier, Tony. *The Battle of Berlin 1945.* London: Jonathan Cape, 1988.

MacIntosh, Malcolm. *Juggernaut: A History of the Soviet Armed Forces.* London: Secker and Warburg, 1967.

Manstein, Erich von. *Lost Victories.* Chicago: Henry Regnery, 1958.

Mellenthin, Friedrich Wilhelm von. *Panzer Battles: A Study of the Employment of Armor in the Second World War.* Norman: University of Oklahoma, 1956.

Meretskov, K. A. *Serving the People.* Moscow: Progress, 1971.

Motter, T. Vail. *The Persian Corridor and Aid to Russia.* Washington, DC: GPO, 1952.

Neipold, Gerd. *Battle for White Russia: The Destruction of Army Group Centre, June 1944.* London: Brassey's, 1987.

Ogarkov, I. V., ed. *Sovetskaia voennaia entsiklopediia, 8 T.* (Soviet Military Encyclopedia, 8 vols.). Moscow: Voenizdat, 1976–1980.

Orenstein, Harold S., trans. and ed. *The Evolution of Soviet Operational Art, 1927–1991: The Documentary Basis.* 2 vols. London: Frank Cass, 1995.

———. *Soviet Documents of the Use of War Experience.* Vol. 1, *The Initial Period of War;* vol. 2, *The Winter Campaign;* vol. 3, *Military Operations 1941 and 1942.* London: Frank Cass, 1991–1993.

Parotkin, I., ed. *The Battle of Kursk.* Moscow: Progress, 1974.

Parrish, Michael. *Battle for Moscow: The 1942 Soviet General Staff Study.* London: Brassey's, 1989.

———. *The USSR in World War II: An Annotated Bibliography of Books Published in the Soviet Union, 1945–1975, with an Addendum for the Years 1975–1980.* 2 vols. New York: Garland, 1981.

Platonov, S. P., ed. *Vtoraia mirovaia voina 1939–1945 gg.* (The Second World War 1939–1945). Moscow: Voenizdat, 1958.

Poirier, Robert G., and Albert Z. Conner. *The Red Army Order of Battle in the Great Patriotic War.* Novato, CA: Presidio, 1985.

Reinhardt, Klaus. *Moscow—The Turning Point: Failure of Hitler's Strategy in the Winter of 1941–42*. Oxford: Berg, 1992.

Rokossovsky, K. *A Soldier's Duty*. Moscow: Progress, 1970.

Salisbury, Harrison E. *The 900 Days: The Siege of Leningrad*. New York: Harper and Row, 1969.

Scherff, Walter. *OKW, WFST, Kriegsgeschichtlichen Abteilung, Kriegstagebuch*. Nurberg: International Military Tribunal Document 1809 PS, n.d., but presumably 1946.

Schramm, Percy E. *Kriegstagebuch des Oberkommandos der Wehrmacht (Wehrmachtfueh-rungsstab)*. 2 vols. Frankfurt: Bernard and Graefe, 1961–1965.

Schroter, Heinz. *Stalingrad*. London: Michael Joseph, 1958.

Seaton, Albert. *The Battle for Moscow 1941–1942*. London: Rupert Hart-Davis, 1971; and New York: Berkley, 1971, 1983.

———. *The Russo-German War 1941–1945*. New York: Praeger, 1971.

Senger und Etterlin, Frido M. von. *Der Gegenschlag*. Neckargemund: Scharnhorst Buchkameradschaft, 1959.

Shaposhnikov, Boris. *Razgrom nemetskikh voisk, pod moskvoi*. Moscow: Voen, 1943.

Shtemenko, S. M. *The General Staff at War, 1941–1945*. Moscow: Progress, 1970.

———. *The Last Six Months*. Garden City, NY: Doubleday, 1977.

Shukman, Harold, ed. *Stalin's Generals*. London: Weidenfeld and Nicolson, 1993.

Sydnor, Charles W., Jr. *Soldiers of Destruction: The SS Death's Head Division, 1933–1945*. Princeton: Princeton UP, 1977.

Tarrant, V. E. *Stalingrad*. New York: Hippocrene, 1992.

Vasilevsky, A. M. *A Lifelong Cause*. Moscow: Progress, 1976.

Velikaia Otechestvennaia voina Sovetskogo Soiuza, 6 T. (The Great Patriotic War of the Soviet Union, 6 vols.). Moscow: Voenizdat, 1960–1965.

Volkogonov, Dmitri. *Stalin: Triumph and Tragedy*. Rocklin, CA: Prima, 1992.

Warlimont, Walter. *Inside Hitler's Headquarters, 1939–1945*. New York: Praeger, 1961.

Whaley, Barton. *Codeword Barbarossa*. Cambridge: MIT, 1973.

Wray, Timothy A. *Standing Fast: German Defensive Doctrine on the Russian Front during World War II*. Research Paper No. 5. Fort Leavenworth, KS: Combat Studies Institute, 1986.

Zaloga, Steven, and Victor Madej. *The Polish Campaign 1939*. New York: Hippo-crene, 1985.

Zhukov, G. *Reminiscences and Reflections*. 2 vols. Moscow: Progress, 1985.

Ziemke, Earl F. *The German Northern Theater of Operations, 1940–1945*. Washington, DC: GPO, 1959.

———. *Stalingrad to Berlin: The German Defeat in the East*. Washington, DC: GPO, 1968.

Ziemke, Earl F., and Magna E. Bauer. *Moscow to Stalingrad: Decision in the East*. Washington, DC: Center of Military History, U.S. Army, 1987.

11   The Battle of the Atlantic

Marc Milner

The Battle of the Atlantic was the longest campaign of the Second World War and covered the length and breadth of the second largest ocean. It involved not only naval and air forces and merchant shipping but also the economic, industrial, and transportation (dockyards, ports, railroads) systems of the participants. The Atlantic war was less about military power projection than about the use of the sea to move basic commodities and to accumulate the resources needed to mount and sustain air and land operations elsewhere. Since 1945 there has been remarkable consensus among historians about the nature, general pattern, and salient points of the Battle of the Atlantic. In many ways this uniformity is indicative of how little modern scholarship has really been done on this remarkable campaign.

Wartime propaganda portrayed the Atlantic war as primarily an engagement of armed forces, and that perception has endured. Changes in import or export rates were attributed generally to direct enemy action, and the prospects for Allied initiatives, like the Second Front, were tied closely to victory over the Germans in the Atlantic. The notion that the Atlantic was essentially a shooting war was fostered by the service histories and memoirs published after 1945. Indeed, the approach was firmly established in British wartime "Staff Histories" and in the United States by Sternhell and Thorndike's enduring *Anti-Submarine Warfare in World War II*, published internally by the Office of the Chief of Naval Operations in 1946. These set the pattern for the official naval histories that followed. The first of these, Morison's *The Battle of the Atlantic*, the first volume of the semiofficial *History of U.S. Naval Operations*, including its air component, concentrated on naval operations up to the collapse of the wolf pack campaign in the spring of 1943. Morison's second volume on the Atlantic (actually volume 10 in his series) covered May 1943 to May 1945 and was even more a simple naval operational history. The important operations of the U.S. Army Air Corps/Force in the Atlantic war were covered—buried?—in Craven and Cate's multivolume history of *The Army Air Forces in World War II.*

Canada played an important role in the Atlantic war, but that story was poorly served by its official historians. Schull's *The Far Distant Ships* was a popular operational "account," weak on context and short on analysis, thus much less useful than Morison's effort. Schull's book was, in fact, the rump of an ambitious plan to produce an official history of the Royal Canadian Navy (RCN) itself up to 1945. That project ended with volume 2 of Tucker's *The Naval Service of Canada,* which covered activities ashore during the war, something unique among the naval histories. However, without a proper operational history to buttress it, Tucker's colorless work was largely neglected. The Canadian air force lacked any official history at all before 1986, and so the Canadian air role in the Atlantic remained completely unknown.

The best of the official histories covering the Atlantic war, Captain S. W. Roskill's *The War at Sea,* was the last to appear. His comprehensive survey of British naval and air operations during the war is built on a strong strategic framework. Roskill accepted that naval intelligence, the system of escorted convoys, and avoidance of the enemy were the foundations of Allied victory in the Atlantic. Victory was not, therefore, simply a matter of beating the U-boats, although that had to be done, and much of *The War at Sea* recounts the action.

It is, perhaps, unremarkable that the service histories of the major combatants concentrated on the fighting at sea. That trend was buttressed by a spate of memoirs from participants on both sides in the generation after 1945. Among these was the crucial volume of Admiral Karl Donitz's *Memoirs,* still the best memoir of a senior commander from either side and good periscopic views of the U-boat war from a number of German submariners. Classic memoirs of the Atlantic war also appeared in Britain. One of the very best and most notorious was by Captain Donald Macintyre, a successful convoy escort and A/S (Anti-Submarine) group commander, who published his wartime exploits, *U-Boat Killer,* in 1956. Macintyre was especially blunt in his comments on the efficiency of the Canadian navy, whose ships were particularly poorly equipped, trained, and led when he saw them in 1941. The RCN he described as bungling and inefficient and its escorts as "travesties of warships." Macintyre reined in his virulent dislike for the RCN in a one-volume popular history called *The Battle of the Atlantic,* but his views on the RCN held the field for the next thirty years.

In the decades after 1945 British and German memoirs captured the field, and the Atlantic war became very much their experience. That left little scope for Easton's *50 North,* a little-known classic that recounts the

Canadian experience, and Waters' *Bloody Winter*, the gripping account of a U.S. Coast Guardsman battling his way through the cruelest winter of the war, 1942–1943. Waters suffered a double jeopardy because he was, by his own reckoning, in the wrong service (U.S. Coast Guard, USCG), doing the wrong duty (convoy escort) in the wrong ocean (the Atlantic) for anyone "back home"—or in the USN—to take much notice either.

Waters' dilemma points to a salient feature of the Atlantic war historiography. Simply put, the Atlantic has been seen as primarily an Anglo-German struggle. America's naval war, nationally, emotionally, and especially from the perspective of the USN, was the Pacific. This is all the more remarkable because the "failure" of the USN adequately to defend shipping in the Atlantic in 1942 remains one of the few genuine controversies in the literature. Even so, there has been little scholarly debate. The British condemned American intransigence over the adoption of escorted convoys in 1942, and Morison (in volume one) agreed. The only other controversies worth the name prior to 1970 were how bad the RCN was and why so few Allied aircraft were available to close the gap in mid-Atlantic air coverage of shipping prior to 1943.

Official histories and memoirs, which dominated the field by 1970, agreed that the Atlantic war was explicable entirely in terms of shifting strategic, operational, and tactical decisions and struggles for new and better equipment. The Allies got the basic strategy right—escorted convoys—and won the battle for more effective equipment, especially ten-centimeter radar, shipborne HF/DF (high frequency direction finder), and long-range airpower. If there was an American view, it was that the whole convoy system was probably a wasted effort: the Allies ought to have sought out and destroyed the U-boats from the outset, instead of "waiting" until 1943 to do it.

What upset this happy existence was Winterbotham's *The Ultra Secret.* Winterbotham revealed that the Allies had systematically attacked and penetrated Axis military ciphers, a revelation that shook the historiography of the Second World War to its very foundations. If the Allies were literally "reading the other guy's mail" routinely, then all the assumptions about cause and effect in the war had to be reviewed. The Atlantic war was particularly dependent on radio traffic, and it was natural to assume, therefore, that it was decisively affected by special intelligence.

Winterbotham's disclosure sent scholars pouring into the archives in the 1970s to review newly declassified documents. First off the mark with a new synthesis of the existing literature and insights from newly released documents, including special intelligence, were Hughes and Costello with *The Battle of the Atlantic.* A lavishly illustrated, large-format book, the work is an excellent and remarkably durable statement on the state of the art by 1977. The authors reflected a solidly British interpretation of the war, in which strategic defense in the form of escorted convoys formed the basis of ultimate Allied victory. They took care to work in the effects of special intelligence and to track the general state of Allied shipping at each stage. Perhaps not surprising, the Americans are portrayed as an enigma: the tremendous efficiency of American mass production of merchant ships is offset against the fundamental and inexplicable failing of the USN along its own coast in 1942, which squandered so much valuable tonnage. As for the Canadian effort, Costello and Hughes dismiss it in two short paragraphs reflecting both the Canadian and Macintyre themes: big and important but misguided.

Since Hughes and Costello's tentative steps at integrating special intelligence into the story, historians of the Atlantic war have been fascinated with Ultra. Their interest was given an enormous push in that same year by two books. Patrick Beesley, who worked at the Government Code and Cypher School at Bletchley Park, published his own account of Ultra and the Atlantic war, *Very Special Intelligence.* A much more detailed exposition of just how Ultra and intelligence operated on a day-by-day basis was also published in 1977 by Rohwer, perhaps the greatest authority on the campaign. Rohwer was among the first to effectively mine the vast Ultra material released to archives, and he laid out his case for the decisiveness of Ultra in an exhaustive account of *The Critical Convoy Battles of March 1943,* the first thorough study of a crucial period of the campaign. The book has been the model for subsequent studies of the links between intelligence and the outcome of battles.

The notion that Ultra was uniquely responsible for the outcome of the Atlantic war was confirmed for many in Hinsley's magisterial official history of *British Intelligence in the Second World War.* Although his massive work covers all aspects of the intelligence war, Hinsley had much to say on the Atlantic campaign. Like Beesley, Hinsley worked at Bletchley Park and so has an insider's feel for the material that lends weight to his work. His final judgment, *Intelligence Revolution,* delivered in the 1988 Harmon Memorial Lecture in Military History, was that without Ultra the Atlantic war might well have lasted another two years.

Most Ultra enthusiasts support Hinsley and remain convinced of the decisiveness of Allied code breaking in shaping the pattern and duration of the Atlantic war. However, not all historians of the Atlantic war agree. Allied reading of German codes was usually intermittent and often not fast enough to affect individual battles. Milner argued in "The Battle of the Atlantic" that Ultra was not singularly decisive, nor did it materially affect the pattern of the campaign itself. Milner's case was based on extensive research on operations and tactics, not on a thorough reevaluation of the intelligence story. That task fell to a distinguished historian of intelligence, David Kahn, who argued in *Seizing the Enigma* that special intelligence helped the Allies but that radar-equipped aircraft and warships beat the U-boats. Ultra intercepts simply allowed that victory to occur with greater certainty. He also suggests that the general pattern of events, the ebb and flow of the broad campaign, was largely unaffected by Ultra.

Kahn's case has recently been supported by another thorough study of the role of intelligence in the Atlantic war, Syrett's *The Defeat of the German U-Boats*, which looks at the role of Ultra in the 1943 Allied victory. The assertions of Kahn, Syrett, and Milner in many ways bring the cycle of cause and effect to where it was before Winterbotham's book: back to basic operational and tactical issues. This was, perhaps, inevitable, given that we now know that the Germans were reading the crucial Allied convoy code until June 1943! Positions in the debate over Ultra have therefore been staked out, but the battle remains a gentlemen's agreement to disagree. In part this stems from the sheer volume of material available on the Atlantic war. With enough money, time, and computer programmers it ought to be possible to pour the data into some vast computer program and then replay the naval campaign day by day.

Until the day when the Atlantic war can be purchased on CD-ROM, students will have to make do with a steadily rising volume of fact-laden books that provide a wealth of primary information. This genre predates the Ultra revelations, but it has mushroomed since 1970. It includes *British Vessels Lost at Sea 1939–1945* and Rohwer's exhaustive *Axis Submarine Successes*, which accounts for every known Axis torpedo fired by a submarine during the war. Much vital raw data on shipping losses, convoys, U-boats at sea, and U-boat sinkings have been available for years in the appendixes of the various official histories (which researchers ignore at their peril). Much of that data has been very usefully drawn together by Tarrant in *The U-Boat Offensive, 1914–1945*. Perhaps the ultimate compilation is Rohwer and Hummelchen's *Chronology of the War at Sea*, a blow-by-blow recounting of action throughout the world.

Ships lend themselves to statistical and factual compilations, and there is available a wealth of profusely illustrated books on various ship types by reputable historians. Some of the old standards, like Silverstone's *U.S. Warships of World War II* and Lenton and Colledge's work on British *Warships of World War II*, remain essential references. The Atlantic war was addressed more directly in Elliott's *Allied Escort Ships of World War II*, which contains much useful information on all Allied building programs. Macpherson and Burgess' *Ships of Canada's Naval Forces* is particularly valuable for the "Operational Status" appendix, which outlines the monthly deployment of each ship in the RCN during the war: a fine example of the raw material readily available and waiting to be sifted.

The Germany side has not been missed in this flood of new material. Lenton covered the German fleet and its fate in *German Warships of the Second World War*. The design and development of the U-boat fleet were presented authoritatively by Rossler in *The U-boat*, the standard technical history of the whole German submarine fleet from its inception until the

1970s. The operation history of the U-boat fleet was finally made widely available in 1989 with the publication of Hessler's *The U-Boat War in the Atlantic*, a confidential British history prepared immediately after the war. Hessler, the former staff officer (operations) of the U-boat fleet, was given access to all captured documents to complete his account, and it is fair to describe his work as the de facto "official" history of the German campaign.

Apart from the Germans, who approach the rewriting of the war with Teutonic thoroughness, much of what is new and innovative in the Atlantic war literature has emerged from Canada over the last fifteen years. The trend started in the 1970s, when the weaknesses of Schull's book, the legacy of Macintyre's stinging rebuke, and the availability of archival material sent scholars and graduate students into the field. Some preliminary findings appeared in Boutilier's anthology, *The RCN in Retrospect*. The first scholarly assessment of the RCN's major role in the main convoy battles, Milner's *North Atlantic Run*, appeared in 1985. Milner put a new spin on the old pattern, arguing that the Canadians were hardly the bungling incompetents that Macintyre suggested and that their operations helped shape events. Further evidence of this came in Hadley's *U-Boats against Canada*, a scholarly account of the inshore campaign in Canadian waters based on exhaustive archival work. Hadley and Milner added new depth and understanding to the Atlantic war, including the American failure to adopt convoys in 1942, the RCN's crucial role in supporting the USN during that dreadful year, and the facts that the RCN carried the burden of U-boat attacks in late 1942 (a period generally dismissed as quiet by British and American historians) and that the victory of early 1943 was more "British" than anyone suspected.

Canadian contributions continued through the 1980s. Douglas' *The Creation of a National Air Force*, Volume 2, *The Official History of the Royal Canadian Air Force*, rescued the significant Royal Canadian Air Force (RCAF) role, a quarter of the Allied squadrons and in British Commonwealth units a further quarter of the aircrew, from utter obscurity. In the process Douglas greatly added to our knowledge of the wider context of the air war over the Atlantic and to the tactical issues wrestled with in Price's earlier *Aircraft vs. Submarine*. Douglas' own anthology on Canadian naval history, *The RCN in Transition*, contains a number of solid chapters addressing the Canadian role in the Atlantic. Finally, Zimmerman's *The Great Naval Battle of Ottawa* took a critical look at the scientific and technical infrastructure that supported the fleet and at the politics of equipment acquisition. Zimmerman's work contributed to a small but important body of science and technical history, such as Hackman's *Seek and Strike*, a history of British sonar development up to the 1950s, that bears directly on the Atlantic campaign.

By the end of the 1980s the Canadian role in the Atlantic war could no longer be easily dismissed, as Hughes and Costello did in 1977, in a few gratuitous sentences. Evidence of that change came in the form of two new syntheses of the Atlantic war, van der Vat's *The Atlantic Campaign* and Terraine's *The U-Boat Wars* (published in Britain as *Business in Great Waters*). It is still possible for major works on the Battle of the Atlantic to appear without giving the Canadian role its proper weight. For example, Law and Howarth's anthology, *The Battle of the Atlantic*, contains fairly comprehensive coverage, even of the modest Italian contribution to the submarine campaign, but evidence of Canadian involvement is noticeably scarce.

The case for including the Canadian role is more than simply one of ensuring completeness. Canadian scholars are engaged in a major reevaluation of the whole Atlantic war, not simply their own role, and new Canadian scholarship brings into question many of the accepted notions about the Atlantic war. Milner's second major monograph on the RCN's role, *The U-Boat Hunters*, covers the last two, generally neglected years of the battle and offers a fresh perspective on the whole campaign. A proper official operational history of the RCN's role is also nearing completion by the Department of National Defence, a project that promises the first major reevaluation of the whole Atlantic war since the 1950s. The same official historians have recently published their final word on the air war in the Atlantic, volume 3 of the RCAF official history, *The Crucible of War*, under the authorship of Greenhous and others, which contains yet more new material on the Atlantic war and Canadian airmen's role.

Canadian work on the Atlantic seems unlikely to slacken for some time to come, and its efforts already point to the last major gap in the historiography of the Atlantic war: the American story. Apart from Morison's two volumes on the Atlantic war the number of major monographs on the American experience in the Atlantic war can be counted on the fingers of one hand. Discounting Farago's rambling and poorly focused book on the origins of modern American antisubmarine organization, *The Tenth Fleet*, the first work of major independent scholarship on America and the Atlantic war appeared only in 1975 with Abbazia's *Mr. Roosevelt's Navy*. Abbazia's superb work focuses on the quasi war fought by the USN in 1941, before the attack on Pearl Harbor and the German declaration of war. His book is unique in its attempt to get at the institutional reaction of the United States and the USN to the Atlantic war.

Significantly, nothing comparable to Abbazia's work on 1941 has ever appeared on the catastrophic events off the U.S. coast in 1942. How this disaster could have happened remains one of the great mysteries of the war. Morison blamed the USN for failing to learn the obvious lessons from the war by the end of 1941, particularly the need for escorted convoys. Cohen and Gooch, in *Military Misfortunes: The Anatomy of Failure in War*, ascribed the disaster to the USN's more general failure to get the operational command, control, and interservice organization right for dealing with a submarine problem. The solution, the Tenth Fleet, was not established until 1943. Gannon's excellent account of the two 1942 cruises of *U-123* off the United States, *Operation Drumbeat*, contains a major subtheme on the more particular issue of why it took so long to convoy shipping. Gannon's conclusions—the misapplication of U.S. destroyer strength, the failure to plan ahead for the small craft needed, and the intractability of Admiral Ernest King—are not new, even if some of the reviewers on the dust jacket seem to have discovered them for the first time. Gannon quite rightly describes this as the single biggest defeat at sea in American history, and yet no scholarly monograph based on a thorough examination of even American documents has ever appeared on the subject.

Rather, American historians have been content to focus on the particular, especially details of the battle off their own shores, by using certain "vehicles" like Gannon's *U-123* episodes. A similar format was followed by Hickam, who recounted the view from the Coast Guard cutter *Dion* in *Torpedo Junction*. Even Y'Blood's study of the operations of small A/S carriers in the Atlantic, *Hunter-Killer*, concentrates on a discrete part of the story, which, in this case, is both an American success story and a nice opportunity to illustrate the powerful influence of Ultra. It says a great deal about American interest in the larger issues of the Atlantic war that Meigs' useful book, *Slide Rules and Submarines*, the closest thing we have to a modern history of antisubmarine warfare in the USN during the Second World War, appeared only in paperback from the obscure presses of National Defence University. U.S. Army Air Force (USAAF) efforts in the Atlantic have fared even worse. For nearly half a century following the appearance of Craven and Cate's official history of the USAAF nothing was published on the Army Air Force's Atlantic war. Schoenfeld's piece of consummate scholarship, *Stalking the U-Boat*, rescued the short history of two USAAF antisubmarine groups serving overseas from utter obscurity. The rest of the USAAF's maritime effort lies forgotten.

Meigs, Gannon, Hickam, Cohen, and others have wrestled with the 1942 disaster off the American coast and only dipped into the vast archival material available in Washington. Perhaps American historians have stayed away from a major assault on their Atlantic war because of the sheer size of the task or the difficulty of using the USN's archival records. Somehow these inhibitions must be overcome. Runyan and Copes' anthology, *To Die Gallantly*, is a promising start. But just as Americans need to get their own story told, they also need to adopt a wider vision of the Atlantic war. The U-boat menace off their coast was not a uniquely American problem that could be fixed by a "made in America" solution. It was an international problem, and it was dealt with at the time, if not subsequently by historians, as a joint Allied problem. Recent Canadian scholarship has much to offer in broadening this perspective. For example, Fisher's " 'We'll Get

Our Own' " describes Canadian oil convoy operations in the U.S. Eastern Sea Frontier during the worst of the 1942 onslaught. They operated without loss, despite at least one German pack operation against them.

American naval historians also must shake their Mahanist roots and stop seeing naval warfare almost exclusively in terms of battles. Indeed, this is a stricture that could be applied to all historians of the Battle of the Atlantic. There is a whole literature available that is germane to the Atlantic story and that remains poorly integrated and often not even acknowledged. These include Behrens' excellent *Merchant Shipping and the Demands of War*, part of the British Civil History Series, Leighton and Coakley's American official history, *Global Logistics and Strategy*, and Doughty's little gem, *Merchant Shipping and War*. All of these deal with the essence of the Atlantic saga: the movement of people and material across the Atlantic for the purposes of war. Remarkably, it is possible to read them and wonder, in many cases, where the Germans have gone. All too often the bottlenecks and problems impeding the movement of ships and material across the Atlantic were inherent in the Allied management of the war itself or stemmed from actions well beyond the purview of U-boats. As Leighton revealed many decades ago in his insightful contribution "U.S. Merchant Shipping," it was as much the invasion of North Africa in November 1942 that threw the Atlantic into crisis over the winter of 1942–1943 as it was the depredations of the U-boats. Many years later Max Schoenfeld demonstrated convincingly that the British shipping and import situation improved in the summer of 1941 *despite* the efforts of Churchill to take direct action in the face of heavy losses in the late winter. Finally, Behrens concluded that American misuse of shipping resulted in the "loss" of some nine million tons annually by 1945: a figure equivalent to nearly *half* of all shipping losses to enemy action (roughly twenty-one million tons) during the whole course of the war and *three times* the total of U.S. flag shipping sunk. All of this suggests that it is time historians stopped concentrating solely on the *Battle* of the Atlantic and begin to reevaluate the Atlantic war itself.

BIBLIOGRAPHY

Abbazia, Patrick. *Mr. Roosevelt's Navy*. Annapolis, MD: NIP, 1975.

Beesley, Patrick. *Very Special Intelligence*. London: Hamilton, 1977.

Behrens, C.B.A. *Merchant Shipping and the Demands of War*. London: HMSO, 1955.

Boutilier, James A. *The RCN in Retrospect, 1910–1968*. Vancouver, BC: University of British Columbia, 1982.

British Vessels Lost at Sea. Cambridge: Patrick Stephens, 1988.

Cohen, Eliot A., and John Gooch. *Military Misfortunes: The Anatomy of Failure in War*. New York: Free Press, 1990.

Craven, W. F., and J. L. Cate. *The Army Air Forces in World War II*. Chicago: University of Chicago, 1948–1958.

Donitz, Karl. *Memoirs: Ten Years and Twenty Days.* London: Weidenfelt and Nicholson, 1959; Annapolis, MD: NIP, 1990.

Doughty, Martin. *Merchant Shipping and War: A Study in Defence Planning in Twentieth Century Britain.* London and Atlantic Highlands, NJ: Humanities, 1982.

Douglas, W.A.B. *The Creation of a National Air Force.* Vol. 2., *The Official History of the Royal Canadian Air Force.* Toronto: University of Toronto, 1986.

———. *The RCN in Transition.* Vancouver, BC: University of British Columbia, 1988.

Easton, Alan. *50 North.* Toronto: Ryerson, 1966.

Elliott, Peter. *Allied Escort Ships of World War II.* London: Macdonald Janes, 1977.

Farago, Ladislas. *The Tenth Fleet.* New York: Richardson and Steirmium, 1962; New York: Paperback Library, 1971.

Fisher, Robert C. " 'We'll Get Our Own': Canada and the Oil Shipping Crisis of 1942." *The Northern Mariner 2,* no. 2 (1992): 33–40.

Gannon, M. *Operation Drumbeat.* New York: Harper and Row, 1990.

Greenhous, Brereton, et al. *The Crucible of War.* Vol. 3, *The Official History of the Royal Canadian Air Force.* Toronto: University of Toronto, 1994.

Hackman, Willem. *Seek and Strike: Sonar, Anti-Submarine-Warfare and the Royal Navy 1914–54.* London: HMSO, 1984.

Hadley, M. *U-Boats against Canada.* Kingston, Montreal: McGill-Queen's; Annapolis, MD: NIP, 1985.

Hessler, Gunter. *The U-Boat War in the Atlantic 1939–1945.* London: HMSO, 1989.

Hickam, Homer H. *Torpedo Junction.* Annapolis, MD: NIP, 1989.

Hinsley, Francis H. *British Intelligence in the Second World War.* Cambridge: Cambridge UP, 1979–1988.

———. *Intelligence Revolution: A Historical Perspective.* Colorado Springs, CO, and Washington, DC: U.S. Air Force Academy, 1988.

Hughes, Terry, and John Costello. *The Battle of the Atlantic.* New York: Dial, 1977; London: Collins, 1980.

Kahn, David. *Seizing the Enigma.* New York: Houghton Mifflin, 1991.

Law, David, and Stephen Howarth, eds. *The Battle of the Atlantic.* London: Greenhill Books, 1994.

Leighton, Richard M. "U.S. Merchant Shipping and the British Import Crisis." In K. R. Greenfield, ed., *Command Decisions,* 199–223. Washington, DC: Office of the Chief of Military History, U.S. Army, 1960.

Leighton, Richard M., and Robert W. Coakley. *Global Logistics and Strategy.* Washington, DC: Office of the Chief of Military History, U.S. Army, 1955–1968.

Lenton, Henry Trevor. *German Warships of the Second World War.* New York: Arco Books, 1976.

Lenton, Henry Trevor, and J. J. Colledge. *Warships of World War II.* London: Ian Allan, 1964.

Macintyre, Donald. *The Battle of the Atlantic.* London: B. T. Batsford, 1961.

———. *U-Boat Killer.* London: Weidenfeld and Nicholson, 1956.

Macpherson, Ken M., and John Burgess. *Ships of Canada's Naval Forces 1910–1981.* Toronto: Collins, 1994.

Meigs, Montgomery C. *Slide Rules and Submarines.* Washington, DC: National Defence University, 1990.

Milner, Marc. "The Battle of the Atlantic." *The Journal of Strategic Studies: Special*

Issue: Decisive Campaigns of the Second World War 13 (1990): 45–66. Later published as *Decisive Campaigns of the Second World War*. London: Frank Cass, 1990.

———. *North Atlantic Run*. Toronto: University of Toronto; Annapolis, MD: NIP, 1985.

———. *The U-Boat Hunters*. Toronto: University of Toronto and Annapolis, MD: NIP, 1994.

Morison, S. E. *The History of U.S. Naval Operations in the Second World War*. Vols. 1 and 10. Boston: Little, Brown, 1947–1962.

Price, Alfred. *Aircraft vs. Submarine: The Evolution of the Anti-Submarine Aircraft, 1912 to 1980*. London and New York: Jane's, 1980.

Rohwer, Jürgen. *Axis Submarine Successes 1939–1945*. Annapolis, MD: NIP, 1983.

———. *The Critical Convoy Battles of March 1943*. Annapolis, MD: NIP, 1977.

Rohwer, Jürgen, and Gerhard Hummelchen. *Chronology of the War at Sea*. Rev. ed. Annapolis, MD: NIP, 1992.

Roskill, S. W. *The War at Sea*. London: HMSO, 1956–1961.

Rossler, E. *The U-Boat*. London: Arms and Armour, 1981.

Runyan, Timothy, and Jan M. Copes, eds. *To Die Gallantly: The Battle of the Atlantic*. Boulder, CO: Westview, 1994.

Schoenfeld, Max. *Stalking the U-boat: USAAF Offensive Antisubmarine Operations in World War II*. Washington, DC: Smithsonian, 1995.

———. "Winston Churchill as War Manager: The Battle of the Atlantic Committee, 1941." *Military Affairs* 52 (1988): 122–27.

Schull, Joseph. *The Far Distant Ships. An Official Account of Canadian Naval Operations in World War II*. Ottawa: Kings' Printer, 1950; reprinted, Toronto: Stoddart, 1987.

Silverstone, Paul H. *U.S. Warships of World War II*. New York: Doubleday, 1965.

Sternhell, C. M., and A. M. Thorndike. *Anti-Submarine Warfare in World War II*. Washington, DC: Office of the Chief of Naval Operations, 1946.

Syrett, David. *The Defeat of the German U-Boats*. Columbia: University of South Carolina, 1994.

Tarrant, V. E. *The U-Boat Offensive, 1914–1945*. Annapolis, MD: NIP, 1989.

Terraine, J. *The U-Boat Wars, 1916–1945*. New York: Putnam, 1989. Published in the United Kingdom as *Business in Great Waters: The U-Boat Wars, 1916–1945*. London: Leo Cooper, 1989.

Tucker, G. N. *The Naval Service of Canada*. Ottawa: Queen's Printer, 1952.

Van der Vat, Dan. *The Atlantic Campaign*. New York: Harper and Row, 1988.

Waters, John M. *Bloody Winter*. Princeton: Van Nostrand, 1967; Annapolis, MD: NIP, 1994.

Winterbotham, F. W. *The Ultra Secret*. New York: Harper and Row, 1974.

Y'Blood, William. *Hunter-Killer*. Annapolis, MD: NIP, 1983.

Zimmerman, D. *The Great Naval Battle of Ottawa*. Toronto: University of Toronto, 1988.

12 Grand Strategy and the "Second Front" Debate

Brian P. Farrell

The Grand Alliance of the Second World War, based on cooperation between the United States of America and the United Kingdom, was, despite serious friction, history's most effective example of coalition warfare. From the start its strategy was that Nazi Germany must be defeated first. That agreement was shaped by a prior event that changed the nature of the conflict: the German victories in Western Europe in the spring of 1940, which forced France to accept an armistice and evicted British forces from the European Continent. The question of how and when Allied forces could return to the Continent, under what conditions and with what objective, steadily became the central issue in Allied grand strategy. The debates animating that grand strategy ran from the spring of 1941 into 1944, when the great Continental campaign of 1944–1945 became the main Allied offensive of the Second World War. This chapter assesses the representative literature and research regarding the formulation of grand strategy revolving around the "Second Front" debate, from the genesis of the American–British alliance in late 1940 to the end of 1943. While most important studies have generally reflected its central contemporary features, there has been no shortage of revisionism on different grounds, and the debate has expanded as archives have opened, and perspectives have lengthened. The main concerns of research remain the central direction of the war; coalition diplomacy; the organization, equipment, and deployment of mass armed forces; the clash of national policies and objectives; problems of command and personalities at the highest levels; and the impact of the course of the war itself.

The first task of a military coalition is finding a common ground for the direction of the war from the different policies and strategies suggested by its members. They must agree on the main objective and how it may best be achieved. The American–British alliance found it relatively easy to define the goal: the unconditional surrender of their enemies, starting with Germany. The problem and the enduring controversy came with the attempt to define the best strategy to accomplish that task. The subsequent literature revolved around the issue of whether or not the best possible military-political result was achieved, and if not, why not. The first and strongest theme was that conflicting national agendas produced and shaped the strategic debate.

In 1946 Elliott Roosevelt, son of the late president, published *As He Saw It*, followed in 1948 by Robert Sherwood's *Roosevelt and Hopkins*, a study of the relationship between the president and his confidant based on the latter's papers. Their theme was similar: clever manipulation by the British prevented the Allies from pursuing the straightforward, American-proposed strategy focused on bringing the German main force to battle and defeating it as rapidly as possible. This launched the great Second Front debate in postwar research and staked out its main theme: the British prolonged the war by fighting with an eye on "ulterior" postwar "political" prospects, that is, the Soviet threat, while the Americans tried to establish an "honest" strategy based on "military" concerns alone. These arguments were dramatically reinforced in 1958, when General Wedemeyer, an American heavily involved in wartime strategic planning, published his outspoken memoir, *Wedemeyer Reports!* Wedemeyer claimed the British maneuvered the Allies into dispersing military power to conduct campaigns on the Axis' periphery; this prevented the concentration of force for an early decisive Continental campaign. The aim was to preserve British influence by preventing the Allies from launching the campaign that the Americans by default must have led. Ironically, American strategy would have left the Allies in a more favorable military-political position.

The counterblast was already under way, with the debate heavily influenced by the collapse of the Allied–Soviet wartime alliance and the onset of the Cold War. The most famous of several works that espoused the "British case" was *The Struggle for Europe* by Australian journalist Chester Wilmot. His argument had a lasting impact on popular perception: whereas the British strategy of operating on the periphery with an eye on the postwar situation might have prevented the Red Army from overrunning Eastern and much of Central Europe, unfortunately, the "narrowly military" American strategy prevailed. The Allies concentrated their might in France, and the Iron Curtain reached the Elbe. This Cold War prism was further reinforced by the publication, from 1948 on, of the six-volume memoirs of the man at the very center of the controversy, Winston Churchill.

Churchill's *The Second World War* dwelt at length on American–British strategy and the invasion of Western Europe. The title of the final volume, *Triumph and Tragedy*, expressed his theme. The Allied triumph over Nazi barbarism was tragically reduced by the failure to reap the full fruits of that victory. The Americans insisted on concentrating forces for a decisive campaign in Western Europe and rejected all British warnings that wartime strategy must not ignore the possibility of a rift with the unpredictable communist giant in the East. With this the battle lines were well and truly drawn. Churchill's theme fit the mood of the time; his wartime position, massive reputation, literary persuasiveness, and access to contemporary sources all brought the debate to a large readership.

Churchill used his privileged position to base his account on the official records of the government and high command—correspondence, reports, minutes—still largely withheld from public scrutiny. He was assisted by a syndicate that included some who served under him in very senior positions during the war. This galvanized the "battle of the memoirs." On the British side the important contributions were General Morgan's *Overture to Overlord* and Bryant's two-volume *Turn of the Tide* and *Triumph in the West*. Morgan supervised the drafting of the Overlord outline plan in 1943 and remained a key man on the supreme allied commander's staff when the plan was revised, and preparations commenced in earnest in 1944. He made two important, if often later overlooked, points: the British were far from unanimous in their skepticism regarding a Second Front in 1944, and the outline of the invasion and subsequent campaign was far advanced by the time the final command team took charge in January 1944. Bryant's account was based on the diaries of the wartime chief of the Imperial General Staff, Alan Brooke. Brooke felt Churchill's claim to have been the architect of British strategy obscured the pivotal role played by the British Chiefs of Staff. This dispute aside, Bryant and Brooke wholeheartedly agreed with Churchill that the fruits of the Mediterranean campaign were wasted by rigid American insistence on concentrating on the invasion of Western Europe, come what may.

The 1950s also saw the emergence of the official histories, a collective effort on the British side and a separate endeavor by the services in the United States. Teams of researchers, some organized during the war itself, enjoyed privileged access to official documents in order to produce an authoritative and didactic interpretation of the many facets of the national or service war experience. While crude, direct interference with the record or the interpretation was not common, the disclaimers could not erase the impression of an "official" stamp of approval. Yet the massive resources employed, the mandate to explore the war experience in painstaking detail, and access to official documents made these works the starting point for serious research and the basis of many later more popular efforts. The American volumes appeared with citations for later reference; the British suffered from their more restrictive attitude to archival material, and no volumes appeared with citations until the general release of the bulk of wartime records in 1972.

On the British side, useful discussions can be found in the Naval Series,

The War at Sea, the Campaign Series, The Mediterranean and the Middle East, the later series on British Intelligence in the Second World War, and in volumes of the Civil Series that dealt with Allied economic organization and cooperation. But the important studies are the disappointing campaign study *Victory in the West* by Ellis et al. and volumes 2 through 5 of the landmark series *Grand Strategy* by Butler, Gwyer, Howard, and Ehrman. In the United States, the multivolume study *History of United States Naval Operations in World War II* by Morison made the most controversial intervention. More important are the relevant volumes of the massive U.S. Army study, listed here in order of importance for this issue: the two volumes of *Strategic Planning for Coalition Warfare* by Matloff and Snell; *Cross-Channel Attack* by Harrison; the two-volume *Global Logistics and Strategy* by Leighton and Coakley; essays in *Command Decisions*, edited by then Chief Military Historian Greenfield; *Washington Command Post* by Cline; and *Supreme Command* by Pogue.

Varying in quality from suspect to landmark scholarship, these volumes gave the debate over strategy in Europe much needed structure and foundation. Together the more than a dozen different series that explored the question in whole or in part produced a very broad three-part consensus. First, few disagreed that Allied debate is best understood as continuous, focusing directly on the invasion of Western Europe to the very end of 1943—with shifts in emphasis reflecting strategic decisions and the course of the war. Second, while the positions of those involved crossed national lines, the basic differences stemmed from a clash between American and British concepts of grand strategy. Finally, the end product was a blend of the two concepts adapted to circumstances. This last point remains the most controversial and certainly the most important, analytical contribution made by official historians.

It was also widely agreed that four factors shaped the wartime debate. First, German military power was the root of the problem. British historians emphasized the concern of the British high command that the German army was strong enough, even while still heavily engaged in the East, to beat off any premature Allied invasion. Second, the United States entered the war only in December 1941, unprepared for the total war its planners envisaged as culminating in a decisive Continental campaign. The long years of the debate were also the period of American mobilization; no study overlooked the connection. Third, nearly all authors agreed that Allied principals always accepted the need for ground forces to return to the Continent; but most stressed the grave differences of opinion over the prerequisites, objective, and nature of any invasion and subsequent campaign. Finally, no official historian neglected to make the point that although influence shifted as American strength grew, the Grand Alliance was, and always remained, interdependent.

The official histories all saw dramatic differences in American and British strategic situations and traditions as a major cause of the long debate. American planners expected to wield abundant military power and accepted a strategic tradition of bringing wars to a conclusion as rapidly as possible by engineering a decisive clash with the main foe on the main front. British planners were haunted by the losses of 1914–1918 and intimidated by their defeats of 1940–1941 and looked forward to declining resources. They believed the Allies must find a way to defeat the main foe by attrition without confronting its main force in a death struggle. Official historians also concurred that this debate was fatally confused by circumstances. In 1942 American plans for concentrating forces for an early invasion seemed hopelessly unrealistic to the British, who alone had the forces that could have led any such effort then or in 1943. This produced a dispute and a subsequent shift in strategy, which affected the course of the war and launched the great debate on this question. Beyond these broad agreements, the official histories became a complex mass of charge, countercharge, and attempted synthesis.

In *Victory in the West,* Ellis made only one contribution. He conceded that although the British never aimed to scrap Overlord altogether, the Americans did have grounds for being uneasy about the British commitment, even in late 1943, to invade Western Europe. But he argued that the British were rightly concerned that the Americans did not understand how imperative it was to meet the prerequisites for launching the campaign. In other respects Ellis accepted the interpretation of the *Grand Strategy* series.

The thrust of the argument, led by Howard and Ehrman, was as follows. The British brought into 1942 a broad but well-developed strategy: to wear down German power by strategic bombing and peripheral campaigns. This was based on a sound appreciation of the formidable combat power of the German army and the unreadiness of the Allies to tackle it. The arguments that produced operation Torch and the Mediterranean offensive were caused by a premature bid by the Americans to concentrate on a Continental campaign. The ensuing campaigns in 1943 sensibly carried the Mediterranean offensive forward, while slowly but steadily the Allies prepared for a Continental invasion when the time was ripe. By late 1943 the Americans were strong enough to oblige the British to accept a redesigned Continental invasion for 1944, with clearly defined and achievable prerequisites. This depicted a British strategy soberly conceived and consistently pursued, based on operational considerations first and foremost—with perhaps a touch of undue hesitation by the end of 1943, overcome by American resolve. Still worth reading is Ehrman's powerful denunciation of claims that the British pursued any hidden agenda in the Mediterranean or anywhere else.

On the broadest lines, American official historians generally agreed among themselves. The U.S. Army was the driving force in shaping the strategy to concentrate for a decisive Continental campaign in Europe. Its first outline, operations Sledgehammer and Roundup, was vetoed by the British as premature. That forced the Americans to redesign their strategy, as the Mediterranean campaign absorbed Allied resources. From spring 1943 they fought to establish Overlord, a somewhat different offensive, as the basis of Allied strategy for 1944. Beyond this point, the debate was enriched by important differences in explaining how and why Roundup became Overlord.

Morison took the most emphatic "national" line. In a direct rebuttal to Bryant, most accessible in the book *Strategy and Compromise*, he bluntly stated that without American pressure there would have been no Overlord. The main Allied advance would have been through Italy, as desired by Brooke. None of the U.S. Army historians went this far, but they did not produce a monolithic interpretation. Harrison's *Cross-Channel Attack* was the first and remains the most comprehensive official history volume to trace the issue from conception through execution. He saw Overlord as a synthesis, stemming from circumstances but also tracing roots back to some British and American strategic ideas of 1940–1941. Nevertheless, Harrison did agree that the Americans consistently fought for a strategy based on a decisive Continental campaign, against British resistance.

Matloff and Snell's *Strategic Planning for Coalition Warfare* became the standard American interpretation. The American doctrine of concentrating forces for the earliest possible decisive campaign was overcome in the summer of 1942 because the United States lacked the military strength to support its plans. At the Casablanca conference in January 1943 the Joint Chiefs of Staff were unable to present a persuasive alternative to a Mediterranean campaign in that year. This forced them to rethink their concept of a strategic offensive. The result was Overlord, a final triumph for the adjusted, but not abandoned, American strategy to bring about a decisive Continental campaign.

The next step was taken by Greenfield, in work culminating in *American Strategy in World War II*. This piece benefited from both the official histories and memoirs and the only academic study of lasting value published to that point, *Churchill, Roosevelt, Stalin* by Feis. Greenfield agreed that the Americans saw British strategy as unsound and unduly "political," while the British saw American strategy as narrow, doctrinaire, and rigid. Yet he insisted that after the decision to launch operation Torch, no fundamental dispute remained between the parties over grand strategy and the invasion of Europe. Both Allies agreed that an invasion must be the "knockout blow." What they disputed were its timing and scale. The final answer was an Allied strategy based on the American concept of seeking decisive military victory on the Continent but executed in a series of compromises shaped by British pragmatism and opportunism. This rejected the "either-or" Cold War construct as ahistorical.

The official histories written by Leighton and Coakley not only offered a truly fresh perspective, treating the production and allocation of war matériel as an integral part of grand strategy, but also spawned a summary of the first wave of the literature on this topic. Leighton's "Overlord Revisited" took Greenfield one step further. Leighton bluntly rejected the stark distinction drawn between an American "sincere military strategy" and a British "devious political strategy." Grand strategy, adjusted on both sides by circumstances, blended two differing basic national strategies until neither survived to dominate. Most important, accusations such as Wedemeyer's regarding the British agenda reflected not British statements and actions but unwarranted American suspicions. Though far from the last word, this marked a new depth to a literature now boasting a substantial body of serious studies based on official records.

Critics nevertheless continued the "we gained the triumph, you caused the tragedy" theme but now found it more difficult to sustain without careful archival research. In this respect, stubborn British retention of official records left an opening. It was seized by Higgins in works published from 1957 to 1968. They propelled a transition from the first wave, dominated by journalistic accounts, memoirs, and official histories, to a more focused literature based on more accessible records, longer and different perspectives, and new questions. Higgins argued that the official histories underestimated the impact of personalities; he challenged this in *Winston Churchill and the Second Front 1940–1943* and *Soft Underbelly*.

Higgins saw British strategy as the product of the drive and personality of Churchill and Brooke and the arguments against Roundup and Overlord as British justifications and rationalizations. He agreed that the British did not make strategy with one eye on a Soviet threat before 1944; nevertheless, untroubled by the lack of a single British document and relying on the recollections of American principals, his conclusion was emphatic. British strategy regarding the invasion of Europe showed a "profound and long-standing British determination . . . to sacrifice the urgent needs of coalition strategy to those of their own traditional policy" (222). To conserve their power, prestige, and social order, the British resisted Overlord and pressed for an all-out effort in the Mediterranean.

Higgins' 1970 essay, "The Anglo-American Historians' War in the Mediterranean," was an indispensable, if idiosyncratic, insight into the debate. The main target was Leighton and his attempt to debunk American charges against the British. The dispute was fundamental, the Americans rightly feared at least the consequences of British arguments for a delay of Overlord, and the British were not opportunists. The Second Front argument was really a clash of national interests and policies. Interpretations of that argument were colored by the political views of the scholar. "Left"-leaning historians opposed the so-called Mediterranean strategy, whereas "right"-wing scholars lamented its replacement. Full circle? Not quite. Higgins failed to drive home his rejection of Leighton without any firsthand evidence regarding British perceptions, and a powerful voice had already rejected simplistic claims that grand strategy was militarily pristine and/or personality-driven.

In 1968, four years before his volume 4 of the *Grand Strategy* series was released, Howard's *The Mediterranean Strategy in the Second World War* began the second "wave" of study of the Second Front debate. Howard picked up where Leighton left off. The British felt the Allies were too weak militarily to pursue any devious strategic blueprint for staking out postwar claims. They formulated their strategy by seizing any opportunity to keep the pressure on the enemy without risking a confrontation with its main force. Sledgehammer and Roundup were rejected because the British believed they would end in disaster. Operations were pursued in the Mediterranean because it was seen as an area where the enemy could be engaged and should be weakened. Fear of the German army, not the Red Army, drove British strategy, even in the difficult arguments of late 1943, when the British looked to delay Overlord until it seemed safe—not scuttle it altogether. This incisive answer to Higgins' sensationalism capped the existing literature. It also helped provoke a new generation to ask more probing questions about how politicians and staff officers formulated Allied strategy and why the Second Front came about as it did.

Howard's work made no impact on the Soviets. Their view of this question remained monolithic for over forty years. A typical account was Issraeljan's *The Anti-Hitler Coalition*. The capitalist powers hoped to see the Nazis and Soviets exhaust each other; that would allow them to dictate postwar reorganization. Therefore they deliberately delayed launching a Continental campaign in Northwest Europe, until direct pressure from Stalin at Teheran in November 1943 forced their hand. Few Western scholars disagreed that Overlord was finally cast in stone at Teheran. Most rejected the claim that there was a united American–British position. Fruitful developments in American scholarship moved things forward in this respect.

This work did not discard the "national dispute" focus. But it asked more critical questions about American strategy. Steele broke an important barrier in 1973 with his *The First Offensive 1942*. The first really blunt criticism of Marshall, hitherto canonized by Americans, it argued that the agenda of American strategy was every bit as "political" as the British. For Steele, domestic and institutional politics drove the crucial arguments of 1942. Roosevelt, seeking the solid support of American public opinion for the "Germany first" policy, readily supported whatever strategy promised to win it in 1942. Marshall and his staff tried to exploit this to advance Roundup, whose ultimate aim was to entrench the strategic doctrine of the U.S. Army as Allied grand strategy. With the British and Americans both concealing their most urgent goals, the American clash of priorities led to a dangerous deadlock. Marshall found himself forced to defend Sledgehammer, the militarily preposterous plan for invasion in 1942, in order to retain the support of the president and force the British to accept the real objective, concentration on Roundup in 1943. The British veto saved the Allies from probable military disaster.

Steele's trenchant observations about whether it made sense to draw distinctions between "political" and "military" concerns in making strategy at the highest level suggested that those involved could not, dare not, ignore one or the other. But Steele overemphasized the personal roles of Roosevelt and Marshall and left the problem hanging in the autumn of 1942. Stoler kept things moving with his *The Politics of the Second Front.* He focused on the Americans but examined the formulation of Allied strategy through its final resolution in late 1943. The whole Second Front question was a "heavily political" issue from the start; and all three coalition partners made their arguments well aware of this fact. Stoler went as far as to argue that American military and political leaders based their whole strategy on this very premise. A Second Front not only best suited the preferred doctrine of bringing about an early decisive campaign on the main front, but would also enable the United States to impose its leadership and policy on the Grand Alliance.

American planners assumed from the start that British arguments concealed a hidden agenda, so they insisted that their own strategy focused only on the "correct" objective of defeating the enemy. Their suspicions of the Soviet agenda matured in 1943 and reinforced the determination to make sure Overlord entrenched American control of Allied strategy. The Mediterranean campaign was resisted not merely because it was "politically inspired" but because it was incompatible with American political goals and interests. All three major Allies tried to use their combined strength to their individual advantage, in a tug-of-war between the common cause and self-interest. Stoler could not resist trying to explain the "real" motives of British strategy, rejecting without any convincing evidence Howard's thesis of opportunism based on perceived military weakness. But he did strip away the self-righteous myths that one side made "honest" strategy while the other played dishonorable games by demonstrating that it was impossible to make grand strategy without weighing a host of factors.

These works made it clear that grand strategy must be seen as a complex problem for all concerned. Yet they did not end the visceral fascination with the question of whether an earlier Second Front was feasible and why it was never launched. The most ambitious study was Dunn's *Second Front Now.* Dunn explained why Roundup gave way to Overlord by first assessing the "actual" strategic situation of 1942–1944 and then comparing it with the diagnosis made and the strategy pursued in London, Washington, and Berlin. His thesis was blunt. The original strategy, to concentrate forces for Roundup, was sound. The global correlation of forces favored the Allies. They changed things by opting for Torch and dispersing their forces, compounding this by the pursuit of a Mediterranean campaign in 1943. This needlessly prolonged the war. Why? Because Dunn believed "the fact that the decision was made supposedly on military grounds that are not supported under close scrutiny leads us to search for other reasons" (268). The British, unwilling to pay the price demanded by the best strategy, suppressed unwelcome intelligence and overrated German power.

Dunn inspired only one serious confederate, Grigg's *1943: The Victory That Never Was*. Grigg made a similar argument, with a few notable twists. The Allies underestimated latent French strength as an asset. The crucial decision was not Torch but the Casablanca compromise, with the Americans as much to blame as the British. Both revived the accusation, based now on more substantial research, that this "error" compromised the postwar situation. Neither put across the counterfactual main argument, mainly because there was no evidence for the key points—an invasion never launched must have succeeded, British or Allied leaders definitely accepted but suppressed this "fact," and, all things considered, this would have been the "best" solution.

Such work prompted critics to develop Howard's thesis: what drove British strategy was a sincere evaluation of the cost of tackling the German army. Bruce's reply, *Second Front Now!*, went too far by reversing the old myths. The Americans pursued a hidden agenda; the British, a realistic strategy focused only on objective facts. This book bogged down in the narrow world of the planners and British archives but made the popular argument that Overlord was the right answer at the right time. In a more substantial work, Strange took up this argument in "The British Rejection of Operation Sledgehammer."

Strange closely reexamined the reasons for the British veto in 1942. He argued that the repeated defeats of British and Imperial armies from 1940 into 1942 convinced British leaders that their forces were unable to challenge German ground forces on anything approaching equal terms. Therefore, an invasion of the Continent must follow the success of, not be the main stroke in, the strategy of attrition. This thesis restored a strong consensus, at least among historians of British strategy, on the main issue. The British resisted all attempts to base Allied strategy on concentrating to invade Western Europe, until they were overborne at the Teheran conference, because they saw this as an excessive risk strategy. Even if it succeeded, they feared being broken in the process.

Such arguments were expanded in Ben-Moshe's *Churchill: Strategy and History*. Specialist studies also joined the queue. Stafford's *Britain and European Resistance* demonstrated how the British concept of invading Western Europe developed from 1940 step by step. Plans moved from dispersed invasions led by armored forces, aiming to set off a resistance uprising, to the conventional campaign envisaged from 1942 on—but always conditioned by the perception of relative military weakness on the ground. Underlining the whole issue was Sainsbury's definitive study of Allied conference diplomacy, *The Turning Point.* At the Teheran conference the blend of Allied strategies was at last completed. Joint American–Soviet insistence overcame British hesitations based on strategic pessimism first, prestige concerns second.

By the 1990s this literature had established as conventional wisdom that "politics" could never be divorced from any party to the Second Front debate. Yet the tendency persisted to see the problem as stemming from a clash of national strategies. More controversy lingered on the British side. Charmley's *Churchill* turned the original accusation upside down. Churchill's narrow and stubborn focus on operational concerns needlessly sapped British strength as a world power by trapping them in a global total war beyond their means; Overlord was the final disaster. But, for the most part, this thesis remained unpopular. The mainstream views regarding the debate were well expressed in a 1994 collection of studies by Soviet, American, and British scholars of the wartime coalition, *Allies at War,* edited by David Reynolds and others. They reflected both the "clash of national strategies" theme and the broader lines of consensus regarding Allied strategy and the invasion of Western Europe.

Written to sum up the "state of the question," this collection made the point that the problem of coalition warfare can be understood only by assessing the views of all three principals. The most startling new development came in the essay by Rzheshevsky, "The Soviet Union: The Direct Strategy," which made no reference at all to the old accusation that for ideological reasons a viable Second Front was deliberately delayed. Danchev's summary, "Great Britain: The Indirect Strategy," underlined the broad consistency of British literature. The essence of British grand strategy was "not to lose the war"; the major contribution was to prevent the launching of a premature Second Front. There never was a "Mediterranean strategy"; British strategy was made by improvisation, based on the guiding principle that the ground forces were overmatched. The Allies could neither have held off a German response to invasion in 1943 nor accepted the broad dangers of remaining inactive while concentrating forces for a reckless main thrust. The British argued in 1943 to delay and modify Overlord, not prevent it, and they got it exactly right.

Stoler's reply, "The United States: The Global Strategy," reflected the greater movement in both American strategy and postwar literature. American grand strategy, always focused on global war, needed to maintain domestic political support, service cooperation, and American dominance in coalition strategy. The final strategy based on Overlord was a marked departure in practice from the original concept, caused as much by the decision to dilute the "Germany First" agreement as by any British actions. Nevertheless, this blend of Allied strategies was a triumph in itself and vindicated American ability to adapt to changing circumstances and the compulsions of coalition warfare.

British scholars now widely agreed that the transition at Teheran was timely. In turn, Stoler indicated that few American scholars now reject British explanations for a delay in 1943. Together their final consensus sums up the state of the literature: with the appointment of Eisenhower and the "first team" in December 1943, Allied grand strategy now settled on a new basis, conditioned not on British weakness but on Allied strength. Allied ground forces would return to the Continent to fight, rather than merely mop up. The literature has thus largely shed itself of the Cold War prism but remains concerned with the central direction of the war and the even larger question of British decline. These issues are best summarized in the context of the event inextricably linked to the great Second Front debate: the Allied campaign in Northwest Europe in 1944–1945.

BIBLIOGRAPHY

Ben-Moshe, Tuvia. *Churchill: Strategy and History*. Boulder, CO: Lynne Rienner and Hemel Hampstead: Harvester Wheatsheaf, 1992.
———. "Winston Churchill and the Second Front: A Reappraisal." *Journal of Modern History 62* (1990): 503–37.
Bruce, George L. *Second Front Now!* London: MacDonald and Janes, 1979.
Bryant, Arthur. *Triumph in the West*. London: Collins; Garden City, NJ: Doubleday, 1959, 1971.
———. *The Turn of the Tide*. London: Collins and New York: Doubleday, 1957, 1965.
Butler, J.R.M. *Grand Strategy*. Vol. 2, *September 1939–June 1941*. London: HMSO, 1957.
Butler, J.R.M., and J.M.A. Gwyer. *Grand Strategy*. Vol. 3, *June 1941–August 1942*. London: HMSO, 1964.
Charmley, John. *Churchill: The End of Glory*. London: Hodder and Stoughton, 1993.
Churchill, Winston S. *The Second World War: The Grand Alliance*. Boston: Houghton Mifflin, 1950.
———. *The Second World War: The Hinge of Fate*. Boston: Houghton Mifflin, 1950.
———. *The Second World War: Closing the Ring*. Boston: Houghton Mifflin, 1951.
———. *The Second World War: Triumph and Tragedy*. Boston: Houghton Mifflin, 1954.
Cline, Ray S. *Washington Command Post: The Operations Division*. Washington, DC: Office of the Chief of Military History, 1951.
Danchev, Alex. "Great Britain: The Indirect Strategy." In David Reynolds et al., eds., *Allies at War*, 1–26. New York: St. Martin's, 1994.
Dunn, Walter S. *Second Front Now—1943*. University: University of Alabama, 1979.

Ehrman, John. *Grand Strategy*. Vol. 5, *August 1943–September 1944*. London: HMSO, 1956.

———. *Grand Strategy*. Vol. 6, *September 1944–September 1945*. London: HMSO, 1956.

Ellis, Lionel F., with G.R.G. Allen et al. *Victory in the West*. Vol. 1, *The Battle of Normandy*. London: HMSO, 1962.

Feis, Herbert. *Churchill, Roosevelt, Stalin*. Princeton: Princeton UP, 1957.

Greenfield, Kent R. *American Strategy in World War II*. Baltimore: Johns Hopkins UP, 1963.

———. *Command Decisions*. Washington, DC: Office of the Chief of Military History, 1960.

Grigg, John. *1943: The Victory That Never Was*. London: Eyre Methuen, 1980.

Harrison, Gordon. *Cross-Channel Attack*. Washington, DC: Office of the Chief of Military History, 1951.

Higgins, Trumbull. "The Anglo-American Historians' War in the Mediterranean." *Military Affairs 34* (1970): 84–88.

———. *Soft Underbelly: The Anglo-American Controversy over the Italian Campaign, 1939–1945*. London: Macmillan, 1968.

———. *Winston Churchill and the Second Front 1940–1943*. Oxford and New York: Oxford UP, 1957.

Howard, Michael. *Grand Strategy*. Vol. 4, *August 1942–September 1943*. London: HMSO, 1972.

———. *The Mediterranean Strategy in the Second World War*. London: Weidenfeld and Nicolson, 1968.

Issraeljan, Victor. *The Anti-Hitler Coalition*. Moscow: Progress, 1971.

Leighton, Richard M. *Global Logistics and Strategy 1943–1945*. Washington, DC: Office of the Chief of Military History, 1968.

———. "Overlord Revisited: An Interpretation of American Strategy in the European War." *American Historical Review 67* (1963): 919–37.

Leighton, Richard M., and Robert W. Coakley. *Global Logistics and Strategy 1940–1943*. Washington, DC: Office of the Chief of Military History, 1955.

Matloff, Maurice. *Strategic Planning for Coalition Warfare 1943–1944*. Washington, DC: Office of the Chief of Military History, 1959.

Matloff, Maurice, and E. M. Snell. *Strategic Planning for Coalition Warfare 1941–1942*. Washington, DC: Office of the Chief of Military History, 1953.

Morgan, F. E. *Overture to Overlord*. New York: Doubleday, 1950.

Morison, Samuel Eliot. *History of United States Naval Operations in World War II*. Vol. 1, *The Battle of the Atlantic 1939–1943*. Boston: Houghton Mifflin, 1964.

———. *History of United States Naval Operations in World War II*. Vol. 10, *The Atlantic Battle Won May 1943–May 1945*. Boston: Houghton Mifflin, 1964.

———. *Strategy and Compromise*. Boston: Little, Brown, 1958.

Pogue, Forrest C. *The Supreme Command*. Washington, DC: Office of the Chief of Military History, 1954.

Reynolds, David, et al., eds. *Allies at War: The Soviet, American and British Experience, 1939–1945*. New York: St. Martin's, 1994.

Roosevelt, Elliott. *As He Saw It*. New York: Duell, Sloan, and Pearce, 1946.

Rzheshevsky, Oleg A. "The Soviet Union: The Direct Strategy." In David Reynolds et al., eds., *Allies at War*, 27–54. New York: St. Martin's, 1994.

Sainsbury, Keith. *The Turning Point*. Oxford and New York: Oxford UP, 1985.

Sherwood, Robert E. *Roosevelt and Hopkins: An Intimate History.* New York: Harper and Brothers, 1948.

Stafford, David. *Britain and European Resistance 1940–1945: A Survey of the SOE.* London: Macmillan, 1980.

———. "The Detonator Concept: British Strategy, SOE and European Resistance." *Journal of Contemporary History* 10 (1975): 186–209.

Steele, R. W. *The First Offensive 1942: Roosevelt, Marshall and the Making of American Strategy.* Bloomington: Indiana UP, 1973.

Stoler, Mark. *The Politics of the Second Front.* Westport, CT: Greenwood, 1977.

———. "The United States: The Global Strategy." In David Reynolds et al., eds., *Allies at War,* 55–78. New York: St. Martin's, 1994.

Strange, J. L. "The British Rejection of Operation Sledgehammer: An Alternative Motive." *Military Affairs* 46 (1982): 6–14.

Wedemeyer, A. C. *Wedemeyer Reports!* New York: Henry Holt, 1958.

Wilmot, Chester. *The Struggle for Europe.* London: Collins; New York: Harper and Row, 1952; Westport, CT: Greenwood, 1972; New York: Carroll and Graeff, 1986.

13 Anglo-American Strategy and Command in Northwest Europe, 1944–1945

D.K.R. Crosswell

Generations of historians, taking their lead from wartime confrontations between Eisenhower and Montgomery and the memoir literature, cast the debate over strategy and command in the 1944–1945 campaigns in Northwest Europe along national and egocentric lines. They generally fell into two camps: defenders of Eisenhower's broad-front approach and those who maintained that a more aggressive, less deterministic application of Allied strength would have ended the war more quickly, at less cost, and on terms more favorable to the Western powers. The controversy served as the leitmotif of all histories of the campaigns in Northwest Europe.

The chief protagonists—Eisenhower and Montgomery—strove to preserve the appearance of Anglo-American cooperation in the immediate postwar years. Alive to the need to preserve the alliance, both men feared the repercussions of "a battle of the books." In 1945 Montgomery asked Eisenhower to adjust his report on operations in Europe to minimize discordant views, particularly whether Montgomery altered the strategy in Normandy. Eisenhower thought success in Normandy derived from Allied flexibility, not from adherence to a predetermined formula, but ordered the report changed to suit the field marshal. The official common front proved short-lived.

The historiography of the European campaign begins with Ingersoll's vitriolic *Top Secret*. Ingersoll, the Ultra officer in Bradley's Twelfth Army Group headquarters, portrayed Eisenhower as a political general, pliable in the hands of Churchill. The British dominated strategy making, through placing their officers in key command and staff positions. Concentrating upon the most divisive issues—Montgomery's command in Normandy; Eisenhower's priority on the northern drive at the expense of Bradley's offensive; the conduct of the Ardennes fighting and the decision to place two American armies under Montgomery's command; the closing and crossing of the Rhine; and the decision not to advance on Berlin—Ingersoll highlighted wartime differences. A best-seller, the book demarcated the historical debate that followed.

Eisenhower's naval aide, Butcher, published the headquarters diary, *My Three Years with Eisenhower*, in 1946. Although Butcher, at Eisenhower's insistence, softened passages dealing chiefly with Montgomery and de Gaulle in the published version, the book, emanating from the supreme commander's inner circle, lent credence to Ingersoll's assertion that the alliance was riven by personality and national divisions.

Eisenhower's reputation suffered further erosion with the publication of the posthumous memoir of Patton, *War as I Knew It*, Montgomery's *Normandy to the Baltic*, and Grigg's *Prejudice and Judgment*. Patton and Montgomery made similar cases: Supreme Headquarters, Allied Expeditionary Force (SHAEF) missed the opportunity to defeat the Germans in the West by clinging too rigidly to the broad front. Montgomery lauded Eisenhower for balancing the Allied team while minimizing the command dispute. The deepening Cold War sharpened criticism of the "incomplete Allied victory" in the West. Grigg, wartime British secretary of state for war, charged that SHAEF prolonged the war within a political context.

Deeply stung by the mounting criticisms, Eisenhower worried that "crackpot" histories would guide future students of the war. He approached his former chief of staff, Walter Bedell Smith, to write an unvarnished history of the campaign. Churchill had earlier made a similar plea. Smith declined, instead authoring six articles for the *Saturday Evening Post* in which he argued that the broad-front strategy evolved in joint planning as early as April 1944, and Overlord, from Normandy to the Elbe, never deviated from that basic plan. Montgomery's chief of staff, Francis de Guingand, offered further support in his balanced defense of Eisenhower's command and the broad-front strategy.

Driven to refute his American critics, Eisenhower published *Crusade in Europe*, defending the broad front. Eisenhower maintained that any shift in command relations during the campaign would have complicated operations, delaying German defeat. A single thrust, whether commanded by Montgomery or Bradley, required the immobilization of too many Allied divisions. Trying to avoid acrimony, he irritated the British with his unfavorable comparison of Brooke with Marshall. Eisenhower reopened the dispute over Normandy by claiming the British intended to spearhead the breakout to the Seine, but, faced by stiff German resistance, Montgomery shifted the center of gravity west, permitting Bradley's forces to break through and inaugurate the advance through France. In discussing Montgomery's single thrust, Eisenhower termed it "pencil like." Worse yet, Montgomery saw the book as a breach of the covenant not to personalize their differences of opinion.

Bradley offered his version in *Soldier's Story*. Laboring to disguise his distaste for Montgomery, Bradley framed his argument in doctrinal terms: British concentration against the American double advance that sought to exploit superiority of Allied ground and air strength and mobility. Interestingly, he sided with his old antagonist's interpretation of Normandy. Montgomery's plan called for the British seizure of Caen—here he differed with Montgomery—while the American forces under Bradley sealed the Cotentin peninsula, took Cherbourg, then executed the breakout and wheeling movements toward the Seine and Loire and into Brittany. Not only did Bradley's rendering of Normandy differ from Eisenhower's, but he thought the supreme commander should have asserted his authority over Montgomery earlier, especially over opening Antwerp. Market Garden, an operation to outflank German defenses, constituted a serious misdirection of Allied resources. Second, he believed Eisenhower seriously erred in giving Montgomery control over Hodges' and Simpson's armies during the Ardennes. Bradley claimed that while Montgomery genuinely believed in his strategic approach, the field marshal's primary focus centered on levering U.S. divisions from American control. In sharp contrast to Eisenhower, Bradley, alluding to Berlin, admitted that the American command, concentrating on the destruction of the German armies as the sole aim, disregarded political interests of enormous importance.

The 1950s historiographical contest became increasingly bitter, hardening along national lines. Wilmot's *The Struggle for Europe* rode on the crest of criticism of Eisenhower, offering a thoughtful and thoroughly researched critique of post-1943, American-steered strategy in Europe. The American direct approach in Northwest Europe demanded the diversion of strength from the Mediterranean through operation Anvil/Dragoon, landings in southern France which prevented the Allies from garnering the fruits of the campaign in Italy; since Marshall dispatched sixty American divisions to Europe, Eisenhower fashioned the broad front, frustrating more imaginative operations to exploit German vulnerability in France in 1944 and seize Berlin ahead of the Red Army in 1945. The decisions of Marshall and Eisenhower prolonged the campaign in Europe and in the process lost the peace and led to Britain's decline as a Great Power. Wilmot's book sidestepped the thorny issue of command relations, instead concentrating on strategic matters. The most frequently cited book produced in the 1950s, *Struggle for Europe*, held center stage in the historiographic debate for the next two decades.

Because Eisenhower then resided in the White House, Churchill's long-awaited *Triumph and Tragedy* exorcised all references to strategic differences in 1944 and the struggle over command. Centering on the failure to take Berlin and Prague, Churchill asserted the Cold War emanated from two decisions forced on the British by American policy makers—Anvil and the halt at the Elbe. The only wartime member of the Big Three to produce a memoir, Churchill's book occupied a uniquely authoritative position in the historiography of the European war.

Montgomery's and Brooke's memoirs generated heat. The field marshal tried to play down strategic divergences, preferring to highlight doctrinal differences and the fact that his caution derived from diminishing British manpower and matériel resources. His American opposite numbers never appreciated the price the British people had to pay for another year of war. As expected, Montgomery attacked Eisenhower's handling of the campaign in Europe: Eisenhower never understood the Normandy strategy, which proceeded exactly as planned; SHAEF, too remote from the fronts, could not exercise operational command. The appropriate model should have been the Mediterranean headquarters where Eisenhower delegated planning and operations to his commanders in chief. Mirroring Bradley, he claimed the American command never grasped the political ramifications of their single-tracked military strategy.

Brooke felt compelled to reply to Churchill's version of wartime decision making. Bryant's edition of Brooke's diaries demonstrated Brooke's low opinion of Eisenhower as a commander, as well as his deprecation of Marshall as a strategist. *Triumph in the West* revealed for the first time the concerted effort made before November 1944 and at the Malta conference to redefine the command apparatus in Europe. Making no effort to be diplomatic, Brooke believed the essential problem in Europe rested in SHAEF and faulty command relations.

Taken together, the British counteroffensive in the 1950s swept the field. Reduced to its simplest form, the common theme in Grigg, Wilmot, Churchill, Montgomery, and Bryant argued that while the British directed decision making, the Allies made no critical mistakes; but when Marshall and Eisenhower asserted their authority, the Allies lost opportunities to end the war quickly at less human and economic cost. If the war-ending single thrust had been executed, the argument went, the Cold War and the division of Europe would have been avoided.

The official histories of the 1950s and 1960s served as balanced correctives to the memoir literature. Arguably, the best in the American official histories (popularly known as the "green series") is Pogue's *Supreme Command*. As a study of a combined headquarters, the official history examining the war through the prism of SHAEF was supposed to be a joint effort. Satisfied with Pogue, the British allowed him to proceed alone. Lacking documentation on conferences in SHAEF and among the principal actors, Pogue relied on interviews. Except for officers in Montgomery's circle and, to a lesser extent, in the War Office, the interviewees roundly dismissed Montgomery's narrow front. In an effort to remain impartial, Pogue censored himself, refusing to use inflammatory observations. Instead he emphasized how the SHAEF machine, geared for a slow and measured advance through France, was thrown off-balance by the magnitude of Allied success. Unable to adjust logistics, SHAEF missed the opening to exploit the German collapse. Similarly, the agreed zonal boundaries and the train of events after the crossing of the Rhine precluded an advance on Berlin, which in any case would have required the intervention of the political heads. On balance, Pogue defended Eisenhower's decisions, but his reluctance to criticize Montgomery muted his efforts.

The second volume of Ruppenthal's *Logistical Support of the Armies* shifted the discussion away from strategy and command. Ruppenthal demonstrated that Eisenhower and SHAEF never properly organized the American side of the logistics command. Without a clearly defined chain of command, SHAEF tried to supersede the Communications Zone, further complicating a command system already thrown into chaos by the headlong rush of the armies eastward from Normandy. By mid-September logistical scarcity overrode operational planning, rendering any single thrust inoperative. Ruppenthal is still the best study on how logistics constrained operations in the crucial period between the crossing of the Seine and the opening of Antwerp.

Other volumes offer accounts of operations in France, Belgium and Luxembourg, and Germany. Harrison's *Cross-Channel Attack* covered D-Day and Normandy through the Cotentin phase. Blumenson followed up from the fall of Cherbourg through the advance to the Seine and beyond with his *Breakout and Pursuit.* MacDonald in *Siegfried Line Campaign* and Cole in *Lorraine Campaign* analyzed the autumn and winter campaigns along the frontiers. Cole's *Ardennes* reconstructed the Battle of the Bulge while MacDonald completed the story of the advance to the Elbe in *Last Offensive.* The last operational official history finally surfaced in 1993 with the release of *Riviera to the Rhine* by Clarke and Smith.

Stacey weighed in with the third volume in the Canadian official history, *The Victory Campaign.* The Canadian contribution to Allied victory in the gritty fighting in Normandy, on the northern flank in the Scheldt, and in the Rhineland frequently goes unacknowledged. The same can be said of Canadian military historians. Stacey's official history supported Eisenhower's decisions; a narrow thrust in the north, without opening Antwerp, could not have succeeded. On the contrary, Montgomery's Twenty-first Army Group could not have accomplished what it did in the Netherlands without Eisenhower's redirection of First U.S. Army northeast, even though this action deviated from Marshall's directives. In accordance with Pogue and Ruppenthal, Stacey posited that logistical shortages offered SHAEF little room for flexibility.

The long-delayed British official history, *Victory in the West* by Ellis, finally appeared in 1968. Having the advantage of time and access to memoirs, Ellis offered a judicious treatment of the strategic controversy. Ellis neither defended Montgomery nor chided Eisenhower, instead claiming both shared blame for failing to open Antwerp, the most critical error of the war in the West. Eisenhower should have asserted himself by insisting that the twenty-first Army Group open the Belgian port preparatory to any drive eastward while Montgomery, preoccupied with his diminished command, lunged at Arnhem, guaranteeing that the whole Allied offensive ground to a halt, owing to logistical shortages. Ellis, like Stacey and the American official historians, concluded that no single thrust could have ended the war in 1944.

Eisenhower left the White House in 1961 with his reputation sinking. The official historians did much to rehabilitate his military record, yet the image of Eisenhower as a vacillating political general persisted. The first signs of a reversal came with the publication of the memoirs of Churchill's chief of staff, Hastings Ismay, and Arthur Tedder, Eisenhower's deputy supreme commander in Europe and senior British officer in SHAEF. Both vigorously defended Eisenhower. Tedder condemned Churchill and Montgomery for distorting history and their machinations, along with Brooke, to impose a British ground commander. But Eisenhower revisionism did not make any real impact until 1970, with the publication of his wartime papers and the appearance of Ambrose's *Supreme Commander*.

Ambrose, an assistant editor of the *Eisenhower Papers*, single-handedly reversed the tide. Armed with an unerring command of the primary documents, Ambrose portrayed Eisenhower as much more than the amiable champion of Allied cooperation. Eisenhower's military diplomacy, more than his strategic capacity, earned him the European command. Having learned from hard experience before taking command of Allied forces for Overlord in January 1944, Eisenhower emerged sure and decisive, determined to exercise command. Ambrose's study made clear how Eisenhower worked through others. Given the clash of personalities and national and political sensitivities and susceptibilities, he spent much of his time balancing his self-willed subordinates. Prepared to compromise, trim, and deflect, Eisenhower often allowed operations to drift at critical junctures but willingly shouldered final responsibility.

Perhaps too generous in his judgments, Ambrose was not uncritical. He admitted that in the vital first two months of his command—September and October 1944—Eisenhower did not exert tight control over operations. Succumbing to the "victory disease," Eisenhower's acquiescence to Montgomery on Arnhem meant delay in opening Antwerp, contributing to the autumn logistical crisis that stalled the advance. The failure of the SHAEF design to advance on both sides of the Ardennes to deliver the knockout blow did not mean Montgomery's plan would have succeeded. As Ambrose pointed out, all the senior officers in SHAEF—British officers chief among them—proved equally dismissive of Montgomery and his scheme. Logistics and the political impossibility of immobilizing American divisions or subordinating them to British command dictated Eisenhower's course. Like Marshall, he thought the fulcrum of success rested on getting the weight of American power into the campaign. He took the cautious approach, which guaranteed eventual victory. Eisenhower and the American armies came of age in the Ardennes. In the final campaigns, the closing to the Rhine and the decision to halt at the Elbe, Eisenhower purposefully executed the last phase of the Overlord plan. For Ambrose, Eisenhower's broad front and the decision not to advance on Berlin served as perfect corollaries to the stated political objectives of the Grand Alliance.

After a twenty-five-year flood of books came the drought of the 1970s. A number of factors came into play. Ambrose's biography of Eisenhower and Blumenson's *Patton Papers* concluded the cycle of memoirs and autobiographies of the principal actors. The war in Southeast Asia deflected interest and diminished respect for the military. These factors forced a fundamental reevaluation of the discipline of military history. As significant, historians required time to digest newly opened archival sources and the Ultra revelation.

The first years of the 1980s witnessed a spate of major new works; many were revisionist, while others extended old orthodoxies. The first and most significant revisionist history emerged in 1981 with Weigley's *Eisenhower's Lieutenants*. The title is misleading. Instead of a composite biographical approach in the tradition of Douglas Southall Freeman's classic study of Lee and the army of northern Virginia, Weigley critiqued Allied generalship and reappraised the performance of the U.S. Army in the greatest campaign of its history. In a masterful combination of synthesis, narrative, and analysis, Weigley discussed all the familiar conditioning frictions that prevented Allied armies from reaping the maximum advantage from German defeat in France in 1944—personality conflicts, the initial inexperience of operational commanders, the difficulties of sustaining the offensive, the strategic and logistic constraints imposed by the British operating on the left, inter-Allied clashes, interservice rivalry, manpower shortages, and the determined resistance and recuperative powers of the Wehrmacht.

For Weigley, the root problem rested less in the differences between Eisenhower and Montgomery and between American and British doctrine than in the inability of the U.S. Army to articulate a coherent concept of war. Asymmetries existed between American strategy—the Grantian tradition of concentrated and direct power to annihilate the enemy—and American operational doctrine, weaponry, and force structures—the Indian-fighting tradition based on speed and mobility without sustained fighting power. Unable to resolve these contradictory legacies, Eisenhower tried to employ both power and mobility, but, lacking sufficient margins of manpower and matériel, he and his generals missed their opportunity to envelop the German armies and found themselves locked in attritional campaigns along the German frontiers. Less deliberate generalship might have reaped greater strategic rewards, but Allied generals, while competent, were "addicted to playing it safe."

Weigley offered a balanced appraisal of Allied generalship, free of the partisanship that mars much of the historiography. He condemned Eisenhower for failing to rein in his headstrong subordinates, producing the divergence of strength that limited Allied gains in France and the Low Countries. Weigley's analysis of the decision to bypass Berlin contrasted sharply with Ambrose's interpretation; he disparaged Eisenhower for allowing Bradley to deflect eighteen divisions from the drive on Berlin to reduce the Ruhr pocket in western Germany. According to Weigley, Eisenhower should have driven on to Berlin, even after the unnecessary delay on the Ruhr. In mitigation, Weigley maintained that the Allied supreme commander, circumspect by nature, wrestled with counterproductive arguments and contentious personalities that obliged him to adopt politically inspired and imperfect plans not of his choosing.

Also controversial was Weigley's analysis of Montgomery, which was not colored by his distaste for the field marshal's personality—at least not until after Montgomery's antics in the Ardennes. Britain's ablest general, Montgomery, in Weigley's estimate, emerged as Eisenhower's best senior lieutenant. Normandy proved Montgomery's ability to defeat the Germans in positional battle, and Arnhem—correct in conception but spoiled in execution—showed the British commander to be a bold and original strategist. Bradley, to whom Weigley ascribes blame for not closing the Falaise pocket and for negatively influencing Eisenhower on Berlin, suffered badly in comparison. Simultaneously argumentative and authoritative, *Eisenhower's Lieutenants* remains the single most significant account of the 1944–1945 campaigns in Europe.

The war between the generals—or at least the historians' struggle—gained momentum in the 1980s. At age seventy-eight, Bradley embarked upon his autobiography. He wanted to defend his sagging reputation by demythologizing the other major figures. Never clever with words, Bradley struggled for eight years before enlisting the aid of Clay Blair. Bradley died two years before the publication of *A General's Life*, having read only the first hundred pages of a seven hundred-page book. Although written in the first person, the result was not a memoir but an authorized biography. In the end, the book succeeded in denigrating Marshall (a poor judge of commanders who failed to carry the strategic arguments against Brooke), Eisenhower (weak, Anglophilic, and incapable of managing a battlefield), Patton (unbalanced by his ambition and warped personality), and, of course, Montgomery, but without securing any corresponding elevation in General Bradley's standing.

Eisenhower revisionism gained momentum in 1983 with the first volume of Ambrose's biography, *Eisenhower*. Directed at a popular audience,

Ambrose's portrayal of Eisenhower as supreme commander deviated little from his 1970 account. As coalition commander, decision maker, and crisis manager, Eisenhower asserted his military authority and presided over one of the greatest campaigns in military history. In an act of piety as his grandson, David Eisenhower offered *Eisenhower: At War.* Centering on Eisenhower's political and diplomatic roles as supreme commander, the book glosses over hotly contested military questions just as it did the general's liaison with his secretary Kay Summersby. The author claimed Eisenhower viewed the war in its broadest political context, particularly the interconnectedness of the western and eastern theaters. Aware the Red Army had won the European war, Eisenhower tailored the operational denouement in Germany to conform to the dictates of preserving the alliance.

The reevaluation of Eisenhower and his command style was further enriched by Crosswell's study of Bedell Smith, *The Chief of Staff.* Eisenhower's affability and willingness to compromise proved both advantage and liability. Marshall recognized this and dispatched Smith to offset it as Eisenhower's alter ego. Smith emerged as Eisenhower's "hatchet man," shouldering many of the complex military and diplomatic responsibilities involved in organizing and running the headquarters, ranging from handling such diverse political leaders as Churchill and de Gaulle and their military subordinates, to orchestrating the Italian and German surrenders. The hard-boiled Smith became Eisenhower's most trusted adviser and troubleshooter, relied on to seize opportunities, put out fires, and enforce decisions. Together with the parallel reexamination of Eisenhower as military commander and later chief executive, Ambrose, Crosswell, and others have produced a more nuanced portrayal of the complex and driven personality that lurked beneath the veneer of the congenial, small-town Kansan.

While Eisenhower's personality and style of leadership remain subjects of discussion, the same cannot be said of Montgomery. Undoubtedly the most controversial Allied commander in the war against the European axis, Montgomery lived long enough to see the worms eat at his reputation. After the outcry accompanying the publication of Brooke's diaries, he withheld his papers. Although his memoirs created a stir, Montgomery never used his more provocative papers. Shortly before his death in 1976 he released them to Hamilton and his son, Nigel, the designated official biographer.

Hamilton's impressive three-volume *Monty* aspired to rehabilitate the field marshal's reputation. Lewin's balanced but critical *Montgomery* had depicted Montgomery as the supremely confident professional who lifted British spirits with victory at Alamein and in following campaigns. The British historian also provided an incisive analysis of Montgomery's abnormal personality. Hamilton could not burnish his subject's personality faults, nor did he try. The field marshal emerged as an emotional cripple, a man frozen with the immature *mentalité* of a mischievous public school bully. Tactless, an ambitious glory seeker faithless to his superiors—Alexander and Eisenhower—Montgomery denigrated competitors and refused to bestow praise on subordinates.

For Hamilton, Montgomery's virtues as a commander far outstripped his failures in personality. Montgomery understood the liabilities under which he labored. He held a universally low opinion of British generals and appreciated the dwindling combat power of British divisions—products of the waning British manpower and resources pool. Montgomery's caution and his mania for building up reserves derived from the realization that the armies he commanded represented Britain's last gambit as a Great Power. He wanted to ensure that all that could be done was done to guarantee the greatest margins of success while minimizing losses; except for Arnhem, the lone deviation from the pattern when he did accept long risks, his forces always won. In Hamilton's estimate, Montgomery was the greatest Allied general in Europe, the victor of Normandy and, with it, France.

Hamilton told the story precisely as Montgomery would have. Montgomery alone knew the secret of how to beat the Germans. Repeating claims made by Montgomery in his memoirs, Hamilton argued that Eisenhower never understood the Normandy plan. Hamilton also maintained that the original plans never miscarried; Montgomery never intended to seize Caen on D-Day and break out into the tank country beyond. The "master of the battlefield" fought the decisive campaign in the West strictly as proposed. Relegated to army group command, Montgomery chafed under Eisenhower's refusal to concentrate on a narrow front. Eisenhower proved unequal to the task; Bradley's deployments invited the German counteroffensive in the Ardennes, and only Montgomery saved the situation. Reproducing Montgomery's war diary, nightly messages to Brooke, and homilies on operations, Hamilton highlighted the clarity of the field marshal's military vision and provided new evidence of British machinations to place a British commander in control of ground operations. In his bid to redeem Montgomery's status, Hamilton went too far. *Monty* remains a case of condemnation by too much praise.

Montgomery's "quasi-paranoid streak" manifested itself in his lack of regard for the truth and his compulsive need always to justify himself. The field marshal habitually exaggerated the advantages of his ideas while minimizing the obstacles in achieving them. This trait also explains why Montgomery sought to provide misleading accounts in his dispatches, news conferences, and memoirs of the planning and direction of his operations. Montgomery could never admit that his battles did not follow his script to the last detail. His obfuscation and manipulation of historical accounts have given the debate over his generalship a life of its own.

Between 1978 and 1984 no fewer than six books appeared reassessing Montgomery in Normandy. Indisputably the best was D'Este's *Decision in Normandy*. He put to rest any question of who planned the Normandy operation. Montgomery not only planned the campaign but conducted it through the fall of Caen. Sifting through American and British sources, many of them just opened, D'Este argued that Montgomery did plan to take Caen while the American forces threatened a breakout on the right. After failing to seize Caen—British and Canadian troops did not live up to expectations throughout the campaign—Montgomery found the forces under his direct command overextended and suffering heavy losses in an attritional battle. Nevertheless, the overall plan succeeded—Caen served as a magnet for German armor, allowing Bradley to break through at St. Lô. Cobra's success was unexpected, and, according to D'Este, no plan existed for an envelopment through Avranches. Montgomery and Bradley deserve equal censure for the failure to reinforce their respective forces to close the Falaise Gap; both remained wedded to the Overlord plan for a systematic advance to the Seine. Montgomery's rigidity and his insistence that all went according to plan created the rifts that affected Anglo-American relations for the rest of the war. His claims also befogged the issue for historians. These clouds have been lifted by D'Este's work.

The last decade has seen the redirection of interest from operational questions toward a focus on grand strategy and the war's consequences. Churchill continues to exert powerful attraction for historians. Gilbert's plodding narrative biography of Churchill, *Road to Victory*, cast his subject as an unerring strategic virtuoso. In sharp contrast, a number of works have challenged the Churchillian legacy. The first was Lamb's innocuous *Churchill as War Leader*, followed by two provocative, but not wholly convincing, revisionist books by Charmley and yet another biography of the prime minister by Ponting.

These British declinist historians blame Churchill for losing the war even while sacrificing all for Allied victory. They see a fatal paradox between Churchill's atavistic Edwardian worldview, aimed at preserving the empire and the precarious British hold on Great Power status, and how the British Empire fought the war—with Churchill throwing every ounce of imperial strength into the struggle, only to see the strategy of the coalition reorient in favor of the Americans and their strategic agenda. Gilbert went too far in arguing for Churchill's sagacity and influence; the revisionists overcompensated in the other direction.

Wilt's comparative study of Churchill and Hitler, *War from the Top*, offset the trend toward a Churchillian-centered universe by reminding us that British policy and strategy emerged as a collective effort, conditioned by coalition politics and the course of the war. The reassessment of how the definition and execution of grand strategy in Europe affected postwar possibilities shows no signs of losing momentum.

As the polemical battle rages over the price Churchill paid for victory, American historians are moving toward a consensus on Roosevelt and U.S. strategic policy making. The Cold War interpretation cast Roosevelt and his advisers as politically naive, preoccupied with narrow military concerns, and variously manipulated by the British or blind to the Soviet menace. In response, Stoler, "The United States: The Global Strategy," and Kimball, *The Juggler*, have claimed that the president possessed a coherent and consistent set of objectives. Winning the war was political, not merely military. As "evangel of Americanism," Roosevelt fought the war to universalize American liberal institutions and values. To achieve his aims, he had to construct support in Congress and in the public mind for long-term U.S. commitments to preserve the new world order. Cooperating with Stalin was not only essential to victory but critical in securing American interests and constructing a lasting peace. More than Churchill, Roosevelt had to find an equilibrium between conflicting strategic and political demands of war in both Europe and the Pacific. Eisenhower's broad-front strategy acted as the appropriate military counterpoise to the doctrine of unconditional surrender and Roosevelt's grand strategic designs. Not sharing Churchill's obsession for taking minutes, Roosevelt's leadership style and his mania for secrecy left historians with a documentary void. In the end, the views of Roosevelt revisionists, although persuasive, remain largely speculative.

What do the debates over Churchill and the history of British decline and Roosevelt as grand strategist have in common with the fifty-year-old controversies over conflicting Anglo-American strategic variants in the campaigns in Northwest Europe? At the heart of the matter rest some unanswerable questions. If Churchill had made a separate peace with Germany between July 1940 and June 1941, what then might have become of the British Empire? If Roosevelt had not made a political command decision to launch Torch and delay a true "Second Front" beyond 1943, or if less doctrinaire strategies had been followed after the breakout from Normandy, could the division of Europe into hostile blocs have been averted? Many other examples could be cited; the point remains an admixture of patriotic myth, ideology, and personal pride that militated against truly objective accounts of the conduct of the war by the Grand Alliance. Yet they also gave historical writing its immediacy and sustained its popular interest.

The passage of time, especially the demise of the Cold War, demands thorough reexaminations of the first fifty years of scholarship. While Anglo-American discord was real, Cold War perspectives, the memoir literature, and national biases distorted historical accounts, giving political factors and personal quarrels an emphasis missing in historical documents. Since the protagonists are long dead and with the archives mostly available, it is time the debate stopped revolving around vindication or damnation, on national or personal levels. Each generation of historians projects its visions of the present and future into the past. The end of the Cold War has created a world much different than envisioned a decade ago. While historic imponderables must continue to fuel debate, the future course of studies will surely be shaped by different questions prompted by the changed reality of the present.

BIBLIOGRAPHY

Ambrose, Stephen. *Eisenhower.* Vol. 1, *Soldier, General of the Army, President-Elect, 1890–1952.* New York: Simon and Schuster, 1983.

———. *Supreme Commander: The War Years of General Dwight D. Eisenhower.* Garden City, NY: Doubleday, 1970.

Blumenson, Martin. *Breakout and Pursuit.* Washington, DC: Office of the Chief of Military History, 1961.

———, ed. *The Patton Papers.* Vol. 2. Boston: Houghton Mifflin, 1974.

Bradley, Omar. *A Soldier's Story.* New York: Henry Holt, 1947.

Bradley, Omar, with Clay Blair. *A General's Life: An Autobiography by General of the Army Omar N. Bradley and Clay Blair.* New York: Simon and Schuster, 1983.

Bryant, Arthur. *Triumph in the West.* London: Collins, 1959.

Butcher, Harry. *My Three Years with Eisenhower: The Personal Diary of Captain Harry C. Butcher, USNR, Naval Aide to General Eisenhower, 1942 to 1945.* New York: Simon and Schuster, 1946.

Chandler, Alfred, Jr., ed. *The Papers of Dwight David Eisenhower.* Vols. 1–5, *The War Years.* Baltimore: Johns Hopkins UP, 1970.

Charmley, John. *Churchill: The End of Glory.* London: Hodder and Stoughton, 1993.

———. *Churchill's Grand Alliance: The Anglo-American Special Relationship, 1940–57.* London: Hodder and Stoughton, 1995.

Churchill, Winston S. *The Second World War: Triumph and Tragedy.* Boston: Houghton Mifflin, 1954.

Clarke, Jeffrey, and Robert Ross Smith. *Riviera to the Rhine.* Washington, DC: Office of the Chief of Military History, 1993.

Cole, Hugh. *The Ardennes: Battle of the Bulge.* Washington, DC: Office of the Chief of Military History, 1965.

———. *The Lorraine Campaign.* Washington, DC: Office of the Chief of Military History, 1950.

Crosswell, D.K.R. *The Chief of Staff: The Military Career of General Walter Bedell Smith.* Westport, CT: Greenwood, 1991.

D'Este, Carlo. *Decision in Normandy.* New York: Dutton, 1983.

Eisenhower, David. *Eisenhower: At War, 1943–1945.* New York: Random House, 1986.

Eisenhower, Dwight. *Crusade in Europe.* Garden City, NY: Doubleday, 1948.

Ellis, Lionel F., with A. E. Warhurst. *Victory in the West.* Vol. 2, *The Defeat of Germany.* London: HMSO, 1968.

Gilbert, Martin. *Road to Victory: Winston S. Churchill 1941–1945.* London: Heinemann Minerva, 1989.

Grigg, James. *Prejudice and Judgment.* London: Jonathan Cape, 1948.

Guingand, Francis de. *Operation Victory*. London: Hodder and Stoughton, 1947.

Hamilton, Nigel. *Master of the Battlefield: Monty's War Years, 1942–1944*. New York: McGraw-Hill, 1983.

———. *Monty: Final Years of the Field Marshal, 1944–1976*. New York: McGraw-Hill, 1986.

Harrison, Gordon. *Cross-Channel Attack*. Washington, DC: Office of the Chief of Military History, 1951.

Ingersoll, Ralph. *Top Secret*. New York: Harcourt, Brace, 1946.

Ismay, Hastings. *The Memoirs of General Lord Ismay*. New York: Viking, 1960.

Kimball, Warren F. *The Juggler: Franklin Roosevelt as Wartime Statesman*. Princeton: Princeton UP, 1991.

Lamb, Richard. *Churchill as War Leader: Right or Wrong?* London: Bloomsbury, 1991.

Lewin, Ronald. *Montgomery as a Military Commander*. London: Batsford, 1971.

MacDonald, Charles. *The Last Offensive*. Washington, DC: Office of the Chief of Military History, 1973.

———. *The Siegfried Line Campaign*. Washington, DC: Office of the Chief of Military History, 1963.

Montgomery, Bernard. *The Memoirs of Field-Marshal the Viscount Montgomery of Alamein*. London: Collins, 1958.

———. *Normandy to the Baltic*. London: Hutchinson, 1947.

Patton, George. *War As I Knew It*. Boston: Houghton Mifflin, 1947.

Pogue, Forrest C. *The Supreme Command*. Washington, DC: Office of the Chief of Military History, 1954.

Ponting, Clive. *Winston Churchill*. London: Sinclair Stevenson, 1994.

Report by the Supreme Commander to the Combined Chiefs of Staff on the Operations in Europe of the Allied Expeditionary Force, 6 June 1944 to 8 May 1945. Washington, DC: GPO, 1945.

Reynolds, David, et al., eds. *Allies at War: The Soviet, American and British Experience, 1939–1945*. New York: St. Martin's, 1994.

Ruppenthal, Roland. *Logistical Support of the Armies, September 1944–May 1945*. Vol. 2. Washington, DC: Office of the Chief of Military History, 1959.

Smith, Walter Bedell. *Eisenhower's Six Great Decisions: Europe, 1944–1945*. New York: Longmans, 1956.

Stacey, Charles. *The Victory Campaign*. Vol. 3, *The Operations in North-West Europe, 1944–1945*. Ottawa: Queen's Printer and Controller of Stationery, 1960.

Stoler, Mark. "The United States: The Global Strategy." In David Reynolds et al., eds. *Allies at War*, 55–78. New York: St. Martin's, 1994.

Tedder, Arthur. *With Prejudice: The War Memoirs of Marshal of the Royal Air Force Lord Tedder*. Boston: Little, Brown, 1966.

Weigley, Russell. *Eisenhower's Lieutenants: The Campaign of France and Germany, 1944–1945*. Bloomington: Indiana UP, 1981.

Wilmot, Chester. *The Struggle for Europe*. London: Collins, 1952.

Wilt, Alan F. *War from the Top: German and British Military Decision Making during World War II*. Bloomington: Indiana UP, 1990.

14 The Anglo-American Bombing Campaign in Europe

Peter R. Faber

Modern historiography typically involves a four-step process. The official version of an event first dominates the historical landscape until revisionists openly question its veracity. The traditionalists who support past "truths" then respond to the iconoclasts, and out of this mutual dialogue appears a new historical synthesis.

What makes the historiography of the Anglo-American bombing campaign so complicated and often troubling is that it has not followed the usual pattern. The scholarly debate over the efficacy and morality of strategic bombardment against the heartland of Germany has been raucous, ideologically tainted, and thoroughly emotional from the start. Claims and counterclaims have collided with each other since 1945, when John Kenneth Galbraith first argued that the Anglo-American bombing campaign had not broken the morale of the German people. Galbraith made this bald assertion as one of the anonymous authors of the U.S. Strategic Bombing Survey (USSBS), *Summary Report (European War)*. The claim wrongly assumed that the destruction of German morale was a strategic end rather than a means to an end. It also dismissed the conclusions of specific USSBS reports, which determined that the bombing campaign had diminished German morale almost to the breaking point. As a result of contentious positions like Galbraith's, the historiographical debate surrounding the Allied air offensive has yet to reach a truly dispassionate synthesis that reconciles the censure of the revisionist with the sturdy, but measured, support of the traditionalist.

Why, Frankland asked in *The Bombing Offensive against Germany*, is the bomber debate so tenacious, and why does it transcend "the normal frontiers of military argument?" (69) Further, Smith asked, why has "the balance of opinion on the value of the Allied air offensive . . . been heavily on the critical side?" ("The Allied Air Offensive," 67). Although there are multiple reasons for these predispositions, three stand out, beginning with the role of failed expectations.

Early airmen like Giulio Douhet, Hugh Trenchard, William "Billy" Mitchell, and members of the U.S. Air Corps Tactical School's "Bomber Mafia" (Robert Olds, Kenneth Walker, Harold Lee George, Donald Wilson, Robert Webster, Laurence Kuter, Haywood Hansell, and Muir Fairchild) promoted air bombardment as a revolutionary tool of war. The strategic bomber promised to leap over an opponent's ground-based defenses and either terrorize whole populations into submission or paralyze the economic foundations of a nation. The bomber was, in short, an apocalyptic instrument of war that was qualitatively different from anything that had come before; it would destroy future enemies from their economic and political center rather than nibble away at their borders. World War II, however, proved that the "Bomber Mafia" and others were wrong; the bomber was not a revolutionary tool of war. Its technology was too primitive to match the dazzling prewar promises made on its behalf. Bombers could not unilaterally defeat an enemy nation without the active cooperation of ground and naval forces. Nor could they defeat an opponent quickly and therefore humanely, as also promised. The Anglo-American bombing campaign was a grinding war of attrition, and only with the defeat of the Luftwaffe in the spring of 1944 did Allied bombers truly begin to destroy German morale and war production.

The gap between ability and promise, however, left a bitter taste in the mouths of some observers. What the air prophets had promised as a painless solution to the carnage and futility of the First World War became only one of several methods used to prosecute an even bloodier conflict, particularly on the Eastern Front, two decades later. Further, the disingenuousness of wartime airmen, who both minimized the failures and exaggerated the successes of strategic bombardment, added to the disappointment felt by postwar analysts. The willful self-delusion of Anglo-American air leaders was not only an expression of their doctrinal beliefs but also a symptom of the continued vulnerability they felt toward army–navy critics. The Americans in particular needed a successful air campaign to legitimate their quest for an independent air force. Not surprisingly, then, the historiography of the Allied air offensive in Europe "has mostly focused on this gap between the aspirations and the achievements of the airmen, in particular on the failings of the apocalyptic concept of air power that underlay the attacks on cities such as Hamburg and Dresden" (Smith, 67).

If failed expectations muddied the critical waters, so did the association of conventional strategic bombardment with nuclear weapons. In the case of the United States, postwar government and military elites largely believed that the theory of high-altitude, daylight, precision bombardment was successful in World War II. As a result, they took the same theory and adapted it—in various guises—to atomic warfare. The adaptation filled a theoretical void, but it did so at a price. The negative emotions associated with atomic warfare became inextricably linked to public perceptions of strategic bombardment in World War II. On the historical continuities between conventional strategic bombing theory and postwar nuclear warfare doctrines, see Kohn and Harahan, *Strategic Air Warfare*; Overy, "Air Power and the Origins of Deterrence Theory before 1939"; Quester, *Deterrence before Hiroshima*; Sherry, *The Rise of American Air Power*; and Watts, *The Foundations of U.S. Air Doctrine*. Not surprisingly, these associations then tainted the works of revisionist historians like Schaffer and Sherry, who deplored—from a retroactive, omniscient, post–Vietnam War perspective—what they saw as the inefficiencies and dubious morality of the Allied air campaign.

Lastly, Frankland argued persuasively that the controversy over strategic bombing had its cultural roots in fin de siècle Europe, when the word "bomb" became associated with revolutionary terror (98). By hurling bombs at hapless aristocrats and other "reactionaries," anarchists shaped public attitudes toward bombing even before the first airplane appeared. According to Frankland in *Bombing Offensive*, "[B]ombs were connected in people's minds with the collapse of authority, the destruction of life and property and the abolition of security" (98). They were also connected with murder rather than killing and with aggression rather than self-defense. As a result, these negative perceptions, when added to unfulfilled expectations and the commingling of nuclear fears with a non-nuclear past, help explain, in Frankland's words, why "people have preferred to feel rather than to know about strategic bombing" (18).

The presence of emotion explains why the historiography of the Allied air offensive remains fractured and contentious. In particular, airpower historians continue to quarrel, with varying degrees of intensity, over two basic points: the effectiveness and utility of air attacks against an enemy's economy and the questionable morality of area or "precision" bombing against civilian population centers. Historiographical debates surround each of these topics, and they, in turn, identify what issues airpower historians need to explore in the future. The following discussion focuses on the utility and morality of strategic bombardment, but since the literature on the Anglo-American bombing campaign is already so vast, it highlights only those texts that have provided a three-dimensional, representative portrait of the campaign or have appreciably influenced scholarly debate. Otherwise, the reader should consult particular synopses, bibliographies, and single-volume studies of the air war. Those interested in a synopsis of the British and U.S. strategic bombing surveys, for example, should refer to Webster and Frankland's *The Strategic Air Offensive against Germany*. For a survey of the literature prior to 1960, one should review Köhler's "Bibliographie zur Luftkriegsgeschichte." For a review of the literature dealing with specific regions or cities attacked in Germany, consult Groehler's *Bombenkrieg gegen Deutschland*. For English-language bibliographies, refer to Smith's *Air War Bibliography*; Daniels' *Guide*; and the U.S. Air Force Academy's *Air Power and Warfare*. Finally, for a sampling of balanced and thoughtful single-volume surveys of the Allied air campaign, see Levine's *The Strategic Bombing of Germany*, which expertly covers both British and American air operations; Fabyanic's *Strategic Air Attack*; Frankland's *The Bombing Offensive against Germany;* Kennett's *A History of Strategic Bombing*; and Overy's *The Air War 1939–1945*.

THE UTILITY OF STRATEGIC BOMBARDMENT IN THE EUROPEAN THEATER

The questions surrounding the utility of the Allied air offensive are familiar enough. Was the bombing effective? Was it worth the cost? What were its actual results? Could military leaders have employed their bombers elsewhere? Over the last fifty years, those who grappled with these largely economic questions have formed into three distinct camps, and only with Overy's *Why the Allies Won* and his "World War II: The Bombing of Germany" have we reached a near synthesis of opinion on the matter of utility. Yet, despite Overy's yeoman efforts, some still argue that the air offensive against Germany was either totally decisive, an indirect and only partial success, or an utter failure. This division of opinion does not primarily exist in the case of British area bombing, which many historians agree enjoyed only limited success, but it certainly exists in the case of the American air campaign.

Not surprisingly, the Americans who planned or prosecuted their portion of the strategic air war subsequently portrayed it as an unalloyed success, as did specific USSBS reports and official "autopsies" like the seven-volume history *The Army Air Forces in World War II*, edited by Cate and Craven. If there were "failures" in the CBO (Combined Bomber Offensive), its supporters argued, they were just misguided efforts or false starts. Second, since the CBO dropped 72 percent of its bomb tonnage *after* D-Day, any talk of how ineffective it was prior to the spring of 1944 was irrelevant. Yes, it was ineffective, airmen admitted, but it had just begun! Finally, although the CBO was no more decisive in 1943 than the invasion of Italy, both operations were necessary prerequisites for later success. Too many people understood this point in relation to Sicily, air leaders argued, and yet hypocritically condemned the CBO for not achieving immediate results. Such complaints were partially valid and helped General Spaatz conclude that strategic bombardment had been decisive in World War II, as illustrated by his seminal article "Strategic Air Power: Fulfillment of a Concept."

In his apologia, which appeared in the April 1946 issue of *Foreign Affairs*,

Spaatz quoted liberally from the USSBS, captured German generals, Professor Willi Messerschmitt, and Albert Speer to "prove" that strategic airpower was economically decisive in Europe. As the senior American airman in the theater, Spaatz sought to destroy the "heart and arteries" of the German war economy and thus paralyze Nazi military power at its core. The lifeblood of the economy eventually included war industries and arsenals, cities, fuel plants and supplies, and transportation targets. According to Spaatz, who continued to advocate the creation of an independent U.S. Air Force, the critical air attacks of Big Week (February 19–25, 1944) not only validated the concept of strategic airpower but marked *the* decisive turning point of the war in Europe. The U.S. Eighth and Fifteenth Air Forces lost 226 bombers during Big Week, but the Germans lost 282 fighters and one hundred veteran pilots. With approximately one-third of the Luftwaffe's operational fighter force thus destroyed, command of the air soon devolved to the Allies. See Murray, *Strategy for Defeat.*

Significantly, Spaatz's conclusions were not radical enough for the USSBS Oil Division's *Final Report*, which claimed that even without a land invasion, German armaments production would have stopped by May 1945, and Wehrmacht resistance would have ceased by June or July. Spaatz's views, however, did resurface in Craven and Cate's *The Army Air Forces in World War II*. Volumes 2 and 3 of the series acknowledged that air planners and combatants made mistakes; that is, they relied frequently on trial and error to identify proper targets, they did not grasp the interrelationships between one target set and another, and they failed to attack Germany in a repeated, sustained, and massive way. Yet, despite acknowledging these failures, the volumes selectively quoted various USSBS reports and other sources to affirm that the victory of Allied airpower was complete—it had defeated the Luftwaffe by April 1944 and incapacitated the German economy by January 1945.

Significantly, the boosterism of General Spaatz and particular government historians was not an ephemeral, short-term phenomenon. Major General Haywood Hansell and Lieutenant General Ira Eaker preserved the "triumphalist" vision of strategic bombardment well into the 1970s and 1980s. As a former member of the Air Corps Tactical School (ACTS) "Bomber Mafia," Hansell transformed theory into practice by directly contributing to AWPD-1 (Air War Plans Division/1) (see Gaston, *Planning the American Air War*) and AWPD-42 (Air War Plans Division/42), two strategic planning documents partly developed for American and Allied air forces in 1941–1942. Hansell later argued in his impressive *The Air Plan That Defeated Hitler* and *The Strategic Air War Against Germany and Japan* that the strategic air campaign performed four critical tasks during World War II—it destroyed the Luftwaffe, deprived the Wehrmacht of increasingly precious fuels, minimized enemy defenses against a cross-Channel invasion, and successfully interdicted enemy counterthrusts after the D-Day landings and breakout. To Hansell, these accomplishments were fundamental, rather than peripheral, to Allied success in war. On the twin "failures" of not destroying German morale or paralyzing Germany's economy until the winter of 1944–1945, Hansell had ready and now-familiar alibis. If long-range P-47 and P-51 escort fighters had appeared before 1944, and if Anglo-American military leaders had not yielded to political pressure and repeatedly disrupted the Allied air offensive to support "diversions" like the North Africa campaign and D-Day, a sustained strategic air campaign would have shattered Germany's economy a year earlier.

Hansell's claims were partially legitimate, especially over the issue of diversions. If one counts the antisubmarine and the V-weapons campaigns, for example, 46 percent of Eighth Air Force sorties did not contribute to the strategic air offensive proper. However, despite the repeated delays and diversions, Hansell sided with Spaatz, the USSBS, and the official U.S. histories—the Combined Bomber Offensive did fatally weaken the Nazi economy prior to a single Allied soldier's setting foot on German soil.

Ira Eaker, in turn, agreed with them all. In Parton's *"Air Force Spoken Here,"* the former commander of the Eighth Air Force not only claimed that strategic bombardment had an overwhelming and crippling effect on Germany's war effort but also observed that it had another salutary impact: it diverted approximately two million Germans into performing purely defensive tasks such as antiaircraft and fighter defense, bomb damage repair, and dousing fires.

It is possible, as Groehler wrote in "The Strategic Air War," to dismiss Hansell, Eaker, and others as posterity-conscious warriors (or their fellow travelers) whose "biased interpretations and explanations . . . served as self-justification and excuses, and therefore got lost in a blind alley at a certain point" (279). Some continued to emphasize the decisive impact of strategic bombardment in Europe. Yes, Lord Zuckerman admitted in *From Apes to Warlords*, the British area campaign was a "mere irritant" prior to the autumn of 1944, but the collateral effects of later attacks against the Ruhr Valley did break down the German steel industry and therefore the Reich's future capacity to manufacture arms.

Boyne, in turn, admitted in *Clash of Wings* that the Allies underestimated German production capacity, performed too many attacks on too many targets, and should have used more incendiary and larger high-explosive bombs. The standard five hundred-pound HE bomb was too weak, for example, to destroy German machine tool industries in one attempt. Yet, Boyne concluded that Allied bombers could have destroyed Germany so completely that a subsequent invasion would have been "a mere walkover." Only the fear of Soviet troops marching into Western Europe robbed the CBO of the time needed to devastate Germany. As it was, Boyne observed, the disruptive air offensive forced the evacuation of six million Germans within their own borders.

Air Vice Marshal Tony Mason, although not as sanguine as Boyne, also stressed the benefits of strategic bombardment during the war. In *Air Power*, he argued that the CBO performed three undeniable (and critical) services—it forced two-thirds of the Luftwaffe to concentrate on aerial defense rather than attacking advancing Russian troops; it forced the Germans to invest time and treasure in wasteful, last-chance "miracle" weapons like the V1 and V2; and, most important, it prevented the Soviet Union and Germany from deciding the ground war on the Continent without Anglo-American involvement; that is, the CBO made D-Day possible, and without D-Day the USSR might have arranged a separate peace with Germany and secured even more territory than it eventually did. For these reasons and many others, the enthusiasts argued, the Allied air offensive was a success. Military and civilian elites could have done things better or differently, but their investment in strategic bombardment was fundamentally sound, especially in the last year of the war. Ultimately, the CBO reaped returns more than commensurate with its costs, which included approximately ninety-nine thousand airmen dead or missing.

However, some historians distanced themselves from what they dismissed as the boosterism of their colleagues. The air offensive against Germany was only an indirect and partial success, these doubters claimed, and they cited the multiple contradictions surrounding it to buttress their arguments. In the latter stages of the war, MacIsaac pointed out in *Strategic Bombing*, the simultaneous activities of all arms "could not be scientifically separated into discrete elements" (162). As a result, the Allies were often unable to distinguish the beneficial effects of strategic bombardment from those of advancing Russian artillery, for example. Nor did they define strategic bombing accurately; report bombing effects honestly (because of political and security restrictions); or clearly distinguish between two distinct categories of assessment—the effects versus the effectiveness of air attacks. Not surprisingly, critics (and British ones in particular) seized upon these problems to question the timeliness (and therefore relative importance) of the CBO and sometimes to argue that the Allies might have used their heavy bombers more effectively elsewhere.

Three obvious dissenters were Murray, Terraine, and Smith. In the first case, Murray suggested in "The Influence of Pre-War Anglo-American Doctrine on the Air Campaigns" that diverting more bombers to the Battle of the Atlantic would have swung the balance of that critical campaign earlier than May 1943 (245). In "Theory and Practice" Terraine claimed that Bomber Command was largely ineffectual up through the Battle of Berlin (November 1943–March 1944) and became a relevant, potentially war-winning weapon only with the defeat of the Luftwaffe in the spring of 1944 (495). Third, Smith, "The Allied Air Offensive," argued that Anglo-American airmen underestimated the social and economic reserves of their enemy, they had a limited ability to acquire and interpret industrial intelligence, and they were bent on preserving a general air offensive at all costs (especially against aircraft production facilities and ball-bearings industries). Still, Smith concluded broadly, "When the time finally came to launch the second front, the bombers were able to play a very significant role in undermining the ability of Germany to resist" (82).

Terraine and Smith's left-handed compliments to strategic bombardment were similar to the ones also provided by Frankland in *Bombing Offensive* and Rostow in *Pre-Invasion Bombing Strategy*. In a darker moment, Frankland wrote that the CBO was not a strategically integrated campaign; it was nothing more than an updated version of *guerre de course*, and its rate of destruction did not, for most of the war, exceed the casualties inflicted by German defenses. As a result, Frankland concluded that through early 1944 the CBO was only partially successful and considerably divided. Rostow, in turn, believed synthetic oil production became *the* German target set soon after Big Week. Allied air forces should have concentrated on this key node with the same vigor as pre–D-Day transportation targets, since an earlier focus on oil would have saved lives and most probably would have permitted Allied armies to push further east than they ultimately did. The postwar result, according to Rostow, could have been a united, democratic, and pacifist Germany.

So, was the Allied air campaign worthwhile? To the majority of the skeptics, the answer was a qualified yes, but only the fortuitous, unplanned introduction of long-range fighter escorts late in the war facilitated airpower's contribution to the defeat of Germany. The defeat of the Wehrmacht, on the other hand, still depended on the fighting spirit of invading Allied armies, as Emerson observed in "Operation Pointblank."

In Emerson's opinion, the CBO was a victory of improvisation and even luck, particularly in the case of the United States. Since "every salient belief of prewar American air doctrine was either overthrown or basically modified by the experience of war," Emerson agreed with fellow skeptics that the air offensive in Europe was a battle of attrition against the Luftwaffe and that it merely complemented, rather than replaced, the decisive role of tactical air–ground operations (470–71).

Lastly, Mierzejewski was even more emphatic than MacIsaac, Frankland, Terraine, Smith, Rostow, and Emerson. In *The Collapse of the German War Economy*, he observed that the early Allied air campaign was doomed from the start. According to Mierzejewski, there were multiple reasons for the initial (and prolonged) failure of the CBO: (1) murky strategic objectives, to include the "destruction and dislocation" of the German war machine and the "fatal weakening" of enemy morale; (2) unclear "measures of effectiveness," especially over expected goals and effects; (3) poor strategic intelligence analysis, including the failure of Allied planners to identify coal as *the* cornerstone of the German economy; (4) political infighting, in which civilian elites wrongly discouraged attacks against enemy transportation networks; and (5) "mirror imaging," whereby Allied targeting groups wrongly assumed that oil lubricated the German economy, as it did in the United States.

In fact, "The lifeblood of the system was coal, and the fate of the entire organism rested on the conduit that ensured its steady flow, the Deutsche Reichsbahn" (34). Allied air planners, however, stumbled upon this fatal nexus only when those who advocated striking transportation and coal networks, including Air Marshal Tedder and Solly Zuckerman, compromised with Air Marshal Portal, General Spaatz, and the Economic Objectives Unit, who claimed that oil-related targets mattered most. As a result, Mierzejewski acknowledged that Anglo-American bombardment ended all "coherent economic activity" in Germany, but not before February 1945 and not before (according to Lord Zuckerman) the unnecessary destruction of Germany's eastern cities. Zuckerman's conclusion naturally points to those historians and pundits who believe that the Allied air campaign was an outright failure.

Of those who doubted the air war had a decisive impact against Germany, either directly or indirectly, only a minority condemned it on utilitarian (i.e., economic) grounds, and when they did, they focused primarily on the British doctrine of area bombing. The nonbelievers include Bidinian, *The Combined Allied Bombing Offensive*, and Possonoy, *Strategic Air Power*. In particular, Bidinian argued that the logistical and training costs of the CBO far exceeded its benefits; that it depressed German morale, but not to the point of paralyzing the Wehrmacht's military efficiency; and that air attacks actually liberated German industry from the consumer sector and thus facilitated the mobilization of the economy for war in 1942 (146, 150, 152). To repeat, however: Bidinian's criticisms focused primarily on the British doctrine of area bombing and thus pointed to what most critics of the CBO believed was the primary, Janus-faced reason it was a failure—both area and "precision" bombing became increasingly barbarous with time and turned the strategic air campaign into an immoral political act. Germans over sixty years old, for example, made up 12 percent of the population, but they largely remained in urban areas. As a result, they totaled 24 percent of the CBO's victims.

AREA AND PRECISION BOMBARDMENT AND THE MORALITY OF THE CBO

On the issue of morality, revisionist historians condemned both the area assaults of the British and the "precision" daylight attacks of the Americans. Both parts of the CBO, critics argued, were increasingly indiscriminate, especially in the brutally inclement winter of 1944–1945. In the case of Bomber Command, however, the controversy centers specifically on the "de-housing" campaign implemented by Air Marshal Sir Arthur

"Bomber" Harris in late 1942. Known also as "Butch" (short for "Butcher") by his own aircrews, Harris already believed in the mid-1930s that nightly incendiary attacks against whole enemy cities would kill or dislocate industrial workers. Those who survived would then concentrate on looking for food and shelter and thus would indirectly subvert Germany's economic capacity to wage war. Unfortunately, the costs of Harris' campaign were horrendous: Bomber Command ultimately lost approximately 8,200 bombers and 55,000 men, while German losses were perhaps 593,000 people, mostly due to area assaults. Yet, as Harris confirmed in *Bomber Offensive*, he never doubted that widespread area bombing was a war-winning strategy by itself.

Harris emphasized area bombing for three reasons. First, he was a social Darwinist who believed the German proletariat lacked the moral fiber to withstand a sustained area assault. Second, he believed that area bombing had previously worked in World War I, despite the sketchy "evidence" actually available. Finally, Harris claimed that Bomber Command lacked the necessary technology to conduct precision strikes against specific target sites. To Harris, precision targets were mere "panaceas." The enemy could always substitute one damaged item or industry for another. In addition, radar aids to bombardment and navigation were not, in Harris' opinion, sufficiently advanced to justify even a post-1943 conversion to precision attacks, either by day or night. The navigational device "Gee" had a limited range; only a small number of aircraft could use "Oboe," a radar blind-bombing system at any one time, and "H2S," another such system, was difficult to interpret. Yes, these technologies made area bombing more accurate (and therefore effective) after mid-1944, but it remained area bombing nevertheless. Yet, as Messenger argued in *"Bomber" Harris and the Strategic Bombing Offensive*, area attacks did improve British morale and restricted the growth of German production, manpower, and munitions. There were, therefore, substantive reasons for Harris' implacable commitment to area bombing throughout the war. If he was guilty of anything, Messenger concluded, it was only the persistence and zeal with which he executed the area bombing campaign.

However, with so much death and destruction involved with the CBO, many historians—including Hastings, *Bomber Command*; Richards, *Portal of Hungerford*; and Terraine, *A Time for Courage*—find Harris and Messenger's apologias unacceptable and yet partially blame others for Harris' behavior! Hastings, for example, argued that the area offensive against Germany was ineffective, that its ineffectiveness was knowable at the time, and that it was therefore immoral. As already stated, Harris wrongly assumed that German morale would break under an area blitz, even though the British people previously had not. When the Germans proved Harris wrong, he remained inflexibly wedded to the idea of area attacks. There were some benefits to Harris' mulish resolve, but they were not the declared objectives of the CBO, and they were purchased, according to Hastings, at too high a price.

Hastings did not, however, place the moral blame of "pure" night area bombing on Harris, regardless of his parochialism and high-handed jingoism. The "butcher" initially followed orders, and when he later resisted a proposed switch to precision bombardment, neither Chief of the Air Staff Sir Charles Portal nor Prime Minister Churchill had the nerve to step in and order a change in policy. As a result, Hastings ultimately blamed them for the cruelty of morale bombing rather than Harris. Richards also exonerated Harris and held Churchill largely responsible for not reining in his subordinate. Portal was blameless because he accepted Harris' assurances that Bomber Command was trying to comply with Royal Air Force (RAF) policy, which insisted on accurate strikes against oil targets in late 1944. Lastly, Terraine blamed neither Churchill nor Portal for what arguably remained a "strategy of massacre." Instead, he blamed the Chiefs of Staff Committee and later the Combined Chiefs of Staff.

If the preceding historians condemn and yet defend Arthur Harris, McCarthy ("Did the Bomber Always Get Through?") and Levine (*The Strategic Bombing of Germany*) represent those who place the odium of area bombing squarely on his shoulders. To this group, Harris was an unmanageable Neanderthal who was a law unto himself. They admit that in the first three years of the war Great Britain had no other way of attacking Germany directly; that the British government needed to restore flagging civilian morale with a show of force; and that weather, wind, inexperience, mechanical problems, German resistance, the size of British bomber formations, and a host of other problems all made precision air strikes impossible. In short, they acknowledge that the early offensive was doomed to failure, but it was all that Britain could do to torment its tormentor.

Nevertheless, McCarthy concluded that area attacks were a waste of energy, effort, and lives. Because there were better targets available, the British portion of the CBO represented nothing less than a misuse of airpower. Levine dismissed the area offensive as a costly failure prior to April 1944, and he also disputed Harris' claim that radar aids to navigation and bombardment were not sophisticated enough to justify a wartime change in British strategy. In Levine's opinion, "Real precision bombing at night, against most important targets, became possible in the latter half of 1943, probably by late summer, even though the capability for it was not exploited until well into 1944" (190). The obstacle to change was a "fanatical" Harris, who believed that shifting his huge organization to precision assaults was impossible, both bureaucratically and technologically. Levine, in contrast, concluded that Bomber Command could have converted to a new doctrine of precision bombardment in late 1943. When it did not, the results were moral stains like Dresden, a war that unnecessarily lasted into 1945, and a contribution to victory that was far less than it could have been.

Although Levine was not sanguine about the legacy of "Bomber" Harris, his censure and moral outrage were mild when compared to those of Garrett, who concluded in *Ethics and Airpower in World War II* that the moral failure of area bombing was not in its purpose, but with its conduct. In other words, Harris and Bomber Command did not run afoul of the *jus ad bellum* precepts found in modern thinking about just war. The area offensive had the right intent, derived from legitimate authority, and was an instrument of last resort. On the other hand, Garrett asserted that Harris and others clearly failed to comply with *jus in bello* restrictions on the conduct of war, especially after September 1944. In the case of proportionality, British targeting of entire cities ignored any reasonable distinction between combatants and noncombatants.

In the case of "double effect," which requires a conscious effort to limit the suffering of the innocent as much as possible, Bomber Command trivialized the principle. Harris' air planners developed a new calculus where brevity equaled mercy, even if an individual attack was indiscriminate, and where "double effect" was acceptable, provided wholesale slaughter was not the stated goal. Lastly, Harris and his disciples argued that "military necessity" justified the temporary neglect of moral considerations in war. A supreme emergency existed, a nation's survival was at stake, and defeat was imminent. Therefore, the Harris faction claimed, unrestrained area bombing was regrettable but necessary under the circumstances.

With the benefit of hindsight, Garrett rejected the preceding argument. The supreme emergency passed, he insisted, with the defeat of the Luftwaffe in the Battle of Britain. British national survival was no longer in doubt, but Bomber Command drew a different conclusion. It continued to invoke "military necessity" while debasing the concept at the same time. What was necessary progressively became what was expedient. As a result, the just ends Bomber Command sought to achieve were compromised by the particular means it used to gain them. In Garrett's opinion, "The melancholy truth seems to be that in combating a great evil, the British . . . condoned evils, i.e., area bombing, that significantly lessened the whole moral purpose of the struggle" (145). That Garrett retroactively attempted to impose late twentieth-century moral standards on an earlier, unsettled era is open to debate, as are other moral critiques of the CBO, but his conclusions do represent a sour consensus on the doctrine of area bombardment.

If there is an unhappy moral consensus about the British strategic air campaign, in the case of the United States there remains a clear division of opinion between authority-doubting revisionists scarred by America's debacle in Vietnam and committed pragmatists. In the first case, we have

Sherry's *The Rise of American Air Power* and Schaffer's *Wings of Judgment.* Both works argued that American policies against indiscriminate strategic bombardment were so broadly interpreted and so frequently violated that they were meaningless. A commitment to precision bombardment may have existed in theory, but it did not exist in fact. According to Sherry, the sources of this schism were racism, technological fanaticism, and "a slow accretion of large fears, thoughtless assumptions, and incremental decisions" (4). Schaffer, in turn, foisted the odium of indiscriminate area bombing onto Henry "Hap" Arnold and other air force leaders. They also yielded to "military necessity" and then disingenuously clothed their pragmatic attempts to destroy urban targets in moralistic clothing. In short, they adopted a group psychology that ignored the problem.

However, there are three alternative explanations to the revisionism promulgated by Sherry and Schaffer. Parks, for example, claimed in "Air War and the Law of War" that American airmen did not think that what they were doing was immoral or inconsistent with traditional morality, as they understood it at the time. As a result, there was no need, in Schaffer's words, for a "collective pattern of psychological defense through avoidance." Second, Crane argued in *Bombs, Cities, and Civilians* that the American commitment to precision bombardment and the minimizing of noncombatant suffering remained firm, despite a growing reliance on radar bombing. This commitment survived because operational and tactical commanders in Europe enjoyed genuine latitude in waging the air war, and they consciously tried to avoid morale-oriented terror bombing even when distant superiors in Washington encouraged the idea. Lastly, Davis, *Spaatz and the Air War in Europe*, admitted that a process of "barbarization" did occur in the American air campaign, but he also claimed it was inadvertent. The radar bombing device H2X did not adequately compensate for the violent winter of 1944–1945, despite American continued commitment to attacking "recognizable and identifiable" targets, even in bad weather. One can therefore claim, unlike the British example, that the morality (i.e., success) of the U.S. air campaign remains largely in the historiographical eye of the beholder.

THE OPPORTUNITIES FOR FURTHER RESEARCH

Popular histories on the strategic air war in Europe remain a cottage industry. However, the need for scholarly, three-dimensional treatments on various aspects of the war remains high. We have, for example, no scholarly study of American, British, and German combat training programs. We also lack rigorous, in-depth biographies on many airmen, including Henry "Hap" Arnold, Ira Eaker, and even the seminal Hugh Trenchard. There are few substantive histories on Luftwaffe fighter defense units; there are no first-rate, scholarly treatments of the Eighth and

Fifteenth Air Forces; nor is there an exhaustive analysis of Big Week. The degree of autonomy local commanders had in directing the air war remains an open question, despite Crane's initial efforts. Did commanders actually shape air doctrine and strategy at the local level? Lastly, the origins and development of strategic air intelligence, with an emphasis on the philosophic foundations of targeting, still require a comprehensive history, despite the work of Hinsley on *British Intelligence* and others. So, is the subject of the strategic air war in Europe exhausted? Hardly; it remains a valid area of inquiry well into the foreseeable future.

BIBLIOGRAPHY

Bidinian, Larry J. *The Combined Allied Bombing Offensive against the German Civilian 1942–1945.* Lawrence, KS: Coronado, 1976.

Boog, Horst, ed. *The Conduct of the Air War in the Second World War: An International Comparison.* New York and Oxford: Berg, 1992.

Boyne, Walter. *Clash of Wings: Air Power in World War II.* New York: Simon and Schuster, 1994.

Crane, Conrad C. *Bombs, Cities, and Civilians: American Airpower Strategy in World War II.* Lawrence: UP of Kansas, 1993.

Craven, Wesley Frank, and James L. Cate, eds. *The Army Air Forces in World War II.* Vol. 2, *Europe: Torch to Pointblank, August 1942 to December 1943.* Chicago: University of Chicago, 1949.

———. *The Army Air Forces in World War II.* Vol. 3, *Europe: Argument to V-E Day, January 1944 to May 1945.* Chicago: University of Chicago, 1951.

Daniels, Gordon. *A Guide to the Reports of the United States Strategic Bombing Survey (USSBS).* London: Offices of the Royal Historical Society, University College, 1981.

Davis, Richard G. *Carl A. Spaatz and the Air War in Europe.* Washington, DC: GPO, 1993.

———. "German Rail Yards and Cities: U.S. Bombing Policy 1944–1945." *Air Power History* 42 (1995): 46–63.

Emerson, William R. "Operation Pointblank: A Tale of Bombers and Fighters." In Harry Borowski, ed., *The Harmon Memorial Lectures in Military History, 1959–1987*, 441–72. Washington, DC: GPO, 1988.

Fabyanic, Thomas A. *Strategic Air Attack in the United States Air Force: A Case Study.* Manhattan, KS: Military Affairs/Aerospace Historian, 1976.

Frankland, Noble. *The Bombing Offensive against Germany: Outlines and Perspective.* London: Faber and Faber, 1965.

———. "The Combined Bomber Offensive: Classical and Revolutionary, Combined and Divided, Planned and Fortuitous." In William Geffen, ed., *Command and Commanders in Modern Military History*, 253–67. Washington, DC: GPO, 1968.

Garrett, Stephen A. *Ethics and Air Power in World War II: The British Bombing of German Cities.* New York: St. Martin's, 1993.

Gaston, James C. *Planning the American Air War.* Fort Lesley McNair, Washington, DC: National Defense UP, 1982.

Groehler, Olaf. *Bombenkrieg gegen Deutschland (1940–1945)*. Berlin: Akademie, 1990.
————. "The Strategic Air War and Its Impact on the German Civilian Population." In Horst Boog, ed., *The Conduct of the Air War*, 279–97. New York and Oxford: Berg, 1992.

Hansell, Haywood. *The Air Plan That Defeated Hitler*. Atlanta: Higgins-MacArthur/Logino and Porter, 1972.
————. *The Strategic Air War against Germany and Japan*. Washington, DC: GPO, 1987.

Harris, Arthur. *Bomber Offensive*. London: Collins, 1947; Don Mills, Ontario: Stoddart, 1990.

Hastings, Max. *Bomber Command*. New York: Simon and Schuster, 1987; London: Papermac, 1993.

Hinsley, Francis H. *British Intelligence in the Second World War*. Abridged version. Cambridge: Cambridge UP, 1993.

Kennett, Lee B. *A History of Strategic Bombing*. New York: Scribner's, 1982.

Köhler, Karl. "Bibliographie zur Luftkriegsgeschichte." In *Schriften der Bibliothek für Zeitgeschichte*, 5. Frankfurt: Bernard and Graefe, 1966.

Kohn, Richard H., and Joseph P. Harahan, eds. *Strategic Air Warfare: An Interview with Generals Curtis E. LeMay, Leon W. Johnson, David A. Burchinal, and Jack J. Catton*. Washington, DC: GPO, 1988.

Levine, Alan J. *The Strategic Bombing of Germany, 1940–1945*. Westport, CT: Praeger, 1992.

MacIsaac, David. *Strategic Bombing in World War II: The Story of the United States Strategic Bombing Survey*. New York: Garland, 1976.

Mason, Tony. *Air Power: A Centenial Appraisal*. London and Washington, DC: Brassey's, 1994.

McCarthy, John. "Did the Bomber Always Get Through?: The Control of Strategic Air Space 1939–1945." In Alan Stevens, ed., *The War in the Air—1914–94*, 95–112. RAF Base Fairbain, Australia: Air Power Studies Center, 1994.

Messenger, Charles. *"Bomber" Harris and the Strategic Bombing Offensive, 1939–1945*. New York: St. Martin's; London: Arms and Armour, 1984.

Mierzejewski, Alfred C. *The Collapse of the German War Economy, 1944–1945: Allied Air Power and the German National Railway*. Chapel Hill: University of North Carolina, 1988.

Murray, Williamson. "The Influence of Pre-War Anglo-American Doctrine on the Air Campaigns of the Second World War." In Horst Boog, ed., *The Conduct of the Air War*, 235–53. New York and Oxford: Berg, 1992.
————. *Strategy for Defeat: The Luftwaffe 1933–1945*. Maxwell Air Force Base, Alabama: Air UP, 1983.

Overy, Richard J. "Air Power and the Origins of Deterrence Theory before 1939." *Journal of Strategic Studies* 15 (1992): 73–101.
————. *The Air War 1939–1945*. New York: Stein and Day, 1980; London: Papermac, 1987.
————. *Why the Allies Won*. London: Jonathan Cape; New York: W. W. Norton, 1995.
————. "World War II: The Bombing of Germany." In Alan Stevens, ed., *The War in the Air—1914–94*, 113–40. RAF Base Fairbain, Australia: Air Power Studies Center, 1994.

Parks, W. Hays. "Air War and the Law of War." *The Air Force Law Review 32* (1990): 1–225.

Parton, James. *"Air Force Spoken Here": General Ira Eaker and the Command of the Air.* Bethesda, MD: Adler and Adler, 1986.

Possonoy, Stefan T. *Strategic Air Power: The Pattern of Dynamic Security.* Washington, DC: Infantry Journal, 1949.

Quester, George H. *Deterrence before Hiroshima.* New Brunswick, NJ: Transaction Books, 1986.

Richards, Denis. *Portal of Hungerford.* London: Heinemann, 1977.

Rostow, Walt W. *Pre-Invasion Bombing Strategy: General Eisenhower's Decision of March 25, 1944.* Austin: University of Texas, 1981.

Schaffer, Ronald. *Wings of Judgment.* New York and Oxford: Oxford UP, 1985.

Sherry, Michael. *The Rise of American Air Power: The Creation of Armageddon.* New Haven, CT: Yale UP, 1987.

Smith, Malcolm. "The Allied Air Offensive." *The Journal of Strategic Studies 13* (1990): 67–83.

Smith, Myron J. *Air War Bibliography, 1939–1945.* 5 vols. Manhattan, KS: Aerospace Historian, 1977–1982.

Spaatz, Carl. "Strategic Air Power: Fulfillment of a Concept." *Foreign Affairs 24* (1946): 385–96.

Terraine, John. "Theory and Practice of the Air War: The Royal Air Force." In Horst Boog, ed., *The Conduct of the Air War,* 467–95. New York and Oxford: Berg, 1992.

———. *A Time for Courage: The Royal Air Force in the European War, 1939–1945.* New York: Macmillan, 1985. Also published as *To the Right of the Line. The Royal Air Force in the European War 1939–1945.* London: Hodder and Stoughton, 1985.

U.S. Air Force Academy. *Air Power and Warfare.* Special Bibliography Series, no. 59, September 1978.

U.S. Strategic Bombing Survey. *Summary Report (European War).* Washington, DC: GPO, 1945.

———, Oil Division. *Final Report.* Washington, DC: GPO, 1947.

Watts, Barry D. *The Foundations of U.S. Air Doctrine: The Problem of Friction in War.* Maxwell Air Force Base, AL: Air UP, 1984.

Webster, Charles K., and Noble Frankland. *The Strategic Air Offensive Against Germany 1939–1945.* 4 vols. London: HMSO, 1961.

Zuckerman, Solly. *From Apes to Warlords.* New York: Harper and Row, 1978.

———. "Strategic Bombing and the Defeat of Germany." *Journal of the Royal United Services Institute 130* (1985): 67–70.

15   British and American Logistics

Kevin Smith

Because the Japanese attack at Pearl Harbor unleashed the American arsenal of democracy's full strength in open belligerency, Winston Churchill celebrated that moment in his memoirs. "So we had won after all. . . . All the rest was merely the proper application of overwhelming force" (*The Grand Alliance*, 606–67).

The United States, the Soviet Union, and the British Empire were now combined in a Grand Alliance that could overpower its foes with its massed industrial production. Evaluations of Churchill's verdict share a basic limitation as these assessments of the diplomatic, strategic, and tactical aspects of Allied cooperation and victory proliferate yearly. Reviewing "the proper application of overwhelming force" leads also to the oft-neglected evaluation of the Allied logistical effort, all too often assumed as a given without close examination.

Logistics' definition is malleable, at times encompassing all aspects of military administration. Any brief definition could mislead and stir controversy, yet logistics is understood herein as efforts to mobilize, procure, transport, and resupply military forces. This scientific art (requiring administrative and inspirational genius) oversees the mobilization of industry as the prerequisite for supplying modern armies, the procurement of military supplies, the transportation of troops and supplies to theaters of operations and to the battlefield, and the organization of continuous resupply of forces. Also relevant are signals, code breaking, recreation, propaganda, and medical services (including establishment of hospitals and evacuation of wounded). Also, civilian logistical needs were, and have been, neglected as a necessary adjunct to military operations in an era of total war. For further reference in defining logistics, see Leighton and Coakley's excellent introduction, "Logistics—The Word and the Thing," to their authoritative two-volume exploration of American *Global Logistics and Strategy*.

Examining the scholarship of British and American logistics in World War II begins with the recognition that scholarly and especially popular writing, in both attention and attitude, has mimicked the attitudes of many wartime officers. Logistics was, and remains, the poor relation of tactics and strategy, as its practitioners and historians have often lamented. A cursory examination of the historiography of the Battle of the Atlantic illustrates this point.

THE BATTLE OF THE ATLANTIC AS ARCHETYPE

That battle was foundational to the Allies' logistical effort, since the sustenance of British imports and acceleration of the U.S. Army's buildup in Britain were basic to the Anglo-American Second Front strategy. Its extensive literature stresses the strategic and tactical issues, from the official historians onward. Morison's volume on *The Battle of the Atlantic* in his *History of United States Naval Operations* and Roskill's *The War at Sea* can now (belatedly) be compared with Hessler's view based on service in U-boats and on Dönitz's staff (Hessler was his son-in-law) in *The U-Boat War in the Atlantic*. Subsequently, historians have thoroughly mined memoirs and integrated code breaking in their largely successful efforts to plumb the tactical depth and strategic breadth of the Battle of the Atlantic. Hughes and Costello offer a useful and succinct overview of the struggle at sea in *The Battle of the Atlantic*, as does Van Der Vat in *The Atlantic Campaign*. Milner portrays the development of the Royal Canadian Navy in *North Atlantic Run*. Rohwer focuses upon one vital segment of the struggle in *The Critical Convoy Battles of March 1943*, while Terraine provides a First World War context in *The U-Boat Wars 1916–1945*, and Y'Blood examines the American contribution in *Hunter-Killer*. Runyan and Copes have edited a collection of the latest scholarship in *To Die Gallantly* (see among numerous outstanding contributions those of Bowling, Steury, and Milner), also represented in Syrett's analysis of the often-neglected summer of 1943 in *The Defeat of the German U-Boats*.

This literature has been unduly affected by a wartime preoccupation with the submarine danger, which has generated an ongoing legacy of disproportionate attention from operations research analysts to antisubmarine warfare, to the detriment of supplemental emphases upon maintaining important (if mundane) infrastructure like shipyards and internal transport. The effort of the Allied navies in the North Atlantic to protect *ships* was often undermined by the wastage of *shipping capacity* in the ports after ships survived dangerous voyages. Still, no official history of American merchant shipping management in World War II exists. No subsequent book-length evaluation exists, either. The title of U.S. War Shipping Administrator Emory Land's memoir, *Winning the War with Ships: Land, Sea and Air—Mostly Land,* indicates his self-absorption and its lack of substance. De la Pedraja's *The Rise and Decline of U.S. Merchant Shipping* makes almost no reference to the World War II era, in which the American merchant fleet expanded to an unprecedented size. The relevant chapters in Browder and Smith's *Independent: A Biography of Lewis W. Douglas* (the U.S. deputy war shipping administrator) are serviceable. Still, there is no counterpart in American historiography to Behrens' official history in the United Kingdom Civil Series on the History of the Second World War, *Merchant Shipping and the Demands of War.*

Behrens thoroughly detailed British endeavors to maintain enough merchant shipping capacity to feed Britons and mobilize imperial military efforts, but her discussion of Britain's efforts to augment that capacity from U.S. sources suffers from a lack of access to American records. She stressed British solutions to problems like reducing internal transport congestion and expediting merchant ship repair, yet these cannot be accounted for without reference to Lend-Lease. Inter-Allied cooperation was crucial to proper management of British logistical resources, including merchant ships. Just as in the other British official histories discussed later, the traditions of preserving the anonymity of civil servants and insisting upon the unanimity of cabinet decisions once reached also limited Behrens' portrayal of internal disagreements at bureaucratic and cabinet level about how best to extract ships from British industries and from the Americans.

Several of the essays in Howarth and Law, *The Battle of the Atlantic,* are promising, though most of these approximately three dozen essays retain the traditional focus. Barnett offers a stimulating indictment of deficiencies in the British shipbuilding industry in *The Audit of War,* wherein he also contrasts British illusions of power with the reality of decline in coal, steel, and other industries vital to logistical prowess. Other overviews of the decline of Britain's shipbuilding industry include Scott and Hughes' official history of *The Administration of War Production;* Jones, *Shipbuilding in Britain;* Parkinson, *The Economics of Shipbuilding in the United Kingdom;* and Hogwood, *Government and Shipbuilding.* Reid's adoring biography of *James Lithgow,* Britain's wartime controller of merchant shipbuilding, has been superseded by Large's more critical brief treatment in *Between Two Fires.*

In "Winston Churchill as War Manager," Schoenfeld integrated logistical issues into an examination of Churchill's dynamic leadership of the cabinet-level Battle of the Atlantic Committee. He reviewed British efforts to improve port turnaround and reduce tonnage under repair, concluding that Churchill sometimes demanded unwise changes and exaggerated the scope of British reforms but imposed a much-needed sense of urgency.

Greenough notes a significant failure of Britain's wider, imperial logistical responsibility amid his treatment of the Bengal famine of 1943–1944, *Prosperity and Misery in Modern Bengal*. Despite such exceptions, this overview of the Battle of the Atlantic literature reiterates that historians' examinations of what was a battle to control lines of communication have all too often neglected the logistical aspects of this struggle in favor of its tactics and strategy.

CONTINUED RELIANCE ON BRITISH CIVIL AND U.S. ARMY OFFICIAL HISTORIES

This emphasis upon tactical and strategic viewpoints has encouraged continued reliance on British and American official histories of logistics that remain authoritative on important issues, though often in need of revisions that have (thankfully) begun. In *Official Histories*, Higham collected some insightful evaluations of the role and limitations of official civil and military histories in establishing patterns of research. Butler and Hancock (respectively, the editors of the United Kingdom Military and Civil Series on *The History of the Second World War*) wrote essays on the origins and conduct of their giant projects. American participants in this effort, including Morton, Blumenson, and Greenfield, offered contrasting assessments of the validity of official history. Greenfield's assessment (the most positive) condensed his longer description of the process of "doing" official history in *The Historian and the Army*.

For the British, the *History of the Second World War* subsumes the United Kingdom Military History Series and the Civil History Series. The first set is not useful for logistical inquiry. Howard's *Grand Strategy*, vol. 4, remains a model for official history, yet he referenced logistical questions only tangentially. The histories of the British army's technical services were therefore not explored as systematically as in the detailed counterparts in *The United States Army in World War II*, which are discussed later, and thus such investigations were usually published outside the Military History Series, usually by the respective service itself (with the requisite lack of perspective). These include Hay's *R.O.F.: The Story of the Royal Ordnance Factories* and Nalder's *The History of British Army Signals*. Thus, the British military perspective on World War II logistical issues needs further exploration.

There are some encouraging developments. Ogorkiewicz offered a provocative transnational analysis of tank development, organization, and equipment in *Armor: A History of Mechanized Forces*, which naturally stresses interwar and World War II developments in giving British tank development plenty of attention. Macksey examined the controversial role of Percy Hobart, a leading British advocate of employment of unorthodox formations, in *Armoured Crusader*. Macksey also published the wide-ranging

For Want of a Nail. Though this long book lacks citations, Macksey offers a necessary breath of fresh air in his terse contextualization of strategic, logistical, and tactical issues in a unified context throughout the last century of rapid technological change, offering significant examples of the impact of logistics upon strategy and tactics from the World War II era. One provocative insight links the relative length of the British army's "tail" in proportion to its teeth to the revelation of heartless administrative practices in the First World War (though one wonders if anything can justify the Americans' far more profligate use of shipping tonnage to supply their troops). Though he may go too far in trying to liberate his army of arguments from its supply line of unending statistical detail, like Sherman he has caught our attention. Still, more justification for his assertions would be useful.

In arguing that Allied logistical superiority compensated for rather clumsy tactics in *Brute Force,* Ellis offers a useful corrective to excessive Allied claims of brilliant generalship amid a sound insistence upon the importance of recognizing comparative economic strength. He does not carefully distinguish production from distribution and is far too insouciant about the Battle of the Atlantic. Yet this provocative work impels further thinking about an integrated historiography of logistics.

Fortunately, many of the British civil histories remain far more useful than the official military histories, from a logistics standpoint. Many retain enduring value, for only occasionally has subsequent research investigated the issues discussed therein. An overall perspective of the economic home front is available in Hancock and Gowing, *British War Economy,* and Postan, *British War Production,* complemented by the Central Statistical Office's *Statistical Digest of the War,* a fountainhead of information about social and economic wartime mobilization and change in a nation that underwent industrial as well as military conscription. Behrens' *Merchant Shipping* remains central to comprehending British administration of this core element of the war effort.

Also relevant to transportation, production, and procurement issues are Savage's *Inland Transport,* which examines port clearance and railway management, Inman's *Labour in the Munitions Industries,* and Parker's *Manpower.* The latter two review British mobilization of human resources. Their conclusions have been superseded by further research into prewar British rearmament by Peden in *British Rearmament and the Treasury,* which sets the context of financial constraints and the motivations for appeasement. In "British Rearmament," R.A.C. Parker reviewed the British government's prewar reluctance to intervene in industrial planning thanks to concern that forcing skilled workers to shift from export-oriented production toward rearmament would inhibit Britain's ability to pay for needed raw materials. Also see Scott and Hughes' discussion of British prewar organization for, and wartime control of, army, air, and naval production under the Admiralty and the Ministries of Supply, Production, and Aircraft Production in *The Administration of War Production*.

Design and Development of Weapons by Postan et al. stresses the background to procurement of aircraft, artillery, small arms, and transport. For a longer-term perspective on the British aircraft industry, see Higham's articles, "Quantity *vs.* Quality" and "Government, Companies, and National Defense." Payton-Smith's study of British efforts to ensure access to *Oil* is superseded by Painter's *Oil and the American Century*, from an American perspective, and Yergin's *The Prize*, which discusses Anglo-American wartime oil rivalry in a grand historical survey. Hammond, *Food*, examined the evolution of British policy and administrative tactics vital to the crucial effort to manage the acquisition and rationing of domestically produced and imported foodstuffs for an industrialized island population heavily dependent on food imports. Hornby, *Factories and Plant*, covers British efforts to sustain production while not replenishing existing plant.

Hall provided in *North American Supply* and in *Studies of Overseas Supply* (with Wrigley) a narrative of British efforts to procure and pay for vital supplies of raw materials, tools, and weapons from Canada and the United States that suggests the extent and limits of Britain's dependence on that assistance as well as the wartime American aircraft industry's debt to earlier British efforts to "prime the pump" of American industry. Hall's analysis is now superseded by Kimball's standard discussion of Lend-Lease, *The Most Unsordid Act*, by works on complex Anglo-American financial dealings in Dobson's *U.S. Wartime Aid to Britain*, by Woods' *A Changing of the Guard*, and by Reynolds' definitive *The Creation of the Anglo-American Alliance*.

The United States and Great Britain formed numerous Combined Boards to administer their coordinated war effort—in particular to adjudicate allocations of munitions production, raw materials, food, and merchant ships. Hall's mildly optimistic examination of the Combined Boards mechanism in *Studies of Overseas Supply* should be contrasted with the American Rosen's vindictive, Anglophobic analysis of the *Combined Boards'* efforts in assigning munitions and adjusting shipping allocations.

The U.S. Department of the Army's "green books" series, *The United States Army in World War II*, has won applause as the finest example extant of official history. It is ironic—and revealing of different American and British attitudes toward civilian involvement in "military" affairs—that nearly all the best and most relevant British official histories of logistic issues in World War II were written under civilian supervision, while on the American side the army retained direction of scholarly reviews of processes it had administered. One unhappy example of a semiofficial American civil history was Rosen's *Combined Boards*. More useful are Lane's *Ships for Victory*, which praises the Maritime Commission's oversight of the gargantuan expansion of merchant shipbuilding production, and the history of the War Production Board in *Industrial Mobilization for War* (listed under U.S.).

For the army series, Adamczyk and MacGregor's updated *Reader's Guide* is an indispensable introduction to the *United States Army in World War II* series and its twelve subseries. It offers a brief synopsis of the seventy-eight volumes available in 1992. Of two dozen volumes in the Technical Services Subseries detailing exploits of the Chemical Warfare Service, Corps of Engineers, Medical Department, Ordnance Department, Quartermaster Corps, Signal Corps, and the Transportation Corps, several representative selections will suffice.

In *The Ordnance Department: Planning Munitions for War*, Green, Thomson, and Rootes discussed prewar and wartime research and development of weapons, stressing efforts to comprehend and implement combat requirements for ground forces (needed firepower, mobility, and protection) into the development process. Development of antiaircraft and of aircraft weaponry is also included. This volume pointed to the interplay between tactical requirements and logistical feasibility, with reference to survivability and maneuverability of American tanks. In a companion volume, *The Ordnance Department: Procurement and Supply*, Thomson and Mayo emphasized provision of transport and combat vehicles, small arms, artillery, and relevant ammunition. This volume is essential to a clear understanding of superior Allied maneuverability in the Northwest Europe campaign compared to a Wehrmacht that had been responsible for restoring that feature to the battlefield.

The Transportation Corps' movement of men and supplies from internal U.S. destinations by rail, road, and ship to distant battlefronts is discussed in two volumes by Wardlow (*Responsibilities, Organization and Operations* and *Movements, Training, and Supply*) and one by Bykofsky and Larson, *Operations Overseas*. These volumes emphasize the link between logistics and strategy in global amphibious warfare, tracing various aspects of the corps' activities and offering a gold mine of information.

The official historians had one tremendous advantage: immediate access to the archives and the principals involved, especially useful, given the improvisational nature of much logistical activity. Thus, the official histories provided a solid foundation, though they do share the common flaw of parochialism in their representation of one department's viewpoint. As Beaver pointed out in his excellent survey of interwar and wartime army truck procurement in " 'Deuce and a Half,' " Green, Thomson, and Rootes omitted procurement of army trucks, likely attributable to the fact that truck procurement had originally been a Quartermaster Corps task. As we await more second-generation scholarship on World War II logistics, historiographical parochialism can be rectified in two ways: by referring to the departmental histories penned by researchers of the other technical services or by consulting "green books" of grander sweep.

For example, R. Elberton Smith presented a wider perspective in *The Army and Economic Mobilization*, discussing determination of requirements and actual procurement of all types of commodities as well as supervision of the mobilization of American industry from peacetime status to war economy. This theme was given historical perspective outside the World War II series in Kreidberg and Henry's *History of Military Mobilization in the United States Army*. Smith emphasized the difficulty of maintaining price stability and the tendency to contract with large, proven businesses at the expense of small business—of interest to corporatist historians. Unlike some of the other volumes, he offered an excellent conclusion. Holley examined similar processes in *Buying Aircraft*. He covered budgeting, design, and industrial development issues and reviewed the transformation of auto assembly plants to aircraft manufacturing and the impact of Roosevelt's 1940 appeal for fifty thousand planes. The companion volumes in Craven and Cate, *The Army Air Forces in World War II*, are volume 6, *Men and Planes*, examining training and procurement, and volume 7, *Services around the World*, discussing, inter alia, air transport, aviation engineering and medicine, and weather forecasting.

Leighton and Coakley's *Global Logistics and Strategy* set the benchmark for a global and top-level perspective of the inter-Allied, interservice "chronic, pervasive competition for resources." Since the provision of cargo shipping to move supplies and assault shipping to launch amphibious operations were vital components in the Allied strategic effort, any study of Allied amphibious operations or the Second Front must consult them to ensure that evaluation of strategic decision making is firmly grounded in logistical reality. They incorporated civilian records and available information from British memoirs and official histories to provide a reasonable and often critical assessment, offering a balanced appraisal of the competing demands posed by American army, army air, and naval commanders in Pacific, European, and Mediterranean theaters as well as by Russian and British requirements. Still, their sources influenced their research, compelling attention to the army perspective and restricting regard to others.

Despite their occasional criticism of the army's disdain for British assessments of civilian import needs, Leighton and Coakley were not privy to detailed motivations for British policy. They comprehended the context of military logistics in a late-mobilizing U.S. civilian society that hesitantly adopted central resource controls but could not achieve thorough understanding of the civilian logistics of a fully mobilized island state dependent on food imports. They could not know of divisions among British bureaucrats and between British civilians and officers that affected policy formulation. The U.S. Army's views of the flaws in Britain's arguments for an expanded import program were available, but internal British assessments were not. Also, the fascinating interplay of such picturesque personalities as Roosevelt, Somervell, Douglas, Averell Harriman, and British Minister of War Transport Frederick (Lord) Leathers necessarily escaped full attention. Their thorough research in American archives and lack of access to British records therefore produced a brilliant, but one-sided, appraisal.

These books should be consulted in combination with Huston's long-term perspective in *The Sinews of War: Army Logistics*, and Matloff and Snell, *Strategic Planning for Coalition Warfare*. One issue relevant to Allied strategic harmony was maintaining adequate supply to Russia. This was addressed at length in Motter, *The Persian Corridor and Aid to Russia*, which placed administration, local contracting and construction, and access to oil in the wider strategic context. Herring, *Aid to Russia*, contextualized such efforts in the origins of the Cold War. Coakley also explored this topic in "The Persian Corridor," an essay appearing in *Command Decisions*, the editor Greenfield's excellent compilation condensing lengthy discussions of important issues reviewed elsewhere (especially in the "green books"). Several refer to logistical issues. Leighton's "U.S. Merchant Shipping and the British Import Crisis" outlined the army's response to British demands for increased imports at the expense of the movement of American troops and supplies to Britain in Operation Bolero preparatory to crossing the Channel. Thus, logistical constraints threatened the Casablanca strategic agreements. I explored this controversy from both sides in Smith, "Logistics Diplomacy at Casablanca" and set it in its context of the logistically unwise decision for Torch in "Constraining Overlord." Ruppenthal set the original standard for logistical analysis of the army's record in supplying its troops in that theater in *Logistical Support of the Armies*. Waddell has critiqued army handling of logistics during planning, landing, breakout, and exploitation of the Normandy landing in *United States Army Logistics* (sadly, there is no logistical counterpart for the Pacific). In *U.S. Military Logistics, 1607–1991: A Research Guide*, Shrader provided the necessary raw materials for a wider assessment of World War II logistics that is firmly grounded in two centuries of American military history.

Turning to the U.S. Navy, Carter and Duvall's glimpse of Mediterranean and Atlantic naval logistics in *Ships, Salvage, and Sinews of War* complements Carter's outline of the exploits of Service Squadron Ten in the Pacific in *Beans, Bullets, and Black Oil*. Their tedious description of bases, organization, and lists of participating vessels enlivened by an occasional anecdote (but lacking analysis) does not stand comparison with Ruppenthal's inquiry into army logistics in the European theater in *Logistical Support of the Armies*. Connery, *The Navy and Industrial Mobilization*, dealt with the navy's efforts to harness the arsenal of democracy to its purposes. Bureau perspectives are seen in Rowland and Boyd, *U.S. Navy Bureau of Ordnance*, and in the U.S. Bureau of Yards and Docks, *Building the Navy's Bases*. Also see Coletta's chapter on Chief of Civil Engineers Ben Moreell

(Vice Admiral after 1944) in Howarth's *Men of War*. Furer, *Administration of the Navy Department*, is superseded by Albion and Connery's study of undersecretary (later secretary) of the navy and his subordinates, *Forrestal and the Navy*, and by relevant chapters in the perceptive and poignant biography of Forrestal by Hoopes and Brinkley, *Driven Patriot*. Ballantine and Eccles offered the best of a limited selection. In *U.S. Naval Logistics*, Ballantine discussed the costs and benefits of the decentralized bureau system amid navy efforts to shift from improvised creation of forward bases to a functioning system that could sustain the operational burden imposed by distance, magnitude, and uncertainty. Given the navy's overall inattention to logistical issues and their historiography, Rear Admiral Henry Eccles' achievement in *Logistics in the National Defense* deserves attention. He studied naval and military logistics in the broadest context, cautioning against the "logistic snowball": the excessive expansion of logistic personnel and activities at the expense of the tactical forces they support. Rather than bolstering opponents of a "longer tail" thereby, Eccles demanded that commanders properly exercise command responsibility: comprehend logistical issues and exercise control of logistical support, avoiding the condescending tendency to assign less competent officers to logistics, which diminishes efficiency and aggravates the snowball. His didactic, presentist approach is enlivened by a rigorous blend of theory and practice in numerous insightful references to examples from World War II. U.S. Navy logistics in World War II still awaits a modern interpreter.

OPERATIONS IN FRANCE (1944) AND THE BROAD-FRONT CONTROVERSY

The most controversial logistical failure of the war was the inability to sustain Allied forces in their 1944 dash across France long enough to enable a decisive thrust into Germany. Logistical shortages prompted conflict over appropriate strategy in September 1944 once the advance across France was completed. Eisenhower controversially rejected Montgomery's advocacy of a narrow thrust in favor of a deliberate offensive along a broad front.

Ruppenthal distilled his comments in *Logistical Support of the Armies* into several articles, "Logistic Limitations on Tactical Decisions," "Logistic Planning for Overlord in Retrospect," and most notably, "Logistics and the Broad-Front Strategy," which appeared in *Command Decisions*. He assessed the impact of theater and global logistical requirements and shortages upon strategic planning for assault and follow-up operations and tactical execution. Since limited British port and internal transport capacity had forced deployment of American troops in western England, supply needs not only influenced the choice of invasion beaches but dictated who assaulted them—with serious consequences. Also, the need to achieve a secure lodgment for an administrative base and the assumption that enemy resistance and logistical problems mandated slow progress shaped the supply network's response to postbreakout operations.

In *Supplying War*, van Creveld usefully questioned whether a Mediterranean strategy could have won the war for Germany (given the logistical constraints of desert operations, including Libyan port capacity) and condemned Allied planners' "logistic pusillanimity." The Allied advance was less a logistical miracle than a rebuke to the planners' refusal to rely on determination, common sense, and improvisation. It is indeed curious that the most prominent book in memory urging increased attention to logistics thus encouraged renewed disdain for the planning process. His review of Montgomery's plan recognized the greater logistical obstacles to the success of this follow-up operation. In any case, a successful "knife thrust" into the Rhine that did not break German resistance invited counterattack.

In "The History of Logistics and *Supplying War*," Lynn raised questions about van Creveld's calculations in other eras and dismissed his assault on the World War II planners for ignoring their tremendous successes in earlier stages of planning that made pusillanimity possible. Weigley offered more restrained criticism in *Eisenhower's Lieutenants*, indicting instead the related siege of Brest as a wastage of supplies needed farther east that might have enabled a breakthrough into Germany in 1944. Mack also condemned the siege of Brest. A supply officer in both wars and chief of movements in the Communications Zone in 1944, he lived long enough to counterattack ferociously in *The Critical Error of World War II*. He indicted Bradley and Patton's failure to force their subordinates to secure easier supply lines through the southern Brittany ports, thanks to their unwise drive westward to the logistically insignificant Brest and the turn east toward Paris rather than south to Quiberon Bay, which was supposed to anchor Patton's supply line.

CONCLUSION

In sum, the "green books" and the British civil series cast a huge shadow over the subsequent historiography of American military logistics in World War II, in the same way as Churchill's *The Second World War* influenced a generation of historians' appraisals of appeasement and the Anglo-American special relationship. Leighton and Coakley ameliorated somewhat the technical services' histories' tendencies to see the trees rather than the forest, but syntheses are still necessary. Since total global war on multiple fronts produced simultaneous demands upon American procurement and distribution of, for example, vital trucks, airplanes, landing craft, and merchant ships, nearly every internal American (and British) controversy over the proper allocation of resources had global and coalition dimensions. Thus, logistics has to be better integrated into our understanding of the wider American war effort, and that comprehension must be internationalized in the context of the Allies' necessarily different perspectives on vital logistical issues.

Just as Behrens' handling of British and American sources was constrained by her defined mission, so also the U.S. Army official histories could include no more than a superficial reference to British civilian import demands opposed by the army. I have endeavored to address the implications of the U.S. Army's wartime refusal to acknowledge the importance of the inclusion of civilian logistics (in a total war in which an island ally proved so crucial as an operational base) in my multiarchival reassessment of the "logistics diplomacy" of Anglo-American negotiations for allocations of merchant ships in Smith, *Conflict over Convoys.*

The process of integrating the study of World War II logistics into the military mainstream is evident in Ohl's *Supplying the Troops,* which offers an encouraging exception to the general reluctance to tackle specifically logistical subjects in an engaging biography of General B. B. Somervell, the commanding general of U.S. Army Service Forces. In bringing logistics to life through Somervell, Ohl surpassed Millett's largely positive assessment of Somervell in *The Organization and Role of the Army Service Forces.* Ohl depicted Somervell as a bureaucratic warrior par excellence who sought the authority needed to impose centralization upon War Department procurement and supply, fight off coalition partners' demands upon American production, and thereby enable Marshall and Roosevelt to utilize American logistical prowess to dictate strategy. Somervell's stubborn ruthlessness, dislike of civilian interference, and quest for power thereby shaped the development of American army procurement and supply.

While Ohl's analysis of Anglo-American disputes would have benefited by reference to British archives, he provided a prime example of how logistical issues can be brought to life and performed a tremendous service by reminding us of the importance of logistics and reintroducing us to this complex, fiery general. Jean Edward Smith's biography of *Lucius D. Clay,* an officer in Somervell's wartime command, also discusses army procurement and assessment of civilian needs. Biographies of other key figures in army and navy procurement and transportation are also warranted, including General Charles P. Gross, Somervell's chief of transportation, who held provocative opinions about the relative importance of shipping U.S. military and British civilian goods into the British Isles. Thus, a field long dormant for nearly all but official historians shows promise of renewal and opportunity.

BIBLIOGRAPHY

Adamczyk, Richard D., and Morris J. MacGregor, eds. *Reader's Guide* (to the United States Army in World War II Series). Washington, DC: Center of Military History, 1992.

Albion, Robert Greenhalgh, and Robert Howe Connery. *Forrestal and the Navy.* New York: Columbia UP, 1962.

Ballantine, Duncan S. *U.S. Naval Logistics in the Second World War.* Princeton: Princeton UP, 1947.

Barnett, Correlli. *The Audit of War: The Illusion and Reality of Britain as a Great Nation.* London: Macmillan, 1986; also published as *The Pride and the Fall: The Dream and Illusion of Britain as a Great Nation.* New York: Free Press, 1987.

Beaver, Daniel R. " 'Deuce and a Half': Selecting U.S. Army Trucks, 1920–1945." In John Lynn, ed., *Feeding Mars: Logistics in Western Warfare from the Middle Ages to the Present,* 251–70. Boulder, CO: Westview, 1993.

Behrens, Catherine Betty Abigail. *Merchant Shipping and the Demands of War.* London: HMSO, 1955; Nendeln, Liechtenstein: Kraus, 1978 (reprint with confidential notes included).

Browder, Robert Paul, and Thomas G. Smith. *Independent: A Biography of Lewis W. Douglas.* New York: Knopf, 1986.

Bykofsky, Joseph, and Harold Larson. *The Transportation Corps: Operations Overseas.* Washington, DC: Office of the Chief of Military History, 1957.

Carter, Worrall R. *Beans, Bullets, and Black Oil: The Story of Fleet Logistics Afloat in the Pacific during World War II.* Washington, DC: Department of the Navy/ GPO, 1953.

Carter, Worrall R., and Elmer E. Duvall. *Ships, Salvage, and Sinews of War: The Story of Fleet Logistics Afloat in Atlantic and Mediterranean Waters during World War II.* Washington, DC: Department of the Navy/GPO, 1954.

Central Statistical Office. *Statistical Digest of the War.* London: HMSO, 1951.

Churchill, Winston S. *The Grand Alliance.* London: Chartwell; Boston: Houghton Mifflin, 1950.

Coakley, Robert W. "The Persian Corridor as a Route for Allied Aid to the U.S.S.R." In Kent Roberts Greenfield, ed., *Command Decisions,* 225–53. Washington, DC: Office of the Chief of Military History, 1960.

Coletta, Paolo. "Vice Admiral Ben Moreell." In Stephen Howarth, ed., *Men of War: Great Naval Leaders of World War II,* 551–61. New York: St. Martin's, 1992.

Connery, Robert H. *The Navy and Industrial Mobilization in World War II.* Princeton: Princeton UP, 1951.

Craven, Wesley Frank, and James Lea Cate, eds. *The Army Air Forces in World War II.* Vol. 6, *Men and Planes.* Chicago: University of Chicago, 1995; vol. 7, *Services around the World.* Chicago: University of Chicago, 1958.

Dobson, Alan P. *U.S. Wartime Aid to Britain, 1940–1946.* New York: St. Martin's, 1986.

Eccles, Henry. *Logistics in the National Defense.* Harrisburg, PA: Stackpole, 1959.

Ellis, John. *Brute Force: Allied Strategy and Tactics in the Second World War.* London: Andre Deutsch, 1990.

Furer, Julius A. *Administration of the Navy Department in World War II.* Washington, DC: Department of the Navy/GPO, 1959.

Great Britain, Central Statistical Office. *Statistical Digest of the War.* London: HMSO, 1951.

Green, Constance McLaughlin, Harry C. Thomson, and Peter C. Rootes. *The Ordnance Department: Planning Munitions for War.* Washington, DC: Office of the Chief of Military History, 1955.

Greenfield, Kent Roberts. *The Historian and the Army*. New Brunswick, NJ: Rutgers UP, 1954.

———, ed. *Command Decisions*. Washington, DC: Office of the Chief of Military History, 1960.

Greenough, Paul. *Prosperity and Misery in Modern Bengal: The Famine of 1943–44*. New York: Oxford UP, 1982.

Hall, H. Duncan. *North American Supply*. London: HMSO, 1955.

Hall, H. Duncan, and Christopher C. Wrigley. *Studies of Overseas Supply*. London: HMSO, 1956.

Hammond, Richard J. *Food*. 3 vols. London: HMSO, 1951–1962.

Hancock, William Keith, and Margaret Mary Gowing. *British War Economy*. London: HMSO, 1949; Nendeln, Liechtenstein: Kraus, 1975 (reprint with confidential notes included).

Hay, Ian. *R.O.F.: The Story of the Royal Ordnance Factories, 1939–1948*. London: HMSO, 1949.

Herring, George C. *Aid to Russia, 1941–1946: Strategy, Diplomacy, The Origins of the Cold War*. New York: Columbia UP, 1973.

Hessler, Günther. *The U-Boat War in the Atlantic, 1939–1945*. Intro. Andrew J. Withers. London: HMSO/Ministry of Defence (Navy), 1989.

Higham, Robin, ed. "Government, Companies, and National Defense: British Aeronautical Experience, 1918–1945 as the Basis for a Broad Hypothesis." *Business History Review 39* (1965): 323–47.

———. *Official Histories*. Manhattan: Kansas State University Library, 1970.

———. "Quantity *vs.* Quality: The Impact of Changing Demand on the British Aircraft Industry, 1900–1960." *Business History Review 42* (1968): 443–66.

Hogwood, Brian. *Government and Shipbuilding: The Politics of Industrial Change*. Westmead, Britain: Saxon House, 1979.

Holley, Irving B., Jr. *Buying Aircraft: Materiel Procurement for the Army Air Forces*. Washington, DC: Office of the Chief of Military History, 1964.

Hoopes, Townsend, and Douglas Brinkley. *Driven Patriot: The Life and Times of James Forrestal*. New York: Knopf, 1992.

Hornby, William. *Factories and Plant*. London: HMSO, 1958.

Howard, Michael. *Grand Strategy*. Vol. 4, *August 1942–September 1943*. London: HMSO, 1970.

Howarth, Stephen, and Derek Law, eds. *The Battle of the Atlantic 1939–1945: The 50th Anniversary International Naval Conference*. London: Greenhill, 1994.

Hughes, Terry, and John Costello. *The Battle of the Atlantic*. New York: Dial, 1977.

Huston, James. *The Sinews of War: Army Logistics, 1775–1953*. Washington, DC: Office of the Chief of Military History, 1966.

Inman, Peggy. *Labour in the Munitions Industries*. London: HMSO, 1957.

Jones, Leslie. *Shipbuilding in Britain: Mainly between the Two World Wars*. Cardiff: University of Wales, 1957.

Kimball, Warren F. *The Most Unsordid Act: Lend-Lease, 1939–1941*. Baltimore: Johns Hopkins UP, 1969.

Kreidberg, Marvin A., and Merton G. Henry. *History of Military Mobilization in the United States Army, 1775–1945*. Washington, DC: Office of the Chief of Military History, 1955.

Land, Emory Scott. *Winning the War with Ships: Land, Sea and Air—Mostly Land.* New York: R. M. McBride, 1958.

Lane, Frederic. *Ships for Victory: A History of Shipbuilding by the Maritime Commission in World War II.* Baltimore: Johns Hopkins UP, 1951.

Large, David Clay. *Between Two Fires: Europe's Path in the 1930s.* New York: Norton, 1990.

Leighton, Richard. "U.S. Merchant Shipping and the British Import Crisis." In Kent Roberts Greenfield, ed., *Command Decisions,* 199–223. Washington, DC: Office of the Chief of Military History, 1960.

Leighton, Richard, and Robert Coakley. *Global Logistics and Strategy.* 2 vols., *1940–1943* and *1943–1945.* Washington, DC: Office of the Chief of Military History, 1955, 1968.

Lynn, John. "The History of Logistics and *Supplying War.*" In Lynn, ed., *Feeding Mars: Logistics in Western Warfare from the Middle Ages to the Present,* 9–27. Boulder, CO: Westview, 1993.

Mack, Harold L. *The Critical Error of World War II.* Washington, DC: National Defense University Research Directorate, 1981.

Macksey, Kenneth. *Armoured Crusader: Major-General Sir Percy Hobart.* London: Hutchinson, 1967.

———. *For Want of a Nail: The Impact on War of Logistics and Communications.* London: Brassey's, 1989.

Matloff, Maurice, and Edwin Snell. *Strategic Planning for Coalition Warfare, 1941–1942.* Washington, DC: Office of the Chief of Military History, 1953.

Millett, John D. *The Organization and Role of the Army Service Forces.* Washington, DC: Office of the Chief of Military History, 1954.

Milner, Marc. *North Atlantic Run: The Royal Canadian Navy and the Battle of the Convoys.* Annapolis, MD: NIP, 1985.

Morison, Samuel Eliot. *The Battle of the Atlantic, September 1939–May 1943.* Vol. 1 in *History of United States Naval Operations in World War II.* Boston: Little, Brown, 1947.

Motter, Thomas Hubbard Vail. *The Persian Corridor and Aid to Russia.* Washington, DC: Office of the Chief of Military History, 1952.

Nalder, R.F.H. *The History of British Army Signals in the Second World War.* London: Royal Signals Institute, 1953.

Ogorkiewicz, Richard M. *Armor: A History of Mechanized Forces.* New York: Praeger, 1960.

Ohl, John Kennedy. *Supplying the Troops: General Somervell and American Logistics in WWII.* DeKalb: Northern Illinois UP, 1994.

Painter, David. *Oil and the American Century: The Political Economy of U.S. Foreign Oil Policy, 1941–1954.* Baltimore: Johns Hopkins UP, 1986.

Parker, Henry Michael Denne. *Manpower.* London: HMSO, 1957.

Parker, R.A.C. "British Rearmament, 1936–9: Treasury, Trade Unions, and Skilled Labour." *English Historical Review 96* (1981): 306–43.

Parkinson, J. R. *The Economics of Shipbuilding in the United Kingdom.* Cambridge: Cambridge UP, 1960.

Payton-Smith, D. J. *Oil: A Study of War-Time Policy and Administration.* London: HMSO, 1971.

Peden, G. C. *British Rearmament and the Treasury 1932–1939.* Edinburgh: Scottish Academic, 1979.

Pedraja, René de la. *The Rise and Decline of U.S. Merchant Shipping in the Twentieth Century.* New York: Twayne, 1992.

Postan, Michael Moissey. *British War Production.* London: HMSO, 1952; Nendeln, Liechtenstein: Kraus, 1975 (reprint with confidential notes included).

Postan, Michael Moissey, Denys Hay, and John D. Scott. *Design and Development of Weapons.* London: HMSO, 1964.

Reid, J. M. *James Lithgow, Master of Work.* London: Hutchinson, 1964.

Reynolds, David. *The Creation of the Anglo-American Alliance, 1937–1941: A Study in Competitive Co-Operation.* London: Europa, 1981; Chapel Hill: University of North Carolina, 1982.

Rohwer, Jürgen. *The Critical Convoy Battles of March 1943.* Annapolis, MD: NIP, 1977.

Rosen, S. McKee. *The Combined Boards of the Second World War: An Experiment in International Administration.* New York: Columbia UP, 1951.

Roskill, Stephen. *The War at Sea.* 3 vols. London: HMSO, 1954–1961.

Rowland, Buford, and William Boyd. *U.S. Navy Bureau of Ordnance in World War II.* Washington, DC: Department of the Navy/GPO, 1953.

Runyan, Timothy J., and Jan M. Copes, eds. *To Die Gallantly: The Battle of the Atlantic.* Boulder, CO: Westview, 1994.

Ruppenthal, Roland. *Logistical Support of the Armies.* 2 vols. Washington, DC: Office of the Chief of Military History, 1953, 1959.

———. "Logistic Limitations on Tactical Decisions." *Military Review 31* (1957): 3–9.

———. "Logistic Planning for Overlord in Retrospect." In Eisenhower Foundation, *D-Day: The Normandy Invasion in Retrospect,* 87–103. Lawrence: UP of Kansas, 1971.

———. "Logistics and the Broad-Front Strategy." In Kent Roberts Greenfield, ed., *Command Decisions,* 419–427. Washington, DC: Office of the Chief of Military History, 1960.

Savage, Christopher I. *Inland Transport.* London: HMSO, 1957.

Schoenfeld, Max. "Winston Churchill as War Manager: The Battle of the Atlantic Committee, 1941." *Military Affairs 52* (1986): 122–27.

Scott, John D., and Richard Hughes. *The Administration of War Production.* London: HMSO, 1955.

Shay, Robert P. *British Rearmament in the Thirties: Politics and Profits.* Princeton: Princeton UP, 1979.

Shrader, Charles R. *U.S. Military Logistics, 1607–1991: A Research Guide.* Westport, CT: Greenwood, 1991.

Smith, Jean Edward. *Lucius D. Clay: An American Life.* New York: Henry Holt, 1990.

Smith, Kevin. *Conflict over Convoys: Anglo-American Logistics Diplomacy in World War Two.* Cambridge: Cambridge UP, 1996.

———. "Constraining Overlord: Civilian Logistics, Torch, and the Second Front." In Theodore Wilson, ed., *D-Day 1944,* 42–62. Lawrence: University of Kansas, 1994.

———. "Logistics Diplomacy at Casablanca: Anglo-American Failure to Integrate Shipping and Military Strategy." *Diplomacy and Statecraft 2* (1991): 226–52.

Smith, R. Elberton. *The Army and Economic Mobilization.* Washington, DC: Office of the Chief of Military History, 1959.

Syrett, David. *The Defeat of the German U-Boats: The Battle of the Atlantic.* Columbia: University of South Carolina, 1994.

Terraine, John. *The U-Boat Wars 1916–1945.* New York: Putnam, 1989.

Thomson, Harry C., and Lida Mayo. *The Ordnance Department: Procurement and Supply.* Washington, DC: Office of the Chief of Military History, 1960.

U.S. Bureau of Yards and Docks. *Building the Navy's Bases in World War II: History of the Bureau of Yards and Docks and the Civil Engineering Corps, 1940–1946.* 2 vols. Washington, DC: Department of the Navy/GPO, 1947.

U.S. Civilian Production Administration. *Industrial Mobilization for War: History of the War Production Board and Predecessor Agencies, 1940–1945.* Washington, DC: GPO, 1947.

van Creveld, Martin. *Supplying War: Logistics from Wallenstein to Patton.* Cambridge: Cambridge UP, 1977.

Van Der Vat, Dan. *The Atlantic Campaign: World War II's Great Struggle at Sea.* New York: Harper and Row, 1988.

Waddell, Steve R. *United States Army Logistics: The Normandy Campaign, 1944.* Westport, CT: Greenwood, 1994.

Wardlow, Chester. *The Transportation Corps: Movements, Training, and Supply.* Washington, DC: Office of the Chief of Military History, 1956.

———. *The Transportation Corps: Responsibilities, Organization and Operations.* Washington, DC: Office of the Chief of Military History, 1951.

Weigley, Russell F. *Eisenhower's Lieutenants: The Campaigns of France and Germany, 1944–1945.* Bloomington: Indiana UP, 1990.

Woods, Randall Bennett. *A Changing of the Guard: Anglo-American Relations, 1941–1946.* Chapel Hill: University of North Carolina, 1990.

Y'Blood, William T. *Hunter-Killer: U.S. Escort Carriers in the Battle of the Atlantic.* Annapolis, MD: NIP, 1983.

Yergin, Daniel. *The Prize: The Epic Ouest for Oil, Money and Power.* New York: Simon and Schuster, 1991.

PART IV

The War Behind the Lines

16 Intelligence: Code Breaking, Espionage, Deception, and Special Operations

John M. Shaw

No one can claim justly to understand what happened and why during the Second World War without an awareness of the role of intelligence in that conflict. For several decades following the Allies' triumph many of the veils of secrecy obscuring intelligence matters remained largely in place, justified ostensibly by the demands of the Cold War. To the benefit of students of the war, however, the declassification of governments' wartime records and continued scholarship by historians have led to regular reappraisals of conventional interpretations. Intelligence is now a recognized and productive field of the war's studies, even if important segments remain comparatively unexamined.

"Intelligence" in the broadest sense consists of several components, with widely varying degrees of scholarship on each. The most extensively researched aspect is signals intelligence, or SIGINT, gained by monitoring the enemy's radioelectronic transmissions and extracting useful intelligence from them. Most works considering SIGINT look at the British-American effort (Ultra) to decode German or the American effort (Ultra and Magic) to decode Japanese, radio messages, both programs marked by general success starting in early 1941. Other aspects of the war in the ether have received comparatively less attention from historians, notably radio direction finding, traffic analysis (to determine unit organizations and missions), and electronic warfare (such as jamming and misleading, or "spoofing," enemy radars and radios). Historians' emphasis on code breaking is appropriate, since the reliability and timeliness of the information it produced were generally superior to those of most other sources. Furthermore, code breaking provided intelligence useful to political and senior military leaders, while the related aspects of SIGINT tended to be most valuable to tactical commanders. The naval wars in the Atlantic and Pacific, particularly among submarines, merchant shipping, and antisubmarine forces, show the effect of SIGINT on military operations most clearly.

SIGINT's poor relations, so far as the literature goes, are human and photographic intelligence. Traditional espionage, relying on spies, produces human intelligence (HUMINT). This genre, along with stories of counterespionage, sabotage, and derring-do, was common during the 1950s and 1960s as the participants sought to tell their stories for a variety of reasons. Many were entertaining and appealed to the general public but lacked either the corroborative evidence or historical context necessary to make them useful for researchers.

Scholarly works concentrating on HUMINT have been few in number when compared to works on SIGINT. Several studies on America's Office of Strategic Services (OSS) are available, thanks to the release of many of the wartime files. Those interested in Britain's Special Operations Executive (SOE, London's organization for sabotage and covert warfare within occupied Europe) gained access to many pertinent files upon their declassification in 1972, but many other records remained hidden until the early 1990s. After five decades most of what will ever see the light of day has probably come out.

The third major component of intelligence, photographic intelligence (PHOTINT), was of particular value for aerial operations, both in picking targets and assessing damage. Since it had little effect on decisions at the national or strategic levels, works on PHOTINT usually emphasize its role in specific operations and campaigns, for example, Allied bombing of Germany.

Greatly complicating PHOTINT and HUMINT during the war was deception, whereby one side tried to trick the other to achieve specific advantages or to raise doubts about the reliability of other information. The Allies triumphed in this area largely due to the Axis leaders' tendency to interpret information through stereotyped images of their enemies, coupled with feedback from code breaking of the deception efforts' successes or failures. These four elements, SIGINT, HUMINT, PHOTINT, and deception, make up the major fields of intelligence. Each has its scholars, but the unquestioned primus inter pares for the foreseeable future will remain code breaking.

Intelligence literature is as unbalanced regionally as it is topically. The Western Allies' intelligence war against Germany and Italy is well covered on land, sea, and air; German historians have published several worthwhile studies on the war from their side. The corpus on the Eastern Front is much less extensive. Most of what is in English comes from either the German perspective, through captured Wehrmacht files or postwar German writings, or from Western experts analyzing Soviet publications in the absence of access to other Soviet sources. During the 1970s there was a surge of new works in Russian, but few have been translated into

English or are readily available in the West. Although *glasnost* (openness) began opening the Soviet archives to Russian and Western historians, actual results are coming very slowly. Still, the Eastern Front seems to offer the best opportunities for future research.

The greatest void in intelligence scholarship on World War II concerns the Pacific. What little is known is almost exclusively from an American perspective, with some additional insights from the British, Australians, and New Zealanders. However myopic this approach, the value of intelligence is generally at least mentioned in discussions of the United States drives against Japan.

SIGNAL INTELLIGENCE

Considering the number and varying quality of works available, several deserve special note as being particularly significant. Foremost is Hinsley's massive and authoritative five-volume *British Intelligence in the Second World War*, written by a team of British scholars with World War II intelligence backgrounds and special access to the British government's wartime files. Volume 4, on security and counterintelligence, is weak in discussing Britain's lapses in these areas in light of the extent of the Soviet Union's penetrations before and during the war; volume 5, by Howard, focuses on strategic deception; it took ten years to receive government sanction for publication, and then only after heavy censorship. While the series is superb, those wanting a more readable account with less detail should look to Hinsley's single-volume abridged edition, *British Intelligence*. Of special value is Hinsley and Stripp's *Codebreakers*, an interesting set of reminiscences by twenty-four colleagues, including two Americans, working at Bletchley Park, Britain's site for decoding German radio traffic. For Canada the thorough and scholarly *Scarlet to Green* by Elliot devotes two-thirds of the text to World War II; it includes twenty-four annexes to "Personnel and Organization."

Two more works in the must-read category are Masterman's *The Double-Cross System* and Winterbotham's *The Ultra Secret*. The former remains an unequaled explanation of how Britain turned Germany's spy network in England to send false information to Berlin. Masterman, head of the committee that controlled this program, wrote the book for internal training purposes, then waged a long battle with Britain's intelligence bureaucracy to publish it. Winterbotham, likewise a veteran of Britain's secret war against Hitler, wrote the first English-language account of London's program to break and exploit Germany's wartime codes. Causing a furor upon its publication, it forced all other historians of World War II to reconsider their interpretations, while the reputations of several leaders also suffered. Although containing several inaccuracies, as do most of the opportunistic histories rushed into print in the mid-1970s, *The Ultra Secret* is a good introduction for those with little background on the subject. Four years later Winterbotham published *The Nazi Connection*, an account of his contacts in the 1930s with Germany's top leaders as he spied on the rearmament of the Luftwaffe.

Another key book is Drea's unmatched *MacArthur's Ultra*. While not in the same category as Hinsley's series on British intelligence or as earth-shaking as Winterbotham's, it, along with Layton's "*And I Was There*," discussed later, warrants mention because of the relative paucity of serious scholarship on the intelligence war in the Pacific. Relying on both American and Japanese sources, Drea concluded that MacArthur was a great commander but one who listened to his intelligence experts with their decoded Japanese messages only when it suited what he wanted to do anyway. The work is a shining example of how to write good history, combining pathbreaking scholarship with an easy style. An earlier but still worthwhile study on American intelligence in the Pacific theater is Lewin's *The American Magic*.

Britain's diligence in the field of SIGINT provided the basis for several of the better histories of the intelligence war. Beesley focused on its naval aspects, as in "Convoy PQ-17" and *Very Special Intelligence*. The former is an excellent case study of how the Admiralty misinterpreted intelligence and ordered a convoy to scatter, resulting in its destruction by German forces. The latter is one of the top two works (the other is Kahn's *Seizing the Enigma*) of how the Admiralty used SIGINT against the Kriegsmarine (navy) and the problems associated with using such intelligence.

Bennett's *Ultra and Mediterranean Strategy* does an excellent job of showing how Western decision makers used or ignored available intelligence in waging the wars in North Africa and Italy. Bennett, a wartime duty officer at Bletchley Park, called upon his experiences to write *Ultra in the West*. From looking at how Ultra affected the Anglo-American war effort in 1944–1945, Bennett has drawn upon material declassified since the earlier book to produce a study anyone interested in the war in the Mediterranean must read.

Ferris, another historian of the British signals intelligence effort, has several solid works deserving mention. Typical of the overall quality is "The British Army, Signals and Security in the Desert Campaign, 1940–42." He concluded that Britain paid a very high price for its prewar neglect of signals security, having to develop a capability while fighting Rommel in North Africa. Barnett's *The Desert Generals* in its later editions used Ultra materials to confirm his view that "Montgomery was needlessly slow and cautious in his pursuit of Rommel from El Alamein to Tripoli" (Preface).

America has produced a few sound SIGINT histories as well. Kahn, dean of English-language historians of cryptography, first made his mark with his popular book, *The Codebreakers*. A very useful general introduction to the topic, it has several solid chapters on the Second World War. Published before the Ultra secret broke in 1972, *Codebreakers* gives relatively more attention to other SIGINT matters than have other works since Winterbotham's exposé. Kahn has examined the war in the Atlantic in *Seizing the Enigma*, showing that the Battle of the Atlantic was closer to being lost by the Allies than people have thought. Code breaking was not a Western alliance monopoly, as he proved in "The Forschungsamt"; Hitler's analysts decoded several of Roosevelt and Churchill's transatlantic phone calls, though with arguable results. For select documents see Gilbert and Finnegan's *U.S. Army Signals Intelligence in World War II*.

Powell and Putney's *Ultra and the Army Air Forces in World War II*, while not definitive, is noteworthy because of Powell's personal involvement and subsequent career as U.S. Supreme Court justice. Deutsch, another veteran of intelligence, wrote several articles on intelligence and the military. In "Commanding Generals and the Uses of Intelligence," he argued that the top Western commanders and Rommel tended to value their preconceptions more than any hard intelligence that conflicted with such beliefs.

German intelligence enjoys less literature in English than do the United Kingdom and the United States. *German Military Intelligence*, published by the Military Intelligence Division of the U.S. War Department, has two valuable declassified works on the "German G-2 Service in the Russian Campaign," written by Germans involved after the war, and "German Operational Intelligence," by an Allied team. Kahn's *Hitler's Spies* is a standard work.

HUMAN INTELLIGENCE

At the opposite end of the spectrum from the rarefied atmosphere of SIGINT and code breaking is that of HUMINT and sabotage. Foot and Cruickshank have written several fine, official histories of Britain's SOE. These were based on records unavailable to most researchers, such as the former's *SOE in France* and the latter's *SOE in the Far East* and *SOE in Scandinavia*. In 1993 and 1994 the Public Records Office published guides by Atherton to many of the newly released documents Cruickshank had used. The war in France being a well-tilled field, these new materials should offer interested students worthwhile avenues for further investigation. One additional significant work by Foot is *SOE: An Outline History*. Written for a popular audience, it gives a solid introduction to the subject that the books just mentioned take for granted.

SPECIAL OPERATIONS

Related to the work of the SOE and OSS but more overtly violent were actions by commando-type forces. Miller's *The Bruneval Raid* is a popular account of a successful 1942 British effort to steal key components of a German air defense radar on the English Channel. Even more gripping is Gallagher's *Assault in Norway*, a tale of a Norwegian SOE team that sabotaged stocks of heavy water, delaying, perhaps fatally, Germany's atomic research. Finally, Young's *Commando*, though intended for a popular audience rather than historians, is useful because of his wartime service as a senior commando officer.

The United States tended to take a back seat to Britain in intelligence for much of the war in Europe, at least until the invasion of France. In most aspects of the intelligence war, the British primacy never seemed to fade. This explains in part the extent to which American works on the OSS and Ultra continue to argue (usually unsuccessfully) that the United States' contributions were greater than generally thought. Some typical examples of this subgenre are Casey's *The Secret War against Hitler*, Dulles' *The Secret Surrender*, Lankford's *OSS against the Reich*, Parrish's *The Ultra Americans*, Persico's *Piercing the Reich*, and Chalou's *The Secrets War*. Most of these works rely heavily on interviews with OSS veterans, who have been waging a decades-long effort to revise assessments of their contribution. Lankford's edition of Bruce's *Diaries* shows the deputy head of the OSS in Europe more concerned with wining and dining his way across France and Germany than fighting the enemy; the war is a minor event somewhere in the background. Such an account, the usual content of diaries, undermines the persuasiveness of the revisionists' arguments.

DECEPTION

Deception is instrumental to success in wartime. Rightly or wrongly, the British hold the reputation of being its masters in World War II. Novelist Wheatley enjoyed the distinction of being asked by the old-boy network to assist in developing such stratagems for London; he recounted their work in *The Deception Planners*. Cave Brown, a popular historian, produced an ambitious tome on the Western Allies' efforts to hoodwink Hitler. His *Bodyguard of Lies* generally succeeds, although scholars have taken issue with several of his assertions in the years since, notably his depiction of the London Control Station. In Operation Mincemeat the British successfully persuaded the Germans in 1943 of plans to invade the Balkans, a story absorbingly told in Montagu's *The Man Who Never Was*.

INTELLIGENCE OUTSIDE WESTERN EUROPE

Rounding out the corpus on the war in Europe and intelligence are those on the Eastern Front and those by German historians. Glantz has contributed numerous studies indispensable for those interested in the Russo-German conflict. In *The Role of Intelligence in Soviet Military Strategy in World War II*, he looked at matters from Moscow's army levels and above. Even more valuable is his *Soviet Military Deception in the Second World War*, the best available on the topic. Glantz's easy mastery extends to case studies, as in "Soviet Operational Intelligence in the Kursk Operation." In it, he concluded that the Soviets knew where German reserves were during the campaign but that German intelligence analysts were at a total loss as to tracking Soviet forces.

Reinhard Gehlen's memoir, *The Service*, devotes many chapters to his years as head of the German army's office that produced the Eastern Front enemy order of battle. Leonard used his doctoral work as the basis for a worthwhile article, "Studying the Kremlin's Secret Soldiers." This is an excellent starting point for further reading. Pavel Sudoplatov's memoir, *Special Tasks*, covers in part his wartime efforts; ostensibly a Soviet spy and assassin, he makes some interesting, if unproven, claims. Finally, the U.S. Central Intelligence Agency's (CIA) study of the *Rote Kapelle*, the major Soviet spy ring in Nazi Germany, is worthwhile; while one may disagree with the agency's actions, its research is usually solid.

To the benefit of students of wartime intelligence, German historians have with great regularity produced studies that help keep interpretations balanced. Boog's "German Air Intelligence" is a well-researched article on how badly the Luftwaffe handled intelligence. Not only did its analysts largely ignore the economic components of airpower, as in airplane production capability, but within its staffs the operations sections controlled the intelligence sections. This led to short-term concerns at the expense of long-range assessments, made worse by the Germans' viewing the British through stereotyped attitudes.

Muller's "A German Perspective on Allied Deception Operations" is best considered in connection with Howard's *Strategic Deception* and Cave Brown's *Bodyguard*. Praun's "German Radio Intelligence" is his postwar report written for the OSS, valuable in light of his wartime service as a two-star general of German SIGINT. He gave an honest appraisal of the various armies' communications security practices during the war. It appears in an eighteen-volume series of original documents edited by Mendelsohn under the general title *Covert Warfare*.

Rohwer's "Ultra and the Battle of the Atlantic: The German View" is a useful, if a superseded, antidote to the spate of material in the 1970s that claimed for Ultra credit it did not deserve. Lastly, Toliver's story of Hans Scharff, *The Interrogator*, shows how dangerous a skilled questioner can be. Eschewing torture, Scharff treated captured Allied pilots with courtesy and respect and, appealing to their enthusiasm as aviators, led them to reveal secrets, tactics, and techniques they did not intend to tell. Together, these and other works from a German perspective round out the Anglo-American myopia.

Three other books deserve mention as worthwhile starting points in their respective areas. Jones, Churchill's principal science adviser, was a key figure in the development of such weapons as radar, sonar, and operational research. In *The Wizard War*, he reviewed the contributions the "boffins" made in defeating Germany. So long as one keeps the size of his ego in mind, the account is worth attention. Also see Clark, *The Boffins*. Babington-Smith's *Air Spy* tells the story of the Royal Air Force's (RAF) photographic interpreters and their contributions to the strategic bombing campaign against Germany. Stanley's *World War II Photo Intelligence* is an excellent, well-illustrated description of what photo intelligence could do; it covers the Allies as well as Germany and Japan. Aileen Clayton, the first woman commissioned into the RAF's Y Service (for radio interception), focused on tactical results in *The Enemy Is Listening*.

Readers who judged the importance of intelligence in World War II in a theater might understandably conclude Europe was the only place it mattered, but they would be wrong. The body of works on intelligence in the Pacific, while smaller, nonetheless contains some very good material, most of it published in the last ten years. One of the better studies is Boyd's *Hitler's Japanese Confidant*, which gives a unique insight into one way the Allies learned of German plans. By decoding and reading General Oshima Hiroshi's encoded reports from Berlin to Tokyo, American and British intelligence officers gained priceless insight into Hitler's intentions, such political-strategic information usually unavailable to European-based radio intercept stations and code breakers. For readers wanting a condensed version, Boyd published the core of his thesis in *Intelligence and National Security*. Still to be seen is the extent, if any, to which such high-level insight had consequences on Allied decisions.

A classic, from the chilliest days of the Cold War, is Wohlstetter's study of the difficulties of distilling intelligence from masses of information. In *Pearl Harbor: Warning and Decision*, she argued persuasively that the United States had so much conflicting evidence as to Japan's likely targets for attack that it was unable to identify the correct indicators until after the fact.

Two works by naval intelligence officers warrant mention when considering Pearl Harbor and the Pacific War. Showing an absence of the balance and detachment Wohlstetter cultivates is Layton's *"And I Was There."* Deeply involved in the intelligence war against Japan from 1941 on, Layton rejected Wohlstetter's thesis. He claimed instead the U.S. government had adequate advance warning to have averted the disaster of December 7, 1941. Layton's efforts fail, diverting attention from a worthwhile book by a fellow officer. Zacharias' *Secret Missions* suffers from having been rushed into print amid the postwar flood but is nonetheless a vital memoir by the deputy director of naval intelligence from 1942 on who had been watching the Japanese since 1920.

If the American victory in the Pacific war was due in large part to the

American ability to read Japanese codes, the man who broke those codes was arguably the one most responsible for that triumph. Clark's solid biography, *William F. Friedman*, examines that individual and the stresses that led to his nervous breakdown. Friedman's work made possible the decrypts forming the basis of Spector's *Listening to the Enemy*. Relying heavily on declassified National Security Agency internal studies of materials produced by the code-breaking efforts in the Pacific, *Listening* gives more information on tactical SIGINT and COMINT than do most other accounts of Magic. Spector's *Eagle against the Sun* is a general history of the war, mentioned here because of Spector's skill at integrating intelligence into his overall story.

Stripp and Van Der Rhoer produced two useful firsthand accounts of the SIGINT effort against Japan, *Codebreaker in the Far East* and *Deadly Magic*. Stripp, a Briton who worked in the United Kingdom and India, was chiefly concerned with Japanese diplomatic and strategic-level codes; Van Der Rhoer, a U.S. Navy officer who translated decoded Japanese messages in the navy's intelligence office in Hawaii, emphasized materials of more immediate value to the fleet's campaigns. Both have many interesting nuggets to contribute, although their assertions are less persuasive than Drea's or Boyd's. The Australians have contributed to the literature on the subject, recently with Bleakley's *The Eavesdroppers*. While the United States was the dominant player in the electronic war in the Pacific, Bleakley reminds readers that the Australian contribution was significant.

One aspect of the Pacific War often overlooked is the Australian coast watchers, sentinels left behind on Japanese-held islands to monitor shipping and radio back their information. Feldt's *The Coastwatchers* is a nice memoir by the officer responsible for the Solomons and New Guinea, while Lord's *Lonely Vigil* helps put Feldt's assessments into a broader context. In a related vein is Hilsman's *American Guerrilla*. However interesting these are, the Pacific War was decided in and above the ocean, not behind the Japanese army's lines.

Japanese works in English are distressingly scarce, due to the Japanese reticence to discuss the war and the deaths of many of the key individuals needed by historians. An exception is Yoshikawa and Stanford's "Top Secret Assignment." A Japanese navy ensign, Yoshikawa was responsible in 1941 for watching the base at Pearl Harbor while on the Honolulu consulate's staff.

SOURCES AND RESEARCH AIDS

For sources on the history of intelligence, the United States' records and portions of the captured archives of the defeated Axis powers are, for the most part, available in the U.S. National Archives and other public repositories. Many were released before the normal thirty- to fifty-year point, giving researchers the opportunity to find and interview participants and produce histories not solely dependent on written records. Britain's penchant for secrecy has hindered comparable progress there, forcing scholars to rely heavily until recently on the excellent official histories for many aspects of the secret war. However, the Waldegrave Initiative, Britain's 1992 decision and effort to make the government's workings more open to the public, has led to more files becoming available for inspection and study. These materials are likely to cause only minor revisions in historical interpretations, but the change in attitude the initiative represents augurs well for the future for rounding out the record on the peripheral fronts and theaters.

Of tremendous value to students are Atherton's two collections on SOE materials mentioned earlier. Another valuable source is Cline et al.'s *Scholar's Guide to Intelligence Literature*, a bibliography of a huge collection at Georgetown University in Washington, D.C. Cochran's *The Magic Diplomatic Summaries* gives a synopsis of the contents of the periodic reports on Magic, rather than of the messages themselves. Constantinides' *Intelligence and Espionage* is the product of an experienced CIA officer particularly interested in HUMINT, while former army officer House's *Military Intelligence* contains 882 citations of books and articles relating to warfare between the Franco-Prussian War and Desert Storm.

Leading journals on intelligence are *Intelligence and National Security, The International Journal of Intelligence and Counterintelligence, Defense Intelligence Journal,* and *Cryptologia;* all are particularly useful for reviews of the most current debates in the field or new titles on intelligence matters. Of these, the first is most likely to contain scholarly essays on topics relating to World War II, but all regularly present worthwhile papers. For an exhaustive compilation of related journals, refer to Peake's valuable *The Reader's Guide to Intelligence Periodicals.*

BIBLIOGRAPHY

Since intelligence played an important role in all aspects of military and naval history, the reader should also consult other chapters; the index comprehensively lists all references to the literature on intelligence.

Atherton, Louise. *SOE Operations in the Far East: An Introductory Guide to the Newly Released Records of the Special Operations Executive in the Public Records Office.* London: PRO, 1993.
———. *SOE Operations in Scandinavia: An Introductory Guide to the Newly Released Records in the Public Records Office.* London: PRO, 1994.
Babington-Smith, Constance. *Air Spy: The Story of Photo Intelligence in World War II.* New York: Harper and Brothers, 1957.
Barnett, Correlli. *The Desert Generals.* Bloomington: Indiana UP, 1960, 1986.

Beesly, Patrick. "Convoy PQ 17: A Study of Intelligence and Decision-Making." *Intelligence and National Security 5* (1991): 292–322.

———. *Very Special Intelligence: The Admiralty's Operational Intelligence Centre, 1939–1945.* London: Hamish Hamilton, 1977.

Bennett, Ralph. *Ultra and Mediterranean Strategy.* New York: Morrow, 1989.

———. *Ultra in the West: The Normandy Campaign of 1944–45.* New York: Charles Scribner's Sons, 1979.

Bleakley, Jack. *The Eavesdroppers.* Canberra: Australian Government Printing Service, 1991.

Boog, Horst. "German Air Intelligence in the Second World War." *Intelligence and National Security 5* (1990): 350–424.

Boyd, Carl. *Hitler's Japanese Confidant: General Oshima Hiroshi and Magic Intelligence, 1941–1945.* Lawrence: UP of Kansas, 1993.

———. "Significance of Magic and the Japanese Ambassador to Berlin." *Intelligence and National Security 2* (1987): 302–19; *3* (1988): 83–102; *4*: (1989): 86–107.

Casey, William. *The Secret War against Hitler.* Washington, DC: Regnery Gateway, 1988.

Cave Brown, Anthony. *Bodyguard of Lies.* New York: Harper and Row, 1975.

Chalou, George C., ed. *The Secrets War: The Office of Strategic Services in World War II.* Washington, DC: GPO, 1992.

Clark, Ronald W. *The Boffins.* London: Phoenix, 1961.

———. *The Man Who Broke Purple: The Life of Colonel William F. Friedman, Who Deciphered the Japanese Code in World War II.* Boston: Little, Brown, 1977.

Clayton, Aileen. *The Enemy Is Listening.* London: Hutchinson, 1980.

Cline, Marjorie W., Carla E. Christiansen, and Judith M. Fontaine, eds. *Scholar's Guide to Intelligence Literature: Bibliography of the Russell J. Bowen Collection in the Joseph Mark Lauinger Memorial Library, Georgetown University.* Frederick, MD: University Publications of America, 1983.

Cochran, Alexander S., Jr. *The Magic Diplomatic Summaries: A Chronological Finding Aid.* New York and London: Garland, 1982.

Constantinides, George C. *Intelligence and Espionage: An Analytical Bibliography.* Boulder, CO: Westview, 1983.

Cruickshank, Charles. *SOE in the Far East.* Oxford: Oxford UP, 1983.

———. *SOE in Scandinavia.* Oxford: Oxford UP, 1986.

Deutsch, Harold C. "Commanding Generals and the Uses of Intelligence." *Intelligence and National Security 3* (1988): 194–260.

Drea, Edward J. *MacArthur's Ultra: Codebreaking and the War against Japan, 1942–1945.* Lawrence: UP of Kansas, 1992.

Dulles, Allen. *The Secret Surrender.* New York: Harper & Row, 1966.

Elliot, S. R. *Scarlet to Green: A History of Intelligence in the Canadian Army, 1903–1963.* Toronto: Canadian Intelligence and Security Agency, 1981.

Feldt, Eric A. *The Coastwatchers.* New York: Oxford UP, 1946.

Ferris, John. "The British Army, Signals and Security in the Desert Campaign, 1940–42." *Intelligence and National Security 5* (1990): 255–91.

Foot, M.R.D. *SOE: An Outline History of the Special Operations Executive 1940–46.* London: British Broadcasting Corporation, 1984.

———. *SOE in France.* London: HMSO, 1966.

Gallagher, Thomas. *Assault in Norway: The True Story of the Telemark Raid.* London: Purnell Book Services, 1975; New York: Warner, 1976.

Gehlen, Reinhard. *The Service: The Memoirs of General Reinhard Gehlen.* New York: World, 1972.

Gilbert, James L., and John P. Finnegan, eds. *U.S. Army Signals Intelligence in World War II; A Documentary History.* Washington, DC: U.S. Army Center of Military History, 1993.

Glantz, David M. *The Role of Intelligence in Soviet Military Strategy in World War II.* Novato, CA: Presidio, 1990.

————. *Soviet Military Deception in the Second World War.* London: Frank Cass, 1989.

————. "Soviet Operational Intelligence in the Kursk Operation, July 1943." *Intelligence and National Security 5* (1990): 5–49.

Hilsman, Roger. *American Guerrilla.* London: Brassey's, 1990.

Hinsley, F. H. "British Intelligence in the Second World War: An Overview." *Cryptologia 14* (1990): 1–10.

————. *British Intelligence in the Second World War.* Abridged ed. New York: Cambridge UP, 1993.

Hinsley, F. H., et al. *British Intelligence in the Second World War.* 5 vols. in 6 parts. New York: Cambridge UP, 1979–1993.

Hinsley, Francis H., and Alan Stripp, eds. *Codebreakers: The Inside Story of Bletchley Park.* Oxford: Oxford UP, 1993.

House, Jonathan. *Military Intelligence, 1870–1991: A Research Guide.* Westport, CT: Greenwood, 1993.

Howard, Michael E. *British Intelligence in the Second World War.* Vol. 5, *Strategic Deception.* London: HMSO, 1990.

Jones, Reginald Victor. *The Wizard War: British Scientific Intelligence, 1939–1945.* New York: Coward, McCann, and Geoghegan, 1978.

Kahn, David. *The Codebreakers: The Story of Secret Writing.* New York: Macmillan, 1967.

————. "The Forschungsamt: Nazi Germany's Most Secret Intelligence Agency." *Cryptologia 2* (1978): 12–19.

————. *Hitler's Spies: German Military Intelligence in World War II.* New York: Macmillan, 1978.

————. *Seizing the Enigma: The Race to Break the German U-Boat Codes, 1939–1943.* Boston: Houghton Mifflin, 1991.

Lankford, Nelson D., ed. *OSS against the Reich: The World War II Diaries of Colonel David K. E. Bruce.* Kent, OH: Kent State UP, 1991.

Layton, Edwin T., Roger Pinean, and John Costello. *"And I Was There": Pearl Harbor and Midway—Breaking the Secrets.* New York: Morrow, 1985.

Leonard, Raymond W. "Studying the Kremlin's Secret Soldiers: A Historiographical Essay on the GRU, 1918–1945." *Journal of Military History 56* (1992): 403–21.

Lewin, Ronald. *The American Magic: Codes, Ciphers and the Defeat of Japan.* New York: Farrar Straus Giroux; Harmondsworth, U.K.: Penguin, 1982.

Lord, Walter. *Lonely Vigil: The Untold Story of the South Pacific Coastwatchers.* New York: Viking, 1977.

Masterman, J. C. *The Double-Cross System in the War of 1939 to 1945.* London: Yale UP, 1972.

Mendelsohn, John, ed. *Covert Warfare.* New York: Garland, 1989.

Military Intelligence Division, U.S. War Department. *German Military Intelligence, 1939–1945*. Frederick, MD: University Publications of America, 1984.

Miller, George. *The Bruneval Raid: Flashpoint of the Radar War*. Garden City, NY: Doubleday, 1975.

Montagu, Ewen. *The Man Who Never Was*. London: Evans Bros. 1953; New York: Lippincott, 1954; London: Transworld, 1969.

Müller, Klaus-Jürgen. "A German Perspective on Allied Deception Operations in the Second World War." *Intelligence and National Security* 2 (1987): 301–26.

Parrish, Thomas. *The Ultra Americans: The U.S. Role in Ultra*. Chelsea, MI: Scarborough House, 1991.

Peake, Hayden B. *The Reader's Guide to Intelligence Periodicals*. Washington, DC: National Intelligence Book Center, 1992.

Persico, Joseph E. *Piercing the Reich: The Penetration of Nazi Germany by American Secret Agents during World War II*. New York: Viking, 1979.

Powell, Lewis F., and Diane T. Putney. *Ultra and the Army Air Forces in World War II*. Washington, DC: Office of Air Force History, 1987.

Praun, Albert. "German Radio Intelligence and the Soldaten-Sender." In John Mendelsohn, ed., *Covert Warfare: Intelligence, Counterintelligence, and Military Deception during the Second World War Era*, 1: 260. Vol. 6, *German Radio Intelligence*. New York: Garland, 1989.

Rohwer, Jürgen. "Ultra and the Battle of the Atlantic: The German View." In Robert W. Love, Jr., ed., *Changing Interpretations and New Sources in Naval History: Papers from the Third United States Naval Academy Historical Symposium*, 420–43. New York: Garland, 1980.

Spector, Ronald H. *Eagle against The Sun: The American War with Japan*. New York: Free Press/Macmillan, 1985.

———. *Listening to the Enemy: Key Documents on the Role of Communications Intelligence in the War with Japan*. Wilmington, DE: Scholarly Resources, 1988.

Stanley, Roy M. *World War II Photo Intelligence*. New York: Scribner's, 1981.

Stripp, Alan. *Codebreaker in the Far East*. London: Frank Cass, 1989.

Sudoplatov, Pavel, and Anatoli Sudoplatov, with Jerrold L. Schecter and Leona P. Schecter. *Special Tasks*. Boston: Little; Brown, 1994.

Toliver, Raymond F. *The Interrogator: The Story of Hans Scharff, Luftwaffe's Master Interrogator*. Fallbrook, CA: Aero, 1978.

U.S. Army Far East Command. *A Brief History of the G-2 Section, GHQ, SWPA, and Affiliated Units*. 9 vols. Tokyo: General Headquarters, Far East Command, 1948.

U.S. Central Intelligence Agency. *The Rote Kapelle: The CIA's History of Soviet Intelligence and Espionage Networks in Western Europe, 1936–1945*. Washington, DC: University Publications of America, 1979.

U.S. Department of Defense. *The "Magic" Background of Pearl Harbor*. Washington, DC: GPO, 1977.

U.S. Strategic Bombing Survey. *Japanese Military and Naval Intelligence (Japanese Intelligence Section G-2)*. Washington, DC: Strategic Bombing Survey, 1946.

Van Der Rhoer, Edward. *Deadly Magic: A Personal Account of Communications Intelligence in World War II in the Pacific*. New York: Charles Scribner's Sons, 1978.

Welchman, Gordon. *The Hut Six Story*. London: Allen Lane; New York: McGraw-Hill, 1982.

West, Nigel. *MI5, British Security Operations, 1909–1945.* London, Sydney, and Toronto: Bodley Head, 1981.

———. *MI6, British Secret Intelligence Service Operations, 1909–45.* New York: Random House, 1984.

Wheatley, Dennis. *The Deception Planners: My Secret War.* Ed. Anthony Lejeune. London: Hutchinson, 1980.

Winterbotham, Frederick W. *The Nazi Connection.* New York: Harper and Row, 1978.

———. *The Ultra Secret.* New York: Harper and Row, 1974.

Wohlstetter, Roberta. *Pearl Harbor: Warning and Decision.* Stanford, CA: Stanford UP, 1962.

Yoshikawa, Takeo, and Norman Stanford. "Top Secret Assignment." *U.S. Naval Institute Proceedings 86* (December 1960): 27–39.

Young, Peter. *Commando.* New York: Ballantine, 1969.

Zacharias, Ellis M. *Secret Missions: The Story of an Intelligence Officer.* New York: Putnam, 1946.

17 German Occupation of Europe, the Axis "New Order," and Collaboration

Gerhard Hirschfeld

GERMAN OCCUPATION OF EUROPE

Between 1939 and 1945, the German Reich dominated large parts of Europe. It is estimated that by the end of 1941 approximately 180 million non-Germans lived under some form of German occupation. Inevitably, the experience and memory of the war for most Europeans are therefore linked less with military action and events than with Nazi rule and the manifold expressions it took: insecurity and unlawfulness, constraints and compulsion, increasingly difficult living conditions, coercive measures, and arbitrary acts of force that ultimately could threaten the very existence of people. For those millions of human beings whose right to existence had been denied for social, political, or racial reasons altogether, the implications and consequences of the German conquest and occupation of Europe became even more oppressive and hounding.

Nazi rule in Europe during the Second World War involved a great variety of policies in all countries under occupation, determined by political, strategical, economic, and ideological factors. While in Eastern Europe, the central purpose of Germany's conquest was to provide the master race with the required living space (Lebensraum) for settlement as well as human and economic resources for total exploitation. The techniques for political rule and economic control appeared less brutal in Western Europe, in accordance with Nazi racial and ideological views. Looking at the map of Europe between 1939 and 1945, there existed a number of political and administrative structures that can be, broadly defined, summarized in three categories: annexed or appended territories, territories under civil administration, and territories under military administration.

The most favored form of occupation was direct annexation. After the defeat of Poland in September 1939, the following areas were annexed by the Reich: western Poland (the old Polish corridor), renamed Warthegau and Danzig-West Prussia, became two formally constituted *Reichsgaue* (Reich districts). Polish-Silesia (Eastern Upper Silesia), despite some special arrangements to include the coal and iron districts of southwest Poland, the mining district of Teschen, and parts of the former Polish provinces of Cracow and Kielce, was placed under Reich governors and heads of Prussian provinces (Reichsstatthalter and Oberpräsidenten). Also annexed were eastern Belgian border areas, the cantons of Eupen-Malmédy, and St. Vith.

Alsace, parts of Lorraine, and the Grand Duchy of Luxembourg, were treated as Reich territories but were not officially incorporated into the Reich. Though Alsace and Baden were combined to form the new Gau Westmark, this was only a party, not a state, administrative arrangement. Two-thirds of Slovenia bordering on the Ostmark (Austria) were also treated as Reich territory, thus bringing Germany's frontier almost to the Adriatic (Untersteiermark, as were occupied parts of Krain and Carinthia) and the district of Bialstok in eastern Poland.

All these territories were attached to their nearest German Gau, and their respective Gauleiter appointed heads of administration. Thus, Erich Koch, the infamous Gauleiter of East Prussia, became chief of administration in Bialstok, while his colleague Robert Wagner was appointed head of the civil administration in Alsace.

Territories under civil administration were chosen for all countries or areas for which Germany expressed a special political interest or for which it had to show special consideration. Denmark was initially placed under German supervision as a protectorate headed by a Plenipotentiary (*Reichsbevollmächtigter*), but by 1942, prompted by increasing resistance, Hitler turned this arrangement into a de facto military occupation. The Germanic countries Norway and the Netherlands were ruled by Reich commissioners (Reichskommissare Josef Terboven and Arthur Seyss-Inquart, respectively). Though native administrations—in the case of the Netherlands, a headless government was composed of permanent secretaries-general of the former ministries—were largely left untouched, constant interference and massive pressure of the German occupation authorities, notably by representatives of the Nazi Party and the SS (Schutzstaffeln, protection squad), increasingly restricted the available room for maneuver.

The same arrangements applied to the Government-General of Poland (under the brutal bureaucrat Hans Frank), the protectorate of Bohemia, and Moravia (first under Konstantin von Neurath, then, from 1942 to 1945, under Wilhelm Frick). Real power, however, lay in the hands of ruthless SS leaders Reinhard Heydrich, deputy Reich protector, and, after Heydrich's death in 1942, Karl Hermann Frank. The Reich commissariats of the Ukraine and Ostland were ruled by Gauleiters from the Reich, though large parts of these administrative areas remained as battle zones under Wehrmacht control.

In the interest of strategic warfare and/or due to lack of political initiatives, the following areas were left under direct control of Wehrmacht commanders: Belgium (until July 1944, when Hitler turned it into a Reichskommissariat under the Cologne Gauleiter Josef Grohe) and the northern parts of France; the Channel Islands; Serbia; Saloniki-Aegis; and southern parts of Greece, with Crete. In addition all theaters and rear areas of military operations were under military administration.

In addition to those territories administered or directly controlled by Germany, a number of pro-German or collaborationist governments existed: in France (Vichy), Slovakia, Hungary, Romania, Bulgaria, and Yugoslavia (where three puppet regimes of varying types were established, Croatia and Montenegro under Italian supervision and the rump state of Serbia). Greece was a tripartite occupation by Bulgars, Germans, and Italians. The fascist Republic of Salo represented an exceptional case in northern Italy between 1943 and 1945. The territories of Austria (Anschluss March 1938), Sudetenland (annexed October 1938), and Memelland (annexed March 1939) should not be seen as occupied areas since a clear majority of the population there welcomed the annexation by the Reich.

Germany's role in the war and the German occupation of Europe are dealt with in the two volumes by Rich in *Hitler's War Aims*, especially *The Establishment of the New Order* with its extensive literature current until the late 1960s. Rich should now be supplemented by Umbreit's "Kontinentalherrschaft" in the series *Das Deutsche Reich und der Zweite Weltkrieg*, prepared by the Military History Research Office (Militärgeschichtliches Forschungsamt, MGFA) of the Federal Republic of Germany. Umbreit's study is largely based on available German records but also makes good use of relevant secondary source material and literature; authored by Deist and others, an English translation, *Germany and the Second World War*, is under way. For a (rather arbitrary) selection of documents, see the third volume of Noakes and Pridham's *Foreign Policy, War and Racial Extermination*. Still useful, though with occasional shortcomings and mistakes, are the earlier studies by Child, "The Concept of the New Order," and Harvey, "The Structure of Economic Controls" in *Hitler's Europe*, edited by the Toynbees. Solid summaries are provided by Durand in *Le nouvel ordre européen Nazi* and Wright in *The Ordeal of Total War* and by Weinberg in *A World at Arms*. An interesting comparative approach can be found in an essay by Madajczyk, "Die Besatzungssysteme der Achsenmächte," and in a sociological monograph by Carlton, *Occupation*.

In terms of individual countries, German occupation policies in Europe are covered in a number of studies. Concerning the state of historical research into the history of the Second World War in general, readers should consult the reports and selected bibliographies (until 1989) presented, however uneven and occasionally from a rather nationalistic point of view, in *Neue Forschungen zum Zweiten Weltkrieg*, edited by Rohwer and Müller, most of which are in English. The most accessible studies on the German administration of individual countries and territories are (in chronological order of war and occupation): for Czechoslovakia (Bohemia and Moravia), Brandes, *Die Tschechen unter deutschem Protektorat*, and Mastny, *The Czechs under Nazi Rule*; Poland (Government-General), Broszat, *Nationalsozialistische Polenpolitik*, Gross, *Polish Society under German Occupation*, and Madajczyk, *Die Okkupationspolitik Nazideutschlands in Polen;* and Denmark and Norway, *Die Okkupationspolitik des deutschen Faschismus in Dänemark und Norwegen*, edited by the German Federal Archives; Denmark, Thomson, *Deutsche Besatzungspolitik*; and Norway, Loock, *Quisling, Rosenberg und Terboven.*

For Luxembourg see Dostert's *Luxemburg zwischen Selbstbehauptung und nationaler Selbstaufgabe*, and Fletcher's "German Administration in Luxemburg"; for the Netherlands read Hirschfeld's *Nazi Rule and Dutch Collaboration* and De Jong's *Het Koningkrijk der Nederlanden* and *The Netherlands and Nazi Germany*. Studies of Belgium under occupation include Wagner's *Belgien in der deutschen Politik während des Zweiten Weltkrieges* and Warmbrunn's *The German Occupation of Belgium*. For the large literature on France see especially Azéma and Bédarida, *Vichy et les Français*; Durand, *Vichy*; Jäckel, *Frankreich in Hitler's Europa*; and Paxton's *Vichy France*. On the British Channel Islands there is a large volume in the After the Battle Series by Bunting entitled *Model Occupation*.

For the German occupation in Yugoslavia see Hory and Broszat, *Der Kroatische Ustascha-Staat*, and Olshausen, *Zwischenspiel auf dem Balkan*; for Greece, Hondros, *Occupation and Resistance*, and Mazower, *Inside Hitler's Greece*; and for Italy after 1943, the Republic of Salo, see Klinkhammer's *Zwischen Bündnis und Besatzung*. For the Baltic states there is Myllyniemi, *Die Neuordnung der Baltischen Länder*, and for the Soviet Union, Dallin's *German Rule in Russia*, Müller and Ueberschär's *Hitler's War in the East*, and Schulte's *The German Army and Nazi Policies in Occupied Russia.*

GERMANY'S "NEW ORDER" IN EUROPE

Initially, the term "New Order" had been solely used to describe the reorganization of the European national economies. Though no complete and comprehensive official program for the establishment of the new economic order was ever published, hundreds of statements, memoranda, and plans were produced by politicians, civil servants, industrialists, and bankers. However, the *Neuordnungspläne*, *Wunschprogramme*, and *Friedensplanungen* worked out by large German industrial firms and economic associations did not provide coherent and systematic ideas on the political and economic integration of national industries into a postwar Europe. Instead, they simply articulated the massive demands of individual companies and branches of industry against the national economies of conquered territories. The nearest approach to an official outline of German intentions was by Walther Funk, Reich minister of economics, whom Göring in June 1940 had given the responsibility for "the preparation and establishment of planning for the reorganization of Europe." Funk told German and other journalists on July 25, 1940 about the forthcoming reorganization of Europe, which was "to overcome national factors," but denied the existence of a concrete and fixed place; see Freymond's "Aspects of the Reich's Ministry of Economics Concept."

A special department in the Reich Economic Ministry under the heading VO (*Vorbereitung und Ordnung,* or Preparation and Order) was set up to deal with technical details, in particular to collect data and information about the industrial capacities of the occupied countries and to function as a clearinghouse. What emerges from these papers and discussions is a rather detailed picture of the new Europe that the Nazis planned after they had won the war: the basis of the new economic order was the formation of a single economic community working under German command. Centralized planning would replace unorganized liberalism, though there would be no nationalization or expropriation of private industries. Government control over industries along the lines existing in the Reich was envisaged, and suggestions were made that international cartels might be enlarged and strengthened. The newly created *Großraumwirtschaft* would ensure free-flowing trade, harmonize the complementary economies of industrial and agricultural countries, and largely free Europe of its old dependence on overseas supplies. The plans can be followed in Carroll's *Design for Total War,* Eichholtz's *Geschichte der deutschen Kriegswirtschaft,* and Freymond's *Le IIIe Reich et la réorganisation économique de l'Europe.*

But the reality was very different. Despite the verbal gloss, German economists and politicians left no doubt as to who would control, and benefit from, the new Europe. In *The German Economy at War* Milward expressed this fact in a simple and concise formula: "[T]here was little that was new and less that was orderly in the New Order" (52). Solely in economic terms, the new German Empire in Europe would have been a large-scale structure organized for, and run on the principles of, a colonialism of the crudest kind. Germany's economic policy toward occupied countries can in essence be summed up in two terms: exploitation and colonization.

In Western Europe, where the techniques of economic exploitation appeared less brutal than in the East, the result in pure financial terms was equally devastating. At the outset, there was a brief period of pillaging, mostly directed against each country's stockpiles of raw materials and other essential goods. This "uncontrolled period" was soon followed by more or less formal arrangements between a number of German agencies (Armament Inspectorates, Central Order Offices, etc.) and local industries and civil administrations, which led to a continous flow of raw materials and goods into Germany.

France, Belgium, the Netherlands, and Norway (later also Greece and Yugoslavia) were saddled with the cost of supporting the occupying authorities, including Wehrmacht troops. The assessments were astronomically inflated. From 1940 to 1944, France paid approximately ten times the actual costs of the military occupation, as did the Netherlands. The occupation costs that Germany gained from all occupied countries during this time amounted to nearly 40 percent of revenues, according to Harvey, "The Structure of Economic Controls in Europe."

One essential resource in all defeated countries was manpower. The growing demand by the Wehrmacht for more soldiers and Hitler's constant refusal to increase the number of women workers in industry (largely based on his ideological belief that a woman's place was in the kitchen and to produce babies) led to a drastic labor shortage, particularly in agriculture. The situation became even worse when Speer stepped up his new armament program in 1942. His lieutenant, the man in charge of labor allocation, Fritz Sauckel, scoured all of occupied Europe for manpower. Between May 1942 and May 1943, Sauckel's representatives and agents in the occupied territories rounded up—often with the help of local civil administrations—some 2.1 million foreign laborers, bringing the total number in Germany to more than 6 million. By 1943, more than 40 percent of the entire workforce of I. G. Farben, Flick, and Krupp consisted of *Fremdarbeiter* (foreign workers) and prisoners of war. Statistical evidence shows that during the last year of war, every fourth plane, tank, lorry, mortar, and piece of ammunition was produced by foreigners. See the works by Herbert on *Fremdarbeiter* and his *Europa und der "Reichseinsatz"* and the earlier work by Homze, *Foreign Labor in Nazi Germany*.

Western countries provided a great many workers, but the largest proportion came from Poland and the Soviet Union. Until 1942, the Nazi leaders showed no interest in conscripting Russians. They even refused to make use of the huge number of Soviet prisoners of war captured during the German advance in Russia. An appalling proportion of these prisoners, crowded into totally inadequate camps during the winter of 1941–1942, died of malnutrition and endemic diseases. Of the 3,350,000 Soviet prisoners who were captured in 1941, 60 percent had died by February 1942, approximately 600,000 during the previous two months. Bartov's *The Eastern Front*, the contributors to Hirschfeld's *Policies of Genocide*, and Streit's *"Keine Kameraden"* have convincingly documented that Hitler's initial orders for the invasion of Russia and the treatment of civilians there, laid down in the Commissar Order and the Barbarossa Directive, paved the way for the direct involvement of the Wehrmacht in this war of annihilation. Eventually, however, practical considerations overcame ideological objections, and a large number of Soviet prisoners worked in Germany along with civilian laborers from the Ukraine and White Russia. By mid-1943, there were more than 1.5 million of these so-called *Ostarbeiter* in the Reich.

A number of Soviet prisoners of war joined General Vlasov's Russian liberation movement after the last fighting German soldier had retreated from Soviet territory, and Hitler and Himmler had finally overcome their ideological prejudices sufficiently to support Vlasov's movement in a minor way—obviously for entirely selfish reasons. For this see Andreyev's *Vlasov and the Russian Liberation Movement* and Volkmann's "Das Vlasov-Unternehmen."

The central purpose of Germany's conquest of Eastern Europe was, according to Hitler, to provide Germany with the apparently necessary lebensraum—land for settlement and resources for exploitation. The chief responsibility for these programs was Himmler's SS and in particular the new Reichskommissariat for the Consolidation of the Germanic People (RKFDV), which Himmler established shortly after the occupation of Poland; Koehl detailed this organization in *RKFDV: German Resettlement and Population Policy.* Roughly a million Poles and Jews were forcibly evacuated from the annexed provinces of Warthegau and Danzig-West-Prussia to a newly created dumping ground, the Government-General.

With the invasion of Russia and the establishment of the two Reichskommissariate Ostland and Ukraine, vast new perspectives opened before the Nazi pioneers. Two additional Kommissariate were created on paper, and their commissioners were appointed: one for the Caucasus and another one for the region around Moscow; both fell victim to the Wehrmacht's withdrawal from these territories. Equipped with Hitler's vague guidelines, Himmler's SS agencies and Alfred Rosenberg's new Ministry for the Occupied Eastern Territories (established in August 1941) began to draft and initiate colonization plans. But it was easier to expel Russians and Poles from their homes than to find suitable German, Dutch, and Norwegian colonists to replace them. With the exception of the so-called *Volksdeutsche* or ethnic Germans (who had a long time ago—some even hundreds of years—migrated from Germany to Eastern Europe and who were now repatriated to strengthen the newly acquired territories) there was no considerable migration from Central and Western Europe beyond the frontiers of the annexed Polish territories.

Despite all his wild table talks and fantastic dreams about a future Greater Germanic Empire, Hitler's immediate aim was to win the war and not to follow some predetermined blueprint of how Europe should be ruled. That is not to say that these ideas and programs were abandoned—Nazi ideologues and Pan-German resettlement experts and functionaries continued to use Eastern Europe as experimental ground for their racist theories. The deportation and extermination of Jews, Gypsies, and other unwanted people even intensified as the military situation became worse, as shown by Aly's *Endlösung*. The presence of hundreds of thousands of *Volksdeutsche* in the Government-General of Poland might have served as an additional rationale for the implementation of the Holocaust.

On the other hand, Hitler made it quite clear that there would be no anticipation of a future political design for Europe. During the later part of the war, the concept of a New Order was largely left to agitators like Goebbels, who then set off in a propagandistic crusade to save Europe from the Bolsheviks. The hopes of political collaborationists for a genuine cooperation with Germany were brusquely brushed aside. There never had been a real chance for a European partnership of all the right-wing, authoritarian, and fascist parties and movements. In this respect, Hitler remained a follower of the nationalistic ideas of the nineteenth century. He always put the emphasis in his "Germanic Empire of German Nations" on the word "German"; see Kluke's "Nationalsozialistische Europaideologie."

COLLABORATION

The term "collaboration" in the specific sense attached to it since the Second World War (i.e., cooperation with the enemy, with the occupying power) was first used after the memorable meeting between Hitler and Pétain in Montoire-sur-Loire on October 24, 1940. Six days later, Pétain went on French radio and declared that "collaboration has been envisaged between our two countries" and that he had "accepted it in principle" (Azéma, *La Collaboration*, 86–88).

The formal acceptance of this political principle gave rise to the modern definition of collaboration and, unfortunately, led to numerous historical misconceptions and misinterpretations. Collaboration was initially seen as a political arrangement between two nations: the victorious one, which had occupied foreign territory, and the defeated nation, which tried to preserve as much independence as possible. This narrow definition automatically excluded all other forms of cooperation between victor and vanquished, which were then left open to moral judgment and, in most cases, moral condemnation. On these points see Lemberg's "Kollaboration in Europa mit dem Dritten Reich" and Hirschfeld's "Collaboration in Nazi-Occupied France."

Collaboration with the enemy or the occupying power is a complex phenomenon. It can take numerous forms and apply to many different cases: political (often ideological), economic, social, and cultural. There were considerable differences between the phenomena of collaboration in Eastern (including East Central) and Western or Northern Europe. For

Eastern Europe, see Armstrong, "Collaboration in World War II"; Broszat, "Faschismus und Kollaboration in Ostmitteleuropa"; and for Western Europe, see Lammers, "Levels of Collaboration," and the bibliographical essay by Collotti: "Il collaborazionismo." Naturally, collaboration was dependent on the aims, quality, and actual course of the occupation.

During the Second World War, every occupied country developed an original pattern of behavior and a similar reaction. This is particulary true for the first part of the war, when the Axis powers seemed to be seeking a quick and decisive victory. Under the impact of German military successes (blitzkrieg), the prevailing attitude in most Western and Northern European countries hovered among a cautious waiting approach, a form of playing for time (*attentisme*), and a growing willingness to come to terms with the supposedly victorious power in the interest of maintaining law and order, thereby accepting that the entire political and military situation had been totally transformed in favor of German supremacy in Europe. See, for example, Hirschfeld: "Collaboration and Attentism in the Netherlands."

Some motives for this form of accommodation, however, were soon eclipsed by motives for collaboration specific to individual institutions and organizations. An example of this is the so-called New Order debate among Dutch, Belgian, and French industrialists and high-ranking civil servants. This debate anticipated collective "reorientation" of national industries to the political economic "realities" created by the Third Reich: the dismantling of a national economic system, the development of new spheres and methods of production, the reorganization of the national social system, and the possible restructuring of the administrative sector after the removal of parliamentary control. The discussion was ultimately dominated by fear of economic and social chaos and concern for the maintenance of industrial production and jobs, even though rudiments of the "political accommodation" of the first phase of the occupation continued to be apparent.

Economic collaboration provides a test case for demonstrating the ambiguity of arguments and attitude during the occupation period. There were both entrepreneurial as well as more general economic reasons for ensuring the continuation of production and intensive economic cooperation with Germany. This included an interest in maintaining companies as viable entities, a desire to safeguard invested capital—including its potential future proceeds—from possible seizure by the occupying power, and the aim of preventing the penetration of the national economies by German big business. The closure of factories might have led to dismantling and deportation of machinery, goods, and whatever raw material was still available. Moreover, the workers who lost their jobs in this process would face the prospect of being sent to Germany. A high level of industrial production, on the other hand, provided a tolerable livelihood and relative security for many employees. Besides, those goods and finished products not intended for export to Germany would benefit the local population.

But there was more than just the aim of maintaining production and keeping enterprises alive. In most of occupied Western and Northern Europe, all major industries increased their output and profits during the first two years of the occupation; some entrepreneurs were even able to expand during the later periods of the war, when general economic decline had become obvious. The process of modernization intensified in some countries, and the monopolization of industries increased as a result of measures taken by the German authorities in cooperation with larger companies and industrial groups. There was certainly something seductive for many businessmen and politicians about linking their country with a vibrant, renovated European economy as an equal or near-equal partner. The reality, however, was quite different, as shown in Gillingham's *Belgian Business in the Nazi New Order*, Hirschfeld's *Nazi Rule and Dutch Collaboration*, and Milward's two volumes, *The New Order and the French Economy* and *The Fascist Economy in Norway*.

Political collaboration with the Nazi occupation in Europe had many faces and resulted from various motives, but nationalism and revisionism were certainly among its more prominent ones. They figured particularly strongly in the Balkans, where a number of authoritarian and semifascist governments tried with German support to recover those territories that had been previously lost to neighboring states. Thus, under the dictatorship of Antonescu, Romania fought in Russia alongside the Wehrmacht, not least for northern Transylvania, while Bulgaria, under the personal rule of King Boris, was allowed to regain Thrace and Macedonia (though the country resisted German pressure to commit Bulgarian troops to the Eastern Front).

Collaborationist governments and administrations were set up by Germany in occupied Greece and also temporarily in the rump state of Serbia under Nedic. Both Axis powers, Germany and Italy, kept harsh control over their territories and were able to draw considerable economic benefit from most of their occupied areas in Southeast Europe, not least with the help from local authorities. In many cases, political concessions and, very often, shabby compromises resulted from territorial arrangements and compensations. This, for example, happened in Albania, where the Germans, after the disappearance of the Italian protectorate in 1943, ostensibly supported the Albanian annexation of Kosovo. In exchange they succeeded in recruiting an entire Albanian SS Division.

Voluntary enlistment for the Wehrmacht or SS units and the recruitment of foreign nationals by German agencies, so-called military collaboration, are a highly complex theme that can only be hinted at here. Attempts to recruit soldiers for Waffen SS divisions were more or less forcibly undertaken at some time or the other during the war in most countries within the range of German rule, with the exception of Poland and some areas of the Soviet Union. While the political and administrative aspects of this mass enrollment—in the Netherlands only between twenty-two thousand and twenty-five thousand Dutchmen joined the Waffen SS—have been dealt with in a number of occupational studies, the origins, social status, and motivations of volunteers have hardly been researched. Some of the police and army units consisting of volunteers, notably from the occupied Baltic states and the Ukraine, also participated in the mass murder of Jews. See, for example, Stein's *The Waffen SS* and Wegner's *Hitlers politische Soldaten.*

Another chapter of the history of collaboration clearly deserving wider examination, preferably in a comparative perspective, is the extent of support for, and cooperation by, local administrators and police with the Nazis' Final Solution, the persecution and mass murder of European Jews. One of the arguments for collaboration (put forward quite forcefully by its practitioners) has always been that things would have been worse if collaboration had not taken place, in other words, that collaboration had a moderating effect on the repercussions of Nazi occupation.

As far as the persecution and deportation of Jews from most occupied countries are concerned, this justification does not hold true. There can be no doubt that, for instance, the administrative compliance of Dutch civil servants effectively contributed to the smoothness and the absence of problems and difficulties with which the German police and authorities carried through the call-up and deportation of Jews in the Netherlands. Marrus and Paxton, *Vichy France and the Jews,* showed that Vichy's anti-Jewish legislation and Aryanization measures were well under way before the Nazis ordered the segregation of Jews in France as the first step toward the Final Solution. Once the Germans secured the overall initiative, the French authorities did everything in their power to support them in their effort to rid the country of unwanted outsiders. Collaboration did not prevent the worst from happening but rather made it possible and, in any case, paved the road to Auschwitz. Also consult Blom, "The Nazis and the Jews in Occupied Western Europe," and the essays in Benz, *Dimension des Völkermords.*

The cooperation of fascists with the Nazi invaders can be regarded as a classic case of collaboration during the Second World War. In no other case is the range of collaborationist behavior more clear; nowhere is it more starkly revealed that both the prospects and the limits of collaboration were always linked with the interest of the occupying power. In most cases, the demarcation line between Nazi occupation policy and fascist collaboration was very narrow, so far as it did not actually overlap as a result of ideological identification. Collaboration with the occupying power was thus regarded, although perhaps with differing intensity and conviction, as an ultimate objective, either as a long-term and unlimited cooperation with Nazi Germany or (for a small radical faction of the fascist movement) as a total absorption into a future Germanic empire, created under the auspices of Himmler's SS. The wartime fascist collaborationists held rather diverse and heterogeneous convictions, which allowed some of them, at times, to appear to be social revolutionaries and modernizers. But despite their progressive rhetoric and often youthful-sounding slogans of "revolution" and "socialism," these "revolutionary fascists" remained strongly reactionary and largely antimodernist. For a general discussion of fascist collaboration, see Durand, *Le nouvel ordre européen Nazi* and Littlejohn, *The Patriotic Traitors.*

Fascist collaboration certainly contained an element of historical continuity, although opportunism and political or even personal corruption also became dominant features. An element of continuity also applied to those like Pétain in France who viewed close cooperation with Germany as the only operational basis for their policies. French politics during the occupation was a logical and, to a large extent, inevitable consequence of the political events and constellation of the 1930s. Vichy's "pluralistic dictatorship" (Stanley Hoffmann's phrase in "Collaborationism") began with Pétain's reactionary-patriarchial regime (1940–1942), was followed by Laval's authoritarian-technocratic rule (1942–1944), and ended with Darnand's openly fascist system (1944). Despite different motives and diverse approaches, all the protagonists of the "Révolution Nationale" agreed that there was no alternative to their collaboration with the Third Reich. For some of the extensive literature on Vichy France, see, in addition to previously cited works, Brender, *Kollaboration in Frankreich*; Dank, *The French against the French*; Gordon, *Collaborationism in France*; Hellman, *The Knight-Monks of Vichy-France*; Rousso, *La collaboration*; and Sweets, *Choices in Vichy France.*

In all cases, however, the potential as well the limits of political collaboration were subordinate to the interests of the occupying power. Nazi Germany was not interested in creating a genuine fascist state in France or elsewhere. The occupation authorities regarded political collaboration (and, incidentally, any other form of collaboration) first and foremost as a useful means of achieving their own selfish and destructive goals. Concessions were only temporary and never constituted any real change of policy. Fascist parties and their leaders in most occupied countries were reduced to mere puppets and useful tools of administration and economic exploitation. Quisling in Norway, Mussert in the Netherlands, Doriot and Déat in France, the Iron Guard in Romania, and the Arrow Cross movement in Hungary—to name but a few of them—all had to realize that Germany's European policy and Hitler's New Order served one purpose only: to establish and strengthen Germany's superiority and power and to give it maximum support for conducting the war.

Only a few fascist leaders and their supporters were prepared to draw the right conclusion. Most remained faithful followers of the Third Reich whether they promised themselves that things would be totally different after the war or that they were already so politically and morally corrupted that they saw no possible escape for themselves. Some were not willing to give up their dreams about a "peaceful" New Order in Europe. The Dutch fascist leader Anton Mussert continued to bombard Hitler with grandiose ideas about a possible "League of Germanic People" in Europe in which the "Greater Netherlands" would take second place after Germany. The last memorandum arrived in November 1944. Hitler did not even bother to read it. For Norway, see Hoidal's *Quisling* and Loock's *Quisling, Rosenberg und Terboven*; for Belgium, Conway's *Collaboration in Belgium*; for the Netherlands, Hirschfeld's *Nazi Rule and Dutch Collaboration*; for Romania, Heinen's *Die Legion "Erzengel Michael"* and Ioanid's *The Sword of the Archangel*; and for Hungary, Szöllösi-Janze's *Die Pfeilkreuzlerbewegung in Ungarn*.

Most fascist leaders and leading political collaborationists committed themselves to such an extent to the policy of the Third Reich that they were not spared Mussolini's fate. Only a handful escaped to neutral countries or to South America, often with the help of authoritarian regimes or secret services, among them the "Poglavnik" (leader) of the Croatian Ustasha-movement, Anté Pavelic, as well as the leader of the Belgian Rexists, Léon Degrelle. Others were not so lucky. The onetime prime minister of Norway Quisling was sentenced for high treason and shot, as were the erstwhile "leader of the Dutch people" Mussert and the former Hungarian prime minister and leader of the Arrow Cross movement Ferenc Szalasi.

Collaboration ended as the German occupation collapsed. What followed were mass arrests and public purges of hundreds of thousands of people, not only the guilty ones. Thousands, particularly in France and Eastern Europe, lost their lives. In many countries, the period of "wild purges" was followed by *épurations* in the public sector and within a number of institutions and organizations. Recent research into the "wild" purges as well as into the judicial procedures challenges the widely held notion that punishment for collaborators was undermined by misplaced mercy, private machination, or political oportunism. It is perhaps time to attempt a synthesis that initiates a full-scale comparative description and assessment of this period, looking into the purge of collaborators in both Eastern and Western Europe. On this topic begin with the essays on Germany as well as on Austria, Italy, France, Norway, the Netherlands, Hungary, and Croatia and Henke and Woller's *Politische Säuberungen in Europa*; for Belgium, see Huyse et al., *La répression des collaborations.*

BIBLIOGRAPHY

Also see the chapters on "Resistance Movements in Europe," "Prisoners of War and Civilian Internees," and "The Holocaust."

Aly, Götz. *"Endlösung." Völkerverschiebung und der Mord an den europäischen Juden.* Frankfurt am Main: Fischer, 1995.

Andreyev, Catherine. *Vlasov and the Russian Liberation Movement.* Cambridge: Cambridge UP, 1987.

Armstrong, John A. "Collaboration in World War II: The Integral Nationalist Variant in Eastern Europe." *Journal of Modern History 40* (1968): 196–410.

Azéma, Jean-Pierre. *La Collaboration, 1940–1944.* Paris: Université de France, 1975.

Azéma, Jean-Pierre, and François Bédarida. *Le régime de Vichy et les Français.* Paris: Fayard, 1992.

Bartov, Omer. *The Eastern Front 1941–45. German Troops and the Barbarization of Warfare.* London and New York: Macmillan, 1985.

Benz, Wolfgang, ed. *Dimension des Völkermords. Die Zahl der jüdischen Opfer des Nationalsozialismus.* Munich: Oldenbourg, 1991.

Blom, Hans. "The Nazis and the Jews in Occupied Western Europe." *Journal of Modern History 54* (1982): 687–714.

Brandes, Detlev. *Die Tschechen unter deutschem Protektorat.* Vol. 1, *Besatzungspolitik, Kollaboration und Widerstand im Protektorat Böhmen und Mähren bis Heydrichs Tod (1939–1942)*; vol. 2, *Besatzungspolitik, Kollaboration und Widerstand im Protektorat Böhmen und Mähren von Heydrichs Tod bis zum Prager Aufstand (1942–1945).* Munich: Oldenbourg, 1969, 1975.

Brender, Reinhold. *Kollaboration in Frankreich im Zweiten Weltkrieg. Marcel Déat und das Rassemblement national populaire.* Munich: Oldenbourg, 1992.

Broszat, Martin. "Faschismus und Kollaboration in Ostmitteleuropa zwischen den Weltkriegen." *Vierteljahrshefte für Zeitgeschichte 14* (1966): 225–51.

———. *Nationalsozialistische Polenpolitik 1939–1945.* Stuttgart: Deutsche Verlags Anstalt, 1961.

Bunting, Madeleine. *Model Occupation. Channel Islands under German Rule; 1940–1945.* London: HarperCollins, 1995.

Carlton, E. *Occupation. The Policies and Practices of Military Conquerors.* London: Routledge, 1992.

Carroll, Berenice A. *Design for Total War. Arms and Economics in the Third Reich.* The Hague: Mouton, 1968.

Child, Clifton J. "The Concept of the New Order." In Arnold J. Toynbee and Veronica Toynbee, eds., *Hitler's Europe*, 47–73. London: Oxford UP, 1954.

Collotti, Enzo. "Il collaborazionismo con le potenze dell'Asse nell'Europa occupata: temi e probleme della storiografia." *Rivista di storia contemporanea 21* (1992): 327–59.

Conway, Martin. *Collaboration in Belgium. Léon Degrelle and the Rexist Movement, 1940–1944.* New Haven, CT: Yale UP, 1993.

Dallin, Alexander. *German Rule in Russia, 1941–1945. A Study of Occupation Policies.* London: Macmillan, 1957, 1981 (rev.); Boulder, CO: Westview, 1981.

Dank, Milton. *The French against the French: Collaboration and Resistance.* Philadelphia: Lippincott, 1974.

Deist, Wilhelm, et al. *Germany and the Second World War.* Vol. 1; *The Build-up of German Aggression.* Vol. 2; *Germany's Initial Conquests in Europe.* Vol. 3; *The Mediterranean, South-East Europe and North Africa, 1939–1941: From Italy's Declaration of Non-Belligerence to the Entry of the United States into the War.* Trans. by P. S. Falla, et al. Oxford and New York: Clarendon Press, 1990–1995.

Die Okkupationspolitik des deutschen Faschismus in Dänemark und Norwegen (1940–1945). Dokumentenauswahl und Einleitung von Fritz Petrick. Unter Mitarbeit von Reinhard Abraham sowie Helma Kaden und Eva Hintze. Berlin, Heidelberg: Hüthig, 1992. Europa unterm Hakenkreuz. Die Okkupationspolitik des deutschen Faschismus (1938–1945). Achtbändige Dokumentenedition. Ed. the German Federal Archives (since 1990). Vol. 7.

Dostert, Paul. *Luxemburg zwischen Selbstbehauptung und nationaler Selbstaufgabe: die deutsche Besatzungspolitik und die Volksdeutsche Bewegung 1940–1945.* Luxembourg: Imprimerie Saint-Paul, 1985.

Durand, Yves. *Le nouvel ordre européen Nazi. La collaboration dans l'Europe allemande (1938–1945).* Brussels: Edition Complexe, 1990.

———. *Vichy (1940–1944).* Paris: Bordas, 1972.

Eichholtz, Dietrich. *Geschichte der deutschen Kriegswirtschaft 1939–1945.* 2 vols. Berlin (East): Akademie-Verlag, 1968, 1988.

Fletcher, Willard Allen. "The German Administration in Luxemburg 1940–1942: Toward a 'de facto' Annexation." *The Historical Journal 8* (1970): 533–44.

Freymond, Jean. "Aspects of the Reich's Ministry of Economics Concept of an Economic Reorganization of Europe (1940)." *Studia Historiae Oeconomicae 14* (1980): 5–14.

———. *Le IIIe Reich et la réorganisation économique de l'Europe 1940–1942. Origines et projects.* Leiden: Sijthoff, 1974.

Gillingham, John. *Belgian Business in the Nazi New Order.* Ghent: Jan Dhondt Foundation, 1977.

———. "The Politics of Business in the Economic Großraum. The Example of Belgium." *Studia Historiae Oeconomicae 14* (1980): 23–29.

Gordon, Bertram M. *Collaborationism in France during the Second World War.* Ithaca, NY: Cornell UP, 1980.

Gross, Jan T. *Polish Society under German Occupation. The General Government 1939–1944.* Princeton: Princeton UP, 1979.

Harvey, Patricia. "The Structure of Economic Controls in Europe." In Arnold J. Toynbee and Veronica M. Toynbee, eds., *Hitler's Europe,* 171–86. London: Oxford UP, 1954.

Heinen, Armin. *Die Legion "Erzengel Michael" in Rumänien. Soziale Bewegung und politische Organisation.* Munich: Oldenbourg, 1986.

Hellman, John. *The Knight-Monks of Vichy-France.* Montreal: McGill-Queen's UP, 1993.

Henke, Klaus-Dietmar, and Hans Woller, eds. *Politische Säuberungen in Europa. Die*

Abrechnung mit Faschismus und Kollaboration nach dem Zweiten Weltkrieg. Munich: Deutscher Taschenbuch Verlag, 1991.

Herbert, Ulrich, ed. *Europa und der "Reichseinsatz." Ausländische Zivilarbeiter, Kriegsgefangene und KZ-Häftlinge in Deutschland 1938–1945.* Essen: Klartext, 1991.

————. *Fremdarbeiter. Politik und Praxis des "Ausländer-Einsatzes" in der Kriegswirtschaft des Dritten Reiches.* Berlin: Dietz, 1985.

Hirschfeld, Gerhard. "Collaboration and Attentism in the Netherlands 1940–41." *Journal of Contemporary History 16* (1981): 467–86.

————. "Collaboration in Nazi-Occupied France." In Gerhard Hirschfeld and Patrick Marsh, eds., *Collaboration in France. Politics and Culture during the Nazi Occupation, 1940–1944.* Oxford: Berg, 1989.

————. *Nazi Rule and Dutch Collaboration. The Netherlands under German Occupation, 1940–1945.* Oxford: Berg, 1988.

————, ed. *The Policies of Genocide. Jews and Soviet Prisoners of War in Nazi Germany.* London: Allen and Unwin, 1986.

Hoffmann, Stanley. "Collaborationism in France during World War II." *Journal of Modern History 40* (1968): 375–95.

Hoidal, Oddvar. *Quisling. A Study in Treason.* Oslo and New York: Norwegian UP, 1989.

Homze, Edward L. *Foreign Labor in Nazi Germany.* Princeton: Princeton UP, 1967.

Hondros, John L. *Occupation and Resistance. The Greek Agony 1941–44.* New York: Pella, 1983.

Hory, Ladislaus, and Martin Broszat. *Der kroatische Ustascha-Staat 1941–1945.* Stuttgart: Deutsche Verlags Anstalt, 1964.

Huyse, Luc, Steven Dhondt, et al. *La répression des collaborations, 1942–1952. Un passé toujours présent.* Bruxelles: CRISP, 1993.

Ioanid, Radu. *The Sword of the Archangel. Fascist Ideology in Romania.* Boulder, CO: East European Monographs, 1990.

Jäckel, Eberhard. *Frankreich in Hitler's Europa.* Stuttgart: Deutsche Verlags Anstalt, 1966.

Jong, Louis de. *Het Koninkrijk der Nederlanden in de tweede wereldoorlog.* S'Gravenhage: Nijhoff, 1969–1988.

————. *The Netherlands and Nazi Germany.* Cambridge: Harvard UP, 1990.

Klinkhammer, Lutz. *Zwischen Bündnis und Besatzung. Das nationalsozialistische Deutschland und die Republik von Salò 1943–1945.* Tübingen: Niemeyer, 1993.

Kluke, Paul. "Nationalsozialistische Europaideologie." *Vierteljahrshefte für Zeitgeschichte 3* (1955): 240–58.

Koehl, Robert Lewis. *RKFDV: German Resettlement and Population Policy, 1939–1945. A History of the Reich Commission for the Strengthening of Germandom.* Cambridge: Harvard UP, 1957.

Lammers, Cornelis J. "Levels of Collaboration. A Comparative Study of German Occupation during the Second World War." *Journal of Social Sciences 31* (1995): 3–31.

Lemberg, Hans. "Kollaboration in Europa mit dem Dritten Reich um das Jahr 1941." In Karl Bosl, ed., *Das Jahr 1941 in der europäischen Politik.* Munich and Vienna: Oldenbourg, 1972.

Littlejohn, David. *The Patriotic Traitors: A History of Collaboration in German Occupied Europe, 1940–1945.* London: Heinemann, 1972.

Loock, Hans-Dietrich. *Quisling, Rosenberg und Terboven. Zur Vorgeschichte und Geschichte der nationalsozialistischen Revolution in Norwegen.* Stuttgart: Deutsche Verlags Anstalt, 1970.

Madajczyk, Czeslaw. "Die Besatzungssysteme der Achsenmächte." *Studia Historiae Oeconomicae 14* (1979): 105–21.

———. *Die Okkupationspolitik Nazideutschlands in Polen 1939–1945.* Berlin: Akademie-Verlag, 1987.

Marrus, Michael R., and Robert Paxton. *Vichy France and the Jews.* New York: Basic Books, 1981.

Mastny, Vojtech. *The Czechs under Nazi Rule. The Failure of National Resistance, 1939–1942.* New York: Columbia UP, 1971.

Mazower, Mark. *Inside Hitler's Greece. The Experience of Occupation, 1941–1944.* New Haven, CT: Yale UP, 1994.

Milward, Alan S. *The Fascist Economy in Norway.* Oxford: Clarendon, 1972.

———. *The German Economy at War.* London: Athlone, 1965.

———. *The New Order and the French Economy.* Oxford: Clarendon, 1970.

Müller, Rolf-Dieter and Gerd R. Ueberschär. *Hitler's War in the East.* London and Providence, RI: Berghahn Books, 1996.

Myllyniemi, Seppo. *Die Neuordnung der Baltischen Länder 1941–1944. Zum nationalsozialistischen Inhalt der deutschen Besatzungspolitik.* Helsinki: Suomen Hist. Seura, 1973.

Noakes, Jeremy, and Geoffrey Pridham, eds. *Nazism 1919–1945.* Vol. 3, *Foreign Policy, War and Racial Extermination. A Documentary Reader.* Exeter, U.K.: University of Exeter, 1988.

Olshausen, Klaus. *Zwischenspiel auf dem Balkan. Die deutsche Politik gegenüber Jugoslawien und Griechenland von März bis Juli 1941.* Stuttgart: Deutsche Verlags Anstalt, 1973.

Paxton, Robert O. *Vichy France: Old Guard and New Order, 1940–1944.* New York: Columbia UP, 1972, 1982.

Rich, Norman. *Hitler's War Aims.* Vol. 1, *Ideology: The Nazi State, and the Course of Expansion.* New York: Norton, 1973. Vol. 2, *The Establishment of the New Order.* London: Deutsch, 1974.

Rohwer, Jürgen, and Hildegard Müller. *Neue Forschungen zum Zweiten Weltkrieg. Literaturberichte und Bibliographien aus 67 Ländern.* Koblenz: Bernard and Graefe, 1990.

Rousso, Henry. *La collaboration.* Paris: MA Editions, 1987.

———. *The Vichy Syndrome. History and Memory in France since 1944.* 2d ed. Cambridge: Harvard UP, 1994.

Schulte, Theo. *The German Army and Nazi Policies in Occupied Russia 1941–1945.* Oxford: Berg, 1989.

Stein, George H. *The Waffen SS. Hitler's Elite Guard at War, 1939–1945.* Ithaca, NY: Cornell UP, 1966.

Streit, Christian. *"Keine Kameraden." Die Wehrmacht und die sowjetischen Kriegsgefangenen 1941–1945.* Stuttgart: Deutsche Verlags Anstalt, 1978.

Sweets, John F. *Choices in Vichy France. The French under Nazi Occupation.* New York: Oxford UP, 1986.

Szöllösi-Janze, Margit. *Die Pfeilkreuzlerbewegung in Ungarn. Historischer Kontext, Entwicklung und Herrschaft.* Munich: Oldenbourg, 1989.

Thomson, Erich. *Deutsche Besatzungspolitik in Dänemark 1940–1945.* Düsseldorf: Bertelsmann, 1971.

Toynbee, Arnold J., and Veronica M. Toynbee, eds. *Hitler's Europe.* Survey of International Affairs 1939–1946: War Time Series No. 4. London: Oxford UP, 1954.

Umbreit, Hans. "Auf dem Weg zur Kontinentalherrschaft." In *Das Deutsche Reich und der Zweite Weltkrieg,* vol. 5, part 1, 1–345. Stuttgart: Deutsche Verlags Anstalt, 1988.

Volkmann, Hans-Erich. "Das Vlasov-Unternehmen zwischen Ideologie und Pragmatismus." *Militärgeschichtliche Mitteilungen* 2 (1972): 117–55.

Wagner, Wilfried. *Belgien in der deutschen Politik während des Zweiten Weltkrieges.* Boppard: Boldt, 1974.

Warmbrunn, Werner. *The German Occupation of Belgium, 1940–1944.* New York: Lang, 1993.

Wegner, Bernd. *Hitlers politische Soldaten. Die Waffen-SS 1933–1945. Leitbild, Struktur und Funktion einer nationalsozialistischen Elite.* 3d ed. Paderborn: Schöningh, 1988.

Weinberg, Gerhard L. *A World at Arms. A Global History of World War II.* Cambridge: Cambridge UP, 1994.

Wright, Gordon. *The Ordeal of Total War, 1939–1945.* New York: Harper and Row, 1968.

18 Resistance Movements in Europe

Bob Moore

Few scholarly works, in any language, have attempted to provide an overall synthesis of resistance to the German occupation of Europe during the Second World War. In part, this has been due to the difficulties of encompassing the wide range of sources, the variety of debates, and the number of countries and languages involved. However, the absence of general texts is also symptomatic of the fact that "resistance" in each of the occupied countries has been perceived as a unique element within national historiography and therefore not demanding of external comparison. The early works on the subject demonstrated that resistance came in many different shapes and forms. Broadly speaking, it has been examined in two ways: as a part of the Allied war effort and as part of the internal response to German occupation. Both perspectives are well represented in the literature, but seldom has there been any attempt to link or contrast the two. As a result, even the term "resistance" can be used to mean very different things. The armed insurrections of partisans and *maquis* and the espionage and escape networks so beloved of novelists and screenwriters can be clearly identified as falling within the term, but more problematic are the unrecorded or unnoticed acts of individuals and groups against the German occupying power or its agents. Between these two perspectives is a third area of research involving the relationships between resistance organizations and the Allied powers.

GENERAL

Resistance as a part of the espionage and sabotage campaign against the Axis powers has been well covered, notably by the works of Foot, whose wartime career in the British Special Operations Executive (SOE) gave him a great many insights into the relationships between the organizations

like MI5 and MI6 working from London and the networks operating in
occupied territory. In *Resistance*, he surveyed the various definitions of
resistance used by other scholars and divided his subject matter into three
functional categories: intelligence, escape, and sabotage, the latter heading further subdivided into sabotage, attacks on troops and individuals,
politics, and insurrection. Although acknowledging the more "civilian"
forms of resistance, such as passive and administrative resistance and the
production of clandestine newspapers, he nevertheless concentrates on
the military aspects of what was done, who was involved, and its relative
importance to the Allied war effort. This latter question has remained an
important element in the debate on resistance. Authors such as Foot highlighted the heroic and sometimes tragic history of the European resistance
but also placed it firmly within the military history of World War II.

For an analysis of the relationships between SOE and the European
resistance movements, Stafford produced a more or less chronological
account, *Britain and the European Resistance*, which highlights the problems
and sometimes tense relationship between the needs of the Allied war
effort, as conveyed by SOE, and the objectives of national or regional
resistance organizations. He also mentioned SOE's greatest failure, the so-
called *Englandspiel*, where agents sent to the Netherlands and captured by
the German Sicherheitsdienst attempted to alert their masters in London
to their true fate but were ignored, leading to the capture of forty-three
agents, of whom thirty-six were executed. This is also afforded extensive
treatment in De Jong's history of the Netherlands in World War II.

The first major international conferences devoted to the history of the
resistance took place in 1958 and 1960, published in two volumes as *European Resistance Movements*. The first dealt with such themes as the psychological war and the role of the clandestine press, Jewish resistance, the
maquis and guerrilla warfare, and the Allied relationship with the resistance. The second concentrated on the resistance and the Allies, as well
as other aspects of national opposition to German rule. In many respects,
these volumes set the agenda for subsequent research. However, the im-
plicitly comparative nature of the conference sessions tended to produce
papers on the international and military importance of the resistance,
rather than its role in the internal history of individual countries. This
trend was continued in a further important conference volume edited by
Hawes and White. White provided a comprehensive introduction, highlighting both the commonalities and diversities of the European resistance
and pointing out that all activity was directed toward the defeat of a common enemy and that resistance in all countries could be not only active
and tangible but also internal and passive. Moreover, it was likely to grow
as the war proceeded, and the possibility of liberation became stronger.

White drew four major conclusions from this comparative analysis. First, the resistance to German rule created alliances of formerly antagonistic groups, for example, between Catholics and communists. Second, resistance had differing objectives; there was conservative resistance directed toward re-creating the traditional order, and there was revolutionary resistance that saw the defeat of Germany as the prelude to a transformation of government and society. Third, there is the question of external links and where resistance movements looked for help. Some had contacts with the Western powers in London, some with the Soviets in Moscow, and one or two looked to both sides for guidance and assistance. Finally, the scale and achievements of the resistance movements across Europe varied enormously, and evaluating their contribution to liberation and postwar reconstruction is a complex process. Specific mention should be made here of Milward's provocative "Economic and Strategic Effectiveness of Resistance," in which he claimed that resistance had little economic or strategic value for the Allied war effort.

This one publication demonstrates the direction scholarship took in the mid-1970s and also highlights many of the problems involved in the study of resistance. However, one further text also demands our attention. In 1972, Henri Michel produced the first and still perhaps the best attempt to synthesize all aspects of the European resistance in one comparative volume. *The Shadow War* starts with the nature of German occupation, then moves on to deal with exile resistance movements, the origins of clandestine organizations, their various types, and the different forms of resistance, and finally assesses the achievements of the resistance throughout Europe. Inevitably, given the scope of the book, the treatment of each country is somewhat brief, but this remains an essential guide to the origins, conduct, and achievements of the resistance. Moreover, it also raised essential questions taken up by other authors, most notably the place of resistance movements in the national historiographies of World War II, the role of illegal publications and newspapers, and the vexed question of the resistance's "contribution" to liberation and postwar reconstruction. Beyond this, there are the more recent study of civilian resistance in Europe by Semelin, *Unarmed against Hitler*; a juxtaposition of resistance and collaboration in Europe by Rings, *Life with the Enemy*; and a survey of partisan movement in *The Partisans of Europe* by Macksey, who concluded that while partisans did have some military successes, the price paid for these in terms of Axis retribution may have been unacceptably high.

Many of these authors deal with the development of resistance organizations and the roles played by geography and topography in conditioning their activities. Rural resistance took very different forms from that in the cities. Some landscapes afforded much better protection than others for clandestine activity. The countryside provided secure hiding places for whole networks in France and whole armies in Yugoslavia but gave little or no protection in the Netherlands. Groups were often engaged in specialist tasks such as the production of forged papers or ration cards or the management of escape and evasion lines, like those into Switzerland, Spain, and Sweden, for Allied servicemen, political fugitives, and Jews. The growth and success of these networks depended on a multiplicity of factors, which makes generalization difficult.

The historiography of resistance in occupied Europe has developed more or less separately in each country. This is in part due to the differences in the organization and nature of German rule, most notably between Eastern and Western Europe, but evident even between neighboring states. Most research has examined resistance as part of the domestic social and political history of the country under occupation. As such, attention has been directed to the origins, participants, structures, organizations, successes, and failures of the resistance and to its role in postwar reconstruction. Only a very few authors have been brave enough to make tentative comparisons between states. The fact that these historiographies are overwhelmingly national (and, for the most part, published in the language of the country concerned) provides the justification for taking each of the major occupied states in turn, both to demonstrate the development of these individual historiographies and also to highlight some of the parallel paths taken by scholars in looking at ostensibly similar problems.

One or two can be mentioned here. Resistance in most Western countries can be divided between military and nonmilitary, among communist, socialist, confessional, and right-wing. The creation (or not) of single, unified movements and the role of key individuals in this process have also remained a major debate, as have the definition of resistance and the difficulties of defining activities at the margins, in the gray areas between passivity and passive opposition, or of people and groups who were apparently collaborating and resisting at the same time. Other problems that seem common to more than one country include the dilemma of national communist parties after occupation but before the collapse of the Nazi-Soviet pact, and their later role in resistance activity; the opposition (or lack of it) to the deportation of the Jews; and the importance of the resistance to the liberation of their countries and their role in restoring national prestige in the postwar era after societies had been fatally divided between those who cooperated with the occupying power and those who were steadfast in their opposition. Finally, there has been an increasing interest in the role of women within national resistance movements. Many of the central debates on this issue can be found in the key work by Rossiter, *Women in the Resistance,* but other authors working on both Eastern and Western European countries have done much to further knowledge of this previously neglected area.

NORTHERN EUROPE

As the first Western European country to be occupied by the Germans and the last to be liberated, Norway experienced a resistance that lasted longer than many of its European counterparts. The standard general text in English remains Gvelsvik's *Norwegian Resistance*, and this can be combined with the specific survey by Kjelstadli, "The Resistance Movement," on the relationship between the Norwegian resistance and the Allies. A brief narrative introduction to the subject can also be found in *Norway* by Riste and Nökleby, which provides a chronological overview and discussion of the major issues.

"Nonviolent Resistance" by Wehr examines various aspects of civilian resistance to Nazi occupation. The most recent book on the subject, *Krig og Okkupation*, comes from Skodvin, who stressed the broad-based civilian opposition to German rule and attempts at Nazification. Certainly, the lack of any popular support for the collaborationist, indigenous Norwegian Nazi Party under Vidkun Quisling seems to have simplified some of the debates about Norwegian society under occcupation, although questions remain over the reaction to the deportation of the Jews and the "economic collaboration" that was an integral feature of the German regime. Skodvin was an active participant in the resistance whose firsthand experiences combined with a detailed knowledge of the archival sources make this an essential text. The best recent literature survey on the occupation of Norway comes in "Forskningen om Krigen," by Sorensen, who concentrated on the tendency toward value judgments in existing works and suggested new perspectives that might be explored.

Danish resistance was complicated by the fact that Denmark was never formally at war with Germany but became a de facto participant in the common struggle alongside the Allies. For a comprehensive overview, one need look no further than the three-volume work of Hæstrup, *Secret Alliance*, which provided a detailed examination of the origins, development, and structure of the Danish resistance. Hæstrup has also commented specifically on its links to the Allied powers, and this external element has been further examined in "The Danish Resistance Movement" by Hillingso, who highlighted the problems and conflicts between the movement in Denmark and the various Allied agencies in London, including SOE and military intelligence. The relationship was clouded by the Allied mistrust of the Danes' will to fight and their inability to mount a sustained campaign. This can be read alongside the specialist study by Bennett of the British Broadcasting Corporation and its relationship with the Danish resistance. However, the Danish resistance is perhaps most famous for engineering the escape of its Jewish community to Sweden from under the noses of the German authorities. Key texts for this particular aspect can be found in the monograph by Yahil, *The Rescue of the Danish Jews*, and the edited collection by Goldberger, *The Rescue of Danish Jews: Moral Courage under Stress*, which includes an extensive chapter by Hæstrup on the Danish Jews and the German occupation. The fiftieth anniversary of the invasion prompted a reappraisal of the existing literature by Roslyng-Jensen in "Den 9 April 1940."

WESTERN EUROPE

The resistance movements in France have attracted more scholarly attention than in any other part of Europe. One reason for this is the importance of the resistance as a factor in restoring French national pride in the years after the war's end. However, this also created problems and the need for historians to overcome the many myths that became associated with the "heroic" view of French actions against the occupier. The first major history of the resistance as a whole and still perhaps the most comprehensive and encyclopedic is the five-volume *Histoire de la Résistance* by Noguères. In spite of his participation as a regional chief of the movement "Franc-Tireur" in Montpellier, the writing is both rigorous and scholarly and has acted as the basic source for many other subsequent works. Divided until November 1942 into occupied and unoccupied (Vichy) zones, the history of the resistance has also tended to be divided along these lines.

The first study in English, *The French Resistance*, by Knight, adopted a more or less chronological approach to the subject. More recently, Kedward contributed two major texts. The first, on *Resistance in Vichy France*, clearly demonstrates the variety of movements and activities that existed and also the uncertainties of the participants, acting, as they were, against a French state. The second analyzes the creation and development of the *Maquis*, the resistance based in the countryside of the south that began with men taking to the hills to avoid labor conscription and ended with some of them organizing a full-scale insurrection against the Germans in 1944. In *The Politics of Resistance in France* Sweets made a substantial contribution to an understanding of motivation behind resistance in central and southern France and its structures. As in every occupied country, there were many different resistance organizations established. One of the best accounts of an individual group is Blumenson's careful reconstruction of the early Parisian network created around the staff at the Musée de l'Homme in 1940 in *The Vildé Affair*.

The role of the French Communist Party (PCF) in the resistance and its dilemmas in the months before June 1941 have been examined by a number of authors, most notably Kedward, Simmonds ("The French Communist Party"), and Pike ("Between the Junes"). A local study, "The Communist Resistance in the Haut-Vienne" by Farmer, is also instructive in showing that success was often based on identifying with local interests and defying or ignoring party orders. Attempts have been made to uncover the role of women in the resistance, most notably by Schwarz in *"Partisanes,"* who looked at female participation in PCF combat groups and showed that in the extreme conditions of underground warfare, women did trespass into "male gender territory."

There have been innumerable texts on the relationships between the resistance movements and the Free French and Allies in London. Apart from the work by Foot on *SOE in France*, there is also the detailed study by Funk, *Hidden Ally*, on the role of the resistance in the Allied landings in southern France in 1944. Finally, at a more general analytical level, the problems of defining resistance within the more general question of civilian behavior during the occupation have been addressed by Sweets in a case study of France, "Hold That Pendulum!" He noted that the traditional view of the French as a nation of resisters has been replaced by an image of them as a nation of collaborators and suggested that reconsideration of both these extremes will lead to a more tempered view of French behavior under occupation.

Perhaps more than in any other Western European country, the resistance in Belgium has been considered an internal matter. Moreover, its historians were slow to move into the field of contemporary history, and not until the 1970s did scholars begin to publish on aspects of the Second World War. Given the high profile of the debate on the conduct of Leopold III during the occupation, the punishment of collaborators, and the continuance of the Flemish question, resistance did not command much attention. Archives remained closed, and oral history was untapped for many years. Probably the most important and the most comprehensive study devoted specifically to resistance is *Het Verzet* (The Occupation) by Vijver and others in the general series on Belgium in the Second World War. In French, but somewhat older, is the survey *La Résistance* by Bernard, which lacks the archival base of later works but benefits from the author's career both as an agent in the field and as a staff officer in London. His more recent work has concentrated specifically on the "secret army" in Belgium, made up of diverse groups of soldiers and ex-servicemen, and on the (civilian) patriotic militias and armed partisans. As with all other occupied European countries, the Communist Party in Belgium was placed in a compromised position by the Nazi-Soviet pact of August 1939. Their response to this dilemma and the internal debates on the various possible courses of action is carefully outlined by van Doorslaer in *De Kommunistische Partij van België.* Beyond this, one has to look at more general works. The most recent of these is *La Belgique Occupée* by the highly respected Verhoeyen and deals with the whole period from the outbreak of war to the liberation.

As with many other European states, scholars in the Netherlands have tended to place their country's resistance movement firmly and exclusively within the national historiography of the Second World War. This has been to categorize all behavior during the occupation as either *goed* (correct) or *fout* (incorrect). The major achievements of the Dutch resistance, the February strike of 1941 against the roundup of Jews in Amsterdam, the April–May 1943 strike against forced labor drafts, and the stoppage of the railways to assist the Allied landing at Arnhem in 1944 have all formed the subjects of individual monographs by Sijes, *De Februari-staking;* Bouman, *De April–Mei Stakingen;* and Rüter, *Rijden en Staken,* respectively.

A brief survey of the resistance can be found in a series of published lectures by the late Louis de Jong, the doyen of Dutch historians on the Second World War. They summarize the resistance's main achievements by measuring them against the successes and failures of German policy. He argued that while the attempt to Nazify Dutch society failed, economic exploitation and the deportation of the Jews succeeded. Thus, the record of the resistance was essentially mixed. On one hand, contacts between the Dutch resistance and the British SOE were compromised by the network's penetration by the German security service, leading to the capture and death of many British agents. On the other hand, the resistance was more or less united into a single entity by the last year of the occupation and successfully hid several hundred thousand people underground. De Jong has published a limited number of papers in English on anti-Nazi resistance and contacts with the Allies. One key work is the collection edited by Roegholt and Zwaan, which surveys the main resistance elements in the Netherlands, including the military, left-wing, and church-based movements. Each chapter also charts the expansion of these groups and their activities, successes, and failures.

An important critique of de Jong's writings has come from Blom, who argues against the use of a *goed/fout* structure to understand Dutch behavior during the occupation. It is especially regrettable that no English version of this exists, although a short summary of the main points can be found in the review article by Moore. Scholarship in English remains scarce. For a brief summary, one can turn to the relevant chapters in the survey works on the occupation period by Warmbrunn, *The Dutch under German Occupation,* or Maass, *The Netherlands at War,* and to the May 1946 series of articles in the *Annals of the American Academy of Political and Social Sciences.* On specific aspects of the debates on resistance, Smith in "Neither Resistance nor Collaboration" examined the strange case of the short-lived but popular *Nederlandse Unie,* which the Germans perceived as an instrument to encourage collaboration but which adherents saw as a statement of continued patriotism and a means of protest against the occupation. Hirschfeld's *Nazi Rule and Dutch Collaboration* covers Dutch collaboration in fuller detail.

SOUTHERN EUROPE

Axis rule in Southern Europe provoked a wide variety of oppositional responses. Yet it should not be forgotten that Italy (as an integral part of the Axis until 1943) produced its own resistance movement. While the story of antifascist resistance to Mussolini's regime prior to the Italian surrender in September 1943 properly falls outside the terms of this survey, the emergence of an armed resistance to German occupation in the northern half of the country has many parallels with counterparts elsewhere in occupied Europe. The earliest comprehensive treatment of the subject came in Battaglia's *Story of the Italian Resistance*, but the most detailed survey in English of the Italian resistance movement remains *Mussolini's Enemies* by Delzell. He outlined the development of the armed resistance of 1943–1945, highlighting the various groups involved, their relationships with the Badoglio government and the Allied powers, and their role in the liberation of northern Italy from the Germans. A more recent, but briefer, summary can be found in Puzzo's *The Partisans and the War in Italy*, which deals specifically with the northern half of the country.

The nature of support given to the partisans against the Germans by Italian civilians has been the subject of much debate. The orthodox line claims that the National Liberation Committee for north Italy had the support of the entire population. This view can be found in the extensive work on the Italian resistance by Quazza, as in *Resistenza e storia italiana*, whereas a more revisionist approach, implying that German occupation produced more *attentisme* and a form of civil war, has its most recent expression in *Una guerra civile* by Pavone. The role of the resistance in the liberation of the north is also explored in *Italy, 1943–1945* by Ellwood, who highlights Allied worries about the partisans, especially the communists, setting themselves up as alternative local or regional governments to those of Badoglio's regime. At a more specialist level, Absalom in "Hiding History" looked at the behavior of peasants in the north of the country who assisted Allied fugitives, such as prisoners of war, escape from the Germans. He pointed out that this type of resistance was separate from partisan activity and represented an entirely different response to the occupation. As long as all Italians were assumed to have supported the Allied/antifascist cause, then their singular behavior was hidden, only to emerge when this particular myth was exploded. As with most of the occupied European countries, the role of women in the resistance is now beginning to be analyzed in more detail; in *Women and the Italian Resistance* Slaughter provided the first comprehensive treatment of their participation in the Italian theater.

The resistance movement in Greece had a particular history of its own, being directed against three occupying powers, Italy, Germany, and Bulgaria. A survey of the omissions and problems of the early historiography can be found in "The Greek Resistance" by Woodhouse, who had been commander of the Allied Military Mission to Greece during the war. However, the most accessible, comprehensive texts come from his later *Struggle for Greece* and *Occupation and Resistance* by Hondros, but the important role of the Greek Communist Party, both as liberators and then as the target for Allied suppression, has been more directly addressed by Kousoulas in *Revolution and Defeat* and by Vlavianos in *Greece, 1941–49*. On more specific aspects, the organization of EAM (National Liberation Movement), the political arm of the Greek resistance, see Stavrianos' "The Greek National Liberation Front." In "The Development of Guerrilla Warfare" Gerolymatos pointed out the conflict between the British Foreign Office and SOE over support for ELAS (National Popular Liberation Army, the military arm of EAM), the largest of the resistance organizations. In addition, recent research carried out by Hart, "Women in the Greek Resistance," shows how female participation in the resistance struggle altered the class and gender constraints of traditional Greek culture.

The struggle against occupation in Yugoslavia took on a far more military aspect than in the countries further west. The Germans' inability to pacify large areas allowed the formation of two separate armed resistance organizations: the chetniks led by Draza Mihailovitch and the partisans led by Tito. The history of the chetniks has received a good deal of recent attention. A full account can be found in Milazzo's *The Chetnik Movement*, while Karchmar's *Draza Mihailovic* surveyed their resistance activity and the reasons for the movement's downfall, pointing out that it was essentially Serbian and premodern in its organization. He also suggested that its virulent anticommunism made any form of accommodation with the partisans impossible. Also important is the extensive *Chetniks* by Tomasevich, which also provides an introduction to the period and the wider historical background.

The best recent survey of the communist partisan movement, its successes, and failures can be found in "Pariahs to Partisans to Power" by Wheeler. The changing nature of British policy toward the chetniks and partisans is well covered by Auty and Clogg, *British Policy towards Wartime Resistance*, and by Wheeler in *Britain and the War for Yugoslavia*, while Roberts in *Tito, Mihailovic and the Allies* looked in detail at the switch in Allied support from Mihailovitch to Tito and suggested that this was prompted by the former's propensity to make deals with the Germans and the latter's ability to hold down large numbers of Axis forces. The scope of British military involvement in the country and its impact on events can be found in McConville's *A Small War* and Deakin et al.'s *British Political and Military Strategy*. For the United States' role, see "In Search of Yugoslavia" by DeSantis and *OSS and the Yugoslav Resistance* by Ford. An early study on the role of women in the resistance by Reed, "The Anti-Fascist Front of Women," shows that although the Croatian Yugoslav communists were eager to involve women in the national liberation movement, their organization, the Anti-Fascist Front of Women (AFZ), possessed little credibility in peasant villages and was further weakened by discrimination against women in the Communist Party itself.

The isolated nature of postwar Albania has meant that it has attracted little attention. However, an important article by Fischer, "Resistance in Albania," outlined British (SOE) policy toward the resistance movements in that country and highlighted how its vacillating attitude to collaborationist groups served to alienate the communists, with important results for the postwar era. A survey of resistance against the earlier Italian occupation by Demiri, "La Résistance," used Albanian sources to show levels of organization and subversion.

EASTERN EUROPE

The very nature of the "war of annihilation" fought by the Germans in Eastern Europe and the policies pursued against Polish and Soviet civilians gave a very different focus to the term "resistance" in those countries. In Poland, attention has been centered on four themes. The construction and history of the underground Home Army has been chronicled by its last commander, Korbonski, in *The Polish Underground State;* his memoirs also represent an important source. The Home Army's link with the Polish government in exile has been explored in Peszke's "The Polish Government's Aid."

The heroic, but ultimately doomed, uprising by the Jews in the Warsaw ghetto in 1943 has been chronicled and analyzed by Gutman in *The Jews of Warsaw.* Among many other issues, he questioned why the rebels received so little help from the Poles. Similarly contentious is the Home Army's attempt to liberate Warsaw through the uprising in 1944 and the nearby Red Army's apparent unwillingness to aid them, allowing the Germans to suppress the Poles before mounting an offensive to occupy the city. The history of the uprising and its ultimate failure, the subject of many memoirs and "popular" works, has been well told in now somewhat old, but nonetheless important, books by Ciechanowski, *The Warsaw Rising,* and Zawodny, *Nothing but the Honour.* A different approach can be found in Hanson, *The Civilian Population and the Warsaw Uprising of 1944,* who looked at morale inside the city and charted the responses of ordinary citizens from initial enthusiasm to later bitter disappointment when the Germans were not driven out, and Allied help failed to arrive. Scholars from Poland, most notably Juchniewicz, *Poles in the European Resistance,* and Okecki, *The Polish Resistance,* have also contributed to our understanding of Polish resistance through general texts on the subject as a whole. The standard text on *Poland, SOE and the Allies* remains Garlinski, but Reynolds in " 'Lublin' " versus " 'London' " looked in detail at the politics of the conflict between the two governments in exile and the consequences for the noncommunist Home Army as the likelihood of Soviet domination became a reality.

Discussion of resistance inside the occupied Soviet Union has inevitably centered on the partisan warfare that made such an important contribution to elements of the Red Army's success. A general history of the campaign on the Eastern Front can be found in the extensive work by Ziemke and Bauer, *Moscow to Stalingrad*. More specifically, Armstrong's *Soviet Partisans* pointed out the partisans' value in psychological terms as well as in practical military matters of sabotage and intelligence gathering. An even earlier work by Howell, *The Soviet Partisan Movement*, provides much useful information. The specialist study of Jewish partisans in Belorussia, *They Chose to Fight* by Tec, is a model of meticulous research. The role of women among the partisans has been given some limited attention by Cottam, "Soviet Women," and a brief description in English from a Soviet source can be found in an article by Zhilin, "The People's Struggle."

BIBLIOGRAPHY

Absalom, Roger. "Hiding History: The Allies, the Resistance and the Others in Occupied Italy 1943–1945." *Historical Journal 38* (1995): 111–31.

Armstrong, John A., ed. *Soviet Partisans in World War II*. Madison: Wisconsin UP, 1964.

Auty, Phyllis, and Richard Clogg, eds. *British Policy towards Wartime Resistance in Yugoslavia and Greece*. London: Macmillan, 1975.

Battaglia, Roberto. *The Story of the Italian Resistance*. London: Odhams, 1957.

Bennett, Jeremy. *British Broadcasting and the Danish Resistance Movement 1940–45: A Study of Wartime Broadcasts of the BBC Danish Service*. Cambridge: Cambridge UP, 1966.

Bernard, Henri. *La Résistance 1940–45*. Brussels: Renaissance du Livre, 1968.

———. *Un maquis dans la ville. Historique du régiment des milices patriotiques de Schaer-beek*. Brussels: Renaissance du Livre, 1970.

———, et al. *Het Geheim Leger 1940–1944*. Ghent: Verbeke, 1986.

Blom, J.C.H. "In de ban van goed en fout? Wetenschappelijke geschiedschriving over de bezettingstijd in Nederland." In G. Abma, Y. Kuiper, and J. Rypkema, eds., *Tussen Goed en Fout: Nieuwe gezichtspunten in de geschiedschrijving 1940–1945*. Franeker: T. Wever, 1986.

Blumenson, Martin. *The Vildé Affair: Beginnings of the French Resistance*. Boston: Houghton Mifflin, 1977.

Bouman, P. J. *De April–Mei Stakingen van 1943*. The Hague: Nijhoff, 1950.

Brandes, Detlef. *Die Tschechen unter deutschem Protektorat*. 2 vols. München: Oldenbourg, 1969–1975.

Bruins Slot, J. "Resistance." *Annals of the American Academy of Political and Social Sciences 245* (1946): 144–48.

Ciechanowski, Jan. *The Warsaw Rising of 1944*. Cambridge: Cambridge UP, 1974.

Cottam, Jean K. "Soviet Women in Combat in World War II. The Rear Services, Resistance behind Enemy Lines and Military Political Workers." *International Journal of Women's Studies 5* (1982): 363–78.

Deakin, William, et al. *British Political and Military Strategy in Central, Eastern and Southern Europe in 1944*. New York: Macmillan, 1988.

Delzell, Charles F. *Mussolini's Enemies. The Italian Anti-Fascist Resistance*. Princeton: Princeton UP, 1961.

Demiri, Mexhit. "La Résistance Antifasciste dans le prisons et les camps de concentration à travers les documents des occupants étrangers en Albanie." *Studia Albanica 25* (1988): 119–30.

DeSantis, Hugh. "In Search of Yugoslavia: Anglo-American Policy and Policy-Making 1943–45." *Journal of Contemporary History 16* (1981): 541–63.

Doorslaer, Rudi van. *De Kommunistische Partij van België en het Sovjet-Duits niet-aanvalspakt tussen augustus 1939 en juli 1941*. Brussels: Masereelfonds, 1975.

Ellwood, David. *Italy, 1943–1945*. Leicester: Leicester UP, 1985.

European Resistance Movements 1939–1945: First International Conference on the History of the Resistance Movements Held at Liege-Bruxelles-Breendonk, 14–17 September 1958. London: Pergamon, 1960.

European Resistance Movements 1939–1945: Second International Conference on the History of the Resistance Movements, Milan 1960. London: Pergamon, 1964.

Farmer, Sarah. "The Communist Resistance in the Haute-Vienne." *French Historical Studies 14* (1985): 89–116.

Fischer, Bernd J. "Resistance in Albania during the Second World War. Partisans, Nationalists and the SOE." *East European Quarterly 25* (1991): 21–47.

Foot, M.R.D., and J. M. Langley. *MI9: Escape and Evasion 1939–45*. London: Bodley Head, 1979.

———. *Resistance: An Analysis of European Resistance to Nazism*. London: Eyre Methuen, 1976.

———. *SOE in France*. London: HMSO, 1966.

Ford, Kirk, Jr. *OSS and the Yugoslav Resistance, 1943–1945*. College Station: Texas A and M UP, 1992.

Funk, Arthur Layton. *Hidden Ally: The French Resistance, Special Operations, and the Landings in Southern France*. Westport, CT: Greenwood, 1992.

Garlinski, Jozef. *Poland, SOE and the Allies*. London: Allen and Unwin, 1966.

Gerolymatos, A. "The Development of Guerrilla Warfare and British Policy towards Greece 1943–1944." *Journal of the Hellenic Diaspora 17* (1991): 97–114.

Goldberger, Leo, ed. *The Rescue of Danish Jews: Moral Courage under Stress*. New York and London: New York UP, 1987.

Gram, Gerada. "Norge under Besaettelsen." *Historie 19* (1992): 351–55.

Gutman, Yisrael. *The Jews of Warsaw, 1939–1943: Ghetto, Underground, Revolt*. Bloomington: Indiana UP, 1982.

Gvelsvik, T. *Norwegian Resistance*. London: Hurst, 1979.

Hæstrup, Jørgen. "Denmark's Connection with the Allied Powers during the Occupation." In *European Resistance Movements*, 282–97. London: Pergamon, 1964.

———. *Secret Alliance: A Study of the Danish Resistance Movement 1940–1945*. 3 vols. Odense: Odense UP, 1976–1977.

Hanson, Joanna K. M. *The Civilian Population and the Warsaw Uprising of 1944*. Cambridge: Cambridge UP, 1982.

Hart, Janet. "Women in the Greek Resistance: National Crisis and Political Transformation." *International Labor and Working Class History 38* (1990): 46–62.

Hawes, Stephen, and Ralph White, eds. *Resistance in Europe 1939–1945: Based on the Proceedings of a Symposium Held at the University of Salford, March 1973*. London: Allen Lane, 1975.

Hegt, W. Noordhoek. "The Resistance of the Medical Profession." *Annals of the American Academy of Political and Social Sciences 245* 1946: 162–68.

Hillingso, K.G.H. "The Danish Resistance Movement and Its Relations with Great Britain." *Revue Internationale d'Histoire Militaire 53* (1982): 105–12.

Hirschfeld, Gerhard. *Nazi Rule and Dutch Collaboration: The Netherlands and German Occupation, 1940–1945*. Oxford: Berg, 1988.

Hondros, John Louis. *Occupation and Resistance: The Greek Agony, 1941–1944*. New York: Pella, 1983.

Howell, Edgar M. *The Soviet Partisan Movement 1941–1944*. Washington, DC: Department of the Army, 1956.

Jong, Louis de. "Anti-Nazi Resistance in the Netherlands." In *European Resistance Movements 1939–1945*, 137–49. London: Pergamon, 1960.

———. "The Dutch Resistance Movement and the Allies 1940–1945." In *European Resistance Movements 1939–1945*, 340–65. London: Pergamon, 1960.

———. *Het Koninkrijk der Nederlanden in de Tweede Wereldoorlog*. 9, 936–1040. The Hague: Staatuitgeverij, 1979.

———. *The Netherlands and Nazi Germany*. Cambridge and London: Harvard UP, 1990.

Juchniewicz, Mieczyslaw. *Poles in the European Resistance Movement 1939–45*. Warsaw: Interpress, 1972.

Karchmar, Lucien. *Draza Mihailovic and the Rise of the Cetnik Movement 1941–42*. 2 vols. New York and London: Garland, 1987.

Kedward, H. Roderick. "Behind the Polemics: French Communists and Resistance 1939–1941." In Stephen Hawes and Ralph White, eds., *Resistance in Europe*. London: Allen Lane, 1975.

———. *In Search of the Maquis: Rural Resistance in Southern France, 1942–1944*. Oxford: Clarendon, 1993.

———. *Resistance in Vichy France*. New York and Oxford: Oxford UP, 1978.

Kjelstadli, S. "The Resistance Movement in Norway and the Allies, 1940–1945." In *European Resistance Movements*, 324–39. London: Pergamon, 1964.

Knight, Frida. *The French Resistance 1940–1944*. London: Lawrence and Wishart, 1975.

Korbonski, Stefan. *The Polish Underground State: A Guide to the Underground 1939–1945*. New York: Hippocrene, 1981.

Kousoulas, D. George. *Revolution and Defeat: The Story of the Greek Communist Party*. London: Oxford UP, 1965.

Maass, Walter B. *The Netherlands at War, 1940–1945*. London: Abelard-Schuman, 1970.

Macksey, Kenneth. *The Partisans of Europe in World War II*. London: Hart-Davis, MacGibbon, 1975.

McConville, Michael. *A Small War in the Balkans: British Military Involvement in Wartime Yugoslavia.* London: Macmillan, 1986.

Michel, Henri. *The Shadow War: Resistance in Europe 1939–1945.* London: André Deutsch, 1972.

Milazzo, Matteo Joseph. *The Chetnik Movement and the Yugoslav Resistance.* Baltimore: Johns Hopkins UP, 1975.

Milward, Alan. "The Economic and Strategic Effectiveness of Resistance." In Stephen Hawes and Ralph White, *Resistance in Europe.* London: Allen Lane, 1975.

Moore, Bob. "Occupation, Collaboration and Resistance: Some Recent Publications on the Netherlands during the Second World War." *European History Quarterly 21* (1991): 109–18.

Noguères, Henri, with Marcel Degliame-Fouche. *Histoire de la Résistance en France.* 5 vols. Paris: Robert Laffont, 1967–1981.

Okecki, Stanislaw. *The Polish Resistance Movement in Poland and Abroad 1939–45.* Warsaw: Polish Scientific, 1987.

Pavone, C. *Una guerra civile. Saggio storico sulla moralità nella Resistenza.* Turin: Bollati Boringhieri, 1991.

Peszke, Michael. "The Polish Government's Aid to and Liaison with Its Secret Army in Occupied Poland, 1939–1945." *Military Affairs 52* (1988): 197–202.

Pike, David Wingeate. "Between the Junes. The French Communists from the Collapse of France to the Invasion of Russia." *Journal of Contemporary History 28* (1993): 465–85.

Puzzo, Dante A. *The Partisans and the War in Italy.* New York: Peter Lang, 1993.

Quazza, Guido. *Resistenza e storia italiana.* Milan: Feltrinelli, 1976.

Reed, Mary E. "The Anti-Fascist Front of Women and the Communist Party in Croatia. Conflicts within the Resistance." In Tova Yedlin, ed., *Women in Eastern Europe and the Soviet Union.* New York: Praeger, 1980.

Reynolds, Jaime. " 'Lublin' versus 'London'—The Party and the Underground Movement in Poland, 1944–45." *Journal of Contemporary History 16* (1981): 617–48.

Rings, Werner. *Life with the Enemy: Collaboration and Resistance in Hitler's Europe, 1939–1945.* London: Wiedenfeld and Nicholson, 1982.

Riste, Olav, and Berit Nökleby. *Norway 1940–1945: The Resistance Movement.* Oslo: Tanum-Norli, 1984.

Roberts, Walter R. *Tito, Mihailovic and the Allies 1941–45.* New Brunswick, NJ: Rutgers UP, 1973.

Roegholt, Richter, and Jacob Zwaan, eds. *Het Verzet 1940–1945.* Weesp: Fibula-van Dishoeck/Unieboek, 1985.

Roslyng-Jensen, Palle. "Den 9 April 1940: Some Halvtredsrsjubilar: En Oversigt." *Historisk Tidsskrift 91* (1991): 154–74.

Rossiter, Margaret L. *Women in the Resistance.* New York: Praeger, 1986.

Rüter, A.J.C. *Rijden en Staken. De Nederlandse Spoorwegen in Oorlogstijd.* The Hague: Nijhoff, 1960.

Schwarz, Paula. "*Partisanes* and Gender Politics in Vichy France." *French Historical Studies 16* (1989): 126–51.

Semelin, Jacques. *Unarmed against Hitler.* New York: Praeger, 1993.

Sijes, Ben. *De Februari-staking.* The Hague: Nijhoff, 1954.

Simmonds, J. C. "The French Communist Party and the Beginnings of Resistance." *European Studies Review* (1981): 517–42.

Skodvin, Magne. *Krig og Okkupation 1939–1945*. Oslo: Norske Samlaget, 1990.

Slaughter, Jane. *Women and the Italian Resistance*. Denver, CO: Arden, 1995.

Smith, Michael L. "Neither Resistance nor Collaboration: Historians and the Problem of the *Nederlandse Unie*." *History* 72 (1987): 251–78.

Sorensen, Oystein. "Forskningen om Krigen I Norge." *Nytt Norsk Tidsskrift 6* (1989): 40–58.

Stafford, David. *Britain and the European Resistance 1940–1945: A Survey of the Special Operations Executive, with Documents*. Toronto and Buffalo: University of Toronto; London: Macmillan, 1983.

———. "The Detonator Concept: British Strategy, SOE and European Resistance after the Fall of France." *Journal of Contemporary History 2* (1975): 185–217.

Stavrianos, Leften. "The Greek National Liberation Front (EAM): A Study in Resistance Organisation." *Journal of Modern History 24* (1952): 42–55.

Suhl, Yuri. *They Fought Back. The Story of the Jewish Resistance in Nazi Europe*. New York: Crown, 1967.

Sweets, John F. "Hold That Pendulum! Redefining Fascism, Collaboration and Resistance in France." *French Historical Studies 15* (1988): 731–58.

———. *The Politics of Resistance in France (1940–1944): A History of the "Mouvements Unis de la Résistance."* De Kalb: Northern Illinois UP, 1976.

Tec, Nechama. *They Chose to Fight: Jewish Partisans in Belorussia during World War II*. Oxford: Oxford UP, 1992.

Tomasevich, Jozo. *The Chetniks, War and Revolution in Yugoslavia 1941–45*. Stanford, CA: Stanford UP, 1975.

Touw, H. "The Resistance of the Netherlands Churches." *Annals of the American Academy of Political and Social Sciences 245* (1946): 149–61.

Verhoeyen, Etienne. *La Belgique Occupée*. Brussels: De Boeck Université, 1994.

Vijver, Herman van de, Rudi van Doorslaer, and Etienne Verhoeyen. *Het Verzet*, vol. 2 of *Belgie in de Tweede Wereldoorlog*. Kapellen: DNB-Pelckmans, 1988.

Vlavianos, Haris. *Greece, 1941–49: From Resistance to Civil War: The Strategy of the Greek Communist Party*. New York: St. Martin's, 1992.

Warmbrunn, Werner. *The Dutch under German Occupation, 1940–1945*. Stanford, CA: Stanford UP, 1963.

Wehr, Paul. "Nonviolent Resistance to Nazism: Norway, 1940–1945." *Peace and Change 10* (1984): 77–95.

Wheeler, Mark C. *Britain and the War for Yugoslavia, 1941–1943*. Boulder, CO, and New York: East European Quarterly, 1980.

———. "Pariahs to Partisans to Power: The Communist Party of Yugoslavia." In Tony Judt, ed., *Resistance and Revolution in Mediterranean Europe 1939–1945*. London and New York: Routledge, 1989.

White, Ralph. "The Unity and Diversity of European Resistance." In Stephen Hawes and Ralph White, eds., *Resistance in Europe 1939–1945*, 7–23. London: Allen Lane, 1975.

Woodhouse, C. M. "The Greek Resistance." In *European Resistance Movements*, 374–90. London: Pergamon, 1960.

———. *The Struggle for Greece*. London: Hart Davies MacGibbon, 1976.

Yahil, Leni. *The Rescue of the Danish Jews: Test of a Democracy.* Philadelphia: Jewish Publication Society, 1969.

Zawodny, Janus. *Nothing but the Honour. The Story of the Warsaw Uprising.* Stanford, CA: Hoover Institution, 1978.

Zhilin, Pavel. "The People's Struggle on Temporarily Occupied Soviet Territory." *Social Sciences 16* (1985): 60–71.

Ziemke, Earl F., and Magna E. Bauer. *Moscow to Stalingrad: Decision in the East.* Washington, DC: Center of Military History, U.S. Army, 1987.

19 Prisoners of War and Civilian Internees: The European and Mediterranean Theaters

S. P. MacKenzie

Amid the vast outpouring of literature over the last half century dealing with the Second World War, the history of prisoners of war (POWs) and civilian internees has received comparatively little attention.

Despite its scale, the story of the thirty-five million military personnel and one hundred thousand or so civilian internees incarcerated between 1939 and 1945 has been overshadowed by events of even greater size and import. This is particularly true of the war in Europe. The fate of Russian and German POWs from the Eastern Front, for instance, is often overlooked in the face of the enormity of the Holocaust and the war against the Jews.

Similarly, the history of the complex and delicate diplomacy between states at war with one another through neutral parties over POW and internee affairs has yet to be written; historians have thus far found the immensely significant negotiations surrounding wartime alliances and the shaping of the peace of greater interest. Over the past two decades in particular, however, interest among both popular writers and scholars in POW affairs has gradually increased to the point where, though much still remains to be explored, a significant corpus exists.

PRISONERS OF WAR

Ever since the last shots died away, memoirs by former POWs have been published in significant numbers year after year, a trend that as yet shows no sign of ending. Many of the more commercially successful memoirs recount successful escape attempts and have been turned into films (e.g., Eric E. Williams, *The Wooden Horse*). All, however, also tend to deal to a greater or lesser extent with the mundane realities of life behind barbed wire in Germany and are useful as historical sources. A representative sample can be found in Enser's *A Subject Bibliography of the Second World War* and the follow-up volume, *Aftermath*, though it is worth noting that a number of accounts by German prisoners, translated into English (and therefore far rarer than accounts by British or American POWs), have tended to appear after Enser's last update, for example, Horner, *A German Odyssey*. A rare example of the perspective from the other side of the wire—that of the guards—can be found in *Colditz: The German Viewpoint* by Eggers.

The secondary sources on the POW experience have tended until the last decade or so to follow the lead taken in memoirs, often the authors' main source base, in terms of subjects examined. Especially in the 1950s, this usually meant biographical escape stories, for example, Burt, *The One That Got Away*, recounting the only successful escape back to Germany of a German prisoner from Allied captivity, or Brickhill, *The Great Escape*, an account of the mass breakout from Luft Stalag III, later popularized by Hollywood. Later works were more expansive, dealing not only with escapes but also with capture, daily camp life, and final repatriation on a collective as well as an individual level. Only quite recently, however, has scholarly attention begun to deal at any length with POW affairs at the policy-making and international level. Exceptions include Vance, "Men in Manacles: The Shackling of Prisoners of War," as well as MacKenzie's "Treatment of Prisoners of War in World War II" and "Shackling Crisis: A Case Study in the Dynamics of Prisoner-of-War Diplomacy."

The general reader seeking a brief introduction to the subject may wish to consult Garrett, *P.O.W.*, a popular work on military prisoners in history by an ex-POW, or Baily, *Prisoners of War*, the relevant volume in the Time-Life history of World War II. Also very useful as an introductory text is *Behind Barbed Wire* by A. J. Barker, which takes a more thematic approach to POW treatment in the twentieth century. For those interested primarily in American POWs, Doyle, *Voices from Captivity*, provides an interesting literary approach to POW narratives from World War II and other conflicts.

More numerous than the general studies are the various works that address how POWs of various nationalities coped with captivity in enemy hands. Perhaps because the Nazis held more prisoners for a longer period than did the Italians, there are no secondary works in English dealing specifically with Allied POWs in Italian camps. Even memoir material is comparatively thin in this area: an example is *Farewell Campo 12* by Hargest. A number of books in English, however, examine how German and Italian prisoners of war were dealt with by the Allies.

The most recent attempt at a general history of Allied POWs, Rolf's *Prisoners of the Reich*, is a popular work that deals, for the most part, with British and Commonwealth prisoners in German hands. Sadly, it does not add much to what can be found in the general works listed earlier. More analysis is present in works dealing with specific nationalities, such as Foy, *For You the War Is Over*, which examines American POWs in German camps, and the excellent volume in the New Zealand official history, Mason's *Prisoners of War*, which is comprehensive and thorough enough to stand as the next best thing to a general history of British and Commonwealth POWs in Axis hands. The Canadian experience is best covered in the relevant sections of Vance's thorough work *Objects of Concern: Canadian Prisoners of War through the Twentieth Century*, which supersedes the memoir accounts contained in Dancocks' *In Enemy Hands*. Australians are dealt with briefly in another popular account, *Prisoners of War* by Adam-Smith.

A number of books examine some of the more famous camps in Germany. These include Reid, *Colditz: The Full Story*, a popular work by a former escapee based on a variety of POW and guard memoirs dealing with Sonderlager IVC, and Arthur A. Durand, *Stalag Luft III*, which despite its rather lurid subtitle, *The Secret Story*, is a scholarly study of some distinction. Attention must also be drawn to an interesting article, Vance, "Politics of Camp Life," which examines the realities of POW existence in two rather more prosaic camps.

Most of the preceding books deal with escape attempts to a greater or lesser degree. Those readers specifically interested in this aspect of the POW experience, however, would do well to consult two studies that deal with British and American attempts to foster successful escapes (Foot and Langley, *MI9*, and Neave, *The Escape Room*, and perhaps also Crawley, *Escape from Germany*, which deals with Royal Air Force (RAF) escape techniques).

Much of the literature of non-English-speaking POWs is, naturally enough, written in the vernacular. Exceptions include two studies of German POWs in Britain during and after the war—Kocham, *Prisoners of England*, and Sullivan, *Thresholds of Peace*—and several works on Axis prisoners in the United States. Krammer's *Nazi Prisoners of War in America* is a well-rounded study that, in contrast to most works in English—Foy is also an exception in this respect—examines captor policy formulation. It supersedes, to a great extent, the relevant chapters in the official history by Lewis and Mewha, *History of Prisoner of War Utilization by the United States Army*, and is superior to Gansberg's *Stalag USA*, though this last work is by no means a bad book as an introduction to the subject. The recent appearance of a study by Robin, *Barbed-Wire College*, which deals with political reeducation efforts among German prisoners, suggests that enough work has now been done on general treatment of German POWs to allow scholars to begin approaching the subject from a more thematic viewpoint.

Italian POWs in Allied hands have until recently tended to receive considerably less attention than the Germans. This has been at least partially rectified by Keefer in his book *Italian Prisoners of War*, a successful attempt to produce a Krammer-like general study of Italian POWs in American custody. Italian POWs held in Australia are covered somewhat less comprehensively in Fitzgerald, *Italian Farming Soldiers*, while Axis POWs in Canadian camps are dealt with superficially in Carter, *Behind Canadian Barbed Wire*.

In recent years studies of Axis POWs in specific parts of America have begun to appear, among them May, *Camp Concordia*, Kansas; Powell, *Splinters of a Nation*, dealing with German prisoners in Utah; Koop, *Stark Decency*, following a group of German prisoners in New England; and Donald Mace Williams, *Interlude in Umbarger*, covering a group of Italian POWs involved in a Texas church community. Such studies exhibit both the strengths and weaknesses of local history.

The rather grim story of the huge numbers of Soviet and German POWs captured on the Eastern Front and transported to camps is not, alas, well served in English. A glimpse at conditions in Soviet camps can be found in Fehling, *One Great Prison*, and at the atrocious treatment of captured Soviet personnel in Schulte, *German Army and Nazi Policies in Occupied Russia*. Serious students, however, should consult Streit, *"Keine Kameraden,"* for the fate of Soviet POWs and the relevant volumes in the Maschke commission series (sponsored by the West German government as a semi-official history of German POWs in enemy hands) for details on treatment of captured Germans in Soviet camps and, indeed, the camps of the Allies.

The very large number of French POWs in German hands also, unfortunately, lacks a chronicler in English. Readers must therefore turn to Yves Durand, *La Captivité*, or his similar book in Hachette's *vie quotidienne* (daily life) series. A sense of how POWs figured into the domestic life and foreign policy of Vichy France, however, can be gained from Fishman's *We Will Wait* and her contemporaneous article, "Grand Delusions." The fate of the over five hundred thousand Italian "military internees" rounded up by the Germans after Italy dropped out of the war in 1943 also lacks a treatment in English. The best foreign-language source is Schreiber, *Die italienischen Militärinternierten im deutschen Machtbereich*.

The importance of POW and "guest" civilian labor to the German war effort—bearing in mind that the Third Reich held more prisoners than any other belligerent—can be gleaned from the relevant pages of Homze, *Foreign Labor in Nazi Germany*. An interesting overview of the labor question can be obtained in Davis, "Prisoners of War in Twentieth Century Economics." The work undertaken by POWs is also dealt with, from the prisoners' perspective, in many of the books previously listed.

A number of philanthropic organizations involved in the welfare of prisoners have published accounts in English of their activities. The International Committee of the Red Cross, heavily involved in both welfare efforts and diplomatic initiatives to keep the 1929 Geneva Convention as the benchmark for POW treatment, not only published an official *Report of the International Committee of the Red Cross* but also made its work between 1939 and 1945 a central feature of the second volume of the official history of the International Red Cross: André Durand's *From Sarajevo to Hiroshima*. The Young Men's Christian Association (YMCA) also brought out an official history of its work on behalf of prisoners during World War II; see Vulliet, *The Y.M.C.A. and Prisoners of War*. These histories can be checked against the memoirs of Red Cross and YMCA representatives who visited camps and later recorded their impressions of how well or otherwise the Geneva Convention was working in various countries. These latter include Junod, *Warrior without Weapons*; Bernadotte, *Instead of Arms;* and Christiansen, *Seven Years among Prisoners of War*.

National Red Cross organizations have also sponsored histories that deal, albeit often briefly, with relief work connected with POWs. In English these general studies include Dulles, *The American Red Cross*, and the rather more detailed *Red Cross and St. John*, compiled by Cambray and Briggs, which covers the activities of the British Red Cross.

War crimes against POWs are extensively documented in the Nuremberg trial records, a summary of which can be found in Datna, *Crimes against POWs*. For the Eastern Front, where atrocities were extremely common on both sides, a number of relevant studies exist in English. Documented Soviet atrocities near the front lines are dealt with in a very interesting translated work based on recently unearthed archival material, Zayas, *Wehrmacht War Crimes Bureau*. A rather more broad discussion of German mistreatment of Soviet prisoners can be found in the excellent study by Bartov, *Hitler's Army*, and in Schulte, *The German Army*, the latest comprehensive look at Nazi policies in occupied Russia.

One atrocity that stands apart, both in scale and in the number of books devoted to the subject, is the secret massacre of thousands of Polish officer POWs by Soviet security forces in the Katyn forest and elsewhere in 1940. The standard work on the subject remains Zawodny, *Death in the Forest*. Though some Soviet revelations are included in Allen, *Katyn: The Untold Story*, a complete history will have to await thorough investigation of material in the Russian archives. Slows, *Road to Katyn*, is one of the few firsthand accounts in English of the experience of Polish POWs in Soviet hands, supplementing the references in Sword, *Deportation and Exile*.

Despite the large number of memoirs and other kinds of literature on POWs in World War II that have appeared since 1945, most interpretations have not aroused much critical debate in English. Over the last few years, however, a number of works have questioned one of the central unspoken assumptions of the existing secondary literature on the war in the West: namely, that both sides treated enemy prisoners more or less in accordance with the Geneva Convention and that governments acted in the interests of POW safety.

This process began with the publication in the mid-1970s and early 1980s of a number of books that examined the fate of Soviet citizens who had changed sides after capture on the Eastern Front, had fought and been captured in German uniform in the West, and were in 1945 facing repatriation by the Allies to the Soviet Union, where they faced certain death as traitors. *The Last Secret* by Bethell approached this controversial episode with some degree of objectivity and balance. The issue itself, however, was highly charged, and the next book on the subject, which dealt with Britain's role in the affair, Tolstoy's *Secret Betrayal,* was noteworthy for its polemical tone. This was followed in 1982 by a rather more dispassionate and accurate study by Elliot, *Pawns of Yalta,* which dealt with American involvement. Tolstoy, however, generated the greatest amount of controversy through being successfully sued for libel.

That forced repatriation had taken place was unquestionably true; but as the courts eventually decided in reference to Tolstoy's 1986 follow-up book, *The Minister and the Massacres,* a penchant for right-wing conspiracy theories had led Tolstoy to make unjustifiable claims concerning British government knowledge of, and collusion in, the fate of White Russian prisoners captured in Italy. After a successful lawsuit, Tolstoy was ordered in 1989 to pay extensive damages to the plaintiff, one of the few living figures he had accused of deliberately orchestrated murder (see Barker, "British Variety of Pseudohistory"). A more balanced account of this episode can be found in Mather, *Aftermath of War.* Readers may also wish to consult Wyman's *DP,* which places repatriation in the wider context of displaced persons.

Just as one conspiracy theory was being undermined, however, another of even greater import appeared. In 1989 and 1990, a best-selling book by a Canadian writer appeared in several countries. The author, James Bacque, asserted that around one million German POWs in American and French camps had died as a result of a deliberate starvation policy in the immediate aftermath of World War II. Bacque's *Other Losses* set off a storm of controversy in the media and within the academic community and generated a number of studies that indicate that the author's conspiratorial claims and questionable research methods needed to be treated with extreme caution (see MacKenzie, "On the *Other Losses* Debate," and Bischof and Ambrose, eds., *Eisenhower and the German POWs*).

The American government has also been attacked by other conspiracy theorists on the grounds of having done nothing to help American military personnel held by malevolent captors and then having covered up the fact. Like *Other Losses,* works such as Bard's *Forgotten Victims,* which examines in part the plight of American prisoners, especially Jews, who found themselves outside the official POW camp system, and Sanders et al., *Soldiers of Misfortune,* which chronicles the desperate situation of American personnel not repatriated by the advancing Soviets, highlight episodes that many would just as soon forget. The conspiratorial assumptions that underlie their analyses, however, as well as the insistence that "the truth has never been told"—also found in Bacque's work—seriously undermine their credibility.

Much of the secondary literature on prisoners of war, though interesting and not insubstantial, remains somewhat superficial. There is therefore plenty of room for further research by historians, sociologists, psychologists, and other interested parties into the nature of POW life. Avenues for further research might include the differences among the respective experiences of captive officers, noncommissioned officers (NCOS), and other ranks and what this reveals about mid-twentieth-century society, as well as the assumptions underlying international agreements dating from earlier in the century. A start has been made in an article by Joan Beaumont, "Rank, Privilege and Prisoners of War."

The really major gap that requires attention, however, concerns POW diplomacy. Very little has been written concerning how states at war with one another did (or did not) deal with the need to negotiate, through neutral states and the International Committee of the Red Cross, with the enemy over the treatment of captured servicemen. The opening of the Russian archives, moreover, offers a chance for the first real study of Soviet POW policy.

CIVILIAN INTERNEES

The literature on civilian internees in the European theater is much more limited than work on POWs. The majority deals with the controversial issue of the general internment of German and Italian civilians in Britain, many of whom were political refugees. In all cases, the conclusion drawn is that internment was a policy hastily implemented in an atmosphere of fifth-column panic in 1940; that living conditions for internees were often less than satisfactory (especially on the Isle of Man); that internees were put at grave risk when transported overseas through U-boat-infested waters (as in the *Arandora Star* disaster); and that, all in all, the whole thing was a costly mistake only gradually rectified in the course of the war.

Worthwhile popular works on the subject include Gillman and Gillman's, "*Collar the Lot!*" and Kocham's *Britain's Internees*. The progressive widening of the internment net in 1940 and the gradual relaxation of internment regulations later in the war are dealt with thoroughly in Simpson, *In the Highest Degree Odious*, a book likely to become the definitive work on the subject of British internment policy. Also of importance is Stent, *Bespattered Page?* A wider context for British internment of enemy aliens is provided in Marrus, *The Unwanted: European Refugees in the Twentieth Century*.

The internment of Italian and German civilians in the United States, both U.S. citizens and enemy nationals, has received far less attention than either internment in Britain or the relocation of Japanese civilians. There does exist, however, a study of German internment at Fort Lincoln, North Dakota (Christgau, *"Enemies"*), and of the relocation and internment of Italians on the West Coast (Fox, *The Unknown Internment*). Both deal with the difficulties internees faced and the iniquities of the relocation program.

The internment and eventual release of about seven thousand enemy nationals and other suspected persons in Australia have also been recently studied. The result is Bevege's *Behind Barbed Wire*, which, in contrast to many other such studies, does not start from the premise that internment was ipso facto morally reprehensible or unnecessary.

Though no specific study has yet been undertaken, a basic understanding of life for Allied internees in enemy hands in Europe can be gleaned from references to the work of the Red Cross in the official history and in Durand. Mason, as well as providing the most useful single study of Commonwealth POWs in enemy hands, also provides some insight into the plight of civilian internees (in this case from New Zealand), as does Bard, albeit in a rather turgid manner, for certain interned Americans in Nazi Germany. The treatment of enemy aliens and internment policy in Axis Europe, however, remains a fertile area for further research.

BIBLIOGRAPHY

Adam-Smith, Patsy. *Prisoners of War: From Gallipoli to Korea.* New York: Viking, 1992.

Allen, Paul. *Katyn: The Untold Story of Stalin's Polish Massacre.* New York: Scribner's, 1991.

Bacque, James. *Other Losses: An Investigation into the Mass Deaths of German Prisoners at the Hands of the French and Americans after World War II.* Toronto: Stoddart, 1989.

Baily, Robert H. *Prisoners of War.* Alexandria, VA: Time-Life, 1983.

Bard, Mitchell H. *Forgotten Victims: The Abandonment of Americans in Hitler's Camps.* Boulder, CO: Westview, 1994.

Barker, A. J. *Behind Barbed Wire.* London: Batesford, 1974.

Barker, Thomas M. "A British Variety of Pseudohistory." In Günter Bischof and Stephen Ambrose, eds., *Eisenhower and the German POWs: Facts against Falsehood*, 183–98. Baton Rouge: Louisiana State UP, 1992.

Bartov, Omer. *Hitler's Army: Soldiers, Nazis and War in the Third Reich.* New York: Oxford UP, 1991.

Beaumont, Joan. "Rank, Privilege and Prisoners of War." *War and Society 1* (1983): 67–94.

Bernadotte, Folke. *Instead of Arms.* London: Hodder and Stoughton, 1949.

Bethell, Nicholas. *The Last Secret: The Delivery to Stalin of over Two Million Russians by Britain and the United States.* New York: Basic, 1974.

Bevege, Margaret. *Behind Barbed Wire: Internment in Australia during World War II.* St. Lucia, Queensland: University of Queensland, 1993.

Bischof, Günter, and Stephen Ambrose, eds. *Eisenhower and the German POWs: Facts against Falsehood.* Baton Rouge: Louisiana State UP, 1992.

Brickhill, Paul. *The Great Escape.* New York: Norton, 1950.

Burt, Kendal. *The One That Got Away.* New York: Random House, 1956.

Cambray, P. G., and G.G.B. Briggs. *Red Cross and St. John.* London: Sumfield and Day, 1949.

Carter, David J. *Behind Canadian Barbed Wire: Alien, Refugee and Prisoner of War Camps in Canada 1914–1946.* Calgary, AL: Tumbleweed, 1980.

Christgau, John. *"Enemies": World War II Alien Internment.* Ames: Iowa State UP, 1985.

Christiansen, Chris. *Seven Years among Prisoners of War.* Trans. Ida Egede Winther. Athens: Ohio UP, 1994.

Crawley, Aidan. *Escape from Germany: The Methods of Escape Used by RAF Airmen during World War II.* London: HMSO, 1985.

Dancocks, Daniel G. *In Enemy Hands: Canadian Prisoners of War 1939–45.* Edmonton, AL: Hurtig, 1983.

Datna, Szymon. *Crimes against POWs: Responsibility of the Wehrmacht.* Warsaw: Zachodnia Agencja Prasowa, 1964.

Davis, G. H. "Prisoners of War in Twentieth-Century Economics." *Journal of Contemporary History 12* (1977): 623–34.

Doyle, Robert C. *Voices from Captivity: Interpreting the American POW Narrative.* Lawrence: UP of Kansas, 1994.

Dulles, Foster R. *The American Red Cross: A History.* New York: Harper, 1950.

Durand, André. *From Sarajevo to Hiroshima: History of the International Committee of the Red Cross.* Geneva: ICRC, 1984.

Durand, Arthur A. *Stalag Luft III: The Secret Story.* Baton Rouge: Louisiana State UP, 1988.

Durand, Yves. *La Captivité: Histoire des prisonniers de guerre français, 1939–1945.* Paris: Federation Nationale des Combattants, 1982.

———. *La vie quotidienne des prisonniers de guerre français, 1939–1945.* Paris: Hachette, 1987.

Eggers, Reinhold. *Colditz: The German Viewpoint.* Trans. Howard Gee. London: Hale, 1961.

Elliot, M. R. *Pawns of Yalta: Soviet Refugees and America's Role in Their Repatriation.* Urbana: University of Illinois, 1982.

Enser, A.G.S. *A Subject Bibliography of the Second World War, and Aftermath: Books in English 1939–1974.* London: Andre Deutsch, 1977; rev. ed. Brookfield, VT: Gower, 1990.

Fehling, Helmuth H. *One Great Prison: The Story behind Russia's Unreleased P.O.W.'s.* Boston: Beacon, 1951.

Fishman, Sarah. "Grand Delusions: The Unintended Consequences of Vichy France's Prisoner of War Propaganda." *Journal of Contemporary History 26* (1991): 229–54.

———. *We Will Wait: Wives of French Prisoners of War, 1940–1945.* New Haven, CT: Yale UP, 1991.

Fitzgerald, Alan. *Italian Farming Soldiers: Prisoners of War in Australia 1941–1947.* Carlton, Victoria: Melbourne UP, 1981.

Foot, M.R.D., and J. M. Langley. *MI9: The British Secret Service That Fostered Escape and Evasion, 1939–1945, and Its American Counterpart.* London: Bodley Head, 1979.

Fox, Stephen. *The Unknown Internment: An Oral History of the Relocation of Italian Americans during World War II.* Boston: Twayne, 1990.

Foy, David A. *For You the War Is Over: American Prisoners of War in Nazi Germany.* New York: Stein and Day, 1984.

Gansberg, Judith M. *Stalag USA: The Remarkable Story of POWs in America.* New York: Crowell, 1977.

Garrett, Richard. *P.O.W.* Newton Abbot, U.K.: David and Charles, 1981.

Gillman, Peter, and Leni Gillman. *"Collar the Lot!": How Britain Interned and Expelled Its Wartime Refugees.* London: Quartet, 1980.

Hargest, James. *Farewell Campo 12.* London: Michael Joseph, 1945.

Homze, Edward L. *Foreign Labor in Nazi Germany.* Princeton: Princeton UP, 1967.

Horner, Helmut. *A German Odyssey: The Journal of a German Prisoner of War.* Golden, CO: Fulcrum, 1991.

International Committee of the Red Cross. *Report of the International Committee of the Red Cross on Its Activities during the Second World War (September 1, 1939–June 30, 1947).* 2 vols. Geneva: ICRC, 1948.

Junod, Marcel. *Warrior without Weapons.* Trans. Edward Fitzgerald. London: Macmillan, 1951.

Keefer, Louis E. *Italian Prisoners of War in America, 1942–1946: Captives or Allies?* New York: Praeger, 1992.

Kocham, Miriam. *Britain's Internees in the Second World War.* London: Macmillan, 1983.

———. *Prisoners of England.* London: Macmillan, 1980.

Koop, Allen V. *Stark Decency: German Prisoners of War in a New England Village.* Hanover: University of New Hampshire, 1988.

Krammer, Arnold. *Nazi Prisoners of War in America.* New York: Stein and Day, 1979.

Lewis, C.G.S., and J. Mewha. *History of Prisoner of War Utilization by the United States Army 1776–1945.* Washington, DC: Department of the Army, 1955.

MacKenzie, S. P. "On the *Other Losses* Debate." *International History Review 14* (1992): 717–31.

———. "The Shackling Crisis: A Case Study in the Dynamics of Prisoner-of-War Diplomacy." *International History Review 17* (1995): 78–98.

———. "The Treatment of Prisoners of War in World War II." *Journal of Modern History 66* (1994): 487–520.

Marrus, Michael. *The Unwanted: European Refugees in the Twentieth Century.* New York: Oxford UP, 1985.

Maschke, Erich, ed. *Zur Geschichte der deutschen Kriegsgefangenen des Zweiten Weltkriegs.* 15 vols. Munich: Ernst and Werner Gieseking, 1962–1974.

Mason, W. Wynne. *Official History of New Zealand in the Second World War: Prisoners of War.* Wellington: Government of New Zealand, 1954.

Mather, Carol. *Aftermath of War: Everyone Must Go Home.* London: Brassey's, 1992.

May, Lowell A. *Camp Concordia.* Manhattan, KS: Journal of the West, 1995.

Neave, Airey. *The Escape Room.* New York: Doubleday, 1970.

Powell, Allan K. *Splinters of a Nation: German Prisoners of War in Utah.* Salt Lake City: University of Utah, 1989.

Reid, P. R. *Colditz: The Full Story.* London: Macmillan, 1984.

Robin, Ron. *The Barbed-Wire College: Reeducating German POWs in the United States during World War II.* Princeton: Princeton UP, 1995.

Rolf, David. *Prisoners of the Reich: Germany's Captives, 1939–1945.* London: Leo Cooper, 1988.

Sanders, Jim, Mark Sauter, and R. Cort Kirkwood. *Soldiers of Misfortune: Washington's Secret Betrayal of American POWs in the Soviet Union.* Washington, DC: National, 1992.

Schreiber, Gerhard. *Die italienischen Militärinternierten im deutschen Machtbereich, 1943–1945.* Munich: Oldenbourg, 1990.

Schulte, Theo J. *The German Army and Nazi Policies in Occupied Russia.* New York: Oxford UP, 1989.

Simpson, A. W. Brian. *In the Highest Degree Odious: Detention without Trial in Wartime Britain.* Oxford: Clarendon, 1992.

Slows, Salomon W. *The Road to Katyn: A Soldier's Story.* Trans. N. Greenwood. Oxford: Blackwell, 1992.

Stent, Ronald. *A Bespattered Page?: The Internment of His Majesty's "Most Loyal Enemy Aliens."* London: Deutsch, 1980.

Streit, Christian. *"Keine Kameraden": Die Wehrmacht und die sowjetischen Kriegsgefangenen, 1941–1945.* Stuttgart: Deutsche Verlag-Anstalt, 1978.

Sullivan, Matthew B. *Thresholds of Peace: Four Hundred Thousand German Prisoners and the People of Britain 1943–1948.* London: Hamish Hamilton, 1979.

Sword, Keith. *Deportation and Exile: Poles in the Soviet Union, 1939–48.* London: St. Martin's, 1994.

Tolstoy, Nikolai. *The Minister and the Massacres.* London: Century Hutchinson, 1986.

———. *The Secret Betrayal.* New York: Scribner's, 1977.

Vance, J. M. "Men in Manacles: The Shackling of Prisoners of War, 1942–1943." *Journal of Military History* 59 (1995): 483–504.

———. *Objects of Concern: Canadian Prisoners of War through the Twentieth Century.* Vancouver: University of British Columbia, 1994.

———. "The Politics of Camp Life: Bargaining Process in Two German Prison Camps." *War and Society* 10 (1992): 109–26.

Vulliet, Andre. *The Y.M.C.A. and Prisoners of War: Preliminary Report of the War Prisoners Aid, Young Men's Christian Associations during World War II.* Geneva: YMCA, 1946.

Williams, Donald Mace. *Interlude in Umbarger: Italian POWs and a Texas Church.* Lubbock: Texas Tech UP, 1992.

Williams, Eric E. *The Wooden Horse.* New York: Harper, 1950.

Wyman, Mark. *DP: Europe's Displaced Persons, 1945–1951.* Philadelphia: Balch Institute, 1989.

Zawodny, Janusz. *Death in the Forest: The Story of the Katyn Forest Massacre.* Notre Dame, IN: University of Notre Dame, 1964.

Zayas, Alfred de. *The Wehrmacht War Crimes Bureau, 1939–1945.* Lincoln: University of Nebraska, 1989.

20 The Holocaust

Richard Libowitz

While Allied and Axis military forces clashed around the world, warfare of another sort was raging in Europe. The Holocaust (in Hebrew, Shoah, called by the German government the "Final Solution") set as its goal the annihilation of every Jewish man, woman, and child. Representing the ultimate act in the long history of anti-Semitism, the Holocaust took place with the full knowledge of the Allies, despite German efforts to conceal their activities in the Vilna, Lodz, and Warsaw ghettos, Dachau, Mauthausen, and Theresienstadt concentration camps, and Auschwitz and Treblinka death camps. Wyman, *The Abandonment of the Jews*, and Laqueur, *The Terrible Secret*, revealed the information possessed by Allied leaders, while Ross, *So It Was True*, demonstrated the extent to which such information both was available to the American public and appeared in the general press.

Argument continues as to the precise beginning of the Holocaust. Some mark its onset at the German invasion of Poland in September 1939, with the subsequent roundups and murders of Jews throughout that country. Others set the date at *Kristallnacht*, November 9–11, 1938, when the SA (Sturmabteilung, Nazi paramilitary organization) was set loose to destroy synagogues, Jewish homes, and businesses throughout Germany. All agree that the prelude to mass murder began January 30, 1933, when Adolf Hitler became chancellor of Germany. The subsequent succession of anti-Jewish laws and propaganda-laden newspapers, novels, films, and children's textbooks, as well as the economic boycotts and random acts of humiliation and terror, were designed to remove Jews from German political, economic, intellectual, and social life. The message was clear: Jews were not wanted in the Third Reich.

The economic realities of a worldwide depression in the 1930s, when added to nationalist tensions and widespread anti-Semitic attitudes, precluded German Jews from being welcomed in other lands. Of those who did emigrate, some reached safety in the United States or Great Britain; others found refuge in British Commonwealth countries, such as Canada and Australia, in South American states such as Argentina and Uruguay, or in Palestine (which was governed by the British under a League of Nations Mandate). The majority of the Jews leaving the Third Reich remained in Europe, however, settling in Denmark, Holland, Belgium, or France, lands that would eventually fall under German hegemony.

Despite the increasing difficulties in their lives, many Jews were reluctant to leave Germany, which had been their home for centuries and was a world center of scientific, artistic, and intellectual life. They felt that the various anti-Jewish attitudes and legislation, no matter how troubling, would be temporary and that life would eventually return to the more harmonious mode they had enjoyed in prior decades. The international refusal to increase any assistance to Jewish refugees—the result of the conference held at Evian, France, in July 1938—followed by the events of *Kristallnacht*, disabused most German Jews of those dreams. While many left in the remaining months before the outbreak of war, for most it was too late.

When Hitler gained power in 1933, there were approximately 528,000 Jews within the total German population of 64,000,000. At least half that number fled prior to war, but, as the Third Reich expanded, it found itself with ever more Jews, particularly after the capture of Poland, whose 3,000,000 Jews composed the largest such population in Europe. Mass murders began almost immediately, as Jews were either burned alive in their synagogues or rounded up, taken into the forests, and dispatched by killing squads, the executions conducted at first by police officers, as discussed by Browning in *Ordinary Men*. The police were soon replaced by the special military units, Einsatzgruppen, which were responsible for the mass killings in places such as Babi Yar. Eventually, these shootings proved too slow, expensive, and contrary to military discipline. Poison gas vans having also been tried but rejected as inefficient, a conference was held in the Berlin suburb of Wannsee on January 20, 1942, to determine the "Final Solution" to the "Jewish Question."

At Wannsee it was decided that in addition to continued expansion of the concentration camps initially opened in Germany in 1933, a series of death camps would be erected, to which Jews (as well as the Rom or Gypsy people, homosexuals, communists, and other enemies of the Reich) would be transported and eliminated in an efficient and cost-effective manner.

For the remainder of the war, the capture and execution of Jews were a state priority equal to that of defeating the Allies. Shipped to Poland in boxcars, the death camps at Auschwitz-Birkenau, Majdanek, Treblinka, Bergen-Belsen, Chelmno, and Sobibor were camouflaged as labor centers to conceal their real purposes. At Auschwitz, a substantial number of prisoners were purchased for slave labor or as experimental subjects by major German business concerns, which built plants at the complex, but most arrivees were selected for immediate execution. The means of killing was a cyanide derivative, Zyklon B, normally used as an industrial insecticide. The victims, as many as three hundred at a time, were herded into a gas chamber disguised as a shower room, its door was sealed, and the gas was released. After twenty to thirty minutes, the room would be ventilated; prisoners called *Sonderkommandos* would untangle the corpses, extract any gold teeth for the German treasury, and remove the bodies for burning, either in crematoria or on outdoor pyres. The ashes would be dumped in rivers or spread on vacant ground. Estimates vary as to the number of people who died in the different camps. For many years, the figure of six million Jewish fatalities has been used.

The public was horrified by Allied troop reports of the death camps and the photographs that began to be published in early 1945, months before Germany's surrender. Revelations about German activities continued during the International War Crimes Tribunals, which began soon after the war and continued through the later 1940s. Public interest waned with the conclusion of the trials and the rising Cold War, however; the Holocaust became a virtual nonsubject for nearly twenty years; only Israel's capture, public trial, and execution of Adolf Eichmann (1960–1962) returned the *Shoah* to center stage for a few moments, soon to be relegated to the fringes of public interest for the remainder of that decade.

The public's apathy for the Holocaust was paralleled by a paucity of academic interest. No college offered a course on the Holocaust until 1959; a small number of scholars were engaged in research, but as late as 1970 it was possible to have read the entire published corpus of Holocaust materials. All this began to change in the ensuing decade, however, in part from the interest in ethnic studies that swept across American campuses, the desire of aging survivors to preserve their stories, and the rise of a new generation of scholars willing to ask the questions and seek the answers.

Today, general and scholarly interest in the Holocaust has grown to unanticipated proportions, manifested not only in the existence of a multimillion-dollar Holocaust Museum in Washington, D.C., but also by the Holocaust memorials and research centers throughout the United States and around the world, the hundreds of courses on the subject offered in secondary schools, colleges, and universities, and the scholarly books, articles, films, art, and works of belles lettres devoted to the topic. Where scholarly materials were once severely limited, it has become a Herculean task merely to scan the literature published in English in a single year. Historical compendia, proceedings from conferences, philosophical and theological works, memoirs, and secondary summaries of initial research, not to mention the novels, plays, and poetry that continue to be produced, have made Holocaust publications a burgeoning industry.

One sign of this explosion of resources is the effort to compile data in secondary compendia, most notably the *Encyclopedia of the Holocaust*, edited by Gutman. Representative of the historical approach to Holocaust studies that is the hallmark of research at Israel's Yad Vashem, the four-volume work quickly became a standard resource for the field. Another aspect of this effort to control the expanded field has been the preparation of annotated bibliographies on the Shoah. These listings vary in content, from catalogues of documents, to bibliographies of texts and/or listings of articles, including volumes devoted to materials in languages other than English.

Among the often multivolume documentary collections are the twenty-three volume *Archives of the Holocaust*, edited by Friedlander and Milton; Hilberg's *Documents of Destruction*, an eight-volume set; *The Holocaust and After*, by Robinson; and Mendelsohn, *The Holocaust*. Finally, Wyman has prepared thirteen volumes of documents, *America and the Holocaust*. Bibliographic collections include *The Holocaust: An Annotated Bibliography* by Cargas; Edelheit and Edelheit, *Bibliography on Holocaust Literature*; and Szonyi, *The Holocaust*. Friedman's *Handbook* has thirty-two essays discussing Holocaust literature on a wide variety of topics.

The following pages offer a representative sample of the available materials for Holocaust study, divided by country and subject. They do not represent a definitive listing of resources, nor should the exclusion of any title suggest it is of inferior quality. This is an introduction to the subject.

COMPREHENSIVE STUDIES

In attempting an examination of the Holocaust, many readers will begin with one of the large and comprehensive historical volumes. Those seeking a more general background should read Shirer's classic *The Rise and Fall of the Third Reich* before turning to Hilberg's three-volume set, *The Destruction of the European Jews; The War against the Jews*, by Dawidowicz; Bauer's *A History of the Holocaust;* Levin's *Holocaust;* or *The Holocaust as Historical Experience* by Bauer and Rotenstreich. Katz has published the lengthy first volume of a projected three-volume series, *The Holocaust in Historical Context;* Marrus offers a useful shorter text, *The Holocaust in History*, while Gilbert has provided a geographic perspective with his *Atlas of the Holocaust*. Each year is now marked by the publication of collections of scholarly papers, including the ongoing *Yad Vashem Studies*, edited by Dinur, Esh, et al., selections from the Annual Scholars' Conference on the Holocaust and the Churches, and the three-volume *Remembering for the Future*, edited by Bauer et al., from the 1988 conference at Oxford and London of the same name. Articles are also to be found in journals devoted to the field, such as *Holocaust and Genocide Studies*, as well as more general periodicals.

THE CAMPS

Many texts have been written about the concentration and death camps, historical researches as well as survivor memoirs. Historical studies include Arad, *Belzec, Sobibor, Treblinka*; Gilbert, *Auschwitz and the Allies*; Gutman et al., *Anatomy of the Auschwitz Death Camp*; Donat, ed., *The Death Camp Treblinka*; and Willenberg, *Rebellion at Treblinka*. Among the best-known memoirs are those of Wiesel, *Night*; Levi, *Survival in Auschwitz*; and Frankel, *Man's Search for Meaning*. Other remembrances include *Seed of Sarah* by Isaacson; *The Survivor* by Eisner; and *Witnesses to the Holocaust*, a compilation edited by Lewin.

Jews who survived by going into hiding or "passing" as non-Jews have also recorded their stories, such as Tec, *Dry Tears*; Zar, *In the Mouth of the Wolf*; and Friedlander, *When Memory Comes*. Thousands of hours of audio- and videotaped survivor interviews are available in collections housed at Yale University and a variety of Holocaust study centers.

EUROPE

Germany

In 1933, Germany was home for approximately 5.5 percent of the nine million Jews living in Europe, making up less than 1 percent of the German population. Their story has been recounted by Barkai, *From Boycott to Annihilation*; and the contributors to Pehle's *November 1938 Pogrom*. Survivor accounts have been compiled by Gross, *The Last Jews in Berlin*.

Great Britain

The leading Allied power in Western Europe, Great Britain represented a refuge for Jews, both upon its own shores and in Palestine, which the British government had controlled under a League of Nations mandate since 1920. In addition to Laqueur's *The Terrible Secret*, British policy is discussed by Michael J. Cohen, *Churchill and the Jews*; Gilbert, *Auschwitz and the Allies*; Hinsley, *British Intelligence in the Second World War*; Sherman, *Island Refuge*; and Wasserstein, *Britain and the Jews of Europe*. British diplomacy and foreign policy have provided the focal point for many additional works, including Bauer, *From Diplomacy to Resistance*; Gilbert, *Exile and Return*; Penkower, *The Jews Were Expendable*; Woodward, *British Foreign Policy*; and Zweig, *British Policy to Palestine*.

France

France, the country to which many refugees fled in the 1930s, was a short-lived sanctuary. The German invasion, the rapid collapse of the French army, and collaboration by the Vichy government left both refugees and citizens confronted by the menace of the Third Reich's anti-Jewish policies. One of the earliest accounts of those years is by Odic, *Stepchildren of France.* More recent historical studies have been prepared by Marrus and Paxton, *Vichy France and the Jews,* and Sweets, *Choices in Vichy France.* Adler concentrates on *The Jews of Paris and the Final Solution,* while Abitbol looks to the Jewish population under French colonial rule in *The Jews of North Africa.*

Resistance took two forms in France: armed revolt and rescue efforts. Latour, *The Jewish Resistance in France,* examines activities of the first variety, while Hallie, *Lest Innocent Blood Be Shed,* tells the story of the village of Le Chambon, a remarkable Huguenot peasant community that provided assistance to five thousand Jews between 1941 and 1944, a number equal to the population of the village.

Holland

Because of the popularity of Anne Frank's *Diary,* the high degree of collaboration by Dutch citizens and a Jewish death rate equal to that in Poland are often overlooked. A more accurate picture is reported by Presser, *The Destruction of the Dutch Jews;* Warmbrunn, *The Dutch under German Occupation;* and Colijn and Littell, *The Netherlands and Nazi Genocide.* The general public retains its affection for the story of the Franks; Anne's account has more recently been supplemented by that of Miep Gies, who recounted her activities on behalf of the people hidden in the secret annex of the building at 128 Prinsengracht Street in *Anne Frank Remembered.* Etty Hillesum's *Letters from Westerbork* represents the literary legacy of another Jewish young woman, several years older than Anne Frank, possessed of a different perspective and whose efforts at survival took another direction.

Italy

The Jewish community of Italy has roots reaching deep into the Roman Empire. That history allowed Jews to be accepted by their neighbors as fellow Italians (or, more specifically, fellow Romans, Neapolitans, Venetians, etc.), a status that, combined with a popular disdain for severe government edicts, led to a general indifference toward government-ordered anti-Semitic actions. Zucotti, *The Italians and the Holocaust,* traces the results of this feeling of live and let live. Other works include Michaelis,

Mussolini and the Jews; Poliakov and Sabille, *Jews under the Italian Occupation;* and Steinberg, *All or Nothing.* Don Segre recalls life under that occupation in his *Memoir of a Fortunate Jew.*

Poland

The largest Jewish community in Europe lived in Poland's cities, towns, and villages, where they were doctors and farmers, manufacturers and woodcutters, scientists and rag sellers. Poland was a center of Jewish scholarship and religious life, home to hundreds of Talmudic academies—yeshivas—and the ultraorthodox movement, Hasidism. Approximately 90 percent of Polish Jewry died between September 1, 1939, and June 1, 1945, beaten, shot, herded into ghettos in cities such as Warsaw and Lodz, the survivors loaded into boxcars and taken to Auschwitz and the other camps.

The story of the Holocaust in Poland is recorded in Apenszlak, *The Black Book of Polish Jewry,* and Schoenfeld, *Holocaust Memoirs.* There are many memoirs as well as scholarly studies of the ghettos in Poland, especially Warsaw and Lodz. Warsaw is recounted by Czerniakow's *Warsaw Diary,* Kaplan's *Warsaw Diary of Chaim Kaplan,* Korczak's *Ghetto Diary,* Ringelblum's *Notes,* and Meed's *On Both Sides of the Wall.* Later studies include Gutman, *The Jews of Warsaw,* and Kermish, *To Live and Die with Honor,* a collection of documents. Trunk, *Judenrat,* examined Jewish communal organization in the ghettos, while Keller, *The Warsaw Ghetto in Photographs,* provided a human face for the historical accounts and statistics. The Lodz ghetto is recalled by Adelson and Lapides, *Lodz Ghetto,* and Dobroszycki, *The Chronicle of the Lodz Ghetto.*

Not every Pole was a murderer or a silent bystander. Tec, *When Light Pierced the Darkness,* and Bartoszewski and Lewin, *The Samaritans,* recount rescue efforts on the part of Poles, while Karski, *Story of a Secret State,* provides observations from the courier who brought firsthand information about the Warsaw ghetto to the Allies.

Czechoslovakia

Czechoslovakia, the last of the republics created by the Treaty of Versailles, not only was the home of a lively Jewish community but also was to be the site of the "Central Museum of the Defunct Jewish Race," a repository of Jewish artifacts to be displayed to the world once their owners had been destroyed. Events there have been recorded by Dagan, *The Jews of Czechoslovakia;* Grant, *A German Protectorate;* Jacoby, *The Common Fate of Czech and Jew,* and Kral, *Lesson from History,* the last a series of documents. Also helpful are Mastny, *The Czechs under Nazi Rule,* and Mamatey and Luza, *A History of the Czechoslovak Republic, 1918–1948.*

Czechoslovakia was the location for the "model" concentration camp, Terezin (Theresienstadt in German). Among the memoirs and studies of life in that camp are Bor, *The Terezin Requiem*; Jacobson, *Terezin*; Lederer, *Ghetto Theresienstadt*; Redlich, *The Terezin Diary*; and Troller, *Theresienstadt*. The cultural achievements within the camp have been recorded by Green, *The Artists of Terezin*; Pechova, *Arts in Terezin*; Karas, *Music in Terezin*; and Volavkova, *I Never Saw Another Butterfly*.

Hungary

Although part of the Axis, the Hungarian government chose to protect its Jewish population until 1944, when administration of the country was taken over by Berlin, and Adolf Eichmann personally supervised the transportation of the Jews to Auschwitz. In the final months of the war, approximately half of the eight hundred thousand Hungarian Jews were killed.

Branham is the leading historian of the Shoah in Hungary; his works include *The Politics of Genocide*, *The Destruction of Hungarian Jewry*, a two-volume documentary account, and *The Hungarian Jewish Catastrophe*, a bibliography. Other resources include Cohen, *The Halutz Resistance in Hungary*; Handler, *The Holocaust in Hungary*; and Katzburg, *Hungary and the Jews*.

No account of the Holocaust in Hungary is complete without the story of Raoul Wallenberg, the Swedish diplomat whose efforts resulted in the rescue of as many as one hundred thousand Hungarian Jews. Studies of Wallenberg, both personal reminiscences and later evaluations, include Anger, *With Raoul Wallenberg in Budapest*; Lester, *Wallenberg, the Man in the Iron Web*; and Werbell and Clarke, *Lost Hero*.

Soviet Union

The German invasion of the Soviet Union brought the Final Solution to many who had hoped to escape its wrath under the protection of Josef Stalin. Dobroszycki and Gurock have detailed *The Holocaust in the Soviet Union*. Although the invasion of mother Russia failed, as did Napoleon's army more than 125 years earlier, the German forces found supporters, particularly within the Ukrainian population, which saw Hitler as their liberator from Stalin, whose 1930s campaign against the kulaks had caused millions of casualties. Many Ukrainians joined special divisions of the SS (Schutzstaffeln, protection squad), while others assisted in every phase of the Final Solution, willing to kill Jews for religious reasons or because Jews were held responsible for the hated communist system. Heike, *The Ukrainian Division Galicia*, and Rudnitsky, *Essays in Modern Ukrainian History*, discuss these events from a Ukrainian nationalist perspective, while

Ehrenburg and Grossman, *The Black Book*, and Sabrin, *Alliance for Murder*, present the Jewish account.

Romania

Material relating to the fate of Romania's Jewish population may be found in *Jews and Non-Jews in Eastern Europe*, edited by Vago and Mosse. Butnaru has authored two texts, *The Silent Holocaust* and *Waiting for Jerusalem*, the latter a personal memoir. A twelve-volume set by Ancel, *Documents concerning the Fate of Romanian Jewry*, is also available. More personal information comes from survivor testimonies such as Dorian, *The Quality of Witness*.

Bulgaria

The stories of the Jewish communities of Southeastern Europe have not been recorded as exhaustively as those of their Ashkenazic kin. Chary, *The Bulgarian Jews and the Final Solution*, traces the two-track record of a Bulgarian government that protected "its" Jews but cooperated with German demands to transport "foreign" Jews to the camps. Miller, *Bulgaria during the Second World War*, provides a comprehensive view of this unique national policy.

Yugoslavia

Freidenreich traced the history of the various Jewish communities within the region that became Yugoslavia in *The Jews of Yugoslavia*, while Lowenthal, *The Crimes of the Fascist Occupants and Their Collaborators against Jews in Yugoslavia*, cataloged their destruction, as did Romano, *Jews of Yugoslavia*. More specific information is also to be found in Paris, *Genocide in Satellite Croatia*.

Greece

The fate of this ancient Jewish community, the oldest in Europe, was sealed by German decree, despite active resistance by many within the local population, encouraged to assist their Jewish neighbors by leaders of the Greek Orthodox Church. The history of these events was first covered by Molho and Nehama, *In Memoriam: The Destruction of Greek Jewry*. Other works include Sevillias, *Athens, Auschwitz*; Menasche, *Birkenau*; and Sciaky, *Farewell to Salonica*.

Scandinavia

The relatively small Jewish communities dwelling within the various Scandinavian countries were targeted for the same fate as in Poland or France. Because of a unique rescue effort—smuggling virtually its entire Jewish population to Sweden—the Danish experience has received great attention from scholars and popular writers alike. Flender wrote one of the first accounts of the Danish action, *Rescue in Denmark*; Yahil's *The Rescue of Danish Jewry* remains the best-known study.

Fewer books are available in English concerning the other Scandinavian countries; among the works about the Holocaust in Norway are Cohen, *Dapim: Studies on the Shoah*, and Abrahamsen, *Norway's Response to the Holocaust*. The situation of the tiny Jewish population in Finland is detailed by Rautkallio in *Finland and the Holocaust*.

Neutral Nations

Several European countries—including Spain, Portugal, Sweden, and Switzerland—retained their official neutrality during World War II. For Jews, those countries' borders represented shelter from the onslaught, havens that, unlike the United States, were not an ocean away but might be reached on foot. Although a fascist state, Spain was one such haven. Avni, *Spain, Franco and the Jews*, and Lipschitz, *Franco, Spain, the Jews and the Holocaust*, trace the convoluted pattern by which Jews able to demonstrate Sephardic (Spanish Jewish) ancestry were assisted by Spanish diplomats in claiming protection from the Nazis.

Switzerland, with its central location and history of neutrality, seemed a more likely place of refuge for many Jews. The Swiss did not prepare an unqualified welcome for Jewish refugees, however. Milton has discussed the situation in *Rescue to Switzerland*, as has Haesler, *The Lifeboat Is Full*.

Sweden was the third haven in Europe. Less accessible than Switzerland or Spain, the most complete work on Sweden is by Koblik, *The Stones Cry Out*. The unique efforts of one particular Swedish diplomat—Raoul Wallenberg—have been discussed earlier.

WOMEN

For many years, the specific experiences of women during the Holocaust were subsumed within general accounts of suffering. More recently, research has discovered that although a woman was less likely to pass the original "selection" upon entry to a camp than a man, once assigned to a barracks, she had a higher probability of survival. Recent works about women include publication of memoirs by individual survivors such as

Isaacson, *Seed of Sarah*, and Fenelon, *Playing for Time.* Laska's *Women in the Resistance and in the Holocaust* contains materials and accounts by a variety of survivors, as does Lixl-Purcell's *Women of Exile.*

The roles women played in the perpetration of the Shoah have now also come under scrutiny in works such as Koonz, *Mothers in the Fatherland*; Bridenthal, Grossman, and Kaplan, *When Biology Became Destiny*; and Owings, *Frauen.*

THE CHURCH STRUGGLE

The overwhelming majority of Europe's population defined itself as Christian, members of churches that often received direct support from their national governments. Most Europeans had been baptized within a Christian denomination, usually the Roman Catholic or Lutheran in the West and the Orthodox Church in the East. Whether they supported their denominations avidly or were content to pay their annual dues in return for baptism, marriage, and funeral rites, few formally left or were expelled from the faith.

Studies of the churches and the Shoah have expanded to focus upon a series of topics, beginning with general examinations of anti-Semitism within Christianity, the wartime experiences of a particular denomination, either throughout Europe or within a specific country, and the role of the denomination in complying with, or resisting, Third Reich policies. Other areas of study include the activities of church leaders or individuals made prominent by their works, as well as postwar theological reflections and reforms, including latter-day criticisms by church members or outside scholars.

Christianity and Anti-Semitism

Parkes' classic study, *The Conflict of the Church and the Synagogue*, remains a starting point for research on general Christian attitudes. More recent advances in the field include Davies, *Antisemitism and the Foundations of Christianity*; Flannery, *The Anguish of the Jews*; and Isaac, *The Teaching of Contempt.* Greater focus on the Third Reich era is supplied by Littell, *The Crucifixion of the Jews*; Rausch, *A Legacy of Hatred*; and Cargas, *Reflections of a Post-Auschwitz Christian*, all of whom rejected the notion that the Holocaust is an exclusively "Jewish" event in history and argued for its particular relevance for Christians and Christianity.

Wartime Experiences

During the past twenty years, a sharp interest developed in the actions and inactions of the various churches within a Europe once known as

Christendom. The collection edited by Littell and Locke, *The German Church Struggle and the Holocaust*, was one of the first texts devoted to this issue. Littell continued his work in the area with *The Crucifixion of the Jews.* Helmreich, *The German Churches under Hitler;* Matheson, *The Third Reich and the Christian Churches;* Gutteridge, *Open Thy Mouth for the Dumb! The German Evangelical Church and the Jews;* and Scholder, *The Churches and the Third Reich,* traced the experiences of the primary non-Catholic denominations, examining conditions of resistance as well as instances of acquiescence or complicity.

Research into the wartime activities of the Roman Catholic Church tends to revolve around two foci, general church actions and the role of Pope Pius XII, in particular, the pope's refusal to issue any public statement decrying Nazi activities or the participation of Catholics in the Shoah. Morley's study, *Vatican Diplomacy and the Jews during the Holocaust,* remains the primary work to have been drawn from otherwise closed Vatican archives. Morley's efforts were preceded by Falconi, *The Silence of Pius XII,* and followed by Friedlander, *Pius XII and the Third Reich.* Other studies of Catholic activities include Lapomarda, *The Jesuits and the Third Reich.*

RESCUERS

An entirely different sort of study is devoted to the men and women known as "righteous gentiles," individuals who sought to assist Jews during this period, whether by leading them across the border to a neutral country or providing false identification, a hiding place, or even a piece of bread that would allow for another day's survival. Each of these efforts was fraught with danger; discovery could mean imprisonment, possibly in a concentration camp, beatings, even execution. Within the district of Poland called the Généralgouvernement, those caught aiding a Jew in any way risked the execution of their entire family. Paldiel draws upon the testimonies maintained at Yad Vashem for *The Path of the Righteous,* an examination of rescuers and their actions throughout the Third Reich. The work by Rittner and Myers, *The Courage to Care,* is smaller in scope and based on more recent interviews. Individual rescuers have received attention in recent years, none more than Oscar Schindler, memorialized by Keneally in *Schindler's List.*

BIBLIOGRAPHY

Also see chapters "German Occupation of Europe," "Resistance Movements in Europe," and "Women in World War II."

Abitbol, Michel. *The Jews of North Africa during the Second World War.* Detroit: Wayne State UP, 1989.

Abrahamsen, Samuel. *Norway's Response to the Holocaust.* New York: Holocaust Library, 1991.

Adelson, Alan, and Robert Lapides, eds. *Lodz Ghetto.* New York: Viking, 1989.

Adler, Jacques. *The Jews of Paris and the Final Solution.* New York: Oxford UP, 1987.

Ancel, Jean. *Documents concerning the Fate of Romanian Jewry during the Holocaust.* 12 vols. New York: Beate Klarsfeld Foundation, 1986.

Anger, Per. *With Raoul Wallenberg in Budapest.* New York: Holocaust Library, 1981.

Apenszlak, Jacob, ed. *The Black Book of Polish Jewry.* New York: Roy, 1943.

Arad, Yitzhak. *Belzec, Sobibor, Treblinka.* Bloomington: Indiana UP, 1987.

Avni, Haim. *Spain, Franco and the Jews.* Philadelphia: Jewish Publication Society, 1982.

Barkai, Avraham. *From Boycott to Annihilation.* Hanover, NH: Brandeis UP, 1989.

Bartoszewski, Wladyslaw, and Zofia Lewin, eds. *The Samaritans.* New York: Twain, 1970.

Bauer, Yehuda. *From Diplomacy to Resistance.* Philadelphia: Jewish Publication Society, 1970.

———. *A History of the Holocaust.* New York: Franklin Watts, 1982.

———, ed. *Remembering for the Future.* 3 vols. Oxford: Pergamon, 1989.

Bauer, Yehuda, and Natan Rotenstreich, eds. *The Holocaust as Historical Experience.* New York: Holmes and Meier, 1981.

Bor, Josef. *The Terezin Requiem.* London: Heinemann, 1963.

Branham, Randolph L., ed. *The Destruction of Hungarian Jewry.* 2 vols. New York: World Federation of Hungarian Jews, 1963.

———. *The Hungarian Jewish Catastrophe.* New York: Columbia UP, 1984.

———. *The Politics of Genocide.* New York: Columbia UP, 1981.

Bridenthal, Renate, Anita Grossman, and Marion Kaplan. *When Biology Became Destiny: Women in Weimar and Nazi Germany.* New York: Monthly Review, 1984.

Browning, Christopher. *Ordinary Men.* New York: HarperCollins, 1992.

Butnaru, I. C. *The Silent Holocaust: Romania and Its Jews.* Westport, CT: Greenwood, 1992.

———. *Waiting for Jerusalem: Surviving the Holocaust in Romania.* Westport, CT: Greenwood, 1993.

Cargas, Harry James. *Reflections of a Post-Auschwitz Christian.* Detroit: Wayne State UP, 1989.

———, ed. *The Holocaust: An Annotated Bibliography.* Chicago: American Library Association, 1985.

Chary, Frederick B. *The Bulgarian Jews and the Final Solution, 1940–1944.* Pittsburgh: University of Pittsburgh, 1972.

Cohen, Asher. *Dapim: Studies on the Shoah.* New York: Peter Lang, 1989.

———. *The Halutz Resistance in Hungary, 1942–1944.* New York: Columbia UP, 1986.

Cohen, Michael J. *Churchill and the Jews.* London: F. Cass, 1985.

Colijn, G. Jan, and Marcia S. Littell, eds. *The Netherlands and Nazi Genocide.* Lewiston, NY: Edwin Mellen, 1992.

Czerniakow, Adam. *The Warsaw Diary of Adam Czerniakow.* New York: Stein and Day, 1979.

Dagan, Avigdor, ed. *The Jews of Czechoslovakia.* 3 vols. Philadelphia: Jewish Publication Society, 1984.

Davies, Alan, ed. *Antisemitism and the Foundations of Christianity.* New York: Paulist, 1979.

Dawidowicz, Lucy. *The War against the Jews, 1933–1945.* New York: Bantam, 1976.

Dinur, Benzion, Shaul Esh, et al., eds. *Yad Vashem Studies.* Jerusalem: Jerusalem Post, 1957.

Dobroszycki, Lucjan, ed. *The Chronicle of the Lodz Ghetto, 1941–1944.* New Haven, CT: Yale UP, 1984.

Dobroszycki, Lucjan, and Jeffrey Gurock, eds. *The Holocaust in the Soviet Union.* Armonk, NY: M. E. Sharpe, 1993.

Donat, Alexander, ed. *The Death Camp Treblinka.* New York: Holocaust Library, 1979.

Dorian, Emil. *The Quality of Witness.* Philadelphia: Jewish Publication Society, 1982.

Edelheit, Abraham, and Herschel Edelheit. *Bibliography on Holocaust Literature.* Boulder, CO: Westview, 1986.

Ehrenburg, Ilya, and Vasily Grossman, eds. *The Black Book.* New York: Holocaust Library, 1981.

Eisner, Jack. *The Survivor.* New York: Morrow, 1980.

Falconi, Carlo. *The Silence of Pius XII.* Boston: Little, Brown, 1970.

Fenelon, Fania. *Playing for Time.* New York: Berkley, 1979.

Flannery, Edward. *The Anguish of the Jews.* New York: Paulist, 1985.

Flender, Harold. *Rescue in Denmark.* New York: Holocaust Library, 1963.

Frank, Anne. *Diary of a Young Girl.* New York: Knopf, 1994.

———. *The Diary of a Young Girl: The Definitive Edition.* New York: Doubleday, 1995.

Frankl, Viktor. *Man's Search for Meaning.* New York: Simon and Schuster, 1984.

Freidenreich, Harriet Pass. *The Jews of Yugoslavia.* Philadelphia: Jewish Publication Society, 1979.

Friedlander, Henry, and Sybil Milton, eds. *Archives of the Holocaust.* 23 vols. Hamden, CT: Garland, 1989.

Friedlander, Saul. *Pius XII and the Third Reich.* New York: Octagon, 1986.

———. *When Memory Comes.* New York: Farrar, Straus, and Giroux, 1979.

Friedman, Saul S., ed. *Holocaust Literature: A Handbook of Critical, Historical, and Literary Writings.* Westport, CT: Greenwood, 1993.

Gies, Miep, with Alison Leslie Gold. *Anne Frank Remembered.* New York: Simon and Schuster, 1987.

Gilbert, Martin. *Atlas of the Holocaust.* New York: Macmillan, 1982.

———. *Auschwitz and the Allies.* London: M. Joseph and Rainbird, 1981.

———. *Exile and Return.* Philadelphia: Jewish Publication Society, 1978.

Grant, Shiela Duff. *A German Protectorate.* London: F. Cass, 1970.

Green, Gerald. *The Artists of Terezin.* New York: Hawthorn, 1969.

Gross, Leonard. *The Last Jews in Berlin.* New York: Simon and Schuster, 1982.

Gutman, Israel. *The Jews of Warsaw, 1939–1943.* Bloomington: Indiana UP, 1982.

———, ed. *Encyclopedia of the Holocaust.* 4 vols. New York: Macmillan, 1989.

———, et al., eds. *Anatomy of the Auschwitz Death Camp.* Bloomington: Indiana UP, 1994.

Gutteridge, Richard. *Open Thy Mouth for the Dumb! The German Evangelical Church and the Jews.* Oxford: Basil Blackwell, 1976.

Hasler, Alfred. *The Lifeboat Is Full: Switzerland and the Refugees, 1933–1945.* New York: Funk and Wagnalls, 1969.

Hallie, Philip. *Lest Innocent Blood Be Shed.* New York: Harper and Row, 1978.

Handler, Andrew, ed. *The Holocaust in Hungary.* University: University of Alabama, 1982.

Heike, Wolf-Dietrich. *The Ukrainian Division Galicia, 1943–1945.* Toronto: Shevchenko Society, 1988.

Helmreich, Ernst Christian. *The German Churches under Hitler.* Detroit: Wayne State UP, 1979.

Hilberg, Raul, ed. *The Destruction of the European Jews.* 3 vols. New York: Holmes and Meier, 1984.

―――. *Documents of Destruction.* New York: Quadrangle, 1951, 1971; London: W. H. Allen, 1972.

Hillesum, Etty. *Letters from Westerbork.* New York: Pantheon, 1986.

Hinsley, F. H., et al. *British Intelligence in the Second World War.* New York: Cambridge UP, 1979.

Isaac, Jules. *The Teaching of Contempt.* New York: Holt, Rinehart, and Winston, 1964.

Isaacson, Judith Magyar. *Seed of Sarah.* Urbana: University of Illinois, 1990.

Jacobson, Jacob. *Terezin.* London: Jewish Central Information Office, 1946.

Jacoby, Gerhard. *The Common Fate of Czech and Jew.* New York: Institute of Jewish Affairs, 1943.

Kaplan, Chaim. *The Warsaw Diary of Chaim Kaplan.* New York: Collier, 1965.

Karas, Joza. *Music in Terezin.* New York: Beaufort, 1985.

Karski, Jan. *Story of a Secret State.* Boston: Houghton Mifflin, 1944.

Katz, Steven T. *The Holocaust in Historical Context: Ancient and Medieval Cases.* Vol. 1. New York: Oxford UP, 1994.

Katzburg, Nathaniel. *Hungary and the Jews.* Ramat Gan: Bar Ilan UP, 1981.

Keller, Ulrich, ed. *The Warsaw Ghetto in Photographs.* New York: Dover, 1984.

Keneally, Thomas. *Schindler's List.* New York: Simon and Schuster, 1982.

Kermish, Joseph, ed. *To Live and Die with Honor.* Jerusalem: Yad Vashem, 1986.

Koblik, Steven. *The Stones Cry Out.* Washington, DC: Holocaust, 1988.

Koonz, Claudia. *Mothers in the Fatherland.* New York: St. Martin's, 1986.

Korczak, Janusz. *Ghetto Diary.* New York: Holocaust Library, 1978.

Kral, Vaclav. *Lesson from History.* Prague: Orbis, 1961.

Lapomarda, Vincent A. *The Jesuits and the Third Reich.* Lewiston, NY: Edwin Mellen, 1989.

Laqueur, Walter. *The Terrible Secret.* Boston: Little, Brown, 1980.

Laska, Vera, ed. *Women in the Resistance and in the Holocaust.* Westport, CT: Greenwood, 1983.

Latour, Anny. *The Jewish Resistance in France.* New York: Holocaust Library, 1981.

Lederer, Zdenek. *Ghetto Theresienstadt.* New York: Howard Fertig, 1953.

Lester, Elenore. *Wallenberg, the Man in the Iron Web.* Englewood Cliffs, NJ: Prentice-Hall, 1982.

Levi, Primo. *Survival in Auschwitz.* New York: Collier, 1958.

Levin, Nora. *Holocaust.* New York: Schocken, 1973.

Lewin, Rhoda, ed. *Witnesses to the Holocaust: An Oral History.* Boston: Twayne, 1989.

Lipschitz, Chaim. *Franco, Spain, the Jews and the Holocaust.* New York: KTAV, 1983.

Littell, Franklin H. *The Crucifixion of the Jews.* New York: Harper and Row, 1975.

Littell, Franklin H., and Hubert Locke, eds. *The German Church Struggle and the Holocaust.* Detroit: Wayne State UP, 1974.

Lixl-Purcell, Andrea, ed. *Women of Exile.* Westport, CT: Greenwood, 1988.

Lowenthal, Zdenko, ed. *The Crimes of the Fascist Occupants and Their Collaborators against Jews in Yugoslavia.* Belgrade: Federation of Jewish Communities, 1957.

Mamatey, Victor, and Radomir Luza. *A History of the Czechoslovak Republic, 1918–1948.* Princeton: Princeton UP, 1973.

Marrus, Michael. *The Holocaust in History.* Hanover, NH: University of New England, 1987.

Marrus, Michael, and Robert Paxton. *Vichy France and the Jews.* New York: Schocken, 1981.

Mastny, Vojtech. *The Czechs under Nazi Rule.* New York: Columbia UP, 1971.

Matheson, Peter, ed. *The Third Reich and the Christian Churches.* Grand Rapids, MI: Eerdmans, 1981.

Meed, Vladka. *On Both Sides of the Wall.* New York: Holocaust Library, 1979.

Menasche, Albert. *Birkenau.* New York: Saltiel, 1947.

Mendelsohn, John. *The Holocaust: Selected Documents.* New York: Garland, 1982.

Michaelis, Meir. *Mussolini and the Jews.* Oxford: Clarendon, 1978.

Miller, Marshall L. *Bulgaria during the Second World War.* Stanford, CA: Stanford UP, 1975.

Milton, Sybil. *Rescue to Switzerland.* New York: Garland, 1982.

Molho, Michael, and Joseph Nehama. *In Memoriam: The Destruction of Greek Jewry.* Jerusalem: Jewish Community of Salonika, 1956.

Morley, John. *Vatican Diplomacy and the Jews during the Holocaust.* New York: KTAV, 1980.

Odic, Charles. *Stepchildren of France.* New York: Roy, 1945.

Owings, Alison. *Frauen.* New Brunswick, NJ: Rutgers UP, 1995.

Paldiel, Mordecai. *The Path of the Righteous.* Hoboken, NJ: KTAV, 1993.

Paris, Edmond. *Genocide in Satellite Croatia, 1941–1945.* Chicago: American Institute for Balkan Affairs, 1961.

Parkes, James. *The Conflict of the Church and the Synagogue.* New York: World, 1934.

Pechova, Oliva. *Arts in Terezin, 1941–1945.* Prague: Memorial Exposition, 1973.

Pehle, Walter, ed. *November 1938 Pogrom: From the Reichskristallnacht to Genocide.* Oxford: Berg, 1990.

Penkower, Monty Noam. *The Jews Were Expendable.* Urbana: University of Illinois, 1983.

Poliakov, Leon, and Jacques Sabille. *Jews under the Italian Occupation.* New York: Fertig, 1983.

Presser, Jacob. *The Destruction of the Dutch Jews.* New York: Dutton, 1969.

Rausch, David. *A Legacy of Hatred.* Grand Rapids, MI: Baker Book House, 1990.

Rautkallio, Hannu. *Finland and the Holocaust.* New York: Holocaust Library, 1987.

Redlich, Gonda. *The Terezin Diary of Gonda Redlich.* Lexington: UP of Kentucky, 1992.

Ringelblum, Emmanuel. *Notes from the Warsaw Ghetto.* New York: McGraw-Hill, 1958.

Rittner, Carol, and Sondra Myers, eds. *The Courage to Care.* New York: New York UP, 1986.

Robinson, Jacob. *The Holocaust and After.* Jerusalem: Israel Universities, 1973.

Romano, Jasa. *Jews of Yugoslavia, 1941–1945.* Belgrade: Federation of Jewish Communities of Yugoslavia, 1982.

Ross, Robert. *So It Was True.* Minneapolis: University of Minnesota, 1980.

Rudnitsky, Ivan L. *Essays in Modern Ukrainian History.* Edmonton: Canadian Institute of Ukrainian Studies, 1987.

Sabrin, B. F. *Alliance for Murder.* New York: Sure Sellers, 1990.

Schoenfeld, Joachim. *Holocaust Memoirs.* New York: KTAV, 1985.

Scholder, Klaus. *The Churches and the Third Reich.* Philadelphia: Fortress, 1988.

Sciaky, Leon. *Farewell to Salonica.* New York: Current, 1946.

Segre, Don Vittorio. *Memoir of a Fortunate Jew.* Bethesda, MD: Adler and Adler, 1987.

Sevillias, Errikos. *Athens, Auschwitz.* Athens: Lycabettus, 1983.

Sherman, A. J. *Island Refuge.* London: Elek, 1973.

Shirer, William. *The Rise and Fall of the Third Reich.* New York: Simon and Schuster, 1960.

Steinberg, Jonathan. *All or Nothing.* London: Routledge, 1990.

Sweets, John. *Choices in Vichy France.* New York: Oxford UP, 1986.

Szonyi, David. *The Holocaust.* New York: KTAV, 1985.

Tec, Nehama. *Dry Tears.* New York: Oxford UP, 1984.

———. *When Light Pierced the Darkness.* New York: Oxford UP, 1986.

Troller, Norbert. *Theresienstadt.* Chapel Hill: University of North Carolina, 1991.

Trunk, Isaiah. *Judenrat.* New York: Macmillan, 1972.

Vago, Bela, and George L. Mosse, eds. *Jews and Non-Jews in Eastern Europe, 1918–1945.* Jerusalem: Israel Universities, 1974.

Volavkova, Hana, ed. *I Never Saw Another Butterfly.* New York: McGraw-Hill, 1964.

Warmbrunn, Werner. *The Dutch under German Occupation, 1940–1945.* Stanford, CA: Stanford UP, 1967.

Wasserstein, Bernard. *Britain and the Jews of Europe, 1939–1945.* Oxford: Oxford UP, 1979.

Werbell, Frederick, and Thurston Clarke. *Lost Hero.* New York: McGraw-Hill, 1982.

Wiesel, Elie. *Night.* New York: Avon, 1972.

Willenberg, Samuel. *Rebellion at Treblinka.* Oxford: Blackwell, 1989.

Woodward, Llewellyn. *British Foreign Policy in the Second World War.* London: HMSO, 1962.

Wyman, David. *The Abandonment of the Jews.* New York: Pantheon, 1984.

———, ed. *America and the Holocaust.* 13 vols. New York: Garland, 1989.

Yahil, Leni. *The Rescue of Danish Jewry.* Philadelphia: Jewish Publication Society, 1969.

Zar, Rose. *In the Mouth of the Wolf.* Philadelphia: Jewish Publication Society, 1983.

Zucotti, Susan. *The Italians and the Holocaust.* New York: Basic, 1987.

Zweig, Ronald. *British Policy to Palestine during the Second World War.* Woodbridge: Royal Historical Society, 1986.

Part V

War and Society in Europe and the English-Speaking World

21 Comparative Economic Mobilization in World War II

Geofrey T. Mills

John Maynard Keynes was once heard to remark that "the purpose of war finance was to ensure that nothing was ever settled on financial grounds." He was referring to the primary characteristic of modern warfare with its movement in the late nineteenth century from a labor-intense to a capital-intense endeavor. Given this shift, national economies were now required to produce untold piles of munitions and other war material, which meant that wars were now fought with the entire economy, not simply the armed forces. Furthermore, given the lead times necessary to produce the sophisticated products of modern warfare, a period of mobilization was necessary before the full weight of armies could be brought to bear on the enemy.

World War II is an interesting case study in comparative mobilization strategies from a number of perspectives. The course of the war demonstrated the obvious fact that larger economies could wage modern warfare better over the long haul than smaller ones; however, it also showed that early preparedness could help achieve initial conquests over bigger foes. Furthermore, dictatorial political systems, such as Germany and Italy, under the control of popular, well-motivated, and focused leaders, can mobilize no faster nor with greater intensity than could democracies. In fact, the data reveal that the four countries studied here had similar problems with respect to economic organization, balancing the needs of the military with the civilian economy, logistical problems, manpower requirements, and so on. To a certain extent all four nations solved many of these problems in a similar fashion. For example, they all eventually had a strong administrator in charge of war production, and they all relied heavily on women who were recruited to the industrial labor force. The literature on mobilization in the Second World War is enormous, so large that it would be difficult to even catalog all of it. Most of the initial literature written before 1960 was in the form of memoirs or official government studies. The fifty-year anniversary of the war has generated a mountain of scholarship, a lot of it analytical/quantitative in character or throwing light on previously dark corners of the war, such as the Soviet Union. This chapter presents in summary form the broad outlines and conclusions of the mobilization efforts for four major belligerents.

This chapter is divided into four sections discussing the major countries in the European theater: Germany, Great Britain, the Soviet Union, and the United States (the Japanese situation is discussed elsewhere). France is not considered because it was effectively out of the war by 1941, and the case of Italy approximately parallels that of Germany. In neither instance were the country's efforts significant to the course of the war or its outcome.

GERMANY

The case of German mobilization in World War II has been a hotly debated subject for some time. Part of this is due to a conflict of German war aims, a confusion between the blitzkrieg as a means of making war and a blitzkrieg economy, plus a lack of reasonable data on the German economy in the war (Kalder, "The German War Economy"; Carroll, *Design for Total War*; Milward, *German Economy at War* and *War, Economy and Society*; and Overy, *War and Economy*).

The German economy, ravaged as it was by the stress of the Versailles Treaty, the hyperinflation of the early 1920s, and the depression, had made great strides since Hitler assumed power in 1933. Part of this was due to his early program of remilitarization and focus on infrastructure projects, such as the construction of the autobahns. Symbolized by the remilitarization of the Rhine, this economic activity had brought a considerable measure of relief to the German population and, even before 1937, had created considerable employment. This early period of German mobilization was at a low level compared to later years and was notable for the strides made in airplane design and development, as well as tank production. Hjalmar Schacht was the most visible individual associated with the gains in civilian employment before 1938. After this date Hitler's intent was to put the German economy on a war footing. The question remains as to how large a war footing and over what time period (Overy, *The Origins of the Second World War, Nazi Economic Recovery*, "Transportation and Rearmament in the Third Reich," and "Hitler's War"; and Klein, *Germany's Economic Preparation for War*).

Recent scholarship indicates that Hitler's strategic vision, founded upon racial purity and international conquest for German "living space," would require a major and lengthy war, most probably on many fronts at once. Germany would not be ready to fight such a war until the mid-1940s. War mobilization in Germany was, therefore, designed around this timetable, and to accommodate this plan Germany needed to acquire additional raw materials and construct or otherwise acquire specialized industrial plants. The conquest and subsequent annexation of Austria, the Sudetenland in Czechoslovakia, and part of Poland can all be seen in this light. This region in conjunction with the industrial areas of Germany proper was then to become the economic heartland out of which the war with the major powers would be fought. In 1939 the blitzkrieg approach to war and economics was adopted because, according to Hitler's logic, the Allies would not go to war over Poland, and it was therefore the cheapest and fastest way to acquire the resources he needed to build his vast war machine (Overy, *Origins of the Second World War* and "Hitler's War and the German Economy"; Carroll, *Design for Total War*; and Thies, "Hitler's European Building Programme").

When England, to Hitler's surprise, backed its pledge to Poland with a declaration of war, Germany's economy was not then ready for a major war of attrition. The economy lacked a workable strategic plan, some of the necessary infrastructure for war production was absent, and there were overlapping and conflicting layers of authority and regulation. Industrialists complained bitterly that the army had too much authority, especially over skilled labor allocation, without the necessary expertise or vision to successfully mobilize the economy on the scale needed. Confusion reigned, and output stagnated. The concept of the "Wehrwirtschaft," a war-headed economy, was developed in the 1930s specifically to prepare the German economy for a long and difficult struggle. However, this struggle was not planned to start until the mid-1940s, and the period before was to be used to build the German war economy. By 1939, although significant advances had occurred, not nearly enough had been done to make the "Wehrwirtschaft" a reality (Overy, *The Air War* and "German Pre-War Aircraft Production"; and Milward, "The End of the Blitzkrieg").

In calling Germany's Polish bluff, France and Britain had caught the German economy not fully prepared for a major war. In reaction Hitler ordered that full mobilization be undertaken immediately. Demand for munitions and, by extension, basic materials mushroomed, and in the winter of 1939–1940 German authorities had to invent a system for fighting an all-out war. Armament production capacity was especially crucial, and current output was nowhere near the production goals set by Hitler. Plans were put in place for the reduction of consumption, a new tax policy, inflation control, production expansion and labor allocation. As a result a huge proportion of German gross domestic product (GDP) was being absorbed by the military, even by 1940. In 1939 fully a quarter of German national income was going to the war effort, and in 1941 it was closer to 40 percent. Actual production lagged behind these grandiose plans and did not peak until 1944, much like the rest of the belligerents

(Harrison, "Resource Mobilization for World War II"; Milward, *The German Economy at War*; Carrol, *Design for Total War*; Kalder, "The German War Economy"; and Speer, *Inside the Third Reich*).

One of the problems facing Hitler in his desire to rapidly mobilize the economy was that both military and civilian authorities had control of certain parts of the economy, leaving no one in overall command. In this he faced problems and frustrations similar to those of the other major powers. Straightforward orders to civilians on what and how much to produce and in what order were simply not forthcoming. The easy and rapid conquest of the Low Countries and France had instilled a sense of relief and relaxation in much of the German business community. They were, of course, ignorant of the plans for invasion of Russia. The army, navy, and air force were drawing up plans and placing orders for huge quantities of armaments, and by the fall of 1940 critical shortages, especially in some categories of labor, were becoming more apparent. Throughout the last quarter of 1940 a number of stopgap solutions were implemented to correct the shortage situation. In particular Hitler personally ordered the army and industrialists to cooperate on their respective demands for skilled labor (Overy, "Hilter's War and the German Economy"; Milward, *The German Economy at War* and *War, Economy and Society*).

Such were the intensity and pressure of mobilization efforts after 1939 that data suggest a mostly mobilized Germany economy by June 1941. Even so, military output was lagging behind demand, and it was becoming obvious that other measures besides simpleminded resource allocation needed to be employed if increased war production were to be a reality. A more rational administrative and allocation organization was needed. Bit by bit, management problems were sorted out, and by early 1942 Hitler had decided his course of action (Harrison, "Resource Mobilization for WWII"; Milward, *The German War Economy*; and Overy, "Hitler's War and the German Economy").

One result of Hitler's new directions was that the military would no longer have exclusive control over the war economy, which was now to reside in the able hands of Albert Speer and his staff and associates of industrialists and other experts. Speer attacked needless duplication, the bureaucracies in both the military and civilian sectors, and, most important, the lack of clear direction on allocation priorities. Acting on the personal orders and with the full confidence of Hitler, Speer worked wonders. Rationalization, a move away from needlessly high-quality production, and a reliance on the business community were key factors in the achievements of German war economy through 1944 (Speer, *Inside the Third Reich*).

German mobilization was at a much higher level than that of America or Britain but somewhat comparable to that of the Soviet Union. By 1943 Germany was devoting approximately three-quarters of its national income to the war effort. Of all the major belligerents Germany's economy was the best prepared going into the war, and therefore problems of over-mobilization continually needed to be solved. The German economy could not have made such a showing without the 16 to 18 percent of national income coming either via imports or resources from other external sources such as conquered territories. This figure matches the imports of the United Kingdom at the peak of its needs. It is about the same as the import requirements of the USSR and follows approximately the same time path; that is, the peak came about 1943–1944 (Harrison, "Resource Mobilization for WWII"; Milward, *The German Economy at War*, Overy, *War and Economy*; and Carrol, *Design for Total War*).

The success of the German economy after 1942 was supported on a number of pillars, but especially the base of investment in core armament industries, which, while not completely to everyone's satisfaction, was in place by 1942. Speer had taken control of the economy away from the armed forces. The generals and admirals had built needlessly competing and duplicative structures to ensure that their needs were met, so much so that enormous gains could be achieved by putting the production system on a more rational basis; labor productivity increased by record amounts, soaring nearly two and a half times in the course of the war. These were the underlying economic sources of the German war machine. Hard work, dedication to the specific task, clear-cut leadership, and the iron will of Adolf Hitler were also contributing factors. Perhaps this last item can be identified as a unique ingredient in the German people's superior effort and willingness to sacrifice anything to win the war. They knew Hitler was leading them down a road from which there could be no retreat. His foreign policy and racial purity goals were so repugnant to the Allied powers that Germany had either to win or to be utterly defeated. The Germans responded to this challenge (Overy, *War and Economy*, and Milward, *The German Economy*).

GREAT BRITAIN

British war production, like that of the other belligerents, was dominated by the convoluted politics of the 1930s, which were, in turn, partly a product of the Treaty of Versailles and the serious economic issues generated by the depression. The continuing series of economic problems in the interwar period—the 1925 gold crisis, the onset of the Great Depression, and the credit problems of the 1930s—conspired to produce in the United Kingdom a political environment focused, as in much of the rest of the world, on internal domestic economic concerns.

With this as background, historians have determined that a recognizable British mobilization process was emerging by 1935. The Treaty of Versailles, with all of its provisions on ship sizes and categories, coupled with (or so everyone thought) the restraint of German military power, produced a planning process in the United Kingdom based on the "Ten-Year Rule." This was the assumption that Britain would face no major war within the next decade. The 1935 military plan named Germany and Japan as probable enemies, but even at that, little was done to rearm. What rearmament was accomplished focused almost exclusively on the Royal Navy and Air Force. The budget for the air force did increase substantially from 1932 onward, but not enough to match the advances of German airpower. This was to be expected, given British geopolitical thinking and the economic confines within which military plans had to operate. Fundamentally, British war plans were constrained to operate on the grounds that nothing they did or proposed should interfere with the recovery of the domestic economy. The net result of these policies was that the British devoted only a limited amount to war mobilization before mid-1939. In essence the policy of the British government was to depend on foreign policy, specifically that not backed by the threat of military force, to deal with the German threat. All of this had to change rapidly after the German invasion of Poland in September 1939 and the decision by Chamberlain to honor the British commitment to Polish security. Estimates suggest that the British economy devoted less than 10 percent of national income to mobilization in 1939 and substantially less in prior years (Hancock and Gowing, *British War Economy*; Harrison, "Resource Mobilization for WWII"; Higham, "Government, Companies and National Defense"; and Postan, *British War Production*).

After the declaration of war Britain found itself in difficulty. With little prior attention devoted to war preparation, dependency on foreign imports for many strategic materials, and location within range of the Luftwaffe the United Kingdom was in serious danger of needing to rearm very rapidly or capitulating to German demands.

The first order of business was serious British national leadership capable and willing to deal with the realities of the German menace. This was accomplished with the ascension of Winston Churchill to the prime ministry in May 1940. Under Churchill's leadership the British people and economy began an impressive response to the demands of war.

Aircraft production was, of course, a key priority in that planes, planes, and more planes were needed to fight in the Battle of Britain. They would also be the only means of inflicting damage directly on Germany for the immediate future. Churchill turned to Lord Beaverbrook for help and appointed him minister of aircraft production in the crucial 1940–1941 years. By contemporary standards Beaverbrook had odd views for managing such a complicated piece of business. An improviser at heart, he managed more by instinct and intuition than by a formal organization. Nonetheless he worked his peculiar magic in the aircraft industry. Beaverbrook's managerial influence was not to be felt beyond aircraft, as the major responsibility for resource allocation for war mobilization was placed upon Sir John Anderson (Hancock and Gowing, *British War Economy* and Postan, *British War Production*).

Under Anderson most major areas of economic life in Britain were subject to regulation and administration. Prices, investment, food supplies, production for war, and production for consumers were all subject to administrative oversight. A major problem was to ensure that the United Kingdom got enough imports to feed, clothe, and arm the country. In the end this was a political issue to be settled personally between Roosevelt and Churchill. The problem was potentially massive in that the American military, by early 1940, did not wish to send precious munitions to Britain if it would soon be out of the war or, worse, conquered by Germany. Churchill had the same concerns in reverse, that without American aid England would most probably be out of the war, sooner rather than later. Success in the Battle of Britain in mid-1940, and the U.S. Lend-Lease program of March 1941 helped to settle this issue, leaving the British economy intact and the polity willing to engage Germany in a fight to the finish (Hancock and Gowing, *British War Economy*, and Overy, *The Air War*).

Much like the Soviet Union, Great Britain was dependent on imports of food and raw materials to sustain its war effort. Until the inauguration of Lend-Lease in 1941 the issue regarding Great Britain's ability to maintain a mobilization effort was very much in doubt. But even after this the British economy was heavily dependent on imports. The peak, in 1940, saw British imports approximately 17 percent of the national income. Although this figure fell in the succeeding years, it was never less than 10 percent for the duration of the war. What remained was for the British to put all of this together to ensure and then maintain a high flow of war material. Churchill helped the economic mobilization agencies by placing a two-million-man limit on the size of the army in 1941. Within this limit Lord Anderson was then able to devise a scheme of labor rationing using a complex system of economic priorities. Under this system the British economy was able to provide a high rate of war-related output, peaking in 1943, at approximately 60 percent of national income. Such results are quite startling, given where Britain started, but reflected the organizational skills of Anderson; the stark realization that the United Kingdom could actually lose the war; and the contributions of the Allies, notably the United States, in supplying crucial imports. All in all, the British pulled off a remarkable recovery and achievement of production during the war (Harrison, "Resource Mobilization for War").

SOVIET UNION

It is difficult to write with confidence about the Soviet experience of war mobilization in that access to its archives and data has been less available than in the other three countries addressed in this chapter. These difficulties notwithstanding, recent scholarship has thrown considerable light on the Soviet case. It is safe to conclude that the Soviet Union gave the most extensive effort economically and militarily of all the belligerents in the war. It lost upward of twenty-two million of its population and had the bulk of its economy subject to a scorched-earth policy as it was nearly overrun in 1941–1942. A vigorous and surprising stand was made, and after the Battle of Stalingrad the Red Army began to reverse the course of the war. Soviet economic achievements, materially aided by imports, were crucial to this effort.

The Soviet mobilization began much earlier than that of its allies. Political leadership in the Soviet Union had, in the 1930s, been sensitive to the threat of an invasion and subsequently began to acquire the arms needed to sustain a mass army. Cutting against this effort were the military purges of the 1930s, which stripped a good proportion of the professional officers corps from the armed services, and an apparent misjudgment by Stalin on the true intention of the Nazis. Nonetheless, by 1940 the Soviet economy was devoting perhaps a fifth of its GDP to defense, albeit on a lower technical base and generally a less sophisticated industrial capacity (Harrison, "Resource Mobilization in WWII" and *Soviet Planning*; and Linz, *The Impact of WWII*).

The June 1941 invasion of the Soviet Union by the Germans did catch the Red Army and the political leadership unaware—not so unaware, however, that they lost the war over it. Almost immediately a large and important segment of the industrial base was evacuated from the path of the German army to the safer regions of the Urals. This effort may well have saved both the armaments production capacity and the nation itself. Responsibility for this effort was spread across many individuals, who responded with energy and insight to this massive problem. In the entirety of World War II the transference of the Soviet industrial base to the East is probably the largest single economic activity that helped to save an Allied power. It was unprecedented in history and still stands, fifty years later, as a colossal achievement.

The war could not be further prosecuted, however, until an industrial system dominated by many centers of authority was streamlined. Like the rest of the major powers, the Soviets eventually realized that they needed to centralize the economic side of their war effort. This was accomplished in late 1942, when Stalin brought together, much as Churchill, Hitler, and Roosevelt had, the disparate elements of war production in a single Operations Bureau. It may have been easier to accomplish these ends in a dictatorial political system under extreme attack by a merciless enemy. Ironically, however, the time period required to achieve a centrally directed war economy was the same for the Soviets, about eighteen months, as it was for the rest of the industrial powers (Harrison, "Resource Mobilization for WWII," and *Soviet Planning*; and Lieberman, "Crisis Management in the USSR").

The Soviets had a particularly nasty labor allocation problem, given the large scale of their battle deaths, the scorched-earth policy of the Germans, and the dislocation of the industrial base. The Soviet civilian population was particularly hard hit, especially in European Russia and the Ukraine. During the teeth of the German threat, before the Stalingrad victory, Soviet armed forces could, and did, claim nearly everyone who could hold a rifle. This exacerbated the industrial labor problem, especially for crucial categories of skilled labor, and necessitated the use of large numbers of women in war-related occupations. This problem was eventually sorted out, but not until early 1943. Data for the Soviet Union are sketchy, but what is available suggests a mobilization effort approximate to that of the Germans. Nearly 75 percent of national income became devoted to the Soviet war economy at its peak in 1943 and 1944. Overmobilization needed to be addressed, as did some monumental logistical problems, but again these roughly paralleled the German problems.

Much like the British, the Soviets also depended quite heavily on the American Lend-Lease program and other imports to their economy. Probably more so than with the British, this U.S. program provided the Soviets with the crucial margin of success that enabled them to just survive in 1942 and then to go on and win the war. Estimates vary, but perhaps as much as 18 percent of Soviet GDP was provided externally in 1943 and 1994. Without these products, especially the planes, trucks, and other mechanized equipment, the Soviet economy would have been hard-pressed to produce what it needed to successfully prosecute the war (Harrison, "Resource Mobilization for WWII").

THE UNITED STATES

Economic mobilization for total war in the United States can be broken into three periods. The first, the defense period, runs from 1939 to Pearl Harbor. The second contains the first twenty months of the war and was characterized by trial and experimentation, followed by the third period, after mid-1943, in which a well-organized and focused economic mobilization scheme emerged. Due to the course of the war in Europe the United States mobilized after the British and Germans. A good portion of what the Americans did to mobilize was based, in part, on the needs of the British. This was especially the case with Lend-Lease (Chandler and Wallace, *Economic Mobilization and Stabilization*; Vatter, *The U.S. Economy in WWII*; Janeway, *The Struggle for Survival*; Catton, *The War Lords of Washington*; and Ketchum, *Borrowed Years*).

Initial efforts at mobilization were dominated by the War Department's

Industrial Mobilization Plan. Developed in the interwar period, this plan sought to avoid the mistakes of World War I by envisioning an agency that would organize war production and be directed by a coalition of business elites in concert with labor, various trade organizations, and agriculture interests. The military's input would come via the Army and Navy Munitions Board. Roosevelt, for reasons that remain somewhat unclear but probably were related to the isolationist political environment, never seriously considered the adoption of this plan and its mobilization implications.

Instead, Roosevelt created in September 1939 the War Resources Board to review the latest (1939) version of the Industrial Mobilization Plan. To a lot of New Dealers, especially labor and agricultural interests, the plan was thought to be retrograde in terms of its social implications and business domination. Meanwhile, the War Resources Board itself was coming under intense scrutiny from isolationists who feared the United States would be led into a war that did not involve its vital interests. With the war in Europe in a dormant phase and with the upcoming election, Roosevelt was not in a position to take bold leadership on economic mobilization (Hawley, *The New Deal and the Problem of Monopoly*; Schlesinger, *The Politics of Upheaval*; and Burns, *Roosevelt: Soldier of Freedom*).

The failed experiment with the War Resources Board led to another innovation, the National Defense Advisory Council, created in May 1940. This agency may have been unique in modern government in that it had no chair and no clear mandate. It was another of Roosevelt's schemes to attempt to drag the economy onto a war footing without really appearing to do so. Staffed by seven commissioners, the National Defense Advisory Council was entirely unable to coordinate military purchases, establish a priority system, or convert peacetime consumer production to munitions. The council was replaced by the Office of Production Management, which was somewhat better than previous organizational attempts to straighten out war production, but not by much, and the economy drifted. This remained the situation with respect to economic mobilization until Pearl Harbor forced America into war. During this period America's mobilization effort was hardly noticeable. In 1940 estimates suggest that the United States committed less than 3 percent of national income to war, and even in 1941 it was less then 15 percent (U.S. Department of Commerce, *Historical Statistics of the U.S.*; Goldsmith, "Power of Victory"; Fearon, *War, Prosperity and Depression*; and Vatter, *The U.S. Economy in WWII*).

All of the prewar efforts at mobilization failed for the same reasons: (1) Roosevelt was adamantly against giving his authority over the economy to any one individual, preferring to appoint either weak individuals or loose coalitions of directors to control these agencies; (2) because participation in the war was uncertain until Pearl Harbor, businessmen saw war production, especially if it required new plants and equipment, as a risky business; (3) fueled by rising incomes, consumer demand was increasing almost daily, and since there were no limits on the profits that could be made from these products, businesses much preferred this market; and (4) none of the agencies, not the War Production Board, the National Defense Advisory Council, or the Office of Production Management, could coordinate the economic priorities put forward by the army and navy (Burns, *Roosevelt: Soldier of Freedom*; Catton, *War Lords*; Janeway, *Struggle for Survival*; and Nelson, *Arsenal of Democracy*).

With the United States finally in the war, the economy entered the second of its three stages, lasting from January 1942 through early May 1943. Roosevelt finally appointed a single administrator, Donald Nelson, and gave a single agency, the Office of Production Management, the necessary power and authority to control war production. However, this new organization faced an economy reluctant to give up the lucrative civilian market, and not until June 1942 was the economy substantially converted to a wartime footing (Nelson, *Arsenal of Democracy*; and U.S. Bureau of the Budget, *United States at War*).

Winning this battle was not the same thing, however, as developing and monitoring a well-oiled effort to turn out the sinews of war. The system for allocating production and acquiring the necessary raw materials was, by late summer 1942, in the process of breaking down. The crux of the problem was that the army and navy were not forced to set any priorities at all in their procurement demands, and as a result the orders arrived at businesses as if they were all top priority, and there was no good method for the crucial raw materials necessary for production to be allocated between competing uses. The managers of the economy found themselves in the odd position of achieving substantial war output while, at the same time, the war economy was getting worse in terms of its ability to successfully absorb the procurement orders.

Scarce materials—mainly aluminum, copper, and steel—were the crucial bottlenecks in war procurement and production. The Controlled Materials Plan was devised in late 1942 to allocate a percentage of these materials among the various war agencies that needed them, and they in turn reallocated them to manufacturers and other end users. In this sense the Controlled Materials Plan allocated crucial materials much like money, or chits, which were then "respent" by the recipient. The plan went into operation in early 1943 and was an immediate success. The Controlled Materials Plan, coupled with improved production scheduling and other logistical arrangements, helped to usher in the third stage of the war effort (Janeway, *Struggle for Survival*, and Nelson, *Arsenal of Democracy*).

By late spring of 1943, with war production and economic organization finally in full gear, Roosevelt made his last change in the domestic economic organization. In May he created the Office of War Mobilization, which was the "superagency" so many had wanted, to coordinate all levels of economic activity. Roosevelt appointed an economic czar, James F. Byrnes, whose responsibilities were over all economic activities. This organizational structure finished out the war and oversaw the greatest achievements in production and economic growth of the entire war effort. The years 1943 and 1944 saw the largest production of munitions. In 1943 the American economy devoted fully half of the national income to the war effort. This was a remarkable increase from the 15 percent so allocated in 1941 and the approximately one-third figure of 1942. Such increases suggest two phenomena at work. One was certainly the use of previously unemployed resources; even as late as mid-1941 the unemployment rate was still at 14 percent. The other is, of course, the more efficient organization of the war effort itself. Roosevelt's trial-and-error process had finally produced results (U.S. Department of Commerce, *Historical Statistics*, and Vatter, *U.S. Economy in WWII*).

CONCLUSIONS

The mobilization scenarios of these four major combatants have much in common and also much that is unique to their particular circumstances. Two of the countries, the Soviet Union and Germany, began to prepare for war relatively early in the 1930s, although the degree of preparation and the intensity of the effort varied between them and over time. They devoted approximately the same proportion of national income to the war effort. Furthermore, the purpose of the mobilization was different, and 1940 found neither country ready to fight the sort of war it wanted to fight. The Germans, who had begun as early as 1934 to rearm, were intending to launch a major war of conquest and attrition sometime in the mid-1940s. By contrast the Soviet Union was mobilizing with the major purpose of protecting its national integrity. The Polish crisis of 1939 had ended differently than the Germans had hoped, and they found themselves in a major war some three to five years before they were completely ready. The German invasion of the Soviet Union in the summer of 1941 caught the Soviets unawares and not completely ready to take on the Germans.

The other two countries, the United States and Great Britain, had done comparatively little to prepare themselves for war, and in the case of America it would be safe to say nothing had been accomplished by 1940. These two nations had, therefore, very little time to convert their industrial bases to munitions production. The British, although somewhat ahead of the Americans, were still woefully unprepared for war. America seemed content to do nothing and to stay out of the European conflict as honest neutrals. When war came, both countries were unready to fight a determined and well-armed foe.

Once each country had committed itself to the war effort, its economy was pressed to produce as much in the way of war material as possible. This was no easy task, given the capital-intensive nature of making war by 1940, with its complex weapons systems and vast industrial substructure. As a result of these demands there was a remarkable similarity among all four countries on the ways and means of organizing output for total war. Each country was led by a charismatic leader who held the confidence and loyalty of the citizenry and armed forces for the duration of the war. Each of these leaders found it necessary to mobilize through a series of ad hoc experiments in material allocation, rationing, labor allocation, and production management. In each instance it required between eighteen and twenty-four months to work out a production and labor allocation mechanism to achieve the highest possible output. All four countries had to rely heavily on women for large portions of the labor force, and skilled labor was always and everywhere in short supply. Lastly, each leader ended up placing the responsibility for this problem under a centralized operation with overall authority for domestic economies. America had the office of War Mobilization under James Byrnes, the British had put their resources under Sir John Anderson, and the Germans had Albert Speer. The Soviets coordinated their war economy through the Operations Bureau. The pace of the war was such that in all cases the years 1943 and 1944 marked the peak of wartime production.

The possibility of overmobilization had to be guarded against in all countries. This was a more acute problem in the Soviet Union and later in Germany as both reacted to invasions of their national boundaries. Overmobilization meant insufficient production of civilian goods in order to allow the domestic economy to successfully produce arms for the war economy. Quantity versus quality of production items was another source of friction. This was initially a concern of the British and Germans, whose industrialists had long and proud histories of producing highly specialized, finely tooled precision instruments. At some point, however, this emphasis on quality had to be tempered against the frank need to get to the front arms and munitions that worked "well enough." The Soviet Union especially relied on a policy of keeping production programs simple and well focused.

The United States, given the level of unused economic capacity available in 1940, and Great Britain, for the same reason, had the easiest time arming themselves for war. After the Battle of Britain both countries rearmed with the assurance that their national integrity was secure. Such was not the case with either Germany or the Soviet Union. Starting from much lower unemployment levels and with the threat (or actuality) of invasion looming, both of these countries needed to mobilize very intensely and rapidly. Therefore, at the peak of their efforts both had a higher proportion of national income devoted to the war effort than either the British or the Americans. Of the two the Soviets were more highly mobilized than the Germans.

BIBLIOGRAPHY

Bergson, Abram. *The Real National Income of Soviet Russia since 1928.* Cambridge, MA: Harvard UP, 1961.

Blum, Jerome. *V Was for Victory: Politics and American Culture during WWII.* New York: Harcourt Brace Jovanovich, 1976.

Burns, James M. *Roosevelt: The Soldier of Freedom.* New York: Harcourt Brace Jovanovich, 1970.

Carroll, Berenice A. *Design for Total War: Arms and Economics in the Third Reich.* The Hague, Paris: Mouton, 1968.

Catton, Bruce. *The War Lords of Washington.* New York: Harcourt, Brace, 1948.

Chandler, Lester. *Inflation in the United States, 1940–1948.* New York: Harper and Row, 1951.

Chandler, Lester, and Donald P. Wallace. *Economic Mobilization and Stabilization.* New York: Holt, 1951.

Chester, Daniel, ed. *Lessons of the British War Economy.* Cambridge: Cambridge UP, 1951.

Ellis, John. *Brute Force: Allied Strategy and Tactics in WWII.* New York: Viking; London: Deutsch, 1990.

Fearon, Peter. *War, Prosperity and Depression: The U.S. Economy 1917–1945.* Oxford, U.K.: P. Allen, 1987.

Flynn, George. *The Mess in Washington: Manpower Mobilization in WWII.* Westport, CT: Greenwood, 1979.

Goldsmith, Raymond W. "The Power of Victory: Munitions Output in WWII." *Military Affairs* (1946): 69–80.

Hancock, William K., and M. M. Gowing. *British War Economy.* London: HMSO, 1949.

Harrison, Mark. "Resource Mobilization for World War II: The U.S.A., U.K., USSR and Germany, 1938–1945." *Economic History Review* (1988): 171–92.

———. Soviet Planning in Peace and War: 1938–1945. Cambridge and New York: Cambridge UP, 1985.

Hawley, Ellis. *The New Deal and the Problem of Monopoly: A Study of Economic Ambivalence.* Princeton, NJ: Princeton UP, 1966.

Higham, Robin. "Government, Companies and National Defense: British Aeronautical Experience, 1918–1945 as the Basis for a Broad Defense." *Business History Review 37* (1963): 323–47.

———. "Quantity vs. Quality: The Impact of Changing Demand on the British Aircraft Industry, 1900–1960." *Business History Review 42* (1968): 443–66.

Janeway, Eliot. *The Struggle for Survival.* New York: Weybright and Tauey, 1951.

Kalder, N. "The German War Economy." *Review of Economic Studies 13* (1946): 33–52.

Ketchum, Richard. *Borrowed Years, 1938–1941: America on the Way to WWII.* New York: Random House, 1989.

Klein, Burton H. *Germany's Economic Preparations for War.* Cambridge, MA: Harvard UP, 1959.

————. "Germany's Preparation for War: A Reexamination." *American Economic Review 28* (1948): 56–77.

Lieberman, S. R. "Crisis Management in the USSR: The Wartime System of Administration and Control." In Susan Linz, ed., *The Impact of WWII on the Soviet Union*, 59–76. Totowa, NJ: Rowman and Allenheld, 1985.

Lingeman, Richard. *Don't You Know There's a War On? The American Home Front 1941–1945.* New York: Putnam, 1970.

Linz, Susan J. *The Impact of WWII on the Soviet Union.* Totowa, NJ: Rowman and Allanheld, 1985.

Mason, Timothy. "Labor in the Third Reich." *Past & Present 33* (1966): 112–41.

————. "Some Origins of WWII." *Past & Present 31* (1964): 67–87.

Millett, Allan, and Williamson Murray, eds. *Military Effectiveness.* Vol. 3, *World War Two.* Boston: Allen and Unwin, 1988.

Milward, Alan. "The End of the Blitzkrieg." *Economic History Review*, 2nd Series *16* (1964): 499–518.

————. *The German Economy at War.* London: Athlone, 1965.

————. *War, Economy and Society.* Berkeley: University of California, 1977.

Nelson, Don. *Arsenal of Democracy: The Story of American War Production.* New York: Harcourt Brace Jouanovich, 1946.

Overy, Richard. *The Air War, 1939–1945.* New York: Stein and Day, 1980; London: Papermac, 1987.

————. "The German Pre-War Aircraft Production Plans: 1936–1939." *English Historical Review 90* (1975): 779–83.

————. "Goring's Multi-National Empire." In A. Teichova and P. Cottrell, eds., *International Business in Central Europe 1918–1939*, 269–93. Leicester: Leicester UP, 1983.

————. "Hitler's War and the German Economy: A Reinterpretation." *Economic History Review*, 2nd Series *35* (1982): 272–91.

————. *The Nazi Economic Recovery: 1932–1938.* London: Macmillan, 1982.

————. *The Origins of the Second World War.* London and New York: Longman, 1987.

————. "Transportation and Rearmament in the Third Reich." *Historical Journal 16* (1973): 389–409.

————. *War and Economy in the Third Reich.* Oxford: Oxford UP, 1994.

Polenberg, Richard. *War and Society: The United States 1941–1945.* Philadelphia: Lippincott, 1972.

Postan, Michael. *British War Production.* London: HMSO, 1952.

Robertson, A. "Lord Beaverbrook and the Supply of Aircraft 1940–1941." In Anthony Slaven and S. Aldcroft, eds., *Business, Banking and Urban History: Essays in Honour of S. G. Checkland*, 80–100. Edinburgh: J. Donald, 1982.

Robinson, E. "The Overall Allocation of Resources." In Daniel Chester, ed., *Lessons of the British War Economy*, 34–57. Cambridge: Cambridge UP, 1951.

Schlesinger, Arthur. *The Politics of Upheaval.* Boston: Houghton Mifflin, 1960.

Schweitzer, Arthur. "Profits under Nazi Planning." *Quarterly Journal of Economics 61* (1946): 9–18.

Speer, Albert. *Inside the Third Reich: Memoirs.* New York: Macmillan, 1970.

Stein, Herbert. *The Fiscal Revolution in America.* Chicago: University of Chicago, 1969.

Thies, J. "Hitler's European Building Programme." *Journal of Contemporary History* 13 (1978): 423–34.

U.S. Bureau of the Budget. *The United States at War.* Washington, DC: GPO, 1946.

U.S. Department of Commerce. *Historical Statistics of the United States: Colonial Times to 1957.* Washington, DC: GPO, 1960.

Vatter, Hal. *The U.S. Economy in WWII.* New York: Columbia UP, 1985.

Weinberg, Gerhard. *Germany and the Soviet Union, 1939–1941.* Leiden: E. J. Brill, 1972.

22 The War and Social Change in Allied Lands, Occupied Europe, and the English-Speaking World

Loyd E. Lee

Scholarly views on the relationship between twentieth-century industrialized warfare and domestic social and political structures vary greatly. Some find little connection between the two. War and its demands are seen as a hiatus, a catastrophic interlude, to be certain, but one neither redirecting social organization nor intensifying prewar trends very much. Nonetheless, mobilizing manpower and economic resources is a key measure of a society's capacity to wage war successfully.

On the other hand, some post–World War I observers discerned war as revolutionary, to be advocated as an agent of radical change or avoided for the same reason. A similar range of opinions is reflected in the writings and research of social historians.

Finally, there is an extensive "home front" literature on "this is the way it was," evoking nostalgia for the drama and heightened sensibility of war, often at the expense of analysis and systematic investigation. Of course, the staggering loss of human lives, the tragic rending of social fabrics, and the geographic shifts in populations and state boundaries, as well as the unprecedented despoliation of centuries of accumulated wealth and cultural artifacts, are clear to everyone. People do not agree on the long-term social significance.

To some extent, all the preceding approaches were present before and during World War II, though immediate postwar historiography generally ignored social history. With the "new social history" of the 1960s and the rise of "war and society" as topics of research, historical writing tended toward closer analyses and less narration, as well as growing disagreement about the consequences of war itself. Ironically, though social historians usually downplay the central role for the state in human affairs, their research has been within the context of national societies and state-directed policies. Little comparative "home front" historiography exists, a reflection of the dissimilar experiences of war by peoples with very different social structures and political institutions, and the many difficulties of international research. Even within national societies, however, previously accepted generalizations have been questioned when matters of social class, geographic location, ethnicity, religion, and so forth are taken into account. Reflecting the state of historiography, this survey is organized by country.

THE UNITED KINGDOM

Three classic studies for a symbiosis between warfare and civil society can be found in Pitirim Sorokin's *Man and Society in Calamity*, Stanislav Andrzejewski's *Military Organization and Society*, and Richard Titmuss' *Problems of Social Policy*, a volume in the official World War II United Kingdom Civil Services Series. Sorokin's 1942 book covered the entire history of disaster during "the greatest crisis in human history" (308) to detail a long list of negative effects on culture, social structure, morality, intellectual life—indeed, all aspects of human experience. Andrzejewski's interests in 1954 were narrower, but he developed a cogent, comprehensive argument that the higher the level of military participation in a society (his military participation ratio, M.P.R.), the greater the extent of social leveling and demands for provision of benefits by the state. Titmuss linked the domestic experience of the Second World War with the advance of the welfare state. Other volumes in the Civil Services Series also covered topics relevant to the study of social history.

Titmuss' later *Essays on the Welfare State* confirmed what many opinion makers surmised during and since the war, that Britain's evacuation of civilians in 1939 from London and other possible targets of aerial bombardment, the near escape from invasion, and the shared ordeal under the blitz revolutionized the government's role in maintaining the population's health and general well-being. In this way, the war experience laid the foundations for the unexpected victory of the Labour Party (unexpected except by the Gallup pollsters) in 1945 and the transformation of wartime measures into the postwar welfare state.

These ideas were given greater scope with the various writings of the prolific Marwick, beginning in 1968 with his *Britain in the Century of Total War*, and with Calder the next year in *The People's War*. Marwick pioneered a mature social history of war (his first book was on British society in the First World War) as well as the comparative social history of war in the twentieth century in *War and Social Change in the Twentieth Century*. For World War II, see his *The Home Front*. Cautious not to be understood to make war the primary motor of social change, Marwick reiterated a decade later in a succinct summary of his approach in *Total War and Social*

Change that he viewed war as only one factor in social change, albeit one previously neglected.

In contrast to Marwick's analytic studies, with their limited interest in laying out the details of popular experience, Calder's *People's War* is an extensive trove based on a wide-ranging bibliography and primary sources, covering and interrelating almost every aspect of society during the war during all its phases. This was a war in which, as he stated, the people were the protagonists, though he concluded that war brought no basic changes in society in spite of the depth and breadth of participation in war making.

Addison's *The Road to 1945* marked a milestone similar to Marwick's. As the first comprehensive, source-based study of politics at the top, Addison detailed the wartime formation of a broad consensus between Labour and coalition Conservatives of the wartime government for a sea change in the state's relationship to citizens. Following this up in *Labour in Power*, Morgan unfolded the first scholarly study extending wartime changes into the postwar arena, though he emphasized the consensus thesis less than Addison.

More recently, Addison's interpretation has been criticized and substantially revised. Jefferys' *The Churchill Coalition and Wartime Politics* denies any wartime bipartisan consensus and notes the absence of major social legislation before 1945. Soon Brooke, having thoroughly examined archival materials for his *Labour's War*, concluded, "The Second World War was not the crucible of lasting political consensus. If such consensus existed at all, it existed after 1945, not before" (342). The revisionists, however, have by no means won the field.

By this time, the debate over consensus got embroiled in the ideological conflict of the 1980s. On the Right Barnett in *Audit of War*, a book receiving few academic plaudits, faulted the wartime coalition, among other factors, for producing unrealistic social expectations that bankrupted society and led to Britain's international decline, a theme of several of Barnett's books. A similar skeptical reception greeted Morgan and Evans, *The Battle for Britain*, who argued that far from producing socialism, wartime politics undermined the true Left and subverted significant social change.

Starting with an analysis of the government's mobilization of civilian morale, Thorpe's "Britain" rolled the consensus thesis back in time. Far from the war's producing a more unified society, he identified several public opinion indexes and other evidence indicating a high level of support for the war effort beginning in 1939, none of it produced by deliberate government morale building. British society was less divided by class before the war than observers from the Left or Right have believed. Placing less emphasis on the effect of censorship, propaganda, and the equalization of wartime burdens by things such as rationing, he argued that the absence of a wartime morale crisis needs little explanation; it largely resulted from the less than anticipated effect of bombing, restricted food supplies, and so forth. Thus, changes wrought by war "could only be limited because, in many essentials, the British people remained the same" (32).

Other studies not sitting well with consensus approaches leading to a left-liberal turn in British society and politics include Smith's *When Jim Crow Met John Bull*, which illustrates the country's first serious introduction to black people (one hundred thirty thousand African Americans) and shows the ambiguity and limitations of Allied official policies and British social tolerance. In his study of the American invasion of Britain, *Rich Relations: The American Occupation of Britain*, Reynolds detailed the full range of Anglo-American interchanges, as well as misunderstandings. In another vein, Simpson, *In the Highest Degree Odious: Detention without Trial in Wartime Britain*, revealed the unseemly confinement of British citizens (not to speak of noncitizens, many of whom were refugees from fascist states) held without trial during the first years of the war.

In an excellent summary of the main scholarship of "Great Britain: The People's War?" Harris attempts to resolve the question posed. Undaunted, she identified comprehensive changes in social administration, expanding state intervention, and disjunctures in the lives of ordinary people. Other changes did not occur or were limited, especially in the personnel of government, the employment of women, and class structure. As she also noted, more research into regional differences, the rise in antisocial behavior, and the large number of strikes will further modify the traditional interpretation of the "home front" as a unifying social force. For other recent summations, with references to more detailed studies, see Brivati and Jones, *What Difference Did the War Make?*, and Smith, *War and Social Change*, as well as the many volumes in the official civil and medical histories.

WESTERN EUROPE

Studies of Continental European wartime domestic history in English are much less available than those of Britain and the United States. Little has been done in any language to synthesize European domestic experiences during the war. Beck briefly summarized *The European Home Fronts*, based on current research (primarily in English, but also in German for Germany) within their national contexts. He includes more than domestic social and political history, however, and less from a European outlook than discrete national perspectives. The more recent *Home Fronts* does not supplant Wright's earlier excellent *Ordeal of Total War*, which, though not consciously a social history, covers the broad impact of war throughout Europe based on the even more limited research available in 1968.

France

The social history of wartime France is not well served in English, except for the resistance, collaboration, and the Holocaust. The fifteen essays in Scriven and Wagstaff's *War and Society*, for example, cover, among others, the preceding topics plus the arts and only indirectly deal with social history. Of course, the wartime discontinuities in French society do not lend themselves to the kinds of issues taken up in unoccupied Britain. Bédarida in "World War II and Social Change in France" provided a brief summary, but it is barely more than an outline. In their "France," Simmonds and Footitt rightly noted that the "creation of a home front during this short period of war . . . was a feeble thing at best" (173). It was complicated in French historiography by the resistance movement and the extent of collaboration.

Italy

Italy's wartime social experience still awaits its English-language historian, though one can reach for Tannenbaum's standard *The Fascist Experience*, which primarily covers the prewar period. While putting Italy's experience within a larger framework of the country's history, Abse's "Italy" argued that "Italy's experience in the Second World War was an extraordinary one and one in which the home front was in many ways far more important than the front line" (104). Asking good questions and utilizing Italian-language historiography, Abse packed much comparative information within a very brief space.

Lamb's *War in Italy, 1943–1945: A Brutal Story* effectively covers the domestic side of that brief chapter in Italian history, from Mussolini's ill-begotten Salo Republic to partisans, prisoners of war, and much else. The standard work on the Anglo-American occupation is Harris' *Allied Military Administration of Italy*.

Scandinavia

To make the wartime domestic experiences of Scandinavia accessible to the outside world, Nissen, *Scandinavia and the Second World War*, edited a comparative history of the very diverse experiences of Finland, Norway, Denmark, and Sweden. Each of seven historians related stories to similar themes such as politics, foreign policy, and economics, as well as resistance and liberation, but with little strictly social history.

EASTERN EUROPE

The Soviet Union

Study of society in the former Soviet Union at war has been difficult because of limited access to archives and the absence of anything more than bogus official data. Nonetheless, Linz and fifteen other distinguished scholars in *The Impact of World War II* made significant contributions to our understanding of many aspects of Soviet society, such as the economy, administration, demography, religion, the party, non-Russians, the experiences of peasants, and literature. They also delineate questions within these topics not yet answered.

Taking up themes beyond those suggested in its subtitle, Barber and Harrison's *The Soviet Home Front* draws primarily upon Russian and English secondary sources to cover party rule, the diplomatic and military background of the Great Patriotic War, and state organization. As did Linz, they concluded that the war's immediate impact was to reinforce the Soviet political system. Also see Harrison's summary, "The Soviet Union," in Noakes' *The Civilian in War*. More recently, the Garrards edited selected papers from a 1990 conference held in the United Kingdom on various aspects of Soviet wartime experience, some of which touch on specific aspects of social history. Finally, Narinsky gave a qualified yes to his question "The Soviet Union: The Great Patriotic War?" a brief summary of the country's social experiences.

Among early classics is *Russia at War* by Alexander Werth, based on his *Moscow War Diary*, published in 1942. A native of Russia whose family emigrated to England during the Russian revolution, he spent most of the war in the Soviet Union as a correspondent for Reuters and the *Sunday Times* (London). Another is the *New York Times* wartime reporter Harrison Salisbury's *The Siege of Leningrad*. He spent eight months during the war and several years afterward in the Soviet Union.

Poland

Poland, the sole European state not only occupied but ceasing to exist, had its western territories incorporated into Germany as the Wartheland. The eastern half became parts of either Ukraine or Belarus (Belorussia) until mid-1941. Gross, *Revolution from Abroad*, covered the two years of Soviet domination. A remnant under German occupation became a reservation, the General Government. A parallel study to *Revolution from Abroad* is Gross' *Polish Society under German Occupation*, a thorough examination of the strains of society under severe repression written informatively within the framework of disciplined social theory. Hanson's "Poland" summarized this still inadequately researched period and explained why that history, given the harshness of occupation, cannot be compared with that of Western belligerent societies.

Greece

Wartime Greece is well served by two recent monographs. Mazower's *Inside Hitler's Greece*, rooted in extensive German and international archival research, authoritatively penetrates relations among the ruthlessly exploitative German army, the collaborationist government, and resistance groups. Going beyond politics, he incorporated the country's social transformation. Hondros, *Occupation and Resistance: The Greek Agony*, is excellent but has less on the social impact of war and occupation.

BEYOND EUROPE

The United States

As in Britain, the study of wartime American society began during the war itself. Three early works still stand out. Francis Merrill, *Social Problems*, unlike most later researchers, worried about the negative impact of the war on family, children, crime, and antisocial behavior, themes less studied since the war. Agnes Meyer, a *Washington Post* correspondent, undertook an extensive tour of the United States in 1942 to examine the social impact of wartime mobilization. Her articles were collected in *Journey through Chaos* and republished as a book in 1944. In concluding, she asked, "Have we learned anything during this world holocaust? If so, the aftermath of this war will not be allowed to culminate in a social retreat on the home front such as took place after the last cataclysm" (361). She was also troubled by negative effects of war (especially the status of the "Negro population" and the "contradictory and indefensible attitude of our society toward childhood"). She thought it would take three generations for society to recover.

Though also researched during the war, Havighurst and Morgan's *Social History of a War-Boom Community* is more attuned to current scholarly interests. In 1942 these two University of Chicago social scientists chose to study the small town of Seneca, Illinois, whose population leaped from 1,235 to 6,600 by 1944 as the site of a shipyard manufacturing Landing ship, tank (LSTs). Their book is valuable both for its balanced conclusions and as an interesting story. Carr and Stermer's *Willow Run* remains a classic account of the best-known American defense town, built by Ford in Michigan to manufacture B-24s, using the most advanced production methods. Its more than thirty thousand workers lived in wretched, overcrowded conditions giving rise to numerous social problems. While not scholarly in approach, the twenty-four essays in Goodman's *While You Were*

Gone are very much worth reading. Written for returning veterans, it reflects the views of diverse American opinion makers and leaders as they grappled with the impact of the war.

The advent of the unexpected Cold War, the unpopular Korean War, and the divisive Vietnam War led many Americans nostalgically to internalize wartime propaganda and look back on "the good war": those who could remember had had new opportunities and better-paying jobs, and the Allies had cooperated and defeated fascism. The world's most destructive conflict and massive bloodletting became identified as America's best years, at least on the home front. Lingeman's *Don't You Know There's a War On?* (1970) reflected this mood. Perret in *Days of Sadness, Years of Triumph* wrote an early comprehensive social history in 1973, arguing that the war produced a social revolution, a watershed legitimating "modern American values and institutions" (12); it also has plenty of "this is the way it was."

The year before, Polenberg, unknown to Perret, launched the transformation of the war's American social historiography with *War and Society*, the first scholarly national survey. Polenberg, more modestly than Perret, found that "[e]verywhere the war acted as a catalyst for social change" (243). Not all domestic experiences were positive (e.g., violation of civil rights, "relocation centers," and continued racism), but many positive changes were accelerated by war. Shortly afterward Blum's *V Was for Victory* complemented Polenberg's book with a cultural history that also filled in more of the experience of Italian Americans, Japanese Americans, and American Jews, as well as African Americans. While both studies remain unchallenged in their comprehensiveness, the distance historiography has traveled since 1972 can be well measured in Winkler's brief summary in *Home Front U.S.A.* and its bibliographical essay. O'Neill's *Democracy at War* covers both the home front and the fight abroad but is stronger on the former, including home politics as well as social history.

In 1992 Polenberg revisited the American home front in "The Good War?" finding that the war in several areas of domestic affairs had undermined democracy and enhanced illiberal attitudes throughout society. Adams went further in *The Best War Ever*. Using secondary sources, he explored the extensive wartime mythmaking, still in his view the dominant popular and semiofficial view. The idea of a "good war" ignores the emotional and physical costs to veterans (whose experience of combat he vividly and caustically describes), the fiascos of the military, disease, institutional and individual racism, gender discrimination, and so on.

The preceding works attempted an overview of America at war, but many significant studies explored particular questions, often stimulated by questions raised in the pioneer studies. For example, Miller's *The Irony of Victory* used contemporary sources, archives, and interviews to conclude that the war changed little in Lowell, Massachusetts. Not only did it have no positive effect, but "Lowell . . . suggests that war actually hinders fundamental social, political and economic progress" (205). In a careful study of Connecticut with implications for national politics, Jeffries' *Testing the Roosevelt Coalition*, while acknowledging some changes, argued persuasively for a continuity in support for the Democratic Party from the 1930s to the 1948 elections.

Labor history has attracted considerable attention, but without agreement on whether the demands of war produced progress. Lipsitz in *Rainbow at Midnight: Labor and Culture in the 1940s* concluded that the war stimulated union members to seek greater social and economic equity. After the war, management and the government, as well as labor leaders, however, thwarted these ambitions. Issues of race and gender became a means of corporate domination. Lichtenstein, *Labor's War at Home*, found no progress for Congress of Industrial Organization (CIO) workers in power sharing with management as union leaders failed to advance their interests. Howell John Harris also concluded that business reasserted its authority over labor during the war in *The Right to Manage*. The retreat of liberalism as the federal government weakened its support for urban reform can also be traced in Funigiello's *The Challenge to Urban Liberalism*.

Looking at particular social classes or different regions of the country has yielded diverging perspectives. Nash, for example, found *The American West Transformed* by the experience of the war, with greater urban and regional planning as well as significant demographic, psychological, economic, and cultural changes.

Johnson's *The Second Gold Rush* centers on Oakland, California, arguing for thoroughgoing change in local society. She reviewed the literature and called for more local studies, recognizing that significant change did not occur everywhere. In "Going among Strangers: Southern Reactions to World War II," Daniel concluded that the "war sent tremors of change throughout the South . . . there would be no return to the rural South that dominated the section's history" (910–11), a theme less assertively argued in the last chapter of Tindall's *The Emergence of the New South*.

Many American state governments established commissions to document their contribution to the war effort. In addition, their archives contain much information relating not only to the government's activities but also to social and economic changes within the state and to the activities of their citizens. Among the best of those is Watters' two-volume *Illinois in the Second World War*, a sober, fact-filled account, though she refrained from drawing conclusions about the long-term impact of war. Clive's study of Michigan, *State of War*, reckoned that while this period had aspects of total war and produced government-fostered prosperity and the institutionalizing of the United Automobile Workers-CIO (UAW-CIO), it also led to suburbanization at the expense of urban centers; in most respects, the gains were ambiguous. Allen's *Hawaii's War Years* is another early authoritative, detailed account, covering domestic social and racial history.

During the fiftieth-year anniversary period (1989–1995), many American state and municipal historical societies and museums mounted exhibits and published guides or devoted issues of state history journals to the domestic side of World War II, a genre not yet studied. Readers should consult local libraries, historical societies, and museums.

Biographies of national leaders usually are of limited value for social history. An exception is James Burns' classic *Roosevelt: The Soldier of Freedom*. Even more worthwhile is Goodwin's *No Ordinary Time*, an extraordinary intertwining of two stories: American society and the life of the Roosevelts in and around the White House. The story unfolds chronologically, not topically, that is, as contemporaries experienced the times.

If American society became less liberal in general during wartime, there is little doubt that veterans received much better postwar treatment than veterans of earlier wars. *Preparing for Ulysses* by Ross explains the politics of the GI Bill of Rights, a sort of socialism for warriors, which gave veterans access to higher education, readjustment perquisites (such as unemployment benefits), cheap mortgages, and other benefits. As Olson's *The G.I. Bill* shows, these benefits transformed the lives of former soldiers as well as higher education.

The war's impact on race relations was noted during the war. Gunnar Myrdal's famous *An American Dilemma* coincided with a new surge of African-American political activism. The pace of research on the war and race relations and the civil rights movement, however, did not really get under way until the late 1960s. Wynn, *The Afro-American and the Second World War*, identified racial progress made during wartime, a progress limited, however, by the postwar contexts of African-American experiences as wartime promises remained unfulfilled or had unanticipated consequences. Migration from the rural South to wartime industrial centers exacerbated racial tensions; see especially Capeci and Wilkerson, *Layered Violence: The Detroit Rioters of 1943*.

The right to bear arms is one basis of citizenship in modern societies, hence the demand for a racially integrated military during the war. Though segregation continued until 1948, the military was the first American institution to end legal segregation, a process detailed in MacGregor's authoritative *Integration of the Armed Forces*. Modell, Goulden, and Magnusson briefly surveyed the historiography of African Americans to suggest that the important wartime changes primarily affected black soldiers, teaching them "how they might succeed in American society" (848). Reed's *Seedtime for the Modern Civil Rights Movement*, a study of the Committee on Fair Employment, shows that this, the most controversial wartime federal agency, was central to ending legal job discrimination

through its cooperation with minority groups and organizations representing their interests.

Native Americans between the 1930s and 1950s went through a turbulent period. Bernstein argued in *American Indians and World War II* that
these overlooked years marked the most profound effect of "turning
American Indians into Indian Americans" (159). She was overly optimistic
in stressing Native American integration into white society, as Holm
pointed out in "Fighting a White Man's War."

If wartime mobilization resulted in gains for some groups, it appears to
have increased repression of gays. In researching *Coming Out under Fire*,
Bérubé interviewed seventy-one gay men and lesbian veterans. He tried to
overcome the limits of anecdotal sources by examining professional psy-
chiatric journals and government reports; he concluded that homophobia
moved from informal discrimination to authorized harassment and persecution.

The impact of the war on children is imaginatively researched and dif-
ferentially presented by class, race, region, and religion in Tuttle's
"*Daddy's Gone to War.*" The war took its toll, as wartime observers had said,
but comprehensive generalizations for children as Americans cannot be
made.

Changes in sexual mores and practices associated with the war are anec-
dotally (perhaps necessarily so) taken up in Costello's *Virtue under Fire*,
which covers the United Kingdom as well as the United States.

In an interesting account based on oral histories and with a well-told
story, Bailey and Farber's *The First Strange Place* examines the cultural contacts between mainland Americans and Hawaiians, as well as those among
Americans uprooted from across the country and thrown into conflict.
While interesting reading, the evidence does not completely support their
conclusion of sweeping cultural transformation.

In sum, at this stage, it is difficult to draw firm conclusions regarding
the war and American society as a whole. Research thus far into ethnic,
gender, regional, religious, and class differences, among others, seems to
show that the domestic impact of war, while significant, does not follow
any clear universal trend.

Canada

Canada entered the war as a diverse society; for this reason the social
experience of the war also varied greatly. Indeed, Coates and Morrison in
"Forgotten Warriors" have recently argued against the view that western
Canada was not affected at all. Their *The Alaska Highway in World War II*
entered the social world of the western provinces, especially the social
interaction with Americans from the South.

In an excellent, but unfortunately rare, case study, Prymak in *Maple Leaf and Trident* examined Canada's citizens of Ukrainian descent. He detailed the distinct periods of this minority's wartime history, rent by its own political divisions (anticommunist nationalists versus communists), to examine the community's growing favorable attitude toward Britain, represented in an increased level of military participation. No similar study exists for Francophone Quebec.

Domestic politics at the federal level is well served by Granatstein's several books. His *Canada's War* is an amalgam of selections from Prime Minister Mackenzie King's extensive official diary and other documents; its theme is the growth of nationalism, and it covers the conscription crises between Anglophone Canadians (who favored it) and Francophone Quebeckers (who opposed it), as well as the wartime extension of public welfare. "The country had irrevocably changed during the 68 months that the war against Hitler had lasted" (419). Granatstein and Morton's *A Nation Forged in Fire*, in spite of its title, concentrates on men in military service, with very little on domestic social history. Douglas and Greenhous in their general summation of Canadian wartime history, *Out of the Shadows*, even in its revised edition, emphasized the need for further research. With only one chapter on the home front, they still concluded that the war did more than any previous experience to weld the country into a unified whole, in spite of the disadvantage Francophones had in the military or the internment of Japanese Canadians. Aster's *The Second World War as a National Experience* is a multinational collection of fourteen essays, with seven on Canada.

Australia and New Zealand

Hasluck's two volumes in the Australian official history on *The Government and the People* is a superb study of government, politics, and civil servants but is not a social history. For that see McKernan, *All In!* Australians initially had less interest in the Second World War than in the First World War because of its European origins and the interwar weakening of ties to Britain. McKernan, however, showed the transformations within Australia of nearly one Australian in seven serving in the armed forces and the impact of American servicemen and servicewomen (relaxation of blue laws, changes in sexual behavior, growing commercialism). Covering similar themes, Darian-Smith, *On the Home Front*, interviewed over a hundred Australians, mostly women, for her social history and history of collective memory of wartime Melbourne. De Maria additionally argued that without the war the welfare state would not have come about in Australia—a common finding in other countries but not one that has remained unchallenged. A heightened race consciousness, even hysteria, also played a large part in wartime Australian society, a theme in Saunders' "The Dark Shadow of White Australia."

CONCLUSION

Even for the historiography of those societies where the literature is rich, many topics remain to be investigated. Class relationships, especially at the regional and urban level, need further investigation, as do their comparison across societies. The same can be said of gender roles, race relations, migration, and the growth of international organizations and bureaucracies. Transnational investigations may show that the war played a significant role as incubator in synchronizing managed economies and the growth of consumerism—or the "Americanization" of the world—with the implied attendant social and cultural transformations. The answers to many of these questions involve topics discussed in several other chapters in this handbook.

Significant comparative social history of the Second World War has yet to be written, even for Europe or the industrialized countries. Noakes' *The Civilian in War* is the only work to cast a net beyond Europe and the United States but includes only Japan. In addition, the ten essays in this volume do not follow a common approach, though the stated theme is the success of belligerents in mobilizing their populations and the effects this had on civilian life. Perhaps because of the variety of national experiences, there is little to compare. In her trenchant essay on British society, Jose Harris asked whether war strengthened collectivism globally. As she noted, many Western European countries emerged from the war with mass social welfare systems, unprecedented migration, increased consumerism, and unparalleled state management of economies, though individual national differences persisted. Whether this is a consequence of the war or of other deeper developments in modern society has yet to be determined.

BIBLIOGRAPHY

Also see the chapters on "German Occupation of Europe," "Resistance Movements in Europe," "Comparative Economic Mobilization," "The Domestic Impact of War and Occupation on Germany," and "Women in World War II."

Abse, Toby. "Italy." In Jeremy Noakes, ed., *The Civilian in War: The Home Front in Europe, Japan and the U.S.A. in World War II*, 104–25. Exeter, U.K.: University of Exeter, 1992.

Adams, Michael C. C. *The Best War Ever: America and World War II*. Baltimore: Johns Hopkins UP, 1994.

Addison, Paul. *The Road to 1945: British Politics and the Second World War*. London and New York: Quartet Books, 1975.

Allen, Gwenfread E. *Hawaii's War Years, 1941–1945*. Westport, CT: Greenwood, 1950.

Andrzejewski (Andareski), Stanislav. *Military Organization and Society.* London: Routledge, 1954; Berkeley: University of California, 1968.

Aster, Sidney, ed. *The Second World War as a National Experience.* Ottawa: Canadian Committee for the History of the Second World War, 1981.

Bailey, Beth, and David Farber. *The First Strange Place: The Alchemy of Sex and Race in World War II Hawaii.* New York: Free, 1992; Baltimore: Johns Hopkins UP, 1994.

Barber, John, and Mark Harrison. *The Soviet Home Front: A Social and Economic History of the USSR in World War II.* London and New York: Longman, 1991.

Barnett, Corelli. *The Audit of War: The Illusion and Reality of Britain as a Great Nation.* London: Macmillan, 1986.

Beck, Earl R. *The European Home Fronts, 1939–1945.* Arlington Heights, IL: Harlan Davidson, 1993.

Bédarida, Francois. "World War II and Social Change in France." In Arthur Marwick, ed., *Total War and Social Change,* 79–94. New York: St. Martin's, 1988.

Bernstein, Alison R. *American Indians and World War II: Toward a New Era in Indian Affairs.* Norman: University of Oklahoma, 1991.

Bérubé, Allan. *Coming Out under Fire: The History of Gay Men and Women in World War Two.* New York: Free, 1990.

Blum, John M. *V Was for Victory: Politics and American Culture during World War II.* New York: Harcourt Brace Jovanovich, 1976.

Brivati, Brian, and Harriet Jones, ed. *What Difference Did the War Make? The Impact of the Second World War on British Institutions and Culture.* Leicester: Leicester UP; New York: St. Martin's, 1993.

Brooke, Stephen. *Labour's War: The Labour Party during the Second World War.* Oxford and New York: Oxford UP, 1992.

Burns, James M. *Roosevelt: The Soldier of Freedom, 1940–45.* New York: Harcourt Brace Jovanovich, 1970.

Calder, Angus. *The People's War: Britain, 1939–1945.* New York: Pantheon Books, 1969.

Capeci, Dominic J., Jr., and Martha Wilkerson. *Layered Violence: The Detroit Rioters of 1943.* Jackson: UP of Mississippi, 1991.

Carr, Lowell J., and James E. Stermer. *Willow Run: A Study of Industrialization and Cultural Inadequacy.* New York: Harper, 1952.

Clive, Alan. *State of War: Michigan in World War II.* Ann Arbor: University of Michigan, 1979.

Coates, Kenneth S., and William R. Morrison. *The Alaska Highway in World War II: The U.S. Army of Occupation in Canada's Northwest.* Norman: University of Oklahoma; Toronto: University of Toronto, 1992.

———. "The American Rampant: Reflections on the Impact of United States Troops in Allied Countries during World War II." *Journal of World History 2* (1991): 201–22.

———. "Forgotten Warriors: War and the Restructuring of Western Canadian Society." *Journal of the West 32* (1993): 5–8.

Costello, John. *Love, Sex, and War: Changing Values, 1939–1945.* London: Collins, 1985. Published in the United States as *Virtue under Fire: How World War II Changed Our Social and Sexual Attitudes.* Boston: Little, Brown, 1986.

Daniel, Pete. "Going among Strangers: Southern Reactions to World War II." *Journal of American History* 77 (1990): 886–911.

Darian-Smith, Kate. *On the Home Front: Melbourne in Wartime, 1939–1945.* South Melbourne, Australia: Oxford UP, 1990.

De Maria, William. "Combat and Concern; the Warfare-Welfare Nexus." *War and Society* 7 (1990): 71–86.

Douglas, William A. B., and Brereton Greenhous. *Out of the Shadows: Canada in the Second World War.* Toronto and New York: Oxford UP, 1977; rev. ed. Toronto: Dundurn, 1995.

Funigiello, Philip J. *The Challenge to Urban Liberalism: Federal–City Relations during World War II.* Knoxville: University of Tennessee, 1978.

Garrard, John G., and Carol Garrard, eds. *World War 2 and the Soviet People: Selected Papers from the Fourth World Congress for Soviet and East European Studies, Harrogate, 1990.* New York: St. Martin's; London: Macmillan, 1993.

Goodman, Jack, ed. *While You Were Gone: A Report on Wartime Life in the United States.* New York: Simon and Schuster, 1946.

Goodwin, Doris Kearns. *No Ordinary Time: Franklin and Eleanor Roosevelt: The Home Front in World War II.* New York: Simon and Schuster, 1994.

Granatstein, J. L. *Canada's War: The Politics of the Mackenzie King Government.* Toronto: Oxford UP, 1975.

Granatstein, J. L., and Desmond Morton. *A Nation Forged in Fire: Canadians and the Second World War, 1939–1945.* Toronto: Lester and Orpen Dennys, 1989.

Gross, Jan T. *Polish Society under German Occupation: The Generalgouvernement, 1939–1944.* Princeton: Princeton UP, 1979.

———. *Revolution from Abroad: Soviet Occupation of Poland's Western Ukraine and Western Belorussia.* Princeton: Princeton UP, 1988.

Hanson, Joanna. "Poland." In Jeremy Noakes, ed., *The Civilian in War: The Home Front in Europe, Japan and the U.S.A. in World War II,* 150–72. Exeter, U.K.: University of Exeter, 1992.

Harris, Charles R. S. *Allied Military Administration of Italy, 1943–1945.* London: HMSO, 1957.

Harris, Howell John. *The Right to Manage: Industrial Relations Policies of American Business in the 1940s.* Madison: University of Wisconsin, 1982.

Harris, Jose. "Great Britain: The People's War?" In David Reynolds et al., eds., *Allies at War: The Soviet, American and British Experience, 1939–1945.* New York: St. Martin's, 1994.

Harrison, Mark. "The Soviet Union." In Jeremy Noakes, ed., *The Civilian in War,* 62–79. Exeter, U.K.: University of Exeter, 1992.

Hasluck, Paul. *The Government and the People.* Vol. 1, *1939–41;* vol. 2, *1942–45.* Canberra: Australian War Memorial, 1952.

Havighurst, Robert J., and H. Gerthon Morgan. *The Social History of a War-Boom Community.* New York: Greenwood, 1968.

Holm, Tom. "Fighting a White Man's War: The Extent and Legacy of American Indian Participation in World War II." *Journal of Ethnic Studies* 9 (1981): 69–81.

Hondros, John L. *Occupation and Resistance: The Greek Agony, 1941–44.* New York: Pella, 1983.

Jefferys, Kevin. *The Churchill Coalition and Wartime Politics.* New York: St. Martin's, 1991, 1995.

Jeffries, John W. *Testing the Roosevelt Coalition: Connecticut Society and Politics in the Era of World War II.* Knoxville, TN: University of Tennessee, 1979.

Johnson, Marilynn S. *The Second Gold Rush: Oakland and the East Bay in World War II.* Berkeley: University of California, 1993.

Lamb, Richard. *War in Italy, 1943–1945: A Brutal Story.* London: John Murray and New York: St. Martin's, 1994.

Lichtenstein, Nelson. *Labor's War at Home: The CIO in World War II.* Cambridge and New York: Cambridge UP, 1982.

Lingeman, Richard R. *Don't You Know There's a War On? The American Home Front, 1941–1945.* New York: Putnam, 1970.

Linz, Susan J., ed. *The Impact of World War II on the Soviet Union.* Totowa, NJ: Rowman and Allanheld, 1985.

Lipsitz, George. *Rainbow at Midnight: Labor and Culture in the 1940s.* Champaign: University of Illinois, 1994.

MacGregor, Morris, Jr. *Integration of the Armed Forces, 1940–1965.* Washington, DC: GPO, 1981.

Marwick, Arthur. *Britain in the Century of Total War: War, Peace, and Social Change, 1900–1967.* London and Boston: Little, Brown, 1968.

———. *The Home Front: The British and the Second World War.* London: Thames and Hudson, 1976.

———. *War and Social Change in the Twentieth Century: A Comparative Study of Britain, France, Germany, Russia, and the United States.* New York: St. Martin's, 1974.

———, ed. *Total War and Social Change.* New York: St. Martin's, 1988.

Mazower, Mark. *Inside Hitler's Greece: The Experience of Occupation, 1941–1944.* New Haven, CT, and London: Yale UP, 1993.

McKernan, Michael. *All In! Australia during the Second World War.* Melbourne: Thomas Nelson Australia, 1983.

Merrill, Francis. *Social Problems on the Home Front: A Study of Wartime Influences.* New York: Harper, 1948.

Meyer, Agnes E. *Journey through Chaos.* New York: Harcourt, Brace, 1944.

Miller, Marc Scott. *The Irony of Victory. World War II and Lowell, Massachusetts.* Urbana: University of Illinois, 1988.

Modell, John, Marc Goulden, and Sigurdur Magnusson. "World War II in the Lives of Black Americans: Some Findings and an Interpretation." *Journal of American History* 76 (1989): 838–48.

Morgan, David, and Mary Evans. *The Battle for Britain: Citizenship and Ideology in the Second World War.* New York: Routledge, 1993.

Morgan, Kenneth O. *Labour in Power, 1945–1951.* New York: Clarendon, 1984.

Myrdal, Gunnar, with Richard Sterner and Arnold Rose. *An American Dilemma: The Negro Problem and Modern Democracy.* New York and London: Harper, 1944.

Narinsky, Mikhail N. "The Soviet Union: The Great Patriotic War?" In David Reynols et al., eds., *Allies at War: The Soviet, American and British Experience, 1939–1945,* 261–83. New York: St. Martin's, 1994.

Nash, Gerald D. *The American West Transformed: The Impact of the Second World War.* Bloomington: Indiana UP, 1985.

Nissen, Henrik S., ed. *Scandinavia and the Second World War.* Trans. Thomas Munch-Petersen. Minneapolis: Minnesota UP, 1983.

Noakes, Jeremy, ed. *The Civilian in War: The Home Front in Europe, Japan and the U.S.A. in World War II.* Exeter: University of Exeter, 1992.

Olson, Keith. *The G.I. Bill, the Veterans, and the Colleges.* Lexington: University of Kentucky, 1974.

O'Neill, William L. *A Democracy at War: America's Fight at Home and Abroad in World War II.* New York: Free; Toronto: Maxwell Macmillan Canada, 1993.

Perret, Geoffrey. *Days of Sadness, Years of Triumph.* New York: Coward, McCann, and Geoghegan, 1973; Baltimore: Penguin, 1974.

Polenberg, Richard. "The Good War? A Reappraisal of How World War II Affected American Society." *Virginia Magazine of History and Biography* 100 (1992): 295–322.

———. *War and Society: The United States, 1941–1945.* Philadelphia: J. B. Lippincott, 1972.

Prymak, Thomas M. *Maple Leaf and Trident: The Ukrainian Canadians during the Second World War.* Toronto: Multicultural History Society of Ontario, 1988.

Reed, Merl E. *Seedtime for the Modern Civil Rights Movement: The President's Committee on Fair Employment Practice, 1941–1946.* Baton Rouge: Louisiana State UP, 1991.

Reynolds, David. *Rich Relations: The American Occupation of Britain, 1942–1945.* New York and London: HarperCollins, 1995.

Ross, Davis R. B. *Preparing for Ulysses: Politics and Veterans during World War II.* New York: Columbia UP, 1969.

Salisbury, Harrison. *The 900 Days: The Siege of Leningrad.* New York: Harper and Row, 1969.

Saunders, Kay. "The Dark Shadow of White Australia: Racial Anxieties in Australia in World War II." *Ethnic and Racial Studies* 17 (1994): 325–42.

Scriven, Michael, and Peter Wagstaff, eds. *War and Society in Twentieth-Century France.* New York: Berg, 1992.

Simmonds, J. C., and H. Footitt. "France." In Jeremy Noakes, ed., *The Civilian in War,* 173–94. Exeter, U.K.: University of Exeter, 1992.

Simpson, A. W. Brian. *In the Highest Degree Odious: Detention without Trial in Wartime Britain.* New York: Clarendon of Oxford UP, 1991.

Smith, Graham. *When Jim Crow Met John Bull: Black American Soldiers in World War II Britain.* New York: St. Martin's, 1988.

Smith, Harold L., ed. *War and Social Change: British Society in the Second World War.* Wolfeboro, NH, and Manchester, U.K.: Manchester UP; New York: St. Martin's, 1986.

Sorokin, Pitirim A. *Man and Society in Calamity: The Effects of War, Revolution, Famine, Pestilence upon Human Mind, Behavior, Social Organization and Cultural Life.* New York: E. P. Dutton, 1942; New York: Greenwood, 1968.

Tannenbaum, Edward R. *The Fascist Experience: Italian Society and Culture, 1922–1945.* New York: Basic Books, 1972.

Thorpe, Andrew. "Britain." In Jeremy Noakes, ed., *The Civilian in War,* 14–34. Exeter, U.K.: University of Exeter, 1992.

Tindall, George B. *The Emergence of the New South, 1913–1945.* Baton Rouge: Louisiana State UP, 1970.

Titmuss, Richard. *Essays on the Welfare State*. London: Allen and Unwin, 1976.

———. *Problems of Social Policy*. London: HMSO, 1971.

Tuttle, William M., Jr. *"Daddy's Gone to War": The Second World War in the Lives of America's Children*. Oxford: Oxford UP, 1993.

Watters, Mary. *Illinois in the Second World War*. Vol. 1, *Operation Home Front*; vol. 2, *The Production Front*. Springfield: Illinois State Historical Library, 1951.

Werth, Alexander. *Moscow War Diary*. New York: A. A. Knopf, 1942.

———. *Russia at War 1941–45*. New York: E. P. Dutton, 1964.

Winkler, Allan M. *Home Front U.S.A.: America during World War II*. Arlington Heights, IL: Harlan Davidson, 1986.

Wright, Gordon. *The Ordeal of Total War*. New York: Harper and Row, 1968.

Wynn, Neil. *The Afro-American and the Second World War*. New York: Holmes and Meier; London: Elek, 1976.

23   Women in World War II

Greta Bucher

The unprecedented level of mobilization of women has given World War II a special place in the historiography of women and war. This is a diverse topic, ranging from women in the military—in combat or support positions—to the women who survived the total war experience—in the camps, in hiding, or in the resistance—to the mobilization of women on the home front and the impact of the war on sexuality and women's equality. Most of the literature concentrates on women in the United States and Western Europe, with a few works on women in the Soviet Union, Eastern Europe, Asia, and Africa. In all of these areas, however, significant gaps remain in our understanding of the impact of the war on women's lives.

WOMEN IN THE MILITARY

Much of this literature consists of a wide range of narratives, based on interviews and personal accounts of wartime experience, that do not examine critically the significance of this event either for women or for the military. Works on the American experience by Gruzhit-Hoyt (*They Also Served*, about women in military and civilian public service), Gordon ("War Stories"), Gunter (*Navy WAVE*), and Cole (*Women Pilots*, on the Women Airforce Service Pilots, WASPs) fall into this category. Granger's *On Final Approach* is one of the few books written by a participant to discuss the negative media image of women in the services, the question of women's "stealing" men's jobs, and sexism as difficulties that women faced and key reasons for the lack of recognition accorded to women pilots of World War II.

Bellafaire's short book on the *Women's Army Corps* (WACs) provides a brief overview of the creation and use of the WAC. Scharr's two-volume

Sisters in the Sky is a dry and highly factual account of the Women's Auxiliary Ferrying Squadron (WAFS) and WASPs, which contrasts sharply with Kiel's overdramatized and sentimental *Those Wonderful Women in Their Flying Machines*; neither analyzes its material. Probably the best work on the WASPs is Verges' *On Silver Wings*; based on archival research and interviews, it covers all aspects of the WASP experience, including the problems they faced with housing, uniforms, sexism, and their media image as "glamour girls." It also discusses the power struggle over who would control the women aviators. Holm's overall view of *Women in the Military* argues that the directors of the women's services believed the changes involved in permanently accommodating women were simply too great, and this, combined with a hate-mail campaign against the WACs, put off plans to extend the WAC until 1949.

None of these works systematically address issues of gender, nor do they discuss the African-American woman's role. Earley's memoir, *One Woman's Army*, and Putney's *When the Nation Was in Need* cover issues of race and gender. Putney systematically looked at the experience of African-American WACs, arguing that institutional prejudice and segregation prohibited most black women from successful careers in the army. Hartmann's larger *Home Front* deals with this issue, but the African-American women's experience in the war remains underresearched. In general, the existing literature on women in the American military provides good factual and impressionistic information on the white woman's experience that now requires analysis and comparison with other countries and other time periods to achieve a useful understanding of the impact of military service on women's place in society, issues of sexual equality, and women's ability to serve in the armed forces.

The literature on women in the services in other countries is not as plentiful but is more useful to the historian. D'Ann Campbell's comparative works "Women, Combat" and "Women in Combat" suggest that the European cultures that put women in combat did so out of necessity, in contrast with the shielded position of the United States, which refused to use servicewomen in combat. Saywell's *Women in War*, covering women in the military in Britain, France, Italy, Poland, and the Soviet Union, is largely anecdotal and has little analysis but is one of the few sources on women in the Polish and Italian resistance movements. Cottam's "Veterans of the Polish Women's Combat Battalion" gives a brief description of the creation of this battalion.

More work exists on women in the Soviet armed forces because the USSR was one of the only countries consciously and actively using women in combat roles. Cottam's translations of Soviet works on women fighter pilots, *Soviet Airwomen* and *The Girl from Kashin*, are laden with Soviet propaganda but provide a fascinating glimpse of women's experiences as combat pilots, including the problems they faced breaking into this male-dominated world. Myles' *Night Witches* provides a slightly more balanced view of the women fighter pilots' experiences but is still merely a narrative of events rather than an exploration of the issues raised by women in combat. Erikson's "Night Witches, Snipers and Laundresses" reviews the various roles that women played in the Soviet Union during the war, including their contributions to the military. Finally, Noggle's *A Dance with Death*, based on interviews with Soviet women pilots, simply narrates each woman's experience in her own words, highlighted by photographs of the women involved. Once again, the purpose of the work is not historical analysis but provision of an interesting story of women's experiences in combat.

Only a few articles explore the Soviet case with a view to analyzing its impact on the military or the society. Griesse and Harlow's "Soldiers of Happenstance" maintains that although the Soviets underplay women's involvement in combat, it is more generally recognized than in other countries. In "Russia: Revolution and War" Griesse and Stites pointed out that Soviet perceptions of women and their status in society did not dramatically change despite their combat experience.

Several works cover British women's experiences in the services, but this body of literature also suffers from a preponderance of narratives and memoirs with little or no historical analysis. The works by Taylor and Jackson, both entitled *Heroines of World War II*, provide stories about the lives of women in both military and civilian areas of war service. Escott's *Women in Airforce Blue* is a factual and impressionistic account of women's experiences in the Royal Air Force, relying on official documentary sources and interviews with women. Goldman and Stites' insightful "Great Britain" looks at women in all areas of the British military, discusses society's attitude toward these women and the concerns over their sexual morality, and investigates the problems women had in integrating into the services.

Three works provide some insight into the Canadian experience during the war. Greer's *The Girls of the King's Navy* is a memoir of the Women's Royal Canadian Naval Service. Gossage's *Greatcoats and Glamour Boots* gives a brief history of the formation of women's services and relates personal experiences of the women she interviewed, told in their voices. Pierson's much more insightful *They're Still Women After All* argues that women were kept out of combat in order to ensure their continuing subordination to the male military hierarchy. She also explored the "whispering campaign" that questioned the sexual morality of female servicewomen as well as the particular social stigma attached to servicewomen who contracted venereal disease and suggested that fears of disruption of gender roles and women's sexual independence combined to prevent women from rising in military service.

Finally, Tuten's "Germany and the Two World Wars" shows that the

Nazis' ideology of separate spheres for the sexes created an atmosphere in which women were not considered for use in combat positions until it was too late to implement the necessary changes. In a similar vein, Wiegand's "Japan: Cautious Utilization" suggests that the total absence of women in the Japanese military reflects Japan's male-dominated social structure. Both make distinct connections among political ideologies, social structures, and the possibilities for women's role in the military that merit further exploration in larger works.

The literature on women in military organizations during World War II is sketchy and often disappointing. Many of these works, by attempting only to describe and praise rather than analyze and evaluate, miss opportunities for great strides in our knowledge of women and war and specifically women in military hierarchies. Given that the Second World War formed the arena in which more women fought for their countries than ever before or since, it is surprising that this topic has not generated more interest among serious historians.

WOMEN IN THE RESISTANCE AND OCCUPIED TERRITORIES

Much of this work also falls into the memoir or narrative category, but a few historians have explored the significance of these experiences for women. Rossiter's *Women in the Resistance* and Weitz's "As I Was Then" on the French resistance make significant contributions to the history of women and war. Rossiter described the various underground movements against the Nazis and women's participation in the movements, with detailed accounts of their exploits and the impact these experiences had on women's political, social, and economic equality and family relationships. She concluded that participation in the resistance profoundly affected French attitudes toward women, as evidenced by women's suffrage and their movement into new career fields. Weitz's *Sisters in the Resistance* is an excellent combination of personal experience as narrated by the women themselves and analysis of that experience. She reached the opposite conclusion from Rossiter, claiming that the birth control pill had more impact on women's lives than did their resistance activities and arguing that contribution to the resistance had little impact on women's enfranchisement. In "Partisanes and Gender Politics" Schwartz concluded that women challenged gender roles most effectively in underground movements, but as the resistance moved above ground, they lost their combatant roles.

Works on women in other occupied territories also explore the impact of resistance activity on women's lives. In "Yugoslavia," Jancar explored the differences between male and female experiences in the resistance and concludes that the gulf between gender roles in Yugoslav society dictated what jobs women could fill in the resistance movement. In "Women in the Yugoslav," she concluded that war is a destabilizing event that may allow traditional hierarchies to break down and force women to make political choices that they had not previously considered, but peace sends politics back to the professionals and reinstates hierarchy, undermining and possibly destroying any gains women may have made. Reed's "Anti-Fascist Front" on Croatia found that while the Communist Party used the Anti-Fascist Front of Women in its resistance movement, it was not willing to tolerate the front's postwar feminist tendencies. Hart argued that traditional gender roles were altered by the participation of "Women in the Greek Resistance" but that these gains were stamped out by the civil war.

Holland and Garett's "The Skirt of Nessus" provides a fascinating demographic analysis of the class and marital status of women resistance workers in Germany and how these factors dictated the types of jobs given them. *Surviving the Fire* by Klug and *Women at War* by Sim relate less useful but quite interesting stories of German women resistance workers. Not all women resisted occupational forces, as described in White's "Prostitution, Identity, and Class Conciousness" on the impact of the British occupation of Nairobi on the types of prostitution practiced and the prostitutes themselves; White's conclusion is that the dominant form of prostitution before the war, in which women discreetly provided domestic as well as sexual services, gave way to the more public form of streetwalking. She also contended that prostitutes prospered and emerged as a petit bourgeois rather than a working-class group. These works constitute a good beginning in these fields for work on women in World War II and open the way for further exploration of the importance of women's participation in their country's liberation and the impact of that experience on their future roles in society.

PRISON CAMPS

Most of the work on women in prison camps concentrates on the European experience, but a few historians have begun working on women in Japanese camps. Rose's *Evidence Not Seen* relates her four years of incarceration in a Japanese camp, providing a unique account of the treatment of female prisoners. Warner and Sandilands' *Women beyond the Wire* is based on interviews and published memoirs. Finally, Frank on American "Army and Navy Nurses Held as Prisoners" by the Japanese merely provides information on where nurses were stationed when they were taken, without delving into the camp experience. None of these works analyze the Japanese treatment of prisoners or the impact of the camp experience on the women involved. This aspect of the war is possibly the most in need of further research.

The Holocaust presents another set of problems for historians. In "The Unethical and the Unspeakable," Ringelheim argues that historians have ignored women in their accounts of the Holocaust and calls for acknowl-edgment of the special abuses women suffered. In "Women and the Ho-locaust," she further suggests that cultural feminist interpretations of the Holocaust glorify oppression by emphasizing women's abilities to cope with the horrors of the camps. Laska's edited volume on *Women in the Resistance and in the Holocaust* contains a graphic account of Nazi atrocities in the introduction and is followed by chapters on various aspects of camp life told in the survivors' words. Despite the lack of analysis, this work provides information on women's particular experience not available else-where. In "Women and the Holocaust" Milton argued that women's link to children, the gender division of labor, different rules for men and women, and women's unique survival skills all created a camp experience significantly different for women and men. With the exceptions of Milton in "Women and the Holocaust" and Ringelheim in her "The Unethical and the Unspeakable," women's historians seem reluctant to apply the same methods of analysis to the Holocaust and prison camp experience used in other fields—perhaps from a fear of minimizing the enormity of the horror of such atrocities. Since this is surely one of the defining events of this century, its impact on the lives of not only Jewish women but also Slavic women, lesbians, and political prisoners demands attention.

SEXUALITY

Women's sexuality was also exploited by some governments during the war. The most extreme case to come to light is documented in Hicks' *The Comfort Women,* who were forced into prostitution to service the Japanese army during the war. This work explores the dynamics of race and sexual exploitation in the Japanese context and details the women's horrific ex-periences. Hillel and Henry's narrative on the Lebensborn in Germany, *Of Pure Blood,* shows how women's sexuality and childbearing capabilities were harnessed not only to ensure the future of the Aryan race but also to serve the sexual needs of select SS (Schutzstaffeln, protection squads) officers. Bock's "Racism and Sexism" delves more deeply into the issue of women's sexuality and explores the interaction of racism and sexism in the Nazi context and its impact on both Aryan and Jewish women as mothers and potential mothers, arguing that all women were profoundly affected by both ideologies. In "The Creation of a Female Assembly-Line Proletariat" Troger asserted that the Nazis used the ideology of biology in moving women around the workforce as necessary and kept women at the bottom of the hierarchy by insisting that their primary function was still motherhood. Summerfield and Crockett argued in "You Weren't Taught That with Welding" that British family and class standards were challenged when women experienced a heightened awareness of their sexuality during the war. Bailey and Farber's book on race and sex in

Hawaii, *The First Strange Place*, includes a chapter on prostitution and explores the experiences of WACs, Women Accepted for Voluntary Emergency Service in U.S. Naval Reserve (WAVES), United Service Organizations (USO) workers, and other women living in Hawaii. This work centers a good deal on the relationships—private, public, and commercial—that women experienced and the impact of the war on race relations.

A few authors have explored the issue of sexuality in the Australian context. Sturma found in "Public Health and Sexual Morality" that unequal penalties imposed on women and men for contracting and spreading venereal disease stemmed from a fear of women's increased autonomy that the war offered. In "War, Sexuality, and Feminism" Reekie examined Perth women's organizations that tried to protect women's sexuality and concluded that they were an attempt by the upper- and middle-class women to control the sexuality of the more permissive working-class women. Lake's "Female Desires" and "The Desire for a Yank" explore the relationship between the presence of American servicemen and the new understanding that women had a right to sexual expression and the emerging emphasis on youth and femininity among women.

THE HOME FRONT AND THE POSTWAR WORLD

The literature on the home front during the Second World War constitutes the bulk of scholarly work on women. The unprecedented numbers of women who entered nontraditional fields of work and the efforts of some governments to support working women have generated questions concerning the impact of war on women's status. Of course, on this topic there are the same histories based on narrative, memoir, or interview. Examples of this type of literature include works by Heacock (*Battle Stations!*), Pearsall (*Women at War*), Wise and Wise (*A Mouthful of Rivets*), and Litoff and Smith on America (*Since You Went Away*), Latta on Canada (*The Memory of All That*), Owings on Germany (*Frauen*), and Saywell on women in Britain, France, Italy, Poland, and Russia (*Women in War*).

The literature on war brides also falls into the narrative or memoir category and includes Shukert and Scibetta's *War Brides*, which concentrates on women in Europe and Britain, Winfield and Hasty's *Sentimental Journey* on both America and Britain, and Hibbert's *War Brides* on Canada. Two works on New Zealand, *Women in Wartime* by Edmond and Milward and *Girls with Grit* by Jean Scott, provide women's firsthand accounts of life during the war, with Scott concentrating solely on the Women's Land Army. These books are entertaining, with interesting information on their respective topics, but do not draw conclusions from the data they provide.

In general, historians agree that women made great strides economically and socially during the war—the debate centers on the postwar implications of these advances. In its simplest form, this topic is centered on the question, Can wartime gains have a significant and lasting impact on the status of women in society? The work on this question operates on a number of levels, ranging from purely political and economic evaluations of the war's impact on women to works that inquire into the psychological implications of wartime freedom and mobility on women's consciousness. The debate began with Chafe's *The American Woman*, which asserts that the war radically changed the economic outlook for American women by introducing them into new fields and altering the traditional ideology that prohibited married women from working. He argued that although women suffered economic losses immediately after the war, they regained ground over the next two years, and women's work became increasingly accepted as a part of middle-class life. Gluck, *Rosie the Riveter Revisited*, agreed with Chafe, arguing that the "feminine mystique" analysis blinded historians to the changes that occurred after the war; the war, she asserted, contributed to women's rising consciousness and expanded freedoms.

In *American Women in World War II*, Weatherford noted the change in the workforce as well as political participation, pointing to women's moving into white-collar jobs and the peace movement as signs of their increased importance in the public sphere. Gregory contended in *Women in Defense Work* that women made great strides during the war as well, although his conclusions are much more tenuous and less well supported. Stephenson showed that the loss of men forced women to become more emancipated in Germany during the war in "Emancipation and Its Problems." In her case study of *Women War Correspondents*, Wagner found that women reporters were given new opportunities during the war to replace men, even going to the front for news. Neither, however, examined the long-term consequences of this phenomenon.

Much of the literature takes issue with Chafe, pointing out that the forces of tradition reasserted themselves after the war. Rupp contended in *Mobilizing Women for War* that the propaganda used to mobilize German and American women was purposely designed to emphasize the temporary nature of women's war work, paving the way for women to go home as men returned to take over their jobs. In "Embattled Femininity" Pierson made a similar argument concerning the Canadian experience. Koonz pointed out in *Mothers in the Fatherland* that while Nazi propaganda emphasized traditional roles for women, women tore the family apart through their organizational activity. In addition, she argued that Nazi ideology took precedence over war needs, resulting in policies that encouraged women to stay home despite the fact that they were needed in the factories. Sachse and Caplan's "Industrial Housewives" also explored the tension between Nazi plans to keep women at home and industrial needs, concluding that women's position in the labor force changed as Germany's war needs changed. As for "Farm Women in the Third Reich,"

Lovin found that women had to assume responsibility for family farms despite the fact that the Nazis did not let them own property.

Scholars have paid most attention to American women. Honey concluded in *Creating Rosie the Riveter* that popular culture differentiated between working- and middle-class women, encouraging only middle-class women—who could return home after the war—to move outside their gender roles, but working-class women—who presented a possible continuing threat to the status quo—were kept in traditional roles. Popular culture for both groups emphasized the overriding importance of family in women's lives and thus encoded messages of women's mobility with the assumption that marriage and family were the best options for all women. Anderson's *Wartime Women* argues that society stressed women's family roles during the war, which prevented the development of a postwar legacy that would help women cope with the contradictions of postwar society, thereby limiting women's choices. In "Last Hired," she concluded the biggest benefit African-American women experienced was the move from rural southern poverty to the industrial economy but that they still occupied the lowest levels of the labor force.

Thomas describes the contributions "Rosie the Alabama Riveter" made to the war effort, consistently differentiating between white and African-American women's experiences in all areas, including work and rationing. Matsumoto explored the issue of race and gender in "Japanese American Women" during the war. In *Women at War with America* Campbell cited the lure of domesticity as the primary reason women did not take advantage of the opportunity to expand their horizons after the war. Milkman concluded in *Gender at Work* that wartime gains could not be maintained due to a conservative backlash spawned by a fear of a renewed depression. Hartmann's *Home Front* argues that while women made some progress into the public sphere—for example, gaining a permanent presence in the military—women as a group did not make great and lasting advances until the 1960s.

Many scholars have examined the British experience. Summerfield's *Women Workers* cites the resiliency of traditional assumptions about women's roles not only as the reason that women could not consolidate wartime gains but also as a limiting factor in the policies of wartime mobilization, while her articles address issues of social services, training of women workers, and the impact of mobilizing women on women's roles at home and at work. Braybon and Summerfield's *Out of the Cage* stresses the continuity over change in women's lives between 1914 and 1945. Smith in "The Problem of 'Equal Pay'" suggested that the British government opposed the equal pay campaign during the war because of fears that it would damage the war effort and concluded that the government prevented gains that might have otherwise occurred. In "The Womanpower Problem," he argued that continued postwar labor shortages prevented women from being entirely forced back into traditional roles, although the state remained dedicated to traditional sex roles. Pedersen and Sklar, "Gender, Welfare and Citizenship," found that women's social entitlements and citizenship in postwar Britain were determined not by their own needs but by their husbands' roles.

Scattered works on other societies consider the same issues. Fishman's *We Will Wait*, on Frenchwomen, asserts that the war was not liberating for women—the grinding hardship they endured resulted in a great desire to return to traditional roles after the war, despite the difficulties in doing so—and that the French government firmly supported this desire. Montgomerie, "The Limitations of Wartime Change," concluded that New Zealand women's labor force participation had limited long-term significance, especially since women were usually employed in traditional female jobs. Johnson contended in "Gender, Class and Work" that although the struggle for equal pay resulted in higher wages for Australian women, they did not achieve equal status with men, pointing out that the movement collapsed after the war. Finally, Stranahan showed in "Labor Heroines" that the women touted as labor heroines in Chinese propaganda to encourage women to increase textile production lived unusual lives, which separated them and their successes from the sphere of most textile workers.

Other authors have concentrated on the support facilities offered women to encourage them to work during the war. Carruthers maintained that British propaganda was out of step with official policy when it encouraged women into " 'Manning the Factories' " before support systems were available; it continued to encourage them to work after the state closed wartime nurseries, following the official policy that women go home. In "Minding Children" Davis argued that pressure from the conservative Catholic Church in Australia prevented the state from supplying enough nurseries to support women entering the workforce; she explored in "Jesse Street" the public discourse on child care for working mothers.

Definitions of gendered activities were one of the primary stumbling blocks to women's continued mobility after the war. In the introduction to *Behind the Lines*, Higonnet et al. portrayed war itself as a gendering activity that privileges the male realm (the front) over the female realm (the home front) and argued that wartime gains for women are encoded with subordination—they may be admitted to traditional bastions of male power, but only as long as the men are no longer the chief actors in these realms. As soon as men return from war, they reassume their old dominance in these areas, limiting and reshaping the changes in women's lives by redefining the parameters of power once again. In "The Domestic Ideal and the Mobilization of Womanpower" Allen asserted that in Britain, the state's decision to conscript only women who did not have family responsibilities allowed it to define housework as something women did for men and children, reinforcing the domestic ideal while ignoring that working-class women were always forced to work and make a home.

Riley maintained in " 'The Free Mothers' " that the pronatalist culture following the war in Britain combined with the efforts to desex the workplace, making it impossible for women to gain the social services they would need to continue working and raising children following the war. Also see her "Some Peculiarities of Social Policy." Most historians agree that the wartime changes in gender roles were severely curtailed in some way in the immediate postwar era, but the question of how these limitations emerged and how severe they were are still under consideration.

In "Rewriting History," Joan Scott recommended an agenda for studying women and war, arguing that we need

> to ask questions not about war's impact on women but about the processes of politics, connections between economic policy and the meanings of social experience, cultural representations of gender and their presence in political discourse . . . [and] questions about the representation of sexual difference . . . [that] link women's history with political history. (25)

She further suggested that it is important not only to assess how the war affected the social and political structures that influenced women's lives but also to ask what the history of women reveals about the politics of war. This is a monumental task, necessitating not only further research but the development of more sophisticated techniques of analysis that will allow a more comprehensive approach to the study of gender in history.

BIBLIOGRAPHY

Allen, Margaret. "The Domestic Ideal and the Mobilization of Womanpower in World War II." *Women's Studies International Forum 6* (1983): 401–12.

Anderson, Karen. "Last Hired First Fired: Black Women Workers during World War II." *Journal of American History 69* (1982): 82–97.

————. *Wartime Women: Sex Roles, Family Relations, and the Status of Women during World War II.* Westport, CT: Greenwood, 1981.

Bailey, Beth, and David Farber. *The First Strange Place: The Alchemy of Race and Sex in World War II Hawaii.* New York: Free, 1992.

Bellafaire, Judith A. *The Women's Army Corps: A Commemorative of World War II Service.* Washington, DC: U.S. Army Center of Military History, 1993.

Bock, Gisela. "Racism and Sexism in Nazi Germany: Motherhood, Compulsory Sterilization, and the State." In Renate Bridenthal et al., eds., *When Biology Became Destiny: Women in Weimar and Nazi Germany,* 271–96. New York: Monthly Review, 1984.

Braybon, Gail, and Penny Summerfield. *Out of the Cage: Women's Experiences in the Two World Wars.* London: Pandora, 1987.

Campbell, D'Ann. "Servicewomen of World War II." *Armed Forces and Society 16* (1990): 251–70.

———. *Women at War with America: Private Lives in a Patriotic Era.* Cambridge, MA: Harvard UP, 1984.

———. "Women, Combat, and the Gender Line." *MHQ: The Quarterly Journal of Military History 6* (1993): 88–97.

———. "Women in Combat: The World War II Experience in the United States, Great Britain, Germany, and the Soviet Union." *Journal of Military History 57* (1993): 301–23.

Carruthers, Susan L. " 'Manning the Factories': Propaganda and Policy on the Employment of Women, 1939–1947." *History 75* (1990): 232–56.

Chafe, William Henry. *The American Woman: Her Changing Social, Economic, and Political Roles, 1920–1970.* New York: Oxford UP, 1972.

Cole, Jean Hascall. *Women Pilots of World War II.* Salt Lake City: University of Utah, 1992.

Cottam, K. Jean, trans. *Soviet Airwomen in Combat in World War II.* Manhattan, KS: MA/AH, 1983.

———, ed. and trans. *The Girl from Kashin: Soviet Women in Resistance in World War II.* Manhattan, KS: MA/AH, 1984.

———. "Veterans of the Polish Women's Combat Battalion Hold Reunion." *Minerva: Quarterly Report on Women and the Military 4* (1986): 1–7.

Davis, Lynne. "Jessie Street and War-Time Child Care." *Lilith* (Australia) *6* (1989): 33–49.

———. "Minding Children or Minding Machines . . . Women's Labour and Child Care during World War II." *Labour History 53* (1987): 85–98.

Earley, Charity Adams. *One Woman's Army: A Black Officer Remembers the WAC.* College Station: Texas A and M UP, 1989.

Edmond, Lauris, and Carolyn Milward. *Women in Wartime: New Zealand Women Tell Their Story.* Wellington, NZ: Government Print Office, 1986.

Erikson, John. "Night Witches, Snipers and Laundresses." *History Today* (Great Britain) *40* (1990): 29–35.

Escott, Beryl. *Women in Airforce Blue: The Story of Women in the Royal Airforce from 1918 to Present Day.* Wellingborough, England: Patrick Stephens, 1989.

Fishman, Sarah. *We Will Wait: Wives of French Prisoners of War, 1940–1945.* New Haven, CT: Yale UP, 1991.

Frank, Mary E. V. "Army and Navy Nurses Held as Prisoners of War during World War II." *Minerva: Quarterly Report on Women and the Military 6* (1988): 82–90.

Gluck, Sherna Berger. *Rosie the Riveter Revisited: Women, the War, and Social Change.* Boston: Twayne, 1987.

Goldman, Nancy Loring, ed. *Female Soldiers—Combatants or Noncombatants? Historical and Contemporary Perspectives.* Westport, CT: Greenwood, 1982.

Goldman, Nancy Loring, and Richard Stites. "Great Britain and the World Wars." In Goldman, ed., *Female Soldiers,* 21–45. Westport, CT: Greenwood, 1982.

Gordon, Eve. "War Stories." *Minerva: Quarterly Report on Women in the Military 7* (1989): 67–89.

Gossage, Carolyn. *Greatcoats and Glamour Boots: Canadian Women at War, 1939–1945.* Toronto: Dundurn, 1991.

Granger, Byrd Howell. *On Final Approach: The Women Airforce Service Pilots of World War II*. Scottsdale, AZ: Falconer, 1991.

Greer, Rosamund "Giddy." *The Girls of the King's Navy*. Victoria, B.C.: Sono Nis, 1983.

Gregory, Chester W. *Women in Defense Work during World War II: An Analysis of the Labor Problem and Women's Rights*. New York: Exposition, 1974.

Griesse, Anne Elliot, and Margaret A. Harlow. "Soldiers of Happenstance: Women in Soviet Uniform." *Minerva: Quarterly Report of Women in the Military 3* (1985): 127–51.

Griesse, Anne Elliot, and Richard Stites. "Russia: Revolution and War." In Nancy Loring Goldman, ed., *Female Soldiers*, 61–84. Westport, CT: Greenwood, 1982.

Gruzhit-Hoyt, Olga. *They Also Served: American Women in World War II*. Secaucus, NJ: Carol, 1995.

Gunter, Helen Clifford. *Navy WAVE: Memories of World War II*. Fort Bragg, CA: Cypress House, 1992.

Hart, Janet. "Women in the Greek Resistance: National Crisis and Political Transformation." *International Labor and Working-Class History 38* (1990): 46–62.

Hartmann, Susan. *The Home Front and Beyond: American Women in the 1940s*. Boston: Twayne, 1982.

Heacock, Nan. *Battle Stations! The Homefront World War II*. Ames: Iowa State UP, 1992.

Hibbert, Joyce, ed. *The War Brides*. Toronto: P.M.A. Books, 1978.

Hicks, George. *The Comfort Women: Japan's Brutal Regime of Enforced Prostitution in the Second World War*. St. Leonards, N.S.W.: Allen and Unwin, 1995.

Higonnet, Margaret R., et al., eds. *Behind the Lines: Gender and the Two World Wars*. New Haven, CT: Yale UP, 1987.

Hillel, Mark, and Clarissa Henry. *Of Pure Blood*. Trans. Eric Mossbacher. New York: McGraw-Hill, 1976.

Holland, Carolsue, and G. R. Garett. "The Skirt of Nessus: Women and the German Opposition to Hitler." *International Journal of Women's Studies 6* (1983): 363–81.

Holm, Jeanne. *Women in the Military: An Unfinished Revolution*. Novato, CA: Presidio, 1982.

Honey, Maureen. *Creating Rosie the Riveter: Class, Gender and Propaganda during World War II*. Amherst: University of Massachusetts, 1984.

Jackson, Robert. *Heroines of World War II*. London: A. Parker, 1976.

Jancar, Barbara. "Women in the Yugoslav National Liberation Movement: An Overview." *Studies in Comparative Communism 14* (1981): 143–64.

———. "Yugoslavia: War of Resistance." In Nancy Loring Goldman, ed., *Female Soldiers*, 85–106. Westport, CT: Greenwood, 1982.

Johnson, Penelope. "Gender, Class and Work: The Council of Action for Equal Pay and the Equal Pay Campaign in Australia during World War II." *Labour History* (Australia) *50* (1986): 132–46.

Kiel, Sally van Wagenen. *Those Wonderful Women in Their Flying Machines*. New York: Rawson, Wade, 1979.

Klug, Lilo, ed. *Surviving the Fire: Mother Courage and World War II*. Seattle: Open Hand, 1989.

Koonz, Claudia. *Mothers in the Fatherland: Women, the Family and Nazi Politics.* New York: St. Martin's, 1987.

Lake, Marilyn. "The Desire for a Yank: Sexual Relations between Australian Women and American Servicemen during World War II." *Journal of the History of Sexuality* (Australia) *2* (1992): 621–33.

———. "Female Desires: The Meaning of World War II." *Australian Historical Studies 24* (1990): 267–84.

Laska, Vera. *Women in the Resistance and in the Holocaust: The Voices of Eyewitnesses.* Westport, CT: Greenwood, 1983.

Latta, Ruth, ed. *The Memory of All That: Canadian Women Remember World War II.* Burnstown, Ontario: General Store, 1992.

Litoff, Judy Barrett, and David C. Smith, eds. *Since You Went Away: World War II Letters from American Women on the Homefront.* New York: Oxford UP, 1991.

Lovin, Clifford R. "Farm Women in the Third Reich." *Agricultural History 60* (1986): 105–23.

Matsumoto, Valerie. "Japanese American Women during World War II." *Frontiers 8* (1984): 6–14.

Milkman, Ruth. *Gender at Work: The Dynamics of Job Segregation by Sex during World War II.* Urbana: University of Illinois, 1987.

Milton, Sybil. "Women and the Holocaust: The Case of German and German-Jewish Women." In Renate Bridenthal et al., eds., *When Biology Became Destiny: Women in Weimar and Nazi Germany,* 297–333. New York: Monthly Review, 1984.

Montgomerie, Deborah. "The Limitations of Wartime Change: Women, War and Work in New Zealand." *New Zealand Journal of History 23* (1989): 68–86.

Myles, Bruce. *Night Witches: The Untold Story of Soviet Women in Combat.* Novato, CA: Presidio, 1981.

Noggle, Anne. *A Dance with Death: Soviet Airwomen in World War II.* College Station: Texas A and M UP, 1994.

Owings, Alison. *Frauen: German Women Recall the Third Reich.* New Brunswick, NJ: Rutgers UP, 1993.

Pearsall, Phyllis. *Women at War.* Aldershot, Hants: Ashgate Editions, 1990.

Pedersen, Susan, and Kathryn Kish Sklar. "Gender, Welfare and Citizenship in Britain during the Great War." *American Historical Review 95* (1990): 985–1006.

Pierson, Ruth Roach. "Embattled Femininity: Canadian Women and the Second World War." In T. G. Fraser and Keith Jeffrey, eds., *Men, Women and War,* 195–210. Dublin: Lilliput, 1993.

———. *They're Still Women After All: The Second World War and Canadian Womanhood.* Toronto: McClelland and Stewart, 1986.

Putney, Martha S. *When the Nation Was in Need: Blacks in the Women's Army Corps during World War II.* Metuchen, NJ: Scarecrow, 1992.

Reed, Mary E. "The Anti-Fascist Front of Women and the Communist Party in Croatia: Conflict within the Resistance." In Tova Yedlin, ed., *Women in Eastern Europe and the Soviet Union,* 128–39. New York: Praeger, 1980.

Reekie, Gail. "War, Sexuality, and Feminism: Perth Women's Organisations, 1938–1945." *Historical Studies* (Australia) *21* (1985): 576–91.

Riley, Denise. " 'The Free Mothers': Pronatalism and Working Women in Industry at the End of the Last War in Britain." *History Workshop Journal 11* (1981): 59–118.

———. "Some Peculiarities of Social Policy concerning Women in Wartime and Postwar Britain." In Margaret Randolph Higonnet et al., eds., *Behind the Lines: Gender and the Two World Wars*, 260–71. New Haven, CT: Yale UP, 1987.

Ringelheim, Joan. "The Unethical and the Unspeakable: Women and the Holocaust." *Simon Wiesenthal Center Annual 1* (1984): 69–87.

———. "Women and the Holocaust: A Reconsideration of the Research." *Signs 10* (1985): 741–61.

Rittner, Carol, and John K. Roth, eds. *Different Voices: Women and the Holocaust.* New York: Paragon House, 1993.

Rose, Darlene Deibler. *Evidence Not Seen: A Woman's Miraculous Faith in the Jungles in World War II.* San Francisco: Harper and Row, 1990.

Rossiter, Margaret L. *Women in the Resistance.* New York: Praeger, 1986.

Rupp, Leila J. *Mobilizing Women for War: German and American Propaganda, 1939–1945.* Princeton: Princeton UP, 1978.

Sachse, Carola, and Jane Caplan. "Industrial Housewives: Women's Social Work in the Factories of Nazi Germany." *Women and History* (1987): 1–97.

Saywell, Shelley. *Women in War.* New York: Viking, 1985.

Scharr, Adela Riek. *Sisters in the Sky.* Vol. 1, *The WAFS*; vol. 2, *The WASP.* St. Louis, MO: Patrice, 1986.

Schwartz, Paula. "Partisanes and Gender Politics in Vichy France." *French Historical Studies 16* (1989): 126–51.

Scott, Jean. *Girls with Grit: Memories of the Australian Women's Land Army.* Sydney: Allen and Unwin, 1986.

Scott, Joan W. "Rewriting History." In Margaret Randolph Higonnet et al., eds., *Behind the Lines: Gender and the Two World Wars*, 21–30. New Haven, CT: Yale UP, 1987.

Shukert, Elfrieda Berthiaume, and Barbara Smith Scibetta. *War Brides of World War II.* New York: Penguin, 1988.

Sim, Kevin. *Women at War: Five Heroines Who Defied the Nazis and Survived.* New York: Morrow, 1982.

Smith, Harold L. "The Problem of 'Equal Pay for Equal Work' in Great Britain during World War II." *Journal of Modern History 53* (1981): 652–72.

———. "The Womanpower Problem in Britain during the Second World War." *The Historical Journal 27* (1984): 925–46.

Stephenson, Jill. "Emancipation and Its Problems: War and Society in Wurtemburg." *European History Quarterly* (Great Britain) *17* (1987): 345–65.

Stranahan, Patricia. "Labor Heroines of Yen'an." *Modern China 9* (1983): 228–52.

Sturma, Michael. "Public Health and Sexual Morality: Venereal Disease in World War II Australia." *Signs 13* (1988): 725–40.

Summerfield, Penny. "What Women Learned from the Second World War." *History of Education* (Great Britain) *18* (1989): 213–29.

———. "Women in the Two World Wars." *Historian* (Great Britain) (1989): 3–8.

———. "Women, Work and Welfare: A Study of Child Care and Shopping in Britain in the Second World War." *Journal of Social History 17* (1983): 249–70.

————. *Women Workers in the Second World War: Production and Patriarchy in Conflict.* Beckenhelm, England: Croom Helm, 1984.

Summerfield, Penny, and Nicole Crockett. "You Weren't Taught That with Welding: Lessons in Sexuality in the Second World War." *Women's History Review* (Great Britain) (1992): 435–54.

Taylor, Eric. *Heroines of World War II.* London: R. Hale, 1991.

Thomas, Mary Martha. "Rosie the Alabama Riveter." *Alabama Review 39* (1986): 196–212.

Troger, Annemarie. "The Creation of a Female Assembly-Line Proletariat." In Renate Bridenthal et al., eds., *When Biology Became Destiny: Women in Weimar and Nazi Germany*, 237–69. New York: Monthly Review, 1984.

Tuten, Jeff M. "Germany and the Two World Wars." In Nancy Loring Goldman, ed., *Female Soldiers*, 47–60. Westport, CT: Greenwood, 1982.

Verges, Marianne. *On Silver Wings: The Women Airforce Service Pilots of World War II, 1942–1944.* New York: Ballantine, 1991.

Wagner, Lilya. *Women War Correspondents of World War II.* New York: Greenwood, 1989.

Warner, Lavinia, and John Sandilands. *Women beyond the Wire: A Story of Prisoners of the Japanese, 1942–1945.* London: Michael Joseph, 1982.

War Wives: A Second World War Anthology. London: Grafton, 1989.

Weatherford, Doris. *American Women in World War II.* New York: Facts on File, 1990.

Weitz, Margaret Collins. "As I Was Then: Women in the French Resistance." *Contemporary French Civilization 10* (1986): 1–19.

————. *Sisters in the Resistance: How Women Fought to Free France, 1940–1945.* New York: J. Wiley, 1995.

White, Luise. "Prostitution, Identity, and Class Consciousness in Nairobi during World War II." *Signs 11* (1986): 255–73.

Wiegand, Karl L. "Japan: Cautious Utilization." In Nancy Loring Goldman, ed., *Female Soldiers*, 179–88. Westport, CT: Greenwood, 1982.

Winfield, Pamela, and Brenda Wilson Hasty. *Sentimental Journey: The Story of the GI Brides.* London: Constable, 1984.

Wise, Nancy Baker, and Christy Wise. *A Mouthful of Rivets: Women at Work in World War II.* San Francisco: Jossey-Bass, 1994.

24 Refugees, Displaced Persons, and Migration as a Consequence of World War II

Otto B. Burianek

THE SECOND WORLD WAR AND THE MOVEMENT OF PEOPLES

The Second World War brought about uprooting of populations on an unprecedented scale. German and Soviet offensives in 1939 and 1940 produced waves of refugees in rapid succession. Then came the deportations of civilians from the occupied countries into the Reich, particularly after the Axis campaigns in the Balkans and the Soviet Union, and impressment of millions of Allied prisoners of war. Added to this were the mass evacuations of Jews from all the territories occupied by the Axis to forced labor camps and extermination camps in the East, the Final Solution. During 1944 and 1945 millions more refugees fleeing the advancing Red Army streamed into Germany, where ten million foreign laborers competed with the native population for food and shelter. According to Malcolm Proudfoot, some sixty million European civilians had been forcibly removed from their homes by reason of the conflict. This number exceeds by tenfold that produced by the First World War. It is not certain whether this sum includes all those who fled fascism in Italy, Spain, and Greater Germany before the war and the millions of ethnic Germans expelled from Eastern Europe after the war. An inestimable number of Chinese, Koreans, and Southeast Asians were driven from their homes by the invading Japanese. When historians consider this, they must reckon that the full extent of the world refugee phenomenon caused by this war may never be known.

In the course of the twentieth century the refugee has become a persistent problem in international relations. For the first time in history the community of sovereign states has had to deal with massive waves of homeless people in permanent exile, and to this day they are unable to offer lasting refuge to all who seek it. Without a doubt the rise of fascism in Europe and the resultant Second World War played a major role in this historical development. In the 1930s Nazism produced refugees in numbers that far exceeded the capacity of the Office of the League of Nations High Commissioner for Refugees as well as private relief societies. The governments of the Western nations were therefore compelled to regard refugees no longer as a temporary problem resulting from specific conflicts; in 1938 they established the Intergovernmental Committee on Refugees, the first permanent organization to provide them aid and protection. During the war the Western Allies gave their military forces the responsibility for the care and repatriation of millions of deportees found in liberated territories, a significant expansion of the military mission for both theater and field commanders. After the war the West ceased to categorize the homeless by national or ethnic origin and adopted a new broader definition of refugee as any person seeking refuge from war or persecution. Furthermore, in its postwar confrontation with the communist bloc, the West learned no longer to entrust the care of refugees to organizations whose ability to respond was stymied by policies of the governments of member states that were producing refugees; instead, they created new organizations that retained a greater freedom of action.

The Second World War also produced the twentieth-century neologism "displaced person." The term originated in the discourse of research and planning for postwar refugee relief carried on by the governments of the Western Allies. The first comprehensive survey of Europe's demographic disruption was *The Displacement of Population in Europe*, published in 1943 by Eugene M. Kulischer, a researcher with the International Labour Office. Kulischer described displacement to include German colonists settled in countries occupied by the Axis, non-Germans who fled their homes or were forcibly deported, and non-Germans recruited for work or military service by the Axis. It is likely that Kulischer's work introduced the term "displaced person" and its abbreviation "DP" into the international vocabulary.

The term received its working definition from military staffs in England planning the Allied invasion of Western Europe. It is important to note the distinction crafted by the officers at Supreme Headquarters, Allied Expeditionary Forces SHAEF. *Refugees* were defined as uprooted persons found within the boundaries of their country of origin. *Displaced persons*, as expressed in an Allied directive issued to the field forces on November 18, 1944, were "civilians outside the national boundaries of their country by reason of the war, who are desirous but unable to return home or find homes without assistance, or [in the case of citizens of enemy or ex-enemy states] to be returned to enemy or ex-enemy territory." This terminology enabled the Allied armies to designate the latter people as those whom they were obliged by wartime pledges to aid and repatriate, as distinct from those whose care could be assumed by the restored governments of liberated countries. Clearly, these terms were fashioned to suit the military mission during and immediately after hostilities, which did not envision care for permanent exiles. But after the war many displaced persons declined repatriation and accepted their domicile in the DP camps as indefinite refuge. Inevitably, the terms came to be used interchangeably and were often confused. In the western occupation zones of Germany and Austria the appellation "DP" became a coveted designation, for it made the bearer eligible for Allied aid and protection. By mid-1946 there were in western Germany over a million exiles designated as DPs by military governments but who were in fact refugees awaiting permanent settlement.

SURVEY OF SIGNIFICANT WORKS

During and immediately after the war the discussion on the refugee and displaced persons problem spawned a large literature, the bulk of which consists of descriptive accounts by eyewitnesses, contemporary surveys of the disposition of refugees throughout Europe or the world (usually commissioned by some agency), some organizational histories, and a large number of journal articles on specialized subjects, such as medical care and child welfare. Few works deal comprehensively with refugees, displaced persons, and migration during and after World War II. The subject is vast and exceedingly complex. Fortunately, some scholars have attempted to relate and document the history of European refugees in its entirety, and a number of others have produced studies of some of its major aspects. Several excellent works can therefore be recommended here. This chapter offers a selective overview of the literature deemed of interest to students of the history of the war. It omits personal narratives and works treating specialized topics; readers wishing to read such works can consult several bibliographies cited later. Except for a few essential works in foreign languages, this purview is confined to works published in the English language.

One may best begin with Michael Marrus' *The Unwanted. European Refugees in the Twentieth Century*. This survey begins with events in the 1880s and proceeds through the Cold War years. The refugee problem produced by World War II is very well explained within this longer span of time, during which refugees became a persistent international issue. Marrus' work focuses upon the evolution of the concept of refugee, the impact of refugee movements on the relations between sovereign states, and the development of the various international agencies founded to aid refugees.

Refugees and Displaced Persons

The welter of migrations, flights, deportations, expulsions, and transfers during the 1930s and 1940s wrought profound changes upon the demographic map of Europe. There are several competent studies commissioned by various national and international bodies in an effort to come to grips with this complex train of events. A description of the situation before the outbreak of the war in Europe is presented in *The Refugee Problem*, a study commissioned by the Royal Institute of International Affairs in 1939 and edited by Sir John Hope Simpson. During the war the International Labor Office took an active interest in the enormous foreign labor program in the Reich; under its auspices Eugene Kulischer produced the aforementioned work *The Displacement of Population in Europe*. This work not only helped popularize the term "displaced person" but also proposed that the liberating armed forces should carry out mass repatriation as soon after the war as practicable as the essential first stage in European recovery. *The Jewish Refugee*, published in 1944 by Arieh Tartakower and Kurt Grossmann, was the first attempt to give a systematic account of the uprooting of the Jewish communities in Europe. Sponsored by the American Jewish Congress, this work utilized an extensive gathering of sources, listed in the bibliography, to take stock of the crisis confronting world Jewry and to propose solutions. It correctly predicted that, for a variety of reasons, the majority of Jewish refugees would not be successfully repatriated to their countries of origin and proposed a number of likely countries and regions of reception, principally Palestine.

In his 1948 work *Europe on the Move: War and Population Changes 1917–1947*, Eugene Kulischer advanced the idea that since the fall of the Roman Empire the prolific Germanic peoples have striven to colonize the East, and the equally fecund Slavic peoples have been pressing westward. The outcome of the Second World War was the almost complete reversal of the Germanic *Drang nach Osten* and the subsequent spread of the "Slavonic settlement area" into Central Europe. To substantiate his thesis he produced a detailed account of Europe's shifting population currents. The Rockefeller Foundation funded a project more ambitious in its scope, if not its theoretical conclusions; a team of investigators under Vernant published in 1953 *The Refugee in the Post-War World* as the first "survey of the number, location and condition of refugees in all parts of the globe." It also traces the history of several international organizations to aid these peoples. The refugee flow provoked by the Soviet repression in Hungary occasioned the publication in 1957 of *Refugee and the World Community* by John Stoessinger. The author devotes much effort to yet another current survey of the situation but is mainly concerned with the persistence of the refugee problem and the apparent inability of international organizations to cope with it. If one theme in all these works can be pointed out, it is the inability of experts to propose effective responses to the worsening refugee plight, now obtaining throughout Africa and Asia.

While international researchers far removed from the situation struggled to comprehend the swelling scene, the Allied armed forces confronted the catastrophe firsthand and made the first concrete efforts to relieve misery on a gigantic scale. Some of the most profitable reading for students of this subject can be found in books dealing with the activities of the occupation forces. One can begin with two publications of the U.S. Army's Office of the Chief of Military History. A work edited by Coles and Weinberg, *Civil Affairs: Soldiers Become Governors*, reproduces military correspondence on a number of aspects of civil affairs, including the care of displaced persons in Italy and Germany. Ziemke's *The U.S. Army in the Occupation of Germany, 1944–1946* records the development of the army's postwar mission and its performance during the early occupation period. It describes activities throughout the entire chain of command, from the War Department down to the tactical units and military government detachments in the field, and is indispensable in showing the evolution of directives governing the army's work with displaced persons.

The Allied governments did not intend for the armed forces alone to care for the DPs. They were to be assisted by the United Nations Relief and Rehabilitation Administration (UNRRA), an international organization chartered in November 1943 to undertake reconstruction in liberated countries. After the first six months of the posthostilities period, UNRRA was to assume full responsibility for all remaining DPs, but it suffered from many organizational weaknesses and was unable to fulfill its mission. It also was torn by disagreements between the Western and the Soviet governments over many issues, such as the care for DPs who declined repatriation, and in 1947 it was dissolved, an early victim of the Cold War. Its work with the DPs was taken up by the International Refugee Organization. In Germany and Austria, where most of the nonrepatriable DPs remained, the military continued its role as guardian until 1949. Despite its checkered career, UNRRA provided many valuable services during its short existence; this story is well set forth in *UNRRA: The History of the United Nations Relief and Rehabilitation Administration*, the three-volume official history edited by Woodbridge.

If a single work should be offered here as the best study on the refugee problem during and after World War II, it would be Malcolm Proudfoot's *European Refugees*. A population geographer by training, Proudfoot served in the Reports and Analysis section of the Displaced Persons Branch of the G-5 Section at SHAEF. This position gave him a unique vantage point from which to observe and record the armed forces' initial encounter with the hordes of uprooted peoples. It surveys the refugee problem in all of its important aspects: wartime movements, escapes and migrations, preparations of the military to deal with the enormous DP problem in Europe, and the establishment of UNRRA. Proudfoot discusses the manifold difficulties associated with civilian relief in areas devastated by war and the armies' extraordinary feat of repatriating ten million displaced persons. He also devotes a chapter each to Jewish postwar refugees in Allied occupied territory and to ethnic German refugees, the expellees. It remains the best English-language source on Europe's war refugees, particularly the response of the Allied military to their plight.

The 1967 book *While Six Million Died* by journalist Arthur Morse was the first substantial study of what would become the most controversial aspect of the history of refugees in the Second World War, the failure of the Western countries, particularly Britain and the United States, to provide haven for European Jews during the Holocaust. Morse criticized the American people for their inaction and blamed certain government officials for refusing to relax restrictions on immigration. The following year David Wyman published *Paper Walls*, which discussed American's response to the growing plight of European Jewry from 1938 to 1941. The effects of the depression engendered a "popular hostility" against foreigners in general and Jews in particular; these "antialien emotions" prevailed among the public and Congress and discouraged government officials from taking stronger measures. In a 1970 study entitled *The Politics of Rescue*, Feingold focused upon Assistant Secretary of State Breckinridge Long; anti-Semitism motivated his stubborn refusal to issue more visas to European Jews seeking refuge in America.

In *No Haven for the Oppressed* Friedman argued that American inaction resulted not as much from antiforeign sentiment or anti-Semitism as from a preoccupation with unemployment and, later, the rigors of global war. This book caused other scholars to consider the many factors that influenced policy before and after America's entry into the war, as well as the weakness of American Jewish leaders in dealing with the emergency. This more sophisticated approach is reflected in Wyman's sequel, *Abandonment of the Jews*. With meticulous research he recorded the reaction of the executive branch, Congress, the media, and many private organizations. Anti-Semitism remained an important cause, in particular the much more prevalent "passive anti-Semitism" that caused so many people to look the other way. But he also blamed the mass media for failing to trust the reports of the atrocities in Poland and arouse public attention and the leaders of American Jewish organizations who allowed feuds to frustrate concerted action.

After the United States, Great Britain was in the most advantageous position to help the Jews. In April 1943 British and American officials held a secret conference in Bermuda on the refugee problem. The declaration issued afterward promised no strong action and brought much criticism to both governments. Wasserstein added to the public's knowledge in his work *Britain and the Jews of Europe* by using recently released

Foreign Office documents relating to the Bermuda conference. Britain stood in far greater danger of defeat than the United States and devoted a greater share of its resources to the war effort; these considerations tended to overshadow initiatives to help refugees. Yet the number of Jewish war refugees accepted by Britain was far larger in proportion to its native population than that taken in by the United States.

There are studies of the responses of other Allied countries to the Holocaust. The Canadian government appears to have maintained the most explicitly anti-Semitic refugee policy, as shown in Abella and Troper's *None Is Too Many*. One can make further comparison by reading Haesler's *The Lifeboat Is Full*, which deals with Switzerland; Avni's *Espana, Franco y los Judios*; and Morley's *Vatican Diplomacy and the Holocaust*.

Many thousands of Axis troops and auxiliaries captured by the Western Allies were found to be Soviet citizens. In addition millions of Soviet civilians and prisoners of war (POWs) were in forced labor in the Reich. At the Yalta Conference in February 1945 the American and British governments pledged to assemble and repatriate all Soviet citizens. But many of these Soviet citizens, particularly those who had entered the ranks of the Wehrmacht to fight against Stalin's regime, preferred death to return. The attempts by the American and British armies to fulfill this agreement produced some of the most sordid episodes of the war. In 1973 Epstein, a researcher with the Hoover Institution, published *Operation Keelhaul*; he campaigned for years for the release of classified documents. Many of the key documents were, in fact, made available by 1972, but not in time to benefit Epstein's book, which suffers from many errors of fact and omission.

In contrast to Epstein's impassioned exposé, Bethell's *The Last Secret* shows more understanding of how leaders in wartime make decisions. It tells a grim story, principally of the role of the British government and activities of British forces in southern Austria, but it, too, has several gaps. Tolstoy's *The Secret Betrayal* sought to bear witness to all known episodes of forced and violent repatriation; it is a severe indictment of His Majesty's government and documents some cases of appalling duplicity. *Pawns of Yalta* by Elliott is based on an enormous collection of sources and is as thorough an account on the American side as is likely to be written.

The best scholarship on displaced persons has come out of the Federal Republic of Germany in the 1980s. Jacobmeyer's *Vom Zwangsarbeiter zum Heimatlosen Auslaender* is the first academic analysis devoted entirely to the subject of displaced persons. It was received in 1985 as a pioneering work. It treats the policies pursued in all three Western occupation zones and in other respects supersedes the work by Proudfoot, Ziemke, and others by drawing upon a large volume of untapped archival sources. It remains the most authoritative reference on this subject in any language.

Jacobmeyer published an English-language summation of his research in Rystad's *The Uprooted. Forced Migration as an International Problem in the Postwar Era.* Other essays dealing with displaced persons can be found in Bramwell's *Refugees in the Age of Total War,* a result of a 1985 symposium cosponsored by the Refugee Documentation Project of York University, Canada, and the Refugee Studies Programme of Oxford University. Many of the papers describe how the DPs were swept up in the political turbulence of the early postwar period, as seen, for example, in the efforts of the Ukrainians to evade forced repatriation and the recruitment of Poles as military auxiliaries. Mark Wyman's *DP. Europe's Displaced Persons, 1945–1951* affords insight into the dreary existence of the DPs in postwar Europe and lists many primary sources in its bibliography.

The majority of the displaced persons under Allied care were forced laborers during the war. To understand the mentality of the postwar DP and the problems of long-term care confronted by military government, one should study the history of Nazi Germany's foreign labor program, particularly the conditions under which foreign workers lived. The outstanding work on this subject by far is Herbert's *Fremdarbeiter: Politik und Praxis.* After the Soviet citizens and the Poles, the largest group under the foreign workers was the French; their story is recorded in Evrard's *La Déportation des Travailleurs Français dans le IIIe Reich.* Those who read neither German nor French can rely on Homze's *Foreign Labor in Nazi Germany;* although dated in some respects, it has much valuable information on the hard existence of Germany's foreign workers, information culled from the reports of the U.S. Strategic Bombing Survey. Readers can also benefit from Herbert's more recent *History of Foreign Labor in Germany,* a survey that condenses the author's pathbreaking research and places Germany's wartime experience within the context of that country's continuing effort to meet its shortage of labor.

European Migration Resulting from the Second World War

Migration is generally defined as the movement of people from one place to settle in another. It is not always easy to distinguish migrants from refugees in this period, as so many migrations were forced. The relatively free emigration of peoples from Europe at the turn of the century had become a thing of the past, and beginning in the 1920s immigration to the New World, America in particular, came under increasingly heavy restrictions. After 1939 nations were motivated by wartime conditions and security considerations to curtail free migration even further. The trend seen here is clear: while the freedom of the individual to move and resettle was disappearing, the totalitarian state asserted its power to move masses of people by force. Flight and deportation and the lot of the refugee and displaced person have already been discussed. With respect to migration, the Second World War presents the example of the population transfer and population exchange.

An important part of Hitler's New Order was the redrawing of the ethnic map of Central and Eastern Europe. The Nazis pursued an ambitious program by which far-flung German settlements in the East were brought "home into the Reich," into territory newly annexed from Poland. There were also some exchanges with Ukrainians and Baltic peoples. These movements, as well as others not involving Germans, are recorded one by one in Schechtman's *European Population Transfers.* Many of these actions were arranged by treaty, imitating the 1921 exchange of population between Greece and Turkey. The author made the observation, so ominous now in hindsight, that European national leaders, frustrated with the failure of the League of Nations, could resort with increasing frequency to the population transfer or exchange to solve their problems with ethnic minorities.

In 1946, when Schechtman's book appeared, the world was already witnessing the reversal of centuries of Germanic colonization to the east and the expansion of Soviet power, as described by Kulischer. The most important element of this postwar migration was the forced removal of the ethnic German minorities from Czechoslovakia and Poland. Most of those Germans who had not already fled before the advancing Red Army into the Reich were systematically expelled; they came to be known as the *Heimatvertriebene* (persons expelled from their homelands).

An estimated twelve million persons were removed into occupied Germany. Unlike the DPs, the expellees received no assistance from the Allies and had to turn to the overtaxed local governments. These transfers had been given international sanction at the Potsdam Conference; although the Allies had called for the movements to be carried out in an "orderly and humane" manner, they could not possibly regulate the transfer of millions of people in the short span of time provided. There were many cases of atrocities and acts of revenge. De Zayas' *Nemesis at Potsdam* first appeared in 1977; in its third revised edition, it remains the most accessible scholarly study in English to document this tragic event.

Other forced population transfers are those of Poles and Ukrainians living in the areas of eastern Poland, such as Galicia, annexed by the Soviet Union, and Ukrainians living in postwar Poland, as well as Hungarians living in Transylvania who were pressured to leave after the area was annexed by Romania. These and other migrations are described in Schechtman's *Postwar Population Transfers in Europe, 1945–1955.*

The memory of the Holocaust summons the image of East European Jewish communities isolated and helpless before the Nazi invaders. But several thousand Jews found refuge in the Soviet Union, and some hardy souls caught in Poland were able to evade extermination and fight on. As the prospect of help from the Allies became more unlikely, Jewish partisans devised escape routes leading out of Europe. These routes later became the pathways to Palestine. Many Jews were received into the U.S. zone of Germany as displaced persons, to obtain food, clothing, and shelter while awaiting the chance to quit Europe altogether. Others migrated through Austria to camps in Italy or left by routes through Bulgaria to the Black Sea. Several books document this remarkable story, among them Yehuda Bauer's *Flight and Rescue: BRICHAH*, the Kimches' *Secret Roads*, and *Underground to Palestine*, a memoir recording the observances of the journalist I. F. Stone during his travels in Germany in 1946. Another journalist, Tad Szulc, published *The Secret Alliance* on the role played by the American Jewish Joint Distribution Committee and the Hebrew Sheltering and Immigrant Aid Society.

This migration is noteworthy in the history of the immediate postwar period, for it took place in defiance of British restrictions as well as the initial opposition of the U.S. Army, which wanted to see a decrease, not an increase, in the number of DPs in its charge in Germany and Austria. Clearly, the tribulations of the Jews did not cease with the end of the war. Survivors who returned to Poland found their homes destroyed and themselves unwelcome. Many undertook another arduous trek into the American occupation zones of Germany and Austria, only to have to wait in DP camps for the opportunity to emigrate. A great number of these "postwar DPs," possibly the majority, wanted to come to America. Unfortunately, the same sentiments that had discouraged strong action to rescue Jews during the war manifested themselves after the war in restrictions on immigration. American attitudes toward the displaced persons, specifically the Jews, and how the way eventually was cleared for DPs to come to America are well documented in Dinnerstein's *America and the Survivors of the Holocaust*. This book is the best study to explain the plight specific to the Jews as a group among Europe's displaced persons, and its scholarship is buttressed by an extensive bibliography.

RECENT SCHOLARSHIP

In 1987 Breitman and Kraut coauthored *American Refugee Policy and European Jewry, 1933–1945*. They took issue with the works by David Wyman and others that attributed the American government's ineffective response to the Holocaust primarily to passive anti-Semitism. They argued that America's refugee policy was a product of restrictive immigration laws, the American public's opposition to increased immigration, and the reluctance of President Roosevelt to risk confrontation by taking extraordinary measures to help foreign Jews. Although there were probably individuals who were biased against Jews, "bureaucratic indifference" was the main culprit; in advancing this argument, the authors laid much emphasis on the characteristic functioning of an entrenched bureaucracy, specifically the Department of State, and even invoked Max Weber. Many reviewers found their argument unconvincing and pointed out the authors' unfamiliarity with the internal affairs of the War Refugee Board as well as the various Jewish organizations. Nevertheless, the book was well received for its meticulous research and careful writing and perhaps, above all, for pointing out the fact that "humanitarian considerations are not easily translated into government policy."

The suffering of the German refugees and expellees has received much scholarly attention in the Federal Republic of Germany, which continues to struggle with the problem of accommodating many exiles. The current state of this research and an agenda for future work are set forth in an anthology entitled *Fluechtlinge und Vertriebene in der westdeutschen Nachkriegs-geschichte.*

The works by Schechtman, Vernant, and Stoessinger have been described as systematic surveys by competent, dispassionate observers. Yet some reviewers have lamented the weakness of their explanations for the causes of mass forced migration and their proposed solutions. These complaints have persisted till the present. The Refugee Studies Programme of Oxford University has taken up the challenge of drawing object lessons from the recent past. In *Refugees and International Relations*, edited by Loescher and Monahan, seventeen essays "examine the general failure to resolve refugee situations" and seek solutions to these problems. This research into the present problem prevailing, above all, in Africa, Southeast Asia, and the Middle East, draws heavily on the experiences of World War II and its aftermath.

Another study group headed by Goran Rystad at Lund University, Sweden, has concentrated its investigation of refugee politics on the period of the Cold War. In addition to the work of Jacobmeyer on the postwar DP problem, Rystad's anthology, *The Uprooted*, contains other essays in English that look at America's postwar refugee policy, the role of UNRRA and the International Refugee Organization (IRO) as predecessors of the Office of United Nations High Commissioner for Refugees, and how experiences in Europe during the Cold War influenced the evolution of the concept of refugee.

Sjoeberg's *The Powers and the Persecuted* sheds valuable light on the meaning of the Second World War in the history of international refugee relief. His study of the much maligned Intergovernmental Committee on Refugees (IGCR) revealed the lessons learned by the Western nations in responding to the refugee problem. The IGCR was created in 1938 to aid German and Austrian refugees, predominantly Jews, from Nazism; it was the first permanent refugee agency and also the first international agency authorized to negotiate directly with a refugee-producing country. But in 1943, when the IGCR was reorganized to work on behalf of refugees from other countries, the organization effectively lost its authority to negotiate with enemy states. This prevented it from aiding Jewish refugees in Germany or Nazi-occupied territory.

By its mandate the IGCR was also prevented from helping refugees from Allied countries without first receiving a formal request from their respective governments. Thus, it could not arrange the resettlement of the nonrepatriable displaced persons, the majority of whom came from the Soviet Union, Poland, and the Baltic countries. After some years of frustrated attempts, Western governments dissolved the IGCR in 1947 and established the International Refugee Organization. The Soviet Union declined to join; without Soviet opposition, the IRO was free to effect the resettlement of over seven hundred thousand displaced persons, the first truly effective refugee aid organization. Yet the work of the IGCR during the war was not without significance. As the first permanent refugee organization, it was a great improvement over the League of Nations. In 1943 it was the first to receive regular funding from member states, and in its effort to expand its mandate the IGCR also caused Western governments to depart from the practice of defining refugees by national and ethnic categories in favor of a broader definition to include all persons seeking escape from persecution.

SUGGESTIONS FOR FUTURE RESEARCH

First, it may be well to note the apparent absence of any major work on war refugees and displaced persons in the Pacific theater. It seems to be a given that the majority of the refugees of the Second World War were Europeans. Perhaps an explanation lies in the fact that few refuges were available in the Far East; Chinese peasants could not easily traverse the vast distances to the USSR, and Southeast Asians had to cross jungle to reach India. It cannot be doubted that the Japanese juggernaut uprooted great numbers of civilians and that there were refugees. In a 1949 article, Kulischer estimated in "Displaced Persons in the Modern World" that from three to five million Chinese fled to Free China, as well as many thousands of Chinese residing in Southeast Asia, the Philippines, and the Dutch East Indies. Romanus and Sunderland's two histories of General Stilwell's campaign allude to the flight of several thousand civilians from Burma along the "Refugee Trail" that led to Assam. Woodbridge's work devotes a chapter to the work of UNRRA in China after the war. Otherwise, there is very little work on refugees and refugee relief in the Far East.

It is also well known that the Japanese ruled their subject peoples harshly. Yet no English-language work has appeared on the deportation and exploitation of foreign labor by imperial Japan. It would be worthwhile to discover if foreign labor was as crucial for Japan in maintaining its total war effort as it had been for Nazi Germany. On another point, recent scholarship has sought to explain the success of the communists in mobilizing the peasant masses in China. One work, by Chong-sik Lee, has argued that the communists gained followers not as much from social and economic appeals as from the depredations of the Japanese invaders. Possibly, Mao's movement recruited many internally displaced Chinese refugees.

The European field invites research in all its aspects, especially in the realm of social history. The "DP problem" in postwar Europe offers the opportunity to examine how a people decimated and dispersed by war gather themselves and rebuild a community in a foreign land. As Jacobmeyer observed, the DP camp functioned as a "surrogate homeland"; study of religious life, education, and employment in the camps should offer many insights. Some work has already been undertaken on the Jewish DPs. There remains much to be done for DPs of other national and ethnic identities, particularly the Poles, the largest national group among the postwar DPs in western Germany.

Social historians can also approach the question, exploring, for instance, the functioning of the underground economy, the black market, among the foreign workers in Nazi Germany. German historians have already done much solid work on the living conditions of the foreign workers; English-speaking scholars may be particularly interested in exploring these works to discover origins of the crime, unemployment, and social alienation that most readily typified the postwar DP in the minds of many military government officers. Another fascinating topic is the enormous effort devoted after the war to reuniting lost family members. Such work is a vital part of refugee relief; the history is yet to be written describing the tracing services carried out by UNRRA and continued today by the Red Cross.

Much can be learned by examining how the armed forces dealt with refugees and displaced persons found within their areas of operations. Only the military was able to quarter the many thousands of uprooted people, feed them, and apply the necessary measures to curb the spread of disease. Exploration of the military unit records in archives can yield many object lessons that may be of signal value today as armed forces face the challenge of carrying out civilian relief missions throughout the globe.

Those who wish to research in depth some aspect of the history of the displaced persons can benefit from several very useful bibliographies. Recommended, above all, is an excellent guide produced by students at the University of Edmonton under the supervision of Boshyk and Balan, *Political Refugees and "Displaced Persons."* This group sent questionnaires to archives and libraries, both public and private, throughout the world. The guide summarizes the archival holdings on displaced persons of many institutions and lists hundreds of articles in specialized journals on many aspects of work with DPs, from medical care to schooling. Although it emphasizes primary materials relating to Ukrainian DPs, it offers many leads for a researcher interested in social history or any national group among Europe's postwar refugees.

Readers interested in surveying the expansive literature produced during the 1940s can consult two guides. *Displaced Persons: A Selected Bibliography 1939–1947*, produced by the Russell Sage Foundation, was the first attempt to catalog the growing body of articles, pamphlets, and books. In the wake of congressional debates over the Displaced Persons Bills of 1948 and 1950, the Library of Congress compiled *The Displaced Persons Analytical Bibliography*, a comprehensive guide to popular and specialized literature as well as official documents, each entry followed by an informative annotation.

Several of the academic works cited in this chapter have excellent bibliographies, particularly those by David Wyman, Elliott, Dinnerstein, and Sjoberg. The study by Marrus lacks a bibliography, but the notes are rich in valuable source material.

Recently, two new research guides have been published by the Refugee Studies Programme of Oxford University. One is a directory of individuals doing research on refugees, *The Directory of Current Research*, classified alphabetically by name and also by discipline; another, *Displaced Peoples and Refugee Studies*, lists bibliographies and research guides as well as addresses of libraries, archives, and research centers. Also worth mentioning is a new catalog, *Refugees: Holdings of the Center for Migration Studies Library/ Archives* in New York.

BIBLIOGRAPHY

Abella, Irving, and Harold Troper. *None Is Too Many: Canada and the Jews of Europe 1933–1948*. 3d ed. Toronto: Lester and Orpen Dennys, 1991.

Avni, Chaim. *Espana, Franco y los Judios*. Madrid: Altadena, 1982.

Bauer, Yehuda. *Flight and Rescue: BRICHAH*. New York: Random House, 1970.

Bethell, Nicholas. *The Last Secret. The Delivery to Stalin of Over Two Million Russians by Britain and the United States*. Intro. Hugh Trevor-Roper. New York: Basic Books, 1974.

Boshyk, Yuri, and Boris Balan. *Political Refugees and "Displaced Persons," 1945–1954. A Selected Bibliography and Guide to Research with Special Reference to the Ukrainians*. Edmonton, Alberta: Canadian Institute of Ukrainian Studies, University of Alberta, 1982.

Bouscaren, Anthony T. *International Migrations since 1945*. New York: Frederick A. Praeger, 1963.

Bramwell, Anna C., ed. *Refugees in the Age of Total War*. London: Unwin Hyman, 1988.

Breitman, Richard, and Alan M. Kraut. *American Refugee Policy and European Jewry, 1933–1945*. Bloomington: Indiana UP, 1987.

Coles, Harry L., and Albert K. Weinberg, eds. *Civil Affairs: Soldiers Become Governors.* Washington, DC: Office of the Chief of Military History, Department of the Army, 1964.

De Zayas, Alfred M. *Nemesis at Potsdam. The Anglo-Americans and the Expulsion of the Germans. Background, Execution; Consequences.* London: Routledge and Kegan Paul, 1977. Rev. 2d ed. 1979.

Dinnerstein, Leonard. *America and the Survivors of the Holocaust.* New York: Columbia UP, 1982.

The Directory of Current Research on Refugees and Other Forced Migrants. Oxford, England: Refugee Studies Programme of Oxford University, 1988.

Displaced Peoples and Refugee Studies: A Resource Guide. Ed. Refugee Studies Programme, University of Oxford. Comp. Julian Davies. London: Hans Zell, 1990.

The Displaced Persons Analytical Bibliography. Washington, DC: 81st Congress, Second Session, House Report No. 1687, February 1950.

Displaced Persons: A Selected Bibliography, 1939–1947. Comp. Felicia Fuss. New York: Russell Sage Foundation, 1948.

Elliott, Mark R. *Pawns of Yalta. Soviet Refugees and America's Role in Their Repatriation.* Urbana: University of Illinois, 1982.

Epstein, Julius. *Operation Keelhaul. The Story of Forced Repatriation from 1944 to the Present.* Old Greenwich, CT: Devin-Adair, 1973.

Evrard, Jacques. *La Déportation des Travailleurs Français dans le IIIe Reich.* Paris: Librairie Arthene Fayard, 1972.

Feingold, Henry L. *The Politics of Rescue: The Roosevelt Administration and the Holocaust, 1938–1945.* New Brunswick, NJ: Rutgers UP, 1970.

Fluechtlinge und Vertriebene in der westdeutschen Nachkriegsgeschichte. Bilanzierung der Forschung und Perspektiven fuer die kuenftigen Forschungsarbeit. Ed. Rainer Schulze, Doris von der Brelie-Lewien, and Helga Grebing. Hildesheim: Verlag August Lax, 1987.

Friedman, Saul S. *No Haven for the Oppressed: United States Policy toward Jewish Refugees, 1938–1945.* Detroit: Michigan State UP, 1973.

Haesler, Alfed. *The Lifeboat Is Full: Switzerland and the Refugees, 1933–1945.* Trans. Charles Lam Markmann. New York: Funk and Wagnalls, 1969.

Herbert, Ulrich. *Fremdarbeiter: Politik und Praxis des Ausländer-Einsatzes in der Kriegswirtschaft des Dritten Reiches.* Berlin and Bonn, Germany: Dietz, 1986.

———. *A History of Foreign Labor in Germany 1880–1980. Seasonal Workers, Forced Laborers, Guest Workers.* Ann Arbor: University of Michigan, 1990.

Homze, Edward L. *Foreign Labor in Nazi Germany.* Princeton: Princeton UP, 1967.

Jacobmeyer, Wolfgang. *Vom Zwangsarbeiter zum Heimatlosen Auslaender. Die Displaced Persons in Westdeutschland 1945–1951.* Göttingen, Germany: Vanderhoeck and Ruprecht, 1985.

Kimche, Jon, and David. *The Secret Roads.* New York: Farrar, Straus, and Cudahy, 1955.

Kulischer, Eugene M. "Displaced Persons in the Modern World." *Annals of the American Academy of Political and Social Sciences 262* (March 1949): 166–77.

———. *The Displacement of Population in Europe.* Montreal: International Labour Office, 1943.

————. *Europe on the Move: War and Population Changes, 1917–1947*. New York: Columbia UP, 1948.

Lee, Chong-sik. *Revolutionary Struggle in Manchuria: Chinese Communism and Soviet Interest, 1922–1945*. Berkeley: University of California, 1983.

Loescher, Gil, and Laila Monahan, eds. *Refugees and International Relations*. New York: Oxford UP, 1989.

Marrus, Michael R. *The Unwanted. European Refugees in the Twentieth Century*. New York: Oxford UP, 1985.

Morley, John F. *Vatican Diplomacy and the Holocaust, 1939–1945*. New York: KTAV, 1980.

Morse, Arthur D. *While Six Million Died: A Chronicle of American Apathy*. New York: Random House, 1967.

Proudfoot, Malcolm J. *European Refugees. A Study in Forced Population Movements*. London: Faber and Faber, 1957.

Refugees: Holdings of the Center for Migration Studies Library/Archives. Comp. Diana Zimmerman, with the assistance of Maria del Giudice. Staten Island, NY: Center for Migration Studies of New York, 1987.

Romanus, Charles F., and Riley Sunderland. *Stilwell's Command Problems*. Washington, DC: GPO, 1956.

————. *Stilwell's Mission to China*. Washington, DC: GPO, 1953.

Rystad, Goran, ed. *The Uprooted. Forced Migration as an International Problem in the Postwar Era*. Lund, Sweden: Lund UP, 1990.

Schechtman, Joseph B. *European Population Transfers 1939–1945*. New York: Oxford UP, 1946.

————. *Postwar Population Transfers in Europe, 1945–1955*. Philadelphia: University of Pennsylvania, 1962.

Simpson, John Hope. *The Refugee Problem. Report of a Survey*. London: Oxford UP, 1939.

Sjoberg, Tommie. *The Powers and the Persecuted. The Refugee Problem and the Intergovernmental Committee on Refugees (IGCR), 1938–1947*. Lund, Sweden: Lund UP, 1991.

Stoessinger, John G. *The Refugee and the World Community*. Minneapolis: University of Minnesota, 1956.

Stone, Isodore F. *Underground to Palestine*. New York: Boni and Gaer, 1946.

Szulc, Tad. *The Secret Alliance. The Extraordinary Story of the Rescue of the Jews since World War II*. New York: Farrar, Straus, and Giroux, 1991.

Tartakower, Arieh, and Kurt R. Grossmann. *The Jewish Refugee*. New York: Institute of Jewish Affairs of the American Jewish Congress and the World Jewish Congress, 1944.

Tolstoy, Nikolai. *The Secret Betrayal*. New York: Charles Scribner's Sons, 1977.

United Nations Relief and Rehabilitation Administration. *UNRRA: The History of the United Nations Relief and Rehabilitation Administration*. Gen. ed. George Woodbridge. New York: Columbia UP, 1950.

Vernant, Jacques. *The Refugee in the Post-War World*. New Haven, CT: Yale UP, 1953.

Wasserstein, Bernard. *Britain and the Jews of Europe 1939–1945*. London: Institute of Jewish Affairs; Oxford: Clarendon, 1979.

Wyman, David S. *The Abandonment of the Jews. America and the Holocaust 1941–1945*. New York: Pantheon Books, 1984.

————. *Paper Walls. America and the Refugee Crisis, 1938–1941.* Amherst: University of Massachusetts, 1968; New York: Pantheon, 1985.

Wyman, Mark. *DP. Europe's Displaced Persons, 1945–1951.* Philadelphia: Balch Institute, 1989.

Ziemke, Earl F. *The U.S. Army in the Occupation of Germany, 1944–1946.* Washington, DC: Center of Military History, U.S. Army, 1975.

25 The Domestic Impact of War and Occupation on Germany

Loyd E. Lee

The central topics in the historiography of German society during the Third Reich have been the social roots of the Nazi Party and its supporters, life under prewar national socialism, and the Nazi racist policies and practices. Questions regarding popular support and the extent of political opposition, or resistance, have also received considerable attention, but other issues in social history during wartime commonly examined in Western democracies have rarely interested historians of Germany. The specific impact of the war, as distinct from the nature of the regime and its subsequent collapse, has been less frequently researched. For the immediate postwar period, scholarship has generally focused on military occupation policy to the neglect of societal changes.

The extensive literature on German society during the Third Reich, especially before the war, cannot be reviewed here. For a recent overview of major topics, see Crew's "General Introduction" in his *Nazism and German Society* and the literature cited there in both English and German. Though not primarily rooted in original research and lacking footnotes, Kitchen's *Nazi Germany at War* authoritatively covers the gamut of social history and much else, noting that national socialism itself left no significant social impact. Roseman's "World War II and Social Change in Germany" is an exception in that it directly addresses the question of war-induced social change, concluding that the war, while not an independent cause, had specific effects preparing Germany for postwar transformation.

GERMAN SOCIETY AT WAR

The pieces in Crew's anthology include nine authoritative essays on key issues, most with some attention to the wartime experience. This and

Kitchen's volume are superior to Beck, *Under the Bombs: The German Home Front*; Engelmann, *In Hitler's Germany* (largely based on personal experiences and interviews); and Grunberger, *A Social History of the Third Reich*. Each casts its net widely, with interesting and sometimes telling details, but with insufficiently rigorous analysis.

Totalitarian societies, lacking complexes of social relations outside official control—that is, having no civil society—are often thought to have no public opinion. Yet the Nazi government spent considerable energy to monitor public opinion in order to heighten morale and loyalty to the regime. Through skillful use of security reports, Steinert, *Hitler's War and the Germans*, concluded that a limited public opinion resistant to official persuasion existed. Kershaw's *Popular Opinion and Political Dissent* examines Bavarians before and during the war; they—the "muddled majority" grumbled and disbelieved propaganda, but society held together and remained supportive. Also see his *The "Hitler Myth"* on how the regime reinforced and sustained the myth that a charismatic führer looked out for "the little man," unaware of his plight when war turned life sour.

Peukert's *Inside Nazi Germany*, first published in German in 1982, attempts to unite *Alltagsgeschichte*, the history of everyday life, with an interpretation of the regime's place in industrial development. The difficulties of this sort of history, aside from its practitioners' reluctance to interpret their findings, as he pointed out, are the spotty and incomplete nature of sources and research and whether life under the "emergency" conditions of Nazi rule can be understood as "everyday" at all. His aim of combining themes such as Nazi racism, terror, and genocide with those of resistance and/or political consent, the relationship of the regime to industrial society, the experiences and mood of the "little man," class relationships, and generational splits makes this an important contribution.

Roseman's "Social Change in Germany" also laments the lack of research concentrating on the war years to justify his focusing only on Nazi wartime social policy (little wartime impact, as the regime was on a war footing from 1933) and the working class (conflicting authorities, uncertainty over the role of women, and the suspension of early Nazi social experimentation). The high mortality among officers and Soviet occupation eliminated the reactionary Junker class, while the importation of foreign labor increased German working-class mobility. The high casualty rates among soldiers (25 percent of males aged thirty-five to fifty years) were, in part, made up by postwar refugees from the East. He concludes, "It is evident that 'total war' is not an independent cause of social change" (75).

Noakes in his essay "Germany" raised the question of how the regime maximized the mobilization of society without the strain of war's lowering morale. The working classes, on whom he concentrates, were generally loyal at the beginning of the war but in time suffered deteriorating living standards and bombing. A labor shortage caused by intensified economic mobilization and attrition at the front was made good by forced-labor prisoners of war, foreign workers, and women. No strikes erupted as in the last years of World War I, either for fear of the Gestapo or from sheer exhaustion. Salter came to much the same conclusion in his "Germany."

The standard work on foreign labor, which made up one-fifth of the German workforce by 1944, is Homze's thorough *Foreign Labor in Nazi Germany*. It focuses on governmental policy, its roots in the German past, Nazi ideology on the proper role of *Untermenschen*, and, more immediately, the desperate need for labor after the failure of Operation Barbarossa in 1941. Like most recent scholars of the national socialist government, he found conflicting policies from the top down—polyocracy, as it is sometimes called. Speer wanted to gear up labor for increased production, a goal undermined by Sauckel's "recruiting" of eight million foreigners and opposed by most Gauleiters. Some of these conclusions are contested in Hancock's *National Socialist Leadership*; that is, Goebbels, Himmler, Bormann, and Speer believed willpower, fanaticism, and propaganda could mobilize society for total war; her evidence also further dents the idea that Germany pursued a short-term blitzkrieg strategy in the early war years.

Clearly, in matters of race the war made a difference, whether seen as a culmination of Nazi social policies or viewed as the opportunity or circumstances for racial radicalization. Burleigh and Wippermann, *The Racial State*, comprehensively survey Nazi race policies (see also their bibliography) for Jews as well as Roma (Gypsies), the mentally handicapped, asocials, and homosexuals, with an emphasis on policy and institutions. This literature is very extensive and is often classified under the topic of the Holocaust. For homosexuals, see Plant's *The Pink Triangle*, titled after the "badge" homosexuals were required to wear in the concentration camps.

The first chapters of Diefendorf's *In the Wake of War* dramatically detail bomb damage and its immediate consequences. The trauma of defeat and occupation in 1945 is treated in Peterson, *The Many Faces of Defeat*. An American army interpreter and interrogator between 1945 and 1947, Peterson culled memoirs and diaries, official archives, and private papers and conducted interviews to build a multifaceted account of the great variety of experiences in immediate postwar Germany.

RESISTANCE

The history of the German resistance is more a part of that country's coming to terms with its own past than of a commonality with other European resistance movements that fought against German occupation and rule as well as sometimes against national socialism. Also unlike occupied countries, resistance to the regime bore the stigma of treason to one's country, a main reason interest in the German opposition was slow to develop and still remains ambiguous. Where it existed (and its depth remains disputed), it was more consciously a political and moral act than a struggle against foreign oppression. Some scholars prefer the term "opposition" to "resistance," though the two words are often used interchangeably.

Other differences suggest the distinctiveness of German resistance. The extent of Nazi co-optation and terror, while not perhaps as total as sometimes depicted, made it difficult for overt, public opposition to develop or even survive. While collaboration flourished outside Germany, its abettors were not as likely to turn against resisters as Nazi supporters were to inform on fellow Germans. Resisters in occupied Europe could count on differences in language, the occupiers' limited ability to coerce cooperation, and residual, if unexpressed, hatred of Germans to provide "space" for resistance.

Though an extensive literature in German on the resistance has developed, this aspect of German history is still relatively unknown in Germany. None of the opposition leaders are generally considered national heroes; though the courage and heroism of many of these men and women may be admired, most belonged to a moral, religious, and political universe far from the secularism and more homogeneous society of the 1990s.

Initial research on the opposition was thwarted by Allied military controls and the amnesia of Germans eager to get on with life. Pathbreaking was Hans Rothfels' *German Opposition to Hitler*, first published in English in the United States in 1948 and reminding Americans that there was "another Germany." A German edition appeared the next year, with a revised edition in English in 1970. Allen Dulles, head of the Office of Strategic Services (OSS) in Europe after 1942, in 1947 wrote a brief account based on his personal knowledge of *Germany's Underground*—"There *was* an anti-Nazi underground working in Germany, despite the general impression to the contrary," whose story "deserves to be told" (xii–xiii).

Rothfels' book, like the other research at the time, focused on the civil bureaucrats, diplomats, and, especially, the military or on outstanding personal acts of heroic resistance, often from these institutions. Carsten's *The German Resistance to Hitler* contains four essays by early German scholars, reflecting a beginning critical reassessment of the goals and social ideas of the conservative-national opposition, as well as extending study to the socialists, the communists (in Berlin), and the churches. Zeller's *Flame of Freedom* is a frequently reprinted classic from the same period.

An important turning point came with Hoffmann's lengthy 1977 *History of the German Resistance* (first published in Germany in 1969), based on more wide-ranging archival materials and more inclusive of the varieties of resistance, individuals, motives, and activities. In forty-eight chapters Hoffmann examined in minute detail not only the plans and ideas of the leading resistance figures but their deeds as well. It includes maps, city plans, documents, and an extensive bibliography. In 1988 Hoffmann, who by then was recognized as one of the field's leading authorities, wrote a short study, *German Resistance to Hitler*, primarily to outline the basic problems in understanding the resistance, its participants, and the dilemmas they faced. Like others whose works are cited earlier and, in fact, like most historians, he accepted the undoubted truth that in a dictatorship only the military can successfully overthrow the government. He also argued, as do most writers, but not their critics, that the opposition was not an opportunistic move undertaken after defeat became apparent.

Before the war, opposition leaders attempted to persuade British and French to resist Hitler's aggression; during the war, they hoped to gain Allied approval for a negotiated end to the war. The story is complex, and the leaders unrealistically believed the Western Allies would junk their Soviet partner and accept a restoration of the Hohenzollern crown and an expanded Germany. Von Klemperer's massive *German Resistance against Hitler: The Search for Allies Abroad*, based on meticulous archival research, with extensive analysis of the leaders, replaces previous studies on this question. He included not only traditional military and bureaucratic resisters but also church leaders and German exiles. This expanded the scope of understanding the variety of men and women in opposition and their motives, though his faulting the Allies for their silence and not aiding the resistance by modifying unconditional surrender and promising not to intervene in a coup is widely questioned.

As the scholarship on the opposition deepened, it became possible for general accounts to supplement and in some cases supplant previous literature. Several recent studies stand out for this reason. Balfour's *Withstanding Hitler* concentrates on two questions: why did not more Germans resist, and why did those who did not succeed? He studied various social groups, from those traditionally considered, to businessmen, youth, and women. Modes of resistance, difficulties, and aims are scrutinized. Nearly half is devoted to a "portrait gallery" of individuals and groups, plus a review of major previous literature.

Now that many of the basic stories of resistance have been written, we are moving into a third historiographic phase, attempting to locate resistance within the nexus of German society and politics as a whole. Three works in particular stand out in this regard.

A Festschrift for Hoffmann edited by Nicosia and Stokes, *Germans against Nazism: Nonconformity, Opposition and Resistance in the Third Reich*, brings together twenty important essays by leading writers on the German resistance, many of them Hoffmann's former students. They are original, authoritative, and current in their scholarship (in 1990) and cover a remarkable variety of themes key to understanding the opposition: Nazi responses to unpopular measures, different social classes, political persuasions, the churches, geographic areas, and individual acts of resistance. Another significant collection from a 1986 conference is Large's brief collection of twelve essays, *Contending with Hitler: Varieties of German Resistance in the Third Reich*, with its appropriate subtitle indicating a major difficulty facing the resistance.

The German communists were ruthlessly suppressed, their leaders arrested, interned, or executed. During the Cold War, their role received scant Western attention, though Merson, *Communist Resistance in Nazi Germany*, attempted to lay out the basic facts. This aspect of the German resistance will receive much more attention with the unification of the two Germanys and the opening of East German archives to all scholars. Gill is undoubtedly right that new sources from the former German Democratic Republic may alter our view of the resistance, but otherwise his *Honourable Defeat* offers little new; while comprehensive, it gives the impression that the army was more committed to resistance than it was.

Critics often argue that all of this represented tiny, isolated, factionalized minorities never close to forming a movement, a charge scholars sympathetic to the opposition have not successfully met. For example, Weinberg in his *World at Arms* gives the resistance only three paragraphs (753–54), mentioning only one individual by name, von Stauffenberg.

In *Resistance against the Third Reich*, Geyer and Boyer edited another group of essays by a distinguished group of resistance scholars from Europe and the United States that breaks new ground. The collection centers around three themes: normality, exceptionalism, and resistance (how ordinary people coped with abnormal, humanity-denying demands); human solidarity and the restoration of politics (destroyed by the atomization of the Nazi regime); and the impact of the resistance on postwar Germany.

One of the more poignant instances of principled, but futile, resistance is that of Munich students Hans and Sophie Scholl, converts to Catholicism. In 1943 they were arrested, arbitrarily tried, and beheaded; over one hundred friends and associates were also executed. Their story can be followed in Dumbach and Newborn, *Shattering the German Night*, and Hanser, *A Noble Treason*, and in their own writings.

ALLIED OCCUPATION AND GERMAN SOCIETY, 1945–1949

The literature on the Allied occupation of Germany is very extensive; however, that on German society during the interregnum is a neglected topic in English. Doerr's selective bibliography, *The Big Powers and the German Question*, includes more than five hundred annotated and descriptive entries drawn from several languages for the period 1941–1949, though the majority deal with diplomacy among the Allies, rather than with the domestic social and political impact of the four military occupations. A useful supplement is Paul's bibliography of English-language materials on the immediate postwar period, *The Germans after World War II*, which concentrates on domestic affairs. With a few sentences describing each, she included 970 entries of personal accounts by Germans and foreign observers, the efforts of civilian relief organizations, fiction by Germans and non-Germans, and films, as well as historical studies, journal articles, and a bibliography of bibliographies consulted.

General Accounts

There is an urgent need for a scholarly synthesis that is more than an account and analysis of the occupation from the viewpoint of the Allies and its relationship to Germany's political future. Bark and Gress' *From Shadow to Substance, 1945–1963*, the first of two volumes, is journalistic, with an annoyingly conservative bias; also, it treats very little outside politics and for this period focuses on "zero hour" and the division of Germany. Alas, it is the only lengthy history in English. Fulbrook's *The Two Germanies*, like Henry Turner's *Germany from Partition to Reunification*, is informed by the best scholarship in English and German, but both are sketchy for the immediate postwar era. Fortunately, recent work is beginning to fill the gap.

The Military Occupations

Though the Allies agreed on maintaining the economic unity of Germany at Potsdam in 1945 and thus its social unity, the four military governments of the United States, Great Britain, France, and the Soviet Union soon managed separate de facto administrations. The bulk of scholarly work has been on the American military government, as is perhaps fitting, given the United States' predominance in economic and military power after 1945. The first complete published study was Zink's *American Military Government*. Based on official reports and documents, it is concerned with the broad range of activities of the Office of Military Government of the United States for Germany (OMGUS) and very little with German reactions. In 1957 he thoroughly revised it as *The United States in Germany*, referring to "the tangled events of the American occupation," for which there "may be some doubt whether a truly definitive single study of the extremely complex and widely ramified aspects of the occupation will ever be forthcoming" (iii).

Ziemke's official *U.S. Army in the Occupation of Germany* thoroughly covered the army's unprecedented task, but only through the first year, during the toughest period for establishing an administration, feeding people, dealing with refugees, and carrying out the program of de-Nazification and democratization. As he explained, however, "[T]he U.S.

authorities in Germany, left without a valid principal objective [Washington's policy in the initial draconian Joint Chiefs of Staff directive (JCS) 1067 being oriented more to the past than the future], were compelled to exploit loopholes . . . and to improvise" (445).

Several studies contemporaneous with Ziemke's tried to measure the impact of occupation. In *A German Community under American Occupation: Marburg*, Gimbel concluded that though the changes Americans sought were not completely realized, the occupation was not simply a confused and mismanaged affair, thwarting German democratization. In *The American Occupation of Germany*, relying on German archives as well as American records, he generalized this view into a revisionist defense of the military government. Covering much the same ground, Peterson faulted the *American Occupation*, emphasizing its limited influence. The papers and reminiscences in Schmitt, *U.S. Occupation*, reflect the same historical perspective of the 1970s.

A conference reevaluating the role of American military government in Germany and Japan resulted in Wolfe's *Americans as Proconsuls*, which showed the mixed opinion among scholars. Backer, an official of the occupation turned scholar, showed in *Winds of History: The German Years of Lucius DuBignon Clay* that the American "proconsul" until 1947 was no cold warrior but an early advocate of giving Germans responsibility for their own affairs.

The "failure" of de-Nazification and American-style democracy brought forth a deluge of criticism in the late 1940s and 1950s. For this see Tent's *Mission on the Rhine: Reeducation and Denazification in American-Occupied Germany*, who found the problem lay not with the Americans' approach, as the British and French with more ambitious plans accomplished no more, but with the intractability of the situation. More recently, Smith compared Allied attempts at reeducating German prisoners of war (POWs) in *The War for the German Mind*, concluding that it had little impact in the West while Soviet control in the East made the question moot.

The published papers of three recent conferences of German and English-speaking scholars provide further insights into the research of the 1980s. Noteworthy is the growing emphasis on Germans' roles in shaping their postwar society, especially by traditional elites. If democracy developed in West Germany, it seems to have been primarily a German product. *American Policy and the Reconstruction of West Germany*, edited by Diefendorf and others, covers traditional questions, but with greater depth based on new archival material. Of the twenty-three essays, only one is on cultural history, none on social history, but all are authoritative, often backed up by full-length monographs. Also resulting from a 1990 conference, but more appropriate for beginners, *America and the Shaping of German Society*, edited by Ermarth, focuses more on social and cultural change, with seven historical essays and seven reminiscences. Similar in scope and purpose and based on a 1993 conference is Pommerin's *American Impact*, with ten essays, half devoted to social and cultural history. Unique in comparing policies of the three western zones, Rogers found that they "regularly interfered in the development of a new German party system" (139), though he could not prove how much difference such interference made.

The other occupation zones have received less attention. For the British zone, see the official *Civil Affairs and Military Government North-West Europe 1944–1946* by Donnison, a thorough accounting of all aspects of occupation that notes its achievements and the "absence of guidance from above" (465). Ian Turner's *British Occupation Policy and the Western Zones* contains twelve essays based on new archival research reexamining basic questions of Britain's postwar goals in Germany, with key essays by Turner on de-Nazification, historiography, and sources.

The French zone has only one monograph in English, but it is a very substantial one: Willis' *The French in Germany*. Reversing earlier critical and negative views of French obsession with security (which helped divide Germany) and reparations, Willis found the occupation to be the prelude to rapprochement, evident especially in French educational policies.

Of the studies on the early years in the Soviet zone, Nettl's *The Eastern Zone and Soviet Policy* stands out; he concluded that official Soviet aims and the economy the Russians created aimed not so much at creating a communist society but at exploiting the zone for Russia's immediate needs. This is a view generally upheld by Naimark's massively researched *Russians in Germany*, what is apt to be the standard work until archival materials are opened. Naimark argued that little new will come from these archives, as research so far confirms work based on Western sources, for example, of widespread rape and looting, of internment camps run by the Soviet secret police (four in former Nazi concentration camps whose inmates in time included socialist and communist critics of the Soviet occupation), and of German scientists and laborers forced into nuclear weapons programs. A good complement to Naimark, Pike's excellent *Politics of Culture*, illustrates in another field the Soviet approach to occupation, the subordination of intellectual and artistic life to immediate political goals.

The most pressing need for students of German society and the Second World War, in addition to filling gaps with specialized studies, is a synthesis of the social impact of the war and the immediate postwar experience under occupation.

BIBLIOGRAPHY

Also see "Women in World War II," "Prisoners of War," "Comparative Economic Mobilization," "The Holocaust," and "Refugees."

Backer, John H. *Winds of History: The German Years of Lucius DuBignon Clay.* New York: Van Nostrand Reinhold, 1983.

Balfour, Michael. *Withstanding Hitler in Germany, 1933–1945.* London and New York: Routledge, 1988.

Bark, Dennis L., and David R. Gress. *From Shadow to Substance, 1945–1963.* Oxford and Cambridge, MA: Blackwell, 1993.

Beck, Earl R. *Under the Bombs: The German Home Front, 1942–1945.* Lexington: University of Kentucky, 1986.

Burleigh, Michael, and Wolfgang Wippermann. *The Racial State: Germany, 1933–1945.* Cambridge: Cambridge UP, 1991.

Carsten, F. L. *The German Resistance to Hitler.* Berkeley: University of California, 1970.

Crew, David F., ed. *Nazism and German Society, 1933–1945.* London and New York: Routledge, 1994.

Diefendorf, Jeffry M. *In the Wake of War: The Reconstruction of German Cities after World War II.* New York: Oxford UP, 1993.

Diefendorf, Jeffry M., Axel Frohn, and Hermann-Josef Rupieper, eds. *American Policy and the Reconstruction of West Germany, 1945–1955.* New York: Cambridge UP, 1993.

Doerr, Jürgen C. *The Big Powers and the German Question, 1941–1990: A Selected Bibliographic Guide.* New York and London: Garland, 1992.

Donnison, F.S.V. *Civil Affairs and Military Government North-West Europe 1944–1946.* London: HMSO, 1961.

Dulles, Allen. *Germany's Underground.* New York: Macmillan, 1947.

Dumbach, Annette E., and Jud Newborn. *Shattering the German Night: The Story of the White Rose.* Boston and Toronto: Little, Brown, 1986.

Engelmann, Bernt. *In Hitler's Germany: Daily Life in the Third Reich.* Trans. Krishna Winston. New York: Pantheon Books, 1986.

Ermarth, Michael, ed. *America and the Shaping of German Society, 1945–1955.* Providence, RI, and Oxford: Berg, 1993.

Fulbrook, Mary. *The Two Germanies, 1945–1990: Problems of Interpretation.* Houndmills, Basingstoke, Hampshire, and London: Macmillan Education, 1992.

Geyer, Michael, and John W. Boyer, eds. "Resistance against the Third Reich." *Journal of Modern History 64*, Supplement (1992).

Gill, Anton. *An Honourable Defeat: A History of German Resistance to Hitler, 1933–1945.* New York: Henry Holt and London: Heinemann, 1994.

Gimbel, John. *The American Occupation of Germany: Politics and the Military, 1945–1949.* Stanford, CA: Stanford UP, 1968.

———. *A German Community under American Occupation: Marburg, 1945–1952.* Stanford, CA: Stanford UP, 1961.

Grunberger, Richard. *A Social History of the Third Reich.* London: Weidenfeld and Nicolson, 1971.

Hancock, Eleanor. *The National Socialist Leadership and Total War 1941–1945.* New York: St. Martin's, 1991.

Hanser, Richard. *A Noble Treason: The Revolt of the Munich Students against Hitler.* New York: G. P. Putnam's Sons, 1979.

Hoffmann, Peter. *German Resistance to Hitler.* Cambridge: Harvard UP, 1988.

———. *The History of the German Resistance 1933–1945*. London: Macdonald and Jane's, and Cambridge: MIT, 1977; Montreal: McGill-Queens UP, 1996.

Homze, Edward L. *Foreign Labor in Nazi Germany*. Princeton: Princeton UP, 1967.

Kershaw, Ian. *The "Hitler Myth": Image and Reality in the Third Reich*. Oxford: Clarendon and New York: Oxford UP, 1987.

———. *Popular Opinion and Political Dissent in the Third Reich*. Oxford: Clarendon and New York: Oxford UP, 1983.

Kitchen, Martin. *Nazi Germany at War*. New York: Longman, 1995.

Klemperer, Klemens von. *German Resistance against Hitler: The Search for Allies Abroad, 1938–1945*. Oxford: Oxford UP, 1992.

Large, David Clay, ed. *Contending with Hitler: Varieties of German Resistance in the Third Reich*. Cambridge: Cambridge UP; Washington, DC: German Historical Institute, 1991.

Merson, Allan. *Communist Resistance in Nazi Germany*. London: Lawrence and Wishart, 1985.

Naimark, Norman. *The Russians in Germany: A History of the Soviet Zone of Occupation, 1945–49*. Cambridge, MA: Belknap, 1995.

Nettl, J. P. *The Eastern Zone and Soviet Policy in Germany, 1945–1950*. New York: Octagon, 1951.

Nicosia, Francis R., and Lawrence D. Stokes, eds. *Germans against Nazism: Nonconformity, Opposition and Resistance in the Third Reich*. New York: Berg, 1990.

Noakes, Jeremy. "Germany." In Noakes, ed., *The Civilian in War: The Home Front in Europe, Japan and the U.S.A. in World War II*. Exeter: University of Exeter, 1992.

———, ed. *The Civilian in War: The Home Front in Europe, Japan and the U.S.A. in World War II*. Exeter: University of Exeter, 1992.

Paul, Barbara Dotts. *The Germans after World War II: An English-Language Bibliography*. Boston: G. K. Hall, 1990.

Peterson, Edward N. *The American Occupation of Germany: Retreat to Victory*. Detroit: Wayne State UP, 1977.

———. *The Many Faces of Defeat: The German People's Experience in 1945*. New York: Peter Lang, 1990.

Peukert, Detlev. *Inside Nazi Germany: Conformity, Opposition and Racism in Everyday Life*. New Haven, CT: Yale UP, 1987.

Pike, David. *The Politics of Culture in Soviet-Occupied Germany, 1945–1949*. Stanford, CA: Stanford UP, 1992.

———, ed. *The Opening of the Second World War: Proceedings of the Second International Conference on International Relations*. New York: Peter Lang, 1991.

Plant, Richard. *The Pink Triangle: The Nazi War against Homosexuals*. New York: H. Holt, 1988.

Pommerin, Reiner. *The American Impact on Postwar Germany*. Oxford and Providence, RI: Berghahn, 1995.

Rogers, Daniel. *Politics after Hitler: The Western Allies and the German Party System*. New York: New York UP, 1995.

Roseman, Mark. "World War II and Social Change in Germany." In Arthur Marwick, ed., *Total War and Social Change*, 58–78. New York: St. Martin's, 1988.

Rothfels, Hans. *The German Opposition to Hitler*. Hinsdale, IL: Regnery, 1948; London: G. Wolf, 1970.

Salter, S. "Germany." In S. Salter and J. Stevenson. *The Working Class and Politics in Europe and America, 1929–1945.* London and New York: Longman, 1990.

Schmitt, Hans A., ed. *U.S. Occupation in Europe after World War II: Papers and Reminiscences from the April 23–24, 1976, Conference Held at the George C. Marshall Research Foundation, Lexington, Virginia.* Lawrence: Regents of Kansas, 1978.

Scholl, Hans, and Inge Scholl. *At the Heart of the White Rose: Letters and Diaries of Hans and Sophie Scholl.* New York: Harper and Row, 1987.

Scholl, Inge. *Students against Tyranny: The Resistance of the White Rose, Munich, 1942–1943.* Middletown, CT: Wesleyan UP, 1970.

———. *The White Rose: Munich 1942–43.* Middletown, CT: Wesleyan, 1983. Published in 1970 as *Students against Tyranny.*

Smith, Arthur Lee, Jr. *The War for the German Mind: Reeducating Hitler's Soldiers.* Oxford and Providence, RI: Berghan, 1996.

Steinert, Marlis G. *Hitler's War and the Germans: Public Mood and Attitude during the Second World War.* Trans. and ed. Thomas E. J. de Witty. Athens: Ohio UP, 1977.

Tent, James F. *Mission on the Rhine: Reeducation and Denazification in American-Occupied Germany.* Chicago and London: University of Chicago, 1982.

Turner, Henry Ashby. *Germany from Partition to Reunification.* New Haven, CT, and London: Yale UP, 1992.

Turner, Ian D., ed. *Reconstruction in Post-War Germany: British Occupation Policy and the Western Zones, 1945–1955.* Oxford, New York, and Munich: Berg, 1989.

Weinberg, Gerhard L. *A World at Arms: A Global History of World War II.* Cambridge: Cambridge UP, 1994.

Willis, F. Roy. *The French in Germany, 1945–1949.* Stanford, CA: Stanford UP, 1962.

Wolfe, Robert, ed. *Americans as Proconsuls: United States Military Government in Germany and Japan, 1944–1952.* Carbondale and Edwardsville: Southern Illinois UP, 1984.

Zeller, Eberhard. *The Flame of Freedom: The German Struggle against Hitler.* Boulder, CO: Westview, 1994.

Ziemke, Earl F. *The U.S. Army in the Occupation of Germany, 1944–1946.* Washington, DC: GPO, 1975.

Zink, Harold. *American Military Government in Germany.* New York: Macmillan, 1947.

———. *The United States in Germany, 1944–1955.* New York: D. Van Nostrand, 1957.

PART VI

The Colonial Heritage and the War

26   World War II and Latin America

Errol D. Jones

Historians reconstructing World War II have focused their attention on the major players, generally ignoring the role and contribution of Latin American nations. With the exception of Weinberg's 1994 study, *A World at Arms* (stating incorrectly that only Brazil sent forces into battle when Mexico did as well), and Henri's older work translated into English and published in 1975 as *The Second World War*, which briefly cover Latin American involvement, most one-volume general studies scarcely mention the role played by Central and South American nations. Ready's two-volume *Forgotten Allies* includes brief mention of the Brazilian Expeditionary Force that fought in the Italian campaign, but there is scant information on political events that brought them there. A single sentence notes that a Mexican air force squadron saw action in the Philippines. Since Latin America's participation in the war was in some way influenced by, or co-ordinated with, the United States, histories of Latin American–U.S. relations describe and analyze the region's participation in the conflict. This chapter discusses the major Latin American countries' involvement in the war and those significant works, mainly in English, that have studied them. No attempt is made to be all-inclusive, nor are minor players or peripheral regions discussed.

LATIN AMERICAN RELATIONS BEFORE THE WAR

Even among scholars of Latin American writing in the English language a comprehensive survey of Latin American entanglement in the conflict did not appear until Humphreys' two-volume study in 1981–1982. Widely acclaimed by scholars in the field, Humphreys' first volume of *Latin America and the Second World War* provides an excellent synthesis of how each Latin American nation responded to the pending world crisis and the U.S.

entry into the war. Volume two closely follows U.S. diplomatic efforts to secure needed raw materials from Latin America while urging regional leaders to break relations with the Axis. The difficult relations with Argentina occupy a significant portion of this volume. Based on a careful reading of British Foreign Office records, U.S. diplomatic papers, participants' published memoirs, and newspapers, the author also demonstrates solid command of the secondary literature on the topic. A close examination of Humphreys' work is essential to an understanding of the major issues and themes surrounding Latin America's participation in the war.

Latin America's role in the war is best understood from an appreciation of prevailing circumstances in the area during the 1930s. A region producing rich raw materials and foodstuffs, Latin America exported essential commodities that went mainly to European and U.S. ports. In turn, most countries depended on imports of manufactured goods, foreign capital, and specific raw materials as the motor force of their economies. U.S. and British investments predominated in the 1920s and 1930s. Latin American dependence on this arrangement proved disastrous when the Great Depression of the 1930s drove down commodity prices, dried up foreign exchange, thereby limiting imports, and shrank foreign investment. Reacting to the crisis, many governments implemented policies to develop home industries, diversify agriculture, reduce dependency, and move toward greater self-sufficiency. This was especially the case in Argentina, Brazil, Chile, and Mexico so that by the end of the decade import substitution industrialization modified significantly the nature of the import trade.

By 1938 the United States and Great Britain accounted for nearly half the trade with Latin America. Two other nations, however, had begun to offer serious competition in the Latin American market: Germany and Japan. Significantly, German trade advanced as that of the British declined. See Frye's fascinating description of Nazi Germany's political and commercial activities in the Western Hemisphere in *Nazi Germany and the American Hemisphere*, but evidence is lacking to support his conclusions that the Americas formed an important part of Hitler's global ambitions. Trade rivalry on the eve of the Second World War is the focus of Hilton's *Brazil and the Great Powers*, with his emphasis mainly on Germany's challenge to Anglo-American preeminence in Brazil. In his *Economic Defense of Latin America*, Bidwell covers German bilateral trade with Brazil, as does McCann's pathbreaking *The Brazilian–American Alliance*. South America accounted for about three-quarters of the value of all Latin American trade prior to the war, and Argentina commanded the lead in importing and exporting. With Argentina British trade was greatest.

Owing to proximity, investment, national strategic interests, and historical ties, Central American and Caribbean nations felt the powerful influence, at times unwanted, of the United States. While American investors had pumped eight hundred million dollars into the region by 1940, Cuba alone received almost three-quarters of it. Colombia's geographical propinquity to the Panama Canal prompted U.S. policymakers to court this Andean nation as a key to defense of the canal. By 1939 Colombia welcomed U.S. naval and aviation missions, and economic and financial relations between the two were close. Bushnell's biography of Eduardo Santos provides excellent coverage for this era. Oil-rich, dictator-dominated Venezuela, on the other hand, did not attract as much North American attention, except perhaps for its growing significance as a petroleum producer. Lieuwen's *Petroleum in Venezuela* and *Venezuela* should be consulted for an understanding of that country in the prewar and war years.

Mexico, deeply influenced by the United States, historically loathed and resented American abuses of power and in the 1930s came to a showdown with its nemesis of the north when the Cárdenas administration expropriated U.S. and British oil companies. President Roosevelt and his ambassador to Mexico at the time, Josephus Daniels, resisted oil company and State Department pressure to punish Mexico and succeeded in resolving the conflict in an amicable way. A test for the new Good Neighbor policy, U.S. willingness to seek peaceful solutions to the problem no doubt enabled the two countries to become allies once both were forced into the war by Japanese and German attacks. Cronon's biography, *Josephus Daniels in Mexico*, and Wood's *The Making of the Good Neighbor Policy* credit Daniels' moderating influence and political acumen for avoiding a diplomatic rupture. Relations with Great Britain, however, became so acrimonious that Mexico severed ties in May 1938, not to be resumed until October 1941.

While U.S. hegemony was unchallenged in Central America and the Caribbean, as one moved south down the Andes, its influence diminished. In both Ecuador and Peru the United States was the single largest supplier of imported goods but did not dominate the export trade. In fact, trade with Japan was sizable, and over seventeen thousand Japanese had made Peru their home by the 1930s. Alarmists warned that Japan planned to increase its influence in the region and to use the existing Japanese community to take over the country. The military government in 1936 imposed limitations on Japanese immigration. Gardiner's *The Japanese in Peru* offers the best coverage for this topic. Elections in 1939, in which the leftist Alianza Popular Revolucionaria Americana (APRA) was banned, brought a government to power that pledged adherence to both Pan-Americanism and world peace.

GERMAN INFLUENCE

German influence in Bolivia increased in the twentieth century. Germans trained the army, owned the major airline, invested in several firms, and immigrated to the capital, La Paz. Tin, however, dominated the export economy, and most of it went to England for smelting. The British minister was pleased to report home in 1938 that "Bolivians do not like Germany or German methods" (Humphreys, volume 1, 21). Unbeknownst to this British official, the Bolivian military ruler, Germán Busch, had stunned the German minister when he privately asked for help in establishing a totalitarian regime. Busch died under "mysterious circumstances" before any changes occurred, and in March 1940 General Enrique Peñaranda was elected president. For in-depth coverage of this era see Klein's *Parties and Political Change in Bolivia.* Blasier's article "The United States, Germany and the Bolivian Revolutionaries" gives a sound account of German influence and this particular episode.

Germans had also trained the Chilean military, held second place to the United States as a supplier of imports, influenced political thinking, although not necessarily national socialist, and numbered almost thirty-five thousand immigrants, mainly in the south. Many of these Germans had been in Chile since the nineteenth century, and while Nazi propagandists were active among them, most were Chileans, first and foremost. Chileans confronted the onset of the European war with a shaky Popular Front government led by moderate Radical Pedro Aguirre Cerda. Stevenson's *The Chilean Popular Front* is the standard work on this period.

ARGENTINA

With minor exceptions, Paraguay and Uruguay played an insignificant role in the Second World War. That was not the case, however, with Argentina. Of a population of nearly thirteen million in 1939, 20 percent of whom were foreign-born, almost two hundred forty thousand Germans had settled in Argentina. In 1930 the military, supported by the landed oligarchy, overthrew a democratically elected government and established a decade of rule by the old conservative elite. To protect their economic interests, the conservative government signed a trade agreement with the British that guaranteed continued sale of its cattle and cereal products in return for purchase of British industrial goods and favorable treatment of English-owned utilities and railroads. The United States, wishing to enter the Argentine market, regarded this arrangement as discriminatory and felt that the British promoted Argentine hostility toward U.S. aims and intentions everywhere in Latin America, but particularly in Argentina.

This economic rivalry continued to a certain degree even after the United States joined Britain as an ally against the Axis, giving rise to conflicting historical interpretations. Numerous books and articles cover the period leading up to the war, but the best contributions can be found in Potash, *The Army and Politics in Argentina,* for his insights on the military; Peter H. Smith, *Politics and Beef in Argentina;* Tamarin, *The Argentine Labor Movement,* on the developing nationalism among the labor class from 1930 to 1945; Conil Paz and Ferrari, for solid background on foreign policy in *Argentina's Foreign Policy*; and Gravil, *The Anglo-Argentine Connection*, on economic relations of the two countries during the 1930s.

LATIN AMERICA AND THE START OF WORLD WAR II

The German invasion of Poland in September 1939 stirred Western Hemisphere leaders to action. Based on consultative procedures established earlier at the Lima Conference, a meeting of all American ministers convened in Panama at U.S. initiative to discuss the situation and decide upon a course of action. The first of many Pan-American meetings throughout the war, the Panama Conference adopted a unified policy that all American republics would remain neutral. The Declaration of Panama also established a security zone around the American republics, excluding Canada and undisputed colonies and possessions of European countries.

Owing to their weaker economic and political position vis-à-vis European industrial powers and the might of the United States, Latin American republics had struggled since independence to maintain their national sovereignty. Jealous of their autonomy, somewhat insecure in their relations with each other as well as with the Great Powers, a growing sense of nationalism led the republics to press the United States to adhere to noninterventionist agreements. While Latin American diplomats were concerned primarily with U.S. intervention into their internal affairs, North American diplomats could interpret these agreements as a reaffirmation of the Monroe Doctrine. A plethora of studies on U.S. relations with Latin America exists, but one would do no better than to start with Connell-Smith, *The United States and Latin America*. Gellman's *Good Neighbor Diplomacy* is excellent for the Roosevelt years, 1933–1945, as is Dallek's *Franklin D. Roosevelt and American Foreign Policy*.

Once German armies overran France, the Roosevelt administration feared that European territorial possessions in the Americas might serve as staging points of aggression against the United States and its neighbors. Urged on by the United States, American ministers met in Havana in July 1940 and agreed to the Declaration of Havana. A victory for the United States in its attempt to multilateralize the Monroe Doctrine, the agreement promoted the idea of "collective trusteeship": Western Hemisphere colonies of European countries occupied by the Nazis would come under Pan-American administration. Humphreys believes that collective trusteeship meant that the United States would take over these possessions. While the Declaration of Havana was ratified by two-thirds of the American states, Argentina and others thought the colonies should become independent. For a discussion on this and other Pan-American conferences, one should consult Langer and Gleason, *The Challenge to Isolation*; Conn and Fairchild, *The Framework of Hemisphere Defense*; Conn, Engleman, and

Fairchild, *Guarding the United States and Its Outposts*; and Mecham, *The United States and Inter-American Security*. Argentine opposition to the United States at the conference set the stage for the diplomatic struggle between the two countries that occurred at the Rio Conference in January 1942.

Latin Americans reacted with surprise and shock to the Japanese attack on Pearl Harbor. Within two days Chile and the United States called for a consultative meeting of American ministers. Gathering at Rio de Janeiro in January 1942, the American foreign ministers sought to strike a unified accord in confronting the aggressors. The Rio Conference is famous in the historical literature for the widening rift that developed between Argentina and the United States when the former objected to the latter's attempts to force an agreement that all American nations would sever relations with the Axis. Argentina pressed for, and won, an agreement that only "recommended" severance. Owing to his inability to force the Latin American foreign ministers to break relations, Undersecretary of State for Latin American Affairs Sumner Welles became the target of Secretary of State Cordell Hull's wrath. Those wishing to study the event should consult Hull's *Memoirs* and Welles' *Seven Major Decisions* for widely differing interpretations of the conference. For the entire conference and the growing conflict between the two men, see Pratt's biography *Cordell Hull*. Woods, *The Roosevelt Foreign Policy Establishment*; Gellman, *Good Neighbor Diplomacy*; and Francis, *The Limits of Hegemony* all offer insights into the episode. Welles, in a burst of self-congratulation, saw the conference as a great success. In his book *The Time for Decision*, he stressed the unity achieved at Rio that he believed created, for the first time, true Pan-Americanism.

Even before the American foreign ministers met in Rio on January 15, 1942, nine Latin American countries had joined the United States, Canada, and fifteen other nations to declare war on the Axis. Costa Rica, Cuba, the Dominican Republic, El Salvador, Guatemala, Haiti, Honduras, Nicaragua, and Panama were technically at war when they met in Rio. Three other Latin American nations, Colombia, Mexico, and Venezuela, had severed diplomatic ties with the Axis, and by the time the conference was over, all but Argentina and Chile had broken off relations.

Naturally, the bulk of historical writing about Latin America and the war emphasizes the years from the 1942 Rio Conference to the Chapultepec Conference held in Mexico City in February 1945. Within that period, U.S. relations with the major economic powers of the region captured most of the attention, as the United States attempted to persuade those countries to place defeating the Axis ahead of their own national agendas. The roles of Argentina, Brazil, Chile, and Mexico during the war account for a significant body of the literature. The remainder of this chapter examines the principal studies that fall into these areas.

U.S. AND LATIN AMERICAN RELATIONS

Roosevelt's implementation of the Good Neighbor policy helped to dilute Latin American resentment toward U.S. imperialism and paved the way for more amicable and even close relations between the northern giant and many Latin American republics, in particular Mexico and Brazil. Dallek's book, while a global study, covers well the relations with Latin America. Wood's *Good Neighbor Policy* is an introduction to the history of the new policy, but Green in his *Containment of Latin America* places emphasis on U.S. efforts to strengthen its economic position in the region without using military intervention. In *Good Neighbor Diplomacy*, Gellman synthesizes the views of the politicians and diplomats involved from a thorough search of their papers. Langer and Gleason's two works are both excellent global studies of American foreign policy during the years 1937 to 1941, but with a wealth of detail on U.S. relations with its hemispheric neighbors.

Although suffering from a number of shortcomings, Haglund's *Latin America and the Transformation of U.S. Strategic Thought* calls attention to the importance of events in Latin America from 1936 to 1940 for the role they played in shaping American foreign policy, especially the growing awareness in the United States of the Nazi influence in the region. On this matter, one should also consult Reynolds, *The Creation of the Anglo-American Alliance.* For economic relations see Gardner, *Economic Aspects of New Deal Diplomacy*, and for the question of security Mecham analyzes the problem from the late 1880s into the Cold War era. In an attempt to increase its security, the United States created an inter-American military system that took form during the war. Child's *Unequal Alliance* is essential reading to understand how that system emerged. Security rationale as well as economic considerations underpinned U.S. moves to dominate commercial aviation in Latin America, the subject of Burden's *The Struggle for Airways in Latin America.* Besides his interesting account of U.S. pressure to eliminate Germans from the airlines in countries like Colombia, Bolivia, and Brazil, thereby benefiting Pan American and Grace, Burden studied U.S. foreign policy during the 1930s as it related to aviation. Laurence Duggan, who was involved in many of the episodes about which he writes, should also be consulted on the security issues; see his *The Americas: The Search for Hemisphere Security.* See, as well, Dozer, *Are We Good Neighbors?*

Brazil

Leslie Bethell in his bibliographic essay "Latin America, Europe and the United States, 1930–1960" may be correct by stating that no general study exists of relations between Brazil and the United States. But fortunately, for the war years such is not the case. An admirable overview of

Brazilian history during the years prior to and during the war can be read in Skidmore, *Politics in Brazil*. Since Brazilian dictator Getulio Vargas played such a pivotal role during this epoch, it is essential to read a few of the numerous biographies about him. Dulles, who has devoted most of his life to an examination of the "Gaucho leader," offers a detailed portrayal in *Vargas of Brazil*. His account of Vargas' repression of the communists in *Brazilian Communism* is informative. Chilcote's study, *The Brazilian Communist Party*, offers contrasting viewpoints and presents a broader overview. Levine analyzed the "critical years" of Vargas' rule, 1935–1939, in *The Vargas Regime*. Peter Seaborn Smith's *Oil and Politics in Modern Brazil* examines the important role the Brazilian military and Vargas played in formulating petroleum policy before, during, and after the war, and Wirth's *The Politics of Brazilian Development* analyzes industrial development, especially the important Volta Redonda steel complex, for the same period.

Roosevelt's policymakers regarded Brazil as a South American balance to the growing opposition of Argentina. Despite taking power by force and establishing a dictatorship, State Department officials supported Vargas' *Estado Nôvo* as preferable to dealing with his opponents: the fascistic Integralist Party, Nazi fifth columnists, the wing of the military led by Army Chief of Staff Pedro Aurélio de Góes Monteiro, or the communists. Jones' bibliographic essay "Brazil" is a useful guide to works on the Brazilian military. For an explanation of fascism's failure to take root in Brazil, see Hennessey's important "Fascism and Populism in Latin America." Hilton's "Fascism in Brazil" capably explains Integralist relationships with labor, state governments, and the military. In his "Ideology and Diplomacy," Seitenfus demonstrates the Italian influence on Brazilian fascism.

McCann's excellent, well-documented examination, the *Brazilian–American Alliance, 1937–1945*, is fundamental, owing to its exhaustive thoroughness and clear description of the events from 1937 to 1945. Several studies by Hilton cover the same era but approach it from different perspectives and emphases. His "Brazilian Diplomacy and the Washington–Rio de Janeiro 'Axis' " takes McCann to task on numerous points, but especially over his interpretation that relations between the United States and Brazil soured because the former sought certain economic and political advantages for itself that would increase the latter's dependency. McCann rebutted some of these charges, holding to his interpretation that U.S. officials sought economic advantages over Brazil that were imperialist. See his "Critique of Stanley Hilton." In "Brazil, the United States and World War II," McCann summarized Brazilian–American relations from 1935 to 1945 and reinforced his earlier conclusions that the United States sought a position of preeminence in Brazil and elsewhere in the hemisphere. Moura's excellent doctoral dissertation, "Brazilian Foreign Relations, 1939–1950," provides an understanding of the Brazilian agenda from that perspective. Focusing on Brazil but including Argentina, Chile, Ecuador, Mexico, and the United States, Hilton's *Hitler's Secret War* reveals the activities of German espionage agents in the region. The author combed the declassified files of the Federal Bureau of Investigation, Federal Communication Commission, and Office of Strategic Services, as well as the memoirs and biographies of various Allied agents, to tell an interesting tale of German intrigue and undercover activity. Rout and Bratzel in *The Shadow War* also provide an interesting overview of German espionage and U.S. counterespionage in Brazil, as well as in Argentina, Chile, and Mexico. Lesser's contribution, *Welcoming the Undesirables*, analyzes elite Brazilian attitudes toward Jews during the rise of European Nazism.

Cordell Hull noted Brazil's significance to the Allied cause when he wrote in his *Memoirs*, "Without the air bases Brazil permitted us to construct on her territory victory either in Europe or in Asia could not have come so soon" (Volume 2, 1423). Craven and Gate's first volume of *The Army Air Forces in World War II* discusses the air traffic that crossed the Atlantic from northeast Brazil, where the United States built bases, to north Africa, which facilitated the Allied invasion of Africa. Brazil was the only Latin American country to send an expeditionary force into the European theater, where it participated in the Italian campaign. History of the Brazilian Expeditionary Force (BEF) has attracted some scholarly attention from Brazilian historians and writers, the most competent and thorough of whom is Castello Branco. His *O Brasil na II Grande Guerra* is a detailed account. Unfortunately, few historians have investigated it in English. An exception is McCann, whose article "The Brazilian Army and the Problem of Mission" looks at the role of the army in the war and the changes produced in the philosophy of the officer corps. See also in this regard his thoughtful article "The Brazilian General Staff and Brazil's Military Situation."

At war's end the Expeditionary Force returned home triumphant, and the Brazilian military emerged from the conflict with the best-equipped armed force in Latin America. By far the largest recipient of Lend-Lease aid of all Latin American nations, Brazilians now took over newly built, enlarged, or modernized naval and air bases. Many in the officer corps developed strong ties with U.S. military brass, a connection that grew stronger as time went on. With a strengthened economy, a new steel industry, large foreign exchange surpluses, and increasing world diplomatic prestige, Brazil gained from the war everything its principal South American rival, Argentina, had hoped for itself. Frank's informative monograph, *Struggle for Hegemony*, ably describes this rivalry and concludes that U.S. aid to Brazil altered the regional balance of power, assuring Brazil's eventual dominance.

Argentina

Argentina pursued a course different from that of Brazil. Rather than closely collaborating with the Allies and thereby being eligible for Lend-Lease and military aid programs, it maintained a neutral position that the United States, especially, perceived to be pro-Axis. As the war progressed, and Argentina resisted British and North American pressure to sever relations, the United States took measures to isolate and punish it. These acrimonious relations have attracted a great deal of attention from historians. Humphreys devotes several solid chapters to the conflict. His account is especially strong for information on motivations, intentions, and objectives of British and North American officials, less so for those of the Argentines. In *The Limits of Hegemony,* Francis researched the decision-making process on the U.S. side but emphasizes domestic politics in Argentina and Chile as well.

Di Tella and Watt edited an excellent collection of essays analyzing the complex relations between Argentina and the Great Powers. Relying on recently available British and U.S. documentation, the most interesting essays in their *Argentina between the Great Powers* promote the view that Argentine neutrality during the war stemmed not from a pro-fascist bias, but from an attempt to serve British interests without provoking U.S. hostility. The principal argument here is that Argentine leaders believed that breaking relations with the Axis would have brought reprisals in the form of torpedoing Argentine ships laden with beef and cereal products destined for British ports. This position further maintains that to the British those supplies were far more important than an Argentine show of solidarity with the Allies, and therefore British diplomats encouraged them to remain neutral, bringing the Foreign Office and the State Department into repeated conflict.

In *The Roosevelt Foreign Policy Establishment,* Woods argues this position, as does Ciria, *Parties and Power in Modern Argentina.* Humphreys, however, faults them for believing what he called a "myth" spread by journalists and certain State Department officers that Britain was "secretly encouraging Argentina to stand out against the United States" (volume 2, 140, n.95, 96). Relying heavily on Foreign Office records, Humphreys cites the strongly worded British communiqué of December 31, 1942, lamenting the Argentine policy of maintaining diplomatic relations "with the enemies of humanity," and Anthony Eden's harsh words to the Argentine ambassador to Great Britain deploring Argentina's attitudes (volume 2, 142). Rapoport's *Gran Bretaña* discounts the significance of the communiqué and appraises the overall British attitude toward Argentina as not negative. See as well his brief *Las relaciones anglo-argentinas.* Newton's "critique" of Rapoport's *Gran Bretaña* should be consulted in this regard.

Tulchin, *Argentina and the United States* stresses the complex internal political situation as an explanation for Argentine policy.

The unpopular, reactionary Argentine President Ramon Castillo's intentions to bequeath the presidency to one of his wealthy cronies moved the major military and opposition political factions to close ranks long enough to remove him from power in June 1943. Led by a group of dissident officers calling itself the Grupo de Oficiales Unidos (GOU), the new military government at first was welcomed by the Allies, believing it meant an eventual rupture with the Axis. Disillusion soon set in, however, as the military regime became more repressive and fascistlike. Not only did it quickly become clear to U.S. and British policymakers that Argentina had no intention of breaking with the Axis, but they, especially State Department officials, were angered by the military's continued request for military equipment. If not already convinced, Cordell Hull now came to believe that Argentina was squarely in the Nazi camp. Hull's and Welles' memoirs have already been mentioned, but one should also consult British Ambassador to Argentina David Kelly's *The Ruling Few* for the Allies' relations with the military government. Journalistic accounts of the June 1943 coup can be found in Josephs' *Argentine Diary* and the Greenups' *Revolution before Breakfast.*

Several excellent, scholarly examinations contribute to our understanding of these events. The contributors to Di Tella and Platt's *The Political Economy of Argentina* attempt to answer the important question of why Argentina went from relative prosperity and political stability to economic decline and political chaos. One group of essayists finds the causes of the Argentine malaise in this period, rather than earlier at the end of World War I or during the Great Depression. Alexander's two works, *The Perón Era* and *Juan Domingo Perón: A History,* are essential to an understanding of the army colonel who conspired to take over in 1943 and then rose on the backs of the workers from his position of secretary of labor to the presidency. Potash's two books on the military in Argentina are also crucial for his insights into the military mind and the factional infighting. In *The Nazi Menace in Argentina,* Newton, after a thorough review of the archival data, concludes that while there were Nazi agents in the country, they did not pose a significant threat to taking control or projecting German power into the region. In this same vein, MacDonald's "The Politics of Intervention" reveals the sensationalistic reports from the Federal Bureau of Investigation (FBI) and Office of Strategic Services files regarding Nazi influence in the Argentine government.

Hull and Edward Stettinius, who had taken Sumner Welles' place as undersecretary, became so angry with the Argentines that they pressed Great Britain to cut off its purchases of meat and grains from the recalcitrant republic. For an authoritative account of this, see volume 3 of Hammond's *Food,* which covers Allied food policies during the war. Peffer's article, "Cordell Hull's Argentine Policy," deals with the same issue but differs with Hammond, who faults her for assuming that Anglo-Argentine discussions over the meat contract were ever formally suspended.

Fearing that Argentina would be left out of the formation of the United Nations at the scheduled April 1945 meeting to be held in San Francisco, the military government on April 4 declared war on the Axis and agreed to the resolutions adopted at the recent Mexico City (Chapultepec) Conference of American Ministers. Great Britain, the United States, and other Latin American governments that had withheld recognition from the military regime now restored diplomatic relations, and the United Nations extended an invitation to Argentina to attend the San Francisco meeting later in the month. Many of the works cited previously provide coverage of these events, but for the Argentine situation in particular and the Latin American role in the formation of the United Nations see Humphreys. Russell, *A History of the United Nations Charter*; Campbell, *Masquerade Peace: America's UN Policy*; Connell-Smith, *The United States and Latin America*; and Houston, *Latin America in the United Nations* all provide information on this topic.

Chile

The historical literature on Chile and Bolivia during the war merits mention in this chapter owing to the latter's turbulent political situation and the former's reluctance to sever relations with the Axis immediately after the Rio Conference. Based on fear for the safety of its lengthy, unprotected coast and Pacific islands, the provisional nature of its government in the early months of 1942, and the important and highly respected German community, Chile chose to ignore the Rio Conference recommendation to break ties with the Axis. A combination of internal political factors, U.S. pressure, and overcoming the fear of the Japanese threat eventually led the Rios administration to change its policy in January 1943. Declaration of war against Japan followed in February 1945 after Chilean leaders learned a few months earlier that only those countries that had declared war and signed the Declaration of the United Nations would be invited to attend the conferences on postwar international organization. The memoir of the U.S. ambassador to Chile during this period, Claude Bowers, *Chile through Embassy Windows*, offers an insider's view of the events. Francis, *The Limits of Hegemony*, while using few Chilean sources and being sketchy on the Chilean context, nevertheless provides a detailed survey of Chilean–U.S. relations from the Rio Conference to the end of the war. In *Chile and the United States*, Pike provided the context and hoped, vainly, in the light of later tragedies, that his study would lead to a better understanding of Chilean social problems and attitudes toward the United States. See, as well, Sater's more recent book, *Chile and the United States: Empires in Conflict.*

Bolivia

Without consulting the Bolivian Congress, President Enrique Peñaranda declared war on the Axis on April 7, 1943. By December 20 of that year a coup led by a group of young military officers backed by the Movimiento Nacionalista Revolucionaria (MNR) overthrew Peñaranda and set up a junta directed by Major Gualberto Villarroel. Aggressively nationalistic, opposed to settlements made with Standard Oil Company after Bolivia had nationalized its local holdings, and ardently critical of Bolivia's economic agreements with the United States and its adherence to the Declaration of the United Nations, the MNR contained a fascist wing that hoped for a Nazi victory. Nevertheless, British, U.S., and Latin American threats to withhold recognition and impose economic sanctions kept the new government on the Allied side for the duration of the war. Internal anger and revulsion at the junta's gross civil rights abuses exploded in a July 1946 revolt in which a mob broke into the presidential palace and killed the hapless Villarroel. The mob hanged him and the two men who had stayed with him, from a lamppost. As an overview of Bolivia's political history from the 1880s to 1952, Klein's survey is unrivaled. For insiders' perspectives on this drama see Ostria Gutiérrez, a former foreign minister of the Peñaranda government, *The Tragedy of Bolivia*, and Víctor Andrade, a member of Villarroel's cabinet and then his ambassador to Washington, *My Mission for Revolutionary Bolivia.*

Labor's increasingly powerful role and the significance of the Catavi massacre as factors in the overthrow of Peñaranda are carefully analyzed by Lora, *A History of the Bolivian Labour Movement.* Blasier's fascinating analysis of the "Belmonte affair" in his article cited earlier shows how the British tried to maneuver the Peñaranda government into the Allied camp, and Hyde, *The Quiet Canadian*, reveals the role played by William Stephenson, who established the British Security Coordination Service (BSC) and was responsible for the "Belmonte affair." For British policies toward Bolivian tin mining and the significance of that resource to the war effort, see Hillman, "Bolivia and British Tin Policy."

Mexico

Although Mexico had become a significant supplier of oil to Germany, especially after 1938, by the summer of 1941 its leaders had shifted their orientation more toward strengthening relations with the United States and Great Britain. In the spring of 1942 German torpedoes sank two Mexican oil tankers, and Mexico declared war in May. Niblo's monograph,

War, Diplomacy and Development, is essential reading for an understanding of the changes Mexico underwent as it moved from an agrarian country, hostile toward, and distrustful of, the United States, to a rapidly industrializing ally in the struggle against the Axis. Emphasizing the economic aspects of those changes, Niblo is primarily concerned with the growing dependency of Mexico's industrial economy on the United States. One should also consult his earlier piece, "The Impact of War," and his article "British Propaganda in Mexico," a description of British agents' manipulation of Mexican public opinion favoring the Allies by placing news stories in Mexican newspapers.

Niblo demonstrated that this kind of activity did not end with the termination of hostilities. Schuler made a solid contribution in "Germany, Mexico and the United States." He concluded that although economic relations between Mexico and Germany were disrupted early in the war, Mexico maintained political connections until June 1941, when doubts set in that Germany probably would dominate Europe. Mexico then quickened the pace of cooperation with the United States. War gave Mexico new possibilities for improving its industry and its status with the United States, according to Torres Ramírez in her political-economic history, *México en la segunda guerra mundial*. Loyola's collection of essays, *Entre la guerra y la estabilidad política*, not only treats the political economy and hemispheric defense but also examines the war's impact on Mexican culture. Betty Kirk, writing from Mexico since 1938, gives a journalistic view of events up to Mexico's entry into the war in *Covering the Mexican Front*.

As Roosevelt's ambassador to Mexico from 1933 to 1941, Josephus Daniels precariously kept Mexico in the U.S. camp even while the Department of State pressed Mexico to cave in to oil company demands for immediate compensation for their expropriated properties. Cronon's biography of the ambassador is essential. In *Das Dritte Reich und Mexiko*, Volland, after a thorough review of Mexican and German archival sources and the diary of Hitler's minister to Mexico, emphasizes the significance of the huge Mexican oil sales to Germany after 1938. His account demonstrates that Mexican oil was a great aid to the German war machine in its invasions of France and the Low Countries.

Several scholars analyzed Mexican–U.S. relations in general, such as Cline, *The United States and Mexico* and *Mexico: Revolution to Evolution*. His overviews, however, should be used in conjunction with the more recent analyses of Vasquez and Meyer's *The United States and Mexico*; Aguilar Camín and Meyer's *In the Shadow of the Mexican Revolution*; and Schmitt's *Mexico and the United States*. Mosk, *Industrial Revolution in Mexico*, writes about the "New Group" of industrialists who emerged with the war and whose importance his critics claim he exaggerates. Mabry's *Mexico's Acción Nacional* is a basic source on the development of the major opposition party from the Right to the ruling party of the revolution and is excellent for opposition party activities during the war. Craig's fine analysis of the Bracero program that brought hundreds of thousands of Mexican workers to the United States to work in the fields and railroads is an essential part of the war story. The right-wing Sinarquistas and events in rural Mexico before and during the war are well covered in Whetten's *Rural Mexico.* Nor can the student ignore the part played by Vicente Lombardo Toledano, the leftist labor leader of Mexico's *Confederación de Trabajadores Mexicanos* (CTM), who urged the government to break relations with the Axis. His activities during this time can be followed in Mellon, *Mexican Marxist: Vicente Lombardo Toledano.*

While Mexico's principal contribution as an ally to the war effort was to supply the United States with increasing quantities of strategic resources and laborers, it also sent an air squadron that saw action against the Japanese in the Philippines and in Formosa. Almost a quarter of a million Mexicans living in the United States entered the American military, and fourteen thousand of them saw combat. Santoro's doctoral dissertation, "United States and Mexican Relations," is an important source for an understanding of these events, while Prewett, "The Mexican Army," discusses the makeup of the Mexican army when it entered the conflict.

The Caribbean

Other regions of Latin America were involved in the war in less direct ways than the countries previously mentioned. Primarily, these states entered into agreements with the United States to supply badly needed resources to the Allies and to provide locales for Allied military installations. In this latter regard Caribbean and Central American republics performed a vital service to the United States and in return received loans, credits, technical aid, and economic and military assistance. As a result, U.S. influence increased dramatically in many of these countries, and that influence, for good or ill, is one of the lasting legacies of the war.

No military engagements involving the Axis occurred in the Western Hemisphere during the war, with the exception of naval combat off the coast of the United States, in the Caribbean, and in the South Atlantic. Scheina reviews the role Latin American navies played during the war in his *Latin America: A Naval History.* The story of the *Graf Spee,* a German pocket battleship that roamed the South Atlantic sinking British merchant ships, suffered severe damage, and was sunk by its German commander, is elaborately told in the immense study by Millington-Drake, *The Drama of Graf Spee.* For the Battle of the Caribbean, during which German submarines in 1942 alone sank 336 ships with a tonnage of more than one and a half million, see the first volume of Morison's *The Battle of the Atlantic.* Morison called the Caribbean the U-boats' "happiest hunting ground" (145). Kelshall's *The U-Boat War in the Caribbean* is useful for information on German activity in the region.

Owing to its strategic significance and the naval combat that occurred there, the Caribbean presented several challenges to Allied diplomats. U.S. influence and intervention in the region created resentment, which the Good Neighbor policy failed to allay. During the course of the war, U.S. presence increased, and with it, new problems arose. While there is no comprehensive study focused specifically on the Caribbean during World War II, Fraser's *Ambivalent Anti-Colonialism* examines the role of the United States in British West Indian independence from 1940 to 1964. Since the nineteenth century the United States had pressed Europeans to end colonial control in the area. During the war British cries for assistance met with demands that they open their colonies to U.S. influence. Lend-Lease agreements secured Caribbean naval bases and market potential for the United States, but, at war's end, Fraser concludes, fear of Russian expansion and the onset of the Cold War resulted in the United States' urging British, Dutch, and French to reassert their control over their colonies. In *Cruising the Caribbean*, Fernandez reaches similar conclusions. Langley's useful synthesis of U.S. activity in the Caribbean, cited earlier, capably summarizes the strategic issues brought on by the war.

The war's impact and increasing U.S. influence in Cuba, the Dominican Republic, and Haiti have been analyzed by some historians. Gellman in *Roosevelt and Batista* showed not only that the United States was able to keep Cuba firmly in the Allied camp (five thousand cigars sent to Churchill over the course of the war reflect Cuba's pro-Allied spirit) but that Roosevelt's administration significantly shaped Cuba's internal development. In their book *The United States and the Trujillo Regime*, Atkins and Wilson provide information on wartime agreements that established a naval mission, sent submarine chasers to assist the Dominican Republic's coast guard, and created a marine air station that trained their pilots. For Haiti, the Heinls' *Written in Blood* recounts the firm support the Haitian government gave the Allies and their disastrous experiment with a rubber-bearing vine that uprooted large numbers of peasants, cost millions of dollars, and yielded little rubber.

CONCLUSION

A growing number of researchers have directed their attention to the immediate aftermath of the war in Latin America in an effort to gauge the relationship between the global upheaval and the political, economic, and social development thereafter. Space allows mention of only a couple here. In *Latin America between the Second World War and the Cold War*, Bethell and Roxborough bring together eleven essays on as many Latin American countries that recorded strikingly similar experiences. With the Allied victory these nations witnessed a process of democratization, a shift toward the Left, and increasing labor militancy. As the Cold War set in, these trends were quickly reversed, however, with the resurgence of the political Right, demands for economic growth, and U.S. pressure to secure the hemisphere from "communism." By 1948, the editors conclude, an opportunity for social democracy was lost, replaced by authoritarian regimes promoting economic growth without equity. Rock's *Latin America in the 1940s* arrives at similar conclusions.

Much still remains to be done for a better understanding of Latin American involvement in the war and the ramifications of the world conflict on individual countries. A few suggestions for future research are therefore in order. The quantity and quality of research already published are uneven: Argentine–U.S.–British diplomatic relations in 1940–1945 have, in some areas, attracted too much attention, but Caribbean and Central American topics have been neglected.

So far no comprehensive analysis has been done of the problems and solutions that emerged from U.S. programs imposed on Latin Americans to further the war effort. A history of the building of the Pan-American Highway and its impact on the economy and society of those regions affected by it would be a contribution. A detailed analysis of the various schemes to obtain rubber in Latin America and the way in which those programs altered the human and natural environment would not only make fascinating reading but help us understand the impact that American-sponsored development programs had on the people where they were established.

There is no shortage of studies done on German, Italian, and Japanese immigration to Latin America, but research is lacking on how these groups fared when their adopted nations broke with, or declared war on, the Axis. We know that businesses and properties were confiscated by some governments, but the picture is not clear as to how families and communities originating from one of the Axis nations fared in the period 1939–1945.

Research showing the impact of the war on women in the United States suggests that similar investigations could be undertaken in Latin America, especially where the exigencies of war drained men from field and factory, such as in Brazil and Mexico. How did the war affect women throughout the region politically, economically, and socially? To what extent was the war disruptive to families and to community organizations?

Finally, as a new generation of historians emerges, and Latin American governments organize and make available more of the documentation of the era, questions as to the meaning of the great conflict for the future development of Latin America can be resolved with greater certainty.

BIBLIOGRAPHY

Aguilar Camín, Héctor, and Lorenzo Meyer. *In the Shadow of the Mexican Revolution.* Trans. Luis Alberto Fierro. Austin: University of Texas, 1993.

Alexander, Robert J. *Juan Domingo Perón: A History.* Boulder, CO: Westview, 1979.

———. *The Perón Era.* New York: Russell and Russell, 1965.

Andrade, Víctor. *My Mission for Revolutionary Bolivia: 1944–1962.* Ed. Cole Blasier. Pittsburgh: University of Pittsburgh, 1976.

Atkins, G. Pope, and L. C. Wilson. *The United States and the Trujillo Regime.* New Brunswick, NJ: Rutgers UP, 1972.

Bethell, Leslie, ed. *The Cambridge History of Latin America.* 11 vols. London: Cambridge UP, 1985– .

———. "Latin America, Europe and the United States, 1930–1960." In Leslie Bethell, ed., *Cambridge History of Latin America,* vol. II, 959–68. London: Cambridge UP, 1995.

Bethell, Leslie, and Ian Roxborough, eds. *Latin America between the Second World War and the Cold War, 1944–1948.* Cambridge: Cambridge UP, 1992.

Bidwell, P. W. *Economic Defense of Latin America.* Boston: World Peace Foundation, 1941.

Blasier, Cole. "The United States, Germany and the Bolivian Revolutionaries, 1941–46." *Hispanic American Historical Review* 52 (1972): 26–54.

Bowers, Claude. *Chile through Embassy Windows, 1939–1953.* New York: Simon and Schuster, 1958.

Burden, W. H. *The Struggle for Airways in Latin America.* New York: Council on Foreign Relations, 1943.

Bushnell, David. *Eduardo Santos and the Good Neighbor, 1938–1942.* Gainesville: University of Florida, 1967.

Campbell, T. M. *Masquerade Peace: America's UN Policy, 1944–1945.* Tallahassee: Florida State UP, 1973.

Castello Branco, Manoel Thomaz. *O Brasil no II Grande Guerra.* Rio de Janeiro: Biblioteca do Exército, 1960.

Chilcote, Ronald H. *The Brazilian Communist Party: Conflict and Integration, 1922–1972.* New York: Oxford UP, 1974.

Child, John. *Unequal Alliance: The Inter-American Military System, 1938–78.* Boulder, CO: Westview, 1980.

Ciria, Alberto. *Parties and Power in Modern Argentina, 1930–1946.* Trans. C. A. Astiz and Mary McCarthy. Albany: State University of New York, 1974.

Cline, Howard F. *Mexico: Revolution to Evolution, 1940–1960.* London: Oxford UP, 1962.

———. *The United States and Mexico.* Rev. ed. New York: Oxford UP, 1963.

Conil Paz, Alberto, and Gustavo Ferrari. *Argentina's Foreign Policy, 1930–1962.* Notre Dame, IN: Notre Dame UP, 1966.

Conn, Stetson, Rose Engleman, and Byron Fairchild. *Guarding the United States and Its Outposts.* [U.S. Army in World War II.] Washington, DC: Department of the Army, 1964.

Conn, Stetson, and Byron Fairchild. *The Framework of Hemisphere Defense.* [The Western Hemisphere. U.S. Army in World War II.] Washington, DC: Department of the Army, 1960.

Connell-Smith, Gordon. *The United States and Latin America.* London: Heinemann Educational, 1974.

Craig, Richard B. *The Bracero Program: Interest Groups and Foreign Policy.* Austin: University of Texas, 1971.

Craven, W. F., and J. L. Gate, eds. *The Army Air Forces in World War II.* 7 vols. Chicago: University of Chicago, 1948–1958.

Cronon, E. D. *Josephus Daniels in Mexico.* Madison: University of Wisconsin, 1960.

Dallek, Robert. *Franklin D. Roosevelt and American Foreign Policy, 1932–1945.* New York: Oxford UP, 1979.

Di Tella, Guido, and D.C.M. Platt, eds. *The Political Economy of Argentina, 1880–1946.* London: Macmillian; Oxford: St. Anthony's College, 1986.

Di Tella, Guido, and D. Cameron Watt, eds. *Argentina between the Great Powers, 1939–46.* Pittsburgh: University of Pittsburgh, 1990.

Dozer, Donald M. *Are We Good Neighbors? Three Decades of Inter-American Relations, 1930–1960.* Gainesville: University of Florida, 1959.

Duggan, Laurence. *The Americas: The Search for Hemisphere Security.* New York: Holt, 1969.

Dulles, John W. F. *Brazilian Communism, 1935–1945: Repression during World Upheaval.* Austin: University of Texas, 1983.

———. *Vargas of Brazil: A Political Biography.* Austin: University of Texas, 1967.

Fernandez, Ronald. *Cruising the Caribbean: U.S. Influence and Intervention in the Twentieth Century.* Monroe, ME: Common Courage, 1994.

Fernández Artúcio, Hugo. *The Nazi Octopus in South America.* London: Farrar, 1943.

Flynn, Peter. *Brazil: A Political Analysis.* London: E. Benn, 1978.

Francis, Michael J. *The Limits of Hegemony: U.S. Relations with Argentina and Chile during World War II.* Notre Dame, IN: University of Notre Dame, 1977.

Frank, Gary. *Struggle for Hegemony: Argentina, Brazil and the U.S. during the Second World War.* Coral Gables, FL: University of Miami, 1979.

Fraser, Cary. *Ambivalent Anti-Colonialism: The United States and the Genesis of West Indian Independence, 1940–1964.* Westport, CT: Greenwood, 1994.

Frye, Alton. *Nazi Germany and the American Hemisphere.* New Haven, CT: Yale UP, 1986.

Gardiner, C. Harvey. *The Japanese in Peru, 1873–1973.* Albuquerque: University of New Mexico, 1975.

Gardner, F. L. *Economic Aspects of New Deal Diplomacy.* Madison: University of Wisconsin, 1964.

Gellman, Irwin F. *Good Neighbor Diplomacy: United States Policy in Latin America, 1933–1945.* Baltimore: Johns Hopkins UP, 1979.

———. *Roosevelt and Batista: Good Neighbor Diplomacy in Cuba, 1933–1945.* Albuquerque: University of New Mexico, 1973.

Gravil, Roger. *The Anglo-Argentine Connection, 1900–1939.* Boulder, CO: Westview, 1985.

Green, David. *The Containment of Latin America: A History of the Myths and Realities of the Good Neighbor Policy.* Chicago: Quadrangle, 1971.

Greenup, Ruth, and Leonard Greenup. *Revolution before Breakfast*. Chapel Hill: University of North Carolina, 1947.

Haglund, David G. *Latin America and the Transformation of U.S. Strategic Thought, 1936–40*. Albuquerque: University of New Mexico, 1984.

Hammond, R. J. *Food*. 3 vols. London: HMSO, 1951–1962.

Heinl, R. D. Jr., and Nancy Gordon Heinl. *Written in Blood: The Story of the Haitian People, 1942–1961*. Austin: University of Texas, 1978.

Hennessey, Alistair. "Fascism and Populism in Latin America." In Walter Laquer, ed., *Fascism: A Reader's Guide, Analyses, Interpretations, Bibliography*, 255–94. Berkeley: University of California, 1976.

Hillman, John. "Bolivia and British Tin Policy, 1939–45." *Journal of Latin American Studies 22* (1990): 289–315.

Hilton, Stanley E. "Ação Integralista Brasileira: Fascism in Brazil, 1932–1938." *Luso-Brazilian Review 9* (1972): 3–29.

———. *Brazil and the Great Powers, 1930–1939: The Politics of Trade Rivalry*. Austin: University of Texas, 1975.

———. "Brazilian Diplomacy and the Washington–Rio de Janeiro 'Axis' during the World War II Era." *Hispanic American Historical Review 59* (1979): 201–31.

———. *Hitler's Secret War in South America, 1939–1945*. Baton Rouge: Louisiana State UP, 1981.

Houston, J. A. *Latin America in the United Nations*. Westport, CT: Greenwood, 1956.

Hull, Cordell. *The Memoirs of Cordell Hull*. 2 vols. New York: Macmillan, 1948.

Humphreys, R. A. *Latin America and the Second World War*. 2 vols. London: Athlone, University of London, 1981–1982.

Hyde, H. Montgomery. *The Quiet Canadian*. London: Hamish Hamilton, 1962.

Jones, Errol D. "Brazil." In David G. La France and Errol D. Jones, eds., *Latin American Military History: An Annotated Bibliography*, 342–484. New York and London: Garland, 1992.

Josephs, Ray. *Argentine Diary: The Inside Story of the Coming of Fascism*. New York: Random House, 1944.

Kelly, David Victor. *The Ruling Few*. London: Hollis and Carter, 1952.

Kelshall, Gaylord. *The U-Boat War in the Caribbean*. Port of Spain, Trinidad: Paria, 1988.

Kirk, Betty. *Covering the Mexican Front: The Battle of Europe versus America*. Norman: University of Oklahoma, 1942.

Klein, H. S. *Parties and Political Change in Bolivia, 1880–1952*. Cambridge: Cambridge UP, 1969.

Langer, W. L., and S. E. Gleason. *The Challenge to Isolation, 1937–1940*. London: HarperCollins, 1952.

———. *The Undeclared War, 1940–1941*. London: HarperCollins, 1953.

Langley, Lester D. *The United States and the Caribbean, 1900–1970*. Athens: University of Georgia, 1980.

Lesser, Jeffrey. *Welcoming the Undesirables: Brazil and the Jewish Question*. Berkeley: University of California, 1995.

Levine, Robert M. *The Vargas Regime: The Critical Years, 1935–1938*. New York: Columbia UP, 1970.

Lieuwen, Edwin. *Petroleum in Venezuela: A History.* Berkeley: University of California, 1954.

——. *Venezuela.* London: Oxford UP, 1968.

Lora, Guillermo. *A History of the Bolivian Labour Movement, 1848–1971.* Cambridge: Cambridge UP, 1971.

Loyola, Rafael, ed. *Entre la guerra y la estabilidad política.* Mexico: Editorial Grijalbo, 1990.

Mabry, Donald J. *Mexico's Acción Nacional: A Catholic Alternative to Revolution.* Syracuse: Syracuse UP, 1973.

MacDonald, Callum A. "The Politics of Intervention: The United States and Argentina, 1941–1946." *Journal of Latin American Studies 12* (1980): 365–96.

McCann, Frank D. *The Brazilian–American Alliance, 1937–1945.* Princeton: Princeton UP, 1973.

——. "The Brazilian Army and the Problem of Mission, 1939–64." *Journal of Latin American Studies 12* (1980): 107–26.

——. "The Brazilian General Staff and Brazil's Military Situation, 1930–1945." *Journal of Inter-American Studies and World Affairs 25* (1983): 299–324.

——. "Brazil, the United States, and World War II: A Commentary." *Diplomatic History 3* (1979): 59–76.

——. "Critique of Stanley E. Hilton's Brazilian Diplomacy and the Washington–Rio de Janeiro Axis during the World War II Era." *Hispanic American Historical Review 59* (1979): 691–701.

Mecham, J. Lloyd. *The United States and Inter-American Security, 1889–1960.* Austin: University of Texas, 1981.

Mellon, R. P. *Mexican Marxist: Vicente Lombardo Toledano.* Chapel Hill: University of North Carolina, 1966.

Michel, Henri. *The Second World War.* Trans. Douglas Parmée. New York: Praeger, 1975.

Millington-Drake, Eugene. *The Drama of Graf Spee and the Battle of the Plate.* London: P. Davies, 1964.

Morison, Samuel Eliot. *The Battle of the Atlantic, September 1939 to May, 1943.* Boston: Little, Brown, 1948.

Mosk, Sanford. A. *Industrial Revolution in Mexico.* Berkeley and Los Angeles: University of California, 1950.

Moura, Gerson. "Brazilian Foreign Relations, 1939–1950." Diss. University of London, 1982.

Newton, Ronald. "Gran Bretaña, Estados Unidos y las clases dirigentes argentinas, 1940–45." *Hispanic American Historical Review 62* (1982): 515. Critique of Mario Rapoport.

——. *The Nazi Menace in Argentina, 1931–47.* Stanford, CA: Stanford UP, 1991.

Niblo, Stephen R. "British Propaganda in Mexico during the Second World War: The Development of Cultural Imperialism." *Latin America Perspectives 10* (1983): 114–26.

——. "The Impact of War: Mexico and World War II." La Trobe University Institute of Latin American Studies, Occasional Paper no. 10. Melbourne, 1988.

——. *War, Diplomacy and Development: The United States and Mexico, 1938–1954.* Wilmington, DE: Scholarly Resources, 1995.

Ostria Gutiérrez, Alberto. *The Tragedy of Bolivia.* New York: R. Welch, 1956.

Peffer, E. Louise. "Cordell Hull's Argentine Policy and Britain's Meat Supply." *Inter-American Economic Affairs 10* (1956): 219–43.

Pike, Frederick B. *Chile and the United States, 1880–1962.* Notre Dame, IN: University of Notre Dame, 1963.

Potash, Robert A. *The Army and Politics in Argentina, 1945–1962: Perón to Frondizi.* Stanford, CA: Stanford UP, 1980.

———. *The Army and Politics in Argentina, 1928–1945: Yrigoyen to Perón.* Stanford, CA: Stanford UP, 1969.

Pratt, Julius William. *Cordell Hull, 1933–44.* 2 vols. New York: Cooper Square, 1964.

Prewett, Viriginia. "The Mexican Army." *Foreign Affairs 19* (1941): 609–20.

Rapoport, Mario. *Gran Bretaña, Estados Unidos y las clases dirigentes argentinas, 1940–1945.* Buenos Aires: Editorial de Belgrano, 1980.

———. *Las relaciones anglo-argentinas: aspectos políticos y económicos; la experiencia del gobierno militar, 1943–1945.* Buenos Aires: Fundación para el Estudio de los Problemas Argentinos, 1979.

———. "The United States, the German-Argentines and the Myth of the 4th Reich, 1943–47." *Hispanic American Historical Review 64* (1984): 81–103.

Ready, J. Lee. *Forgotten Allies: The Military Contribution of the Colonies, Exiled Governments, and Lesser Powers to the Allied Victory in World War II.* 2 vols. Jefferson, NC, and London: McFarland, 1985.

Reynolds, David. *The Creation of the Anglo-American Alliance, 1937–1941: A Study in Competitive Co-Operation.* London: Europe, 1981.

Rock, David, ed. *Latin America in the 1940s: War and Postwar Transitions.* Berkeley: University of California, 1994.

Rout, Leslie B., and John F. Bratzel. *The Shadow War: German Espionage and United States Counter-Espionage in World War II.* Frederick, MD: University Publication of America, 1986.

Russell, Ruth B. *A History of the United Nations Charter: The Role of the United States, 1940–1945.* Washington, DC: Brookings Institution, 1958.

Santoro, Carmela Elvira. "United States and Mexican Relations during World War II." Diss. Syracuse University, 1967.

Sater, William F. *Chile and the United States: Empires in Conflict.* Athens: University of Georgia, 1990.

Scheina, Robert L. *Latin America: A Naval History, 1910–1987.* Annapolis, MD: NIP, 1987.

Schmitt, Karl M. *Mexico and the United States, 1921–1973: Conflict and Coexistence.* New York: Wiley, 1974.

Schuler, Friedrich. "Germany, Mexico and the United States during the Second World War." *Jahrbuch für Geschichte von Staat, Wirtschaft und Gesellschaft Lateinamerika 22* (1985): 457–76.

Seitenfus, Ricardo Silva. "Ideology and Diplomacy: Italian Fascism and Brazil, 1935–38." *Hispanic American Historical Review 64* (1984): 503–34.

Skidmore, Thomas E. *Politics in Brazil, 1930–1964.* New York: Oxford UP, 1967.

Smith, Peter H. *Politics and Beef in Argentina; Patterns of Conflict and Change.* New York: Columbia UP, 1969.

Smith, Peter Seaborn. *Oil and Politics in Modern Brazil.* Toronto: Maclean-Hunter, 1976.

Stevenson, J. R. *The Chilean Popular Front.* Philadephia: University of Pennsylvania, 1942.

Tamarin, David. *The Argentine Labor Movement, 1930–1945: A Study in the Origins of Peronism.* Albuquerque: University of New Mexico, 1985.

Torres Ramírez, Blanca. *México en la segunda guerra mundial.* Mexico City: Colegio de México, 1979.

Tulchin, Joseph S. *Argentina and the United States: A Conflicted Relationship.* Boston: Twayne, 1990.

Vázquez, Josefina, and Lorenzo Meyer. *The United States and Mexico.* Chicago: University of Chicago, 1985.

Volland, Klaus. *Das Dritte Reich und Mexiko.* Bern, Switzerland: Verlag Peter Lang, 1976.

Weinberg, Gerhard L. *A World at Arms: A Global History of World War II.* Cambridge: Cambridge UP, 1994.

Welles, Sumner. *Seven Major Decisions.* London: H. Hamilton, 1951.

———. *The Time for Decision.* New York: Harper and Brothers, 1994.

———. *Where Are We Heading?* New York: Harper and Brothers, 1946.

Whetten, Nathan L. *Rural Mexico.* Chicago: University of Chicago, 1948.

Wirth, John D. *The Politics of Brazilian Development, 1930–1954.* Stanford, CA: Stanford UP, 1970.

Wood, Bryce. *The Making of the Good Neighbor Policy.* New York and London: Columbia UP, 1961.

Woods, R. B. *The Roosevelt Foreign Policy Establishment and the Good Neighbor: The United States and Argentina, 1941–1945.* Lawrence: University of Kansas, 1979.

27   World War II and the Middle East

John M. Vander Lippe

Within the global framework of World War II, the Middle East, stretching from Egypt to Iran and from Turkey to the Arabian Peninsula, was of vital strategic importance, due to oil reserves and other raw materials as well as its geographic location. For the warring powers, the significance of its position between Europe, Africa, and Asia was enhanced by the waterways of the Suez Canal, the Turkish Straits, and the Persian Gulf. The belligerents fought on the battlefields as well as at the table for diplomatic, economic, and military predominance throughout the region. Ultimately, supremacy in the Middle East helped to determine the outcome of the war.

For the people of the Middle East, World War II intensified the struggle to obtain, regain, or maintain their independence from the domination of European imperialism and to build the institutions of sovereign nation-states. Thus, the overall regional role of the Middle East in the war and the impact of the war on Middle Eastern societies represent two distinct, but inseparable, issues. One reflects the importance of the strategic struggle between the warring powers for control of the region, while the other points to the relationship between the war and specific political, economic, and social developments within the region itself. For scholars of World War II, the Middle East has not been a major area of concern, while for scholars of the Middle East, the impact of World War II on the region has not been of major concern, since they interpret the war as influencing events but not playing a primary role in Middle Eastern history. For example, Yapp argues in *The Near East since the First World War* that for the region as a whole the Second World War had none of the importance of the First World War, which brought the downfall of the Ottoman Empire and fundamental political change. According to Yapp, in the Second World War the Germans never considered the region to be vital; thus, it remained at the fringes of the larger struggle. The war served only to hasten certain changes in the region that were already developing and had the effect of raising the strategic importance of the region in the postwar Cold War period.

Thus, extant scholarship, stressing either Great Power influence on the Middle East or the historical development of the region since World War I, places World War II within the broader context of the continuum of Middle Eastern history in the twentieth century, with a focus on nationalist movements, state building, and the struggle to overcome the political and economic constraints of Western domination. Actually, Kirk's *The Middle East in the War*, published in 1952, is the only major work to deal specifically with the Middle East as a whole during World War II. Kirk divides the war into three periods: September 1939 to the fall of France, the Italian invasion of North Africa to the Battle of El Alamein, and the period 1943 to 1945, when war receded from the region, and Axis influence decreased. Kirk stresses the economic impact of the war on the region: the disruption of trade patterns, the reduction of foreign investment, the economic and political demands of the Allied occupation of Arab and Iranian territory, and the impact of general mobilization of the Turkish military.

For Kirk, economic dislocation was at the center of demands for radical change that emerged throughout the Middle East during and after the war. In the Arab territories, particularly Egypt, Palestine, Syria, and Iraq, demands for the end of British and French control were combined with nascent movements aimed at replacing the old ruling elites, compromised by their collaboration with the European imperialist powers. In Turkey, the economic difficulties stemmed from the diversion of resources to prepare for defense against German or Soviet invasion, while Iran experienced hardship as the British and Soviets commandeered materials and labor to supply the Allied war effort on the Eastern Front. Thus, for Kirk, World War II profoundly influenced economic relations in the Middle East, permeating domestic affairs as well as regional and international relations.

In the general absence of works that specifically examine the regional impact of World War II on the Middle East, this chapter is a study of scholarship examining international complexities confronted by the Middle East during the war period. It explores both the struggle that took place between the Great Powers in the Middle East and regional and national struggles that influenced Middle Eastern history.

THE GREAT POWERS AND THE MIDDLE EAST

With the destruction of the Ottoman Empire after World War I, Britain and France gained control over much of the territory occupied by the

Arabs through the mandate system, while the Turks successfully fought for independence and formed a republic in 1923. The interwar period, particularly the 1930s, saw growing efforts by the Europeans to consolidate and increase their influence and control in the region.

For the British, the Suez Canal and the Persian Gulf were of vital concern, seen as the keys to oil, raw materials, and markets in the Arab territories and essential for communications with India, Australia, and colonies in Asia. Monroe in *Britain's Moment in the Middle East* argues that concern for a secure passage to India shaped all British policy in the region throughout the nineteenth and twentieth centuries. In this context, Britain's continuing control of Egypt, its role in creating Iraq after World War I, and the establishment of the Palestine Mandate were all aimed at controlling and maintaining the land and sea bridges from the Mediterranean to the Indian Ocean. Monroe argues, however, that enthusiasm for formal and direct control of the region had flagged significantly by 1939. World War II helped prolong British control for a few more years to keep the rivals away from its power sources, but the major impact of the war on British policy was to heighten awareness of the increasing financial responsibility that came with direct control.

Silverfarb in *The Twilight of British Ascendancy* explored British attempts to control indigenous political opposition during World War II. One of the major fears of the British administrators and policymakers was the spread of Nazi influence among military and political leaders in Iraq and the region. In May 1941, the British crushed a coup in Iraq by apparently pro-German forces led by Rashid Ali al-Gaylani. The 1941 deposition of Reza Shah of Iran and the British ultimatum to King Faruq of Egypt in February 1942 were other incidents in which the British felt they had to take action to curtail German influence and to ensure continued cooperation with the Allies. Each of these events had repercussions after the war, with the emergence of Muhammad Musaddiq in Iran, the 1958 Iraqi revolution, and the 1952 Free Officers coup in Egypt, all aimed at ousting political and military leaders who were seen as collaborators with Britain.

Along with attempting to combat German political influence in the Arab Middle East during the war, the British tried to block German trade by controlling the economy of the region. This effort by the British was introduced as a way to alleviate the negative impact of the war while they hoped to gain favorable status among the Arabs. Wilmington, *The Middle East Supply Centre*, and Lloyd, *Food and Inflation in the Middle East*, discuss the role of the Middle East Supply Centre, created in Cairo in 1941 through Anglo-American cooperation, in purchasing commodities and raw materials and in supplying needed foodstuffs for the domestic economies of the Arab countries. According to Wilmington, as well as Lloyd, the first years of the war saw tremendous inflationary pressures as hoarding, price gouging, and the diversion of transportation to the war effort disrupted the already weak economies of the region. British planners hoped to solve their own problems of supplies as well as establish goodwill through the strategic purchase of large quantities of certain crops. For instance, the British purchased the entire Egyptian cotton crop for 1940 at favorable prices. The center served as a means to control economic activity in the Arab Middle East and formed the basis for subsequent Anglo-American cooperation in the region following the war.

Besides efforts in the Arab countries, British policymakers considered Turkey a bulwark against the spread of German as well as Soviet influence in the Middle East, and also considered it a potentially important ally in the Balkans. Evans, *The Slow Rapprochement*, and Zhivkova, *Anglo-Turkish Relations*, both deal with the restoration of Turkish–British relations during the 1930s. Following World War I, after an initial conflict with the Turkish nationalist regime led by Mustafa Kemal Ataturk, the British concluded that a formal alliance would help offset continuing pro-German sentiment in Turkey. They also believed that the alliance could sway Turkey from joining Germany in another European war and restrict delivery of chromium ore and raw materials to German industry. Turkey's neutrality or alliance was seen as essential to preventing the Germans from forming a land bridge to the Persian Gulf or gaining control of the straits. Negotiations for an alliance culminated in the Anglo-Turkish Treaty of May 1939. Although the treaty formally committed Turkey to war against the Axis, Turkey resisted declaring war until February 1945.

The question of Turkish neutrality during the Second World War is the subject of Weisband, *Turkish Foreign Policy*, and Deringil, *Turkish Foreign Policy during the Second World War*. Both Weisband and Deringil are in general agreement that Turkey remained neutral despite its alliance with Britain, largely because the Turkish president Ismet Inonu and his advisers were convinced that the British would, or could, not deliver the military and financial assistance necessary for Turkey to contribute to the war effort and fight off a German or Soviet attack. Without considerable help from the Allies, Turkish leaders feared involvement in the war would drain the treasury, result in massive destruction, and ultimately weaken Turkey's military capability. Thus, they decided to delay entry into the war for as long as possible without breaking completely with either the Axis or the Allies. But at the same time, Turkish leaders pursued Turkish interests, even at the risk of Allied or Axis animosity. Shaw, *Turkey and the Holocaust*, discussed the efforts of the Turkish government to protect Jews with Turkish citizenship from Nazi persecution before and during the war.

Overall, British policy toward the Middle East before, during, and after World War II stressed keeping strategically important resources under British control and out of the hands of the Germans and the Soviets and away from the control of the governments of the region. This view led to conflict and competition not only with enemies but with supposed allies as well. Gaunson, *The Anglo-French Clash in Lebanon and Syria,* and Rosh-wald, *Estranged Bedfellows,* provide excellent insight into the conflicts between the British and French over policy toward Syria and Lebanon. In 1941 Rashid Ali's coup in Iraq prompted the British to invade Syria to stop the transport of arms by the Vichy French government. The Free French endorsed the invasion, but the Allies soon quarreled over policy toward the Arabs. The Free French, who gained official political control, accused the British military occupation forces of encouraging an anti-French Arab nationalist movement in Syria. The British grew impatient with De Gaulle's insistence that the empire was vital to the national existence of France and that Arab nationalism had to be crushed. By 1945 De Gaulle felt betrayed by the British, who used their military superiority in the region to force the end of the French mandate.

As the war began, just like the Allied European powers, the Germans intensified their own efforts to gain diplomatic primacy in Turkey, as well as in the Arab lands and Iran. German policymakers believed that influence in the Middle East could work to restrict British access to the strategic waterways, gain control of much needed oil reserves and strategic minerals, and ultimately help isolate the Soviets. The German campaigns in North Africa and the Dodecanese Islands proved unsuccessful in dislodging the British and French from the area, but throughout the war they continued diplomatic and economic pressure.

In 1939, as British–Turkish negotiations were proceeding, Franz von Papen arrived as the German ambassador. Von Papen was well known to Turkish leaders from World War I, and he devoted much effort to reminding the Turks of historical German–Turkish "friendship" against the "hostility" of the British and Soviets. Howard, "Germany, the Soviet Union and Turkey during World War II," and DeWilde, "German Trade Drive in Southeastern Europe," discuss the importance of Turkey for German war plans: first, it was a supplier of raw materials, such as leather and foodstuffs, and a potentially important supplier of chromium, essential for steel. Turkey was also seen as a buffer against the British in the Middle East. Third, when the Germans prepared their invasion of the Soviet Union, the military planners felt Turkey's continued nonbelligerency would stabilize the right flank of the invasion. In this context, much of the struggle between the Germans and British for dominance in the Middle East was waged covertly, particularly in Turkey. The covert war between the Axis and Allies is discussed in Rubin, *Istanbul Intrigues,* and Moyzisch, *Operation Cicero.*

The Germans also worked to encourage anti-British and anti-French feeling among the Arabs and Iranians. Before and during the war the Germans claimed to support the Arab cause in Palestine, and the mufti of Jerusalem and leader of the Supreme Muslim Council, Haj Amin al-Husayni, expressed pro-German sentiments. According to Hirzowicz, *The*

Third Reich and the Arab East, the roots of pro-German sentiment among the Arabs were based more on the definition of mutual enemies than on historical or cultural friendship. After all, German planners considered the Middle East important for overall war aims but never felt that control of the area was of essential strategic value. When Iraqis revolted against British control in 1941, the Germans attempted to supply arms through Vichy-controlled Syria and through Turkey but allowed the revolt to collapse rather than divert resources from the imminent invasion of the Soviet Union.

For the Allied powers, in particular Britain and the Soviet Union, Iran was a strategically vital area, due to oil and its proximity to the Indian Ocean. After the German invasion of the Soviet Union in 1941, Iran became the primary route for Allied arms and supplies. Lenczowski, in *Russia and the West in Iran,* stressed the Great Power competition for control of Iran. Throughout the first half of the century Britain and Russia alternately competed and cooperated for this end. In 1941 the British and Soviets jointly occupied Iran and justified their removal of Reza Shah as a German sympathizer. Ramazani, *Iran's Foreign Policy,* discusses the efforts of Reza Shah and his successor, Muhammad Reza Shah, to maintain Iranian independence against both the Russians and the British. At the time, for Muhammad Reza Shah, it seemed that an alliance with America, a distant power, would be the only way to end Iran's domination by Europeans.

The two superpowers that emerged out of World War II had had limited interests in the Middle East before 1945. American concerns in the region had traditionally been defined in terms of missionary activities, trade, and maintenance of open seas. With the discovery of large oil reserves in Saudi Arabia in the 1920s, American attention increased and began to reflect a more determined policy of economic and political as well as cultural expansion. DeNovo, *American Interests and Policies in the Middle East,* and Baram, *The Department of State in the Middle East,* both trace the development of American involvement in the region prior to World War II. According to DeNovo and Baram, the Office of Near Eastern Affairs of the U.S. State Department was the main advocate of increased and direct involvement in the Middle East, especially in the Arab countries, after World War I.

With the postwar devastation of the British economy, America took on the role of protector of the strategic raw materials and waterways of the Middle East. Louis' *The British Empire in the Middle East* is a detailed study of the diplomacy of British decolonization and the emergence of the United States as the strongest Western power in the region. Kuniholm, *Origins of the Cold War in the Near East,* and Rubin, *The Great Powers,* provide studies of the transition from British to American power in the region in the aftermath of World War II. By 1945, oil had become an even more important commodity for the restoration of the Western industrial complex. Hence, American postwar support for Turkey and Iran against the Soviets was aimed at preventing communist incursion into the Persian Gulf and the Arab countries.

Soviet policy toward the Middle East has received considerable attention from Western scholars, centering on the spread of communism as well as questions of traditional Russian interests in the region. The Soviets saw the Middle East as a natural area in which to expand their political influence, while maintaining it as a buffer against other imperial powers. Laqueur, in *The Soviet Union and the Middle East*, argued that Soviet policy was shaped by the ideological concerns of communist expansion enunciated by Lenin and Stalin. Thus, he stressed the discontinuity between Great Power competition in the Middle East prior to World War I and the situation of the region in international affairs in the post-1945 period. The Soviets pursued the goals of increasing Soviet influence, spreading communism, and gaining access to markets and materials through informal as well as formal diplomatic channels. During the interwar years, Soviet policy was pursued largely through the activities of the Comintern, which offered covert support to communist parties and sympathizers in Turkey, Iran, and the Arab lands. Only after World War II and the end of the British and French mandates were the Soviets successful in expanding their influence through official diplomatic relations with Arab regimes in Egypt, Syria, Yemen, and Iraq.

In contrast to Laqueur, Spector, in *The Soviet Union and the Muslim World*, underlined the continuity of Russian and Soviet policy toward the Middle East as a region and the Muslim world as a whole. That policy has always been expansion of territory and influence, emerging from the experience of the Russian Empire and infused into the foreign policy of the Soviet Union.

World War II and the emergence of the Soviet Union as a superpower led to its involvement in regional conflicts in the Middle East, which the Soviets viewed as an important arena in which to challenge American hegemony. In this context, Behbehani, *The Soviet Union and Arab Nationalism*, discusses Soviet views of Zionism and the dilemmas of Soviet policy in supporting Zionism and Israel while also supporting Arab nationalism as an anti-imperialist and anti-Western ideology.

Control of Middle Eastern oil was a dominant aspect of the struggle between the Great Powers before and during the war and became a domain of the superpower struggle after the war. Kent, *Moguls and Mandarins*, traced British oil policy from the late Ottoman period up to World War II, while Anderson, *Aramco, the United States and Saudi Arabia*, examined the making of American oil policy from the 1930s through the war. In the wake of World War II, oil and other mineral resources in the Middle East, along with agricultural commodities, became even more vital for postwar Western industry, especially the reconstruction of Europe.

THE MIDDLE EAST AND THE IMPACT OF WORLD WAR II

For the societies of the Middle East, the war had profound implications. Most of the Middle East was under the direct or indirect control of the Allies for at least part of the war, and the entire region experienced severe dislocations as trade routes were cut off, and global investment was directed toward the military. Domestic economies reflected war shortages and inflation, exacerbated by the demands of mobilization, as in Turkey, or support of foreign troops, as in Egypt, or diverting resources for Allied use, as in Iran.

Politically, the war intensified European domination in the Arab lands, which increased the struggle for power. The war weariness and financial predicament of France and Britain following the war combined with demands for independence to pave the way for the end of colonial control. In Iran and Turkey, curbs on domestic political activity and expression, justified as a wartime necessity, fueled growing demands for reform and democracy, albeit in different ways. This period, in and outside the region, also defined the struggle for Palestine. The various economic and political trends that developed during the war continued, shaping postwar changes in the Middle East.

Throughout the war, Turkey maintained a mobilized army of more than a million soldiers against a possible German or Soviet invasion. According to Karpat, *Turkey's Politics*, the single-party government, restrictions on political debate, censorship of the press, rationing of food, and requisitioning of transportation and supplies for the war effort combined to create tremendous inflation, shortages, and a growing sense that the government must change. In 1945 President Ismet Inonu called for the creation of a multiparty political system, which many observers, such as Ahmad, *The Turkish Experiment in Democracy*, and Tamkoc, *The Warrior Diplomats*, have attributed to the growing public discontent with wartime problems. Keyder, *State and Class in Turkey*, argued that wartime conditions spurred the emergence of a commercial bourgeoisie, which led a successful challenge for political power against the military-bureaucratic elite that had ruled since the beginning of the republic. In 1950 Inonu's Republican People's Party handed power to the Democrat Party, with its platform of laissez-faire economics and free speech, following its victory in a free, multiparty election. According to Leiser, ''The Turkish Air Force, 1939–1945,'' and Edwards, ''The Impact of the War on Turkey,'' the war also led to a massive increase in military spending, which served to make Turkey a regional military power and strategically important to the post-1945 Cold War struggle.

During the war, Turkish policymakers had been careful to avoid close ties to either side, convinced that Turkey would have to fight the Soviets after the war. Thus, after World War II, Turkish foreign policy shifted in favor of a close relationship with the United States as a counter to Soviet pressure for territorial concessions. Two prominent members of Turkey's Foreign Ministry, Acikalin, in "Turkey's International Relations," and Sadak, in "Turkey Faces the Soviets," both argued the strategic importance of Turkey for the Western powers and the need to prevent the Soviets from monopolizing the Black Sea and the straits. Alvarez, "The *Missouri* Visit to Turkey," and Leffler, "Strategy, Diplomacy and the Cold War," pointed out the strategic value that American policymakers placed, in turn, on Turkey as a forward base for operations against the Soviets and as a Western ally in the Muslim Middle East.

Unlike Turkey, Iran and the Arab lands experienced direct foreign control during the war; this encouraged popular movements against both European domination and collaborationist regimes. Though Muhammad Reza Shah Pahlavi worked to reassert the legitimacy of the throne and regain control of Iran's foreign and domestic policies, the emergence of the leftist Tudeh Party and the nationalists under Muhammad Musaddiq challenged the Shah. Musaddiq came to power at the head of the National Front, on the promise of nationalizing Iran's oil and ending British as well as Soviet dominance. The rise and fall of Musaddiq are well documented in Bill and Louis' *Musaddiq, Iranian Nationalism, and Oil* and Cottam's *Nationalism in Iran*.

American and British leaders, fearing communist influence and suspecting Musaddiq of being "Moscow's agent," engineered a coup to return the shah to power by removing Musaddiq. According to Zabih, *The Mossadegh Era*, the coup fueled popular resentment of continuing Western dominance and irreparably damaged the throne's legitimacy, preparing the way for the Iranian revolution of 1979.

Arjomand, *The Turban for the Crown*, Bakhash, *Reign of the Ayatollahs*, and Hiro, *Iran under the Ayatollahs*, trace the emergence of a post-Musaddiq coalition of religious leaders, merchants, workers, and students who were united by their hostility to the shah's regime and became increasingly strident in their opposition to Western domination and Western hostility to Islam.

In Egypt, Iraq, Syria, and Lebanon, World War II ended direct European control as the movements emerged to replace the existing regimes, tainted by association with the British and French. According to Gershoni and Jankowski, *Redefining the Egyptian Nation*, Egyptian nationalism was inspired partly by the struggle against the British and partly by an internal redefinition of the Egyptian nation that developed during the interwar years. Following the war the nationalist movement, dominated by the Free Officers, seized power in a revolution in 1952, ousting King Faruq and ending the monarchy created by Britain. Gamal Abdel Nasser soon became leader of a movement based on the principles of nationalism and socialism, which aimed to overcome the exploitative relationship with Europe and establish the Arabs as a powerful and united community. According to Berque, *Egypt: Imperialism and Revolution*, the popularity of the 1952 revolution and the Free Officers stemmed from tremendous popular resentment of British "arrogance and domination" during and after the war and from the corruption and perfidy of King Faruq.

In Egypt, as in other Arab countries, nationalism not only meant liberation from Europe but also called for revolutionary change, particularly the overthrow of collaborationist regimes, nationalization of resources, and redistribution of wealth. Iraq, like Egypt, was officially independent prior to the war. Continued British presence, under the pretext of national defense, was a constant source of tension within Iraqi politics and society. British suppression of the revolt of 1941 and British support of Nuri al-Said and King Faysal II after the war served as rallying points for nationalist officers and intellectuals. Khadduri, *Independent Iraq*, and Longrigg, *Iraq*, both trace the rise of nationalist sentiment within the Iraqi military and society. Published in the early 1950s, both predate the 1958 revolution.

The coup and the rise of Arab socialism and the Ba'th Party in Iraq are examined in a number of works, including the massive study by Batatu, *The Old Social Classes and the Revolutionary Movements of Iraq*. Batatu argued that the revolutionary movement and involvement of the Iraqi military in politics stemmed from, and were a reaction against, British occupation. Khadduri, *Republican Iraq*, and Sluglett and Sluglett, *Iraq since 1958*, explore the militarization of Iraqi politics in the postwar period in the same context.

The experience of occupation profoundly shaped the political, economic, and cultural development of Syria and Lebanon. French occupation of Syria and Lebanon, under the guise of the League of Nations mandate, differed from British control of Egypt, Palestine, and Iraq in that the French believed the Arab lands to be permanent additions to the "French civilizational arena." According to Khoury, *Syria and the French Mandate*, the French adopted policies specifically designed to impede political development, in order to prevent the emergence of groups that could challenge French supremacy. The French creation of Lebanon with its large Christian as well as Muslim communities was intended to increase dependency on France as arbiter and ruler. Syrian and Lebanese politics in the mandate period depended on the activities of urban notables who mobilized urban masses and economic resources to compete for influence in the French administration. According to Longrigg, *Syria and Lebanon under French Mandate*, and Seale, *The Struggle for Syria*, the problems of World War II, especially Anglo-French conflict after 1940, played a significant role in the popularization and strengthening of Arab nationalism after the war and in the rise of the Syrian Ba'th Party.

Prior to World War II, Standard Oil of California (later, ARAMCO) discovered significant oil reserves in the Arabian Peninsula, the only part of the Arab world to escape direct European intervention. This ensured American interest in Saudi Arabia during and after the war. In 1945, Franklin Roosevelt met King Ibn Saud on his return from Yalta. Demand for oil during the war meant that profits from oil exports continued to grow after the war, as did American involvement. As billions of dollars in revenues flowed in, and thousands of American technicians and advisers arrived, Saudi Arabian society was transformed. Armstrong, *Lord of Arabia*, and Howarth, *Desert King*, explored the role of Ibn Saud in forming the kingdom during the interwar years, while Lacey, *The Kingdom*, traced the impact of oil revenues on Saudi society after World War II.

Of the entire Middle East, no region underwent more change because of World War II than Palestine. The Palestine Mandate during the interwar years is the subject of a multitude of works; the following are key. Stein's *The Land Question in Palestine* examines the role played by the Jewish Agency and absentee Arab landlords in the transfer of land to Jewish immigrants before the war. The edited volume by Louis and Stookey, *The End of the Palestine Mandate*, and Cohen's *Palestine, Retreat from the Mandate* and *Palestine and the Great Powers* concentrate on British policy in Palestine throughout the period.

By the 1930s the Supreme Muslim Council, led by Haj Amin al-Husayni, and the Jewish Agency, led by David Ben-Gurion, were locked in a battle for control of the territory. The rise of the Nazis in Germany had increased international pressure on the British to lift restrictions on Jewish immigration, while Palestinians called for it to end and for immediate independence for Palestine.

In 1936 Arabs began militant resistance to British policy, in hopes of ending Jewish immigration and land transfers and in an effort to gain international recognition of Palestinian rights. The Arab revolt is the subject of a recent work by Swedenburg, *Memories of Revolt*, which examines the long-term impact of the revolt on historical memory among both the Palestinian and the Israeli communities. Two other works, Kupferschmidt, *The Supreme Muslim Council*, and Mattar, *The Mufti of Jerusalem: Al-Hajj Amin al-Husayni and the Palestinian National Movement*, concentrate on the role of the Supreme Muslim Council and Haj Amin al-Husayni in shaping Arab policies toward the British and the Zionists.

When the Arab revolt began, much of the Palestinian leadership was under arrest or in exile, including the mufti. Ben-Gurion and leaders of the Jewish Agency and its military wing, the Haganah, decided to cooperate with Britain against Germany, even while opposing British restrictions on immigration into Palestine. Porat, in *The Blue and the Yellow Stars of David,* focused on the efforts of the Jewish Agency to save European Jews from the Holocaust by smuggling them into Palestine against British policy. At the same time, the Haganah organized Jewish military units in Palestine, including a Jewish Brigade, to fight for the Allies.

Jewish cooperation with the British and Palestinian resistance and lack of central organization played decisive roles in later developments. Khalidi, *From Haven to Conquest,* and Morris, *The Birth of the Palestinian Refugee Problem,* both focus on the forceful dispossession of the Palestinian Arabs by Jewish forces after World War II. The Arab–Israeli wars and the ongoing conflict, as well as efforts to establish peace between Israelis and Palestinians, have been a central aspect of regional and international politics in the Middle East ever since.

CONCLUSION

The definitive study of the overall impact of World War II on the Middle East as a region has yet to be published. Few scholars of the Middle East have concentrated specifically on the experience of World War II, and few would argue that World War II was the most important event in the twentieth-century history of the region. Yet some conclusions regarding the Second World War and the Middle East can be drawn from the broader concerns of existing studies. First, World War II brought two struggles in the region, one between the Great Powers and the other by peoples of the Middle East for independence and sovereignty. Both struggles were part of a larger historical continuum in the Middle East. Thus, World War II is treated not as a distinct or separate period in the history of the Middle East but as a time of transition that encouraged some already existing trends, such as Arab nationalism, and brought pressure for changes, such as the end of formal European rule or transition to multiparty politics. World War II laid the ground for the new struggles of the Cold War.

For the people of the Middle East, World War II presented a number of problems as well as possibilities. Wartime inflation, dislocation, and foreign domination caused enormous and lasting problems but also served as forces for change. After 1945, movements for national liberation, redistribution of wealth, and reassertion of cultural autonomy swept across the region. While these movements have produced uneven results and in most places led to authoritarian regimes, they had profound implications for Middle Eastern societies and for the future of the region.

BIBLIOGRAPHY

See also the chapter on "North Africa and the Mediterranean Theater."

Acikalin, Cevat. "Turkey's International Relations." *International Affairs 23* (1947): 477–91.

Ahmad, Feroz. *The Turkish Experiment in Democracy, 1950–1975*. Boulder, CO: Westview, 1977.

Alvarez, David. "The *Missouri* Visit to Turkey: An Alternative Perspective on Cold War Diplomacy." *Balkan Studies 15* (1974): 225–36.

Anderson, Irvine. *Aramco, the United States and Saudi Arabia: A Study of the Dynamics of Foreign Oil Policy, 1933–1950*. Princeton: Princeton UP, 1981.

Arjomand, Said Amir. *The Turban for the Crown: The Islamic Revolution in Iran*. New York: Oxford UP, 1988.

Armstrong, H. C. *Lord of Arabia, Ibn Saud: An Intimate Study of a King*. London: A. Barkey, 1934.

Bakhash, Shaul. *Reign of the Ayatollahs: Iran and the Islamic Revolution*. New York: Basic, 1984.

Baram, Phillip. *The Department of State in the Middle East, 1919–1945*. Philadelphia: University of Pennsylvania, 1978.

Batatu, Hanna. *The Old Social Classes and the Revolutionary Movements of Iraq*. Princeton: Princeton UP, 1978.

Behbehani, Hashim. *The Soviet Union and Arab Nationalism, 1917–1966*. London: KPI, 1986.

Berque, Jacques. *Egypt: Imperialism and Revolution*. Trans. Jean Stewart. New York: Praeger, 1972.

Bill, James, and William Roger Louis, eds. *Musaddiq, Iranian Nationalism, and Oil*. Austin: University of Texas, 1988.

Cohen, Michael. *Palestine, Retreat from the Mandate: The Making of British Policy, 1936–1945*. New York: Holmes and Meier, 1978.

————. *Palestine and the Great Powers, 1945–1948*. Princeton: Princeton UP, 1982.

Cottam, Richard. *Nationalism in Iran*. 2d ed. Pittsburgh: University of Pittsburgh, 1964.

DeNovo, John. *American Interests and Policies in the Middle East, 1900–1939*. Minneapolis: University of Minnesota, 1963.

Deringil, Selim. *Turkish Foreign Policy during the Second World War: An "Active" Neutrality*. Cambridge: Cambridge UP, 1989.

DeWilde, John. "German Trade Drive in Southeastern Europe." *Foreign Policy Reports 12* (1936): 214–20.

Edwards, A. "The Impact of the War on Turkey." *International Affairs 22* (1946): 389–400.

Evans, Stephen. *The Slow Rapprochement: Britain and Turkey in the Age of Kemal Ataturk, 1919–1938*. London: Eothen, 1982.

Gaunson, A. B. *The Anglo-French Clash in Lebanon and Syria, 1940–1945*. London: Macmillan, 1987.

Gershoni, Israel, and James Jankowski. *Redefining the Egyptian Nation, 1930–1945*. Cambridge: Cambridge UP, 1995.

Hiro, Dilip. *Iran under the Ayatollahs*. London: Routledge and Kegan Paul, 1987.

Hirzowicz, Lukasz. *The Third Reich and the Arab East*. London: Routledge and Kegan Paul, 1966.

Howard, Harry. "Germany, the Soviet Union and Turkey during World War II." *Department of State Bulletin 19* (1949): 63–78.

Howarth, David. *Desert King: Ibn Saud and His Arabia.* New York: McGraw-Hill, 1964.

Karpat, Kemal. *Turkey's Politics: The Transition to a Multi-Party System.* Princeton: Princeton UP, 1959.

Kent, Marian. *Moguls and Mandarins: Oil, Imperialism and the Middle East in British Foreign Policy, 1900–1940.* London: Frank Cass, 1993.

Keyder, Caglar. *State and Class in Turkey.* London: Verso, 1987.

Khadduri, Majid. *Independent Iraq, 1932–1958.* New York: Oxford UP, 1960.

———. *Republican Iraq: A Study in Iraqi Politics since the Revolution of 1958.* New York: Oxford UP, 1969.

Khalidi, Walid. *From Haven to Conquest: Readings in Zionism and the Palestine Problem until 1948.* Beirut: Institute for Palestine Studies, 1971.

Khoury, Philip. *Syria and the French Mandate: The Politics of Arab Nationalism 1920–1945.* Princeton: Princeton UP, 1987.

Kirk, George. *The Middle East in the War.* New York: Oxford UP, 1952.

Kuniholm, Bruce. *The Origins of the Cold War in the Near East.* Princeton: Princeton UP, 1980.

Kupferschmidt, Uri. *The Supreme Muslim Council: Islam under the British Mandate in Palestine.* Leiden: E. J. Brill, 1987.

Lacey, Robert. *The Kingdom.* New York: Harcourt Brace Jovanovich, 1982.

Laqueur, Walter. *The Soviet Union and the Middle East.* New York: Frederick A. Praeger, 1959.

Leffler, Melvyn. "Strategy, Diplomacy and the Cold War: The United States, Turkey and NATO, 1945–1952." *Journal of American History* 71 (1985): 807–25.

Leiser, Gary. "The Turkish Air Force, 1939–1945: The Rise of a Minor Power." *Middle Eastern Studies* 26 (1990): 383–95.

Lenczowski, George. *Russia and the West in Iran, 1918–1948: A Study in Big-Power Rivalry.* Ithaca, NY: Cornell UP, 1949.

Lloyd, E.M.H. *Food and Inflation in the Middle East, 1940–1945.* Stanford, CA: Stanford UP, 1956.

Longrigg, Stephen. *Iraq, 1900–1950.* New York: Oxford UP, 1953.

———. *Syria and Lebanon under French Mandate.* New York: Oxford UP, 1958.

Louis, William Roger. *The British Empire in the Middle East, 1945–1951: Arab Nationalism, the United States, and Postwar Imperialism.* New York: Oxford UP, 1984.

Louis, William Roger, and Robert Stookey, eds. *The End of the Palestine Mandate.* Austin: University of Texas, 1986.

Mattar, Philip. *The Mufti of Jerusalem: Al-Hajj Amin al-Husayni and the Palestinian National Movement.* New York: Columbia UP, 1988, 1992.

Monroe, Elizabeth. *Britain's Moment in the Middle East, 1914–1971.* 2d ed. London: Chatto and Windus, 1981.

Morris, Benny. *The Birth of the Palestinian Refugee Problem, 1947–1949.* Cambridge: Cambridge UP, 1987.

Moyzisch, L. C. *Operation Cicero.* New York: Coward-McCann, 1950.

Porat, Dina. *The Blue and the Yellow Stars of David: The Zionist Leadership in Palestine and the Holocaust, 1939–1945.* Cambridge: Harvard UP, 1990.

Ramazani, Rouhollah. *Iran's Foreign Policy, 1941–1973: A Study of Foreign Policy in Modernizing Nations.* Charlottesville: University of Virginia, 1975.

Roshwald, Aviel. *Estranged Bedfellows: Britain and France in the Middle East during the Second World War.* New York: Oxford UP, 1990.

Rubin, Barry. *The Great Powers in the Middle East, 1941–1947: The Road to the Cold War.* London: Frank Cass, 1980.

———. *Istanbul Intrigues: Espionage, Sabotage and Diplomatic Treachery in the Spy Capital of WWII.* New York: Pharos, 1991.

Sadak, Necmeddin. "Turkey Faces the Soviets." *Foreign Affairs* 27 (1949): 449–61.

Seale, Patrick. *The Struggle for Syria: A Study of Post-War Arab Politics, 1945–1958.* 2d ed. London: Tauris, 1986.

Shaw, Stanford. *Turkey and the Holocaust: Turkey's Role in Rescuing Turkish and European Jewry from Nazi Persecution, 1933–1945.* New York: New York UP, 1993.

Silverfarb, Daniel. *The Twilight of British Ascendancy in the Middle East: A Case Study of Iraq, 1941–1950.* New York: St. Martin's, 1994.

Sluglett, Marion Farouk, and Peter Sluglett. *Iraq since 1958: From Revolution to Dictatorship.* London: KPI, 1987.

Spector, Ivar. *The Soviet Union and the Muslim World.* Seattle: University of Washington, 1959.

Stein, Kenneth. *The Land Question in Palestine, 1917–1939.* Chapel Hill: University of North Carolina, 1984.

Swedenburg, Ted. *Memories of Revolt: The 1936–39 Rebellion and the Palestinian National Past.* Minneapolis: University of Minnesota, 1995.

Tamkoc, Metin. *The Warrior Diplomats: Guardians of the National Security and Modernization of Turkey.* Salt Lake City: Utah UP, 1976.

Weisband, Edward. *Turkish Foreign Policy, 1943–1945.* Princeton: Princeton UP, 1973.

Wilmington, Martin. *The Middle East Supply Centre.* Albany: State University of New York, 1971; London: University of London, 1972.

Yapp, M. E. *The Near East since the First World War.* New York and London: Longman, 1991.

Zabih, Sepehr. *The Mossadegh Era: Roots of the Iranian Revolution.* Chicago: Lake View, 1982.

Zhivkova, Ludmila. *Anglo-Turkish Relations, 1933–1939.* London: Secker and Warburg, 1976.

28 The War and the British Commonwealth

Ritchie Ovendale

THE BRITISH COMMONWEALTH AND THE ORIGINS OF THE SECOND WORLD WAR

Most of the general histories of the origins of the Second World War—indeed, of the war itself—ignore the roles of the Commonwealth and empire. A possible reason for this is an explanation offered for Neville Chamberlain's policy of the "appeasement" of Europe by those who endorsed the prime minister's policy: the reluctance of the Dominions to fight in September 1938. The antiappeasers dominated political life in Britain in the 1950s, and only with the change of the political climate in the 1960s—symbolized perhaps by the appointment of Chamberlain's private secretary, Alec Douglas Home, as prime minister, aided by the modification of the fifty-year closure rule of British documents to thirty years by Harold Wilson and the subsequent opening of many of the documents in January 1968, followed by most of the 1939–1945 materials in 1972—did scholars begin to consider the roles of the Commonwealth and empire more seriously. This literature is discussed in Ovendale, *"Appeasement" and the English Speaking World* (4–9).

THE TWO SCHOOLS

There are two distinct approaches discernible in the writings in the field: one school is concerned with the Commonwealth and empire in terms of their influence on British foreign policy; the other emphasizes the extent to which the events leading up to the Second World War and the war itself influenced developments within the countries themselves, initially in relation to the growth of the British Commonwealth and, later on, the independence movements and decolonization.

Beloff in *Imperial Sunset,* volume 2, *Dream of Commonwealth,* published twenty years after the first part of his study of imperial decline, pointed to the argument that a major line of division between policymakers in London was between "those who saw the maintenance of the Commonwealth as mainly a source of extra weight to Britain's own international diplomacy and those who saw the maintenance of the Commonwealth itself and its evolution as the primary concern of British policy." Beloff mentioned the traditional separation between the study of foreign policy and that of Commonwealth affairs as the reason the importance of the Commonwealth factor in the making of British policy has been difficult to assess. He concluded that with a merging of the approaches "it would seem that the imperial or Commonwealth factor was a more powerful one than has often been allowed" (13).

Mansergh almost forty years earlier, in his *Survey of British Commonwealth Affairs: Problems of External Policy,* a work that not only examined developments within the Dominions but also stressed that an understanding of their attitudes was essential to a proper appreciation of British policy before the Second World War, had upbraided the curious indifference of "the predominant school of contemporary English historians" to the importance of the Dominions (xviii). In a work published six years later, Miller, *The Commonwealth in the World,* suggested that reluctance of the Dominions to fight at Munich had become "one of the stock arguments" in favor of Chamberlain's policy of "appeasement" (43). D. Cameron Watt in *Personalities and Policies* tackled head-on the question of whether the Dominions influenced or were responsible for the policy of the appeasement of Europe (159–74). Mansergh in *The Commonwealth Experience,* published in 1969 but written before the relevant documents in the Public Record Office, London, became available, suggested that on the question of the success of Dominion pressure on Neville Chamberlain, the then-available evidence put the issue "in the borderline between speculation and proven historical fact" (282).

When the fifty-year rule became the thirty-year rule, and the British documents started being opened up in January 1968, the primary sources were scrutinized in an attempt to answer this question. Ovendale's *"Appeasement" and the English Speaking World* examined the course of events within the individual Dominions as well as their influence on British policy and considered this in the context of relations with the United States. Parker in 1993 claimed in *Chamberlain and Appeasement* that "the Dominions had little or no influence on British policy except in supplying added justification to policies that Chamberlain and his supporters would have wished to pursue anyway" (296).

THE DOMINIONS AND THE CONDUCT OF THE WAR

Taylor has pointed out that the Second World War was "an Imperial war":

It was fought by the British mainly in Imperial zones of the Mediterranean and the Far East. It was fought by Imperial armies serving in almost complete unity, and it ended in victory for every Imperial cause. The Commonwealth demonstrated its strength and spirit. The English-speaking peoples might have been expected to draw the moral that the Commonwealth alone provided the foundation for their greatness and security. This did not happen. (12–13)

Similarly, Mansergh, in his *Survey of British Commonwealth Affairs: Problems of Wartime Co-operation and Post-War Change*, mentioned that the theme of his coverage of the Second World War was "the capacity of the Commonwealth system to sustain unity of purpose and effort among Commonwealth governments and peoples in war." Mansergh emphasized the dangers of generalization about cooperation: imperialists in wartime might have wanted a centralized machinery that could survive the end of hostilities; the more nationalist Dominions with their "anti-Downing Street complex" were wary of any such proposal. He suggested that Commonwealth co-operation in wartime "cannot be understood by a meticulous study of constitutional or conventional arrangements but only by the unravelling of a relationship as it worked and as it developed during the war years" (xv, 26–27).

Writing a decade later Miller in *Britain and the Old Dominions* singled out two problems that complicated the relations between Britain and the Dominions during the Second World War, and he saw both as being bound up with the character of Winston Churchill's leadership: first was the control of the forces that the Dominions committed to the fight; "the second was how the Dominions were to influence decisions made about the war by Britain and the United States" (130). The role of the Dominions' forces was covered in the British official military history of the Second World War: Gibbs' *Grand Strategy* and Kirby's *The War against Japan*, volume 1, *The Loss of Singapore*.

The Dominions' own viewpoint is, however, more often contained in the series of official histories commissioned by the Dominion governments. About New Zealand's history, Wood's *The New Zealand People at War* was the first volume in a fifty-volume series completed in 1986. Also included in this series were Gillespie's *The Pacific*, Ross' *Royal New Zealand Air Force*, and Waters' *The Royal New Zealand Navy*. The War History Branch of the New Zealand Department of Internal Affairs published in 1959 *Documents Relating to New Zealand's Participation in the Second World War*. The domestic front was covered in Sutch, *The Quest for Security in New*

Zealand 1840 to 1966 (281–388), but his work has been described as reflecting dissenting views and is not always considered central. These years
have also been viewed through the eyes of the New Zealand statesman
who was at various times minister of finance and minister in Washington
in Sinclair, *Walter Nash*.

There are also specific monograph studies on Canada: Stacey, *Arms, Men
and Governments: The War Policies of Canada*; and Granatstein, *Canada's War:
The Policies of the Mackenzie King Government*, which emphasized that the
"achievement of the war and the war effort was that Canada entered the
peace as a nation" (420). The role of the Canadian prime minister was
specifically examined in Pickersgill, *The Mackenzie King Record*. Canada's
official record of these years was published between 1974 and 1990: Murray and Hilliker, *Documents on Canadian External Relations*.

Fisk, *In Time of War: Ireland, Ulster and the Price of Neutrality*, considered
Anglo-Irish relations during the Second World War. Prime Minister Ea-
mon de Valera's view that Ireland's neutrality was based on prudence and
not cowardice was examined by Bowman in *De Valera and the Ulster Question*
(206–66); similarly, Dwyer, in *De Valera: The Man and the Myths*, argued
that the prime minister's perception of Ireland's interest was the determining factor of his policy (226).

Andrews in *Isolationism and Appeasement in Australia: Reactions to the European Crises* provided a study of Australian governmental and public opinion covering the period from the Abyssinian crisis to the outbreak of war
in 1939; this complemented the coverage of those years by a government
official, Alan Watt, in *The Evolution of Australian Foreign Policy* and the official history by Hasluck, *The Government and the People*, two volumes. The
Documents on Australian Foreign Policy, volumes 1 and 2, edited by Neale on
the origins of the Second World War, include a great deal of material
from the Public Record Office, London, on the meetings of the high
commissioners in London.

Millar, *Australia in Peace and War: External Relations*, and Ward, *The History of Australia: The Twentieth Century*, considered the interwar years in
relation to domestic developments in Australia. There is also an important
study of individuals by P. G. Edwards, *Prime Ministers and Diplomats: The
Making of Australian Foreign Policy*. Significant biographical and autobiographical material includes the account by the wife of Prime Minister
Joseph A. Lyons, in office from 1931 to 1939, Enid Lyons' *So We Take
Comfort*, and the biography of Stanley M. Bruce, who served as high commissioner in London, by Cecil Edwards, *Bruce of Melbourne, Man of Two
Worlds*. Long, in his overall account of Australia's participation in the Second World War, *The Six Years War: A Concise History of Australia in the 1939–
45 War*, pointed to the "early effects within Australia" of the war years as
being "a drive towards more rapid and adventurous development and
more assertiveness, a weakening of the political and economic links with

Britain and a strengthening of the links with the United States, and increasing diversion of trade towards the Asian countries" (480).

In the late 1980s and the 1990s, at a time when Australian Labor governments raised the question of the severing of the links with the British Crown, the issue of the defense of Singapore and Britain's commitment to Australia's defense just before and during the early stages of the Second World War became a live political issue that stimulated academic controversy. Two decades earlier, at the time of debates over Australian participation in the Vietnam war, Reese, in *Australia, New Zealand, and the United States*, had examined the extent to which the Pacific Dominions moved out of a British orbit into an American one.

In 1991, Bridge in his introduction to *Munich to Vietnam: Australia's Relations with Britain and the United States since the 1930s* pointed out that the popularly received version of the British Pacific fleet's ignominiously leaving the Australian scene with the fall of Singapore, never to return, and with Australia and New Zealand's moving into the United States' informal Pacific empire was an exaggeration and that the transition was "not nearly so simple or absolute" (2). Bridge argued that "Australians' perceptions of their country's relationship with Britain and the United States in World War II are hopelessly distorted by hindsight and by Labor patriotic myths." The received version, widely spread in textbooks and on the television screen, pointed to the "inexcusable betrayal" of the fall of Singapore in February 1942 and the case that while Britain was prepared to exploit Australia, it was not prepared to defend it. The pro-British appeaser, Robert Menzies, had gone, and the heroic and nationalist Labor leader John Curtin recalled Australian divisions from the Middle East, looked to the United States, and saved Australia in New Guinea and at the Battles of the Coral Sea and Midway. Bridge exposed these "myths" as a "travesty of the truth." As early as 1977 Barclay in his article "Australia Looks to America: The Wartime Relationship, 1939–1942" had pointed to the extent to which Curtin had become disillusioned with the United States and after 1942 had become dedicated to the restoration of traditional British colonial influence in the Pacific and the Far East.

Other Australian scholars have also challenged the myth that Australia switched its national allegiance from Britain to the United States during the Second World War. Day, for instance, in his essay "Pearl Harbor to Nagasaki" posed the case that Australia pursued three different policies: the first, a nationalistic one, aimed at increasing independence in foreign and defense policy; another policy designed to increase links with the United States; and a third to preserve the links with Britain. This school is in line with the case made by Bell in 1977 that "Australia's close war time military collaboration with the U.S. was not developed at the permanent expense of continuing defence co-operation with Britain or close post-war Imperial relations, especially in the political and economic spheres.''

Hamill in *The Strategic Illusion* also pointed to Australia and New Zealand's continuing attachment for the imperial connection even after the symbol of Singapore had collapsed (314). Singapore as a symbol, McIntyre argued in *The Rise and Fall of the Singapore Naval Base*, was not one that deluded the Australians, "who were the most importunate in their demands for the presence of a battle fleet" (216). Louis, however, in his article "The Road to Singapore: British Imperialism in the Far East" concluded that "the sinking of *Prince of Wales* and *Repulse* together with the fall of Singapore brought an end to the illusion of both the power and prestige of the British Empire in the Far East" (385).

Other monograph studies of the background to, and Australia's participation in, the Second World War include McCarthy's *Australia and Imperial Defence*, John Robertson's *Australia Goes to War*, Gillison's *Royal Australian Air Force*, and Horner's *High Command: Australia and Allied Strategy*. There are five series of official histories, *Australia in the War of 1939–1945*, as well as the published *Documents on Australian Foreign Policy*, volumes 3–8.

The South African documents have not yet been published. There are, however, biographies that cover South African domestic, imperial, and foreign politics. Hancock, in his biography of Jan C. Smuts, the South African imperial and world statesman, *Smuts: The Fields of Force 1919–1950*, suggested, perhaps mistakenly, that Smuts became disillusioned with Chamberlain's policy of "appeasement." Paton's *Hofmeyr* is an account of the years as seen by J. H. Hofmeyr, who during the Second World War acted as prime minister during Smuts' frequent absences abroad. Hofmeyr was, in South African terms, a liberal on the race question.

The Afrikaner nationalist position, sympathetic to Germany, was examined in the biographies of the South African prime minister in the late 1930s: van den Heever, *Generaal J.B.M. Hertzog*, the Afrikaans version; *General J.B.M. Hertzog*, an abridgement in English; and the biography by his minister of defense, Pirow's *James Barry Munnik Hertzog*. Pirow, twenty years after the event, with good reason, wrote of the South African cabinet meeting of September 3, 1939, and South Africa's subsequent entry into the war (covered in detail by Ovendale's *"Appeasement" and the English Speaking World*) that it made it a certainty "that when the political pendulum swung back again, as it was bound to do, Malan's extremists would take over and the English speaking South Africans would become bywoners [aliens] in their own country" (246). Furlong, in *Between Crown and Swastika*, examined the relationship between national socialism in Germany and the development of the Nationalist Party in South Africa during the Second World War and pointed to the links between a number of South African leaders after the 1948 election in South Africa, which initiated the apartheid era and the European radical Right. The development of South Africa's economy during the Second World War was covered in H. M. Robertson et al., "The South African Economy during the Second World War."

THE SECOND WORLD WAR AND INDEPENDENCE MOVEMENTS

The approach of the school that emphasizes the influence of the Second World War on developments within the countries themselves, initially in relation to the growth of the British Commonwealth and, later on, the independence movements and decolonization, is crystallized in the popular work by Cross, *The Fall of the British Empire.* This book considered the war's importance for the emergence of independence movements, particularly the reverberations of the fall of Singapore in India and on British prestige throughout Asia, as well as the experience for many black Africans of serving abroad and their subsequent role in independence movements—the latter also was covered in Killingray and Rathbone, *Africa and the Second World War.*

Pearce, in his overall analysis of Britain's position in Africa, *The Turning Point in Africa: British Colonial Policy,* pointed to the inroads made into indirect rule during the Second World War. Pearce also examined the extent to which the war changed Britain's image of itself: the "cult of 'Imperialism' was almost wholly extinguished; what had once been a high-minded political doctrine passed into a term of vulgar reproach." At the end of the war a relatively impoverished Britain was in debt to its African colonies, a reversal of roles that complemented the granting of self-government.

Moves toward independence in the African colonies were specifically analyzed in a number of texts. Olusanya in *The Second World War and Politics in Nigeria* showed how various activities engendered by the war led to a political awakening in that country "led by a group of young, educated nationalists under the leadership of Nnamdi Azikiwe, whose newspaper, the *West African Pilot,* became the medium of nationalist expressions." Olusanya also demonstrated that in response to the Allied propaganda that emphasized that the war was being fought to preserve democracy and ensure freedom, Nigerians came to expect that "the freedom which was being fought for should be extended to them" (51–53). Similarly, Smyth in her article "Britain's African Colonies and British Propaganda during the Second World War" pointed to the expectations aroused in Africa by British Ministry of Information propaganda. Bourret's study of the Gold Coast, *Ghana: The Road to Independence,* also noted the increased opportunities for technical and administrative training the Second World War afforded to Africans, "which resulted in a deeper self-confidence and determination to take a more active part in the country's development'' (155). Another aspect, the contribution to the British war effort, is emphasized in Clayton and Savage, *Government and Labour in Kenya*; these authors pointed to the East African territories' contributions in terms of food, raw materials, and even manpower (235).

Owen in his article ''War and Britain's Political Crisis in India'' considered the position from the point of view of the metropolitan power and pointed to the extent to which the British were ''deprived of the initiative and ability to control the events which was the vital underpinning of their plans to advance India to the status of a Dominion'' (108). India's contribution to the war effort was covered by Mason's *A Matter of Honour* and Cohen's *The Indian Army: Its Contribution to the Development of a Nation.* Prasad edited the *Official History of the Indian Armed Forces in the Second World War*, a collaborative venture undertaken by the armed services historical sections of both India and Pakistan. Hauner's monumental and scholarly study of *India in Axis Strategy* also examined the role played by the Indian National Army in the war and in the independence movement and in particular the contribution of Subhas Chandra Bose, as well as the extent to which the Second World War and the pressure from Washington ensured India's independence.

Moore's *Churchill, Cripps and India* was sympathetic to the British Labour and Indian Congress Parties, whereas Tomlinson's *The Indian National Congress and the Raj* emphasized what he describes as the ''negative'' and ''extreme positions'' sustained by both Congress and the raj (157). The account of the role the viceroy played during the first years of the war, by his son, Glendevon, *The Viceroy at Bay: Lord Linlithgow in India*, was sympathetic; Rizvi's *Linlithgow and India* was, however, more critical. The standpoint of Linlithgow's successor, Field Marshal Sir Archibald Wavell, has been efficiently edited by Moon, *Wavell, the Viceroy's Journal.* Jawaharlal Nehru's position and his relationship with other Indian leaders were covered in Sarvepalli Gopal, *Jawaharlal Nehru.* Brown *in Gandhi: Prisoner of Hope* concluded that the war years showed Gandhi ''the grievous problems associated with deploying non-violence in public life'' and indicated that ''there were aspects of relationships between Indians where non-violence seemed to be ineffective'' (358). Paul Scott's *The Raj Quartet*, televised as *The Jewel in the Crown*, presented a fictitious account of the relationships between the raj and the various communities in India that was widely acknowledged to offer important insights. The volumes of documents published as *The Transfer of Power*, Mansergh, editor in chief, covered the moves toward independence in India during the Second World War.

Developments in Burma were documented in Tinker, *Burma: The Struggle for Independence.* Allen, in his analysis of the Burma campaign, *Burma: The Longest War*, pointed to the ''tragic twist'': by the time that the Burma road was safely pushed through to China, the war was nearly over; furthermore, Burma was the first country, after the grant of independence, to leave the British Commonwealth, only three years after the Fourteenth Army had driven the Japanese from it (xv).

A work that specifically offered two lines of approach—understanding both the decline and fall of the British Empire and the emergence of new Southeast Asian politics in the twentieth century—was Tarling, *The Fall of Imperial Britain in South-East Asia*. In particular it examined the extent to which the ideologies of self-determination and nationality were encouraged in the area by the Second World War.

THE ROLE OF THE FOREIGN AND COLONIAL OFFICES

Colonial issues, alongside those of League of Nations trusteeships and mandates, have attracted particular examination. These works showed the divisions between the Foreign and Colonial Offices, as well as the importance of the United States in the equation. Louis in *Imperialism at Bay 1941–1945: The United States and the Decolonization of the British Empire* examined American and British wartime planning for the future of the colonial world. Louis took as his themes "American anti-colonialism and American expansion; and British reactions to American 'informal empire' as well as American ideas about the future of the British Empire." He examined the divisions between the Colonial and Foreign Offices and the extent to which "the Colonial Office regarded the trusteeship scheme, among other things, as a Foreign Office device to appease the Americans." He suggested that the emphasis Australia and New Zealand placed on the concept of a trusteeship that took into account the welfare of the inhabitants, as well as the security of the Great Powers, "cracked the facade of the Commonwealth" (vii, 66, 511).

Ovendale in *Britain, the United States, and the End of the Palestine Mandate* considered the divisions between the Foreign and Colonial Offices during the Second World War as to whether Britain should pursue a policy of partition, which would mean the creation of a separate Zionist state, or trusteeship, which could safeguard British security interests in the Middle East, as well as the extent to which the United States attempted to dictate a policy to Britain for Palestine in the interests of its own domestic politics.

Particular attention was paid to the management of the war effort by the Colonial Office on the part of the colonies, together with the distinct effect that this had on the metropolitan conceptions of what could be done from the "center" in Lee and Petter, *The Colonial Office, War, and Development Policy Organisation and the Planning of a Metropolitan Initiative*. These authors offered the thesis that "this positive experience of the 'lessons of war' was a key element in all subsequent handling of the traditional constitutional patterns in central-local relations" (16).

THE OVERALL ASSESSMENT

In making an overall assessment of the significance of the Second World War for the Commonwealth and empire, some scholars have offered profit-and-loss accounts. Porter, for instance, suggested in *The Lion's Share* that in the period just before the outbreak of the Second World War those responsible for the security of Britain saw the empire as a "strategical and military burden, an impossibly extended frontier which stretched Britain's resources further than they would go." He pointed out that "defence of the empire tied up more British troops than the war in Europe used colonial troops, so that the total military account of the empire was in debit" (103). Gallagher, however, in his posthumously published essay "The Decline, Revival and Fall of the British Empire" dismissed the idea of looking at the fall of the British Empire in "a briskly functionalist way" and concluded that the damage of the Second World War brought it down. He insisted that the British world system had been showing signs of decay long before 1939 and that the Second World War reversed the trend, observable at the end of the First World War, of Britain's moving from a system of formal rule toward a system of influence, back toward empire. Gallagher argued that in military terms, India exploited Britain during the Second World War. But Britain's decision to quit India was not intended to mark the end of empire: "Quitting India has to be seen in the light of the simultaneous decision to push British penetration deeper into tropical Africa and the Middle East." It is possible to make a case that by the end of the Second World War, India had become an economic liability rather than an asset, whereas Africa was still viewed by London as being profitable.

BIBLIOGRAPHY

Allen, Louis. *Burma: The Longest War 1941–45*. London: J. M. Dent, 1984.

Andrews, E. M. *Isolationism and Appeasement in Australia: Reactions to the European Crises, 1935–1939*. Canberra: Australian National UP, 1970.

Australia in the War of 1939–1945. 4 volumes. Canberra: Australian War Memorial, 1952–1968.

Barclay, G. St. J. "Australia Looks to America: The Wartime Relationship, 1939–1942." *Pacific Historical Review 42* (1977): 251–71.

Bell, Roger J. *Unequal Allies: Australian–American Relations and the Pacific War*. Carlton Victoria: Melbourne UP, 1977.

Beloff, Max. *Imperial Sunset*. Vol. 2, *Dream of Commonwealth 1921–42*. Basingstoke: Macmillan, 1989.

Bourret, F. M. *Ghana: The Road to Independence 1919–1957*. London: Oxford UP, 1960.

Bowman, John. *De Valera and the Ulster Question, 1917–1973*. Oxford: Clarendon, 1982.

Bridge, Carl, ed. *Munich to Vietnam: Australia's Relations with Britain and the United States since the 1930s.* Carlton, Victoria: Melbourne UP, 1991.

Brown, Judith M. *Gandhi: Prisoner of Hope.* London: Yale UP, 1989.

Clayton, Anthony, and Donald C. Savage. *Government and Labour in Kenya 1895–1963.* London: Frank Cass, 1974.

Cohen, Stephen P. *The Indian Army: Its Contribution to the Development of a Nation.* Berkeley: University of California, 1971.

Cross, Colin. *The Fall of the British Empire 1918–1968.* London: Hodder and Stoughton, 1968.

Day, David. "Pearl Harbor to Nagakasi." In Carl Bridge, ed., *Munich to Vietnam: Australia's Relations with Britain and the United States since the 1930s,* 52–69. Carlton, Victoria: Melbourne UP, 1991.

Documents on Australian Foreign Policy. 7 vols. Canberra: Australian Government Publishing Service, 1975–1988.

Documents Relating to New Zealand's Participation in the Second World War. Wellington: Department of Internal Affairs, War History Branch, 1959.

Dwyer, Ryle. *De Valera: The Man and the Myths.* Swords, Dublin: Poolbeg, 1991.

Edwards, Cecil. *Bruce of Melbourne, Man of Two Worlds.* London: Heinemann, 1965.

Edwards, P. G. *Prime Ministers and Diplomats: The Making of Australian Foreign Policy, 1901–1949.* Melbourne: Oxford UP in association with the Australian Institute of International Affairs, 1983.

Fisk, Robert. *In Time of War: Ireland, Ulster and the Price of Neutrality 1939–45.* London: Paladin, 1983.

Furlong, Patrick J. *Between Crown and Swastika: The Impact of the Radical Right on the Afrikaner Nationalist Movement in the Fascist Era.* Hanover, NH: Wesleyan UP, published by the UP of New England, 1991.

Gallagher, John. "The Decline, Revival and Fall of the British Empire." In Anil Seal, ed., *The Decline, Revival and Fall of the British Empire. The Ford Lectures and Other Essays by John Gallagher,* 73–153. Cambridge: Cambridge UP, 1982.

Gibbs, N. H., et al. *Grand Strategy,* Vols. 1–5. London: HMSO, 1956–1976.

Gillespie, O. A. *The Pacific.* Wellington: Department of Internal Affairs, War History Branch, 1952.

Gillison, Douglas. *Royal Australian Air Force 1939–1942.* Canberra: Australian War Memorial, 1962.

Glendevon, John. *The Viceroy at Bay: Lord Linlithgow in India 1936–1943.* London: Collins, 1971.

Gopal, Sarvepalli. *Jawarharlal Nehru: A Biography.* Vol. 1, *1899–1947.* London: Cape, 1975.

Granatstein, J. L. *Canada's War: The Policies of the Mackenzie King Government, 1939–1945.* Toronto: Oxford UP, 1975.

Hamill, Ian. *The Strategic Illusion: The Singapore Strategy and the Defence of Australia and New Zealand 1919–1942.* Singapore: Singapore UP, 1981.

Hancock, W. K. *Smuts: The Fields of Force 1919–1950.* Cambridge: Cambridge UP, 1968.

Hasluck, Paul. *The Government and the People,* Vol. 1, *1939–1941.* Canberra: Australian War Memorial, 1952.

———. *The Government and the People,* Vol. 2, *1942–1945.* Canberra: Australian War Memorial, 1970.

Hauner, Milan. *India in Axis Strategy: Germany, Japan and Indian Nationalists in the Second World War.* Stuttgart: Klett-Cotta, 1981.

Horner, D. M. *High Command: Australian and Allied Strategy, 1939–1945.* London: Allen and Unwin, 1982.

Killingray, David, and Richard Rathbone, eds. *Africa and the Second World War.* Basingstoke: Macmillan, 1986.

Kirby, S. Woodburn. *The War against Japan,* Vol. 1, *The Loss of Singapore.* London: HMSO, 1957.

Lee, J. M., and Martin Petter. *The Colonial Office, War, and Development Policy Organisation and the Planning of a Metropolitan Initiative, 1939–1945.* London: Published for the Institute of Commonwealth Studies by Maurice Temple Smith, 1982.

Long, Gavin. *The Six Years War: A Concise History of Australia in the 1939–45 War.* Canberra: Australian War Memorial and Australian Government Publishing Service, 1973.

Louis, William Roger. *Imperialism at Bay 1941–1945: The United States and the Decolonization of the British Empire.* Oxford: Clarendon, 1977.

———. "The Road to Singapore: British Imperialism in the Far East, 1932–42." In Wolfgang J. Mommsen and Lothar Kettenacker, eds., *The Fascist Challenge and the Policy of Appeasement,* 352–88. London: George Allen and Unwin, 1983.

Lyons, Enid. *So We Take Comfort.* London: Heinemann, 1965.

Mansergh, Nicholas. *The Commonwealth Experience.* London: Weidenfeld and Nicolson, 1969.

———. *Survey of British Commonwealth Affairs: Problems of External Policy 1931–1939.* London: Oxford UP, 1952.

———. *Survey of British Commonwealth Affairs: Problems of Wartime Co-operation and Post-War Change 1939–1952.* London: Oxford UP, 1958.

———, editor in chief. *The Transfer of Power.* Vols. 1–5. London: HMSO, 1970–1974.

Mason, Philip. *A Matter of Honour: An Account of the Indian Army, Its Officers and Men.* London: Cape, 1976.

McCarthy, John. *Australia and Imperial Defence 1918–39.* St. Lucia, Queensland: University of Queensland, 1976.

McIntyre, W. David. *The Rise and Fall of the Singapore Naval Base.* London: Macmillan, 1979.

Millar, T. B. *Australia in Peace and War: External Relations 1788–1977.* London: C. Hurst, 1978.

Miller, J.D.B. *Britain and the Old Dominions.* London: Chatto and Windus, 1966.

———. *The Commonwealth in the World.* London: Gerald Duckworth, 1958.

Moon, Penderel, ed. *Wavell, the Viceroy's Journal.* London: Oxford UP, 1973.

Moore, R. J. *Churchill, Cripps and India, 1939–1945.* Oxford: Clarendon, 1979.

Murray, David R., and John F. Hilliker, eds. *Documents on Canadian External Relations,* Vols. 7–11. Ottawa: Department of External Affairs, 1974–1990.

Neale, R. G., et al., eds. *Documents on Australian Foreign Policy 1937–49.* Canberra: Australian Government Publishing Service, 1975–1976.

Olusanya, G. O. *The Second World War and Politics in Nigeria 1939–1953.* London: Evans Bros for University of Lagos 1973.

Ovendale, Ritchie. *"Appeasement" and the English Speaking World: Britain, the United States, the Dominions and the Policy of "Appeasement," 1937–1939*. Cardiff: University of Wales, 1975.

———. *Britain, the United States, and the End of the Palestine Mandate, 1942–1948*. Woodbridge, Suffolk: Royal Historical Society, 1989.

Owen, Nicholas. "War and Britain's Political Crisis in India." In Harriet Jones and Brian Brivati, eds., *What Difference Did the War Make?*, 106–30. Leicester: Leicester UP, 1993.

Parker, R.A.C. *Chamberlain and Appeasement: British Policy and the Coming of the Second World War*. Basingstoke: Macmillan, 1993.

Paton, Alan. *Hofmeyr*. London: Oxford UP, 1964.

Pearce, R. D. *The Turning Point in Africa: British Colonial Policy 1938–48*. London: Frank Cass, 1982.

Pickersgill, J. W. *The Mackenzie King Record*. Vol. 1, *1939–1944*. Chicago: Chicago UP, 1960.

Pirow, Oswald. *James Barry Munnik Hertzog*. London: Allen and Unwin, 1958.

Porter, Bernard. *The Lion's Share: A Short History of British Imperialism 1850–1970*. London: Longman, 1975.

Prasad, B., ed. *Official History of the Indian Armed Forces in the Second World War*. 5 volumes. Delhi: Combined Inter-Services Historical Section India and Pakistan, 1952–1960.

Reese, Trevor R. *Australia, New Zealand, and the United States: A Survey of International Relations 1941–1968*. London: Oxford UP, 1969.

Rizvi, Gowher. *Linlithgow and India: A Study of British Policy and the Political Impasse in India, 1936–1942*. London: Royal Historical Society, 1978.

Robertson, H. M., et al. "The South African Economy during the Second World War." *Official Year Book of the Union 29* (1956–1957): 809–97.

Robertson, John. *Australia Goes to War, 1939–1945*. Sydney: Doubleday, 1984.

Ross, J.M.S. *Royal New Zealand Air Force*. Wellington: Department of Internal Affairs, War History Branch, 1955.

Scott, Paul. *The Raj Quartet*. 4 vols. London: Heinemann, 1966–1975.

Sinclair, Keith. *Walter Nash*. Oxford: Oxford UP, 1976.

Smyth, Rosaleen. "Britain's African Colonies and British Propaganda during the Second World War." *The Journal of Imperial and Commonwealth History 14* (1985–1986): 65–82.

Stacey, C. P. *Arms, Men and Governments: The War Policies of Canada, 1939–1945*. Ottawa: Queen's Printer, 1970.

Sutch, W. B. *The Quest for Security in New Zealand 1840 to 1966*. London: Oxford UP, 1966.

Tarling, Nicholas. *The Fall of Imperial Britain in South-East Asia*. Singapore: Oxford UP, 1993.

Taylor, A.J.P. "Lament for a Commonwealth." In Winston Churchill, *History of the English Speaking Peoples 1*, 12–13. London: Purnell, 1969, 1971.

Tinker, Hugh, ed. *Burma: The Struggle for Independence 1944–1948*. Vol. 1, *From Military Occupation to Civil Government 1 January 1944 to 31 August 1946*. London: HMSO, 1983.

Tomlinson, Brian Roger. *The Indian National Congress and the Raj 1929–1942: The Penultimate Phase*. London: Macmillan, 1976.

van den Heever, C. M. *Generaal J.B.M. Hertzog.* Johannesburg: Afrikaanse Pers-Boekhandel, 1943.

———. *General J.B.M. Hertzog.* Johannesburg: Afrikaanse Pers-Boekhandel, 1946.

Ward, Russel. *The History of Australia: The Twentieth Century 1910–1975.* London: Heinemann, 1978.

Waters, S. D. *The Royal New Zealand Navy.* Wellington: Department of Internal Affairs, War History Branch, 1956.

Watt, Alan. *The Evolution of Australian Foreign Policy. 1938–1965.* Cambridge: Cambridge UP, 1967.

Watt, D. Cameron. *Personalities and Policies.* South Bend, IN: University of Notre Dame, 1965.

Wood, F.L.W. *The New Zealand People at War. Political and External Affairs. Official History of New Zealand in the Second World War, 1939–45.* Wellington: Department of Internal Affairs, War History Branch, 1958.

29 Sub-Saharan Africa

Thomas Ofcansky

The Second World War marked a turning point in the history of Sub-Saharan Africa. By 1939, European colonialism had reached the apex of its power in the region. Moreover, the colonial state in Sub-Saharan Africa had gained an unprecedented degree of legitimacy not only among the indigenous populations but also among the various electorates in Europe.

Much of the international community also had accepted European colonial rule in Sub-Saharan Africa as a political and strategic necessity. However, the Second World War unleashed forces that weakened and ultimately brought an end to the European colonial empires in Sub-Saharan Africa. The factors that contributed to this extraordinary turn of events included growing African agitation for self-government, the diminishing lack of political and economic commitment to empire among the colonial powers, and increasing international support for self-determination.

Unlike World War I, when Allied armies battled German forces in East, West, and Southern Africa, there were no significant military confrontations in Sub-Saharan Africa during World War II. Nevertheless, the region played a vital role in the Allied war effort. Great Britain, for example, mobilized nearly five hundred thousand men from its African colonies, the general impact of which is discussed in Killingray's "Labour Mobilization in British Colonial Africa." Helmreich analyzes the important and historically critical role played by the Belgian Congo (now Zaire) in the development of the atom bomb in "The Uranium Negotiations of 1944." Also, the war had significant political, economic, and social ramifications for the region. Most existing scholarship on these subjects focuses on the war's impact on African, rather than European, communities.

One of the most popular topics is whether the war facilitated a political awakening among Africans in general and African soldiers in particular and in turn stimulated decolonization.

THE WAR AND DECOLONIZATION

Two of the best general works about the decolonization process are Crowder's "The Second World War" and "Prelude to De-Colonisation." The first argues that the war created a new international environment in which the colonial powers were put on the defensive and forced to introduce political, social, and economic reforms that ultimately led to the demise of their empires in Sub-Saharan Africa. The latter essay, which is confined to West Africa, demonstrates that the war brought forth a new generation of African politicians who refused to accept the pace of political change laid down by the colonial governments. According to Crowder, politicians in British West Africa agitated for self-government while their French West African counterparts wanted an equal place in the French Community.

Expectations of change in French Africa were accelerated by the Brazzaville Conference (January 30–February 8, 1944), a turning point in French colonial rule in Sub-Saharan Africa. Benoist's "The Brazzaville Conference, or Involuntary Decolonization" examined the reasons for, and ramifications of, General Charles De Gaulle's promise that a postwar France would recognize French Africa's right to manage its own affairs. Similarly, Marshall's "Free France in Africa: Gaullism and Colonialism" suggested that the conference contributed to the desire for independence and to the need for the creation of a political system to achieve that goal. Crowder, on the other hand, argued that the conference refused to recognize French Africa's right to self-government but acknowledged that French colonies should have representative governments. In "The 1939–45 War and West Africa," Crowder showed that because of the region's importance to the Allied war effort, Great Britain and France felt obliged to institute a series of political, economic, and social reforms. "A Colonial State in Crisis: Vichy Administration in French West Africa" by Giblin makes a stronger case, arguing that French colonial officials sought to preserve a presence in Africa despite their misgivings about American and British postwar intentions. A sympathetic assessment of the effect the 1939–1945 conflict had on the entire region is contained in "The Turning Point: The Impact of the Second World War on Africa" by Mazrui and Tidy.

There is a paucity of material about how the Second World War facilitated the decolonization process in individual countries. However, some work has been done on Ghana, Nigeria, Kenya, Uganda, and Zambia. In "Soldiers, Ex-Servicemen, and Politics in the Gold Coast," Killingray rejected the notion that veterans developed a new political awareness that played a significant role in the decolonization process. Instead, he contended that ex-servicemen performed a limited role in nationalist politics throughout the 1945–1950 period. Schleh's "The Post-War Careers of Ex-Servicemen in Ghana and Uganda," which agrees with Killingray's assessment, asserted that there is no connection between the recruitment of Africans into British forces and the emergence of post-1945 nationalist movements. Conversely, Israel's "Ex-Servicemen at the Crossroads: Protest and Politics in Post-War Ghana" maintained that nationalist leaders channeled the political and economic grievances of ex-servicemen into popular demonstrations against the colonial government. Israel made a similar argument in "Measuring the War Experience," by claiming that the shared overseas experiences of veterans, particularly in Asia, which also was seeking to free itself from colonial rule, helped to justify growing demands for Gold Coast independence. Nwaka's "Rebellion in Umuahia, 1950–1951" presented an even stronger argument for a link between veterans and anticolonial activities. However, Olusanya's "The Role of Ex-Servicemen in Nigerian Politics" and *The Second World War and Politics in Nigeria* insisted that Nigerian veterans made no significant contributions to the rise of nationalism in the post-1945 era. "The Impact of World War II on Kenya" by Okete is an exhaustive analysis of how veterans facilitated the growth of the anticolonial movement.

There also is no consensus about the relationship between the war and the rise of African nationalism in other Sub-Saharan countries. For example, Lawler's "Reform and Repression under the Free French: Economic and Political Transformation in the Côte d'Ivoire" argued that the harshness of French colonial policy during the war gave rise to post-1945 demands for self-government. Fetter's "Changing War Aims: Central Africa's Role," on the other hand, maintained that Allied demands for African raw material poisoned relations between Belgian officials and their colonial subjects, especially after the former crushed a 1941 African labor strike at Union Minière and a 1943–1944 rebellion in Kasai. Once World War II ended, African workers formed an important support base for the anticolonial movement. "African Soldiers in World War II" by Headrick rejected both of these interpretations, claiming that there is little evidence that wartime service led to a massive political awakening among Africans in British or French Africa. Indeed, Headrick contended that with the exception of Ghana and Kenya, there was no connection between veterans and the decolonization movement.

ECONOMIC AND POLITICAL IMPACT OF THE WAR

Another topic that has generated considerable interest among scholars concerns the war's economic and political impact on Sub-Saharan Africa. There is a diversity of studies on the former subject, particularly insofar as the war affected agricultural production. For example, "Africans and Agricultural Production in Colonial Kenya" by Anderson and Throup asserted, unlike many other authors, that African producers such as the Kikuyu and Abaluhya enriched themselves by capitalizing on the wartime economic boom. Other useful materials about the economic dimensions of the Second World War include Bhila's "The Impact of the Second World War on the Development of Peasant Agriculture in Botswana," which studied how the British colonial government increased agricultural production by requiring Africans to grow crops on tribal lands for the war effort. Olurunfemi's "Effects of War-Time Trade Controls on Nigerian Cocoa Traders and Producers" investigated the impact of economic controls in southwestern Nigeria.

On a broader level, Pearce's "The Colonial Economy: Nigeria and the Second World War" and Rodney's *World War II and the Tanzanian Economy* evaluated how the war affected the entire economies of two of Britain's more important African colonies. Spencer's "Settler Domination, Agricultural Production and the Second World War in Kenya" explored how many European settlers profited from increased wartime demands for wheat, maize, and dairy products. Similarly, Westcott's "The East African Sisal Industry" examined how increased wartime demands stimulated sisal production and led to a conflict among the growers, who created associations to wrest control of marketing from merchant companies that wanted to maintain a free market.

"British Imperial Economic Policy during the War" by Cowen and Westcott advanced a more comprehensive view of the economic ramifications of the war by examining the extent to which it reduced colonial autonomy and centralized imperial economic policy around the British national economy. Close to the end of the conflict, Fortes wrote "The Impact of the War on British West Africa," which insisted that the military struggle would represent the most significant instrument of social progress in the region for at least the next fifty years. Lonsdale's "The Depression and the Second World War in the Transformation of Kenya" declared that the combination of economic collapse and military conflict transformed Kenya from a segmentary to a centralized, but ungovernable, state. Lastly, one of the more innovative studies, Mokopakgosi's "The Impact of the Second World War," compared oral data with archival material to determine the conflict's long-term effect on farmers, traders, and women and children left behind by the soldiers who had joined the Allied struggle. "The Economic Origins of Decolonisation in Zambia, 1940–1945" by Henderson assessed how wartime economic problems stimulated postwar challenges to British colonial rule. Cornelis evaluated the war's economic impact on Belgian Africa and explained the colonial economy's dependence on African resources in "Belgisch-Congo en Ruanda-Urundi Tijdens de tweede Wereldoorlog. De Economische en Financiële Situatie."

The other economic subject receiving extensive coverage is the mobilization of African labor, whether for military service or for forced civilian work. Much of this literature examined the implications of large-scale mobilization on individual countries or specific regions. For example, Grundlingh has written several articles about how the war affected black South African soldiers. His "Recruitment of South African Blacks for Participation in the Second World War" reviewed the policies and practices used by the South African government to encourage African enlistment in the armed forces. Grundlingh also examined how the war affected the common soldiers in "Aspects of the Impact of the Second World War on the Lives of Black South African and British Colonial Soldiers." Additionally, his "Soldiers and Politics" studied the ways in which the war helped to arouse African yearning for a new political order. Despite their wartime service, Grundlingh stated that Africans suffered from numerous forms of discrimination in his " 'Non-Europeans Should Be Kept Away from the Temptations of the Town' " and "Prejudices, Promises and Poverty." Easterbrook's "Kenyan Askaris in World War II" is a useful inquiry into the Kenyan experience. Sadly, there is a paucity of material written by African veterans. One of the more useful exceptions is Kakembo's *An African Soldier Speaks*. Similar coverage is needed for other countries in British, French, and Belgian Africa with regard to how military service affected the lives of ordinary African soldiers.

Other relevant studies concerning the labor mobilization issue include Bessant's "Coercive Development: Land Shortage, Forced Labor, and Colonial Development in the Chiweshe Reserve," which insisted that chronic land shortages and the mobilization of tens of thousands of Africans so alienated Chiweshe citizens that they formed a nucleus of anticolonial sentiment during the post-1945 period. Sekgoma's "The Second World War and the Sierra Leone Economy" asserted that the British colonial authorities used wartime emergency powers to crush the development of an independent labor movement. "Labour Mobilization for the War Effort in Swaziland" by Simelane investigated the mobilization process and the African reaction to being called up for nonmilitary government service. An examination of some documents issued by the Congolese colonial government regarding the problems affecting the domestic labor situation is contained in "The Conditions of Indigenous Workers in the Belgian Congo in 1944." The materials in this article are a good starting point for anyone who wants to understand the reasons for the labor unrest and strikes that plagued parts of the Belgian Congo. Vickery's "The Second World War Revival of Forced Labour in the Rhodesias" stated that European settlers succeeded in using increased wartime food requirements to convince the colonial authorities to reinstitute a forced labor policy. Other helpful articles about the impact of labor mobilization include Duncan's "State Bureaucracy and African Labour in South Africa"; Higginson's "Piston Box without Steam"; and Johnson's "Settler Farmers and Coerced African Labour in Southern Rhodesia, 1936–46."

The materials that examine the political impact of the Second World War on Sub-Saharan Africa also encompass an array of other topics. "Bechuanaland and the Second World War" by Kiyaga-Mulindwa affirmed that the territory's most important chiefs supported the British during the war to make political capital for the Botswana in the post-1945 period. "The Impact of the Second World War on the Gold Coast" by Holbrook is a comprehensive assessment of how the conflict affected all aspects of Ghanaian society.

Apart from reviewing the African military contribution to the French war effort, Lawler's *Soldiers of Misfortune* contains considerable information about the political dilemma the common soldier faced in deciding whether to support the Vichy government or the Free French forces. "Tragedy at Thiaroye" by Echenberg analyzed the events that led to one of the most politically significant African challenges to French colonial rule during the war years. His "Morts pour la France" also has some material pertaining to the political grievances of African soldiers.

On a broader level, Beecher's "The Second World War and the U.S. Politico-Economic Expansion" investigated how various American officials maneuvered the U.S. government into a post-1945 program to modernize Liberia socially and economically. "Closer Union and the Future of East Africa" by Westcott evaluated the factors that caused the British Colonial Office to oppose the federation of Kenya, Tanganyika, and Uganda as the best way to decolonize Great Britain's East African territories. More general overviews of the war's impact on individual countries include Gordon's "The Impact of the Second World War on Namibia"; Zeleza's "Kenya and the Second World War"; and Westcott's "The Impact of the Second World War on Tanganyika, 1939–49." Nyambariza examined one of the more tragic aspects of the war in "Les Efforts de Guerre et la Famine de 1943–1944 au Burundi, d'Après les Archives Territoriales." Readers interested in how war affected the Belgian Congo should consult Léon de Saint-Moulin's "L'Effort de Guerre, 1940–1945" and "La Population du Congo Pendant la Seconde Guerre Mondiale."

Little scholarly work has considered the war's impact on European communities in Sub-Saharan Africa. Indeed, the recent works concern only the response of colonial civil servants to the conflict. Interested readers should consult Baker's "Civil Response to War" and Pearce's "Morale in the Colonial Service in Nigeria during the Second World War."

PROPAGANDA

During the 1939–1945 period, the colonial powers published scores of books, pamphlets, and articles extolling the virtues of African participation in the Allied struggle against Germany and Japan. Clearly, much of this material was designed to facilitate African support of the wartime policies of the colonial powers. Additionally, it can be argued that even the post-1945 items were not so much military histories as political tracts to convince Africans that rather than creating a gulf between colonizer and colonized, the common wartime experience represented the postwar basis of a continued acceptance of colonial rule. Bent's *Ten Thousand Men of Africa*, for example, recounted the heroic deeds of the Africans who fought in Syria, Egypt, Palestine, Sicily, and Italy. This book also has thirteen appendixes that contain useful information about the organization, staffing, and performance of various Bechuanaland units. Additionally, there are numerous references to African loyalty "to the King and the Commonwealth."

Gray's *Basuto Soldiers in Hitler's War* is similar in style and content to the *Ten Thousand Men of Africa*. Bourdillon, who served as governor of Nigeria during the 1935–1942 period, outlined the importance of the African contribution to the struggle against the Axis powers in "Nigeria's War Effort." Apart from discussing the exploits of African soldiers in Ethiopia, the lavishly illustrated *Belgian Congo at War* explored the various nonmilitary contributions the colony made to the Allied war effort. *Belgian Congo, Reservoir of the Allies* by Wauters showed the importance of that country to the Allied war effort. Laguerre's *Free French Africa*, published primarily for an American audience, provided an emotional assessment of the importance of the partnership between French Africa and Free French military forces in the region. Oftentimes, a colonial power would rely on foreign journalists or academics to present their case. Burman's *Miracle on the Congo* sought to convince readers of the political and military importance of the American-sponsored Free French movement.

The appearance of these and numerous other similar works reflected a wider Allied propaganda effort in Sub-Saharan Africa. However, with a few exceptions, little work has been done on this subject. For a simple discussion of one aspect of this campaign, interested readers should consult Dickson's "Studies in War-Time Organisation." Several more scholarly contributions have been made by Smyth, including "Britain's African Colonies and British Propaganda during the Second World War" and "The British Colonial Film Unit and Sub-Saharan Africa," both of which showed how British propaganda succeeded in turning the Africans against the Germans and how the British use of concepts such as freedom, self-determination, and independence helped to lay the groundwork for postwar African nationalism. Similarly, her "War Propaganda during the Second World War in Northern Rhodesia" analyzed how British propaganda enabled Africans to engage in political dialogue about the war and the postwar status of British colonial rule. Smyth's "Propaganda and Politics: The History of the *Mutende* during the Second World War" explained how an important vernacular government newspaper, the *Mutende*, supported the war effort. Lastly, she also wrote a more exhaustive, essential study entitled "The Development of Government Propaganda in Northern Rhodesia Up to 1953."

Other useful examinations of this topic include Gadsden's "Wartime Propaganda in Kenya," Holbrook's "British Propaganda and the Mobilization of the Gold Coast War Effort," and Clarke's *West Africans at War: 1914–18, 1939–45*, which contained numerous illustrations of propaganda photographs and posters. Ihator took a more comprehensive approach with regard to the conflict's impact on the print media in "The Impact of the Second World War on West African Press and Politics." For French Africa, two important works are "La France de Pétain et l'Afrique" by Blanchard and Boëtsch and Kingston's "A Study in Radio Propaganda Broadcasts in French from North and West African Radio Stations."

Smyth also analyzed the war's impact on British Africa's post-1945 mass media in "The Post-War Career of the Colonial Film Unit in Africa" and "The Central African Film Unit's Images of Empire." Marx's " 'Dear Listeners in South Africa': German Propaganda Broadcasts to South Africa" is one of the few studies of Berlin's propaganda efforts in Sub-Saharan Africa. Giblin's "The Image of the Loyal African during World War II and Its Postwar Use by the French Communist Party" showed how French politicians used an obvious propaganda portrait for political purposes. On a broader level, Furlong's *Between Crown and Swastika: The Impact of the Radical Right on the Afrikaner Nationalist Movement in the Fascist Era* inspected the influence of fascism on white South Africa before, during, and after the Second World War.

AREAS FOR FURTHER RESEARCH

Further research is required in several important areas. For example, the role played by foreign missionaries during the conflict remains a relatively untouched subject. Apart from Gustav Bernander's *Lutheran Wartime Assistance to Tanzanian Churches 1940–1945*, a tract written largely for the faithful, there are only a few other recent studies, including Bontinck's "Les Missions Catholiques à Leopoldville Durant la Seconde Guerre Mondiale" and Ndi's "The Second World War in Southern Cameroon and Its Impact on Mission–State Relations, 1939–50." Among other things, the former explored the Catholic missions' attitudes and policies toward the Africans and the colonial authorities during the war, while the latter examined wartime relations between the colonial government and the various Baptist, Catholic, and Lutheran (Basel) missions active in southern Cameroon.

With the exception of Ekoko's "Britain and the Divided French Empire in West Africa" and Norton's "Belgian-French Relations during World

War II as Seen by Governor General Ryckmans," there has been little recent work on the attitudes and policies among the colonial powers in Sub-Saharan Africa. With the ongoing declassification of some wartime government documents in Britain, France, and Belgium, scholars undoubtedly will be able to undertake at least a partial examination of this subject. However, an in-depth study will have to await the day when researchers have greater access to relevant official documentation.

There are very few studies about the Second World War's impact on women in Sub-Saharan Africa. One exception is White's "Prostitution, Identity, and Class Consciousness in Nairobi during World War II," which contended that Nairobi's prostitutes enjoyed relatively prosperous lives by owning and operating profit-making enterprises (i.e., sale of sex, domestic skills, and rental of rooms) for which they provided the labor. "Women and the Second World War in Swaziland" by Simelane provided a useful overview of the conflict's impact on women who played a vital role in the country's agriculture.

Humanitarian issues also have received inadequate coverage. Indeed, Pennington's "Refugees in Tanganyika during the Second World War," which merely recounted the ramifications of the colonial government's decision to grant temporary asylum to war refugees and displaced persons from numerous places in Europe, represents a rare example of the kind of topics that need to be addressed. Some others include how the war affected human rights practices and medical policies throughout Sub-Saharan Africa.

Lastly, the environmental ramifications of the war have been largely ignored by scholars. There are two government-produced studies—Bechuanaland Forest Department's *Uganda Forests and the 1939–45 War* and *Forestry and the War Effort*—but both fail to address fully the environmental impact of increased timber production for the war effort. Another environmental issue that warrants an examination concerns the tremendous destruction of wildlife in countries like Kenya during the 1939–1945 period. At the time, colonial authorities justified such devastation because of the necessity of feeding large numbers of Allied soldiers.

BIBLIOGRAPHIES AND RESEARCH SOURCES

Although there are no book-length bibliographies devoted to the Second World War in all of Sub-Saharan Africa, interested readers can consult several useful items, including Gardinier's "The Second World War in French West Africa and Togo: Recent Research and Writing," Heyse's *Bibliographie du Congo Belge et du Ruanda-Urundi (1939–1951)*, Mertz's "South African Historiography on the Second World War," and Ofcansky's "A Bibliography on the Second World War." *Africa and the Second*

World War: Report and Papers of the Symposium Organized by UNESCO at Benghazi is a useful introductory study guide.

Scores of public and private institutions would be of use to scholars interested in conducting research on the Second World War in Sub-Saharan Africa. Space limitations prevent mentioning all of them. However, some of the more important ones in Britain include the Public Record Office, the Imperial War Museum, Rhodes House, Cambridge University Library, the Foreign and Commonwealth Office Library, and the National Army Museum. In France, relevant materials can be found at the Centre Militaire d'Information et de Documentation sur l'Outre-Mer, the Service Information et Historique de la Légion Etrangère, Service Historique de l'Armée, the Musée des Troupes de Marine, the Archives Nationales, and the Service d'Information et de Relations Publiques des Armées. Useful Belgian sources are located in Archives Africaines, Bibliothèque Africaine, Centre de Recherches et de Documentation Africaine (CEDAF), and the Archives Générales du Royaume. Although there has been no recent work on the impact of the Second World War on Portuguese Africa, scholars interested in conducting research on Portugal's African colonies may want to consult the holdings in the Arquivo Histórico Militar, Arquivo Histórico Ultramino, or Arquivo Nacional da Torre do Tombo.

In Sub-Saharan Africa, there are national archives in every country. A few of the more significant such facilities include the Kenya National Archives, Tanzania National Archives, Zimbabwe National Archives, Archives du Côte d'Ivoire, and the Archives du Sénégal, which contains the records of the Government-General of French West Africa (1895–1959). For non-Africans, it would be valuable to consult David Easterbrook's "Recent Bibliographic and Development Trends in Archives South of the Sahara and Their Impact on the Expatriate Researcher" prior to making arrangements to conduct research about the Second World War in African archives.

For those unable to conduct research in Europe or Sub-Saharan Africa, numerous libraries in North America contain extensive Africana collections. Some of the more useful include Indiana University, Michigan State University, University of Wisconsin (Madison), Northwestern University, Boston University, Hoover Institution, University of Toronto, University of Florida (Gainesville), University of California (Berkeley), University of British Columbia, Syracuse University, West Virginia University, and the Library of Congress. Before embarking on a research trip, individuals should write to the appropriate institutions inquiring about any special regulations or requirements pertaining to the use of specific archival and general collections.

BIBLIOGRAPHY

Africa and the Second World War: Report and Papers of the Symposium Organized by UNESCO at Benghazi. Paris: UNESCO, 1985.

Ajayi, J.F.A., and Michael Crowder, eds. *History of West Africa.* Vol. 2. New York: Columbia UP, 1973.

Anderson, David, and David Throup. "Africans and Agricultural Production in Colonial Kenya: The Myth of the War as a Watershed." *Journal of African History 26* (1985): 327–46.

Baker, Colin. "Civil Response to War: The Nyasaland Civil Service 1939–1945." *Society of Malawi Journal 1* (1985): 38, 44–61.

Bechuanaland Forest Department. *Forestry and the War Effort: Statement of the Bechuanaland Forest Authority.* Morija: Morija Printing Works, 1946.

Beecher, Lloyd N. "The Second World War and the U.S. Politico-Economic Expansion: The Case of Liberia, 1938–45." *Diplomatic History 3* (1979): 391–412.

Belgium Government Information Center, New York. *Belgian Congo at War.* New York: Belgian Government Information Center [1942].

Benoist, Joseph Roger de. "The Brazzaville Conference, or Involuntary Decolonization." *Africana Journal 15* (1990): 39–58.

Bent, Rowland A. R. *Ten Thousand Men of Africa: The Story of the Bechuanaland Pioneers and Gunners, 1941–1946.* London: HMSO, 1952.

Bernander, Gustav. *Lutheran Wartime Assistance to Tanzanian Churches 1940–1945.* Lund: Gleerup, 1968.

Bessant, Leonard Leslie. "Coercive Development: Land Shortage, Forced Labor, and Colonial Development in the Chiweshe Reserve, Colonial Zimbabwe, 1938–1946." *The International Journal of African Historical Studies 25* (1992): 39–65.

Bhila, Hoyini H. K. "The Impact of the Second World War on the Development of Peasant Agriculture in Botswana, 1939–1956." *Botswana Notes and Records 16* (1984): 63–71.

Blanchard, Pascal, and Gilles Boëtsch. "La France de Pétain et l'Afrique: Images et Propagandes Coloniales." *Canadian Journal of African Studies 28* (1994): 1–31.

Bontinck, Frans. "Les Missions Catholiques à Leopoldville Durant la Seconde Guerre Mondiale." In J. J. Symoens and J. Stengers, eds., *Le Congo Belge Durant la Seconde Guerre Mondiale,* 399–418. Brussels: Académie Royale des Sciences D'Outre-Mer, 1983.

Bourdillon, Bernard H. "Nigeria's War Effort." *Journal of the Royal African Society 39* (1940): 115–22.

Burman, Ben Lucien. *Miracle on the Congo: Report from the Free French Front.* New York: John Day, 1941.

Clarke, Peter B. *West Africans at War 1914–18, 1939–45.* London: Ethnographica, 1986.

"The Conditions of Indigenous Workers in the Belgian Congo in 1944." *International Labour Review 53* (1946): 340–48.

Cornelis, Henri A. A. "Belgisch-Congo en Ruanda-Urundi Tijdens de tweede Wereldoorlog. De Economische en Financiële Situatie." In J. J. Symoens and J. Stengers, eds., *Le Congo Belge Durant la Seconde Guerre Mondiale*, 51–88. Brussels: Académie Royale des Sciences D'Outre-Mer, 1983.

Cowen, Michael, and Nicholas Westcott. "British Imperial Economic Policy during the War." In David Killingray and Richard Rathbone, eds., *Africa and the Second World War*, 20–67. New York: St. Martin's, 1986.

Crowder, Michael. "The 1939–45 War and West Africa." In J.F.A. Ajayi and Michael Crowder, eds., *History of West Africa*, vol. 2, 596–621. New York: Columbia UP 1973.

———. "Prelude to De-Colonisation: The Second World War." In Michael Crowder, *West Africa under Colonial Rule*, 482–511. Evanston, IL: Northwestern UP, 1968.

———. "The Second World War: Prelude to Decolonisation in Africa." In Michael Crowder, ed., *The Cambridge History of Africa*, vol. 8, 8–51. Cambridge: Cambridge UP, 1984.

———. "Second World War." In Michael Crowder, *Colonial West Africa: Collected Essays*, 268–82. London: Frank Cass, 1978.

Dickson, A. G. "Studies in War-Time Organisation: The Mobile Propaganda Unit, East Africa Command." *African Affairs 44* (1945): 9–18.

Duncan, David. "State Bureaucracy and African Labour in South Africa: The Milling Workers' Strike of 1944." *Canadian Journal of African Studies 25* (1991): 361–77.

Easterbrook, David L. "Kenyan Askaris in World War II and Their Demobilization, with Special Reference to Machakos District." In B. Myrick, David L. Easterbrook, and J. R. Roelker, *Three Aspects of Crisis in Colonial Kenya*, 27–58. Syracuse: Syracuse University, 1975.

———. "Recent Bibliographic and Development Trends in Archives South of the Sahara and Their Impact on the Expatriate Researcher." *Africana Journal 11* (1980): 289–98.

Echenberg, Myron. "Morts pour la France: The African Soldier in France during the Second World War." *Journal of African History 26* (1985): 373–80.

———. "Tragedy at Thiaroye: The Senegalese Soldiers' Uprising of 1944." In Jean Copans Cohen and Peter C. W. Gutkind, eds., *African Labor History*, 109–28. Beverly Hills and London: Sage, 1978.

Ekoko, A. E. "Britain and the Divided French Empire in West Africa, 1940–1942." *Odu: A Journal of West African Studies 31* (1987): 140–60.

Fetter, Bruce. "Changing War Aims: Central Africa's Role, 1940–41, As Seen from Leopoldville." *African Affairs 87* (1988): 377–92.

Fortes, Meyer. "The Impact of the War on British West Africa." *International Affairs 21* (1945): 206–19.

Furlong, Patrick J. *Between Crown and Swastika: The Impact of the Radical Right on the Afrikaner Nationalist Movement in the Fascist Era.* Hanover, NH, and London: Wesleyan UP, 1991.

Gadsden, Fay. "Wartime Propaganda in Kenya: The Kenya Information Office, 1939–1945." *International Journal of African Historical Studies 19* (1986): 401–20.

Gardinier, David E. "The Second World War in French West Africa and Togo:

Recent Research and Writing." *Proceedings of the French Colonial Historical Society 10* (1985): 261–72.

Giblin, James L. "A Colonial State in Crisis: Vichy Administration in French West Africa." *Africana Journal 16* (1994): 326–40.

———. "The Image of the Loyal African during World War II and Its Postwar Use by the French Communist Party." *Canadian Journal of African Studies 14* (1980): 319–26.

Gordon, Robert J. "The Impact of the Second World War on Namibia." *Journal of Southern African Studies 19* (1993): 147–65.

Gray, Brian. *Basuto Soldiers in Hitler's War.* Maseru: Basutoland Government, 1953.

Grundlingh, Louis W. F. "Aspects of the Impact of the Second World War on the Lives of Black South African and British Colonial Soldiers." *Transafrican Journal of History 21* (1992): 19–35.

———. " 'Non-Europeans Should Be Kept Away from the Temptations of the Town': Controlling Black South African Soldiers during the Second World War." *The International Journal of African Historical Studies 3* (1992): 539–60.

———. "Prejudices, Promises and Poverty: The Experiences of Discharged and Demobilized Black South African Soldiers after the Second World War." *South African Historical Journal 26* (1992): 116–35.

———. "The Recruitment of South African Blacks for Participation in the Second World War." In David Killingray and Richard Rathbone, eds., *Africa and the Second World War,* 181–203. New York: St. Martin's, 1986.

———. "Soldiers and Politics: A Study of the Political Consciousness of Black South African Soldiers during and after the Second World War." *Historia 36* (1990): 55–66.

Headrick, Rita. "African Soldiers in World War II." *Armed Forces and Society 4* (1978): 501–26.

Helmreich, Jonathan E. "The Uranium Negotiations of 1944." In J. J. Symoens and J. Stengers, eds., *Le Congo Belge Durant la Seconde Guerre Mondiale,* 253–84. Brussels: Académie Royale des Sciences D'Outre-Mer, 1983.

Henderson, Ian. "The Economic Origins of Decolonisation in Zambia, 1940–1945." *Rhodesia History 5* (1974): 49–66.

Heyse, Théodore. *Bibliographie du Congo Belge et du Ruanda-Urundi (1939–1951): L'Afrique Centrale dans le Conflit Mondial.* Brussels: G. Van Campenhout, 1953.

Higginson, John. "Piston Box without Steam: Strikes and Popular Unrest in Katanga, 1937–1945." *International Journal of African Historical Studies 21* (1988): 97–118.

Holbrook, Wendell P. "British Propaganda and the Mobilization of the Gold Coast War Effort, 1939–1945." *Journal of African History 26* (1985): 347–61.

———. "The Impact of the Second World War on the Gold Coast, 1939–1945." Diss., Princeton University, 1978.

Ihator, Augustine Sunday Inyeseh. "The Impact of the Second World War on West African Press and Politics: The Case of Nigeria." Diss., Howard University, 1984.

Israel, Adrienne M. "Ex-Servicemen at the Crossroads: Protest and Politics in Post-War Ghana." *The Journal of Modern African Studies 30* (1992): 359–68.

———. "Measuring the War Experience: Ghanian Soldiers in World War II." *The Journal of Modern African Studies 25* (1987): 159–68.

Johnson, David. "Settler Farmers and Coerced African Labour in Southern Rhodesia, 1936–46." *Journal of African History 33* (1992): 111–28.

Kakembo, R. H. *An African Soldier Speaks.* London: Livingstone, 1946.

Killingray, David. "Labour Mobilisation in British Colonial Africa for the War Effort, 1939–46." In David Killingray and Richard Rathbone, eds., *Africa and the Second World War,* 68–96. New York: St. Martin's, 1986.

———. "Soldiers, Ex-Servicemen, and Politics in the Gold Coast, 1939–1950." *The Journal of Modern African Studies 21* (1983): 523–34.

Killingray, David, and Richard Rathbone, eds. *Africa and the Second World War.* New York: St. Martin's, 1986.

Kingston, Paul J. "A Study in Radio Propaganda Broadcasts in French from North and West African Radio Stations, 8 November 1942–14 December 1942." *Revue d'Histoire Maghrebine 11* (1984): 127–41.

Kiyaga-Mulindwa, D. "Bechuanaland and the Second World War." *Journal of Imperial and Commonwealth History 12* (1984): 33–53.

Laguerre, André. *Free French Africa.* New York: Free French Movement in America, 1942.

Lawler, Nancy Ellen. "Reform and Repression under the Free French: Economic and Political Transformation in the Côte d'Ivoire, 1942–45." *Africa 60* (1990): 88–110.

———. *Soldiers of Misfortune: Ivoirien Tirailleurs of World War II.* Athens: Ohio UP, 1992.

Lonsdale, John. "The Depression and the Second World War in the Transformation of Kenya." In David Killingray and Richard Rathbone, eds., *Africa and the Second World War,* 97–142. New York: St. Martin's, 1986.

Marshall, Bruce D. "Free France in Africa: Gaullism and Colonialism." In Prosser Gifford and William Roger Louis, eds., *France and Britain in Africa: Imperial Rivalry and Colonial Rule,* 713–48. New Haven, CT, and London: Yale UP, 1971.

Marx, Christopher. " 'Dear Listeners in South Africa': German Propaganda Broadcasts to South Africa, 1940–1941." *South African Historical Journal 27* (1992): 148–72.

Mazrui, Ali, and Michael Tidy. "The Turning Point: The Impact of the Second World War on Africa." In Ali Mazrui and Michael Tidy, *Nationalism and New States in Africa,* 10–30. Nairobi: Heinemann, 1985.

Mertz, Peter Bolko. "South African Historiography on the Second World War." In Jürgen Rohwer and Hildegard Müller, eds., *Neue Forschungen zum Zweiten Weltkrieg,* 461–63. Koblenz: Schriften der Bibliotek für Zeitgeschichte, 1990.

Mokopakgosi, Brian. "The Impact of the Second World War: The Case of Kweneng in the Then Bechuanaland Protectorate, 1939–1950." In David Killingray and Richard Rathbone, eds., *Africa and the Second World War,* 160–80. New York: St. Martin's, 1986.

Ndi, Anthony. "The Second World War in Southern Cameroon and Its Impact on Mission–State Relations, 1939–50." In David Killingray and Richard Rathbone, eds., *Africa and the Second World War,* 204–31. New York: St. Martin's, 1986.

Norton, William B. "Belgian–French Relations during World War II as Seen by Governor General Ryckmans." In J. J. Symoens and J. Stengers, eds., *Le Congo Belge Durant la Seconde Guerre Mondiale*, 285–312. Brussels: Académie Royale des Sciences D'Outre-Mer, 1983.

Nwaka, Geoffrey I. "Rebellion in Umuahia, 1950–1951: Ex-Servicemen and Anti-Colonial Protest in Eastern Nigeria." *Transafrican Journal of History 16* (1987): 47–62.

Nyambariza, Daniel. "Les Efforts de Guerre et la Famine de 1943–1944 au Burundi, d'Après les Archives Territoriales." *Cahiers CRA Histoire 4* (1984): 1–18.

Ofcansky, Thomas. "A Bibliography on the Second World War." *Africana Journal 16* (1994): 423–49.

Okete, James Ellysham Shiroya. "The Impact of World War Two on Kenya: The Role of Ex-Servicemen in Kenya Nationalism." Diss., Michigan State University, 1968.

Olurunfemi, A. "Effects of War-Time Trade Controls on Nigerian Cocoa Traders and Producers, 1939–45: A Case Study of the Hazards of a Dependent Economy." *International Journal of African Historical Studies 13* (1980): 672–87.

Olusanya, Gabriel Olakunle. "The Role of Ex-Servicemen in Nigerian Politics." *The Journal of Modern African Studies 6* (August 1968): 221–32.

———. *The Second World War and Politics in Nigeria, 1939–1953*. London: Evans Brothers, 1973.

Oyemakinde, Wale. "Michael Imoudu and the Emergence of Militant Trade Unionism in Nigeria, 1940–1942." *Journal of the Historical Society of Nigeria 7* (December 1974): 541–61.

Pearce, Robert D. "The Colonial Economy: Nigeria and the Second World War." In B. Ingham and C. Simmons, eds., *Development Studies and Colonial Policy*, 263–92. London: Frank Cass, 1987.

———. "Morale in the Colonial Service in Nigeria during the Second World War." *Journal of Imperial and Commonwealth History 11*, no. 2 (January 1983): 175–96.

Pennington, A. L. "Refugees in Tanganyika during the Second World War." *Tanganyika Notes and Records 32* (January 1952): 52–56.

Rodney, Walter. *World War II and the Tanzanian Economy*. Ithaca, NY: Cornell African Studies Center, 1976.

Saint-Moulin, Léon de. "L'Effort de Guerre, 1940–1945." *Zaïre-Afrique 25* (February 1985): 91–106.

———. "La Population du Congo Pendant la Seconde Guerre Mondiale." In J. J. Symoens and J. Stengers, eds., *Le Congo Belge Durant la Seconde Guerre Mondiale*, 15–50. Brussels: Académie Royale des Sciences D'Outre-Mer, 1983.

Schleh, Eugene P. A. "The Post-War Careers of Ex-Servicemen in Ghana and Uganda." *Journal of Modern African Studies 6*, no. 2 (August 1968): 203–20.

Sekgoma, Gilbert A. "The Second World War and the Sierra Leone Economy: Labour Employment and Utilisation, 1939–45." In David Killingray and Richard Rathbone, eds., *Africa and the Second World War*, 232–57. New York: St. Martin's, 1986.

Simelane, Hamilton Sipho. "Labor Mobilization for the War Effort in Swaziland,

1940–1942," *The International Journal of African Historical Studies 26* (1993): 541–74.

———. "Women and the Second World War in Swaziland, 1941–1945." *Uniswa Research Journal 3* (1990): 35–44.

Smyth, Rosaleen. "Britain's African Colonies and British Propaganda during the Second World War." *Journal of Imperial and Commonwealth History 14* (1985): 65–82.

———. "The British Colonial Film Unit and Sub-Saharan Africa, 1939–1945." *Historical Journal of Film, Radio and Television 8* (1988): 285–98.

———. "The Central African Film Unit's Images of Empire, 1948–1963." *Historical Journal of Film, Radio and Television 3* (1983): 131–47.

———. "The Development of Government Propaganda in Northern Rhodesia Up to 1953." Diss., University of London, 1983.

———. "The Post-War Career of the Colonial Film Unit in Africa." *Historical Journal of Film, Radio and Television 12* (1992): 163–77.

———. "Propaganda and Politics: The History of the *Mutende* during the Second World War." *Zambia Journal of History 1* (1981): 43–60.

———. "War Propaganda during the Second World War in Northern Rhodesia." *African Affairs 83* (1984): 345–58.

Spencer, Ian. "Settler Domination, Agricultural Production and the Second World War in Kenya." *Journal of African History 21* (1980): 497–514.

Uganda Forest Department. *Uganda Forests and the 1939–45 War.* Entebbe: Government Printer, 1947.

Vickery, Kenneth P. "The Second World War Revival of Forced Labour in the Rhodesias." *International Journal of African Historical Studies 22* (1989): 423–37.

Wauters, Arthur. *Belgian Congo, Reservoir of the Allies.* London: Belgian Office of Information, 1942.

Westcott, Nicholas J. "Closer Union and the Future of East Africa, 1939–1948: A Case Study in the 'Official Mind of Imperialism.' " *Journal of Imperial and Commonwealth History 10* (1981): 67–88.

———. "The East African Sisal Industry, 1929–1949: The Marketing of a Colonial Commodity during Depression and War." *Journal of African History 25* (1984): 445–61.

———. "The Impact of the Second World War on Tanganyika, 1939–49." In David Killingray and Richard Rathbone, eds., *Africa and the Second World War*, 143–59. New York: St. Martin's, 1986.

White, Luise. "Prostitution, Identity, and Class Consciousness in Nairobi during World War II." *Signs: Journal of Women and Culture in Society 11* (1986): 255–73.

Zeleza, Tiyambe. "Kenya and the Second World War, 1939–1950." In W. R. Ochieng, ed., *A Modern History of Kenya 1895–1980*, 144–72. London: Evans Brothers, 1989.

Author Index

See also Subject Index for participants who were also authors.

Aandahl, Fredrick, 60
Abbazia, Patrick, 185
Abella, Irving, 389
Abitbol, Michel, 318
Abrahamsen, Samuel, 322
Absalom, Roger, 293
Abse, Toby, 353
Acheson, Dean, 89, 90
Acikalin, Cevat, 446
Adair, Paul, 172
Adam-Smith, Patsy, 304
Adamczyk, Richard D., 64, 240
Adams, Michael C. C., 356
Adams, R.J.Q., 36
Adamthwaite, Anthony, 35–36
Addington, Larry H., 147
Addison, Paul, 351–52
Adelson, Alan, 319
Adler, Jacques, 318
Agar, Augustus, 104
Agar-Hamilton, J. A., 148
Agerton, Arthur A., 90
Aguilar Camín, Héctor, 428
Ahmad, Feroz, 445
Aimone, Alan C., 60
Albee, Parker Bishop, 74
Albion, Robert Greenhalgh, 47, 243
Alexander, Don W., 127

Alexander, Martin, 36
Alfieri, Dino, 140
Allard, Dean C., 60
Allen, Franklin, 101
Allen, Gwenfread E., 358
Allen, Louis, 460
Allen, Margaret, 376
Allen, Paul, 124, 306
Allen, Thomas B., 48
Allen, W.E.D., 171
Alper, Benedict S., 102
Alvarez, David, 446
Aly, Götz, 274
Ambrose, Stephen, 111, 209–12, 307
Ancel, Jean, 321
Ancell, R. Manning, 50
Anderson, David, 470
Anderson, Irvine, 444–45
Anderson, Karen, 375
Anderson, Terry, Jr., 106
Andrade, Víctor, 427
Andrews, E. M., 456
Andreyev, Catherine, 273
Andrzejewski, Stanislav, 350
Angell, Norman, 27
Angelucci, Enzo, 47, 144
Anger, Per, 320
Ansel, Walter, 129, 131, 143, 148

Anthérieu, Étienne, 126, 131
Apenszlak, Jacob, 319
Apple, Nick P., 77
Arad, Yitzhak, 317
Ardery, Philip, 100
Arendt, Hannah, 33
Argyle, Christopher, 50
Arjomand, Said Amir, 446
Armstrong, Anne, 150
Armstrong, H. C., 448
Armstrong, John A., 275, 280
Armstrong, Richard N., 171
Arnold, Henry H., 65, 91
Ash, Bernard, 126
Aster, Sidney, 62, 360
Astor, Gerald, 111
Atherton, Louise, 62, 257
Atkins, G. Pope, 430
Auphan, Paul, 142
Auty, Phyllis, 294
Avni, Haim, 322, 389
Azeau, Henri, 129
Azéma, Jean-Pierre, 270, 274

Babington-Smith, Constance, 260
Backer, John H., 407
Bacque, James, 307–8
Badoglio, Pietro, 140
Baer, George W., 58
Bagnasco, Erminio, 144
Bailey, Beth, 359, 372–73
Baily, Robert H., 303
Baker, Colin, 472
Bakhash, Shaul, 446
Balan, Boris, 395
Baldwin, Hanson W., 121
Balfour, Michael, 404
Ballantine, Duncan S., 243
Ballard, Robert D., 74
Bamm, Peter Kurt Emmrich, 106
Banks, Arthur, 50
Bankwitz, Philip C. F., 128
Baram, Phillip, 443
Barber, John, 132, 354
Barclay, G. St. J., 457
Barclay, George, 104
Bard, Mitchell H., 307
Bark, Dennis L., 406

Barkai, Avraham, 317
Barker, A J., 303
Barker, Thomas M., 307
Barnard, Roy S., 100
Barnes, John, 84
Barnett, Correlli, 62, 149, 236, 256, 351
Bartoszewski, Wladyslaw, 319
Bartov, Omer, 163, 272, 306
Batatu, Hanna, 447
Bates, Richard W., 60
Bateson, Charles, 6
Battaglia, Roberto, 293
Baudot, Marcel, 49
Bauer, Eddy, 124
Bauer, K. Jack, 49
Bauer, Magna E., 161, 163, 296
Bauer, Yehuda, 316–17, 392
Baumbach, Werner, 130–31
Baumont, Maurice, 36
Bausum, David, 45
Bausum, Henry S., 45
Baxter, Colin F., 48, 141
Bayerlein, Fritz, 142
Bayliss, Gwyn M., 45
Beach, Edward L., 108
Beaumont, Joan, 308
Beaver, Daniel R., 240
Beck, Earl R., 352, 401
Bédarida, Francois, 124–25, 270, 353
Beecher, Lloyd N., 472
Beesley, Patrick, 182, 256
Beevor, Antony, 132
Behbehani, Hashim, 444
Behrendt, Hans-Otto, 141–42
Behrens, C.B.A., 186, 238, 245
Bell, Philip M., 6, 38
Bell, Raymond E., 128
Bell, Roger J., 457–58
Bellafaire, Judith A., 367
Bellamy, Chris, 172
Beloff, Max, 454
Ben-Moshe, Tuvia, 199
Bendiner, Elmer S., 100
Benes, Eduard, 92
Bennett, Jeremy, 289
Bennett, Ralph, 141, 256
Benoist, Joseph Roger de, 468

Frohn, Axel, 407
Frost, Charles Sydney, 105
Frye, Alton, 416
Fugate, Brian I., 172
Fulbrook, Mary, 406
Fuller, J.F.C., 3–5, 8, 15–19
Funigiello, Philip J., 357
Funk, Arthur Layton, 45, 291
Furlong, Patrick J., 458–59, 474
Fussell, Paul, 103

Gabel, Kurt, 101
Gabreski, Francis, 101
Gadsden, Fay, 474
Gailey, Harry A., 18
Gallagher, John, 462
Gallagher, Thomas, 258
Galland, Adolf, 87
Gamelin, Maurice G., 128
Gander, Terry, 144
Gannon, M., 186
Gansberg, Judith M., 304
Gardinier, David E., 475
Gardner, F. L., 417, 421
Garett, G. R., 371
Garlinski, Józef, 296
Garrard, Carol, 354
Garrard, John G., 354
Garrett, Richard, 303
Garrett, Stephen A., 229
Garzke, William, 144
Gaston, James C., 222
Gate, James L., 423
Gaulle, Charles de, 92
Gaunson, A. B., 442
Gavin, James M., 91
Gebhardt, James F., 172
Gehlen, Reinhard, 86, 259
Gelb, Norman, 149
Gellman, Irwin F., 419–21, 430
Gemzell, Carl-Axel, 125
George, Mary, 61
Gerolymatos, A., 294
Gershoni, Israel, 446
Geyer, Michael, 405
Gibbs, N. H., 455
Giblin, James L., 468, 474
Gibney, Frank, 111

Gibson, T. A., 75
Gies, Miep, 318
Gilbert, Felix, 63
Gilbert, James L., 257
Gilbert, Martin, 11, 32, 63, 316–17
Giles, Henry, 102
Gill, Anton, 405
Gillespie, O. A., 455
Gillingham, John, 276
Gillison, Douglas, 458
Gillman, Leni, 308
Gillman, Peter, 308
Gimbel, John, 407
Giorgerini, Giorgio, 145
Giuliano, Gerard, 126
Glantz, David M., 166, 258–59
Gleason, S. E., 419, 421
Glendevon, John, 460
Gluck, Sherna Berger, 374
Goebbels, Joseph, 86, 163
Goerlitz, Walter, 162, 172
Goldberger, Leo, 290
Goldman, Nancy Loring, 369
Goldsmith, R. W., 342
Gooch, John, 142, 185
Goodenough, Simon, 50
Goodman, Jack, 355–56
Goodwin, Doris Kearns, 358
Gopal, Sarvepalli, 460
Goralski, Robert, 51
Gordon, Bertram M., 278
Gordon, Eve, 367
Gordon, Robert J., 472
Gossage, Carolyn, 369
Gott, Richard, 32
Goulden, Marc, 358
Gowing, Margaret Mary, 238, 338–39
Granatstein, J. L., 360, 456
Granger, Byrd Howell, 367
Grant, Shiela Duff, 319
Gravil, Roger, 419
Gray, Brain, 473
Gray, J. Glenn, 103
Grechko, A. 171
Green, Constance McLaughlin, 240
Green, David, 74, 421
Green, Gerald, 320
Green, William, 49

Subject Index

See also Author Index for wartime participant authors.

About the Editor and Contributors

GRETA BUCHER is an Assistant Professor at the U.S. Military Academy at West Point. Her research centers on the impact of the Second World War on Soviet women.

OTTO B. BURIANEK teaches at Georgia College. He continues research on the U.S. Army's work with displaced persons in Europe after World War II.

ROBERT J. CAPUTI's interests are European diplomatic and military history and global history.

D.K.R. CROSSWELL is the author of a biography of Walter Bedell Smith. He has taught at Kansas State, James Madison, the National University of Singapore, and the National Institute of Education.

PETER R. FABER, recently Director of American History at the U.S. Air Force Academy, is an Air Force officer currently assigned to the Naval War College.

BRIAN P. FARRELL is Lecturer in Military History at the National University of Singapore, recently completing a study of British grand strategy in World War II.

DAVID M. GLANTZ is editor of the *Journal of Slavic Military Studies* and a member of the Russian Academy of Natural Sciences and author of a number of books on the Soviet military.

GERHARD HIRSCHFELD, Director of the Bibliothek für Zeitgeschichte (Library for Contemporary History), and Honorary Professor at Stuttgart University, Germany, chairs the German Committee for the History of the Second World War. His numerous publications include the German occupation of Europe and other topics.

JONATHAN M. HOUSE, Associate Professor of History at Gordon College, Georgia, and former career army officer, is the author of *Towards Combined Arms Warfare: A Survey of 20th Century Tactics, Doctrine, and Organization* and coauthor with David Glantz of *When Titans Clashed: How the Red Army Stopped Hitler.*

ERROL D. JONES is Chair of the History Department at Boise State University. In addition to publications in Mexican history, he is coeditor of *Latin American Military History: An Annotated Bibliography.*

LOYD E. LEE is Professor of History and Chair of the department at the State University of New York, the College at New Paltz. He is the author of *The Politics of Harmony: Civil Service, Liberalism and Social Reform in Baden, 1800–1850*; *The War Years: A Global History of the Second World War*, and other publications on German and global history.

RICHARD LIBOWITZ is on the faculties of Saint Joseph's and Temple Universities. Vice President of the Philadelphia Center on the Holocaust, Genocide and Human Rights, his publications include *Methodology and the Academic Study of the Holocaust*, with Zev Garber and Alan Berger.

S. P. MACKENZIE, Associate Professor of History at the University of South Carolina, is author of *Politics and Military Morale* and *The Home Guard* and various articles on prisoners of war.

GEOFREY T. MILLS is currently Associate Dean and Associate Professor of Finance at the University of Northern Iowa. His research interests center on the economics of war, especially issues surrounding mobilization and economic stabilization.

MARC MILNER has published widely on the Battle of the Atlantic, including *North Atlantic Run* and *The U-Boat Hunters*. He is Professor of History and Director of the Military and Strategic Studies program at the University of New Brunswick.

BOB MOORE is Senior Lecturer in Modern History at Manchester Metropolitan University (U.K.) and has published extensively on the Netherlands in the twentieth century and on the Second World War.

THOMAS OFCANSKY is Senior Analyst on East Africa for the Department of Defense. He has written numerous books and articles about Africa.

RITCHIE OVENDALE is a Professor of International Politics at the University of Wales, Aberystwyth. His publications include, as editor, *British Defence Policy since 1945*.

STEPHEN T. POWERS is currently Professor of History at the University of Northern Colorado. He is the coauthor of *The March to Victory: A Guide to World War II Battles and Battlefields from London to the Rhine*.

EUGENE L. RASOR is Professor of History, Emory & Henry College in Virginia. He has published many bibliographic surveys, including several relating to World War II.

JAMES J. SADKOVICH has published widely on Italian and Yugoslavian history, including the *Italian Navy in World War II*.

DONALD G. SCHILLING is Professor of History at Denison University, where he teaches modern European and German history, including a course on the Second World War.

JOHN M. SHAW, a career army officer, taught military history at the U.S. Military Academy from 1991 to 1995.

KEVIN SMITH is Associate Professor of History at Ball State University. He wrote *Conflict over Convoys: Anglo-American Logistics Diplomacy in the Second World War*.

JOHN M. VANDER LIPPE, Assistant Professor of Middle Eastern and Soviet History at the State University of New York at New Paltz, is completing a book on Turkish political discourse during the presidency of Ismet Inonu, 1938–1950.

ISBN 0-313-29325-2

90000>

EAN

9 780313 293252

HARDCOVER BAR CODE